Snow Widows

Snow Widows

Scott's Fatal Antarctic Expedition Through
the Eyes of the Women They Left Behind

Katherine MacInnes

WILLIAM
COLLINS

William Collins
An imprint of HarperCollins*Publishers*
1 London Bridge Street
London SE1 9GF

WilliamCollinsBooks.com

HarperCollins*Publishers*
1st Floor, Watermarque Building, Ringsend Road
Dublin 4, Ireland

First published in Great Britain by William Collins in 2022

2023 2025 2024 2022
2 4 6 8 10 9 7 5 3 1

ISBN 978-0-00-839465-3

Typeset in Dante MT Std by Palimpsest Book Production Ltd, Falkirk, Stirlingshire
Printed and bound in the UK using 100% renewable electricity at CPI Group (UK) Ltd

MIX
Paper from
responsible sources
FSC www.fsc.org **FSC® C007454**

This book is produced from independently certified FSC™ paper
to ensure responsible forest management.

For more information visit: www.harpercollins.co.uk/green

'No man is an island'
John Donne, 1624

The story of Captain Scott's adventure, of five men who trekked to the South Pole, has been told from a male perspective so many times that it would take a book to list them. This is not that book. For the first time, this group biography looks at the expedition from a fresh perspective, through the eyes of the women they left behind.

This book is dedicated to five heroines – five real women with flaws and foibles who are to me, and I hope to you, no less impressive than the 'knights' who flew their colours.

'Stop the garden party? My dear Laura, don't be so absurd. Of course we can't do anything of the kind. Nobody expects us to. Don't be so extravagant.'

Laura protests: 'But we can't possibly have a garden party with a man dead just outside the front gate.'

'Oh, Laura!' Jose began to be seriously annoyed. 'If you're going to stop a band playing every time someone has an accident, you'll lead a very strenuous life.'

'The Garden Party' by Katherine Mansfield, 1922

New Zealand novelist Katherine Mansfield called the dead man in her short story, 'The Garden Party', Mr Scott. Mansfield was familiar both with the *Terra Nova* expedition (her brother-in-law, geologist J. Mackintosh Bell, had applied to Captain Scott for a place) and with Kathleen Scott, through their close mutual friend, Gilbert Cannon.

CONTENTS

PART THREE *Allegro molto*

'The Lady Question'

The figurehead is descending slowly from the shelf, high up in the National Museum of Wales storage unit just north of Cardiff. It is January and the shed is unheated, but she wears a snow-white, off-the-shoulder dress, a serene expression on her half-smiling face. Her right hand is held across her chest, over her heart; her left holds her dress out of the waves, or in this case, the arms of the forklift. Looking at her from the side, I notice what looks like the scrolled top of a violin where she was attached to the prow of Captain Scott's expedition ship, the *Terra Nova*, over a century ago.

The figurehead is taller than me, at least on castors. Her elegance is undeniable, her stoicism second to none. One hundred and ten years ago this wooden lady arrived at the Ross Ice Shelf fully expecting to bring Captain Scott and his four companions back home. While she was at the bottom of the globe, many weeks' sailing from the nearest cable head, five women waited anxiously at home for news.

Back then she was the only female allowed to the Antarctic. This story is set against 'The Lady Question', as it was referred to in the imperialist, anti-suffrage Royal Geographical Society in London at the time. 'Can a lady be a Fellow?', asked the patriarchal hardliners rhetorically. Of course not, unless of course they were the 'third sex', namely militant suffragettes who the Society were at pains to exclude. After a protracted tussle, over half the 163 women admitted as members in 1913 were explorers and travellers, of the others, a small group were appropriately connected wives or widows: 'These women,' according to a recent paper published in *The Geographical Journal*, 'included Mrs Oates, wife of Captain L.E.G. Oates who accompanied Captain R.F. Scott on the expedition to the South Pole.'[1] Which is all very well except that Captain Oates didn't have a wife. He wasn't married. So who was she? Who was this Mrs Oates? Who were the hitherto invisible wives (and mothers) – the 'Snow Widows' – behind that most famous 'selfie' of five doomed men lined up at the South Pole on 18 January 1912?

Scott of the Antarctic still drags his sledge through eponymous archives, official diaries and authorised biographies, but in order to answer that question, I have chased the Snow Widows through dusty attics and auction rooms, and sifted them from history's cutting room floors. My aim has been not to analyse, but to try to place the stories in their historical context and let the women speak for themselves. Out of choice, I would take a seat that gave me a clear view into the wings of the theatre, the dancers warming up, the actors mastering their nerves. I want to see the back of the embroidery, an x-ray of that famous picture, the 'making of' at the end of a film. To that end, the story you are about to read is full of contradictions (many of which I have deliberately left in) and it is built on the premise that the minutiae of everyday life reveals as much as the major historical events that shape our lives.

Kathleen Scott wrote an autobiography. The others did not. Caroline Oates kept accounts and Emily Bowers's daughter May, a diary. Lois Evans exists in interviews with her living relatives and archived sound recordings in Gower, South Wales. Oriana Wilson and I are well acquainted – researching my biography of her revealed this bigger story. It also prompted me to interview those who knew the Snow Widows personally (all but one now deceased), which has been invaluable.

This story is set just over a century ago when attitudes to the role of women, to class, education, religion, parenting, marriage, race and sexuality were very different; when the most women could hope for was to be, as even Scott acknowledged they often were, 'the real power behind the throne'.[2] But human bodies are just as vulnerable, as are human hearts. In an effort to make the book you are about to read 'too readable', as Emily Bowers might say, I have told it through scenes in present tense, and for clarity – and brevity – I have occasionally conflated events and dates. Instead of superimposing modern values, this historical context invites you to time travel to a bygone era, to understand a mindset that is completely alien to us now. And so this is written with an awareness of meta-biography – it will not be a comfortable ride. It is too easy both to be wise in retrospect, and to be swept up by the glamour of adventure without having to consider the collateral impact for those on the shelf.

My appointed time with the figurehead is over. She is wheeled back to cold storage where she will be re-crated and begin her slow ascent back to invisibility. I do not want to say goodbye. This lady is the sailor's muse, but also a metaphor for resilience. She has swum with killer whales, leopard seals and penguins, she has been used as a battering ram in sea ice, but most importantly for me, she has met the Snow Widows. What has she seen, what has she heard? If she could speak, what would she say? For now, perhaps she can lead us to that mid-air liminal place, that foreign country of a century ago where the most famous epic in the history of exploration has yet to begin.

The Five Dots

What drives a man through storm and snow over ice . . .
into a world of cold misery? The real pivot upon which all
his efforts are based is the desire to be rated well among his
colleagues, and inseparably linked with this is the love of some
feminine heart. Is not this also the inspiration of all the world?
Frederick Cook, North Pole explorer, 1893

10 NOVEMBER 1910

QUEEN'S HALL, LONDON, ENGLAND

As England slides into winter, the London theatres are getting ready
to offer warmth, light and diversion from the long, dark nights. English
composer Edward Elgar's star is in the ascendant. He has just been
commissioned to write a march for King George V's coronation. But
tonight his Violin Concerto in B Minor, Op. 61, is to be premiered
at the Queen's Hall on Langham Place. The soloist, Austrian Fritz
Kreisler, is known as 'the violinist of Vienna'. Elgar, a violinist himself,
was prompted to write this concerto when Kreisler told an English
newspaper that Elgar was the 'greatest living composer' and wished
that 'he would write something for the violin'. Kreisler may be the
reason for the concerto, but he is not Elgar's inspiration. On the
printed score Elgar has written: 'Herein is enshrined the soul of
. . . . .' Five dots. He is precise about it, five dots not the usual three.
There is wild speculation. Who is '. . . . .'? A woman? A man? Five
women? Five men? Will they be in the audience tonight? So far, Elgar
refuses to say.

Sir Edgar and Lady Speyer descend the sweeping staircase to the hall
of their mansion, which straddles 44 to 46 Grosvenor Square in Mayfair.
Their chauffeur has the motorcar under the porticoed carriage entrance.
Uniformed footmen wield umbrellas against the rain as the Speyers

climb into the back seat. Sir Edgar, a German-born financier and philan-
thropist, wields the power of a Renaissance prince. His wife, formerly
Leonora von Stosch, was a concert violinist. Sir Edgar underwrites
Henry Wood's Promenade concerts, the Proms. He does this, so he
says, 'to please my wife'. Together they sponsor composers, among
them Elgar, Debussy and Richard Strauss.

The Speyers' patronage is broad. In addition to underwriting the
Queen's Hall, they sponsor Antarctic explorer Captain Robert Falcon
Scott of the Royal Navy. (In letters to Captain Scott, Leonora refers to
Mount Speyer in the Antarctic as 'our mountain'. Scott named it for
them on his first *Discovery* expedition.) For Scott's second *Terra Nova*
expedition, Sir Edgar is not only the major donor, but he has agreed
to be the British Antarctic Expedition treasurer.

As the Speyers' car moves off towards Langham Place, Kreisler
enters his drab dressing room backstage at the Queen's Hall. He is
dressed in a black tailcoat and stiff white shirt. He sets a hard leather
case on a wooden table at right angles to an upright piano. He clicks
the clasps, opening the lid to reveal the 'Hart' Guarneri del Gesù.
Holding the violin up, he strokes the tailpiece with the fingers of his
bow hand, tracing the maker's initials. He feels the rough surface of
'B.G.' picked out in diamonds. But the audience have not come to
admire precious stones and, as usual before a premiere, Kreisler feels
sick with nerves.

Ever since he was a boy, he's loathed practising. Now he wishes
he'd overcome his aversion. He breathes deeply and falls back on familiar
actions. He tunes the A, the second-top string, down to the piano's A.
He tunes the D with the A, the G with the D and finally the E, the
top string, with the A. He thinks of traditional violinists shifting notes
on gut strings that had to be warmed up, coaxed. Now, with metal
strings, Kreisler is pushing back frontiers. In the second movement he
must play the leap of a twelfth on a G string from a low A flat – by
any standards, an amazing feat. Elgar is an accomplished violinist
himself, but Kreisler is better, the grit in the pearl. Elgar cannot compete
with Kreisler on the violin, but he can write music that is only just
possible to play. The stakes are high. Kreisler has his reputation, his
career on the line. There is the very real risk of failure . . .

ORIANA WILSON – WELLINGTON, NEW ZEALAND

Oriana Wilson strolls through the Bishopscourt gardens in Wellington. They are alive with fantails swerving like swallows to catch insects on the wing. Inside, Bill is discussing his post-expedition future with the bishop, his old dean at Caius College, Cambridge. It is a good time to come to the southern hemisphere again and avoid the English winter, but Oriana, 'Ory', misses the culture. This is a new country where settlers are still trying to establish themselves – 'they are so starved of art and music' down here.[3] Everywhere there is evidence of slash and burn, clearing land for pasture – sheep are the new gold. 'In a century, or less,' Ory's husband Dr Edward Wilson, 'Bill', estimates, 'all or most of this unique fauna and flora will be extinct, they are dying out before one's eyes.'[4]

Tonight the Wilsons are staying with Lady Bowen at Middleton, just outside Christchurch in South Island. Lady Bowen has deliberately reproduced a little England to insulate herself against the rougher edges of settler life. She is the sister of ex-Royal Geographical Society (RGS) president Sir Clements Markham – the man who first appointed Captain Scott to the *Discovery* expedition. While she may not be able to hear Elgar's new concerto as it is premiered, she's made sure that the upcoming Christchurch Musical Union's second subscription concert programme includes Elgar's *Imperial March*, *Chanson de Matin* and his romantic *Chanson de Nuit*.

Bill is one of seven *Discovery* expedition veterans going back for more. He intends to enjoy his last days at home to the fullest, knowing precisely what lies before him. There is no doubt that some music allows a private retreat, in which each man can think of a particular person, '. . . . .', left at home. Bill tells Ory that he hopes to be chosen for the honour of the Polar Party, the final group of men who will go all the way 'for your own dear sake'. But really she knows he does everything for God.

EMILY BOWERS – BUTE, SCOTLAND

William Maxwell has just published a history of the co-operative movement, and Emily Bowers sometimes feels, as she shrugs on her overcoat against the *dreich* Scottish weather and climbs the external stairs to the Maxwells' apartment, that their living arrangements at Caerlaverock embody its best principles. In the already well-thumbed newspaper, Emily can see that Elgar's Violin Concerto will be premiered in London that night. The 4th Marquess of Bute's stately home in the southeast of the island hosts public performances of Elgar's work which Emily and her two daughters can attend.

Truthfully, Emily prefers hymns. 'The Sankey hymns are really splendid,' wrote her son, Lieutenant Henry Bowers, 'Birdie', when he encountered them on his travels around the world with the Royal Indian Marine, 'wherever I hear them I think of the dear old family time again.'[5]

But why has Elgar dedicated the piece to an anonymous person? Who do the five dots represent? In his last letter home from the *Terra Nova*, Birdie wrote: 'Lady Somebody at lunch said, "Have you nobody who cares about your going to the Antarctic?"' apparently prompted by 'my callous pleasure at going'. Birdie merely smiled. He had, like Elgar, declined to give a name, but he told Emily that he thinks not of a 'Lady Somebody' so much as he thinks of 'the honour of my mother who deserves to have something more than a rolling stone for a son'.[6]

LOIS EVANS – PORTSMOUTH, ENGLAND

Lois Evans leans down to blow into the base of the grate. Coals flicker in the small kitchen – sliced laverbread (laver seaweed dipped in oatmeal and fried in bacon fat) sizzles in the pan. Has she heard about Elgar's five-dot dedication? Lois is an amateur musician, a singer. She can read free newspapers in the Temperance libraries set up around the docks to steer sailors from the temptation of the public houses. The *Cardiff Times* feels that the music of Elgar's Concerto 'seem[s] in its wildness to have come streaming down into England from the Welsh mountains'.[7]

Lois reaches down and riddles the coals. When will her husband Petty Officer Edgar Evans, 'Taff', taste laverbread again? Taff is one of Scott's former *Discovery* men, and Captain Scott is the only person in the world who could persuade him to return to that bleak place. Taff may be Scott's favourite bluejacket, his own 'Jack Tar', but Lois is sure he will not be chosen for the prestigious final journey to the Pole. He is not an officer, he is a petty officer, the top of the ratings class but still lower deck.

The pulley squeaks as Lois releases the rope from the cleat and lowers the children's clothes on the dolly. Long shorts for Norman, flannel bloomers for Muriel and rompers for Ralph. Since she has no gramophone, Lois must sing or hum familiar tunes – the *Terra Nova*'s record collection includes some Norwegian folk tunes and a bit of music hall fun like 'Stop Yer Ticklin', Jock', as well as a few popular songs by the classical singers Lois admires: Clara Butt and Enrico Caruso. As she begins the familiar domestic race to beat the infant school bell, Lois knows that she is not the only mother of Taff's children – not the only woman getting his children's tea – but she is his only wife. If Taff wrote a violin concerto, or more likely, a lower-deck ditty, would he dedicate it to her?

CAROLINE OATES – LONDON

The crisp white card of the Queen's Hall Winter Programme is on Caroline Oates's desk in Evelyn Mansions and beside it, a freshly ironed newspaper with its warm, papery scent. She prefers to stay in her London residence for the winter, though she keeps her servants on at Gestingthorpe Hall in Essex. Caroline notes that tonight's premiere of Elgar's Violin Concerto will be performed by virtuoso violinist Fritz Kreisler. The evening has been sold out for months, but she is a regular and valued patron of the Queen's Hall and perhaps she will see Sir Edgar Speyer while she is there.

Like Speyer, Caroline has a vested interest in both the Queen's Hall and the Antarctic. Caroline's son-in-law is a singer at the Queen's Hall and her son, Captain Lawrence Oates, 'Laurie', is a paying guest on Captain Scott's expedition. If her thoughts glance to tonight's programme and Elgar's enigmatic dedication, Caroline might think of pretty Florence Chambers from the West Riding, the only girl a youthful Laurie wrote to as an ardent admirer. Florence, now married, is still his ideal, the knight's lady. Rumour has it that he carries her 'colours', a photograph of her in his wallet, even now.[8] When will he settle down and bring home a wife?

Before tonight's official premiere, Caroline has business to attend to. The local servants her son has retained at his Inniskilling Guards base in Mhow, British India, must be paid. She needs to organise beaters for the Gestingthorpe village shoot. A servant, Ivy Finch, is in hospital – medicines cost money. Separate to all these transactions she writes: 'Expenses in London' in her accounts book. Beside it she writes an amount that is more than all the previous expenses combined. She does not choose to be more specific.

KATHLEEN SCOTT – CHRISTCHURCH, NEW ZEALAND

There have been balls (including a masquerade, all powder and patches) and Kathleen loves dancing, but ye gods, New Zealand's Little Englanders can be prim. All afternoon she has been sitting on a wooden packing crate on the *Terra Nova*, sewing on nametapes just like 'the good-mannered nice little wife of a junior officer'.[9] It doesn't suit her. She can only sustain the illusion for so long.

When Scott leaves their garden hammock in Te Hau each morning for expedition business, Kathleen shakes her long hair out and takes her shoes off, sinking her bare toes into the perfectly manicured 'English' lawn. Christchurch is stiflingly provincial, but somehow Te Hau, expedition agent Joseph Kinsey's summer house perched on a windy cliff above Sumner beach, is an oasis of privacy where she can be herself. The papers are delivered by bicycle boy. Between callisthenics, sunbathing and occasional sketching, Kathleen has time to catch up on events at home. Elgar has dedicated his Violin Concerto to five dots. Is it brilliant or absurd?

Kathleen wonders who her husband will choose to accompany him on the final push to the South Pole. Partly it will depend on who is fit enough physically and mentally at the time – but only partly. The explorers have a long, sunless winter to get through, and real and metaphorical crevasses to cross along the way. Besides, it's better to keep the men on good behaviour, guessing. She's told Scott many times that the Pole is 'a little thing to be done'. He must do it and 'leave no stone unturned'.[10] 'Capt South Pole Scott', as she refers to him, is the one she selected as the genetic donor, the 'father for my son'.[11] Now he must risk his life in white warfare to prove himself worthy of her choice.

QUEEN'S HALL, LONDON

Outside the Queen's Hall, gusts flap the flimsy awnings that cover the walkway from the street to the foyer doors. In the circle of light around the street lamps, fine rain blizzards. Guests walk quickly from their cars up a strip of sodden red carpet towards the light falling through glass foyer doors. Inside, men brush diamond droplets off their top hats. Women hand their damp fur coats to cloakroom staff, revealing sparkling opera jewels.

In the auditorium, there is the buzz of conversation. As the London Symphony Orchestra tune their instruments, whispers are exchanged behind a flutter of white programmes – 'Who is ". . . . ."?' Apparently Elgar has given the impression that it is 'a feminine spirit'. Is she here?

'Crowd enormous', notes Elgar's stalwart wife, Lady Elgar, taking her seat. 'Excitement intense'.[12] The atmosphere crackles with anticipation. Lady Elgar is a poet herself, familiar with the muse, and she is the inspiration behind her husband's famous *Salut d'Amour*. Tonight she knows that his enigmatic dedication has conjured intense interest, and this can only be a good thing.

Sir Edgar Speyer, taking his seat nearby, seems preoccupied. Lady Elgar knows that he sponsors Captain Scott – the newspapers report daily that Scott's ship is leaking, so is that what he's thinking about? Scott's orchestra is made up of over sixty men, thirty-three dogs and nineteen ponies. How will Sir Edgar keep abreast of expedition news once Scott leaves New Zealand in a few days' time? The press are suggesting there isn't space on the *Terra Nova* for Marconi's bulky ship-to-shore radio.

Lady Leonora Speyer knows that although there will not be a shellac 78-rpm record of tonight's Concerto ready before Captain Scott's ship leaves New Zealand for the Antarctic, she can play most of the themes for him when he returns. (During the process of composition, she helped Elgar with the fingering – she's possibly more familiar with it than Kreisler.) And although Scott will not have this Concerto, she has made sure that the *Terra Nova* is equipped with a piano, a pianola, two Monarch gramophones and several hundred records to boost morale.

As the Speyers glance around the auditorium, acknowledging their friends, Leonora might observe quietly to her husband that by the time Scott returns triumphant sometime in 1912, they could solve two mysteries: Elgar's '. . . . .' and who Scott has chosen to accompany him on the final leg of the journey to the South Pole. Though thirty-one men will overwinter in Antarctica, only Scott's chosen party will reach the Pole itself, an honour that is fiercely coveted.

Sir Edgar is preoccupied by money. As a banker, it is his business, but as the treasurer of Scott's latest expedition he has been party to recent negotiations for an exclusive news contract in return for much-needed funds. Central News will have exclusive rights to any expedition news for twenty-four hours after it's received. In order to honour this contract, the *Terra Nova* will have to sail from the Antarctic to New Zealand secretly, send a coded telegram across the world and then hide from view. The dimming lights might remind Sir Edgar that while it is relatively easy for Elgar's '. . . . .' to hide in the audience of the Queen's Hall, it is very difficult to hide a ship on the open sea.

Now Elgar walks to the conductor's position at the centre of the stage to a burst of applause. As he bows to the audience, some in the stalls observe that his gaze hovers briefly over Block A. Looking up from their press seats near the stage, the music correspondents notice that the composer is 'very much strung up', and no wonder.[13] From the wings, Fritz Kreisler walks briskly to his mark downstage left 'looking as white as a sheet'.

As the orchestra embarks on the opening bars, Kreisler holds his violin vertically in his left fist, his bow in his right. He looks down at the stage just in front of his feet and listens as waves of music pass through him – two flutes, two oboes, two clarinets, horns, trumpets, trombones, a tuba, timpani and strings. Already it is stirring, heroic, elevating. Instead of a gradual build-up, the music seems to perform a deep dive into the epicentre of the piece. The outside world falls away.

INTRODUCTION

Cherchez la Femme

ORIANA – DUNEDIN, NEW ZEALAND

Oriana Wilson is expected for dinner downstairs at Vernard, the Moores' home on the corner of Jubilee Street and Hawthorn Avenue. William Moore is in shipping, the success of his business requires connectedness, but as the time for her husband's return approaches, every ring of the telephone makes her jangly. It is as if her nerves are strung out like the telegraph wires. Taking advantage of the long February evenings, she likes to sit on the tough, papery flax that covers the Otago Peninsula and watch yellow-eyed penguins as they waddle to their burrows in the dunes. If she pauses and picks up the precious Zeiss binoculars that were an engagement gift from Bill, she can sometimes see albatrosses around Taiaroa Head, shags from Stewart Island, even sea lions swimming round from Sandfly.

She is practising drawing the 'yellows' to improve her signature emperor penguin thank-you sketch in the visitors' books of the many people who have hosted her during her wait in New Zealand. The Antarctic emperors of Cape Crozier are her husband's special subject. They endure long separation and yet their migratory instincts lead them back inexorably to their mate.

Straight after she met Bill, then a medical student at Cambridge, he wrote home to his parents in Cheltenham: 'Perhaps I will write a paper on Marriage someday with all the symptoms and signs of acute love. They are very interesting when you come to think of them.'[14] But he confessed to his father that try as he might to reduce the thing to 'symptoms' and 'signs', he felt 'like Mowgli at the time of "The Spring running"'. Ory thinks of herself as 'scraggy and thin', but her husband describes her as 'tall and elegant'.[15] Her quick, bird-like movements make her appear shorter than her true height, just shy of six foot, and her features are classical, complete with a Roman nose. Her startling iceberg-blue eyes can freeze anyone (except Bill) from twenty paces.[16]

What is the emperor reunion like, the tapping of beaks, the flash of yellow cheek? Bill always said when he saw his wife on the deck of the harbour tug in April 1904 – after that first *Discovery* expedition with Scott to the Antarctic – Oriana looked 'not a day older and far more beautiful'. That reunion 'beat a wedding hollow'.[17] The anticipation of another reunion like that helps to sustain Ory through this second trial. She looks down at her sketch. For some reason she always finds herself drawing one of the penguins with its back turned, walking away. Instead of the Antarctic landscape (which she has never seen), she sketches a few horizontal lines under each penguin to indicate foreground and background, leaving blank space for the gap between.

Back at the Moores', Ory dresses for dinner. From the guest bedroom window she can see the horizon beyond the Nugget lighthouse. She could be the first person to see the top masts of the *Terra Nova* as she sails home. But the ship is not due for six weeks. Perhaps tonight Bill will come to her in her dreams and when she wakes she will feel his presence in the room. She appears to him in much the same way: 'I dreamt of you singing at a piano,' he wrote 'impromptu, to a number of people'[18]. It is the portrait he carries in his mind as he trudges the weary distances, her image insulating him against the monotony, the pain and the cold. 'You looked lovely,' Bill said, 'because you were sitting with your back to a large window through which was a perfect glory of buttercups in a lovely hayfield in bright sunshine.'

. . . . .

Although they do not know it, around the time Ory and the Moores finish dining in Dunedin, Captain Scott's expedition ship is sailing past. The ship does not carry navigation lights. Leaving the Nugget lighthouse behind, the *Terra Nova* moves north across the mouth of Dunedin harbour on her way up the coast of South Island to Oamaru.

EMILY – ROME, ITALY

Emily converses with God in much the same way that she conducts her pen and ink conversation with her temporarily invisible son. As she sinks laboriously onto the kneeler in All Saints Anglican Church, her prayers for his safety ascend like the unravelling prayer scrolls in frescoed pictures around the city. After the service, she emerges into the glittering brightness of Rome and heads towards the British Library on Via Gramsci. She goes there every day to see the latest news telegrams, the long strips of type glued onto single sheets and pinned up on the noticeboard on the *piano nobile*, the first floor.

Emily prefers not to walk – she is short, with a tendency to be 'fairly plump' (she blames Jester's tea room in Rothesay for this).[19] She hides thinning strawberry-blonde hair with a prettily angled hat, under which her round face defaults to smiles. She hails a horse-drawn cab. Around her the landscaped gardens of the Villa Borghese sparkle, like an illustration from Hans Christian Andersen's 'Snow Queen'. She passes palm fronds weighted with snow, and she hears the 'whumpf' as it slides off the branches, and in the distance the jangling harness and the muffled sound of hooves. Even the park's centrepiece, Giovan Battista Embriaco's hydrochronometer, is frozen in time.

Emily knows that snow positively excites her son, Birdie, as it did his father. 'The snow takes my eye more than anything', Birdie tells her. 'How I would wallow in it if I could! If ever you find me preferring heat to cold, please hit me with the nearest thing to hand.'[20] Unlike Birdie, his mother can resist the urge to start a snowball fight these days, but she is naturally well covered and does not mind the cold as long as it is dry. The Roman climate suits her best and her rheumatism is always better here. The damp winters of Bute on the Scottish west coast leave her stiff and sore, and the humidity in British Malaya, where Emily married her husband and gave birth to two daughters, could be oppressive. In her mid-sixties now, Emily feels too old to go 'knocking about the world', but Rome, the crucible of western civilisation, is the exception.[21] Here in Italy, the air is generally crisp and the sun shines.

Back home in Bute it is an hour behind; what will her daughters be doing now? And Birdie, in the Antarctic? What is the time at the South Pole, that ultimate latitude, where all time zones, all the lines of longitude, merge? Emily likes an academic problem. Rome is where the educational revolutionary Dr Maria Montessori lives, and Emily can attend her lectures. As an ex-headmistress, Emily still has a passion for education and the kind of brain that earned her a top scholarship in the Queen's Certificate. To start with, Emily applied the traditional teaching techniques she had learned at the Teacher Training College in Cheltenham. Now there are other alternatives: child-led Montessori and teacher-led Steiner. Emily tends towards the Montessori approach, while Mary, 'May', her eldest, also a teacher, appreciates Steiner's interest in spiritual matters. Edith, 'Edie', the second-born, is a down-to-earth nurse. Emily had prayed that her youngest (her 'male investment', as Birdie jokingly refers to himself) would make a safe career choice.[22] It was a forlorn hope. With a missionary teacher for a mother and roving mariner for a father, adventure is in his blood.

Emily's carriage stops outside the British Library and she reaches into her purse for lire to pay her fare. In truth, going to the Antarctic was the 'last thing' she wanted her son to do. She told him, in no uncertain terms, that she would rather 'be dead'. It was not an attempt at dissuasion. It was a statement of fact. But she is not dead, although as she places her hand on the marble banister and starts up the long flight of stairs, she soon might be. There are only so many times seams can be double stitched. Stairs at least offer an antidote to that iconic Roman quartet: *carbonara*, *cacio e pepe*, *amatriciana* and *gricia*. Perhaps by the time her son comes home – sometime at the end of March or beginning of April – she will be able to see her toes.

. . . . .

Off the east coast of New Zealand, on the other side of the world, it is the middle of the night. The men of the *Terra Nova* are summoned to a meeting below deck. Plans are made to land two of them at Oamaru harbour shortly after midnight. No one on the mainland must see them. They must send a telegram to London in the morning and then take the train north to Christchurch. The *Terra Nova* will hide over the horizon to give the Central News Agency the contracted twenty-four-hour exclusive.

CAROLINE – QUEEN'S HALL, LONDON

Caroline Oates always favours the Grand Tier. It is 9 February 1913, so over two years since she was here at Queen's Hall for the premiere of Edward Elgar's now famous Violin Concerto back in November 1910. This time, she has come hear her son-in-law, the Irish baritone Frederick Ranalow, perform in the Proms. The democratising of music means there is the distinct whiff of inexpensive perfume in the Hall these days. Perhaps it's the new female violinists. The Queen's Hall Symphony Orchestra has just employed five – the first major orchestra to employ women. Whatever next? But whoever is playing, concerts, operas and plays help to distract Caroline from thinking about her son Laurie. She is expecting him back soon – April probably. She wonders how much he will have changed – what he will have missed most. Probably not culture.

Caroline has tried to raise her children with an appreciation of the fine arts, but with limited success. In his early twenties Laurie had written home after seeing *Othello*: 'It was very good but I am afraid I did not appreciate it.'[23] Caroline persisted. A refined appreciation of culture defined aristocracy. If one didn't 'appreciate it', one better jolly well try harder. It was rather like persuading a hunter to take a fence. The greener the horse, the bigger the approach circles. Caroline would, at any rate, prefer a larger circle than a lower fence. She tries to make her son act the part, but Laurie seems to take a perverse pleasure in 'slovenly dress and slouching gait' – he is often mistaken for a farmer.[24] Laurie can scrub up fairly well in the line of duty and cuts quite a dash in his Inniskilling Dragoons uniform. It is when that line blurs – 'the duty of lord of the manor of Gestingthorpe' – that his clothes seem to wilt on his frame. Caroline, on the other hand, is never less than immaculately presented, corset tightly laced and dark hair scraped back in a bun. She wears fashionably long chain necklaces and belts bristling with keys. Only her two eldest children can coax a loosening, a smile, a whimsical pose for the camera.

The lights dim and Caroline's son-in-law begins his oratorio. Caroline first set eyes on Ranalow in her study at Gestingthorpe Hall, his curriculum vitae in her hand. He'd answered Caroline's advertisement for a singing teacher for her eldest daughter Lilian. For a society girl, destined for a good marriage, singing is almost obligatory and

Ranalow's job was to enhance Lilian's eligibility before she did the London Season. It was not in the job description for him to marry her himself.

When Ranalow asked for her daughter's hand, Caroline was appalled. It went without saying that there were lines that one simply did not cross. Appreciating theatre, as she explained to Lilian, does not mean marrying into it. P.L.U.s, People Like Us, do not walk the boards. Caroline asked Ranalow how much he earned. When he told her, she declared, 'But Lilian spends that much on hats each year!'[25] Ranalow was tenacious and Caroline is not stupid. Keeping them apart would only have given the relationship Romeo and Juliet's credentials. She resigned herself to subsidising Lilian's lifestyle herself and the pair were duly married at St Mary's Gestingthorpe in January 1909. Shortly afterwards, her youngest son Bryan, aged twenty-six, became engaged to Alma, daughter of the local vicar at Pebmarsh, also a step down in society but without the dubious glamour of the stage. Laurie was 'wildly surprised' at the news, telling his mother, 'I feel quite out of it, all the family getting married. I suppose Violet [Caroline's youngest daughter] will be fixing herself up next.'[26]

Caroline tries to concentrate on the oratorio – Ranalow has toured Australia with Nellie Melba and there is no doubt he has a fine voice. But why do her children treat their class, their Oates inheritance, so lightly? The Gestingthorpe squire prefers horses to heraldry and snowy wastes to the green and pleasant land that is his ancestral home. Caroline's thoughts fly often to the Antarctic. She suspects that if Laurie were here in the Queen's Hall, he would eschew the 'fainting souls' and 'storms of bewilderment' on offer, in favour of his 'special' song: 'The Vly Be on the Turmut [The Fly Is on the Turnip]'.[27] She longs for her son's return when she will, as he asks, 'boil the fatted rabbit' – poacher-speak for 'fillet of beef, if you please'.

. . . . .

As Caroline's chauffeur drives her back to dine at her apartment in South Kensington, on the opposite side of the globe, the *Terra Nova* steams slowly east like a phantom ship towards Oamaru harbour. In the moonless night, men stand silently on deck sniffing the air.

Petrichor is the Latin term that the university men aboard use to describe this smell and the sensation it evokes: 'With what mixed feelings we smelt the old familiar woods and grassy slopes, and saw the shadowy outlines of human homes.'[28] One of the men describes the reason for their unease: 'It was of the first importance that the relatives should be informed of the facts before the newspapers published them.'

LOIS – RHOSSILI, GOWER, WALES

From the saddleback tower of the church, a bell rings out six miles over snow-covered fields to the north and far out over the Bristol Channel to the south. Lois knows that bell. Since the fourteenth century, St Teilo's bell has marked beginnings and endings, weddings, funerals and emergencies – wreckings and drownings. For Lois, it is the Rhossili messaging system. She and her cousin – now husband, Taff – were the first generation of children to be subject to the 1870 Elementary Education Act. Sitting side by side in the village school, they learned reading, 'riting and 'rithmatic to the rhythm of that ancient bell. But for all that learning, recently, in Portsmouth, she has known real hunger.

In the little stone church of St Mary the Virgin, Lois and her three children take their place among a congregation of relations: Beynons, Evanses and Tuckers. They were all christened in the Norman font here, all apart from Muriel, Lois's middle child, who was baptised 'abroad' in Portsmouth. Beyond the rector in his pulpit, the wooden choir stalls frame the altar. It was here in the St Mary's choir, singing duets with the previous rector's daughter Miss Lucas, that Lois had first been talent spotted. The rector's wife had given them both lessons in the large classical rectory down towards Rhossili beach, and there Lois was exposed to a genteel, servanted lifestyle with the expectation of secondary education. She also learned how to read sheet music and to sing an independent treble melody in duets. Lois's subsequent singing career was modestly successful, and she is sometimes identified locally as Lois 'The Voice'. She is a tiny woman – Taff can pick her up in one arm – by day a machine of perpetual motion, but at night, when the chores are done, she sings with the grace, clear confidence and good looks of a film star. Now in Rhossili church, among literate and illiterate (the congregation know the liturgy by heart), Lois can still hold the difficult long notes in 'Afferte Domino' (Psalm 29) without singing flat.

That evening, the Feast of St Teilo, patron saint of fruit trees and horses, is an excuse for a party in the bleakest time of year. There will be singing and mummers and wine (the vine is a fruit tree after all), and perhaps Lois's brother Enoch will involve the Gower Princess, their prize mare in the festivities. St Teilo's falls towards the end of a long winter; it is a good reason to get together and celebrate the return of spring. Lois knows that Taff relishes a good celebration. He has been King Neptune aboard the *Terra Nova* for the ritual of crossing of the Equator – the Lord of Misrule indeed. But it is difficult for Lois to feel very regal as she and her mother serve a modest cockle pie. They killed the pig as usual with the onset of winter, but roast pork is a luxury and the Beynons must be careful while their daughter and grandchildren are staying with them at West Pilton Cottage – four more mouths to feed is no small thing.

In letters home to Chapel Street in Portsmouth, where Taff still imagines Lois is living, he tells her, 'my belly fairly rumbles'. They all know he dreams of 'a glorious feed' on his return to Gower.[29] Last time Taff went to the Antarctic with Scott in 1901, he arrived back in New Zealand on April Fool's Day, 1904. From there the *Discovery* sailed back round the world, arriving in London in September. Lois hopes that her straightened circumstances are just a temporary belt tightening. Taff and his best friend, the Irishman and fellow Petty Officer Tom Crean, plan to buy a pub when they retire from the navy. For Lois it will mean a return to the familiar routine of her childhood, her parents owned the Ship Inn in Middleton when she was a girl. For Taff, food and a ready audience for his growing fund of anecdotes. Lois's father William Beynon says the grace and the meal begins. If Taff is back in September, perhaps they'll kill the next pig early and just live off cabbages and cockle pie.

. . . . .

On the other side of the world it is 2.30 in the morning. Three men climb over the side of the *Terra Nova* into a dinghy. When they reach Sumpter's Wharf on the south side of Oamaru harbour, they are confronted by the night watchman. The ship they have come from has failed to answer the lighthouse message: 'What ship?'. He tells the men that he could have them arrested. One of the men takes the oars and rows back, leaving the other two to negotiate. Once back on board the *Terra Nova*, the rower is asked what happened. 'We was attacked on the wharf by a man, Sorr,' he says, 'we came away quick & I told him nothing, Sorr.'[30]

KATHLEEN — THE PACIFIC

It is just before midnight on 9 February 1913 and Kathleen Scott is in her cabin aboard the passenger steamship SS *Aorangi*. The ship is christened after the Maori name for Mount Cook, but Kathleen is unimpressed, noting in her diary: 'This ship, smells.'[31] She is chronically seasick. She holds her hair out of the way as she vomits into the tin bucket provided. Instead of coming out to New Zealand via South Africa, as she did last time, she has chosen to cross the mercifully 'dry land' of America before sailing west from California across the International Date Line. They will lose a whole day. The *Aorangi* is due into Wellington, New Zealand on 27 February so that Kathleen will be recovered and ready to meet her husband Captain Scott when the *Terra Nova* returns there from the Antarctic.

Kathleen has dismissed any female passengers on the *Aorangi* on sight. Apart from her best friend, the celebrated contemporary dancer Isadora Duncan, women bore and irritate her in equal measure. The suffragettes, those women referred to by the RGS as 'bounders', are particularly bad. Men, on the other hand, are to be flattered and adored until they fall in love with her. Kathleen's thick, dark hair sets off a blue gaze that is direct, disarming and eloquent; she will not suffer fools. She believes she has 'bad legs' (hidden under a long skirt) but whenever a man enters the room, she positively sparkles.[32] She tries to decline their inevitable advances, however, aspiring to be a 'completely faithful wife', though at times Kathleen admits to an almost overwhelming urge to 'go out and love'.[33] On the *Aorangi* she has sought out the company of a discreet 'young South American'. She does not name him in her diary, but captions photographs of a brooding Latino with the Uruguayan surname: 'Gallinal'. It is not about conversation. He doesn't speak English. It is about worship.

Earlier that day Kathleen had ventured inside to the wireless room. The room is located just below the main deck, the shortest distance between the radio equipment and the aerials. It is a masculine domain, the sort of place in which she thrives. With the South American waiting patiently outside, she had watched the Irish operator at work. The wireless pioneer Guglielmo Marconi is a friend – radio waves, he tells her, offer invisible lines of communication that render physical cables obsolete. But the cable companies are not convinced. The Eastern and Associated Telegraph 'All Red Line' links up the pink-mapped countries of the British Empire. But a new Pacific network has laid this invisible line along which her boat sails. As Kathleen watched the uniformed radio operator pluck invisible messages out of thin air, his automatic pencil put her in mind of the 'planchette' in a séance, a method of communicating with spirits.[34]

Gallinal will not leave her side. If she'd had him in her studio at the bottom of her garden on Buckingham Palace Road, she would have had clay to mould into an ideal male form, dumb worship, Rodin's *The Thinker* in his prime. All she needs is an armature, but before that a wire mesh to form the shape on which to press the clay and, of course, the clay itself. Kathleen's hands are masculine, her thumbs bend backwards from the knuckle – the pliability of clay is almost like flesh, the sensuous pressure of touch. Before she left England, she had been working hard at her sculpture – four bishops for niches in Winchester College chapel, her first public monuments – but it wasn't quite enough. Since Scott has relinquished his expedition salary, along with some of the other officers, in order to afford to extend the expedition, her earnings have been absorbed into paying the cook and their son Peter's nurse, the dull necessities of daily life. As Scott constantly reminds her, it is important to keep up appearances.

'I bought a frock which cost fourteen pounds,' Kathleen tells Scott in her diary. 'It really is a stupid thing to have to do . . . but I feel I owe it to the cause to look decent, and they tell me I am looking very decent these days. That's because I am well and pay fourteen pounds for my frocks.'[35] Her husband is probably even now on board the *Terra Nova*, pressing creases down the front of his Royal Navy trousers in readiness for his return to New Zealand and press photographs. It is, Scott has told her, 'a serious consideration . . . you mustn't only look nice (which you can't help) but you must look as though there isn't any poverty at all . . . Kathleen dearest, I am dreadfully sensitive to appearances.'[36] The writer James Lees-Milne described the result of her 'trying to dress well' as 'a sort of aggressive no-taste'. Kathleen Scott is the 'worst-dressed woman' he knows.[37]

On this trip, she has tried to look presentable to dine at the captain's table, where those who have sea legs and healthy appetites eat with the confidence that their suppers will stay down. The mailboat fare: grape nuts for breakfast and beef tea served at 11 a.m. Despite bottles of Mothersill's (pink and brown seasickness tablets derived from belladonna that allow Britain to 'Rule the Waves'), dinner is more of a challenge. Kathleen is fine in a gale, it's insipid weather that turns her insides out. As she climbs into her bunk at the end of another nauseous day, she imagines thousands miles more of this to go with brief reprieves for a day ashore in Tahiti and Rarotonga. The tin bucket is beside her, the box of wave-ruling Mothersill's beside that. Roll on the 27th.

. . . . .

Far across the Pacific to the southeast, her husband's expedition ship, the *Terra Nova*, is steaming east to hide over the horizon from the New Zealand mainland. The distances are so vast that although the two ships are steaming towards each other, they cannot see one another round the curvature of the earth. In Oamaru, the lights go on in the harbour master's house on Arun Street. It is three o'clock in the morning. The harbour master's wife offers the two seabooted men a bed. They thank her politely but say that if it's all the same to her, they'd rather sleep on the floor.

PART ONE

Allegro

QUEEN'S HALL, LONDON

As the orchestral introduction draws to a close, the violinist Fritz Kreisler, slightly less pale now, feels more prepared for what is to come. He has heard the five themes that Elgar has woven into the warp and weft of the score. The mystery of '. . . . .' is still being discussed in whispers, but now there is a hush.

Kreisler knows that although the audience have glimpsed the future, he has to take them back to the beginning and carry them forward with him to the finish in approximately fifty-five minutes' time. At least with a narrative composer like Elgar, the structure takes charge. He focuses on the five themes. He must keep faith with the 'Hart', the voice with which to tell the story.

Kreisler raises his violin and places it between his left collarbone and chin. He lifts his bow and holds it hovering just above the strings. Ahead of him there is constant double-stopping, chords, virtuosic passage work, athletic leaps and sustained lyrical passages. The stamina needed is phenomenal. It's like an Olympic hurdle race and the starter has raised his flag.

Kreisler braces himself for the first movement, the Allegro. He waits as the orchestra funnels the vast heroic soundscape down towards a single musical note. Setting his bow across the strings, Kreisler catches that note and flings it out into the audience.

I

'I Hate Those Awful Goodbyes'

I JUNE 1910

WEST INDIA DOCKS, LONDON

High on the main mast, a flag flutters out – a white firework bursting against a brilliant blue sky. A cheer erupts, making the air tremble. The Ensign is broken. The white rectangle with its red crosses lifts in the roof-skimming breeze. It is the most prestigious flag in the Royal Navy, the red cross of St George with a miniature version in the upper canton. At this moment, it is the starter gun to the Pole. At the bottom of the mast is Lady Bridgeman, the admiral's wife, who now hands the flag halyard back to her husband.

Among the crowd jostling and cheering on West India Docks, there are five women. At this moment in the summer of 1910, the five have no idea that they share a common future. And yet, as the flag breaks, they move in unison, faces lifting to the sky, their wide hat brims cross-hatching the heat-shimmered surface. But there is another woman who has her back turned to the flag. She is looking in the opposite direction.

This woman has no hat, no gloves. She wears an impassive expression, cool and calm. In her old-fashioned decollete dress, she resembles a chaste Botticellian Venus. The woman's head is tipped back towards the bow of the wooden barque. Her long throat is exposed, her loosely streaming hair decorated with roses. It is nothing to her whether she cleaves the clean, cold waters of Newfoundland or flotsam and bloated rats.

She is the *Terra Nova*'s figurehead, the protectress but also the muse, the witch, the siren call of adventure, the song leading them on. Whatever the secret hopes and fears fluttering through full hearts on the crowded dock today, this wooden beauty is the only woman going all the way to the Antarctic.

The men from the Royal Geographical Society who have come down to the docks for the *Terra Nova*'s christening admire the elegant figurehead with her serene expression. She will take the expedition men, all of whom apart from Bill Wilson are here, basking in the adulation of the crowd, down to the Antarctic coast. But she will not stay. The men of the RGS stand apart from the 'unwashed' cheering crowd. They are nearly all agreed that no flesh and blood woman would, could or should ever explore, particularly the far south. Lord Curzon, the president-elect, is most decided. The RGS should not admit females.

> We contest in toto, the general capability of women to contribute to scientific geographic knowledge. Their sex and training render them equally unfitted for exploration; and the genus of professional female globe-trotters with which America has lately familiarised us* is one of the horrors of the latter end of the nineteenth century.[38]

Douglas Freshfield, Curzon's vice president, disagrees. He is all for women. Might he refer Lord Curzon to Mrs Freshfield's publications *Alpine Byways* and *A Tour of the Grisons*? There's little point. Women, Curzon assures Freshfield, will contribute nothing but their guineas to geography.[39]

Sir Clements Markham, the father of Antarctic exploration, is standing beside his wife on the deck of the *Terra Nova*, where she has just raised the ship's burgee. Sir Clements hopes that this expedition will restore credibility to a Society 'lost by the mismanagement of the female trouble'.[40] The Sixth International Geographical Congress agrees that exploration of the Antarctic region is the greatest piece of geographical exploration still to be undertaken. Scott's *Terra Nova* expedition must erase, not just the taint of ignorance from the map at the bottom of the world, but ignominy and dissent in the dispute over women. The British Antarctic Expedition must realign the RGS behind an ideal Britannia. Amid the noise and summer heat, the *Terra Nova*'s figurehead remains unflinching in the face of that vast responsibility.

ORIANA – LONDON

Oriana Wilson stands on the *Terra Nova*'s deck, looking out at the crowd. She has spent four years on Lord Lovat's remote Scottish moor

---

* One of the female globe-trotters in question was Josephine Peary (1863–1955), wife of Robert Peary, claimant of the North Pole. 'Jo' accompanied her husband to the Arctic several times and was the first white woman to give birth to a child within the Arctic circle.

in Fort Augustus with only her husband and black grouse for company, and now this. At least there is a breeze somewhere. It is cooler here than down below in her husband's cabin, where she has just finished stowing his gear. The London smog is almost fresh in comparison to the heavy reek of whale oil and shag smoke down there.

The ship pitches and yaws lightly on the rising tide. Fortunately, Ory is a good sailor. She boasts a stomach of solid iron (reinforced appropriately in the present context by a whalebone corset). A long skirt and a corset are not ideal working clothes aboard, but she has standards. Even dressed as a lady, she would not normally presume to work alongside the sailors unless it was necessary, but it is. As head of the scientific staff, Bill, her husband, must arrive in the Antarctic with the correct equipment. (He is, at this moment, in the Orkneys, learning how to catch whales in order to restock the larder in the Antarctic.) As her husband's unofficial scientific assistant, she knows what the correct equipment is.

While Bill has been embracing the character-building discomfort and drenching seas, Oriana, who his family have nicknamed his 'U.H.' (Useful Help), has provisioned his cabin to cover everything from art to ornithology via medicine. She has stowed Bill's watercolour paint-brushes with the scalpels, arsenic preserving fluid with antiseptic (both clearly labelled) and a stack of his favourite cartridge paper with gelatine sizing. In pride of place she has placed the page proofs of their precious grouse enquiry report, the culmination of four years' harmonious fieldwork together.

If Ory tries to pinpoint the exact moment her husband had agreed to return to the Antarctic, she would cite the invitation that arrived in Fort Augustus. It was sent by an exultant Scott immediately after he heard that Shackleton's Nimrod expedition had failed to reach the Pole. 'If I should go South again,' wrote Scott to Bill, 'you know there is no one in the world I would sooner have with me than you, though I should perfectly understand the ties which might make it impossible.'[41] Ory does not want to be that tie. But when she expressed her concerns for her husband's safety (and perhaps her ability to endure another long separation with an uncertain outcome), Bill responded emphatically, 'I cannot bring myself to think that you would fail.' It would be failure if he had to 'be afraid on her account' and it would be failure if he had to 'desert Scott if he goes'.[42]

Shackleton, now Sir Ernest Shackleton, apparently told his wife that he turned back within a hundred miles of the South Pole because he thought she would prefer 'a live donkey to a dead lion'.* Ory still wonders, which would Bill choose? Donkey or lion? Life or death? Bill's deep Christian faith means a tendency to prefix 'life' with 'this', 'this life': 'This is not our rest, and the sooner it's over, the sooner to sleep.'[43] Bill compares Christian life to a building – Ory and he must be vigilant for cracks or 'signs of settling'. Now on the West India Docks as Ory watches Lady Markham hand back the burgee halyards to her husband, she can at least confirm that there are no signs of settling down yet. She has not failed.

A brass band strikes up on the dockside. After breaking the flag there was a lull but now there is a renewed surge of energy, crowds jostling for a view, children on shoulders swinging rattles and streamers, in the harbour hooters, cheers, claxons, and the slap and splash of the heavy hemp ropes as they fall from the stanchions into the water below. The diminutive three-masted whaler, dwarfed by great liners and cargo-carrying ships, eases away from the dockside, out into the flood tide. The noise of the crowds behind is gradually replaced by the even rhythm of the steam engine, the slap of silty waves against the bow where the figurehead leans out, her right arm extended towards the unknown, towards *terra nova*.

When the flurry of departure settles and the ship's routine resumes, the logbook is brought for Ory's examination. She finds, to her surprise, that her name is entered on the first pristine page as the 'Officer of the Watch'. It is touching to find that her hard work below deck has not gone unnoticed. As Officer of the Watch, she wonders what her duties entail. There has never been a reason to write 'her' in the Royal Navy

---

* Shackleton had first gone to the Antarctic as a junior member of Captain Scott's *Discovery* expedition. He was invalided home with scurvy. In 1907, he published his intention to return to the *Discovery* base and try for the South Pole himself. Scott had kept his own plans to return private. Bill persuaded Shackleton to write to Scott to confirm that he would not use 'our old *Discovery* base' but find his own base, leaving the territory Scott had mapped to him (Shackleton to Scott, 17 May 1907, MS 1456/24 SPRI). When Shackleton arrived in the Antarctic a year later, he had to 'break my word to Scott and go back to the old base' (Shackleton to his wife Emily, 26 January 1908, MS 1537/2/16/3 SPRI). Bill told Shackleton that he wished Shackleton had done 'any mortal thing in the whole world rather than break the promise you made' (Bill to Shackleton, undated 1909, 28 SPRI). Bill later admitted to his friend John Fraser that he had broken with Shackleton over the matter.

rule book, but 'his duty [is] to keep watch on the Bridge . . . as the representative of the ship's master, to accept total responsibility for safe and smooth navigation'. Ory watches the sailors' practised movements as they work the ship smoothly and safely. The tidal flats slip away on either side: Surrey Quays, Greenwich and Woolwich. At 8 p.m. the ship docks at Greenhithe for the night and Ory disembarks. Tomorrow it will carry on to Portsmouth en route to Cardiff. It has been a thrilling time – alive with possibility. It seems entirely in keeping when, the next day, Charles Rolls completes the first continuous cross-Channel return flight in his Wright Flyer from Dover to Sangatte in ninety minutes.

3 JUNE 1910

BILL WILSON – ORKNEY ISLANDS, SCOTLAND

In the fishing grounds of Orkney, unaware of 'Mrs Wilson O.O.W. (RN)' or Rolls's feat of aviation, Ory's husband Bill stands on the firing platform of a whaler, the heavy gun loaded. His whaling instructor is Henriksen, a young Viking of thirty-three years. 'Often I tink,' Henriksen assures Bill, 'I know vat dat vhal tink in my het.'[44] In his letter to his wife, Bill narrates Henriksen's pigeon-English for her entertainment: 'I tink I know vhat dat val will tink – dat chap – he tink, ven I go down, I go dis way – ja – den I tink, ja, dis way; den I tink again, dat vhal he go dis vay, but den he go dis vay, 'gain I tink – so I go not dis vay, but dat vay – so – dat feller he come and blow an' I shoot – ja!'

As the Orkney whale feints this way and that, trying to shake his nemesis, on Friday 3 June another Norwegian, the explorer Roald Amundsen, slips quietly out of Christiania (present-day Oslo). He has borrowed his friend and mentor polar explorer Fridtjof Nansen's ice ship, the *Fram*. He has made sure that the general assumption is that he is heading north, embarking on an Arctic drift. Unlike the continental Antarctic, the Arctic is a frozen sea, so Amundsen and the team aboard the *Fram* will drift across the Arctic, moving with the ocean current.

Days after Amundsen's unobtrusive departure, Bill returns to the *Terra Nova* for the journey to Cardiff. He notices his wife's name in the ship's log. A private joke is one thing, but the log will be inspected in every port so he feels he has to insure against misinterpretation – she is not a 'globe-trotter' and he does not want her to be mistaken for one. 'Ory was on board but not I,' he writes at the beginning of his expedition journal. 'Ory's initials may be seen in the *Terra Nova* log as one of the Officers on Watch . . . I did not put them there or suggest it, but they are there.'[45]

Bill has tried to impress upon the men of the *Terra Nova* that anything they write down could be used by a journalist looking for a story. His experience on Scott's previous *Discovery* expedition has made him wary – the unscrupulous press stop at nothing for sensational headlines and it disgusts him. In the Antarctic, when they can only send and receive letters once a year when the supply ship gets through the sea ice, a misunderstanding might take a year to correct. Scott has produced an official 'confidentiality notice' to be included in every letter home as a precaution.

If Bill was really worried that 'Watch Officer Ory' might be mistaken for a 'New Woman' or worse, a hunger-marching suffragette, he might have referred to her as 'Oriana', or even 'Mrs Wilson'. But the 'joke' was being written into the *Terra Nova* log about the same time that he was pidgining the telepathic Norwegian whale captain to Ory in his letters. Part of him realises that the sailors meant it as a piece of harmless fun, as flattery even, and besides, she deserves appropriate recognition:

> These were days of very hard work for Ory, as she has had all the London packing to do while I was really making holiday . . . She has had no holiday, and the weather has been very hot . . . [She] got all my clothes ready for the whole voyage and had them packed for Madeira, the Cape, Australia, New Zealand and the Antarctic. Left all to her, and she managed it perfectly. Then when I got back and had to work late every night writing and drawing, she would not be sent to bed until I was near coming, and so we both got tired out with very short sleep, but happily not irritable with it, and I shall always remember these days as days of perfect companionship, the best of all good things that a wife can bring at such times.[46]

6 JUNE 1910

EMILY – LONDON

To the right of the main entrance to Waterloo Station there are two horse-drawn cabs with their backs to the station's entrance. Beyond them stretches a line of black motorcars, their cabs open. The uniformed porters, who have been leaning on their luggage trolleys, straighten up and adjust their peaked caps. The station is in the throes of what the London and South Western Railway company call 'the great transformation'. The chaos works to the porters' advantage. They are in demand to navigate passengers from the street outside to the correct platforms for their trains. Birdie, his mother Emily and sister May want the Portsmouth train.

'The porter who took our things thought it would go from number two platform, while another porter, with whom he discussed the question, had heard a rumour that it would go from number one. The station-master, on the other hand, was convinced it would start from the local.' Jerome K. Jerome's *Three Men in a Boat* had found themselves in exactly the same situation when leaving Waterloo to catch their boat, eleven years earlier. Characteristically, Birdie attempts to keep things light. He took the train up from Portsmouth on the 3rd and they have had a precious few days. May looks across at her brother. To her, Birdie seems worried and overworked and much older in his ways. 'Told me the last time we dined together at the Strand Palace that he had a feeling he had left the R.I.M. [Royal India Marine] for ever but that he was absolutely confident of returning from the Antarctic.'[47] Their few days together puts May in mind of a line from Robert Browning: 'Never the time and the place / And the loved one all together!'[48] May is here to support Emily. Both she and Birdie know how upset their mother can become with what May calls the 'recurring sadness of farewells'.[49] The three of them follow behind the station porter at a steady pace.

Inside, the station seems to trap the summer sun like a greenhouse. The ambient noise level is loud, echoing with the sound of footsteps, the metal trolley wheels and the kiosk hawkers shouting their trade. Emily proceeds not unlike the portly pigeons that strut the crowded concourse. Birdie's sister May, feeling 'very nervous & highly pitched', follows her mother to a two-storey structure like a bookcase with a clock.[50] It is a mahogany noticeboard, divided into three unequal columns. From left to right metal plates reveal the time of the train, the destination and the platform. The information plates are adjusted on a rolodex that purrs as the plates flick around.

Emily purchases two platform tickets and they pass through a pair of ornate metal gates. They have followed the porter as instructed but when he does eventually alight on a platform, they can't help wishing he'd chosen another. From where they are standing, they can see that the opposite platform is stacked with coffins. Emily does not need coffins to remind her. She has forgiven Birdie his 'thunderbolt', that four-word telegram: 'Arrive 27th. Appointed Antarctic.'[51] But only because Christians forgive. Birdie has never 'forgotten that you once said you hoped you would be dead before I started on anything so foolhardy'.[52]

For all Birdie's optimism, Emily has a growing sense of conviction that this is the end. That this is the last time she will ever see her son. Birdie protests that 'life is just as precarious up the Gulf, where I was going, as in the Antarctic'.[53] Emily is not convinced. At least as an officer in the Royal Indian Marine he is posted to places that are on the map. Places, mostly coloured the pink of the British Empire, with place names that she has either visited or taught or, in some cases, both. She knows that the Empire needs men like her son to do their imperial duty, to 'found colonies and settle them', as John Ruskin put it, making send-offs like this one her selfless obligation.

If Emily pauses for breath, shuts her eyes and thinks back to when she was Birdie's age, she would remember a young woman with sea spray in her face standing on the deck of a ship sailing out to Further India. She left the charted waters of the school in Sidmouth where she had risen to headmistress for the uncharted waters of a missionary school in Penang. There she met Captain Alexander Bowers, a fifty-year-old merchant sea captain. Alexander's father was a carpenter from Greenock, but Alexander was ambitious – while working for the Burma Steamship Company, he'd earned a fellowship of the RGS for charting the 1,000-mile Irrawaddy River. Together Emily and Alexander sailed all over Further India, opening up new trading posts and mapping coastline. Now as Emily battles to hold back tears, she knows that although she wants her children safe at home, she had, at their age, embraced high adventure. Apart from her rheumatism, Emily still has a robust constitution, but May has a weak chest, and recently left London in hopes of improving a (possibly tubercular) cough. Now in the fresh air of Bute, she is determined to outswim her brother's distance record beyond the pontoon.

'I can't bear seeing people crying,' Birdie told his mother once, 'and so I am keeping well clear of the wives of some of our sailors.'[54] For those for whom tears threaten, he suggests that it only requires a deliberate change of attitude to see the thing in a positive light. Emily concentrates on the train. Behind the blackened funnel of the steam engine is a line of carriages from first to third class. It is the iron representation of England's social structure. One must never descend from the 'lower middlers' of second class to the wooden benches of third. One must never assume that one can buy a plush first-class ticket, without having earned it through marriage or knighthood or, in the case of the recently lionised Sir Ernest Shackleton, both. And if one is Emily, who has come a long way from the humble tailor shop on St George's Place, Cheltenham where she spent the first few years of her life, one must leave the past completely behind in order to rise.

Birdie tells Emily that he will be sailing under the White Ensign of the Royal Yacht Squadron. From modest beginnings as a naval cadet on the training ship HMS *Worcester*, Birdie is taking their Bowers name to these heady heights. With heavy hearts, the three Bowerses follow the porter down the platform to the middle of the train.

In Emily's experience, most things improve with practice. It is the failsafe technique taught her at the Cheltenham Teacher Training College – a technique she has applied with considerable success to times tables, spelling, algebra. Now, as she steels herself to say goodbye yet again to her only son, she must acknowledge that the exception proves the rule.

Birdie has been chosen from 8,000 applicants. 'To imagine such a thing is mere chance is out of the question,' he tells her. 'It simply had to be – nothing could be clearer.'[55] It is the term they use in letters to each other: 'D.V.' (*Deo volente*) – God willing. Surely Emily must agree that this is a perfect example of D.V. In the back of his mind Birdie suspects that he has not been quite 'fair to his mother', but she cannot blame him for accepting the opportunity.[56] He hopes to make her proud.

Besides, the main focus of the expedition is his mother's second religion, Education. The British Antarctic Expedition (BAE) is taking equipment to make observations in biology, geology, glaciology, meteorology and geophysics. They will be making new copy for the schoolbooks, not just reciting them.

The Portsmouth train makes to depart. Bareheaded seamen lean from the third-class windows waving caps, sailors' wives weep openly. Birdie, averting his eyes, steps onto the train. With a grating sound he pushes the window of the train door down and looks out. The shrill note of the guard's whistle. Doors clunk shut along the train.

Emily sees the 'Dear Boy' before her. It is the face of her only son, the child she and her late husband Alexander christened 'Henry'. He has her reddish fair hair, her husband's long, beaky nose, her downwards-slanting eyes and his very own cheery smile. He promises her he will write before he leaves. He will send her a letter from Cardiff. He will start the letter right now in the train.

As the train pulls out, her suspicion becomes a certainty. She knows this is the end. It is a definite presentiment and she is frozen, powerless. She wants to be already dead. The noise of the train is deafening, the hiss of the brakes releasing, the metal wheels on the track. Birdie is leaning out of the window, his words getting fainter as the train moves away: 'I am perfectly confident without a shadow of doubt that I shall come back to you . . . no worse and I hope a better man . . . God bless and keep you, my dearest mother, till our certain meeting a year or two hence, as we [leave] each other to-day.'[57]

15 JUNE 1910

LOIS – GOWER

Nearly everyone in South Gower seems to be streaming towards the Worms Head. Lois Evans and her three young children join her parents, the Beynons, and Aunt Sarah Evans, who is also her mother-in-law, as they filter into the crowd. Sarah's white widow's bonnet bobs on the back of her tight grey bun as she strides purposefully south. Sarah is as broad as Lois is slender, but both move quickly over the familiar terrain, their two fields planted with turnips and swedes.

They are heading for the promontory shaped like a giant sea serpent, the 'wurm' that marks the most westerly tip of the Gower peninsula. They should be able to see the *Terra Nova* steam past on its way from Cardiff to Madeira. Taff has told her he will look out for them. To get there they must walk across the rocky causeway along the large, flat-topped 'Inner Head' over a natural rock 'Devil's Bridge' and over a 'Low Neck' out to the 'Outer Head'. It is a mile long. Lois's older children can walk with their cousins if they promise to take care over the bridge, but baby Ralph is tied to her back in a woollen shawl. Lois's niece Sarah stayed in Cardiff to see the *Terra Nova* off, but Lois has chosen to be here on the Worms Head, away from the publicity, good and bad, that surrounds any group of sailors on a binge before a long voyage.

The Welsh have excelled themselves. There are two men with the Welsh surname Evans in the *Terra Nova* crew. One is an officer, Lieutenant Edward Evans, 'Teddy'. The other is Taff, a rating, Lois's husband. Teddy is Scott's second-in-command. He will captain the *Terra Nova* out to Cape Town, where Captain Scott will meet them and continue on to Melbourne and then New Zealand. Teddy's wife Hilda is from New Zealand. Along with the other officers' wives, Oriana Wilson and Kathleen Scott, Hilda will take a liner to the South Island, the *Terra Nova's* final port before it sets off to Antarctica. Taff's wife Lois has never been abroad, but the expedition funds do not extend the privileged liner ticket to her.

The Evans name means that dignitaries of Cardiff have fallen over themselves to identify Wales with the expedition. They've offered free docking, free coal, defects made good, an office and staff placed at their disposal. They have donated 100 tons of Insole's best Welsh steaming coal, 300 tons of patent fuel and the bulk of their lubricating oils. But when Lois visited the *Terra Nova* at the docks earlier in the week, she noticed that the ship was so heavily laden it settled deeply in the water. Seams in the forepeak, usually well above the water line, were leaking. Taff predicted that unless they could locate those leaky seams, it would mean half an hour to an hour's pumping every watch.

Rumours have already reached Lois that Taff sat between the mayor and Captain Scott at the send-off dinner and was the only one outside the officer class asked to make a speech. Lois doesn't like to think of how much 'lubricating oil' he had taken on board before he did that. Some of the folk who have just arrived from Cardiff decline to answer her tentative enquiries into the state of Taff's head that morning. But they tell her that when the sailors hoisted the Cardiff flag at the fore and the Welsh flag at the mizzen, someone pointed to the flag and asked them why they didn't have a Welsh leek. They were told that they didn't need one, they already had a leak in the forepeak!

Taff's quick wit and his good humour endeared him to Captain Scott. The letter of appointment wasn't so much an invitation as a foregone conclusion. Taff had served under Scott in the Antarctic on the *Discovery* expedition. Although the letter was a surprise, Lois is proud that her husband has been singled out. In March the previous year, Taff was given two weeks to report to the West India Docks in London to begin refitting the *Terra Nova*. Within a fortnight, Lois lost her husband and the security of his full navy salary. Unlike the *Discovery* expedition, funded chiefly by the Royal Society and the Royal Geographical Society, this would be a private venture. This time Taff's salary, and therefore Lois's allowance, is largely dependent upon Scott's fundraising skills. But Taff trusts Scott and answered the Captain's summons without hesitation, moving into shared lodgings in London's docklands. Transforming a whaler into an expedition ship in two months was all-consuming work and Lois has hardly seen her husband since he left, nor the children their father.

When they arrive at the furthest point of the Worm, they rest in the thick grass. The sky is swirling with breeding seabirds: herring gulls, guillemots, razorbills, kittiwakes and the whirring puffins. When Lois and Taff were young they used to find the small cleft that forms a blowhole, the wurm's nostril. A small handful of sand thrown into it is blown back into the air. If you put your ear to the ground, you can hear the deep noise of bellows in motion. They all know the old Gower saying: 'The old Worm's blowing, time for a boat to be going.'[58]

Watching now through the shared binoculars, Lois sees the *Terra Nova* steaming towards the Breaksea Light Vessel in a flotilla of smaller boats. After a while, the pilot boat peels off. That will be the officers' wives, who sailed the first 30 miles with the ship before disembarking. She had not been invited to join their party. Lois continues to watch them out past Lundy Island, where they begin to face the headwind and the Atlantic swell. To the sailors in the group, it seems that in spite of her deeply laden condition, the *Terra Nova* is breasting each wave in splendid form. With her deck cargo, she reminds them of 'a little mother with her child upon her back'.[59]

The ship is almost over the horizon. They must return before the rising tide cuts them off. Wilfred Beynon, Lois's cousin, remembers that 'I don't know what it is, but once you put a sheep out on Wurm's Head, it can't be kept away from there . . . Once they've had a taste of the grass out there, they'll never be safe again.'[60]

16 JUNE 1910

CAROLINE – GESTINGTHORPE

Caroline Oates's uniformed butler, Oscar Minchin, brings the post to the morning room at Gestingthorpe Hall. The room is square, with one side almost entirely taken up by full-height, south-facing sash windows. The windows, shaded by striped awnings that can be wound out from the facade, look onto the south lawn towards the Belvedere and on to the newly planted avenue of lime trees. She has planted the trees to screen Hill Farm and focus on Laurie's favourite view: the Leys, a foxy coppice. With the windows open, tendrils from the Virginia creeper that covers the south facade escape across the sill.

Caroline and her son parted privately after the ceremony in London. She did not go to Cardiff to see him off. Laurie had deliberately told her how much 'I hate those awful goodbyes'.[61] Two days before he left, she sent him a cheque for £50 (£2,500 today). That was the kind of unsentimental goodbye one couldn't hate. She knew he would not be able to spend it in Antarctica, but at the rate he got through money, it would probably be gone before he ever set foot on that icy shore.

Caroline is meticulous. She opens the letter with a silver paper knife. She will add it to the pile. There are letters in that pile from his army postings in Egypt, South Africa and India, but this one has a Cardiff postmark. According to Laurie, the official *Terra Nova* send-off had been a trial. First there were the visiting women, 'a great nuisance as we can't get really dirty', and then the mayor and his cronies. 'I never saw such a mob – they are Labour Socialists,' he told her. 'The only gentleman I have seen come aboard is the telephone operator.' But Caroline can tell that Laurie is enjoying himself. He stayed with a Colonel Herbert near Cardiff to avoid the 'nibs and nobs', and Herbert's young daughter asked him if he was a pirate. 'She was quite disappointed when she heard that I was not.'

There is something faintly rakish about 'pirate' and it is surely better than 'farmer'. Laurie insists on wearing his bowler on the back of his head and his most battered Aquascutum suit. He wears his brown hair shaved almost to the scalp. No wonder Herbert's daughter was confused. She is not alone. Caroline is still trying to come to terms with the rapid turn of events that have led to this moment. She still has Laurie's 'confession' letter neatly filed in her desk:

I have now a great confession to make. I offered my services to the Antarctic expedition . . . under Scott . . . Now I don't know whether you will approve or not but I feel that I ought to have consulted you before I sent in my name. I did not do so as I thought there was very little chance of my being taken (as cavalry officers are not generally taken for these shows) . . .

Points in favour of going. It will help me professionally as in the army if they want a man to wash labels off bottles they would sooner employ a man who had been to the North [sic] Pole than one who had only got as far as the Mile End Road. The job is most suitable to my tastes . . . The climate is very healthy although inclined to be cold . . .

Points against. I shall be out of touch for some considerable time. It will require a goodish outlay of about £1,500 as I have offered to subscribe to the funds . . .

P.S. I am sorry this letter is so disgracefully written but I am in bed.[62]

There was always an amusing excuse for Laurie's disgraceful letters, but for all the disarming humour and self-deprecation, the central message is crystal clear – he had not consulted her. It is the first time he had ever 'offered funds' of this magnitude without doing so. Going to the Antarctic, he argued, though not absolutely necessary, would, in his opinion, be well worth the outlay.

Hitherto, Caroline has kept a tight hand on Laurie's 'outlays'. She has an excellent head for figures, he does not. Laurie failed his exams at Eton, his Cambridge tests and the army entrance. He still cannot spell or add, and he has a weakness for buying thoroughbreds, but in spite of it all, the leavening humility to recognise that 'if you were the same way with your money as I am with mine we should soon be in the soup'.[63] And yet he offered Scott a fortune. What could Caroline have done? Refused? Forced Laurie to retract his offer, to go back on his gentlemanly word? It is his money. He is nearly thirty and lord of the manor of Gestingthorpe. There was nothing she could do. She could not even say goodbye.

Horses are a comfort, riding is the Oates family cure-all. Caroline is aware that she must keep up appearances. She reaches for the servant's bell to the right of the mantelpiece to summon her lady's maid, Isabella Longhome, for her lightest summer riding habit to wear over her corseted summer dress. She looks her best in her tailored riding clothes, small bowler riding hat tipped slightly forward from the crown of her greying head. George Baker, the groom, might bring the grey mare to the front door where she can climb the stone mounting block and lower herself into her side saddle.

Leaving the large Georgian house behind her, Caroline rides out of the semi-circular carriageway. If she chooses to go left, she will pass the Gestingthorpe lodge, if right, she will go through the dappled shade of the great beech and lime trees out into the main road. On the opposite side of the unmetalled road, the brick tower of St Mary the Virgin rises from its grassy graveyard. To the left is the village school, a squat building of two rooms which abuts the Reverend Bromwich's vicarage garden. Increasingly, Caroline has noticed that some of the village children forget to doff their caps to her. If she does not recognise the offender, she asks for their name in order to register her disapproval in a letter to the school.[64]

She rides past fields of yellowing barley, a hazy sea of alternately folding valleys receding into a blue distance. There are about a hundred men employed on the land across the fifteen farms of the parish to plough, drill and harvest. Gestingthorpe is totally dependent on the power from heavy horses – the size of each farm business is gauged by its number of horses. The kings of the land are the Suffolk Punches, so sturdy with their thick necks and feathered feet, brasses clinking. Caroline rides past cattle grazing along Belchamp Brook, past the shining surface of Brundon Mill's pond until she reaches East Anglia's oldest grazed common pastures, the Auberies Estate, where Thomas Gainsborough's now ancient oak tree spreads its branches.

Caroline is interested in art. She is involved in commissioning a statue of Gainsborough for his nearby hometown of Sudbury. His masterpiece, *Mr and Mrs Andrews*, which features this very oak tree, exudes an easy landowner's confidence that eludes Caroline. (She wasn't born to this life, though that's a secret she guards fiercely.) A young squire, like Laurie, wearing a rakish tricorne hat, shotgun cocked over his arm, stands nonchalantly beside a lady in a sky-blue silk dress. The area where the lady's left hand should be is raw canvas, unfinished. An artistic puzzle. The blank area represents what Caroline calls 'life's perplexities'.[65] Kicking her mare up the small rise to the oak, she can see the wide branches spread benevolent and yellow-green. The shady earth is dry and bare, and there is the animal smell of cattle that have sheltered here. Some say the oak is a living example of the old order.

Together with Laurie's sudden assertion of independence, Caroline is concerned about the state of the country. The People's Budget has introduced unprecedented taxes on the lands and incomes of the wealthy landowning classes. Is the Oates family immune from the politics of Westminster? Are they safe within the ornate gold frame of their oil-painted countryside? Caroline suspects not. Now, more than ever, they need that tricorned squire to be visible, reinforcing his manorial position. For even here in ultra-conservative Gestingthorpe, in the depths of the country, the children do not doff their caps.

16 JULY 1910

KATHLEEN — LONDON

In the nursery on Buckingham Palace Road, Kathleen Scott lifts the tiny fingers from around her index finger. Peter is a blond, tousled, ten-month-old toddler crawling around the nursery on fat, bandy arms and legs. This is the most heart-wrenchingly awful thing she has ever done. 'In agonies and ecstasies of reciprocated love', Kathleen releases the pressure of his pudgy grip, unstitching the strongest bond she has ever known.[66]

When she married Captain Scott just under two years ago on 2 September 1908, she had not been in love with him. His love was not requited. He had been the right man to be the father for her son, he had the requisite 'lion' genes. But after Peter's birth, 'I fell for the first time gloriously, passionately, wildly in love with my husband . . . He became my god; the father of my son and my god. Until now he had been a probationer, a means to an end. Now my aim, my desire, had been abundantly accomplished.' Until that moment she had wondered why she had saved herself. 'Now my determined, my masterful virginity, sustained through such strong vicissitudes, seemed not, as I had sometimes feared, mere selfish prudery, but the purposeful and inevitable highway to this.' And yet, there was a cost. The price of passion was the agony of unstitching from Peter. 'Looking back over my life I can think of nothing that hurt more hideously.'[67]

Kathleen is a woman. It is all very well for her maternal instincts to soften her resolve but she must not allow them to soften her husband's. Days before her marriage and before Peter's birth, she endorsed notices published in newspapers to the effect that neither would affect his plans for the South Pole. The man she refers to as 'Capt South Pole Scott' cannot renege on their unspoken agreement.[68] While she will ensure the continuation of his name biologically, he will create their historical name, based on his reputation. If he wavers, she's ready: 'You shall go to the Pole. Oh dear me, what's the use of having energy and enterprise if a little thing like that can't be done?'

The cab arrives at the front door. Scott's mother Hannah is ready to take Peter to stay in Henley-on-Thames, where she lives with her married daughter. Kathleen is worried that they will feminise her baby son – give him warm baths, Lord Fauntleroy-curls and petticoats. It will be 'four months of enchanting growth that I should be shut out from and would never come back again'.[69] Kathleen realises that he would not know her when she came back. She even forces herself to imagine that he might 'look to someone else, maybe, for protection from me'.

At least if she accompanies Scott to New Zealand – to the last port before Antarctica – she can ensure that he does not suffer from what he calls his 'black moods', or at least not so much that his men lose respect for him as a leader.[70] She can also try to get pregnant. By the time she returns she wants to offer Peter the best present of all, a brother. In the meantime she will write letters and telegrams to Hannah, and through her try to maintain communication with her babe. She leaves photographic portraits for Hannah to show Peter his parents so that their faces, at least, will be familiar to him. There is nothing more she can do. Outside the cab meter is ticking around. They need more money, not less. She must go. Kathleen walks herself down the garden path, closes the gate behind her and gets into the cab. 'I followed my husband.'[71]

In the first daze of separation, the Scotts emerge from their cab onto the echoing concourse at Waterloo Station. As the station porters begin loading their luggage onto rattling trolleys, Kathleen leads the way through the crowd of press to the platform for the 11.35 a.m. boat train to Southampton. On the far side of the ticket barrier, Mrs Oriana

Wilson and Mrs Hilda Evans (wife of Lieutenant 'Teddy' Evans, who is captaining the *Terra Nova* at present) are waiting beside a passenger carriage with the new London & South West Railway livery, mint green lined with chocolate brown. Since 1910, the LSWR has begun electrifying some suburban services, but at the far end of this platform, the boat train engine belches black coal smoke. From Southampton they will go to Cape Town in comfort aboard the mail steamboat HMS *Saxon*. Scott has given Teddy instructions to save coal and to use the sails as much as possible, so Scott and 'the harem' will arrive first. Kathleen and the others are ushered towards the train by the waiting crowd – Sir Edgar and Leonora Speyer are among the well-wishers – when suddenly a familiar voice echoes through the concourse:

'Three cheers for Captain Scott.'

It is Ernest – now Sir Ernest – Shackleton who is, in Kathleen's opinion, 'rotten; bad blood and no good at all'.[72] How typical of him to make a public show of sportsmanship. But it seems he has not finished.

'Three cheers for Mrs Scott.'

All thoughts of Peter are forgotten. Kathleen rushes for the open door of the train carriage. She has a leatherbound diary with a brass lock and key – she will confide her feelings about Shackleton to its pages: 'I would willingly assist,' she writes, 'at that man's annihilation.'[73]

2

Pen & Ink Conversations

I JULY 1910

EMILY – BUTE

In her ground-floor flat in Ardbeg, Rothesay on the Isle of Bute, Emily receives her weekly letter from Birdie. Ever since he boarded the naval training ship HMS *Worcester* at the age of fourteen, he has rarely missed the weekly 'pen & ink conversation'.[74] Birdie started the letter on 22 June before the *Terra Nova* reached Madeira, where it will stock up before continuing to Cape Town. He is in charge of stores and knows that once they dock, he will be too busy to write properly. He hopes that Emily too has had little time to think and that the change of atmosphere from London smog to Western Isles 'bucked you up in every way'.[75] Continuing, Birdie tells his mother:

> The person who has most impressed me among us is Dr Wilson, whom you will remember to have just seen – a tall clean-shaven chap. He is the soundest man we have, a chap whom I would trust with anything. I am sure he is a real Christian – there is no mistaking it – it comes out in everything. He also has his *Discovery* experience, and though he is not ready to talk, can be squeezed for information at odd times. People like myself always have their tongues hanging out for information on the Antarctic.[76]

Emily sits in the garden they share with the Maxwells upstairs and thinks of her son with his 'tongue hanging out'. Birdie has always had an unquenchable thirst for anything Antarctic. He is an enthusiast by nature and cannot even affect the laconic indifference of the upper classes. Sometimes Emily could kick herself around the room. From a gunboat in Burma, Birdie, his feet blistered from sunburnt decks, begged her for news about icy wastes and longed for the chance to 'worry' the Pole – 'If only they will leave the South Pole itself alone for a bit,' he said, 'they may give me a chance.'[77] Emily now realises that she fanned the icy flames by sending newspaper cuttings about the American explorers Cook and Peary arguing over which of them had first discovered the North Pole, book reviews of Scott's *The Voyage of the Discovery* and even Shackleton's *The Heart of the Antarctic*.

With her son's letter on her lap, she looks up. Her eyes travel around her wrap-around panoramic view: to the north, the intense blue of Loch Striven, east past the rocky promontory with the white finger of Toward lighthouse, the mouth of the Firth of Clyde and Wemyss Bay ferry port and on southwards the bright green island of Great Cumbrae and the Irish Sea. She glances at the *Terra Nova* headed paper – the penguin logo has a protruding beak, calling her son's prominent nose fondly to her mind: 'I was Polly at Sidcup,' Birdie notes academically, 'Beakie at Streatham, Kinkie on the *Worcester*, Bosun Bill on the *Dufferin*, Nosie on the *Fox*', and now he is 'Birdie'.[78] As an ex-headmistress, Emily is clear about the distinction between name calling and nicknaming. All his life Birdie has referred to his people as 'Bower birds' and his home as the 'nest of Bower birds'.[79] And so Henry becomes Birdie, even to her.

The letter has been franked with a circular mark 'Funchal' over the top, 'Madeira' at the base and across the circle a lozenge shape with the date. Ships to the Straits Peninsula, or Further India, as Malaya was sometimes called, stopped over on the island to replenish food and fresh water, so it's likely that Emily has been there as well. The Catholic Portuguese are not her natural bedfellows. Emily raised her children in her evangelical Christian faith – she has no time for high church with its musky incense and secret confession: 'I can't stand the nonsense.'[80]

But Birdie has obviously met a fellow Christian, which can only be a good thing. Emily's memory is excellent; of course she remembers Dr Bill Wilson. She also remembers his wife, as tall and thin as him. Perhaps it is something to do with Edward Lear's popular nonsense poem 'The Jumblies' (a useful rhythmic text for teaching reading), and Birdie will come back taller from the 'Torrible' Antarctic too. But Emily is worried about recent press reports about leaks in the ship's hull – the *Terra Nova* seems almost as leaky as the Jumblies' sieve 'in which they went to sea'.[81]

Emily has just received a photograph of Birdie on the *Terra Nova*, taken from the dockside looking up. It is already in a frame in the front

room. If she wants to see it, she can climb the steep steps that lead up
from the shared garden to the galley kitchen on the right of the building.
From the back of the kitchen, a narrow corridor leads left to her front
room with its coal fire. In the frame, Birdie is posing in his Royal Indian
Marine uniform, two lieutenant's stripes around his wrist. He leans with
his left hand on one of the ship's lifeboats, the fingers of the other in his
pocket. With his peaked cap pulled down almost to the bridge of that
wonderful nose, and without the other officers towering over him, he
looks every inch the handsome naval officer. Will she ever see that face
again? 'Your photo is looking at me. I wish it was your own self but
please God the day will soon come when I see you.'[82] Her daughter May,
who has moved home to Ardbeg, has recently become interested in
spiritualism as a logical extension of Christianity. Could Emily's presentiment at Waterloo Station be the result of a spiritual second sight?

Emily rearranges the boxes of Ceylonese butterflies that Birdie, a keen and
knowledgeable lepidopterist, has entrusted to her care. They are brightly
coloured like the petals of flowers in Malaya. In Malay culture there is a
belief that at the time of every birth on earth, a flower is supposed to grow
up in heaven and to live a life parallel to that of each person. If the flower
continues to grow well, the person enjoys good, robust health; if it droops,
the person droops. Emily sets the butterfly collection in pride of place. The
surfaces of the glass boxes attract dust, but she will not allow one mote to
fall on this. Emily has always kept a tidy house, even in the days of scholar
lodgers who seemed to think it their duty to create mess. Birdie's collection
is still the brightest thing in the room, a spot of cheerful colour.

I must admit that my journey down [to Portsmouth] to-day was
hardly what one might call cheery,' [Birdie wrote after that farewell.]
'Still, life is made up of these things and thus it must go on till we
never more shall part and God shall wipe away all the tears from
our eyes. It seems a strange paradox in nature that those who have
many sons may have them always with them, while so often the
single ones are taken. My love for you and the desire to remain
with you always tempers my natural desire for a roving life, which
was born in me. As the knowledge that I had to go to sea grew
and grew, I always fought it for your sake but for my own loved it:

it was my calling. It had to be, but God has given me the love of
it mixed with the bitter that must fill all earthly cups. For you it
seems to me that the bitter alone is left, but He knows, and does
and will compensate you . . . You know at all events that your son
loves and honours his mother above all things on earth.[83]

It is a relief to be able to continue communication even after that
dreadful parting. If Emily wonders what Birdie thinks of how she
behaved, his letter to Edie tells her: 'the dear old Mother was very
upset but held up'.[84] Now Emily tries to readjust to her 'pen & ink'
son – Birdie's description of sailing through the Royal Navy fleet of
dreadnoughts is evocative. Emily pictures the little wooden whaler, its
white, square-rigged sails flying, its chivalric figurehead, right arm
extended, off to 'battle' – white warfare in the Antarctic.

'I must say I was never so impressed in my life with hideous strength,'
wrote Birdie of sailing through the ironclads. 'The new monsters are
ugliness itself, but for sheer diabolical brutality in ship-building some
of the Dreadnought cruisers take the cake. The look of them is enough
to scare anyone.'[85]

She remembers seeing Kaiser Wilhelm II from Horse Guards Parade
with Birdie at King Edward VII's funeral on 20 May earlier that year. The
Kaiser disguised his withered left arm well. May thought him 'very
imposing' but Emily, less impressionable, is concerned with his desire to
build up the German fleet.[86] None of the dreadnoughts have figureheads,
their bows being reinforced battering rams. 'When you pass close enough
to look into the muzzles of their guns', says Birdie, 'the effect is something to be remembered. Much as I love ships and especially H.M. Ships,
there was something about the look of this squadron that was Satanic.'[87]

The dreadnoughts are Admiral Jackie Fisher's brainchild. Emily keeps
abreast of all entitlements. Six months earlier, when Fisher was created
Baron, he had taken as the punning motto: 'Fear God and dread nought'.
Emily fears God but she is often consumed by anxiety when Birdie is
away. He cannot worry like that; his sex, he says, precludes him. He
exhorts her to check her anxiety. It can't be good for her. Emily tries
to calm her nerves by reading out loud, which helps to bring the 'pen
& ink conversation' alive. In Birdie's Madeira letter, he tells her, they'd
been offered lunch at the sumptuous hotel owned by a Mr Reid. Emily

probably knows the hotel. If her eyes run ahead of her, she might censor the next part before it reaches May's ears. For Mr Reid, it turns out, has a locked drawer in which he keeps 'a collection of the filthiest and most disgusting repulsive curiosities I could ever imagine. I never believed such things could exist or that the hand of man could be employed in constructing such crude examples of filth. To the surprise of my companions I told him straight . . . that I thought it was the most disgusting exhibition I had ever seen. The mind of that man must be a cesspool.'[88] Emily is proud of Birdie's moral courage but will this be interpreted as innocent prudery? Will it make Birdie vulnerable with the saltier members of the crew? It is all very well to bring a boy up to Christian behaviour, but perhaps, boys like Birdie who could not remember a father, are more sensitive when it comes to 'man's talk'?

I JULY 1910

CAROLINE – GESTINGTHORPE

Three days earlier, on 28 June, the Postmaster General, Mr Herbert Samuel, was asked to explain the excessive postage rates to Madeira in parliament. He confirmed the postal rate for a parcel not exceeding 3 lb as 1 shilling 6 pence. Laurie is keen on parcels. Caroline has received 'heads', hunting trophies from Mhow in India, 'from the hounds as a token of their esteem', and carpets from Port Said in Egypt, but this situation is different and, perhaps owing to excessive postal rates, Laurie has not sent anything but news.[89] Caroline inserts her silver paper knife into the top of the envelope. The logo on the flap is a black circle with 'British Antarctic Expedition' around the top and 'Terra Nova R.Y.S.' around the base. In the middle a rather bewildered-looking penguin stands on an inverted globe. The penguin cannot distract her from the Madeira postmark, stamped 26 June 1910. How much does Laurie remember of his trip there fifteen years ago?

1896

It was March 1896 and Laurie was fifteen. The Oates family – William, Caroline and their four children, Lilian, Laurie, Violet and Bryan, together with a skeleton retinue of servants – had decided to meet the summer by going out to the island for Easter. Willie took his camera, his watercolours and sketchbook. He was particularly keen on a neoclassical water fountain in Funchal that the locals used as a meeting place.

Caroline still has his sketches of that fountain. Easter was on 5 April that year, but three weeks before, after the Oateses' arrival in Madeira, there was an outbreak of typhoid. Willie and Caroline decided to stay, but they were scrupulous. They made their children drink boiled water and wash their hands thoroughly with soap. In the end it was not the children but Willie who fell ill.

Caroline immediately sent the children home with their nurses and governesses and stayed on to look after her husband. Madeira was connected by undersea cable to Porthcurno in Cornwall, and from there messages were relayed within minutes to the family in London. Caroline sent cables from the Carmo Hotel nearly every day. Laurie was sixteen on 17 March when Caroline, still at her husband's bedside, wrote in her diary: 'A shocking morning of anxiety. I really believe my darling is sinking.'[90] The symptoms of typhoid made sufferers feverish, often vomiting blood. Caroline had married her cousin partly to marry back into the landed side of her parental inheritance, but it was not just for the status. She adored him. Their relationship was often compared to that of Victoria and Albert. Albert died of typhoid fever on 14 December 1861, when William Oates was sixteen years old.

William Oates died of typhoid fever on 3 April 1896, when his son Lawrence Oates was sixteen years old. Caroline's brother-in-law had just arrived in Funchal to support her. Willie was buried by the British chaplain W. Graham at first light on the morning after his death, in line with the island's regulations on contagious diseases. The regulations seemed harsh, but until recently the mortal remains of foreigners dying of contagious diseases, especially if they were not Roman Catholic, were thrown from the cliffs at Garajau. The Oateses were Nonconformists and Caroline was told that she was lucky that a place had been found in the British cemetery. Perhaps it was partly the influence of her brother-in-law, as the cemetery had a special section for German Protestants. Caroline returned to England in deep mourning. At sixteen, Laurie had become squire to the hundred or so villagers of Gestingthorpe and yet he was still at Eton.

Now, a decade and a half on, thirty-year-old Laurie writes to Caroline from Madeira. He has left the crew of the *Terra Nova* behind and climbed the rocky amphitheatre above the town. In the corner of the cemetery he finds his father William's grave: 'It was quite tidy, I thought, but the lilies on it were of course a little faded and the roses had finished blooming. I had four dogs with me and they played about while I was in the cemetery. It was most quiet and nice.'

In Caroline's study she keeps a photograph of the gravestone, white marble with plain lettering. The lettering is not as beautiful as she would like. Willie was a stalwart supporter of William Morris and the Arts and Crafts, but the typeface is disappointing, baldly mechanical. She did not choose it. She had returned to England immediately to be with her children before the stone was made, the lettering set. But every year, just before the anniversary of Willie's death, she sends £1 to a Mr Miles in Funchal for maintenance. She was forty-one when she was widowed. She has never married again.

To compensate for the utilitarian grave, Caroline commissioned a memorial stained glass from Heaton, Butler & Bayne of 14 Garrick Street, Covent Garden. She and Willie loved that workshop, warmed by the glass furnaces in the basement, each room a magical wonderland of flickering jewelled light. Willie created a memorial window for his brother Frank, a St Francis surrounded by exotic animals. Now St Francis is joined by St Peter, his hands reaching so far out of the lead boundary between tinted panes of glass that he seems to touch Jesus as he strolls across the waves. Caroline has done her best to transport the sensational colours of Garrick Street to St Mary the Virgin, Gestingthorpe. Together with their design for the Oates family of heraldic beasts that roar from the mezzanine window in Gestingthorpe Hall, Willie's immortal name is alive in lights.

By her desk Caroline keeps her favourite photograph of her 'darling' Willie. He sits in a deck steamer en route to South Africa. Laurie was a sickly child and they'd gone to South Africa for his health. In the photograph Willie is moustachioed, loose limbed and with Laurie's slight pout of his lower lip to the right. It is the Oates family's subtle version of the 'Hapsburg jaw'. Now fifteen years after his father's death Laurie is following the same route, and then on to where there are no fountains, and drinking water is obtained by hacking at icebergs.

AUGUST 1910

KATHLEEN – JOHANNESBURG, SOUTH AFRICA

Kathleen wears her whitest dress full-length and patterned with intricate needlework. She knows that her artist's overalls would be more suitable attire for going down a mine, but she is trying to follow her husband's instructions. White is only worn by the leisured upper classes and the 'English embroidery' is so labour-intensive that it indicates that 'there isn't any poverty at all'.[91] Perhaps she would not have to make such an effort if South Africa had already produced the expected £5,000 expedition sponsorship they hope to extract.

The *Terra Nova* has not yet arrived. When it does, they will need to make repairs, replenish supplies and get mail before they go on to Australia and then New Zealand, where the men will leave for the Antarctic. Instead of waiting, the Scotts are touring the 'Randlords' with their 'begging cap'. As they rattle towards the mine in a Randlord's motorcar, Kathleen learns that one of them, Lionel Philips, has his eye on a Rodin sculpture for a gallery in Joubert Park. Kathleen, who studied under Rodin in Paris, proceeds to charm Lionel into commissioning her for a statue for a niche in the stoop of his new Dutch-style mansion. Scott knows that his mother is not convinced about his choice of wife. He will write to her to tell her that 'I find I am quite in the background! . . . Kathleen is popular everywhere.'[92]

They go out of the brilliant sun 1,500 feet down into the red earth, to an echoing cavern of stifling heat and darkness where miners kneel beside the rock face, candle stubs dripping wax. The smell of tallow and sweat mixes with the dry, metallic taste of pulverised rock dust that hangs in the air. The miners are stripped to the waist, 'breathing at a horrible rate, coughing that cough'.[93] It is phthisis, pulmonary tuberculosis, a wasting disease.

At Lionel's command, the miners lift their heavy rock hammers and begin to pound with hammer and chisels. These are also the sculptor's work tools, and Kathleen watches fascinated as the dim cavern echoes with the sound of metal on stone. In her notebook, she keeps careful notes of the whole process: gold rock pulverised, poured, bound with alloys and made into gold bars worth £3,000 – too heavy to lift. The man who is showing them round has 'that cough', and likely knows he has only a few months to live, but insists on working to be able to feed his wife and children. This 'do or die' attitude resonates. Major Leonard Darwin, outgoing president of the RGS, has just taken up chairmanship of the British Eugenics Society. Darwin's view of the expedition is that 'they mean to do or die – that is the spirit in which they are going to the Antarctic . . . I have not the slightest doubt that a rich harvest of facts will be reaped . . . Captain Scott is going to prove once again that the manhood of the nation is not dead, and that the characteristics of our ancestors, who won this great empire, still flourish amongst us.'[94]

The act of raising the stone hammer makes a row of ancient classical statues, 'Laocoöns', reaching back over their shoulders for the snake. That ancient masterpiece is white marble, this is shining black – the heavy biceps, the thick forearms, the pectoral muscles and the ridges of muscle down the ribs. These miners are risking their lives of necessity rather than choice. Kathleen must incite her husband to risk everything like these miners. Some things are worth dying for.

Kathleen can remember her early twenties at the Colarossi art school in Paris at the turn of the century: 'Passing an open door of one of the studios, I saw [a friend] at the back of the room . . . and went to join her. [She] was standing composedly with her head critically on one side. At the end of the studio passed, one by one, a string of nude male models. Each jumped for a moment on to the model throne, took a pose, and jumped down. The model for the week was being chosen. Before reason could control instinct I turned and fled, shut myself into the lavatory and was sick.'[95]

It was only ten years ago. How could she have been so vulgar, so naïve? The nude was not sexual, it was about texture, articulation of form, light and shade. Back then she was still fairly fresh from her convent orphanage where the nuns insisted that the girls bathe in a shift lest they catch sight of their own nakedness. At that time, the nakedness of men was quite beyond her. Now it is the vandalism of the white plaster fig-leaves that she resents. Exquisite Greek marbles ruined by restorations.

Across her thoughts, a sonorous male voice brings her back from Paris and London to the African mine. The whole cavern resonates like the inside of a drum. In Henley-on-Thames, Peter's nurse will be singing nursery rhymes not tribal chants, she will be filling his head with functional nanny's idioms and claustrophobic Victorian cautionary tales. When she returns, Kathleen will write to Scott's sister, Rose: 'We love every detail you can tell us about that fat son of ours. I'm so glad he's not being a trouble.'[96] She must not betray her class by inappropriate sentiment, by cosseting. She must be stoical about the separation. It will be weeks before she gets news, 'but I doubt not he will be none the worse for that'.

These miners don't sing of caution, they sing of courage. This is not an entertainment, it is the sound of survival, of reinforcing the bonds between men facing danger together. When the *Terra Nova* blows into Cape Town later that week, Bill Wilson will assure her that 'I doubt if a class of the Ladies College could be more unselfish in looking after each other's interests, even if they were all preparing for confirmation.'[97] The *Terra Nova* crew is close knit under Lieutenant Teddy Evans, who captained the boat out from England. Teddy is obviously a popular leader. She will have to make sure that the 'Ladies College' don't favour him over her husband 'Capt South Pole Scott'.[98]

28 AUGUST 1910

ORIANA – SALDANHA BAY, SOUTH AFRICA

Oriana takes her place in the stern. The owner of a little white-washed house in Hoetjes Bay where she and Bill are staying has arranged for some Saldanhavaarder boys to row them out. The small wooden pier creaks as the boat's painter is untied. The boys grin. How do they see Ory? An impeccably dressed memsahib with kid gloves? Would they suspect that those gloved hands have eviscerated and dissected over a thousand birds from the family Phasianidae in the order Galliformes?

Friends who trekked up to their grouse moor in Fort Augustus, where she and Bill had set up a temporary laboratory, found her 'surrounded by a halo of feathers and entrails'.[99] She'd become so adept that she once declared a recently delivered brace entirely free from disease.[100] The sender hoped so. They were intended for consumption not dissection. Now Ory is half a world away from those slippery entrails, heading out into the crystal clear waters of Saldanha Bay. This stopover in South Africa is the nearest her workaholic husband will get to a holiday. Previously Bill had visited sanatoriums for his tubercular lungs and complained that it was the enforced inactivity rather than the disease that nearly killed him. Holidays are death. He doesn't want a holiday.

What do the Wilsons make of Leonard Darwin's 'do or die' assessment of the expedition? Both believe that this second trip to the Antarctic is God's will and that 'rich harvest of facts' is Bill's duty, his proper work. Her duty is to make his duty possible – she must not fail him. If the Pole isn't worth dying for, what is? 'It looks,' says Bill, 'almost as though in real love anything short of death is insufficient; and yet, though death for one's best and truest love is the highest thing of all, it is to be avoided by every means.'[101]

The helmsman is taking them close past Marquis Island. Bracing herself against the gunnel, Ory hopes she can trust her husband to avoid death 'by every means'. She tries to hold her binoculars steady, peering through to see the penguin nests among the stones. These are black-footed penguins, *Spheniscus demersus*. The locals call them 'salted penguins' – preserved in barrels as food, along with eggs from the nesting sites. The smell of guano, buff-coloured excrement that seems to cover the island, is pungent.

Ory wonders if the odour will precipitate one of her migraines. She is not as robust as she would like to be, and she must look after herself while Bill isn't around to do it. Last time he left she suffered a bout of pneumonia, but Leonard Darwin's 'do or die' is not about him doing and her dying. Bill promises her that he will not leave the expedition's winter quarters to begin the journey south to the Pole until he hears that she is well.

A gannet streaks vertically out of the sky and skewer-dives, piercing the shiny surface of the sea with a white flash. It reappears near them holding a large fish in its beak. Tipping its head back, it flicks the fish lengthways down its gullet headfirst. They are so close Ory can see the bird's throat swell as the fish slips down, she can see the beautiful blue rings around the gannet's yellow eyes. The nearest rower flicks his oar, stuns the gannet and hooks it into the boat. It is unusual for Ory to hold a live bird, strangely warm. She notes that the head is buff, the bill whitish and the feet pale greenish white with a black line down each toe to the nail. The bird begins to flap. Bill asks her if she has seen enough to memorise the detail. She has. They let it go.

Ory knows that Bill and Shackleton wrestled with large emperor penguins on the *Discovery* expedition. Shackleton would tell his lecture audiences that if you wanted an emperor egg, all you had to do was squeeze a bird and the egg dropped out. But the Wilsons are scientists not entertainers. Bill believes penguins might hold the key to the secret of evolution. Specifically he thinks that their embryos might go through all their species' stages of evolution inside the egg, based on the popular theory 'ontongeny recapitulates phylogeny', or ORP, posited by the German biologist Ernst Haeckel. For Bill, proving this theory is the chief draw and justification of Antarctica.

After two wet, wavy hours, they tie up at the whaling station, which reeks of the sickly sweet stench of blubber. Ory has exchanged one set of entrails for another. Captain Steen, who gives the tour of the station, is a sceptic: 'He disbelieves everyone, even [Norwegian explorer Fridtjof] Nansen, whose story he calls a nonsense story, a great joke! . . . Peary and Cook [North Pole claimants] he entirely discredits.'[102] Ory learns that they have an average catch of five whales a week, sometimes eight, but they cannot deal with them before the heat renders them partly rotten and the oil deteriorates. Steen shows them the filleting station where each plate of bone has to be separated, washed with soda, dried and packed into barrels. Whalebone corsets are popular but the scraping, washing and cleaning leaves little profit. As they thank Steen for his tour and take their leave, she looks down to find 'splodges of blubber on my skirt and on my gloves as a memento!'[103]

By five o'clock Ory and Bill are back at the hotel on Hoetjes Bay. One of the guests walks into the hotel dining room with a bunch of rare scented lilies that can only be found in one place. He presents them to Ory. It is proof, as if Bill needs it, that Ory 'looked well to other eyes than mine'.[104] By embarking on this second Antarctic expedition, he is trusting her not to 'fail' him. How many years of men with rare lilies can she resist? What is 'failure'?

After dinner the Wilsons set out up the hills behind the hotel through 'a perfect wealth of flowers'.[105] Climbing the slope, they tread carefully: 'One's foot crushed new beauties at every step.' There is a blazing sunset with the scent of flowers stronger in the cooling air. Just before they return they find the 'gem of the day', a sunbird's nest. 'Ory put the hen off and in it were two delicate little bluish eggs with brown spots, new laid and looking lovely in the pure white lining of cotton wool. It was the prettiest nest I have ever seen.'

Although it is August, it is the beginning of spring and nesting time in the southern hemisphere. The Wilsons have been married for nine childless years and yet they are still in love and have not quite given up hope of having a family.[106] Their bedroom is large and dark but their bed linen crisp and clean with beautifully embroidered pillowcases. In the morning they open the window wide: 'As we lay in bed we could watch a colony of orange coloured weaver birds building their compact grass nests singing at the very ends of long gum tree branches. They were ridiculously funny in their chattering eagerness and the cocks were continually being scolded for bringing the wrong stuff to the nest, or for gadding from one nest to the other to visit friends.'[107]

AUTUMN 1910

CAROLINE – GESTINGTHORPE

Caroline covers every beeswax-polished surface of Gestingthorpe Hall with family photographs. The men in her life are dead or absent so the photographs represent them in two-dimensional form. Two of the photographs are of moustachioed men of a similar height and build to Laurie. One sits shyly on a steamer beside his five-year-old son, the other strikes a dramatic pose in a photographer's studio: her husband and his older brother Frank, both gentlemen explorers. William gave up the explorer's life, satisfied with being elected a Fellow of the Royal Geographical Society and becoming the quintessential paterfamilias. Frank, also FRGS, died of fever in Africa, having become one of the first white men to see the source of the Nile. William and Frank. Which one of them is Laurie's most powerful role model? His sensitive, artistic father or his glamorous, swash-buckling uncle? In Laurie's latest letter he tells Caroline that he is having 'a top hole time' aboard ship: 'We shout and yell at meals just as we like, and we have a game called Furl Topgallant Sails which consists in tearing off each other's shirts . . . the whole place a regular pandemonium.'[108]

Once they landed at the Cape, however, Laurie made straight for the hills. He hired horses in Simon's Town and enjoyed some hard riding with his new friends, Dr Edward Atkinson, 'Atch', and Apsley Cherry-Garrard, 'Cherry'. The only problem is the women. Mrs Kathleen Scott turned up at the Cogshill Hotel after a weekend's hack and they had to transform from dishevelled horsemen to 'suits' in a hurry. The image of Laurie imperfectly 'shevelled' is not something on which Caroline wishes to dwell. She always insists that Laurie wear a starched white collar at Gestingthorpe to keep up manorial appearances. And as for the shouting, yelling and tearing shirts – in the past she has written to him about his manners. His reaction is gracious and conciliatory, thanking her for the two lectures: 'To the first I plead guilty, to the second I also plead guilty.'[109]

At her desk in Gestingthorpe on the other side of the world, Caroline hears the bells of St Mary the Virgin as the change ringing sounds out over the gleaned Essex stubble. It is the time of the full orange harvest moon. Four of the bells were cast by Miles Gray of Colchester and among them is one she'd had recast in Bury St Edmonds in 1901. Around the base is the inscription, 'In gratitude to God for the safe return with honour of my beloved son Lawrence E. G. Oates from the dangers of war in South Africa.'[110]

Caroline takes the *Geographic Journal* – she never cancelled her late husband's subscription – so she has read Major Darwin's 'do or die' speech. Laurie has already done and not died. As a Victorian, that phrase conjures Tennyson's poem, 'The Charge of the Light Brigade', with its thundering hooves of chivalric cavalry officers like her son, who galloped into the Valley of Death obedient to the orders of a bungler. Caroline fervently hopes that Captain Scott is not a bungler. He did not lose any men on his last trip, she has that comfort, but when she'd met him in London at West India Docks she didn't like him, an intuitive mistrust: 'I never cared for him.'[111] Now he has her precious son's life in his hands.

Laurie had returned 'with honour' from that war in South Africa, but more importantly, he had returned alive. He was known in the regiment as 'No Surrender Oates'. It took Caroline some time to find out why. The first she heard was a telegram sent back in 1901: 'Wounded in the leg not dangerously.'[112] Caroline knew, from experience, that extreme taciturn stoicism was almost lying. When, on 17 March 1880, she presented Willie with his son and heir, she noted the event in her diary with just three words: 'Baby boy born'.[113]

1901

Perhaps extreme stoicism is one of Darwin's list of 'inheritable characteristics'. When that same 'baby boy', aged twenty-one, found himself exposed and massively outnumbered on a riverbank in South Africa, he refused the Boers' note offering 'an immediate surrender. Life and private property guaranteed.' Who did the 'Boer' think he was? 'We came here to fight,' Laurie wrote right back, 'not to surrender.'[114] After a while, the Boers just got up and walked away. Their marksmen were horribly accurate and yet instead of shooting the mad English officer in the head, they made sure he couldn't follow them by placing a bullet in his thigh. The legend of 'No Surrender Oates' was born. He had narrowly missed a Victoria Cross for gallantry but was settled instead with the Queen's Medal – Caroline would never forgive the army that. Soon after, Lord Kitchener made the act of surrendering a court martial offence. 'Putty heroes', as Laurie called them, would be outed now.

AUTUMN 1910

Laurie's bell is still tolling 'honour' across the stubble as Caroline prepares to go to church at the end of harvest. The carriage is announced at the front door. Beside the coachman in new livery (a recent purchase from Browns of London – an exorbitant £5.5), stand the Gestingthorpe Hall retinue in descending rank, from Oscar Minchin, her trusted retainer, to the Maid of All Work. She has different servants in London. (One of them, the housekeeper at Evelyn Mansions, is called 'Mrs Death'. It will amuse Laurie on his return.) She has never met his Indian servants in Mhow but they seem loyal. Keeping three sets of servants is expensive. Caroline keeps a tight hold of her budget through her beloved accounts book. In a world of uncertainty it is her most trusted companion.

Now Caroline takes her time. She must act her part as lady of the manor or Lloyd George and his cronies will make sure that Laurie has no manor to come home to. The villagers file along the street, past the Gestingthorpe gateway. There is Walter Downs, the wheelwright, and his family who live at Number 1 on the Sudbury Road, the Taylors from Hill Farm (who keep a servant), the Rippingales from the Barracks – all nine ordinary agricultural labourers – and Maria Cansell, who is supported by Outdoor Poor Relief. Most of the village are involved in the harvest. Even the tile-maker and the potter go gleaning.

As Caroline crosses the hall, the first and second bells stop pealing. Caroline climbs into her carriage and the procession moves towards the church. The bells of St Mary's pealed Laurie's triumphant return from Cape Town in 1901. After his recovery, Gestingthorpe village turned out 'en fête' for the day of celebration – flags, bands playing, a hundred children given tea in the school room, and swings and round-abouts which Caroline had arranged. The celebrations concluded with 270 adults sitting down to a feast.

The bells have stopped ringing. Caroline walks into the church, decorated with corn dollies and scented with apples in straw and loaves of fresh plaited bread. She is a little late. It is important to be a little late. Once she is seated in the family pew, the Reverend C.T. Bromwich reads out the parish notices. The collection today will go towards the Tower Fund. This is the second of five services of the day – the reading is taken from Genesis 8:22: 'While the earth remaineth, seedtime and harvest, and cold and heat, and summer and winter, and day and night shall not cease.' At some point in the service, Caroline notices that Bromwich does not seem himself. He is a sandy-haired, square-built man, a tower of strength, and yet today he seems frail.

Caroline remembers Bromwich's speech on Laurie's return from South Africa. He told the congregation that their squire had shown himself to be 'a genuine soldier, a true Englishman, loyal to his King and to his country', concluding with a pithy character summary. Here was a man who had 'done his duty with no swagger and no fuss, but in that simple, natural way as if he were doing something in the ordinary events of everyday life'.[115] The applause that followed – while Laurie handed out packets of German tobacco to the men of Gestingthorpe in the feudal manner – had been loud and heartfelt. But today Bromwich cannot find his rhetorical rhythm – he seems to be struggling.

The Reverend Bromwich (she has never used his Christian name 'Charles') is not the second son of a peer treating his 'living' as a sinecure. Bromwich was one of the first curates to train at Lincoln Theological College, set up by Edward Benson to enable working men to become priests. Bromwich's father is a master builder, a gilder and decorator from Warwickshire, and he and Caroline's late husband William shared an appreciation for fine craftsmanship expressed in the restoration of Gestingthorpe's then-dilapidated church. If Bromwich is not able to attend on her at the Hall, she can cross the street to the rectory behind the school.

Bromwich is really ill. Quite apart from her fondness for him, Caroline cannot risk this critical link between her and the estate's agricultural working class. On 12 October 1910 she enters 'Rev C T Bromwich (Nurse) £10.0.0' in her accounts book. She does not expect him to pay for his own medical care out of the tithe of £5.8.2 she paid him on 8 October. By 1 November she transfers a second amount –

'Rev C T Bromwich £1.5.0 (Largesse)' – it is Caroline's way of showing her affectionate appreciation.[116]

SEPTEMBER 1910

LOIS – OLYMPIA, LONDON

Back in 1906, when Norman was just starting to walk and Lois was pregnant with Muriel, Taff performed at Olympia. He led an eighteen-man crew in a re-enactment of the Jack Tars' victory at Ladysmith on 30 October 1899 during the Second Boer War. On the train up to Olympia now, Lois can prepare the children. She tells them that during the war, a South African town was surrounded by rebel Dutch farmers, 'you see' (Lois's Gower patois means she ends almost every sentence 'you see'.) Jack Tars, Royal Navy ratings, like their father, dragged heavy guns from HMS *Powerful* right across the land to Ladysmith to defend it. And yes, they were successful.

Taff had not been part of the original manoeuvre, but as a bemuscled naval P.T. instructor on HMS *Majestic* he was instrumental in reconstructing it as entertainment. Taff is known for being a strict disciplinarian who gives due credit to hard workers but has no time for shirkers.[117] When he issues instructions, 'every word snap[s] like a north eastern in the . . . shrouds.'[118] For the re-enactment, Taff led the team that dismantled and reconstructed the guns, each one weighing a full ton. The parts had to be hoisted over artificially constructed walls, chasms and bridges in the arena. The display was an overnight sensation but someone – was it Taff? – decided that it would be even better as a competition, a race. It was a race he'd gone on to win several times.

Those arriving from Portsmouth by train have only had one change to get right to the concourse of the stadium. The Olympia exhibition hall looks like a palace containing a very large half-submerged glass barrel on its side. In grounds of Olympia, hawkers call out their wares. They hold up packets done up in cheesecloth, green and brown glass bottles with 'Jack Tar' labels and jars of cockles in brine. The atmosphere is jolly – this is a holiday that the Royal Navy, alongside the army, encourages to boost recruitment. Around Lois, the sailors want news of their friend, the field race legend. Has he remembered them in his letters home? Lois can assure them that he has because he has written home, 'a few lines to let you know that I am in the best of health and I hope this will find you all the same'.[119] For present purposes, they are 'all'.

She loves his letters. Even writing at sea, Taff's copperplate is almost perfectly formed, his lines as straight as if ruled. He makes an artistic broken line under the address on the top right, two long lines either side of a short one, and he always starts right at the top of the paper and finishes right at the end of the second side with a flourishing signature of his real name 'Edgar', ending in two circular loops.

The winds had been against them nearly all the way to Madeira and they had a job to get things 'a bit square' before port. That blessed leak was no better but the main purpose of his letters is to put down his 'programme of our movements' so that she can send letters ahead to be there to greet him.

Some of the sailors around Lois and her young family know of Taff's impromptu gun-run training session in Corfu – perhaps some were there too. With six fellow ratings, Taff hired a four-wheeled cart to take them into the countryside. One of them, probably Taff, had the bright idea of dismantling the cart and taking it over a couple of walls to keep their eye in for the Olympia competition back in London later in the year. They were halfway through when an official turned up. 'What is this tomfoolery?' he asked. 'Gun practice, Sir,' replied Taff. 'Dismounting and retiring with gear.' 'We couldn't make the bleeding fool see how important it was,' explained Taff when he related this particular anecdote, 'and he sent us back to the ship without letting us set the gun up again.'[120]

Now horse-drawn carriages pull up at the grand entrance on the other side of the Olympia building from the station entrance. Lois and her young family can see the wide hats of the fashionably dressed and the striped awnings over walkways leading to the most expensive seats. (Caroline Oates still refers to the Royal Tournament as the 'pageant'. The cavalry displays and the level of horsemanship make it an annual treat, a show not to be missed.)

The cheapest 'seats', standing room only, are up a metal staircase just inside the entrance opposite the station. Inside, semi-circular girders arch up like the gantries of dockyard cranes and shafts of sunlight fall through the glass roof. Vast areas of raked seating rise away from a central arena covered in sand. Around it are large potted plants, trees and hedges. The smell is like the inside of a stable: horses, hoof oil and sweat.

The bands strike up. The Evans children can recognise the Royal Marines from the Royal Tournament poster up around Portsmouth. It has a picture of a man in a white helmet, his foot on the Portsmouth sea wall, looking out at a dreadnought. The white helmets are part of the tri-service massed band – there are drums, shining brass instruments, scarlet jackets and the pounding of marching feet. Finally, it is the field-gun race that they have all been waiting for. Bareheaded sailors in their white shirts, navy trousers and white puttees emerge from the entrance gap to the arena dragging their guns. Among the families on the balcony, a hush settles.

The eighteen Portsmouth sailors are on the near side of the start line by the royal box. They await their signal. As the flag drops, the crews explode into action and heave the heavy iron guns and wooden limbers to the end of the arena. The crowd are cheering them on. The noise bounces back off the glass ceiling in a roar. Both crews turn quickly and carry themselves and the equipment over a 5-foot wall. The dismantled guns are carried to the top of a ramp on the 'home side' of a 28-foot 'chasm'. The crew set up a wire and traveller so all eighteen men and their equipment zip wire across – to the children they seem to be literally flying. Lois has seen the bruises. Those wheels weigh 120 lb each and there have been many dislocated shoulders in the past.

The team and equipment must pass through a hole in the 'enemy wall' at the end of the arena. Each crew must reconstruct their gun and fire. That is only the first part, the 'run out'. The average time is eighty-five seconds. Taff would be monitoring this on a navy-issue stopwatch. How have the Portsmouth lads done? Lois must write it all for her husband in proper detail.

The second part of the competition is the 'run back'. The flag drops, the cheering starts. Sometimes it seems that the stadium roof will burst right open like a bubble with the pressure of sound. The average time for the 'run back' is sixty seconds. How do the Portsmouth team compare? In the final stage, the 'run home', men, guns and limbers pass back through the hole in the home wall. The average time for the 'run home' is twenty-one seconds. What is the aggregate? Have they won overall? Is someone totting up the total? Taff will want the result but he will also want all the splits.

It will take the Evans family more than twenty-one seconds to come down off the ceiling, let alone 'run back home' to 52 Chapel Street in Portsmouth. Around her, Taff's naval colleagues assure her that if he can pull a sledge like he can pull a gun, he'll throw that South Pole in

the air with one hand and twirl it like a bandsman's baton. Taff is a
competitive man. He is a winner. He always has been. Lois knows that
the officers admired the Jack Tars at Ladysmith for their 'do or die'
attitude. Would Taff rather die than lose? Perhaps one day they'll work
out a way of covering the arena with snow and do a field sledge re-
enactment of the trip to the Pole – the run out, the run back and most
importantly that run home.

21 SEPTEMBER 1910

EMILY – BUTE

The sun is setting in the west – the long coast of Ayrshire to the east
is bathed in its waning glow. The short, rotund figure of Emily Bowers
emerges from the front door of the downstairs flat at Caerlaverock and
turns right at the garden gate. Her arm is stiff. Her rheumatism still
troubles her at night but generally Rothesay on the Isle of Bute is a
healthy change from London – if only it weren't for the damp winters.

She takes up her place at the tram stop. It is next to that nice classical
house, Aros na Mara, on the front, with the pretty iron fretwork that
she's always coveted. The tram arrives. The uniformed attendant greets
Mrs Bowers by name. She settles down for the rattling ride south along
the seafront to Rothesay. Opposite her there are two posters: one has
'The Danger of Promiscuous Spectacle Buying' written in capital letters
across the top, with a drawing of some hapless, bespectacled child.
J. Lizars Opthalmic Optician, Buchanan Street Glasgow is using parental
fear to their advantage, denouncing 'quack eyesight specialists'. The
other poster is larger:

The Palace Hall, Rothesay
Wednesday Evening September 21st at 8.30

Mr C. Wade has the honour to announce that
Sir Ernest
SHACKLETON
Will give his
POPULAR LECTURE
ENTITLED
'NEAREST THE SOUTH POLE'

Emily recalls one of Birdie's early letters, about Shackleton from 1909: 'Thank you for the cuttings about the [Shackleton's *Nimrod*] South Polar Expedition, I thought it splendid. My only regret was that I was not one of them . . . Don't laugh!'[121]

Emily is not laughing, but she remembers that during those last few days in London, Birdie and May went to Burberry's expressly to buy a coat identical to the one Shackleton wore on his expedition. Now his opinion has changed: 'After the *Discovery* expedition Shackleton did not play the game by Scott . . . & made hay . . . during the second year when Scott was in the Antarctic,' Birdie tells her, 'Marston [Shackleton's] artist who was aboard [the *Terra Nova*] in London told Wilson that [Shackleton] appropriated all his work & would not let him have any of it back . . . Shackleton's failing seems to have been that he worked for his own hand at the expense of others.'[122]

May's diary is blank for the 21st.[123] Perhaps, despite having finished Shackleton's *The Heart of the Antarctic* and 'enjoyed it immensely' a month earlier, May feels now that attending would be somehow disloyal to her brother.[124] Emily likes to make up her own mind. Has May considered that if both Bowers women 'boycott' the lecture, their absences might be remarked upon? Whatever they say or do not say about Shackleton, Emily must reach her own unclouded conclusion and do 'the right thing'.[125]

As the tram nears Rothesay, the harbour odours drift on the southerly breeze. The tide is out. A smell arises from the scum, rotten wrack and dead fish. The tides are awkward and cleansing carts cannot get down. She is sure that Sir Ernest Shackleton is used to harbour odours, but she is always keen that her adopted island makes the best possible impression on visitors. She wants them to marvel at the view, at the mild climate and the modest law-abiding community with their Sunday closing laws. She does not want them to have to hold their noses and pick their way carefully through the fish.

In the flesh, Shackleton is not tall, but he is handsome and square jawed, his hair neatly parted in the middle and slicked down with cream. The lecture is introduced by their Bute MP, Harry Hope. Birdie has warned his mother that 'To have publicity at home would destroy the charm of home life.'[126] Emily doesn't need to be told twice. She will keep a low profile, as she would hate to jeopardise 'home life'. But Sir Ernest is obviously keen on publicity. As the gaslights bracketed on the walls of the Palace Hall are turned down, he approaches the lectern bathed in incandescent calcium light and walks round to stand in front of it. He has no notes.

If Emily was concerned that this 'intellectual treat' would go over the heads of Rothesay Academy, or Ardbeg Primary, she need not have worried. Shackleton does not attempt rhetorical or oratorical flourishes but tells a simple story peppered with droll remarks. He had received a letter from 'three sporty girls', he tells the audience, who claimed to be 'healthy, gay and bright and willing to undergo any hardship', who would 'just love to don masculine attire' and join the expedition.[127] Rothesay, he has correctly judged, is a conservative crowd.

Most pertinent for Emily is Shackleton's reason for his decision to turn back 97 miles from the South Pole – to push on would have meant certain death. As it was, the four men were lucky to return alive. Emily, too, has read Major Darwin's haunting words of 'do or die', in the library's copy of the *Geographical Journal*. Fortunately, she can remind herself that Birdie is only in the ship's party, not in the landing party – no death or glory there. He will drop off the landing party in Antarctica and then return to New Zealand before the ocean freezes over. He will be safe there, in a popular corner of the British Empire. Plenty of families from Bute have emigrated there. It will be a home away from home.

From the lecture Emily realises that the status conferred by Shackleton's part in Scott's first *Discovery* expedition enabled this average sailor to marry considerably above his own modest class. Their children, Raymond and Cecily, are nearly six and nearly four, with another one on the way. Emily remembers life with three small children. 'I never wittingly hampered his ardent spirit,' Lady Shackleton is quoted as saying, 'or tried to chain it to the domestic life which meant so much to me.'[128]

How does Lady Shackleton manage while her man is away? Her spinster sister, Daisy Dorman, comes to stay. Does Emily have family to support her? Siblings that might come and stay and add their private income, their 'allowance' to hers? The hall is emptying out. It must be time to go home. Emily Bowers has many friends, but she will not be drawn out on her siblings or her parents and her Bute friends are too tactful to enquire.

3

The Influence of the Petticoat

9 SEPTEMBER 1910

ROALD AMUNDSEN – MADEIRA, PORTUGAL

Norwegian explorer Roald Amundsen has just informed his men that he is actually planning to go to the Antarctic.* He stands on the deck of the *Fram*, long legs apart, braced against the movement of the deck. His long face is expressionless, eyes flicking to each member of the team. He recruited this team under the pretext that they were heading for the Arctic. Now that they know his true purpose, anyone who wants to may leave. Do any of them want to leave? His announcement is greeted with stunned silence. They are already aboard the *Fram* with sledges, huskies and provisions, but they realise that while the North Pole has already been claimed, the South Pole is up for grabs. Nobody leaves.

It takes a few minutes for Amundsen's telegram to Scott to be transmitted as electrical pulses through the 'Eastern' cables laid along the sea floor. Travelling underwater via the same route that the *Terra Nova* sails on the surface – Madeira, Cape Town, Melbourne – seven words cover months of sailed distance in minutes. The telegram that will be waiting for Scott in Australia reads:

'Beg leave inform you proceeding Antarctic. Amundsen.'

EMILY – BUTE

Birdie's letter is dated 2 September 1910. The Boer War means that the Army Post Office Corps has speeded up connections between the UK and the Cape, so Birdie's letter arrives in Bute in early September. Emily

---

* Back in March 1910, when Scott was in Norway conducting snow trials of his motor sledges, Scott called upon Roald Amundsen at his house. When he and Tryggve Gran (who'd arranged the visit through Roald's brother Leon Amundsen) arrived, Amundsen could not be found. 'If Scott was deeply disappointed,' Gran writes, 'I was deeply embarrassed, and I can only add that the solution to the mystery emerged almost a year later.' (Smith, 1984, p. 12)

learns that Birdie has been whooping it up with two 'bewitching maidens' at Houw Hoek in the Cape. He and his new friend Apsley Cherry-Garrard (a twenty-four-year-old gent who is 'rich beyond the dreams of avarice') had taken them there for a picnic. On the return journey their hire car threw 'the romantic touch' and broke down. Birdie was impressed with the girls, who, though dressed 'formally', agreed to a cross-country trek to the village of Elgin. They 'stuck it out most pluckily' and had a 'nice little sing song'.[129]

Birdie knows that, lacking private means, he cannot afford to keep a wife, to 'get spliced' yet. His sisters tease him that if only he'd marry rich-beyond-avarice himself, they could all go home to tea. No more teaching, nursing, lodgers or 'knocking about the world' with the Royal Indian Marine. But it is all talk.

'Why did you give me this nature that loves & longs more than anything to be at home,' Birdie asks 'the Mater' after dropping the maidens back to their respective castles at some ungodly hour, 'and yet once away glories in the fact that [he is] cast in the midst of the unceasing racket of a ship's routine, without peace, without privacy & yet revelling in it . . . everything in me longs for the Great White Land to the South.'[130] Even if an heiress presented herself on a plate, for the moment Birdie would choose his 'good salt lady' the sea and now, beyond that, the South Pole. But en route to Nirvana, it is bewitching fun to break down with maidens in the middle of the veldt now and then.

Emily reads Birdie's letter out to May as the last of the summer tourists are parading along the promenade or venturing, still dressed to the nines, onto the beach at Ettrick Bay. She has been worried about the *Terra Nova*. It leaks, according to the press, and there have been 'panic stories'. Birdie thinks the panic merchants are 'blighters' – he does not mince his words. The newsmen 'who do that sort of thing to make money ought to be fried in their own fat'.[131] Hoteliers for the sewer and journalists for the frying pan, as far as Emily's son is concerned. She should not expect them to arrive by 3 October in Melbourne as advertised; at least she should not begin panicking then.

But Birdie has not finished with his observations yet. Second-in-command Lieutenant Teddy Evans who captained the *Terra Nova* from England to Cape Town, has a curious attitude to marriage that fascinates Birdie. Apparently Teddy is a keen advocate, because it gives a man a licence to do anything. Emily has to assume that since her son seems to respect him, 'anything' does not involve breaking his marriage vows. Teddy is obviously a joker. He organised entertainments on the voyage out. Birdie found himself cast in a singing role in the uniquely all-male music hall number 'The Sister's Hardbake' with their 'goo-goo eyes'.[132]

Birdie tells her about the women, the wives who have sailed out on HMS *Saxon* with Captain Scott. There is Mrs Oriana Wilson, 'coldly genuine to a fault, impatient of nonsense & without a particle of frivolity', a 'woman of strong will & fertile brain', 'thoroughly good' and 'the right wife for Dr Wilson'.[133] Next he describes Kathleen Scott: 'To start with I like Mrs Scott & admit her many excellent qualities – for myself I can honestly say she has been kindness always . . . invited herself to tea with me over & over again.' Some of Emily's parenting has obviously percolated through into her son. He is attempting to look at the thing disinterestedly but he's leading up to something. Teddy's wife is obviously his favourite.

> [Hilda] is a person apart – in my esteem – She is not my style in most ways but for a womanly woman of remarkable beauty & general charm she stands out of the crowd as almost everything a wife should be. Unfortunately her excellent qualities have laid her open to much jealousy & that's where the trouble has been between Scott & Teddy. In minor ways the influence of the petticoat has raised that uneasy feeling among a party of men.

Later Birdie concludes: 'Mrs Evans . . . is popular with everyone. Mrs Scott is another sort. I don't like to see women out of their provinces (don't tell May this). Mrs S. is very ambitious and has too much say with the expedition for my liking . . . She appears to influence her husband & to make this apparent is a crime.'[134]

Is Emily still reading out loud when she arrives at '(don't tell May this)'? May is Birdie's favourite sparring partner. He sometimes jokes, 'I wish her much immunity from lockjaw.'[135] May is as clever as her brother, better by far at hitting a ball. But what has she got to look forward to? 'Summer is over!' writes May in her diary, but it is only just beginning for her brother.[136] For Emily, accustomed to negotiating this particular sibling relationship, it is important that they are not distracted – Kathleen Scott's influence is endangering the organisation of the expedition. Kathleen's meddling, whether motivated by jealousy or ambition, is obviously bad for the expedition and what is bad for the expedition is bad for 'my own dear laddie'.[137] What is the worst that could happen? Mutiny?

II SEPTEMBER 1910

KATHLEEN – RMS *CORINTHIC*

The only way to get to New Zealand is by boat. They must leave the dry land of the Cape and go to Melbourne to get money from the Australian government and replenish supplies, and then it is on to New Zealand. Kathleen braces herself for the next leg of the seasick journey. Scott is sailing with the *Terra Nova* this time, she is going by liner, the RMS *Corinthic*. The downside, as far as she is concerned, is that she must be lumped together with the wives again. She uses the collective noun 'herd' – there is something bovine about them. Kathleen walks up the gangplank followed by Hilda and Oriana. In charge of the harem, on wife duty, is a reluctant-looking Bill.

They are all trying to get used to the sudden change of plan. On their return from Johannesburg, Scott had announced that he would be taking over the captaincy from Teddy and giving Oriana's husband the expedition begging cap. Everyone is surprised and disappointed except the Scotts. Even Oriana realises that her husband would have been happier with the men on the *Terra Nova*: 'It is pleasant for me and for Ory too,' says Bill, 'to know that the people on the ship have done all they could to persuade Scott to let me come.'[138]

Kathleen does not mind that her husband is not with her. 'I was very glad,' she writes. 'We felt that he ought to be with his Expedition, & it was very lucky that it was possible. [Teddy and Hilda] were much upset at this decision, fearing it would look as tho' he had not been [a] sufficiently capable [captain on the voyage from Cardiff], but this was more petty of them than was their wont. [Scott] was unaware of this foolish sentiment & would never have dreamt of crediting them with it.'[139] This is disingenuous. Hilda bores Kathleen. She seems childish, just the kind of simpering little wife Kathleen loathes.

The ship has hardly left port when Kathleen begins to feel seasick. She tries to discuss expedition affairs with Bill, out of earshot of the other women, but he will not be drawn. It is intensely irritating. 'I gather he thinks women aren't much use,' she writes in her diary, having retreated to her cabin with the sick bucket. '[I] expect he is judging from long experience so I bear him no malice.'[140]

Later she recovers her sense of humour: 'I'm a woman. Damn! I make myself frocks. I wash frocks. I read novels. I am apathetic. I shall presently become hysterical.'[141] Sewing, washing, reading romance, apathy, hysteria, that's what little girls are made of. Yet it irks her to be lumped together with females who aren't 'much use'. If the point of women is to produce babies, Oriana and Hilda have singularly failed in this purpose. Both have been married for longer than she has and yet neither has yet guaranteed their husbands' genetic inheritance. She, however, has produced children (or at least one child with immediate plans for more). She is beginning to realise that 'My hatred of women is becoming a monomania and must be curbed.'[142]

On a cerebral rather than biological level, she discusses expedition affairs with Scott and he often acts upon her advice. 'Being treated [by Bill] as an outsider as regards expedition affairs is very unfair.'[143] She is her only exception to her rule: 'There is no consistency about her,' wrote one of her husband's future biographers approvingly. Inconsistency, that delightful feminine attribute: 'She will argue by the hour on the personal inferiority of woman, yet in practice can seldom refrain from confuting her own argument.'[144]

But it is not only women who can be inconsistent. What did the men of the Terra Nova want? Simpering wifelettes, 'pathetic grass widows', or robust, outspoken champions like her? Even they could not decide. Kathleen knows that one day Dr Simpson 'was seen standing in the door of his cabin haranguing Mr Lillie & in a complete state of nudity announcing, "When I get married, I shall marry a really intellectual woman."'[145] Kathleen does not aspire to be 'really intellectual' but her husband appreciates her intelligence. The all-male acceptance of nudity aboard her husband's Terra Nova is in sharp contrast to his requirement for Kathleen to 'dress well' to keep up appearances right now on board the Corinthic.

Without the full complement of husbands on the liner, the implication is that the wife takes her husband's rank. Hilda, Teddy's wife, is nominally the second-in-command to Captain Kathleen. But Hilda is from New

Zealand, she is heading home and with every mile her confidence increases. Oriana has the edge on Kathleen by virtue of her experience. She is the only one who has been 'here' before. When Scott returned from Antarctica in 1904, it was Oriana who acted as 'Mrs Scott', his co-host at the legendary post-expedition *Discovery* ball in Christchurch.

From her position at the rail, handkerchief at the ready, Kathleen watches all the other women in their preposterously broad-brimmed *Merry Widow* hats. The Austrian Franz Lehár's operetta has made the hats fashionable and the *Merry Widow* waltz the most hummable tune in the Empire. Oriana and Hilda keep active: deck quoits, table tennis, deck golf, but Bill moans about the 'impossibility of keeping as fit'. What he needs is a jolly good game of Furl the Topgallant Sails.

Kathleen eschews deck games but practises callisthenics in her cabin. Catharine Beecher adapted the German exercises for women, based on the principle of using the person's own body weight as resistance. They are slow and toning and designed to keep one *kállos* (beautiful) and *sthenos* (strong). On land Kathleen always dances to keep up her vitality, but the sick bucket is an indifferent partner for the two-step waltz, and worse for the tango.

As Kathleen becomes accustomed to an ever-present sense of nausea, she notices that the Wilsons are teaching Hilda how to identify sea birds. Bill is a noted ornithologist. Oriana, it seems, is a decent bird spotter. She is better on Southern Ocean gulls than her husband – the rare occasions when he is able to identify a bird first are remarked upon. Kathleen does not alter her 'not much use' opinion. As the three stare through the twin tunnels of their binoculars at the sky, Kathleen looks to make the acquaintance of other passengers.

Her irreverent observations on a similar trip read like a novelette blurb: 'Captain Shannon, Captain Maitland and 3rd ADC Captain Hamilton who loves a Miss Elgar with pretty red hair. Captain Shannon loves Miss Boyle but there's no money.'[146] Kathleen makes the acquaintance of a 'boy', Mr Hull.[147] He is the 'nice son' of Mr Henry Charles Hull, the South African finance minister. Mr Hull junior has no immediate plans to follow his father into the government and is off to learn sheep farming near Sydney. Mr Hull junior is romantic and impressionable. He is the only thing between Kathleen and death by boredom.

SEPTEMBER 1910

ORIANA – RMS *CORINTHIC*

Oriana Wilson has brought some natural canvas, textile tape and a metal buckle to make a sketchbook pouch for Bill to wear over his parka. She places his sketchbook on the canvas and draws round it with a soft pencil. It soothes Bill to see her busy. He believes that the hum of her Singer sewing machine knocks anyone out of the blues because it has got such a very 'busy buzz'. They avoid the issue of Kathleen Scott's developing intimacy with the young Mr Hull. The Wilsons have already established that if people choose to go wrong, they are best avoided. Bill diplomatically observes that 'Mrs Scott is a bad sailor. I saw little of her.'[148]

Bill loathes business. As Ory stitches, Bill outlines his plan for extracting the required £5,000 from the Australian government. This is all Shackleton's fault. After Shackleton raised his own sponsorship for the *Nimrod* expedition, Scott was obliged to do the same. Bill fears that Douglas Mawson, the Australian geologist who covets Bill's position as head of the scientific staff, might put a spanner in the works. Mawson and Shackleton were planning an expedition together. Ory says nothing, but sews on. 'Mawson,' Bill tells the top of his wife's head, 'will no doubt have Shackleton to back him.'[149]

These comments on Shackleton's attempts to thwart Scott's expedition are precisely the sort of thing Bill urges the rest of the expedition, wives included, not to commit to paper. Although Kathleen may have felt that Bill treated her as 'an outsider as regards expedition affairs', Oriana is his sounding board. She stitches and listens, but the lines are blurring.

Together with Hilda Evans they are enchanted by the dancing petrels that 'come down to look at stuff that might be food – the feet drop & they paddle [dancing] quickly along the surface.'[150]

By the end of the trip Bill bestows his biggest compliment upon Hilda. She is 'exceedingly nice . . . as well as being always ready for active games all the voyage'. Ignoring Kathleen's very public *à deux* with young Mr Hull, both Ory and her husband conclude that 'on the whole [they were] very glad to get to know [Hilda] so well, for she is a real brick'.[151]

EARLY OCTOBER 1910

LOIS − PORTSMOUTH

At the end of a day of cooking and washing and cleaning, Lois lights a candle and leads the way upstairs. Without Taff coming home in the evening with his stories and shanties, it can be strangely quiet. Lois might sing to her children. She will never forget the songs learned in her teens when her voice had first come to public notice, and the nerves in the Middleton schoolroom on 21 August 1895 when she was just sixteen. The performance began with the trio − Lois together with Flora Lucas the rector's daughter and Olive Bevan − singing Gilbert and Sullivan's 'Three Little Maids'. This was followed by a duet, with Lois and Flora singing 'Blow, Gentle Wind', and finally Lois's solo, 'O'er Life's Dark Sea'.[152]

If a Swansea artiste was held up on the unmetalled roads on the way out to a venue, usually an inn, in Gower, the locals including 'Lois the Voice' could step in. The Beynon's pub, the Ship Inn, became popular with tourists, especially on feast days like Mapsant Day. When the Methodist minister called Mapsant on 12 November 'an ungodly gathering . . . meeting of the Devil for drinking and dancing', Lois's horizons narrowed. The Temperance movement and the Methodists got together with the local landowners. The Ship Inn required a licence. Without it the Beynons could not trade.

Years later, in the bedroom at 52 Chapel Street, Portsmouth, Lois might put Norman, Muriel and Ralph to bed with a song or a story. Taff's favourite is *The Three Musketeers* by Alexandre Dumas, a swash-buckling drama in which heroic swordsmen fight for justice. Or Lois can read them one of Taff's letters home. Taff was Neptune in a play onboard the *Terra Nova*, a naval tradition of initiation for those who'd never crossed the Equator. He thoroughly enjoyed his brief moment as king, with authority over the officer class.

Norman, aged five, can imagine himself a handsome Neptune. Neptune's wife was Queen Amphitrite. Muriel, aged just four, will make an excellent Amphitrite. (Amphitrite's voice, Lois tells her children, is the only thing that can soothe her husband's mighty rages and lull him into a deep slumber so that the ocean can be at peace.)

Lois reads through the cast, many of them Taff's fellow ratings, his friends: the Doctor (Seaman James Paton); the Barber (Bosun Alfred Cheetham); the Clerk (Petty Officer George Abbott); two Policemen

(Tom Crean and Petty Officer Thomas Williamson) and finally two Bears, the only officers involved – Captain Oates and Dr Atkinson.

Lois can tell that Taff had scripted Neptune's address. It shows his quick wit, sailing just shy of insubordination. As an opening remark, Neptune had observed that the ship still had a bad leak. Neptune wondered whether the leak was due to the tuneless singing of sea shanties at the pumps that his royal ear was forced to endure. Neptune said that the stiff breezes he had sent them seemed to have veered around and blown up the hawse pipes, which meant the sails had to be furled in the middle watch in the early hours of the morning. Neptune wondered at the progress of the ship. Were they towing a sea anchor? Was the rudder lying athwartships? In summary, Neptune declared that the *Terra Nova* 'would go a long way in a long time'.[153]

After prayers, Lois blows out the candle. The Captain, Teddy, had apparently decorated Taff for his services as Neptune before splicing the main brace and ordering port for everyone. Taff thought it was a bit dry – he'd hoped for more than a dram after all his exertions. 'A little of what you fancy,' music-hall star Marie Lloyd sang, 'did you good,' after all.

12 OCTOBER 1910

ORIANA – MELBOURNE, AUSTRALIA

Sitting in the backseat of a motorcar, Ory watches the tea trees rush by. They are being driven out into the bush for a spot of birding, a welcome break from the harem at the Menzies Hotel. Kathleen has been determined to get hold of their husbands' mail, even marching up to the Melbourne Post Office herself to demand it. Ory leaves all that unseemly carry-on behind, noting that these trees are not trees any more than tree ferns are trees. They are *Leptospermum scoparium*, an upright evergreen shrub with small white or pink flowers that have an elegant scent of jasmine. Bill has promised Kathleen that he will check in with the hotel by telephone. At the last village before they enter the bush, he makes a call back along the telegraph wires that loop alongside the road. There is a telegram. The *Terra Nova* is expected in about six hours. Ory had hoped to drive on to Dandenong, with luxurious 'intact' native bush. Instead they picnic awkwardly, standing by the side of the dusty road.

Trying not to let her binoculars bump into the bone around her eye sockets, Ory looks for birds on their return drive. She spots crow-shrikes, kookaburras and 'the most magnificent parakeets and wonderfully coloured lorikeets'. Trying to rescue Ory from her disappointment, Bill notes that 'It is an epoch in one's life, I think, to see these beautiful long-tailed lorikeets on the wing in their own country . . . their wonderful colouring yellow, orange, crimson, blue and green.' Too soon they are back at the Menzies Hotel, where Kathleen and Hilda are waiting. They pick up a sackful of mail and take the train to Port Melbourne, arriving at about 5 p.m. There is no sign or word of the *Terra Nova*. They have tea at an inn and wait at the petrol-canning factory that is supplying the expedition with Shell motor spirit for the motor sledges. It begins to drizzle.

Bill gets hold of a launch and, having loaded the three wives, motors out into the bay to see if they can see the ship. They get as far as the lighthouse, where they are told the *Terra Nova* is still four miles out. They return to shelter and wait. They sally forth again through the dusk and the now pouring rain, motoring towards the swinging anchor lights on each ship. None of the ships is the *Terra Nova*. They return to the canning factory.

The wind is getting up and everyone in the boat is 'soaked through'. The sea has become distinctly more dangerous for the 'crank little motor launch'. Bill tries to persuade the three wives to return to the hotel, while he makes one final attempt. Oriana is not going to 'fail' her husband. She will drown before she complains.

The lighthouse finally telephones the canning factory at 9 p.m. to say that the *Terra Nova* is anchored half a mile outside their light. Once more they set out, 'the wives with [Bill] and the mail bag'. By now it is pitch dark. The sea is 'very bad indeed for our beastly little boat'.[154]

12 OCTOBER 1910

KATHLEEN – MELBOURNE

Kathleen, sitting at the other end of the 'beastly little boat', realises that Bill is angry. She laments the fact that the 'other women's needs must come too'. Factoring 'pathetic grass widows' into her plans is unbearably limiting: '[Bill Wilson] was furious with me & protested, the women were cold & hungry.'[155]

Kathleen acknowledges reluctantly: 'It was very dark & very wet & humours were questionable; but I knew my man would expect me &

in spite of a very difficult opposition I persisted . . . At last we arrived at the ship, & as we came along the weather side our little launch got in a bad swell & the ladies thought it was capsizing & wanted to return without going to the ship, but I had heard my good man's voice & was sure there was no danger.'

It is, all of them are aware, highly irregular for a woman to board the ship. Hilda and Oriana stay in the launch, drenched and shivering and gripping on to the seats lest they be catapulted out. Kathleen climbs out and up the ladder into the *Terra Nova*. She 'went down to the wardroom – so snug it looked, filled with beaming brown faces & pipes – A cheery scene after the hours of coldness & churlishness. So I went to [Scott]'s & Teddy's cabin for they had all but finished changing to come ashore with us & I changed my drenched stockings with a pair of [Scott's] socks, & so ashore – a very happy meeting.'

Kathleen is probably aware of the effect of changing her stockings in a boat bursting with men who have not seen a woman for a month, but she pretends innocence. Dr Simpson, who emerges from his cabin (this time with his clothes on), makes no recorded comment. At a time when it was scandalous for women to 'show a bit of ankle', Kathleen, who regards herself as an 'insider' as regarded expedition affairs, writes again as if the rules do not apply to her.

Perhaps Kathleen knows about Amundsen's telegram, which has been waiting in Melbourne ever since they arrived. She would like to be able to say that her husband's first reaction is to send Amundsen a good luck telegram.[156] Somehow, Scott quickly masters the disinterested gentlemanly response: 'I decided long ago to do exactly as I should have done had Amundsen not been down here. If he gets to the Pole, he is bound to do it rapidly with dogs,* but one guesses that success will justify him, and that our venture will be out of it. If he fails, he ought to hide.'[157]

---

* Scott's curiously resigned reference to dogs offers insight into what many consider his greatest failure. He was not ignorant of the advantage of dog-sledging, rather he thought it akin to cheating: 'No journey made with dogs', he wrote 'can approach the sublimity of a party of men who succeed by their own unaided efforts. Surely in this (latter) case, the conquest is more nobly and splendidly won.' (Quoted in Cameron, 1980, p. 148)

12 OCTOBER 1910

ORIANA – MELBOURNE

Nursing their cups of cocoa in bed back at the Menzies Hotel, Bill tells Ory that she 'behaved like a brick all through our difficulties in the bay, but in the future I hope it will never fall to my lot to have more than one wife at a time to look after, at any rate in a motor launch, in a running sea at night time'.[158]

It is all right to laugh about it now. Before he turns out the paraffin lamp, he finishes his journal entry: 'It was for [the husbands] on board to say whether I should risk drowning their wives now, so as they seemed in favour of it I went in.' One wife was really enough for him. Though, obviously, if they had children he would 'look after' them too.

Earlier that week, Ory had introduced Bill to 'John', the four-year-old son of Major Wilson and his wife Mabel, distant relatives who lived in Melbourne. John is 'a splendid little chap, cram full of fun'.[159] Bill watched his childless wife enchanted by a child. Back in England his niece Ruth calls him 'Uncle Toad'. He sends her amphibian kisses. Why are he and Ory childless? Which of them is infertile?

Is it him, after his treatment for tuberculosis in his early twenties? The Davos sanatorium in Switzerland was extreme. Or is it Ory with her 'bad headaches' and her unreliable appetite, perhaps a form of anorexia nervosa? Both of them come from large Victorian families. It would be easier to leave for the expedition if he knew she had part of him to comfort her. Ory is in her mid-thirties. Is it conceivable that God will yet smile on their union and Bill will be greeted on his return from the Antarctic by a little boy like John, wearing a *Terra Nova* ribbon in his straw hat?

But Ory is still reeling from the shock of Amundsen. She knows the rules, all she has to do is keep quiet. While the rest of the British Antarctic Expedition fume silently, Ory writes that 'Scott had a cable from [RGS secretary] Scott Keltie to say that Amundsen was on his way to McMurdo Sound! It is really very mean of him.'[160]

LOIS – PORTSMOUTH

Roald Amundsen's challenge is published in the newspapers. Since the *Terra Nova* expedition is seen as a naval enterprise, the Portsmouth docks buzz with righteous indignation. When Lois learns the news, she hears it in the knowledge that, ever since they were children, Taff has risen to a challenge. He thrives on competition.

CAROLINE – GESTINGTHORPE

Caroline Oates receives an unusually expensive telephone call from her son-in-law Frederick Ranalow. Their conversation costs an exorbitant 5 shillings. This is followed a few days later with 2 shillings' worth of telegrams. What is happening to Europe? England was Norway's chief supporter in gaining independence from Sweden. Queen Maud of Norway is the late King Edward VII's youngest daughter. Caroline sallies forth with her chequebook. On 21 October she spends 13 shillings 6 pence on a pair of boots from Jaeger for Laurie. It might not solve Amundsen, but at least Laurie will go into 'battle' well shod.

From Melbourne, Laurie's first reaction is to tell Caroline – by a combination of telegram and letter – that:

> If he [Amundsen] gets to the Pole first we shall come home with our tails between our legs and make no mistake. I must say we have made far too much noise about ourselves, all that photo-graphing, cheering, steaming through the fleet etc. etc. is rot and if we fail it will only make us look more foolish. They say Amundsen has been underhand the way he has gone about it but I personally don't see it is underhand to keep your mouth shut. I myself think these Norskies are a very tough lot. They have 200 dogs and Yohansen [sic] is with them and he is not exactly a child, also they are very good ski-runners while we can only walk. If Scott does anything silly such as underfeeding his ponies he will be beaten sure as death.[161]

17 OCTOBER 1910

KATHLEEN – MELBOURNE

Having battled seasickness from England to Australia, Kathleen does not want to have to ask if there is a 'ladies' powder room' on the warship HMS *Powerful*. She intends to enjoy herself. The *Powerful* is at least at anchor in the relatively still waters of Melbourne Bay. The warship is more than three times the length of the *Terra Nova* and beside it the whaler looks like a bath toy. Hilda and Oriana are safely

tucked away at the Menzies Hotel. It is 'a very nice party of men &
myself – All parties should be like that.'[162]

They have been to the Melbourne races, where Captain Oates wore
an 'indescribable hat', and Kathleen asked every enfranchised Australian
woman she met if they voted differently to their husbands. Most did
not, a straw poll confirming her anti-suffrage sympathies: men can vote
for their women.*

Kathleen nearly confesses to a 'monomania of woman hating', but
Admiral Poore is of the old school.[163] One's wife hosted the wives of other
naval officers and took an interest in the welfare of the wives of lower
deck, that is how one became an admiral. Kathleen has a vision of obligatory all-female Antarctic lunches and visits to ratings' wives – it does not
fill her with joy. She will write to the rating's wives if there is good news
and only visit if the news is bad. Antarctic lunches with the officer class
wives in London while the *Terra Nova* is away must be endured.

The Scotts are taken back to land in the admiral's launch, but they miss
the last train back to the Menzies Hotel. They decide to walk up the
train tracks into town. The rails gleam in the light of a pale moon.
They discuss Kathleen's future 'from my own little feminine point of
view, which was pleasant'.[164] The discussion covers old ground lightly
– faithfulness, sex and fertility.

The Scotts are most decided about sex and their opinions are formed
by Marie Stopes. Scott met her by chance during one of his fund-raising
lectures. At the time she was interested in geology, fern fossils and the
emerging theory of continental drift. Coal from the Antarctic might
prove the theory. She would like to get that coal. But Stopes is not only
interested in geology. She is compiling notes for a book that she will
call *Married Love*. The assumption, historically, is that men are biologically obliged to release sperm even by 'buying another body'. She
maintains that this biological imperative is a myth and that they are
selling their health and honour, and running a real risk of contracting
venereal disease (and, more importantly, passing the disease on to their
chaste brides).[165] To give her argument credibility among men, Stopes

---

* By 1908, two years before Kathleen's straw poll, all white Australian women over the
age of twenty-one had been given the vote. Fifteen years earlier in 1893, all New
Zealand women of age became enfranchised.

quotes Professor Forel's *The Sexual Question*, published in 1908: 'It is quite possible for a normal man to contain himself much longer and it is his duty to do so, not only when his wife is ill, but also during menstruation and pregnancy.' The Forel–Stopes principle must apply in the Antarctic. After Marie Stopes met Scott, she wrote repeatedly to him, asking to be considered for the British Antarctic Expedition team – perhaps to geologise while testing the principle of celibacy? She was so insistent and Scott so polite in his refusal, that she really believed he was considering her request.

As Kathleen and Scott walk along the rail tracks towards the Menzies Hotel, they discuss *The Sexual Question* and Marie's theory of faithfulness. Does Scott realise that male worship is rocket fuel for Kathleen? Is he aware that she is considered to be a curiously moral creature among her artistic set – the Beardsleys' *Yellow Book* crowd – who regard marriage as an open affair? The Scotts walk their parallel tracks trying to establish a convergence – the future of their marriage is in the balance.

Kathleen has always kept a record of when her monthly 'periodical tribulations' (as Scott calls them) are due, with a cross and 'came' or 'right' if they did.[166] Conceiving Peter was a scientific mission. She summoned her husband home at the appropriate times. Now, while she follows him across the world, it is more difficult to coordinate her fertility with his availability. He needs to be with her but also with his men aboard the all-male *Terra Nova*. As gum trees rustle their sickle leaves in the shadows on either side of the rail track, the Scotts try to find a modus operandi that will allow them both to fulfil their biological potential and their dreams. Finally Scott agrees that Kathleen can 'Do anything you like but don't get talked about.'[167]

21 NOVEMBER 1910

EMILY – BUTE

'Captain Scott sent for me,' writes Birdie from his bunk in the *Terra Nova* en route to Melbourne.[168] Emily, beside the coal fire in the front room of her downstairs flat in Ardbeg, peers at this missive from the southern hemisphere through her half-moons. Back on the first day of October, her son had been summoned before the headmaster. What had he done? Birdie too wondered what on earth he had done wrong and really believed he was in for a 'wigging'. But the headmaster had other plans: '[Scott]

said "I have decided to have you ashore with me."' Birdie would be
spending the winter in Antarctica after all, and even had a chance of being
chosen for the party that would make the final push south to the Pole.

As usual, Emily's desire for unconsciousness is inversely represented
in Birdie, who is cock-a-hoop. 'I could jump up & turn a somersault in
the air with joy . . . It is the stores more than anything else that brings
me ashore. At least that is Scott's excuse for changing me with Rennick.'
What is it about her children? If only they weren't so capable. (May, who
had been in the Ardbeg tennis finals that August, has just been elected
'Lady Convener'. Edie is now sister of her ward.) Why can't they just
be 'normal' sailors, tennis players, nurses, etc.? Why all this promotion?
It is like a Midas curse. Emily supposes that whoever this Lieutenant
Rennick may be (the man whom Birdie will replace in the land party),
he is less capable than Birdie. Most people are. Even through her initial
panic she recognises that however unglamorous a job 'stores' may be, it
is the difference between life and death in the Antarctic.

'I am longing to get down to the ice now & to build our house &
then go on the great depot journey which will prepare us for the forth-
coming year . . . rather a Hurrah show altogether,' continues Birdie.
The English Church, the New Zealand versions of 'bewitching maidens',
the relative safety of taking soundings and what-have-yous off the coast
in order to make good use of the time – all dust.

'I am as pleased as punch. I am sure you will be glad too when you
come to reflect on all the possibilities of being ashore,' says Birdie.
'Thank the Lord for His many mercies . . . If any incident prevented
me from going now it would be the greatest blow to my life.'

Emily tries to recover from the blow to *her* life. She remembers the
initial 'bombshell' telegram: 'Appointed Antarctic'. She and May got
the good news telegram that the *Terra Nova* had arrived safely in
Melbourne, after a day in Glasgow seeing Mr Mann's pictures. (She
had enjoyed Mr Mann's pictures – he was one of the famous Glasgow
Boys.) And when she returned home from the gallery, to be greeted
by Birdie's telegrammed message 'All Well', it just added to her feeling
of satisfaction. But it was not well.

After sending his initial appointment telegram at the beginning of
the year, Birdie apologised. '[I] do regret that cablegram, but that is no
good now.'[169] He has deliberately avoided a cablegram this time and

Emily finds that she has been living for a month in false comfort. 'We have mixed feelings,' observes May diplomatically.[170] But the insidious sensation of presentiment returns to Emily with full force – the terrible sense that she will not see her son again.

In his letter, he at least has the decency to respond to theirs, brought, rather damp, by Bill that night in Melbourne harbour. Birdie is careful not to trivialise home lives by comparison with his 'national show';[171] in Edie's case it is not hard: 'Nursing at best must always be a difficult job I am sure,' he writes, trying to imagine how he would feel with 'my patient kicking the bucket & having a death at my doors, on the other hand it would be a great pleasure to bring someone who had nearly gone. You will have experienced both things of course.'[172]

He acknowledges that it will be 'strange to be left all alone on a vast continent with not a single woman and no civilised land nearer than 2,000 miles across the great Southern Ocean. Needless to say I would not forego it for anything and am tremendously bucked at being one of the landing party.'

Birdie has sometimes wondered at his lack of interest in parties and girls: 'I think in some respects I am not mature yet – quite different from most chaps of my age, and looked upon as a sort of conundrum.'[173] Birdie admitted to May that he did not seem to feel the need for 'the physical side or animal side of love', like his father who only married late in life.[174] Emily wouldn't mind if their son followed suit. George Fouchar, whom she had all but raised in her Casa di Bambino in Sidcup, has recently eloped, causing his mother no end of anxiety. Emily can trust Birdie not to do that. Birdie cannot guarantee that he will marry rich, but he has promised, 'The day is coming when I am going to make up everything to you, you can depend upon that . . . you will yet be jolly glad you have had a son, although he has cost you a lot!'[175]

So Birdie doesn't rule out 'getting spliced'.[176] Some 'peculiar fellows', he observes, manage to persuade 'nice girls' to be their wives somehow, and he has just met one in Christchurch: 'I cast my eyes on a little girl named Dorothy . . . ridiculously small . . . extraordinarily pretty with a delightful self-awareness & will of her own.' Dorothy ticks all the boxes, but when her parents whisk her away to the country Birdie makes a conscious effort to see it as a blessing: 'I was spared what otherwise would have been an unhappy or not unmixed parting had things gone on for another week.'[177] And to be honest, the lure of Dorothy soon pales beside the lure of the ice.

Still 'bucked' and with Dorothy already a vague memory, he asks his womenfolk back home to sew him a sledging flag and sends the precise dimensions and design: 'From antiquity in Polar Exploration an unwritten law has been that officers in charge of sledges shall have a flag mounted on their sledge. These in our case must consist of a pennant about 2 ½ feet long by 1 foot broad made of silk with Saint George's cross at the hoist and the owner's private crest, colours or device on the other part marked X.'[178] Birdie has sketched a diagram. He knows that his mother could sew a wedding dress with her eyes shut but he is enjoying himself. 'Thus, I shall have to think of a device though the other chaps who had theirs made at home had them done to proper heraldic form.'

Emily feels sure that the heroes of antiquity were focused mainly on sunny sailing trips around the Mediterranean and steered well clear of what she cannot help thinking are 'foolhardy' forays to icy waste-lands. But Birdie's 'shall-ing' and 'thus-ing' reveal that he still has his 'tongue hanging out' with enthusiasm. He doesn't tell Emily that his friend, Captain Oates, can't see the point of flags – Oates has had heraldry 'up to here' – but Birdie knows that Emily will be pleased to hear that the Bowerses are going to become 'crested'. And besides, if this were a sewing bee, his mother would beat Captain Oates's mother hands down. Emily might even throw a couple of stitches to pretend that sewing has always been a hobby and never a trade.

Emily is aware of the subtext. Birdie is telling her to take the 'pig's ear' of the situation and make it into a 'sow's purse', or at least a sledging flag with the motto *Esse quam videri* – 'To be, rather than to seem'.

NOVEMBER 1910

KATHLEEN – CHRISTCHURCH

Among the many things that irritate Kathleen are the 'stuffy little house[s]' of settlers in New Zealand.[179] Why come halfway round the world to recreate a Little England – what a waste of an opportunity. She recognises that the New Zealanders are trying to be kind, 'but I felt stifled.' Stuffiness both of air and attitude are not things she can put up with for very long. 'The atmosphere of the house is physically and mentally bad,' she observes of Mrs Rhode's hospitality; there is 'no air & petty scandal & nothing more . . . [Scott] & I were paraded & dissatisfied & things went badly.' As an alternative, Joseph Kinsey, the British Antarctic Expedition agent, has offered a hammock in the garden of Te Hau, his summer house just outside the city. The hammock is slung between trees in a corner of the garden facing east, with the edge of the cliff just a few yards away, and beyond that the Pacific Ocean. Surely even Kathleen cannot feel stifled there.

All day Scott has to be in Christchurch at the expedition office but in the evening he walks back across the Port Hills to his wife's embraces. He leaves the administration behind, and in this 'wholly enchanting' Eden indulges in the animal sensations it evokes and in 'feelings of inexpressible satisfaction with all things'.[180]

Despite the fresh air sleeping arrangements, the previous evening had gone worse than badly. They were at a dance, yet another, and Scott had come in with a letter from a Mr Hull, claiming that he and Kathleen had become close on the sea passage over from the South African Cape. 'He didn't like it,' writes Kathleen in her diary, '& it certainly did read stupidly.'[181]

For Kathleen, Mr Hull had been a distraction from seasickness and the herd of wives on board the RMS *Corinthic*. But Mr Hull, it transpired, had received a different impression. Kathleen realised that to leave the dance would have been an admission of guilt. What would the Little Englanders' 'petty scandal' merchants make of that? She did not think she was guilty, nor did she want to waste a perfectly good invitation to dance. 'I was not going to spoil the evening on account of this tiresome mistake. I danced till the end . . . & enjoyed it enormously.' As she danced, she was aware that the evening could have gone very differently.

As dawn breaks on the eastern horizon, creeping over the garden to the hammock where they lie, she acknowledges that '[Scott] took my word. If he had not I don't know what might happen.' Back in 1908, during their engagement, she'd worried about shackling herself to conventional ideas of fidelity but Scott reassured her. Kathleen was relieved – 'Knock a few conventional shackles off me, and you'll find as great a vagabond as you.'[182] The morning after the Christchurch dance, a hammock away from stuffiness and convention, Kathleen reaffirms her choice of mate. Among the pressures and politics of preparation, their task is deliciously simple.

Before Peter was born, Kathleen referred to her bump by the most despicable female name she could think of, 'Griselda' from Chaucer's *Canterbury Tales*. Griselda was a woman who was so subordinate to her man that she erased herself entirely. Kathleen could not bear to have a girl, she could not, surely, 'bear' a girl. She did not want to worry about it: 'We are agreed it is not wise to make life into Hell by anticipating things that may never happen,' she told Scott, but to address 'Griselda' head-on was like taking snake venom to cure a bite.[183]

Kathleen's mother had given birth to eleven children but died shortly after Kathleen, the eleventh, was born. Kathleen has no mother to ask if there is a way of ensuring that one conceives a male. Instead she asked Scott to report back from a talk on sex at the British Association. Someone has told her that a cushion should be placed under the pelvis after sex, to tip it backwards for the best chance of the egg being fertilised. She does that. She feels instinctively that optimism and wild food will beget an optimistic child who is healthy as well as happy. Scott puts her right: 'Hereditary tendencies were considered to play a very large part [but] there was much to prove the absence of influence on the embryo by the physical or mental condition of the mother.'[184]

Kathleen is not deterred. She must prevent Scott's 'black moods', his pessimism, from percolating into their yet-to-be-conceived child. 'Dear, are you still and always an unhappy man?' she sometimes asks him. 'Oh what's the matter . . . What is the matter?'[185] If he is depressed in the Antarctic, he will surely lose the confidence and perhaps even the respect of his men. She must be careless and confident, optimistic and risk-taking enough for both of them.

25 NOVEMBER 1910

CAROLINE – GESTINGTHORPE

Caroline is helped out of her carriage into the bustle and hawkers of Sudbury's Friday market. She alights in the cobbled square opposite the fifteenth-century church of St Peter. It is a cold morning, and as she wraps her fur stole around her she can see her breath. It is on this spot, in this square, that she and the great and good of Sudbury intend to erect a statue of Thomas Gainsborough. Australian sculptor Bertram Mackennal has been commissioned. Sketches awaiting approval reveal a Renaissance contrapposto pose, a paintbrush in the right hand hovering over a paint palette in the left. Caroline and the other patrons will invite Princess Louise, Queen Victoria's daughter, to come to Sudbury to unveil it.

Caroline knows Mackennal's work – everyone does. Mackennal has made a profile of George V for the Coronation Medal and the same profile is now on thousands, millions even, of red Three Halfpennny postage stamps. Caroline enters the post office on Sudbury's cobbled square to send a telegram to Laurie, who is about to set sail for Antarctica. On the red stamp, she notices that below Mackennal's excellent profile of the monarch is a turbulent sea, abounding with toothy, heraldic, whale-like creatures. What does the future hold? Gainsborough only had to stroll out across a few fields with a paintbox to satisfy his thirst for adventure.

It is Friday and the post office is busy with soothing, purposeful activity. There are constant comings and goings, collections and despatches of mail both locally, by horse-drawn vans, and further afield by train from Sudbury Station. Caroline, her fur stole wrapped tightly around her neck, approaches the booth. She is handed a rectangular piece of buff-coloured low-quality paper and a pencil. The letter is headed 'Post Office Telegram', with the Crown logo between the first two words. Underneath is the subheading 'Prefix, Time handed in, Office of Origin, Words', with a blank space for her message.

It is impossible to contract all that she feels into the few words her thrifty nature, and the space on the telegram form, require. Laurie's telegram to her is free, compliments of Guglielmo Marconi. When Caroline finishes writing and hands her telegram back to Mr Hill, the Sudbury Postmaster, he writes £1.1.0 in the top left corner. She will have to pay.

Laurie's reply will be brought to Gestingthorpe by horse-drawn van, but she might have glanced at the ABC Universal Commercial Electric Telegraphic Code for help with decoding. Laurie told her that he had gathered all the officers and scientists of the *Terra Nova* on the deck to toast his hero, Napoleon Bonaparte, as an antidote to those Labour Socialists in Cardiff. In the 'ABC', the code includes:

Nalezing – Do only what is absolutely necessary
Nallary – It is not absolutely necessary, but it would be an advantage
Naloopen – It is not absolutely necessary, but well worth the outlay

On the drive home through the frosty November landscape, Caroline has time to reflect on her dyslexic son and his unlikely hero 'Napoleon'. Caroline knew that Laurie had been reading the same book on Napoleon for years now.* The ABC of it is that while this Antarctic expedition is not 'absolutely necessary', it is, in his opinion at least, well 'worth the outlay'. Until now, Caroline's 'tight rein' on Laurie's substantial inheritance has been an effective way of forcing her reluctant correspondent to communicate. She always says yes. Yes to a yacht, *The Saunterer*, yes to a hunter and a pair of polo ponies, and yes to sending that pack of hounds out to enable him to hunt even in Mhow.

Back at the Hall, Caroline seeks privacy in her morning room where a wood fire has been kindled in the grate. She takes out her accounts book, that reliable cut and dried response to 'life's perplexities', and enters the cost of Laurie's telegram.[186] She has just paid 15 shillings as a retainer to Laurie's Indian servants, patiently awaiting Captain Oates's return to Mhow. She enters an amount nearly half as much again just to advertise for servants for herself.

She remembers a time when domestic service accounted for just under half of the employment for all the working women in Britain. In Gestingthorpe, as in the rest of the country, many young women have migrated to the towns and cities. They prefer to work in factories with unions than behind the green baize door. Domestic service was once a job to be proud of, but now there is socialism and unrest, and faithful staff must be solicited – 6 shillings an advertisement.

Generally speaking, Caroline says 'yes' to Laurie. He is, after all, the man of the house. There was one occasion when she may have said 'no'. One day Caroline mentioned, in passing, that a servant, Jemima, at Gestingthorpe had landed herself in 'the usual trouble'; Laurie responded that he felt sorry for her – she was more to be pitied than blamed.[187] Why? Why had Caroline mentioned the servant's 'trouble' to him? Was it just general news or was it to test his response? He did not seem to believe the conventional upper-class wisdom that the servant is always entirely to blame.

In a past Caroline chooses not to remember, Henrietta (Etta) Learmont

---

* The term 'dyslexia' had been coined in 1883 by Professor Berlin, an ophthalmologist in Stuttgart, but it is unlikely that Oates ever knew why he was a slow reader or hated writing letters.

McKendrick, the daughter of a master builder and a domestic servant, got herself into 'the usual trouble'.[188] She'd lived for a time near Meanwoodside, the Oates family seat outside Leeds. The man responsible may have been Laurie. 'The squire and the servant girl' has ancient precedents with equally ancient protocols. Etta was shipped off to Ireland to have the baby, which arrived on 24 March 1900, a few days after Laurie's twenty-first birthday. The baby, a girl, was then removed to the Wright-Kingsford refuge, established in 1898 as a special home for the unwanted children of unmarried mothers. If he was responsible, and there is still some doubt, does Laurie know or at least suspect that he may be a father when he tells his mother that servant girls should be pitied not blamed? If he does know, those best placed to judge his character believe he would have been 'scalded'. The Antarctic, a place without women, would be a welcome refuge. There is no evidence that the discussion about 'Jemima' progressed. Caroline and Laurie are both agreed that 'it is no crime to keep your mouth shut'. Perhaps there are some things that, if left entirely unspoken, can effectively cease to exist.

26 NOVEMBER 1910

TAFF EVANS – LYTTLETON, NEW ZEALAND

Taff has been getting ready for a dry voyage in the usual manner – a pub crawl through Lyttleton, before they move on to the port town of Port Chalmers. When the *Terra Nova* left Cardiff six months before, it took six men to get him aboard. From the deck he'd called out to the crowd at Cardiff in a thunderous whisper, 'Goodbye, we shall always remember you.'[189] Drink makes Taff sentimental not aggressive. The six men who 'helped' him aboard were his friends. But Lieutenant Birdie Bowers has observed that 'a little less of that spirit which did not do us credit on our departure from Cardiff' would lead to more dignified send-offs.[190]

Today is another send-off day, this time from Lyttleton. Mercifully Taff has not been required to give a speech, as he was at the mayor's banquet in Cardiff, but that is not to say that the occasion is without dignitaries. The bishop is due at 2.30 p.m. to take a final service in the ship's stern. Lieutenant Teddy is captaining the ship to Port Chalmers. Teddy's desire for a perfect turnout knows no bounds. He has the added pressure of the editor of a New Zealand newspaper hovering. His wife Hilda has invited her family. Hilda's father is Mr Russell, a rich and prominent member of

Christchurch society and a respected solicitor. He is looking forward to seeing his son-in-law captaining a ship.

The wives and the bishop are expected at 2.15 p.m., but Taff is postponing his hangover. The officers will stand in the stern, the ratings and petty officers will stand further towards the bow. It will be near enough to hear the bishop, but perhaps not near enough for the officers to smell the alcohol on their breath. Now Taff is about to leave the comfort of female company, he is about to leave comfort of any kind – 'grog' is the naval anaesthetic.

At 2 p.m., the stern is full of Royal Navy officers, dressed for the last time for many months in gold-laced uniforms, awaiting the arrival of the bishop for the parting service. In the crowd are Kathleen, Oriana and Hilda. The newspaper editor stands with the Russells. Beyond the *Terra Nova*, in the harbour is a flotilla of ships ready to cheer them out of the harbour. The ships have bunting and streamers, but they are aware of the bishop's service and will not sound their hooters or fire flares until it is over.

The bishop arrives, climbs on board and is ushered to the stern. His text is Luke 12:6: 'Are not five sparrows sold for two copper coins? And not one of them is forgotten before God. But the very hairs of your head are numbered. Do not fear therefore; you are of more value than many sparrows.'

After the service the bishop leaves the ship. Suddenly there is a loud splash. Everyone on the *Terra Nova* hears it. On the quay three wives hear it, the editor hears it, Teddy's relations the Russells hear it. All the boats in the harbour that are waiting for the signal that the service is over see a white splash appear on the *Terra Nova*'s waterline. A moment later, Taff's head bobs up out of the harbour.

LOIS – PORTSMOUTH

On the other side of the world it is three in the morning, and Lois and the children are all deeply asleep. In the photograph propped beside Lois's marital bed, Taff is in his first 'square rig' sailor's uniform. He is a teenager and has just been accepted into the navy as a cadet. He has already earned his proficiency badges. He is not smiling. His eyes are fixed on a point behind her. He is clean shaven and bare headed, his neatly brushed hair parted over his left eye. His neck, even then, is as wide as his head. His features are strong boned and symmetrical – he is a good-looking man.

Jack Tars are often used in advertising, and Taff looks a bit like the man in the popular advert for Brooke's soap – 'Tis used in every clime'. In the advert, a clean-shaven sailor leans over a stone wall and looks at a maiden in Welsh costume, black flower-pot hat over a perfectly white linen bonnet. In the photograph, the ribbon on Taff's uniform, which hangs at the bottom of his sternum, is tied in a perfectly symmetrical 'Brooke's soap' bow.

Navy stipulations allow that a boy under the age of seventeen can have seven bad teeth. Taff had eight but passed. He has been the exception to the rule ever since. Partly it is due to Captain Scott. They have served together in the navy and in the Antarctic. Taff is Scott's own Jack Tar, his talisman. Lois is confident that Scott will allow Taff one more 'tooth' than the other ratings in recognition of this.

Taff fits the popular image of the Tar: 'Properly led . . . [Taff] . . . would go anywhere and do anything and do it with a will.' He was 'always in good humour . . . and if you understood how to manage him, he would do anything he was asked to do – whether he could or not! He would make brooms, milk the cow, play at cricket, march, fight, run, dance sing, play the fiddle, smoke a pipe, drink a glass of grog (or more!).'[191] It was the 'or more' that concerned Lois.

'Go to Sea Once More' is a popular sea shanty about a sailor who, once ashore, gets so drunk that he loses all his clothing and hard-earned money when a prostitute steals them. The song is popular in Portsmouth among Royal Navy Temperance Society members – a warning against strong drink. There is no mention in the navy stipulations of the ability to hold drink, but candidates should have no disease or malformation of the genital organs and a good heart and lungs, without any tendency to hernias. Taff, is 5 foot 10 inches tall and nearly 14 stone. In his recent medical before leaving on the *Terra Nova* he has, once again, been declared in excellent health – no genital malformation due to venereal disease like many of the other sailors. He is a good husband.

Lois is still in bed fast asleep when Taff, on the other side of the world, is called to appear before Captain Scott in full uniform and dismissed.

26 NOVEMBER 1910

ORIANA – CHRISTCHUCH

Harold Stemmer, the Kinseys' gardener, has been watering with the hand-pumped sprayer. The hollyhocks in the flowerbeds of Warimoo,

Kinsey's town house, have survived the five-month drought due to his careful ministrations. The grass is not what Mr Kinsey would call a luxuriant English lawn. That is what he misses most about England. Ory's father was headmaster of Bradfield College, Kinsey, a school-master at Dulwich College – but Kinsey has swapped the British public school for Kinsey & Co., his shipping company. Kinsey wears his boater at a jaunty angle but still misses the rowing and the rugger and most of all the Dulwich College cricket strip. The Warimoo sward, despite Stemmer's best efforts is hard packed and balding.

At the bottom of the garden, Kinsey's 'shed', a Bolton & Paul prefab-ricated wooden hut, is currently being used by expedition photographer Herbert Ponting. The hut smells of warm wood and chinks of weak evening light come through the gaps. On the walls there are two levels of wooden shelves bending under the weight of jars of developing fluid with labelled lids. Under the shelf a loose string is tied between metal hooks. On the string are black-and-white photographs, pegged out to dry.

Pulling a blind down over the window, Kinsey moves to a central table, flicks the switch to the lantern slide projector and inserts a post-card-size glass. A large emperor penguin hits the wooden wall on the opposite side. It is so lifelike. The surface on which the bird is standing is muddy brown – Ponting has been teaching Kinsey how to place colour tint on the slide. Ory knows her husband's colour memory to be 'photographic'. He scribbles precise notes – 'lemon, ochre, royal blue' – all over his sketches for colouring up afterwards. Do these tinted slides render his skill obsolete?

Ory only knows dead emperors, the ones she helped Bill to prepare on his return from the *Discovery* expedition. Some of these still stand in the Canterbury Museum, but the stuffed penguins are not the sleek animals of Bill's watercolours. Their feathers are ruffled, the webs receding from dry toes. Back in 1904 the science of specimen preservation was still a mystery to Ory, cyanide and formaldehyde, magical and deadly. She'd watched from the sidelines. She'd never dissected a bird. Six years on and cyanide and formaldehyde are tamed – with the sweet scent of heather, they take her straight back to the field laboratory at Fort Augustus.

An impromptu lecture on the emperor for their hosts Joseph and Sarah Kinsey? Bill is always better like this. Lecturing to big crowds makes him nervous – this time he will not need to inject himself with a mild sedative. The emperor, Bill tells them, is a fascinating bird. It lives between land and ocean in a place where time is measured in latitude and longitude, the angle of the sun, wind speed and the proximity of an iceberg. The Latin, *Aptenodytes forsteri*, means 'featherless diver'. The emperors' ability to endure harsh conditions and long separation is legendary, their lives a shining avian example of faith, of extreme faithfulness. Sarah Kinsey pronounces that it is high time for dinner.

Back in the main house it is now dark, but in the candlelight the silver sparkles. Oriana chews deliberately while around her the conversation lifts and settles. Science and schools. The Kinseys have servants to serve at table but they are not the same as English servants – they have to be 'petitioned to come'. Back in England, Ory and Bill decided not to have servants. The Kinseys wonder how on earth they manage. Sarah and the Goddess of Domesticity, Mrs Beeton, both know that 'there are few families from the shopkeeper . . . to the nobleman . . . which do not contain servants.'[192] Bill explains:

> O. does all the cooking and house-cleaning, and I do the kitchen-grate and light the fire and clean the flue . . . So you must forgive O. if she shocks you, because she will pick up such horrible expressions. Sometimes she says 'Oh bother' and sometimes she says, 'Well, never mind,' but it's awful to hear her when she breaks things washing up – luckily not our own things – she seems very careful about all our own things.[193]

When they were at home in England, Bill the explorer transformed into something akin to Coventry Patmore's 'Angel in the House': 'I don't smoke and I don't drink, and I have to swear horribly to prevent myself from becoming a little angel and flying away.'

But he will have quite a different task in the Antarctic. He proposes to collect some of those emperor penguin eggs in the middle of the Antarctic winter when the embryos are half formed. Kinsey wonders if a winter journey in the Antarctic is physically possible. Can humans survive those temperatures? Bill admits that since it has never been attempted, it has not been proved impossible. Ory wonders whether Bill is, in fact, the experiment.

The following day they are all at Christchurch station early, waiting for the train south to Dunedin, the nearest proper town to the port at Port Chalmers. 'A 'sweet old lady, Mrs Anderson, came all the way from Opawa to see my Ory off', observes Bill, 'and to give her some lovely flowers which were full of scent'.[194] With the flowers in one hand and her suitcase on the other, Ory climbs into the separate carriage allocated to them on the Christchurch to Dunedin train. The dismissed Taff has come up from Lyttleton to wait on the southbound platform. He enters the Scotts' carriage.

Last time Bill left for the Antarctic, he'd made a plan for the first days of Ory's 'temporary widowhood'. She'd gone to Switzerland with her sister Constance to 'try to forget me'.[195] This time Ory is going to 'stay with the Dennistons [sic]'. Bill has never been to Peel Forest, the Dennistoun's home back up north towards Christchurch. He cannot even spell their name. Saying 'widowhood', albeit prefixed with 'temporary' is a way of disempowering fate. He has often referred to Ory as 'the poor left behind one', or 'his 'grass widow', and now as a 'temporary widow', but he never referred to himself as a 'temporary widower'.[196] He is the active one, the one doing the widowing. Sometimes he worries about what will happen to her. She is the 'very breath of my existence'. In his experience so far, such precious things are often the first taken.[197]

They reach Dunedin at 4 p.m. to find Nelson and Lillie, two of the *Terra Nova* officers, waiting on the platform. Something is wrong. Lillie takes Ory to the hotel. Nelson takes Bill on to Port Chalmers, where the ship is docked. 'Ory knows, and knew then, why.'[198] Bill does not want to write what 'Ory knows' in his diary, an official expedition record. He doesn't even write it in a private letter. He trusts Ory's discretion. It is important that no one realises the truth of the situation. The only thing that is obvious to everyone is Taff climbing out of the Scotts' train carriage as if nothing had happened.

27 NOVEMBER 1910

KATHLEEN – PORT CHALMERS, NEW ZEALAND

At the Port Chalmers wharf, Kathleen finds both Teddy and Hilda 'in a tearful condition' over the situation with Taff. Kathleen concludes that it is all Hilda's fault. Hilda has been working Teddy up to insurrection over this and other perceived slights, '& a volley of childish complaints was let fly. Such as that [Scott] had cut [Teddy's] wife's dance! & many others too puerile to recount, & that therefore he must retire. If ever [Scott] has another expedition the wives must be chosen more carefully than the men, or better still have none.'[199]

Kathleen insists that Hilda come with her to the hotel. She intends to 'bring her to order' and leave Teddy, the 'poor little man', to Scott to deal with. It is 'Capt South Pole Scott' who dictates the terms. If Scott has chosen to retract Teddy's dismissal of Taff, that is his prerogative as leader. He has reinstated Taff after an apology, because he knows that in the Antarctic Taff is worth his weight in solid gold. Scott and Taff have two years of experience of living in the Antarctic. Has Teddy? Though he recognises that Teddy has a grievance, Scott should not have to justify himself to his second-in-command. He believes that in spite of the odd drunken episode before a voyage – typical Jack Tar behaviour – Taff can be trusted.

LAWRENCE OATES – DUNEDIN

The telegram Oates has just received from his mother no longer exists, but it was probably sent from Sudbury via the new Pacific Cable, which is offering cheaper rates than the traditional 'Eastern'. The Pacific Cable has just been laid. It goes under the Atlantic, overland from St John's, Newfoundland to Vancouver and then southwest across the Pacific to the northernmost point of North Island, New Zealand. The New Zealand newspapers have been full of complaints from postal employees of the Eastern, who complain that the new route is undercutting them. It is rather like the fuss Teddy is making now about Scott.

The letter Oates is about to write will take a lot longer than it takes an electric signal to zip along the Pacific Cable. This is partly because he is a slow writer and partly because of sea and tides – things you never have to worry about on a cavalry horse. The hotel's ink sucks up through the nib of his fountain pen. He screws the top and draws a sheet of paper from the stack provided. If all goes well, it should get there shortly after the annual Gestingthorpe Christmas party they host in the huge stone flagged hall. He can picture the Sudbury brass band in the minstrels' gallery on the mezzanine, the Yule log burning brightly in the fireplace, and his mother and his mounted Mhow heads looking on. Although back

home he is responsible for the wellbeing of the whole village, he sometimes wonders if it is less onerous than the responsibility he has now:

> I don't know how long it is since I have been so anxious about
> anything as I am about these ponies. Scott has left everything to
> me in connection with them. When I look at the stalls [built on
> the deck of the *Terra Nova*] sometimes I think they are too small
> and the ponies won't go in and sometimes I think they are too
> big, next minute I think we shall never get them out again if we
> do get them in until I feel positively sick with anxiety . . . I had a
> great struggle with Scott about the horse forage . . . he said, 'not
> 1 oz over 30 [tons] so it's no use arguing' however we argued for
> one hour and he has given way which shows he is open to reason
> . . . he told me I was something of a nuisance.[200]

Scott insists, when asked, that all the animals are in good condition.
It is a lie. The only exam Oates has ever passed with flying colours was
the equine veterinary assessment in the cavalry. He's applied the same
technique to these expedition ponies, running his hands down their
coarse white haired legs, opening their eyes with his thumb and forefinger and lifting their feet to look under their hooves:

> Victor . . . Narrow chest, knock knees . . . suffers with his eyes.
> Aged windsucker.
> Snippets . . . Bad wind sucker. Doubtful back tendons off fore,
> legs. Pigeon toes. Aged.
> James Pigg . . . Sand crack near hind. Aged.
> Bones . . . Aged.
> Snatcher . . . Black marks under eye. Aged.
> Chinaman . . . Has ringworm just above the coronet on near fore.
> I think the oldest pony of the lot which is saying a good deal.
> Christopher . . . Aged. Ringbone off fore. Slightly lame off fore.
> Jehu . . . Aged. Suffering from debility and worn out.
> Nobby . . . Aged. Goes with stiff hocks. Spavin near hind. Best
> pony we have.
> In mentioning the ponies' blemishes I have only mentioned those
> which appear actively to interfere with their work or for identification.[201]

In short, they are a load of 'old crocks'. Scott dismisses Oates as a 'cheery pessimist', while giving the distinct impression that any more negative detail might amount to insubordination. Oates is a paying guest, but he has signed on as a Midshipman – pay: 1 shilling per month – thereby agreeing to abide by naval rules.

Oates is nearly two sheets down (much as he was after he'd drunk 'a skin full of beer' to drown his concerns over those ponies).[202] The letter is finished, it is time for a signoff. Out of the window, he notices two women approaching the hotel. There are so few stone buildings he has forgotten what privacy feels like. Oates can hear Kathleen's voice in discussion with a female New Zealand accent, presumably Hilda. The discussion does not sound light-hearted like the ditty Teddy, Hilda's husband, made up at his expense:

'Who doesn't like female society?
I said Captain Oates
I prefer GOates.'[203]

Oates chooses not to defend himself – with the initials L.E.G. Oates, there have been 'le goat' jokes in the past. He will not be drawn on women. The 'female society' in the hotel lobby has no appreciation of keeping one's mouth shut. Oates remembers refereeing a boxing match in India where the soundtrack was grunting and the slap of flesh on flesh. This is a verbal boxing match with Kathleen's English accent competing with Hilda's colloquial and finally a third. It seems that Kathleen feels that 'There is not a vestige of doubt that [Hilda] is the root of most such troubles, poor little ignorant one.'[204] Now they are all at it.

Later Oates finishes his letter:

Mrs Scott and Mrs Evans had a magnificent battle, they tell me it was a draw after fifteen rounds,' he tells Caroline, grateful for the excuse to keep things light. 'Mrs Wilson flung herself into the fight after the tenth round and there was more blood and hair flying about the hotel than you see in a Chicargo [sic] slaughterhouse in a month, them husbands got a bit of the backwash and there is a certain amount of coolness which I hope they won't bring into the hut with them, however it won't hurt me even if they do.[205]

KATHLEEN – DUNEDIN

The ballroom is already full. The musicians strike up a waltz when the BAE party, having dined with the Moores, are ushered in. An open bay window looks over Otago Bay towards the Yacht Club on the far side – tall masts silhouetted against a deep blue midsummer night, where Taff and the ratings are waiting soberly with the ship. Inside, exotic flowers in cut-glass vases twinkle in specially designed alcoves. Their deep scent mixes with that of the beeswax polished floor – the smell of civilisation already with nostalgic overtones. The ladies are in ball dresses and jewels, the *Terra Nova* men are in anything they hadn't already packed and left in Christchurch, 'tennis shirts, flannels, or whites'. The Edmonds, their hosts, welcome them with bowls of fruit and punch, politely ignoring their unconventional attire.

They all are dazed but careful, lest any of the other guests suspect the truth. Kathleen wants to dance to distract her from the pathetic and to her, transparent, attempts by the other women to 'make the best' of the situation, their fragile courage worn like a medal for all to see.

'None can foretell our luck,' Scott tells anyone who asks. 'We may get through, we may not. We may have accidents to some of the transports, to the sledges, or to the animals. We may lose our lives. We may be wiped out. It is all a question that lies with providence and luck.'[206] This, agrees Kathleen, is the right kind of careless courage. The pathetic expedition wives here tonight seem intent upon ruining the whole programme with their terrible selfishness. The point of women is to incite men to high endeavour, not to shackle them with being safe. Can't they see that they must be proactive to be empowered, rather than this Griselda-like passive acceptance.

The Scotts might start within the safety of the waltz. Kathleen believes that part of Hilda's grievance lies in petty not-niceties of 'social cutting'. Teddy seems determined that 'Scott had cut his wife's dance' and for the sake of peace on earth, Scott had better dance with Hilda tonight.'[207]

There is something martial about the Mazurka music, with a hint of knightly gallantry. Oates's face is unreadable. He does not go in for dancing much himself, much to his mother's disappointment at the Christmas party they give at the Hall, but he had been rather a mean Cossack dancer before the Boers put paid to his squat kick with a bullet in his thigh.

Oriana and Bill are dancing. Captain Scott notices that they always stand out from a crowd. Bill is at a loss: 'Either we must be strikingly beautiful or else very ugly . . . which was it, do you think?'[208] But he answers his own question. When Oriana accepts dances, for propriety's sake, with other men, Bill steps back to watch her. 'I could only stand in the crowd and admire her, and wonder how the deuce such a girl came to give herself to me.'[209] Kathleen doesn't share Bill's appreciation. To her mind Oriana is 'a drab female'.[210]

Birdie Bowers is attempting the two-step with Hilda, who, like the heroine of a modern novel, is divinely tall and always drawing herself up to her full height. Birdie has to stretch up to place his hand on Hilda's right shoulder blade, his nose dangerously near Hilda's decollete. Kathleen is more Birdie's level, but he seems to want to dance with Hilda, or perhaps, since she is after all just a 'poor ignorant one', it is more about pity.[211]

28 NOVEMBER 1910

BIRDIE BOWERS − DUNEDIN

Birdie is writing to Emily. The hour may be late but he has to have a last 'pen & ink' conversation, he has to unburden himself of the shocking events of the past few hours:

'[Oriana] has not been about much owing to the strained relations between [Kathleen] & [Hilda],' Birdie tells Emily. 'I don't know who to blame but somehow don't like [Kathleen] I don't trust her − though I have always been prepared to give her due. Nobody likes her in the expedition & the painful silence when she arrives is the only jarring note in the whole thing. There is no secret that she runs us all now & what she says is done − through [Scott]. Now nobody likes a schemer & yet she is undoubtedly one. We all feel that the sooner we are away the better. She will go home to her small son & will sow no more discord.'[212]

When Emily receives this letter, six weeks later, she wonders when Birdie is going to try to balance his argument, to make an attempt at objectivity, to stand back. 'I am sorry for her as she has tried hard to be one of us & always does anything she can for any of us. She actually brought our initials & came down & sewed them on our winter clothes for us. Very nice of her, was it not − I wish I could like her but I am suspicious.'

His candle is burning low. In his narrow bunk on the *Terra Nova*, he tries to collect his scattered thoughts. Has he ever appreciated how reasonable and rational his women are? They cry, they are anxious, wish to be dead, etc., etc., but in spite of everything, they never pitch a spanner right into the centre of the works. Birdie is shocked at the lengths 'one woman jealous of another can go to . . . That's where the trouble has been between Scott & his second-in-command. If you knew as I do how Teddy Evans has upheld his leader through thick & thin you would marvel . . . The hand behind Capt S. could be seen in many minor ways not against anybody but at [Hilda] through Teddy . . . Through it all Teddy has never criticised [Scott] or run down his wife on the contrary he has been wonderful in his loyalty . . . [but] it was no marvel to us that after the continuing thrusting back of her husband – the man who had made the Expedition – he announced privately to us that he intended to resign unless a clear understanding was established and certain demands acceded to. I never saw a man so determined to throw up all his hopes as [Teddy] was then & rank feeling spread rapidly.'

Birdie is unburdening himself without restraint, marshalling his thoughts, his loyalties. 'May it never be known how very nearly the *Terra Nova* came to not sailing at the last few hours.' Emily will realise how important it is that she keeps this confidential. 'May it never be known' indeed. Birdie knows that his family won't 'quack'.[213]

He has just changed out of the imaginative interpretation of formal clothes he wore for the Edmondses' ball. 'With hearts far from gay we went to dance . . . I was very half hearted about filling a programme at all,' but he had asked Hilda for the two-step, whatever she might have felt of having rather more 'down' than 'up' around the floor.

Birdie and his mother, the mother he sees in his mind's eye as he writes, are nearing the end of the 'pen & ink'. He is tired but he forces his pen across the page. It will not be Emily's turn to speak for another year. Somehow talking to her has allowed him to master his shock, gain a valuable insight into what Rudyard Kipling calls 'the female of the species'. Birdie suspects that Kipling may be right, she may indeed be 'more deadly than the male'.[214] He is in less of a rush to get 'spliced' than ever and is 'longing to get down to the ice'.

'How petty it seems, does it not? – when one thinks of the spirit of us all towards each other – never was a happier selection for mutual good feeling in any ship that ever sailed on a difficult enterprise & yet how nearly all that was destroyed.'[215]

28 NOVEMBER 1910

ORIANA – DUNEDIN

As the Wilsons climb between the sheets of yet another unfamiliar hotel bed, Bill asks Oriana whether, in her honest opinion, he is wrong. Is there 'a place for [him]' on the expedition? Is it to be a scientific expedition to which he felt sure he has been called by God, or a cauldron of petty politics and low down ambition?

Ory knows that her husband has a theory, lifted straight from biblical precedent, that all God requires is willingness. 'He does not like us to look back after putting our hands to the plough, He often takes the plough away as soon as He knows we mean to carry through.'[216] Both Wilsons have their hands, shoulders and backs very firmly to that plough. Will God take it away before Bill has to leave for the Antarctic the following morning? It would be very like him to surprise them with a 'bolt from the blue'. God does things like that, right at the eleventh hour. Look at Genesis 22. God ordered Abraham to offer his son Isaac as a sacrifice, then, when Abraham had the knife raised, sent a ram so that Abraham could sacrifice that instead. Where is that ram now?

Bill's expedition nickname is already 'Uncle Bill the Peacemaker' (she is rather flattered to be called 'Aunt Oriana' and hopes the 'peacemaker' suffix is implied).[217] Even Bill is beginning to realise that he is their chief, their only effective negotiator. If he does not go and the mutiny takes hold, Scott will be ridiculed for failure to see the expedition through. Teddy might be accused of fomenting mutiny. Taff might face disciplinary action in Portsmouth. Everyone else might go home.

How far can he and Ory allow themselves to imagine a future where he stays? Bill has always lusted after a position as a field scientist recording 'species that are dying out before your eyes' as the New Zealand settlers clear the native bush for sheep grazing. He has already applied to Sir Joseph Ward about this once or twice. In the last days before leaving Christchurch, they spent a lot of time on religious retreat at Bishopscourt. Frederic Wallis was Dean of Caius for the first four years that Bill studied medicine at Cambridge back home, but he has now been elevated to Bishop of Wellington here. Perhaps all this is God's circuitous way of leading Bill to a job in the church – is Ory heading back to the vicarage from whence she came?

Ory is a practical woman. If Bill asks her opinion, in the early hours of the morning, she will offer him practical reassurance. There is a place for him. She has prepared his 'place', his cabin, in the heat of the English summer as 'Officer of the Watch' at West India Docks. Besides, his scientific aims are inviolate. The emperor penguin eggs would have to be harvested by someone in order to discover whether they proved, or indeed disproved, Haeckel's ORP theory that he has so often told her about. He is vital to the smooth running of the expedition. Science and peacekeeping are both noble purposes.

As dawn breaks, Bill's sentimentality, his insecurity, is leavened by Ory's practicality. She reminds him that they agreed that he would try not to die. But what if, despite his best efforts, he dies, 'passes over', from what he calls 'this life' to the next? What then? The sun has come up, they have only hours left, she needs to know. 'Whatever happened I know I should come back to you.' Dead or alive, she will be married to Bill. If he dies, he will be permanently with her.

He tries to lighten the atmosphere by applying studied chivalry: 'Anyhow you will do your duty, my brave kind lady, and your "kind sir" will do his.'[218] It is morning. They begin to dress carefully.

After breakfast with Hilda and Teddy, they leave the hotel to call in at the Dunedin Museum. They do some 'small shopping' and board the 1.17 p.m. train, crowded with people who have been given a special half-day holiday to see them off at Port Chalmers. The Scotts, with Hilda and Teddy, are also on the train. Relations are still strained.

29 NOVEMBER 1910

TERRA NOVA – PORT CHALMERS

One moment, 'we were happy and good' and then, Kathleen tells her diary, 'Teddy's . . . tantrums spoiled the day . . . he told me a string of lies and hot air.'[219] In spite of this she entrusts him with four private 'love' letters – inspirational and incendiary – to be given to Scott on his birthday, Christmas and two other significant dates throughout the winter.

Light reflects off the pleated sea, playing on the shiny paint of the steeply angled stern of the *Terra Nova*. A white wooden tender bobs on a long line. On the quay, men in office clothes stand with their hands in their pockets – they have been at work all morning, but they are here now with their families. Across the bay, small boats flutter with regatta bunting and ladies' hats. Plumes of smoke from funnels of coastal steamers blow out over the water.

Kathleen is standing amidships by the wheel, her fur coat loose. She peers from under the broad brim of a light-coloured hat. It is not quite as broad as the *Merry Widows* but it is broader than Oriana's modest half net and Hilda's boater. Kathleen is talking to a hatless man balanced on a stanchion. Captain Scott, his back turned to her, has one foot up on the lower gunnel. He talks to a uniformed man leaning on the rail near the quay.

Behind Kathleen, Hilda leans with her back to the ship's cabin. She faces the stern. Teddy faces her, standing close, so they are less than a foot apart. The sun is bright on the white top of his navy cap, Hilda is in shadow.

Bill and Oriana are huddled on the far port corner of the stern – his left side touching her right from knee to shoulder. Her face is serious. Her arms are crossed over her lap. Looking down the port side of the boat past Teddy and Hilda, she can see the hills on the north side of the harbour obscured occasionally by billows of black smoke from the ship's funnel.

It is 2.20 p.m. Captain Oates and Birdie Bowers are keeping well out of the way of potentially weeping women and photographers. From the port bow, they look out over the deck, invisible beneath its cargo. There are three deck houses on the poop, including all laboratories, which are as full of gear as it is possible to be, five boats and the ice-house. Then there are 162 carcasses of sheep and two of beef, three enormous cases containing the motor sledges chained down to the deck, about 128 cases of petrol, oil and paraffin, in two and three layers tied down to the deck; nearly 50 tons of horse fodder in compressed bales; 33 dogs chained out of biting distance of each other all over the deck and, in timber stables, 19 ponies.

Oates and Birdie have a special bond over these ponies. Oates wanted expensive linseed meal, though Scott was keen on the compressed variety Shackleton had used. 'Finally my opinion was asked (knowing nothing of horse-fodder),' Birdie tells his mother. 'I got in a wink from Oates & said I was sure nothing could equal the linseed meal, and to O's great delight the motion was carried there & then.'[220]

They have just taken 30 tons of coal in sacks thrown in at the last moment, wherever there is space.[221] Taff has told Captain Scott that he and the other ratings will 'pig it anyhow'.[222] The coal can be put in their quarters. It is a noble and very sober gesture. There will be no loud whispering from him as he and the other sailors climb over the ship's rail to loosen ropes that tie the ship around the white-tipped bollards on the dock. The ship pulls away from the side. In the harbour, a flare rips up through the summer sky. Ships' horns sound in different pitches. On the dock, the crowd cheer and turn to run along to the far end where a man is already waving, high up on the cross trees of a lamppost.

As the gap between the ship and shore widens, Kathleen continues to speak to different sailors, smiling, animated. She sees her husband busy and authoritative in his masculine world. She must not let these men see him sad. Sadness is a contamination. She can control herself, she feels strangely serene, but can she trust him? The ship gathers pace. The wives hold their positions, Oriana in the stern, her right side joined to her husband, Hilda holding her husband's gaze as Port Chalmers grows smaller behind him. The flotilla gradually peels away, leaving the tug, the *Plucky*, the only ship to accompany the *Terra Nova* as they round the Heads.

At 3.30, the wives are transferred from the *Terra Nova* to the tug. Kathleen waves from the *Plucky*. She has not said goodbye. She does not want Scott's men to see him sad. Kathleen's voice gives nothing away as she rattles on, but she is 'watch[ing] his face radiating tenderness as the space between us widen[s]'.[223]

'On the bridge of the tug [Hilda] looked ghastly white and said she wanted to have hysterics,' wrote Kathleen later, 'but instead we took photos of the departing ship.'[224] Hysterics is precisely what Kathleen would have expected from the 'poor ignorant one', all sentiment, 'a tearful condition', and yet Hilda seems to be controlling the urge with surprising dignity.

All the time that Kathleen has been encouraging the other wives to look through the viewfinder of the camera, she has not taken her eyes off her husband's. She wants to be quite sure that '[she has] fixed the memory of that upturned face', if necessary 'for a lifetime'.

'Mrs Wilson was plucky and good,' continues Kathleen.[225] She is Captain Kathleen again, these 'pathetic grass widows' her responsibility. 'I mustered them all for tea in the stern and we all chatted gaily.' Oriana knows that her husband expects a 'happy goodbye' for a memory. She was 'plucky and good' for his sake but as the *Terra Nova* passes out of sight, the expression slips. Kathleen looks round and notices that while Hilda is chatting and accepting tea, '[Oriana is] looking somewhat sphinx-like.'

Bill is standing on the bridge of the *Terra Nova*, his binoculars trained on the *Plucky*. 'Ory was with us on board to the last, when she had to go off on a tug and there on the bridge I saw her disappear out of sight waving happily a goodbye that will be with me till the day I see her again in this world or the next. I think it will be in this world and sometime in 1912.'[226]

Just around the corner, Hilda's husband speaks for the other men, for Scott, Taff, for Birdie and for Oates: 'Personally I had a heart like lead, but . . . there was work to be done . . . and the crew were glad of the orders that sent them from one rope to another and gave them the chance to hide their feelings, for there is an awful feeling of loneliness at this point in the lives of those who sign on the ships of the "South Pole trade" – how glad we were to hide those feelings and make sail – there were some dreadfully flat jokes made with the best of good intention.'[227]

The *Plucky* draws up to the dockside recently vacated by the *Terra Nova*. Hilda's family, the Russells, walk her to the station and take the train back home to Christchurch. Hilda hopes she is carrying Teddy's child, but she is concerned that she might not see him again.

Kathleen has promised to send a telegram to Kinsey. She goes to the post office: 'Just back from heads all gay & cheerful everything excellent love to Mrs Kinsey Kathleen Scott.'[228] She has a ticket for Australia, where she will stay in Sydney with Admiral Poore's wife at Admiralty House. 'Poor little Kathleen!' she writes, in an attempt at romantic self-pity. 'My babe at one end of the earth, my lover just off to the other.'[229] She prays to 'all the gods' that she is pregnant.

Oriana is off to Peel Forest, the Dennistouns' homestead near Christchurch. She will hide in the forest and go birding. She will notice the wind in the trees but she will not realise that it indicates a terrible storm, building to a hurricane, heading straight for the *Terra Nova*.

4

'Ice and the English Imagination'*

BILL – *TERRA NOVA*, SOUTHERN OCEAN

Deep turquoise waves are peeling off the surface of the sea. The *Terra Nova* pitches and rolls. Two carrier pigeons are going through their pre-take-off checks on the edge of their wicker crate. The Great Barrier Island standard pigeon post allows each bird to carry five messages written on a lightweight writing stock attached to its leg. It is difficult for the pigeons to preen their feathers into good flying condition with their wicker perch tilting through 30 degrees and sea spray raining down, but eventually they launch up into the threatening sky: 'I watched the two go off today,' observed Bill, surfing the deck, 'and they looked strong enough on the wing.' With his Zeiss binoculars in one hand and the deck rail gripped firmly in the other, the head of the scientific staff tries to look for the science. Why did these domestic birds fly in pairs? Other migratory birds, flying between 'homes', conserved energy by flying in V formations, but carrier pigeons flew best in unaerodynamic pairs. Why pay such a substantial energy cost to fly together? Braced against the rail, Bill can only observe that 'They flew round and round the ship in increasingly wider circles, rising to a good height and gradually disappeared somewhere in a sort of circular direction. It was impossible to say that they had gone in any particular direction. They ought at any rate to reach Campbell Islands one would think.'[230]

Perhaps the seamen who brought the pigeons will be able to make better 'scientific' observations. The fancier has a bell in the loft trap so that he can log the time that the message arrives and take it to the Central Telegraph Office. The record pigeon speed is 44 mph but in the unsettled weather the seamen are not sure. The officers have to

---

* An homage to Francis Spufford's peerless title.

admit that without a Marconi ship-to-shore radio on board, the seaman's Pigeon Gram is not to be sniffed at. A 'sort of circular direction' is the best that the fastidiously truthful Bill can do. The barometer is 'very threatening'.

Six hours after they have been 'playing about with carrier pigeons', the waist of the ship becomes a surging swimming bath, anyone who ventures there at risk of being drowned alive in their clothes.[231] While the seamen furl sails, tighten ropes and secure the deck cargo, Bill's landlubber staff of scientists vomit and bail.

They all know the theory – physical endurance is highly valued for its own sake because it proves manhood, stoicism ennobles the spirit and in the crucible of suffering, the pure gold of honour will appear.[232] Bill spurs them on – they mustn't just tolerate it, they must 'enjoy it from beginning to end'.[233] The scientists appreciate that Antarctica may be the perfect setting for such 'enjoyable' exertions, but surely that depends upon making it there alive?

ORIANA – PEEL FOREST, NEW ZEALAND

Holding her binoculars carefully, Oriana walks through Peel Forest in South Island and tries to notice detail in nature. The air is green and still in the understorey of matipo, konini, ribbonwood and houhere, but the tips of the massive totara trees reach up into a turbulent sky. She wonders whether the carrier pigeons have homed with their messages from the *Terra Nova*. What would prevent them? A stiff northerly?

Ory has always sought solace in the natural world but she is a scientist, not a romantic. Henry David Thoreau's *Walden; or, Life in the Woods* has become almost as popular as the Bible as a text for spiritual development in recent years. But nature is not idyllic, it can be cruel. Bill once had a pet eagle owl that killed his pet buzzard. At first Ory was shocked, but Bill refused to look at the thing emotionally. Nature isn't emotional. There is no such thing as tragedy in the natural world.

Ory climbs carefully up beside the stony stream bed that leads to a 46-foot-high waterfall – the water splashes over the rocky cliff. She is already looking forward to her husband's message of reassurance, though she knows that even if the carrier pigeons fly fast, he could have drowned by the time she receives it.

BIRDIE BOWERS – *TERRA NOVA*, SOUTHERN OCEAN

Birdie is diving across the deck after petrol cans, trying to rugger tackle them before they career over the side. Scott tells him calmly that they do not matter. 'This was our great project for getting to the Pole,' Birdie tells his absent mother in exasperation, 'the much advertised motorised sledges or "motors" that "did not matter".' But he checks himself: 'These incidents must be taken as "confidences" to be told in [Scott's] own way & later on.'[234] However mad it seems at that moment, Captain Scott's summary dismissal of the fêted motors must not be picked up in the press. Besides, Birdie assures Emily that Scott's account will be modest rather than sensational. Throughout the storm, Scott is 'simply splendid, he might have been at Cowes'.[235]

EMILY – BUTE

In Ardbeg, the Bowers women are preparing for what they call 'The Party'.[236] It is an annual event but always seems to involve the 'usual scramble' of preparations. As May rushes from their galley kitchen to the front room with 'eatables', she observes: 'Fools make feasts & wise men eat them.' But Birdie does not think it is foolish to be generous; he is proud of what he refers to as the legendary Bowers hospitality. By all accounts his father was big-hearted and unstinting, and so should they be. The party is a great success. Edie, always keen on her meals, agrees that the food is 'top hole'. Emily, exhausted at the end, collapses into a chair in front of the coal fire in the front room.

OATES – *TERRA NOVA*, SOUTHERN OCEAN

Captain Oates, who has been with the ponies, risks his life to come to the ship's bridge to report that another one has drowned in the stalls. He forces his way back through the swimming pool all the way to the stalls, where he has to watch out for corpses floating on their tether chains, banging into the walls. 'I can't remember having a worse time,' Oates confesses to Caroline.[237] 'The motion up in the bows was very violent and unless one had been through it one would not believe any pony could keep its feet for five minutes. I was drenched all night, the water continually forcing the skylight up and pouring over the focsle in a regular torrent.' It was when he found a loose dog that he began to worry, 'as I knew they would not let dogs about loose unless things were bad'.

CAROLINE – GESTINGTHORPE

Is exploration safer than war? Caroline does not want to think about the perils of the Southern Ocean, but the daily newspapers reveal that the Russian minister for war plans to invade Manchuria. What will this mean for the army, for Laurie's regiment, the Inniskillings? Putting the paper aside, she consults her butler – is everything in hand for the annual Christmas party they hold at the Hall? The Sudbury band? The Yule log? The joints of meat to hand out to the villagers? These are not trivial things. Caroline's largesse is insurance against the storm clouds of revolution gathering on the continent.

TAFF – *TERRA NOVA*, SOUTHERN OCEAN

Taff has spent most of his life at sea, he's familiar with these southerly latitudes, the 'Filthy Fifties', but he's never imagined this. The officers and men form a chain gang at the pumps and Taff yells out shanties to keep rhythm above the screaming, diabolical wind.

LOIS – PORTSMOUTH

Norman and Muriel Evans are nearing the end of the autumn term at their school in Portsmouth. As Taff had predicted in his letters to Lois, they are keen to get back to Gower for the Christmas holidays. Lois isn't so sure. The talk among the sailors' wives is of the strikes at the Naval Colliery Company at Ely Pit in Penygraig. Taff's fellow seamen, the 'Swansea Jacks', are particularly angry that Winston Churchill, the home secretary, has taken the decision to send in troops to take the Colliery Company side.

BIRDIE – *TERRA NOVA*, SOUTHERN OCEAN

After thirty-six hours, Captain Scott approaches Birdie Bowers. Along with Taff, Birdie probably has more sea miles than any man aboard.

'I am afraid it's a bad business for us,' he says. 'What do you think?'[238] Birdie is not really thinking. His reactions are more instinctive, but somewhere in his subconscious is the man against whom he judges himself. The man has hit a cyclonic hurricane just east of the Horn of Africa and huge waves batter his ship, the *Mergui*. The man has asked his crew to lash him to the wheel in order to fight to save the lives of those aboard, his ship, cargo and his livelihood. He succeeds. Birdie, his son, who never had the privilege of sailing with his father, must prove that he is also capable of a 'man's work'.

'We are by no means dead yet,' Birdie replies to Captain Scott.

BILL — *TERRA NOVA*, SOUTHERN OCEAN

Suddenly, after three days of hurricane, there is a rainbow blinking on and off like a Morse signal. 'If ever there was a moment at which such a message was a comfort,' says Bill, 'it was just then.'[239] They have survived the storm, but only just. As the sea becomes calmer, Oates winches dead ponies out of the stable hatch and buries them at sea along with one husky, strangled on its chain. Ten tons of coal have been lost overboard, along with sixty-five gallons of petrol and a case of the biologists' spirits. But they have not lost a man. It is a kind of miracle.

TAFF — *TERRA NOVA*, SOUTHERN OCEAN

Captain Scott has told the ratings that he is particularly impressed with them. They are in a wet, lightless locker under the ponies' stalls. The floor leaks horse urine and worse. Taff has tacked oilskins and canvas to the ceiling from the inside, 'but without sign of complaint'. Scott thinks 'their cheerful fortitude is little short of wonderful.'[240]

Taff does not mention the horse shit when he writes home to say that it has been 'pretty bad weather, which did some damage to the ship . . . but we got over that allright [sic].'[241]

KATHLEEN — SYDNEY, AUSTRALIA

Huddled on the metal balcony in a blanket, Kathleen is watching the stars' twinkling reflections in the Sydney harbour. The first thing she'd done after Scott left New Zealand was to visit a babies' home to cheer herself up, but they were all very ill-looking and it did not. Now she has come to Australia and is staying with Lady Poore at Admiralty House, awaiting her P&O liner back to the UK. Turning her head, she can look back into the elegant bedroom Lady Poore has had prepared for her – silk upholstery, cut flowers, dressing tables and fresh towels. It makes her want to run for the hills, an urge she has decided to indulge.

She is aware of Admiral Poore's thoughts on the role of the naval wife. Kathleen is at the sharp end of duty and lunches and dressing tables and cut flowers. It bores her to suffocation. How much self-sacrifice will be demanded of her before Scott is made an admiral?

With 'speed and stealth', she stands and folds the blanket. She puts it into a sack with a mackintosh sheet and sequestered dining-room food for a few days. Quietly, she opens the bedroom door and, with her 'swag' over her shoulder, descends the sweeping stairs to the dark hall. She has taken a 'vagrant decision' to go Waltzing Matilda in the Blue Mountains – hesitation is only a symptom of suburbanitis. Pulling the great front door shut behind her, she breathes the free air. A shadow detaches from the opposite side of the street. It is the young South African, a man whose devotion makes him a reliable timekeeper. He has organised a getaway car. Kathleen climbs in.

Looking round behind her as they turn out of the street, she is fairly sure that none of the Poore's neighbours have seen her leave. 'I shall not be talked about,' Kathleen tells Scott in her diary, 'this time anyhow.'[242]

CHRISTMAS DAY 1910

BIRDIE – *TERRA NOVA*, SOUTHERN OCEAN

It is midnight and the bright sun reflects off the ice floes. With his right eye against the monocular of the sextant, Birdie takes a sight, calculating the altitude of the sun against Greenwich Mean Time and the observed longitude. After a moment he concludes that they are some of the first people to be celebrating Christmas 'on this round Earth'.[243] He spends the early hours of Christmas morning watching penguins wandering the solid sea in their dinner suits. There is the hiss of fissuring ice against the hull, ponies stamping in their cramped stalls, clinking dog chains and the thin whistle of wind around the bare masts.

MAY BOWERS – BUTE

May, Birdie's sister, is just pinning on her church hat. She leaves the house and walks down the steep hill at Ardbeg to the Reverend Dewar's 8.30 a.m. service at St Ninian's up at Port Bannantyne. On the way the Buchanans give her a lift in their car. After church she will dine with the Maxwells in the flat above theirs. As Birdie has observed, it has become a family tradition. Emily is away, probably in Europe avoiding the Scottish *dreich*. Edie is nursing in Manchester and May is determined to enjoy the independence.

Later, as William Maxwell carves the co-operative goose, they discuss the Christmas service. Birdie is firm friends with 'old Mr Dewar', a 'top hole' clergyman who lives up to his convictions. May hopes that this Christmas there will not be a call from the little island of Inchmarnock. Two years ago when Birdie was back for Christmas, Dewar received a summons to go there in rough weather and Birdie rowed him across the turbulent strait when no one else would. May's arms are tennis-player strong but she has an irritating tendency to catch cold. Her 'bad cough' worries her mother.

They all remember the Christmas that Birdie was home, 'the joy of household decorations fired [him] with such ardour' that when he had finished filling the downstairs flat with evergreens, he proceeded to create a forest in the Maxwells' flat upstairs too.[244] The Bowers–Maxwell Christmas lunch was conducted in a dining room that resembled a wildwood. After lunch May thanks the Maxwells for their hospitality and walks down the external stairs to their ground-floor flat. Christmas with Birdie was a time filled with joy and laughter. Although she does not admit as much to him in her letters, this year there has been no dancing till the 'wee sma' 'oors'.[245] Instead May has been obliged to seek company in books. With naughty ambiguity she writes: 'Spent a night with [Thomas King] Fitchett author.'[246]

BILL – *TERRA NOVA*, SOUTHERN OCEAN

'Still in the pack ice and still immovably fixed,' writes Bill in his journal.[247] The pack ice extends a lot further north than six years earlier. Scott wants to get the depots to 80 degrees latitude south. To do that they need to reach the coast, build their new hut and begin sledging depots of food and fuel south along the route to the Pole. Bill climbs the mast ladder to the crow's nest. 'It is not very warm in a bitter wind,' he writes to Ory, crouching low in the wooden barrel, 'but as private as can be, and therefore a very easy place to find you.'[248] He takes his sketchbook out of the canvas pocket she sewed him and tries to capture the changing light – cobalt shadows and rainbow refraction.

TAFF – *TERRA NOVA*, SOUTHERN OCEAN

Taff's children might like to know that, below deck, 'Uncle' Tom Crean's rabbit has just kindled over twenty 'kittens'. Like Taff, Irish Petty Officer Crean is a veteran of Scott's first *Discovery* expedition. The Welshman and the Irishman are close friends. Captain Scott was with Crean when the news of Shackleton's failure came through – 'I think we'd better have a shot next,' he told Crean.[249]

Crean is still single – he has no 'kittens' waiting for him back home. And these 'kittens' are born with their eyes and ears shut, unlike Taff's lusty brood, which emerged bawling into the world in the bedroom in Portsmouth. Taff's father, Lois's uncle, Charles Evans, was a Cape Horner who sailed on the 'widow makers', big square-riggers that brought copper from Chile round Cape Horn and across the Atlantic to 'Copperopolis', as Swansea was nicknamed. Since it takes three to four tons of coal to smelt one ton of copper ore, it made sense to bring the ore to the coal. Taff knows that when his father returned from trips to Chile, he often came back to find his brood of twelve diminished. Sarah, Taff's mother, buried them alone in the Rhossili churchyard. Lois and Taff only have three – there is no margin. Lois is a good cook, she will keep them strong. On the *Terra Nova*, Scott is nervous about how much people are eating but the cold makes them hungry.[250] Taff is delighted that Clissold, the cook, is preparing a mouthwatering roast, even if it is penguin rather than turkey.

ROBERT FALCON SCOTT – *TERRA NOVA*, SOUTHERN OCEAN

Captain Scott calls all hands on deck. He takes out a blue canvas Common Prayer and reads the Christmas service. Neither he nor Kathleen believe in God, but they got married in a church and baptised their son in another church. Partly it's about maintaining those appearances he's so sensitive about, but partly Christmas on the *Terra Nova* lends structure and civilisation to this floating ice desert at the bottom of the world.

Only the penguins are dressed for church. As Bill has observed, 'They will always come up at a trot when we sing to them and you will often see a group of explorers on the poop singing to an admiring group of Adélie penguins.'[251] The dog driver Cecil Meares is the star performer. His 'God Save the King' never fails to send them into the water.

'We have been wondering,' wrote Scott the last time he was in the

Antarctic for Christmas, 'what Christmas is like in England – possibly very damp, gloomy and unpleasant, we think; we have been wondering too, how our friends picture us.'[252] With little to do, it is easy to fall to imagining what Kathleen will be imagining while he is imagining her. Today of all days, those aboard the *Terra Nova* and those at home are all locked in ice and imagination.[253]

At eight in the evening they divide into officers and ratings, and have a 'sing-song'. Everyone has to take their turn. Bill sings, Herbert Ponting, the expedition photographer, plays the banjo, Griffith Taylor, the geologist, plays the piano and so on. They wonder what their homefolk will be doing at eight o'clock on Christmas morning. 'One's thoughts are naturally with you all at home,' writes Bill, speaking for them all, 'bless you all!'[254]

KATHLEEN – CEYLON

Kathleen is sketching on the shore of a lake in Kandy, Ceylon (present-day Sri Lanka). It is hot and lush, and mercifully the ground does not roll, pitch or yaw. She looks at the textured bark of the banyan tree with its aerial prop roots that have matured into thick, woody trunks. Mr Hull is already a distant memory, but she has just ticked off Mr Wesche, a fellow passenger who has been following her about like a lovesick youth. She explained to him 'very carefully and finally how very distasteful it is to me to have him make love★ to me. He was very nice about it and there should be no further difficulty.'[255] There is smallpox in the local area so their visit will be brief. At dinner back on board the P&O Kathleen avoids Mr Wesche and sits next to a Captain Blair. 'It seems rather absurd for me to drink this soup,' he tells her, 'because I'm going to drown myself directly.' They never found him.

NEW YEAR'S DAY 1911

BILL – *TERRA NOVA*, SOUTHERN OCEAN

Bill is awakened by a 'hurrah party' and the steam siren at midnight. Five hours into the first day of 1911 after a cup of cocoa, he climbs to the crow's nest to read the Holy Communion service. He thinks of

---

★ 'Making love', as Kathleen uses the term, was an extreme form of flirting that was not always linked to the consummation the term now implies.

Ory on her homebound ship. Has she set her watch for his time? Is she sitting in the lee of the ship's funnel, reading the same service in her Common Prayer with him now? Later there will be a New Year's feast, and Bill has discovered a plum pudding planted in his luggage. He has already sampled some. It is, he believes, 'the best plum pudding I have ever eaten – which is saying a good deal'.[256]

SCOTT – *TERRA NOVA*, SOUTHERN OCEAN

That evening, Scott paints the scene in words for his artistic wife: 'On all sides an expanse of snow-covered floes, a dull grey sky shedding fleecy snowflakes, every rope and spar had its white deposit like the sugaring on a cake . . . on the white curtain of feathery crystals I tried to picture your face.' He misses her physically, her face a vision hovering just out of his reach, but 'somehow I know that you would rather I was striving for big, interesting things whatever the cost was'.[257]

MAY – BUTE

There are Butemen celebrating New Year in the heat of the Indian plains, in the shade of the pagodas in Burma, in the sheep stations of colonial grasslands around the globe, but May is thinking only of Birdie. Their island in the Clyde will soon be in the unusual position of being better served telegraphically than by letter post. (Until now it has been deemed not financially worthwhile to run a cable to the Scottish islands on the west coast.) Both the top- and bottom-floor flats at Caerlaverock agree that the Post Office's 'for-profit' attitude to such an important public service is iniquitous. Perhaps one day it will be possible to send a New Year telegram to the Antarctic?

May imagines Birdie 'in the Pack Ice & wondering very much how he is getting on under the strange conditions.' Outside Caerlaverock it is sleeting. Although she was born in the Straits Peninsula, it is difficult to keep the north and south hemispheres with their opposite seasons in her head. She is concerned about her brother '& what it can be like in such sunless desolation'.[258]

Birdie, basking in twenty-four hours of sunlight aboard the *Terra Nova*, is wondering whether to take his coat off. He is as fat as a seal, and 'as a generator of heat in myself' prides himself on his immunity to cold.[259] He is, however, particularly enjoying the socks Emily has knitted him: in the Antarctic 'gambling men bet not in money but in socks'.

TAFF – *TERRA NOVA*, SOUTHERN OCEAN

As they finally break free of the pack ice and spy land, Taff spots the old *Discovery* post office pole sticking up on a rocky promontory by Cape Crozier, just as they'd left it almost a decade before.[260] The postal 'posts' or 'dead drops' are the same method Taff's father, Charles Evans, would have used on his copper trips round Cape Horn. Men would leave details of their position and intentions in a tin cylinder for relief ships that might be sent in quest of them. Some jokers left letters too. Charles Evans was held in high esteem in Gower, but born the wrong side of the Education Act, he'd never been taught to write, nor had his wife Sarah. Sarah is proud of her son's beautiful copper-plate script; his letters are precious. They are precious not only because they are a piece of him, but because they are intrinsically valuable. Taff has told her that the British Antarctic Expedition has issued special 'Victoria Land' stamps. It seems absurd to include stamps on letters sent by dead drop. Taff assures his mother that the stamps will increase in value. Sarah must keep them in the safe box, the Evans 'bank' where she used to keep Taff's salary. As for the content of the letters, Sarah's niece Lois is a good reader, softly spoken with a musical voice that makes people listen. Each letter reading is a modest performance, to be anticipated.

LOIS – PORTSMOUTH

Lois takes the octagonal silver medal down from the nail where it hangs over the fireplace to keep it safe. The paper that goes with it declares that it is awarded for 'extreme human endeavour against appalling weather and conditions that exist in the Arctic and Antarctic'. There is a weight and heft to it. She is used to domestic duties, to cleaning, but this is precious. Silver requires special attention. She can use two methods: mixing chalk, ammonia, alcohol in warm water before a dry polish or, if it is beginning to tarnish, using 1 tablespoon of salt, 1 of baking soda, and soaking in warm water for about an hour.

Lois is proud of Taff's inherited ability to endure 'extreme human endeavour' – his father Charles was the same. Lois knows how hard life has been for her aunt Sarah, but she also knows that it allowed Uncle Charles to provide for his family, for Taff. Uncle Charles only retired after an accident during unloading when a crate of cargo crushed his leg and he had to have it amputated. Taff's father was wonderful company but as tough as they come. When the *Discovery* medal is shining brightly, it hangs in pride of place in the front room of Chapel Street.

Beyond the window, she can see men huddled against the January cold in small groups along Chapel Street. They are mostly shipwrights working round the clock in the dreadnought construction yards. They are probably discussing a campaign to build eight new dreadnoughts: 'We want eight,' is the public cry, 'and we won't wait.' The British navy must be the best in the world. Sir Arthur Conan Doyle claims to be speaking for 'the man on the street' when he says, 'We can pass the eight Dreadnoughts, if we are sure of the eight Shackletons.'[261] One explorer equals eight ironclads? Whatever that man on Baker Street supposes Sir Ernest Shackleton to be capable of, someone has to build those blessed ironclad beasts, and they run on coal not courage!

19 JANUARY 1911

KATHLEEN – EGYPT

Much as Kathleen longs to hold Peter, she just cannot (she has told her mother-in-law) set foot in Egypt without seeing the Pyramids. The P&O will go home without her. She will have to catch another. Peter must wait. Hannah can hold onto him for a little longer, can't she?

She might not yet have had a reply from Henley-on-Thames, but she has just met a friendly archaeologist, a Mr James Quibbell, who tells her 'quite casually that morning he had come upon a 2nd dynasty tomb, probably the earliest ever found.'[262] He has left the sarcophagus untouched as he thought she might like to help him uncover it. 'I was of course most awfully excited.'

Together they descend a dark, dusty shaft, 'rather a climb', and there is the sarcophagus, a large wooden box, 'much eaten by white ants'. They prop the sides up with sods before lifting the lid. Kathleen, daughter of a vicar, is not sold on God. She is not that impressed by occultists either. The evidence suggests that humans are just the sum of their parts – any attempt to pretend otherwise is a kind of cowardice. These ancient Egyptians were 'poor ignorant ones', but there is no excuse for that kind of nonsense now. Only one's name outlives death. Immortality must be earned.

There are three mummies in the tomb and Kathleen has the jawbone of one of them in her hand. It is light and fragile and the teeth are loose. 'As I was lifting out one of the heads Mr Quibbell said, "I suppose you know how to prevent the teeth falling out of the lower jaw?" As though I'd been at it all my life!' Holding the skull in her left hand, she uses her right to stroke the surface lightly with a paintbrush. The mummified skin has the texture of rice paper. Setting the skull down carefully, she passes a strip of cloth under the jaw and over the top of the skull like a headscarf and rests it carefully in the springy bed of dried grass at the bottom of a wooden specimen box.

Who are these mummies either side of the main desiccated corpse? Is it true that in Ancient Egypt retainers were sacrificed in order that the pharaohs could have staff to attend to their comfort in the afterlife? It is true. Retainers and wives.

5

Balancing Lionesses

TAFF — CAPE EVANS, MCMURDO SOUND, ANTARCTIC

Taff is relieved that the pack of killer whales has moved on, but floe fragments are still rocking after their assault, whale after whale having smashed into the ice from below. He doesn't like the look of the intact ice that the *Terra Nova* is tied up against either; it must be getting thin underneath them. No one has slept for forty-eight hours. The unloading must be finished as quickly as possible. With ropes and pulleys, they heave the last of the three motor sledges up from the deck, hand over hand. The gantry is swung out over the edge of the ice to which the ship is moored. They begin to lower it, but without warning one of Taff's fellow petty officers, Thomas Williamson, goes through to his thighs. The motor sledge has just touched down when suddenly it dips, the ice gives way beneath it and it falls with all its weight vertically on the rope. Twenty men on the rope brace themselves in a deadly tug of war, the machine on one end, the humans on the other. A man of Taff's bemuscled physique is the navy's anchor man of choice. He knows the drill. You keep your arms and body almost straight as you lean back, rope held over the shoulders, heels dug deeply into the snow. Man after man is forced to let the rope through his grip – when only five of them are left, 'she took charge at a gallop and is now resting on the bottom at a depth of 120 fathoms'.[263] That motor cost £1,000. It would take Taff thirty years to earn that sum.

'A day of disaster', says Scott. 'R.I.P.', says Bill.[264] Taff supposes it could have been worse. Geologist Raymond Priestly had gone back to the ship for the motor engineer Bernard Day's goggles, but abruptly disappeared through the ice in the commotion. He was swept under by the fast-freezing current, but popped up through the rotten brash some way down: 'Day,' he said, 'here are your goggles.'[265] Taff knows that playing about on the ice edge at the height of the polar summer is a dangerous (and expensive) game. They must hurry and drag the new pre-fabricated hut across to solid ground or that'll go through too. On the *Discovery* expedition they'd overwintered on the ship frozen into the ice and used the *Discovery* hut a few miles down the coast at Hut Point as a workshop. This time the ship is going back to New Zealand and Taff is looking forward to greater comfort. If it's all the same to the others, he intends to spend this winter in the new hut with triple-layered seaweed insulation and gramophone records. Over the next few days, the men build their winter abode on the beach, 12 feet up from the waterline. Scott deems the hut 'in every respect the finest that has ever been erected in the Polar regions: 50 feet long by 25 feet wide and 9 feet to the eaves'.[266] It is christened 'Cape Evans hut', after Teddy rather than Taff, but Taff is pleased as punch with it nevertheless.

27 JANUARY 1911

BILL – *DISCOVERY* HUT, HUT POINT, ANTARCTIC

It is 'perfectly filthy'.[267] A man has just squeezed through the iced-up window frame of the old *Discovery* hut, 15 miles south of their base at Cape Evans. He tries to make his way to the front door from the inside, but the hut is filled with hard-packed snow up to the roof. 'It is sad though to see the place in such a state,' Bill notes, acknowledging that clearing it out will use precious depot-laying time. There are only a few months before the onset of Antarctic winter, when travel becomes all but impossible, so to have any hope of reaching the Pole next summer, the men must lay caches of supplies along their planned route quickly. Then, when the sun appears over the horizon and the temperature rises, the Polar Party will race against time to travel 1,800 miles in four months. They must get to the Pole and back before the sub-zero winter sets in, with its darkness, blizzards and katabatic winds. Bill and eleven others are depot-laying, while the other members of the expedition have broken into smaller parties to start exploring and collecting samples. The *Discovery* hut will be useful as a research station as well as a base in the push for the Pole, so they must make it fit for use before moving on.

They are not the last occupants of Scott's *Discovery* hut. Ernest Shackleton used it to overwinter from April to October 1908 on his *Nimrod* expedition. He used it without permission, in fact expressly against a promise that Bill had brokered between Shackleton and Scott.

Scott is furious. It is difficult not to see the state of the hut as deliberate sabotage. Bill suggests that perhaps someone left the window open by mistake, or perhaps the wind blew it open and that is how the hut filled with snow.

There is the sound of an ice pick hacking at the ice behind the door and the rasp of the men outside shovelling. Finally, taking care not to break the door, they force it open. Inside the hut, the men continue to work, chipping away at the snow and ice. There are wooden boxes frozen to the centre of the floor. Metal tools ring off the hard ice on the floor, splintering it into shards and pounding it into white powder until eventually the boxes come loose. They are filled with a dark substance. Bill looks at it. It is shit. It is not animal shit, not shit from the dogs or ponies; it is human excrement.[268]

ORIANA – SOUTHAMPTON, ENGLAND

Having a vicar for a father – albeit a vicar-headmaster – means a Pavlovian tendency to recall religious phrases. Just the words 'home' and 'clean' conjure the 790th of the *Hymns Ancient and Modern*: 'Who sweeps a room, as for thy laws, makes that and the action fine'. But all the same, if Ory were going to sweep a room, she'd rather do it for Bill: 'It's rather deadly work arranging a home for oneself.'[269]

She begins to descend the gangplank following behind her modest leather suitcase and the porters assigned to the boat train waiting to take passengers to London. As she sits on the deeply sprung seat in the carriage, her luggage safely stowed, she wonders. She will lose her mind unless her in-laws' cook at Westal lets her loose in the kitchen. After six servant-less years in rented accommodation with Bill, she has come to rely on the restorative act of kneading dough, the yeasty smell of baking bread: 'If bread-making be the test of culinary skill, her homemade loaves [are] the perfection of bakery!' exclaimed one delighted guest.[270] Homemaking as a perma-guest involves stealth: hyacinths, blue scented, on window sills; Bill's watercolours exchanged for generic pictures in the guest bedroom; framed family photographs dotted about, mostly of Bill or Fanny, her late mother. From their first married home in the suburbs of London, to the remote shooting lodge in the middle of a Scottish moor, she has perfected a symbiotic takeover of other peoples' homes.

Westal in Cheltenham and her father's rectory in Hilton outside Cambridge are both handsome classical villas, detached in large, airy gardens. But it is not so much about the building as the freedom. The freedom to rise before dawn, the freedom to chew her food slowly or pick at it, or throw it all into the bin and scribble onomatopoeic words to help her remember the exact phrasing of the bird singing outside the dining room window. It is also about the safe space within a marriage in which to 'grouse', to exercise her acerbic critical wit without being judged. However elegant the houses, however welcoming the hosts, she would far rather be in a shack on New Zealand's Chatham Islands recording wildlife and beholden to nobody but Bill. As the guard blows his whistle and the steam brakes release, she reflects that she will spend a lot more time in train carriages like this one, but perhaps, like boat cabins, they are the 'home' that suits her best. Her desire to be useful is given relief by perpetual motion and the illusion of filling Kipling's unforgiving minute: 'With sixty seconds' worth of distance run'. Of course, if she were pregnant, she could be 'usefully' creating a new life just standing still. But she is not. Bill will not be greeted by a child upon his return.

Before travelling on to Cheltenham, she will probably spend some time on Green Street in what she calls 'my London home', the Mayfair house of Reginald and Isabel Smith.[271] The Wilsons and the Smiths became best friends five years earlier when Smith & Elder published Scott's *Voyage of the Discovery*, illustrated by Bill. And in another tie, Reggie is Apsley Cherry-Garrard's cousin. He is not as wealthy as Cherry, but he is a man who can afford to make principled rather than commercial publishing decisions. He has decided to invest in making Bill's *The Grouse in Health and in Disease* as colourful and beautiful as present printing technology will allow and damn the expense. With Bill in the Antarctic, Ory is the only expert available to check details. Apart from her expert knowledge of ornithology, her copy checking is fastidious, her technical drawings excellent and she has a good eye for detail. But that is where her involvement stops. Reggie is a traditionalist. Science should be left to the (real) scientists.

Ory's father and brothers all have degrees from Cambridge. Women have been at Girton College since five years before Ory was born in 1874, but they are still not permitted degrees. Philippa Fawcett, six years older than Ory, scored top in the Maths Tripos, but with a suffragist for a mother – the male Cambridge mathematicians set to calculating the angle of the thin edge of a wedge. Ory would not have passed the entrance exams anyway. It's not that she lacks ability; Birdie has noted her 'fertile brain', others observe her 'strong intellect' and 'zest for philosophical debate'.[272] It is simply that she was only thirteen when her mother died, her childhood and education simultaneously ceasing as she became the sibling parent of the household. Now, with Bill's scientific colleagues, her foreshortened schooling makes her self-conscious.

Isabel Smith gives Ory backlist publications covering philosophy and art via natural history, enabling her to make up lost academic ground. Over the years, their increasingly close friendship has become a safe place in which Ory can discuss intimate secrets. Why have neither Ory nor Isabel ever been able to conceive a child? Even as a medic, Bill's opinion is that such things should be left to *le bon Dieu*. If he were here, in Isabel's morning room, he would advise them to leave it to God. But he is not here, and if Ory and Isabel look out of the sash window onto Green Street they can see the front door of Gustavus Murray's house – once London's pre-eminent obstetrician's practice.

9 MARCH 1911

TAFF – MCMURDO DRY VALLEYS, ANTARCTIC

Apart from the card game, it's not much of a birthday. The whole day all Taff has eaten is cold 'make believe' meals.[273] Six biscuits, half a stick of chocolate, 1 ounce of cheese and 1 ounce of butter. After cribbage is over, he has to look forward to four biscuits, the other half of the stick of chocolate, 1 ounce of cheese and half an ounce of butter. Now he focuses on the card game and the prize for the winner – a 'hot dinner' back in Blighty. At that moment in a draughty tent, the mirage of a proper Gower breakfast – cockles, bacon and laverbread – is almost more than Taff can endure.

Theirs is a mission of exploration, a geological survey of the McMurdo Dry Valleys, a row of largely snow-free valleys within Victoria Land, west of McMurdo Sound and Cape Evans. They've been out in the field since 27 January, while the other men of the Southern Party have been laying depots for the Pole push. Although the four men had dragged a cooker to the snowy edge of the moraine, the scientists want to map new territory and the sledge runners won't work on gravel, so they have left it behind and taken lighter dry rations into the Dry Valleys – it adds up to a sobering 'dry' corrective for the man who toppled into Lyttleton harbour just two months earlier. But Scott has not sent him here as a punishment. Scott recognises Taff's value to the geologists. They are green, Taff is not.

Taff seldom talks about the last time he was in the Dry Valleys with Scott on the *Discovery* expedition. He is tactful, respectful. 'We got into one or two tight spots on the journey but when we did,' says geologist Frank 'Deb' Debenham, '[Taff] never showed any alarm and usually made a joke in the middle of what looked like being a very risky job.'[274] A few days before, they'd been in one of those spots. They'd found a frozen river and the scientists christened it the Alph, from Samuel Taylor Coleridge's poem 'Kubla Khan'. However prettily named, the Alph flooded in the night and they woke drowning in meltwater. Taff is good in a freezing flood but he is also very good at cards, and today on his birthday he is extremely motivated ('my belly fairly rattles'), although the university men are concentrating a shade too hard.[275]

It is Wales and Canada (Taff and Charles Wright) versus Australia (Debenham and Griffith Taylor). Taff asks Deb and Taylor if they've ever proposed to a woman. That is a distracting word in this tent in the middle of nowhere and Taff is not above tactics. 'Woman'. He knows he has to keep it clean and the word 'proposal' does that. Would they like to know how? The thing is, Taff says, that rather as with sledging, you need to make sure the woman can pull her weight, 'you see'. So when the moment comes to pop the question, this is what they should say: 'Kin you keep yourself and help me a bit too?'[276] He hams up his Gower accent.

At the start of this geological expedition, the scientists were in a 'flabby condition' in comparison to their lower-deck tent mate.[277] Taff is a source of 'mighty strength' but despite his muscle, pulling the sledges is 'a bugger' – enough to 'break the heart of the sledge, never mind the party pulling'.[278] Carrying the canvas tent, tent poles, ground sheet, etc. on his back is even harder than pulling it on a sledge, and Taff's considerable muscle bulk requires fuel. Taff continues with his distraction. If the woman 'bit', what you said next was, 'You're the "pizened critter" for me.' If, however, the woman doesn't 'bite', the next line is, well, there is no next line, but he can assure them that 'you're better off without her.' If she agrees to marry you on those terms, 'then you're richer instead of poorer.'[279] That night Taff is up a few hot dinners and the young gentlemen have learned what a 'pizened critter' might do when cornered.

The next day they are reunited with the sledge and the cooker. Taff cooks double hot pemmican hoosh (thick soup made of dried beef), and double hot cocoa, with the inevitable terrible stomachaches as a result. As a rule he does not swear in front of gentlemen, but his favourite, since they ask, is: 'May the curse of the seven blind beggars of Egypt be upon you.' It has always worked for him, although he concedes that it is a bit of a tongue twister. If that doesn't cure the ache, he would prescribe a massage with an ice axe 'or an operation for appendicitis with the same'.

9 MARCH 1911

LOIS – GOWER

A cold, dark night of glittering frost and stars. Lois and her extended family huddle around the kitchen range playing cribbage to while away the time. Aunt Sarah, Taff's mother, wonders which of his birthdays her son will be celebrating. She registered Edgar 'Taff', her fourth child, as born on 7 March, but somewhere between the sub-district of Gower Western and the Royal Navy Certificate of Service, Taff has grown younger by two days. When he entered the navy in April 1891 his birth date was stated as 9 March. Probably he thought it best to go along with the error in the navy rather than question it, and he adopted 9 March thereafter.[280] Taff identified closely with the Royal Navy; it was like his family.

Lois and Taff only have three children, but there is still time, and it would be prudent to have more. Aunt Sarah and Uncle Charles had twelve, and Sarah has already buried eight of them. But she is not worried about Taff. Whenever Taff says he was born, she was there and she knows that from the off, he's been as strong as a plough horse.

After this expedition and navy pension, Taff wants to come back home and run a pub like Uncle William Beynon, Lois's father. The older generation remember that Taff had always been sweet on his cousin Lois. Their wedding – covered in several columns of the *Cambrian*

Daily Leader – has passed into the status of legend. Jane Beynon, Lois's mother, has kept the newspaper cutting with a report of the event entitled '*Discovery* man married at Rhossili'.[281]

1904

It was 13 December 1904 and the village 'was agog with excitement'.[282] 'The bride looked very charming in crempoline silk, trimmed with chiffon, with picture hat to match, and carrying in her hand an ivory-bound prayer book, the gift of the bridegroom'. Lois was just as popular as Taff in her own sphere, 'possessed of a good voice and fond of singing . . . [in] the local concerts held from time to time in this Parish and the surrounding parishes'. For Lois, one of the best things about the wedding service was the singing, 'fully choral with Mrs Henry Richards at the organ'. After the wedding breakfast at the Ship Inn (at which there were two sittings), the newlyweds were driven to Swansea in a pony cart. By then it was dark and all along the route, coast-guardsmen and farmers fired flares and guns in a *feu de joie*.

Taff always knew he could rely on his slim, pretty cousin to graft – she was the 'pizened critter' for him, but now with three children his BAE salary is stretched. On Gower everyone earned their keep: 'I couldn't understand [people] who didn't want to work. That is the difference between the country man and the town man,' says cousin George Tucker; 'That is the way they were brought up, work from morning till night.'[283] It's a hard life, and during the long winter nights it is particularly important to have some entertainment. As well as cribbage, on Taff's thirty-fifth birthday, word has it the Mari Lwyd is abroad.

When Lois talks about the Mari Lwyd in Portsmouth, they think she is talking about Marie Lloyd, the bawdy music-hall singer famous for her song: 'A Little of What You Fancy Does You Good.' (Lois hopes that, now that her husband is in the Antarctic, he is out of the way of the kind of temptation the music-hall Marie Lloyd is suggesting. Does Taff regret his infidelities or does he see them, in the same way as his pre/post-voyage bouts of drunkenness, as an inevitable part of the life of a healthy male?) But their Mari Lwyd is a ribbon-bedecked horse's skull on a broomstick – a mummers' prop peculiar to Gower.

Now, from the frosty doorstep in Gower, the Mari Lwyd gives out a riddle. Inside the house, they try to solve it. It gives them a rhyme. They try to match it. It gives them a song to sing. Is this when the Mari Lwyd realises that Lois 'The Voice' Evans is home? The competition over, the Beynons invite the revellers in for homebrew spiced with nutmeg. The children are relieved to find that it has not been a speaking skull but a man under a sheet with a string pulley working the jaw.

16 FEBRUARY 1911

OATES – ONE TON DEPOT, ANTARCTIC

Captain Lawrence Oates is about to be insubordinate. He will still address Captain Scott correctly as 'Sir', but he cannot stand by and watch this happen. It is very cold and windy, around minus 20, and everyone is getting frostnipped. Two days ago, Weary Willie, the weakest of the ponies, got stuck in a snowdrift. The dogs, scenting an easy meal, fell upon him like a pack of wolves. After the men got the pony back on his feet, covered in blood and bite wounds, Scott asked Oates how much further Weary Willie could go. He answered 15 miles, but it turns out that Scott doesn't believe him.

Before Oates left Cape Evans hut, he told Caroline that 'Scott and [Teddy] boss the show pretty well and their ignorance about marching with animals is colossal, on several points Scott is going on lines contrary to what I have suggested.'[284]

It has taken twenty-four days of struggle to lay fourteen depots, stretching from the edge of the Barrier (the Ross Ice Shelf) to reach this point, and now Scott has ordered that the final depot be left here at 79 degrees, 28.5 minutes south instead of the planned 80 degrees – they are 16 miles short. Instinctively, Oates feels that 16 miles might make a crucial difference to men dragging themselves back from the South Pole. It is worth driving Weary Willie on to 80 degrees, he argues, then shooting him there and adding pony meat to their most southerly depot.

On paper Scott describes the dogs and ponies as expendable; they are a 'wasting asset'.[285] But faced with the reality of the wounded Weary Willie struggling through deep snow, he cannot bear to push further, in spite of Oates's opinion to the contrary:

'I have had more than enough of this cruelty to animals,' replies Scott, 'and I am not going to defy my feelings for the sake of a few days' march.'

'Sir,' says Oates, 'I am afraid you'll come to regret not taking my advice.'

'Regret it or not,' Scott replies, 'I have taken my decision as a Christian gentleman.'

Scott, religion and class notwithstanding, is at least a Britisher, which is more than can be said for Tryggve Gran. Gran is the Norwegian Scott has hired to teach them skiing. On the return journey from 79 degrees, 28.5 minutes south, Oates will have to share a tent with the Norwegian foreigner.

'Oates said straight out that it was not my person he had anything against,' said Gran later, 'but that I was a foreigner. He hated all foreigners from the bottom of his heart, because all foreigners hated England. The entire rest of the world, with Germany at the head, in Oates's view, were only waiting for a pretext to throw themselves on his country and destroy it if they only could.'[286]

Birdie, the other man in their tent of three, is no lover of 'furriners' either. Putting his personal feelings to one side, he tries to act as his mother Emily would to diffuse the situation.

'There may be something in what you say [Oates] but still I'll bet you anything you like that [Gran] will be with us if England is forced innocently into a war.'

'Would you?' asks Oates.

'Naturally,' says Gran. Immediately, Oates reaches across the tent and clasps his hand.[287]

FEBRUARY 1911

CAROLINE – GESTINGTHORPE

The cold makes Caroline's cheeks tingle as she stands with her hands deep in her new mink muff. She watches the stable boy walk around the edge of the pond with a long rein. The cob blows twin plumes of steam from its nostrils, but it has a steady disposition and they have scattered straw and loosened the nails in its shoes to give it some grip.

It is better to risk an animal than a human life, even the lowliest. The ice on the ornamental pond in the walled garden is certainly thick, but this pond is larger and spring-fed and it may not be strong enough to support much weight. The village children on the bank lace their skates and talk excitedly. Caroline cannot distinguish between them, the ones that remember their manners and the others that forget to doff their caps. She prefers the word 'forget', a passive oversight rather than 'revolution'.

At the Antarctic lunches in London, wives and mothers read each other judiciously selected excerpts from their letters. Caroline can use the opportunity to ascertain what kind of a sportsman Captain Scott is. She learns, probably from Kathleen, that Scott held his own at the Sandringham shoot with King Edward VII, whence he was invited after the success of the *Discovery* expedition. Oriana has known Captain Scott the longest, and she remembers that when he came shooting in Scotland he let a stag go because he said it was too beautiful. Caroline hopes that Captain Scott will not allow sentiment to cloud his judgement with animals in the Antarctic.

These lunches are awkward – the wives and mothers have only their menfolk in common, but both Oriana and Caroline subscribe to the Society for the Protection of Birds. The practice of killing birds to decorate ladies' hats (sometimes they used whole stuffed birds) is insupportable. Caroline's daughter Lilian has a weakness for hats, but society milliner Madame Emile abides by Society for the Protection of Birds rules. Feather boas are 'allowed' – it is only feathers that involve killing the bird providing them that are really off limits.

Caroline looks after her livestock carefully – or at least her tenant farmers, her grooms and her kennelmen do. She buries her pets on the far side of the east wall. (They were particularly fond of a dog called 'Scot', but with one 't', not that Laurie would notice.) It was 'Dandie', however, who earned the whole epitaph:

Dumb creatures we have cherished here below
Shall give us joyous greeting when we pass the Golden Gate
Semper Fidelis

Animals are straightforward and faithful; humans, in Caroline's experience, can be difficult. Guests to Gestingthorpe Hall are reminded 'not to shiver, not to ask "what fish?" and not to stay too awfully long, like more than a week'.[288] But they are welcome to visit the stables at any time and select a mount. Again, there are rules. Once, when Laurie had been hunting in Mhow, he'd witnessed a lady riding astride, 'the first I have ever seen.'[289] It went without saying that that sort of nonsense was not expected from any guest at Gestingthorpe.

21 FEBRUARY 1911

SCOTT – ANTARCTIC

Ice pancakes are beginning to join together as the sea freezes over again. The ship and the land parties said their goodbyes back in January as the depot-laying teams struck out south. By now the *Terra Nova* is a day's sailing north of the coast of Antarctica. The ship's party must make haste and return to overwinter in New Zealand. They'll come back down in the southern hemisphere summer in late November or early December, bringing letters from home, news from the outside world, food and fuel.

To the south it is getting colder, and the depot-laying teams are racing north, retracing their footsteps back from Camp 15, One Ton Depot. As they head for home, Cape Evans hut, they find themselves in a landlocked area of mistily outlined pressure ridges. Bill is running beside the dog sledge in front when his leg slips into a crevasse. He calls back, 'Hold on to the sledge!'

Suddenly the middle two dogs disappear. Osman, the lead dog, exerts all his strength to keep a foothold as the traces tighten around his neck with the weight of the invisible dog team hanging in the crevasse. Scott drops to his knees and, lying flat on his stomach, wriggles to the edge and looks down into a luminous blue howling void. He sees that two huskies have slipped out of their traces into the bottom. He hears choking sounds. Looking round, he sees that Osman is being strangled.

The men quickly remove all the essential things from the sledge and then, using an alpine rope, they relieve Osman just before he loses consciousness. Slowly, they haul up dogs two by two. After some time, they have eleven of the thirteen. Is it worth risking a man's life for the remaining two? They lower the alpine rope to 90 feet. It doesn't touch the bottom, but the two dogs appear to be on a snow bridge 65 feet down.

Scott makes a bowline knot with a large loop and steps inside it.

With three men on the other end, he walks backwards over the lip of the crevasse. Slowly he is belayed down past smooth-sculpted ice walls. He spins on the thin rope, the only thing keeping him from a nasty death spiked on the icicles that stretch up to meet him. The rope chafes, slicing into the ice with his weight. He is halfway between the snow bridge and the surface, spinning slowly like the mobile over Peter's cot. Will he ever see his wife and child again?[290]

Scott survives his dog rescue but the next day, 22 February, he receives unwelcome news. The *Terra Nova* has found Amundsen's base nearby in the Bay of Whales. Amundsen has more than 100 dogs and, from his base, a shorter distance to the Pole by 60 miles. Dogs can work in colder temperatures than ponies, which means that Amundsen will have a head start. Without Kathleen's tempering presence, Scott pitches into an incandescent rage. They'll have it out with Amundsen in some undefined way. 'Scott said we could go and fight Amundsen. There was no law south of sixty.'[291] It was Ory's husband Bill who calmed him down. There may be no law south of sixty, but they would be called to account north of sixty, in latitudes he and the others are very much hoping to get back to.

21 FEBRUARY 1911

KATHLEEN – LONDON

It is 10.30 p.m. and Kathleen works 'like a Trojan' in her bare wooden studio. In order to create her first public statue she stands high up on a scaffold: 'I am getting quite used to standing on a plank in mid-air,' Kathleen tells Scott in her diary. Beneath her on the studio floor stands the twenty-three-year-old Mr Basil Blogg (a suitably tall clerk in the Lord Chamberlain's office). He is a good model.[292] 'Once rigged up in [Charles] Rolls's clothes [Mr Blogg] looked quite like enough to be very useful.'

Kathleen climbs down from the enormous iron armature put up by Sheen, her studio man, working from her first statuette of Rolls. 'I can work much better on big things,' she tells Scott. 'I like it.' In the break, Kathleen encourages Mr Basil Blogg to move around the studio naturally while she makes quick sketches in clay. Blogg is not as graceful as Charles Rolls but at least he is about the same height and he doesn't seem to mind wearing the bloody cap.

Lady Llangattock, Rolls's mother, gave Kathleen Charles's clothes.

Her son had died when the tail of his Wright Flyer broke off during an air show in Bournemouth. He was just thirty-two. 'It was horribly grim,' says Kathleen. 'I came away with his coat, trousers, leggings and cap – the cap has bloodstains on it.'[293] But Kathleen is determined to immortalise Lady L's 'dead lion' properly and there is the added benefit of 'forty beautiful pounds'.[294]

As Kathleen ushers Mr Blogg quietly out of the dark house, careful not to wake the sleeping Peter, she wonders if this will get her 'talked about'. No one on Buckingham Palace Road is likely to think it seemly that she has a single man in her house at nearly eleven o'clock at night. But perhaps no one would believe that she first met 'Capt South Pole Scott' in an artiste's salon.

1907

It was a Thursday afternoon in Pimlico in early spring of 1907. A twenty-nine-year-old Kathleen, deeply tanned, with bright blue eyes, walked off the London street and into the company of Mabel and Aubrey Beardsley's *Yellow Book* people – London's cultural elite.

Mabel's red hair had, rumour had it, gained her artistic brother Aubrey entry into Pre-Raphaelite Edward Burne-Jones's studio. Kathleen's mother (from whom Kathleen had inherited her impressive mane) had been painted by Pre-Raphaelite Dante Gabriel Rossetti.

It was a tenuous link. Kathleen's mother died shortly after Kathleen, her eleventh child, was born, but the artistic connection endured. Kathleen arranged her hair into a suitably Proserpinesque abundance and accepted an invitation to a luncheon as part of a deliberate strategy. She wanted two things, neither of them money. She wanted to be recognised as a sculptress. She wanted to fulfil her biological potential, to give birth to a baby Hercules. In order to do the first, she needed to be recognised. (She was already pretty sure of her talent.) In order to do the second, she needed a donation. All her life she had been looking for 'the father for my son'.[295]

There were place names at the luncheon table – it was a 'party of Lions', Kathleen observed, with no 'balancing lionesses: the hostess herself was only a vicarious lioness, not really a lion hunter. She was the very charming sister of a dead lion [the artist Aubrey Beardsley], and her luncheon party was chiefly for his close friends: but lions they were, and to me very splendid ones indeed.' Kathleen sat between Max Beerbohm and J. M. Barrie, and 'wished they would roar a little louder'.[296]

On her left was Beerbohm, six years older than her, with receding hair and a moustache. Deliberately controversial, he maintained that 'There is much to be said for failure. It is more interesting than success.' Kathleen was not so sure about successful Max observing failure from a disinterested distance. He had no skin in the game. Besides, physically he was more like the effete undergraduates he parodied. She needed something more robust. This was not 'the father for my son'.

On her right was Barrie: five foot three and, in his late forties, still physically immature, a childlike figure. His play *Peter Pan, or The Boy Who Wouldn't Grow Up* premiered in 1904. Peter Pan was an enchanting boy, the kind of boy Kathleen would like to give birth to. Barrie's Scottish accent is familiar to Kathleen from the part of her childhood she can remember living in Presbyterian gloom with her Great Uncle in Edinburgh. But this is not 'the father' either.

Far down the other side of the table was a naval officer, Captain Scott. He was not very young, perhaps forty, not very good looking; but he looked very healthy and alert, and I glowed rather foolishly and suddenly when I clearly saw him ask his neighbour who I was. I was nobody, and I knew his neighbour, my hostess [Mabel Beardsley] would be saying so.[297]

Kathleen had already heard about 'Capt South Pole Scott'. From what she knew, he had just returned from a 'very heroic and rather sensational exploit [the *Discovery* expedition], and for the last few months had been subject to the torture of intrusive popularity. I was introduced to him after lunch and he wanted to know where I had got my wonderful sunburn. I was of the richest brown which made my eyes a very startling blue. I told him I had been vagabonding in Greece, and he thought how entrancing to vagabond like that.'

After lunch Mabel appeared. Did Kathleen know that she, Mabel, had met her husband George Bealby as a fellow member of the theatrical cast in *The Lion Hunters* in 1903? Kathleen did not but, looking at her watch, she suddenly realised she had a train to catch. Scott made his apologies and left two minutes later, 'but he saw me just ahead carrying a rather large suitcase,' Kathleen found out later, 'and his "English gentlemen don't carry large objects in the street" upbringing was too much for him. He did not catch me up.'

Ten months later, she went back to Mabel's for tea and met him again: 'With my invariable instinct to avoid what was attracting me, I moved to the furthermost corner of the party, and allowed myself to be diverted by the gay comedy of Ernest Thesiger and the heavy disdain of Henry James. What an unexpected setting for a simple, austere naval officer!'[298]

All of a sudden Kathleen found herself sitting in a stiff, uncomfortable chair with an ill-balanced cup of tea 'being trivially chaffed by this very well dressed, rather ugly and celebrated explorer'. He was standing over her, and apart from the breadth of his shoulders and the smallness of his waist, the thing that struck her were his eyes, 'eyes of a quite unusual dark blue, almost purple. I had noticed these eyes ten months before. I noticed them again now, though by electric light. I had never seen their like. He suggested taking me home . . . Life followed up the decision it had made ten months earlier.'[299]

But it was not as simple as Kathleen implied. Scott later cast himself as the Austenesque 'Darcy'. It was not about class – Kathleen's uncle was an Irish baronet – it was about money. 'I want to marry you very badly,' Scott wrote during their engagement, 'but it is absurd to pretend I can do it without facing great difficulty and risking a great deal for others as well as myself.'[300] The Antarctic was dangerous, but marrying for love rather than marrying money was risk indeed.

30 FEBRUARY 1911

BIRDIE – ANTARCTIC

Birdie, Cherry and Tom Crean are sledging back to the Cape Evans hut across the sea ice, so nearly home after weeks of depot-laying. They make camp, tether the ponies, climb into their sleeping bags and go to sleep. In the middle of the night Birdie wakes to a creaking, a shuffling. Perhaps one of the ponies has found its way into the fodder? 'I cannot describe either the scene or my feelings,' he tells Emily. 'We were in the middle of a floating pack of broken up ice . . . heaving up down with the swell . . . The floe on which we were [camped] had split . . . Gus [the pony] himself had gone & a dark streak of water alone showed the place where the ice had opened up under him.'[301]

Birdie shouts to his sleeping companions and rushes out in his socks to rescue the sledges. The floe splits but with all the men on one piece. Birdie grabs his finnesko (reindeer-hide boots), remarking that they have been in a few tight places but this is about the limit. The currents are taking their floe out to sea. With great difficulty, they manage to persuade the ponies to jump between the floes trying to get back towards the land. Suddenly there is the sound of a hollow blow and another and another. A pack of killer whales begins circling, 'their huge black & yellow heads with sickening pig eyes only a few yards from us'. Cherry is short-sighted, so Birdie fills Petty Officer Crean's pockets with food and sends him off. Crean, who 'like most bluejackets, behaved as if he had done this sort of thing often before', leapt off on his deadly game of hop-scotch with a message for Scott in his pocket.

'I don't care a damn about the ponies & the sledges,' Scott shouts across to Birdie fourteen hours later when he and Oates arrive at the edge of the ice. 'It's you that I want, & I am going to see you safe up here on the Barrier before I do anything else.'[302] The men are able to make a bridge from their sledges and climb back to solid ice. The three ponies drift back out to sea, surrounded by whales.

Through binoculars Birdie realises that the ponies' floe is being brought back in further along the bay. Over the crash of floes and the blows of circling killer whales, Birdie and Oates run back out to try to get the ponies to jump to safety. The animals, now stiff with cold, skid and fall into the water. Now it is a choice between deaths. Oates dispatches a pony with a pickaxe through the skull rather than let the whales play with it. 'I shall be sick if I have to kill another horse,' says Oates, 'like I did the last.'[303] Birdie picks up the axe and dispatches the other, following Oates's shouted instructions.

After the deadly game, both men, covered in blood, are surprised to find themselves alive. Scott tells Birdie that he, particularly, is 'quixotic' not to have abandoned the ponies to save his life from the first. Birdie tells Emily that while he was immersed in solving the problem, it honestly never occurred to him.[304]

MARCH 1911

EMILY – BUTE

The teachers from Rothesay Academy and Ardbeg Primary begin their preparations for Empire Day in early March. They have an army of volunteers. There are floats to assign, papier-mâché helmets for 'Britannia' and hymns, poems and H. E. Marshall *Our Empire Story* assemblies to arrange. An ex-headmistress is a useful volunteer. To the sound of children chanting, 'Remember the Day – 24th May', Emily could cut four long-sleeved dresses from one single bed sheet.

Everyone knew that Mrs Bowers had lived overseas where making one's own clothes was a necessary skill, but they probably did not know that she had been practising this skill since she sewed her own crinoline, as wide as she was tall, which made her look every inch the middle-class professional in the Cheltenham Teacher Training College year group photograph. Now at the Academy and Primary in Bute, Emily might even add that the quality of her sewing lessons was particularly remarked upon. After all, the best place to hide is in plain sight. Besides, volunteering to sew the maypole dresses allows Emily to distract herself from the traumatic memories of 'Empire' in the flesh. She will never forget that night in October 1885 . . .

1885

Emily remembers the flames. Heavily pregnant with May, her first child, she was on board her husband's merchant ship, the *Peah Pekhat*. A message was delivered by boat, summoning them to the rescue of their neighbours in Perak, British Malaya.

It was never clear exactly what happened, but as Emily related it to her children later, the Lamut coolies believed that Captain Lloyd was withholding their wages and that he kept the money in a trunk in his house. Captain Lloyd was brutally murdered and his wife beaten unconscious. To Emily's relief, the children slept through the attack, unharmed, though the building had been set on fire. The murderers were still at large, but instead of leaving, the Bowerses used the floorboards of their own Perak home to make Captain Lloyd's coffin.[305] Emily often wondered afterwards at her involvement, risking May's life in utero. Survivors were taken to safety in Penang where a doctor treated Mrs Lloyd and Emily could help look after the children and ayahs. The incident became a cause célèbre. Back then, anything seemed possible. It was only after they were safely back out to sea watching the smoke rising from the Lloyds' house that the rational side of her brain took over, and she could hardly believe her fearlessness.

Nowadays Emily is reduced to accusations of 'foolhardy[ness]' to put Birdie off taking similar risks, to make sure that he is not as 'quixotic' as she had been back then when it comes to saving his own beloved skin. 'At any rate in the Antarctic, one has no treachery to fear', as Oriana Wilson observes upon hearing the story of Perak.[306] The Bowerses are cheerful, capable, clever and, when danger threatens, strangely careless of their own safety. It is the kind of personality that – once outed – secures fast promotion. Birdie differs from his now middle-aged mother in that he is also resilient. Emily must have been resilient once – how else did she survive the rougher edges of Perak? Perhaps Winston Churchill's doctor, Dr Charles Moran, was right in saying that courage is a finite resource, and she has exhausted hers.

27 MARCH 1911

KATHLEEN – LONDON

Kathleen has filled vases, jugs and glasses with daffodils, and the vanilla scent fills her studio with spring. There is the buzz of conversation – fifty-two guests invited to help her celebrate her thirty-third birthday. Among the guests are a few reporters whom she hopes will comment favourably upon her statue of Florence Nightingale, her latest commission. She has begun to exploit the 'goldmine' of portraiture and not just dead people, live ones too. Sir Edgar Speyer and Lady Wemyss have commissioned portraits – they will begin sitting for her in April. Kathleen is expecting news of the *Terra Nova* daily but is determined 'not to make life into Hell by imagining things that may never happen' and goes through with the party as a point of principle.[307] Her servant Brand comes into the room with a tray of drinks and tells her, discreetly, that she should follow.

Out in the quiet hallway, Kathleen picks the Bakelite earpiece off the table and holds it to her ear. 'I was so excited.'[308] It is the Central News Agency. Their agent, stationed in the south of South Island, has called with the message: 'Ship sighted all well.' The *Terra Nova* has just returned to New Zealand with the news that all is well. Kathleen replaces the receiver carefully and rejoins the party, where no one suspects her news. 'A nice birthday message', and satisfying to have outwitted the reporters.

But she woke to new cables from New Zealand the following day: 'A state of frenzy all day. [*Terra Nova*'s official] message was such a muddle that no one could make head or tail of it.' The text seemed to suggest that a party of Scott's had met Amundsen and visited his camp. The race was on. 'I was of course bombarded with reporters . . . I told them we still wanted money!!! and nought else.'

PART TWO

Andante

QUEEN'S HALL, LONDON

After the first movement, Kreisler lifts his bow from the strings and puts it in his left hand, holding it along the neck of the Hart. He runs the fingers of his right hand through his thick, upright hair. The next movement, the Andante, has a brief orchestral prelude, a chance for him to breathe. The audience adjust their positions in their velvet seats and there is the flutter of white programmes, like a resettling of moths in the dark space beyond the stage.

In the dim light of the auditorium, whispered gossip favours Alice Stuart Wortley, who Elgar calls 'Windflower', as the prime candidate for '. . . . .'. She is the daughter of the Pre-Raphaelite painter John Everett Millais, and she is currently sitting in Block A of the theatre. 'I have never heard Elgar speak of the personal note in his music,' offers Elgar's friend Charles Sandford Terry, seated along from the Speyers, 'except in regard to [this] concerto, and of it I heard him say more than once, "I love it. It is emotional, very emotional but I love it."'[309]

Speyer knows that not all Elgar's music is emotional. Some of it is satirical. (Instead of a thank you, Elgar composed the Smoking Cantata, Op. 1001, an irreverent send-up of his anti-smoking patron.) But tonight Elgar is stern, serious and still nervous, much as Captain Scott was when Speyer last saw him as he set off from Waterloo Station on 16 July. For both Speyer's friends – the composer and the explorer – the second movement is key. The audience will recognise something of its deep dive from the initial introduction, but this time, in the Andante, the context is more detailed and they are more familiar with the music.

6

Sympathetic Equivalence

BILL — CAPE EVANS HUT, ANTARCTIC

The pace of life changes. Overwintering is andante, unhurried. Each man has time to reflect. They have just made it back to the hut after depot-laying and exploring as the sun sets for good. It will not rise above the horizon again until 23 August, 'but it gave us a grand sunset to finish up with'.[310] In contrast to the deeply hostile environment, the hut at Cape Evans gives the impression of domestic routine – a sympathetic equivalence with those at home. The natural environment of the Antarctic compels men to wait, to be patient, to sew, to paint, to live within limits in the same circumscribed way as their women.[311]

Bill starts the four months of darkness with a big stack of sketches to work up into watercolours. 'In comfort once more . . . Acetylene gas jets everywhere, stoves, clothes lines, clocks, telephones, electric gadgets, and scientific apparatus, all in full working order . . . Had a hot bath – shaved off my beard and moustache after Ponting had perpetuated them in a photo. Thoroughly enjoyed the gramophone.'[312] His favourite records are 'A Night Hymn at Sea' by Clara Butt and K. Rumford, and 'Tis Folly to Run Away from Love' by Margaret Cooper.[313] It allows a welcome female voice into the hut now and then. But he also likes the piano, less crackly, though only a few men can play. Those like him who can't try their hand at the pianola, a self-playing piano worked by feeding a roll of punctured paper, like braille music, into a turning drum.

Keeping a strict timetable allows them to maintain a normal circadian rhythm despite the lack of sunlight. Bill starts the day by organising his desk. He sets a large paint box – Ackermann & Co., 'By Royal Appointment' – to one side. At the back of the box lie small, flat, rectangular blocks of pure watercolour pigment – turquoise, ultramarine ochre and yellow gold – all on top of each other. In the top drawer are the sharpeners, tortillon smudgers, copper-handled sable brushes and pencils. In the last layer are various small, rectangular, white ceramic palette trays for mixing colour.

He takes out one of the watercolour sketchbooks Ory 'depoted' for him back in the English summer of West India Docks. On the Antarctic depot-laying journey he sketched with a pencil and wrote the names of colours to add later. He had to remove his smoked-glass goggles to see those colours. Together with the threat of immediate snow blindness, there was the risk of frostbite to the ungloved hand that held the pencil. Sketching is a high-risk activity in the Antarctic and watercolours, at least outside, downright dangerous.

Bill puts a small vial back into the medical case on a shelf by his right elbow. He uses cocaine drops in the eyes to treat the excruciating pain of sunburnt corneas, but he will not need them in the sunless winter. The nearest they will get to bright light is Ponting's magnesium camera flash, a moment of 'snow blindness'. Bill has his engagement picture – a joint portrait photograph of him and Ory taken in Thomson's studio on Bond Street, London. Ory has just blinked from the glare. It captures a moment of instinct, of vulnerability, and reminds him of his temper.[314]

It was shortly after their marriage, when, in an effort to capture the moment, they'd taken a cab to Thomson's studio. Bill knew of a Thomson's Studio in Pimlico. The cabbie thought Bond Street. Like a 'pigheaded ass', Bill insisted. The cabbie had been right, damn it. Bill lost his temper. The resulting image, a double portrait, Ory with her eyes shut, reminds him not to 'give way' to it in the Antarctic. Only Ory knows how hard it is: 'God knows it is just about as much as I can stand at times, and there is absolutely no escape. I have never had my temper so tried as it is every day now, but I don't intend to give way . . . It's a hard school down here.'[315] He sees it as a test of Christian self-control.

For all of them in this hut full of men, self control is about mastering human impulses – everything from tempers to sexual frustration. They must not give way. One of Wilson's junior scientists, Dr George Levick, has found the Adélie penguins capable of 'astonishing depravity'. He observed (in Greek, lest a woman should chance across his scientific notes when he got home) that the 'hooligan males' had sex with anything from other males to chicks and even females that had died the previous year.[316] But for Bill the hut is a welcome test, a chance to practise the asceticism of Christian monastic life. His days are a Benedictine honorarium, with Ory and God the joint focus of his devotions.

Bill looks at his photograph of Ory, the one from Bond Street. He can imagine her opening her eyes. The first thing he'd noticed about her was her 'iceberg eyes', impossibly blue, penetrating and different. 'Nothing is more extraordinary,' he confessed to Ory, 'than the feeling one has of loving people at first sight, and without a word being spoken. You know what I mean.'[317] He'd first met her in 1897 when he was a Cambridge medical student working in a mission in the Battersea slums, and he'd been shot through with electricity by those incredible eyes. He'd just bought some narcissi on impulse as defence against the thick sulphurous smog (and he could never pass a flower seller). The memory of that moment is clean-scented and fresh.

ORIANA — CHELTENHAM, ENGLAND

Ory's feet crunch along beech mast paths weaving between tree trunks buttressed by time. Above her, the lettuce leaves of the beech trees unfurl. Either side, an ocean of bluebells flows down the scarp slope, frozen in spring sunshine. She can hear the soft sound of the wind through the new leaves and, on the 'Kestrel's playground', a thicket of blackthorn fluttering with blossom and birdsong. From St Peters at the foot of the hill, church bells sound out across the valley. Nothing Ory has seen in her four crossings of the world compares to the English bluebell woods, especially this one at the Crippets on the scarp slope above Cheltenham.[318] 'Once or twice I have seen heaven,' said Bill of this place. 'I painted a primrose there . . . upon my soul, the glory of God in Nature has never been so continually before me as it is now and no-one to tell of it all.'

Ory finds their birding tree stump and sits with her binoculars and sketchbook at the ready. As Bill had schooled her, one has to sit 'as still as an old stump' until the wildlife forgot you were there.[319] If Bill were here, sitting beside her on the stump, he would not describe the bluebells as blue. He would probably write cobalt/violet on a pencil sketch before returning to Westal to add watercolour. She tries to sketch a picture 'to tell of it all'. In front of her rolls a chessboard of green fields to the silver Severn and beyond it, the blue remembered hills of Wales – Gloucester Cathedral, a giant chessman off centre of the board. She wants to render it through his artistic filter, but it is no use. Her efforts leach significance in comparison with his extraordinary talent. Her sketches are an aide-mémoire. She is a practical type, his 'Useful Help', not a creative.[320]

She'd first been introduced to this wood on days off from her first real job as matron in the James' school in Cheltenham. Back then she'd been delighted with the independence but devastated by Bill's diagnosis. Tuberculosis – half the sufferers died. 'With heaven in measurable distance,' he told her, 'I feel remarkably calm.'[321] But after his recovery, his convalescent hobby of painting birds took over from medicine. A doctor had status and stability, but Ory, by then his fiancée, helped to facilitate his career change, like picking the thorns off a rose: 'My maid, my maid, you picked them all off for me.'[322]

At the Crippets a kestrel spirals in the updraft. Ory raises her binoculars. There is something about birds of prey that has always appealed to Bill. They are detached, graceful, swift and 'different from the very first', just like Ory. But if he is ever asked to cite the zenith of her essential 'usefulness', he'd tell the story of that time during their grouse enquiry. Ory had just taken a perfectly risen soufflé out of the oven, when he called her to their laboratory. She abandoned the soufflé and, still in her oven gloves, obeyed without question. Bill asked her to hold the pencil exactly as he had it while he ran to fetch a tube of spirits. Ory removed her right glove and held the pencil absolutely still. While the soufflé deflated, Bill tapped the pencil she was holding over a tube of formaldehyde. He was glad to see that Ory had her priorities right. That flea was 'no common flea, but a rare and precious species of its tribe'.[323]

And yet now in the bluebell wood Ory is rudderless, there are her in-laws in Westal, her family at Hilton and yet nobody to 'tell of it all'.

SCOTT – CAPE EVANS HUT, ANTARCTIC

Scott sits at the foot of his bed with one leg across the other. His cubbyhole in the new hut is a large tongue-and-groove wooden box, with one wall open towards Bill and Teddy's bunks at the back of the hut. His right hand holds a sharpened pencil. His journal is open on his collapsible desk, propped out on a wooden arm from the outside wall. He lights his pipe and sucks the stem until the tobacco glows. He holds it in his left hand, like a cigarette between his index and third finger. On his feet he has his indoor finnesko. With his pipe and slippers, Scott confesses to Kathleen that he is hut-proud; he calls their wooden prefab a 'truly seductive home'.

Scott is wary of a tendency to 'indolence' he believes he has inherited from his unheroic father, but wiggling his toes in his fur-lined slippers, he just cannot help himself being comforted by the domestic routine they have established. Kathleen knows this side of him and teases him in letters: 'Don't forget to brush your hair and don't smoke so much, my ducky darling.'[324] After breakfast he retires to his cubbyhole with hair brushed and, lighting his pipe, begins writing his journal. Teddy goes to his cartography, Bernard Day to his 'make and mend' for the motors, Meares to his harness-making for the dogs, Oates to his horses, Ponting to his darkroom to prepare his photographic plates, Debenham to his rock specimens, and Taylor and Gran to their geographical studies. At noon someone goes up the ramp to take meteorological readings. Lunch is cocoa, coffee, cheese, marmalade and honey. The afternoon is like the morning, except that after five the pianola starts up. Then there is supper, and the meal ends with the lighting up of cigars and pipes. Someone puts the gramophone on. They play dominoes or chess till ten and then read in bed till nearly midnight.

Scott has begun a long letter to Kathleen, which he will add to all winter. By the head of his bed he has pinned three photographs of his son in a pair of rompers and two close-ups of Kathleen. Behind him on the right is a row of tobacco pipes with a little Union Flag stuck upright in the rack. The expedition library consists of old storage boxes on their sides. The most popular authors seem to be Tennyson, Dickens (particularly *David Copperfield*) and Robert Browning. He also has Shackleton's *The Heart of the Antarctic*, with all the dates and distances. He is determined to march faster and further when the sun returns to the Antarctic sky.

30 APRIL 1911

KATHLEEN – NEUILLY, PARIS, FRANCE

Kathleen is lighting candles in coloured glass holders around the dark, echoing room. Beside her is a large gramophone, its fluted brass horn points towards the centre of the 'stage'. Isadora Duncan is changing into her dancing dress. Her celebrity status means that she is besieged by men at the stage door of the Opéra Comique. But they have shaken them all off and Isadora has announced that she shall now dance just for Kathleen.

Kathleen needs Isadora to guard her lest her 'nice little naval wife' behaviour becomes a habit. In spite of her resistance, 'I am growing house-proud,' she tells her husband. 'Isn't that comic? I shall settle down into the most conventional of middle-aged matrons with immaculate house-linen and polished silver and stair-rods.'[325] Isadora does not think it is comic. She has invited Kathleen to Paris to find herself again, to find the art student at Rodin's sculpture studio, the girl dawn-swimming in the Seine and afterwards taking part in salons with Gertrude Stein. 'You were wild once,' says Isadora, 'don't let them tame you.' Her motto is *Sans Limite*. There will be no stair rods if Isadora has anything to do with it.

For Isadora, dancing is not just entertainment but art. Her contemporary dance is based on the chorus of Ancient Greece, which ensures tragedies produce a rousing affirmation of life in the spectators. It is also sensual, and humans are sensual beings. 'I may not be much to look at,' Isadora claims, 'but I am very good to feel.'

Now she emerges from behind a screen in her knee-length Greek tunic. She stands on one leg and lifts the other behind her, bent at the knee. She raises her arms, one in front, one behind, and begins to tip her head back. Realising that this is her cue, Kathleen lowers the needle on the gramophone and lies back down on the divan. Isadora's head is so far back that her profile is horizontal. In order to balance, she is leaning forwards at the waist. The music starts and Kathleen watches as the classical statue comes to life, the light silk echoing her movements. She weaves in and out of the coloured lights to the crackling sound of the gramophone. 'Oh dear me!' says Kathleen with an ecstatic sigh, 'very wonderful indeed.'[326]

TAFF – CAPE EVANS HUT, ANTARCTIC

Every morning Clissold bakes bread for the day, taking Taff straight back to 52 Chapel Street. A Tuesday, Lois's baking day, is like inhaling a warm blanket. But they don't have a gramophone back home and Taff does love a good tune. 'Stop Yer Ticklin', Jock' brings a smile to his face and perhaps 'A Little of What You Fancy' a tear. Taff dreams of the music halls round the docks, though none of the shellac gramophone singers are a patch on 'The Voice', obviously.

The hut is divided into officers and men by a wall of wooden packing cases. If he removed the large box of Colman's Cornflour, he would see Lieutenant Birdie Bowers' cheery self in his bunk on the other side. The cooking stove in the galley heats Taff's side of the hut, between the outside door and the wall. As the boss of this particular domain, Taff's bunk is furthest from the outside door, hard up against the packing-case wall opposite Clissold's galley. Stacked in tins on shelves they have their 'gallery'. There are two types of everything donated from sponsors of the expedition. Henry Tate & Sons cubed loaf sugar and Abram Lyle & Sons golden syrup. There is Rowntree's 'Elect' cocoa powder and Fry's chocolate. There are colourful boxes of Huntley & Palmers 'Captain' biscuits and greaseproof paper packets of Fern Leaf butter. Bright blue containers of Griffiths McAlister & Co. malt sit beside round red tins of Dutch Edam cheese. All this food for the winter, and yet Taff knows that there will also be seal meat. It is a dark meat, at once gamey and fishy, with a texture between veal and duck. The others are all over Clissold's crab-eater seal soup but Taff would rather a bucket of cockles.

Ponting has asked Taff and Crean to sit side by side sewing reindeer-skin sleeping bags for a photo of domestic life at Cape Evans hut. Taff pulls his sleeping bag to his left to make sure that 'the lady' is visible between them. Can Ponting see her? She isn't a typical sailor's pin-up, she wouldn't make a very good tattoo, but she is as pretty as a picture – a lot like Lois if Lois had dressed expensively. Lois did in fact have a bolero jacket rather like the lady's, but Taff's wife is not as curvy as Our Lady of the Tea Box. The tea-box lady had probably never done an honest day's work in her life, after all.

Crean and Taff push their needles into the reindeer hide. Neither of them wear their sailor's leather palm thimbles; they may be sewing but they are not women. Ponting tells them to carry on sewing, looking down at their work. The flash bursts into the dimly lit hut – a light like that would be easier to sew by than the acetylene they had. Perhaps Ponting would care to stay flashing there all day while they finished repairing the bags?

Taff is responsible for all the 'housewifes', the sewing kits that each man carries to keep their gear in good repair. He and Crean are not the only seamstresses, but Ponting seems to have picked the two burliest men for the ladies knitting circle. Lois will love this photograph, but right now there is something else bothering Taff. He puts down his 'knitting'.

Where is Dr Atkinson? Taff keeps a weather eye on who goes in and out of the outside door. He counts them out, he counts them back, but Dr Atkinson has been gone some time, too long, Taff reckons, for comfort. He alerts Captain Scott – they must scramble a search party. Quickly Taff gets dressed in his outdoor layers. A blizzard has got up. It is 'black as your hat – that is pitch dark'.[327] Taff calls into the darkness before stepping out, holding a rope tied to the hut. He cannot see his hand in front of his face. Other men tumble out. They must hold onto the ropes otherwise they will turn a disaster into a catastrophe. They shout and call into the whirling drift. Finally, Atkinson stumbles in.

Dr Atkinson's right hand is badly frostbitten, three fingers are unrecognisably swollen. Back home when folk ask Taff what frostbite feels like he tells them. 'Ever sat on a wasp nest? No? Well it's like that, only worse. You don't feel any pain at the time but when the blood begins to circulate . . . I was all right in a week, though.' Now Taff places a bandage gently on Atkinson's right hand while rolling it out. He knows that even the heat from his fingers will be excruciating for the doctor, who is biting hard on the stem of his pipe. If the officer class could restrain themselves from rushing out into every passing blizzard and let Taff think for a moment, he would turn his mind to more technical matters: sledges and boots.

LOIS – PORTSMOUTH

In the afternoons, when the children come home from school, women can open their front doors to the late spring sunshine. It is nearing the Coronation and there have been sports matches in Portsmouth inspired by the Inter-Empire Championships in London. Taff's fellow PT instructors follow them closely. In the newspapers there are reports that the Championships will become a regular event, to be renamed the Commonwealth Games, but for now, the children can have their own championship match in the street.

Lois's Portsmouth neighbours are from all corners of the Empire. When Lois grew up in Gower, everyone spoke with the same dialect except for the schoolmaster and his housekeeper. The schoolmaster was from Northumberland, the housekeeper, Somerset – they were considered to be exotics. The church is the centre of Lois's community, the curate, the recognised authority. Gower is separated North and South – the English speakers in the south are Conformists and therefore 'Church' like Lois, and the Welsh speakers in the north are 'Chapel'. They never talk to each other. Once their Reverend Ponsonby gave a North Gower Chapel girl a lift in his pony cart; he never spoke a word.

Portsmouth, however, is a melting pot. At Binstead Road School in Buckland, Norman and Muriel are educated alongside people who are not even Christian let alone 'Church'. When the men return from the dockyards at six o'clock, their feet beating time on the pavement, the mothers collect their children back into the house. There is one girl that Lois does not want to see – a girl who looks very like Muriel, about the same age. Her name is Lillian Kathleen. Her birthday is 31 July 1906. Her mother is a teacher called Beatrice Pharaoh.[328] Lois suspects that Beatrice sometimes uses the surname Evans, but at school her daughter Lillian's surname is Glazier or perhaps Amsden. When Beatrice of-many-surnames walks down Chapel Street to collect her child, there is a silence, conversation ceasing until they have passed. Lois knows that sailors are supposed to have a 'wife in every port', but she and Beatrice are in the same port and Muriel and Lillian are the same age.

Lillian looks well looked after, but Lois probably knows that Lillian's twin sister died – complications with 'dentition'. Lillian was conceived when Lois was pregnant with Muriel, and yet Lois and Taff have gone on to have Ralph. Whatever Beatrice writes on her census form, she must write 'one' in the column 'Number of Children Dead'. She writes 'P.O. Edgar Evans R.N.' under 'Father' on the girl's death certificate.[329] Does Taff support Beatrice and his remaining daughter? Lillian is not a mudlark – the very poorest children who wait on the mudflats by the wharf for passersby to flick coins into the filthy tidal flats. It is cheap entertainment for the people who flick the coins, but the mud stinks of sewage and the mudlarks emerge so covered that only the whites of their eyes show they are human.

The children in Chapel Street are neither rich nor barefoot. After the local 'Inter-Empire' games, Lois will have some darning and washing to do, some bandaging of grazes on scabbed knees. Lois looks after her three carefully. She will heat water in the copper kettle in the corner of the kitchen and wash them at least once a week. She does not want her children to be mistaken for mudlarks or bastards.

20 MAY 1911

OATES – CAPE EVANS HUT, ANTARCTIC

In the middle of the hut, Oates sits at the wardroom table on the officers' side. To his left is the huge round iron stove, the beating heart with its arterial flue reaching up over his head to disappear through the ridge of the roof. Over his left shoulder is the gallery – the dividing wall of Scott's cubbyhole – hung with a collection of framed 'art'. Beside a picture of George V and Queen Mary, which came down in the *Terra Nova*, Oates has just hooked a framed portrait of Napoleon onto a nail. Napoleon rather than Nelson, mind. Napoleon may have been defeated by 'us' in wellies, but he only lost seven out of seventy battles. Some soldier.

Twisting right, Oates can see his bunk in an area they've dubbed 'The Tenements', where the creed is: 'Down with Science, Sentiment and the Fair Sex'.[330] He has fixed his bunk up like an army camp bed with planks of timber inexpertly nailed and an extra plank nailed diagonally across to Birdie's bunk to keep it from capsizing.

Oates's anti-Fair Sex stance is part comedy and part convenience. *My Secret Life* (an anonymous autobiography published in 1890 graphically describing the pursuit of servant girls) was, unofficially, required reading during his teenage years at Eton. Sex was spoken of as an upper-class sport in the language of a horse-fancier or stableman: 'a nice fresh servant' (free from venereal disease) who is 'clean, well-fed, full blooded' and has not been 'used, ridden or raced' is ready for service. The author even claims that servant girls are proud of having gentlemen to cover them. Whatever Oates makes of all that, one of the attractions of the Antarctic is that although inclined to be cold, there are mercifully no servant girls, no girls at all – Down with the Fair Sex indeed.

Oates strokes the back of his cropped head and sniffs the fetid air

– as his mother might say, the smell of 'The Great Unwashed'. At least he can get 'really dirty' down here in the Antarctic, away from women and their expectation of cleanliness. Away from feminine insistence on a starched white collar, he can luxuriate in good, clean, masculine dirt. Packets of Sunlight soap donated to the expedition promise to produce 'a rich, free lather in hard or soft water', but they will seldom be tested on his clothes. There's a nod to personal hygiene in the round wire-cage wash bag with a sponge and bone-handled toothbrush he has slung from the post of his makeshift bunk, but the area under it is what really matters – a saddle-soap-scented tack room with hemp pony halters, harnesses, his thigh-length guardsman boots and supple chestnut-coloured leather bridles.

After lunch, Oates goes to the stables and lights the blubber stove to warm the pony mash. With his woollen balaclava tucked under his chin, he pokes the blubber fire with a tong. Soon the sweet reek of seal is overlaid with porridge. The ponies begin stamping their feet. Cecil Meares, the dog handler, sits beside Oates on the packing box that serves as a bench. They talk little, but when they do, they discuss working animals. Ponting is also out here in the dark, setting up his tripod and flash. Meares removes the stem of his pipe from between his lips and declares that Scott 'should buy the shilling book on transport'.[331] Scott, who has just emerged from the hut, hears the remark. There is a blinding magnesium flash and then silence.

Oates says nothing but follows Ponting back into the hut, leaving Meares to his fate. Oates has the reputation of getting on with Scott but he agrees with Meares. In fact he has gone further in letters to his mother, Caroline. Scott, he tells her, 'would fifty times sooner stay in the hut seeing how a pair of Fox's spiral puttees suited him, than come out and look at the ponies' legs or a dog's feet'.[332] Listening to the 'row' outside, Oates realises that if Scott ever saw his letters to Caroline, he'd be hanged, drawn and court-marshalled.

As light relief, Oates enjoys a visit to 'Ponker's Emporium' – the photographic darkroom at the far end of the hut. It is a place that invites the sharing of confidences out of the acetylene glare of the communal space. Oates is looking forward to Ponting's show of Japanese slides that evening. When a chastened Meares returns, Oates offers a breezy: 'Coming to the pictures, dearie?'[333]

Once in the dark of the darkroom, Oates watches Ponting performing his alchemy by the light of a green-tinted lantern. After some time, the portrait of him and Meares in the stable emerges in the basin. Ponting has captured the moment of Meares's transgression – the photographic atmosphere could be cut with a knife.

Ponting likes Oates but he is aware of his Inniskilling reputation: 'No Surrender Oates'. They all are. As they peg the wet paper images up to dry on strings above the basin, Ponting asks what will happen if anyone breaks a leg on the southern journey when the sun returns. Oates replies that they will take a revolver. If anyone on the team becomes incapacitated, 'he should have the privilege of using it.'

CAROLINE – GESTINGTHORPE

Caroline, president of the Gestingthorpe Cricket Club, sits in a deck chair in the meadow-scented shade. It is difficult to recline in a corset and the starch in her collar forces her chin up, but looking down her nose, she observes that the 22-yard pitch could be smoother. In the long grass, oxeye daisies are growing. She is keeping half an eye on the game and the other on Leys Wood behind Tinn Meadow. In letters, Laurie always asks if she's seen any foxes there. The woods are a reliable source for the East Essex Hunt. She will have to tell him, 'They have started poaching in the Leys in an awful way, so I am going to put a man in there to pick up snares, mend hedges etc.'[334] It is difficult to keep on top of everything – she imagines there will be a few Gestingthorpe conies gracing the dinner tables of some of those fielding tonight.

Most of the eleven players are locals, with the Essex accent punctuating the sound of leather on willow. But there is Etonian colloquial from Laurie's younger brother Bryan and the distinctly Germanic accents of his cousins. As the Gestingthorpe servants wrestle with the cricket tea, the conversation centres around 'horseflesh' and 'what Laurie is doing now' and, if Frederick Ranalow is there, music. Perhaps they can take the gramophone out to the south terrace and play Elgar after dinner?

This cricket match is just one of the village celebrations that Caroline has organised to reinforce her patriotic position. Her son may risk advertising his loyalty to the Napoleons of Europe. She does not. This very cricket match is held in honour of the upcoming coronation of George Saxe Coburg Gotha and Mary of Hess. It has the added advantage of putting the villagers in mind of their absent squire. Laurie's prowess on the cricket ground is almost as legendary as his 'No Surrender'. Striding out to bat for Gestingthorpe, he'd earned his reputation as 'a great hitter'. As one witness remembered: 'One gigantic, enormous six hit from the south end of "Tinn Meadow" right over the far boundary to an elm tree, where an oak post was driven into the ground to commemorate the feat.'[335]

Caroline tots up her expenses: £10 for the Gestingthorpe coronation fête. The village is looking its best, she has had some cottages re-thatched and ordered special flowers for the church from the Scilly Isles from M. Watts at £2.7. Bromwich has organised a service. Miss Heth has completed £20 worth of research into the Oates genealogy and their entitlement to the manor. The timing suggests some kind of heraldic display for the coronation. It looks as if it will be a hot day and Caroline makes a mental note to organise some shade.[336]

BIRDIE — CAPE EVANS HUT, ANTARCTIC

As he stands 'in a state of nature', with Bill at the hut door, Birdie rubs snow all over his body until he glows a bright, shining pink.[337] Snow bathing, a marvellous curative for the winter ennui, don't you know? 'The advantage of being plump down here,' he tells Emily, 'is tremendous, as you keep warm when others are perished – at least I do – and on a long journey you draw on your supply and don't come down to skin and bone till weeks after the lean ones have their clothes hanging on them like sacks.'[338] And it is not only his rotund figure that is finally working to his advantage. His short stature is advantageous too: 'In a tent . . . I think it is an advantage not to be too tall. You can fit into a corner and sleep in comfort where a big man would be cramped.' Captain Scott attributes Birdie's extraordinary buoyancy to the amber glass in Birdie's snow goggles, which gives him a rose-tinted view of life. 'Most chaps wear green,' Birdie tells Emily, 'but I find amber suits my green eyes best.'[339]

Birdie has not had his 'colours done' in the Antarctic, but he has an avatar that surely has. What will his mother make of Birdie as 'Madame Berde' in the expedition's magazine, the South Polar Times? Madame's ample proportions are corseted in a fetching petticoated little number, finished off with his signature green felt hat. Madame is a cartoon illustrating a spoof letter addressed to 'My Cynthia dear', an imaginary lady in Sydney, Australia, with tips for next season's fashion – because we are 'naturally ahead of you in Fashion's fancies, a whole 20 degrees'.[340]

When his fingers have thawed from his 'bath', Birdie dresses and goes to his bunk. His is the top bunk in The Tenements, on the other side of the packing-case wall from Taff. Hanging from the post on bits of string are a dinner knife, the woollen socks Emily knitted him, fur mitts and a shirt. Birdie knows exactly where everything is. The menagerie acts as a sort of curtain, giving him a bit of privacy from Taylor, Debenham and Gran in their cubicle on the opposite side of the wardroom.

Gran has already begged a more conventional curtain from 'Ponker's Emporium' to screen it from The Tenements. Oates, scorning privacy and such 'effeminate luxury', refers to the cubicle as the 'ladies' boudoir'. The 'ladies' reply that he needn't be jealous just because he hasn't got the only curtain in the Antarctic for himself. The banter continues all day, starting from the moment Birdie wakes in the morning with a yawn and asks Oates, 'How's the hay this morning, Farmer?' and Oates hesitates before delivering a crushing reply.[341] Bill, listening from further up the hut, remarks that 'the way thoughts flash through [Oates's] mind . . . reminds me of a snail climbing a cabbage stalk.'

There is a diagonal piece of wood between the top of Birdie's bed post and Oates's precarious bunk, but since Birdie is only a stocky 5 foot 4 inches tall, he clears it easily. When the table in the centre is busy, he puts a plank of wood on his bunk and, standing on a chair, uses the plank as a desk. Scott is a good leader, he tells Emily, scribbling a note on his plank. Seeing him 'only under the wing of his ambitious & energetic wife made me forget for a moment, [but] I know now that my first impressions were right'.[342]

Birdie is happy to be teased. He likes his nickname and he likes his portrait as 'Madame Berde'. Standing at the plank with his needle and silk, Birdie begins to backstitch red ribbon to form the cross of St George on his sledging pennant. He is not sure that his mother's will get here before they have to leave for the south. Though if the *South*

Polar Times's contributors knew the trade into which his mother was born, perhaps they wouldn't feel so free to caricature him. But they don't. So they do. And besides, Cynthie dear, 'Perhaps nowhere is it possible to have a more pronounced tailor success than here.'[343]

MAY AND EMILY – BUTE

In 1903 Beatrix Potter's *The Tailor of Gloucester* was published, a fairy story about a penniless tailor assisted by mice. It was an instant success and a good text for encouraging primary school children to read. May can read it to the Ardbeg Primary when she is not busy with her sewing.[344] Although May is not officially a tailor or a seamstress, the quantity of sewing she has indicates that she takes in outside work, perhaps to supplement their income.

If she is curious, May can find her grandparents in 'The Royal Cheltenham & County Directory', under 'Commercial and General: 'Webb, Frederick, tailor, 29 St George's Place'. Her grandfather is sandwiched between butchers and brushmakers. It is not a place in society that Emily chooses to advertise or even to discuss with her children. She knows that Birdie's 'Bill' is actually Dr Edward Wilson, whose family also live in Cheltenham. His father, also Dr Edward Wilson, is listed under 'Gentry and Private Residents: Wilson, E. Thomas, physician, Westal'.

May does not ask questions. She will never know that when her mother was young, she was not allowed into the Cheltenham Promenade, an exclusive area behind elegant wrought-iron railings for middle and upper classes only. May has never been literally outside the railings, looking in. Smart tailors like Stucke and Humphreys 'Riding Habits' had their establishments on the Promenade, but Emily's family worked from home. Whenever the conversation veers towards Emily's childhood, May focuses elsewhere. On some level she doesn't want to know more. Now she knits as if her brother's life depends on it. She has an almost morbid fascination with thick socks. Birdie has tried to tell her he has enough, but can one have 'enough' socks in the Antarctic? In her diary May writes: 'He hopes to be at the South Pole. What does the future hold for us all? Shall we be united again on Earth?'[345]

Emily adjusts her spectacles. It is the time of year for strawberries. There is something about the taste of strawberries – juicy, sweet, with a slight sour taste and the aroma of sweet caramel. It was the last thing they'd eaten with Birdie in London – a farewell tea of strawberries.[346] Her arthritis is always much better in the summer, but occasionally her arm is stiff. She peers at the fine needlework around the pierced leg on Birdie's sledging flag. Her stitches are small and neat: 'The stitches of those buttonholes were so small – *so* small – they looked as if they had been made by little mice!'[347]

7

Midwinter: Midsummer

KATHLEEN – LONDON

Kathleen's American lodger has already been to the Festival of Empire, which opened on 12 May at the Crystal Palace. But it is the coronation of George V and Mary, the pageant, she has really come to see. Advertising for a lodger was easy with an address like 'Buckingham Palace Road', and fortunately the American is too polite to notice the Victoria Station shunting yard opposite. If only raising funds for the expedition were as easy, but what could be more obvious than a ship called *Terra Nova*? At least Kathleen is making money, though having a lodger, and a woman at that, is a test of patience.

The 6,000 guests invited to the Abbey arrived at 8.30 that morning. The fixed pews have been replaced with Chippendale-style chairs, each carved with a royal coronet inscribed with the guest's name. Guests will be given the opportunity to purchase the chairs as souvenirs. Another money-making opportunity. Souvenirs. If royalty could stoop to this level of commercialism, why not the British Antarctic Expedition?

LOIS

Beside the Mall, people in the crowd climb the trees, boughs dipping towards the ground as they find their perches. It is free entertainment. If Lois were there, she and the children could watch the Royal Navy passing in two squares towing two field guns a piece. The Jack Tars wear their square-necked shirts, peakless caps and bell-bottom trousers. Either side an admiral in a bicorne walks, trying to keep step. Next the Marines and after them a troop of cavalry with knightly banners held on lances secured to the saddle, pennants fluttering high.

The *Discovery* crew met old King Edward VII when Taff received his medal back in 1904. That medal is shining brightly on its broad white

ribbon in pride of place in the front room of Chapel Street. Will King
George V be as interested in Antarctic affairs?

A mounted band. The lead horse is a grey, upon which a man with
an impossibly shiny cavalry trumpet is mounted. Elgar's *Pomp and
Circumstance* blasts from the trumpet's horn. This is a concert performance for the everyman. It is the sound of pageantry, of Empire
– stirring and patriotic. Most of the band's instruments can be played
with one hand, the other left free to grab the rein. It's a trick, like Taff's
party piece, his one-handed knot tying. The breeze is getting up. The
coronation swags strung between the lamp posts swing out at 45 degrees
right over the procession, lifting and falling with each gust.

ORIANA

People begin waving their handkerchiefs – the whole crowd, a flock
of gulls. They have seen the golden coach. Men remove their hats.
Either side of the coach, footman in gold and scarlet livery walk beside
the doors. Apparently, the king is on their side, Queen Mary on his
left. It is all over in a flash of gold. Ory has noticed stands of scaffolding
poles that seem to have grown up all along the route like trees, and
rows and rows of public toilets. The infrastructure to support the
pageant will take more than a flash to dismantle and the parks (where
thousands of Empire troops have been stationed) will take a while to
come green again.

MAY – BUTE

May had watched the late king's funeral the year before from Horse
Guards Parade. She'd had a good view of the new King George V, nine
crowned heads of Europe and the late king's dog Caesar, which trotted
along in the wake of the royal gun carriage. She and Emily are now
in Bute, scattering exclamation marks: 'Busy preparing for the Aldridges'
[family friends] visit, cleaning! Cleaning!'[348] But they have acknowledged
the coronation through a donation from 'all the Marys of Bute and
Cumbrae', organised by the Marchioness of Bute.

May is really 'Mary', like the queen. To start with, when the
marchioness had called for everyone called Mary who lived on Bute to
come forward, there had been some excitement in the Bowerses' bower.
Perhaps May would be presented. What did one wear to the Palace?

But it was soon clear that the marchioness's ideas were less ambitious. She just wanted donations in order to buy the magpie queen something shiny in the form of (another) new brooch: 'a suitable emblem of [the Marys of Bute's] loyalty in honour of their kinship in name with the Queen' on the day of her coronation.[349] And so instead of curtseying to royalty at a Buckingham Palace tea party, May lights the gas stove in their galley kitchen and puts the kettle on.

CAROLINE – GESTINGTHORPE

Caroline eases herself into her usual chair on the right of the mantel-piece. The village coronation fête was a success and now she is in her evening gown, dressed for dinner. Her eyes sweep down the palatial drawing room to the grand piano at the far end. There is the scent of summer flowers and wood polish. What will Lilian and Ranalow dream up for tonight's musical entertainment? Rumour has it that Elgar refused his invitation to the coronation service because he was insulted to be offered a restricted-view seat near the back of the Abbey. Right now, Laurie would probably embrace 'restricted view' if the venue were as spacious as Westminster Abbey. Caroline notes that this drawing room at Gestingthorpe is about the same size as Scott's hut, a rectangle of 50 feet by 25. She tries to imagine this space, but with a lower ceiling, filled with twenty-five unwashed men. Some of them are gentlemen, some of them are not, all of them would by now be 'really dirty'.

There are many not-gentlemen living in Gestingthorpe Hall, but they are clean and all but invisible. The servants have a separate entrance, giving onto a modest network of rooms that roughly parallels theirs. From the drawing room, Caroline can sometimes hear the servants' bells ringing on the opposite side of the hall in the corridor outside the kitchen. Each bell is labelled with a room in the house. With a full house party for the coronation, those bells never stop ringing.

Even on the family side of the house, there is segregation. Nephews and sons lurk in the masculine billiard room, smoking and chalking their cues. Caroline, her daughters Violet and Lilian and visiting sisters Mary and Marion, stick to the more feminine apartments, the morning room, the music room and tonight before their private coronation feast, the drawing room.

Now that the coronation itself is over, Kaiser Wilhelm II, the son of Victoria's eldest daughter, will make his way home, and so will Caroline's sisters. Mary and Marion Buckton married German brothers, Hermann and Georg Kremnitz respectively, and they live in Dusseldorf. Caroline chose to go there to be with her sisters for the birth of her first child, Lilian.

In the Antarctic, Oates has already admitted that he 'hated all foreigners'. Perhaps he does not class his relations as foreigners. If there is a war, which side would his cousins fight on? How long can the Kremnitz sisters continue to come to Gestingthorpe? The coronation of two people with Germanic titles, and the Kaiser's attendance, legitimise their visit for now.

When Oscar Minchin announces that dinner is ready, the men each escort a lady across the flagstone hall to the candlelit panelled dining room. Dinner is served invisibly from the butler's pantry behind the room. From the head of the table, Caroline surveys her family. This life of aristocratic luxury is all her children have ever known. It is an inheritance they take for granted – she never does. Laurie chose to exchange it for savagery in the Antarctic. He might, right now, be gnawing on a joint of New Zealand mutton. She looks down the white tablecloth laid with the family crested silver, silver candelabra, silver soup tureen. . .

22 JUNE 1911, MIDWINTER'S DAY

OATES – CAPE EVANS HUT, ANTARCTIC

. . . tureen embossed with the BAE penguin emblem and a silver salt and pepper. Down the centre of the crisp white tablecloth are silver soda siphons, bottles of wine, and champagne with the gold foil wrapper frayed at the neck. Oates has finished his champagne, but his port glass is still half full. He puts his bone-handled cutlery together on his plate and picks up his crystal wine glass. It may be June, but it's halfway through the Antarctic winter and Clissold the cook has done them proud for their midwinter feast: 'consommé – seal, roast beef & Yorkshire pudding, horseradish sauce, potatoes a la mode & Brussels sprouts; plum pudding; mince pies; caviar Antarctic'.[350]

Oates is replete. Oscar Minchin, his mother's butler, would be proud – Minchin is always trying to feed him up. (Oates has that effect on people. The villagers of Gestingthorpe seem to think that he looks as if he could do with a good meat pie.) At the end of the table, Ponting is counting down. A blinding magnesium flash later and it is over.

For Oates, the camera is Caroline, his mother, her window onto his life. On his right, a clean-shaven Debenham wears an improbably clean white woollen Jaeger jacket. Oates has elected to wear a dark jacket. It is difficult to keep up appearances when one spends most afternoons tending the animals in sub-zero temperatures, warmed only by burning blubber, but that will not 'wash' with Caroline.

Opposite Oates sits Day, the man in charge of motors. Between Meares with his dogs, Day with his motors and himself with those crocks in the stable, they are in charge of getting this show onto the road. Sometimes the responsibility is overwhelming. Sometimes, particularly after a few glasses of Madeira, it seems possible. They have opened presents on Birdie's 'Christmas Tree' made of sticks and feathers. Oates's is a popgun. 'If you'd like to please me very much you'll fall down dead,' he declares, popping the gun.[351] They need no encouragement; suddenly reintroduced to alcohol they are all slurring and the floor looks frankly comfortable.

Oates looks up at the sledging pennants strung over the table in full Arthurian splendour. His is noticeable by its absence. Are his sisters making one or has he ducked another maternal lecture on his manorial ancestry and responsibility? His mother's plans to marry him off seem to have become widely known. Oates's expedition nickname is 'Titus' and in the South Polar Times, Titus Oates is 'the only man who counts', as 'ladies' attempt to 'bring him to a proposal'. 'Cynthie dear' learns that Mappin & Webb are making a dress with mascots that will appeal to him: a silver horse snowshoe, a popgun, a silver blazon, Per Mare Per Terram Pro Tito (By Sea, By Land, For Titus). In the cartoon a disinterested man strokes a horse, his back turned to the 'woman' who is being rolled along the ground by a Victorian matron (surely Caroline?) in a long black dress and black laced-up shoes, only her lower half visible. Oates goes along with it in the knowledge that Caroline's desire centres around legitimacy – a legitimate heir. But everyone in the hut knows General Sir William Bellairs's unofficial rules: 'A subaltern may not marry, captains might

marry, majors should marry and lieutenant-colonels must marry.'³⁵²
Once a man married he was thought to become soft and incapacitated
as a man of action because of the conflicting claims on his energies
and sense of duty. Laurie's next promotion will be to major. 'Should'
marry? Really? Surely it's like a job? For now he's busy looking after
the 'crocks' and Caroline. His mother is his only real confidante – he
trusts her with treasonable truths.

But the midwinter's day feast is a celebration. Afterwards he surprises
everyone, himself included, with a full-blooded rendition of 'The Vly
Be on the Turmut' with a flourishing finish: 'But of all the jobs as Oi
loike best, gi'e Oi the turmut 'oein'. The others are generous in their
praise – it is the first time he has sung, after all – but he's pretty sure
that is not what Frederick Ranalow would call it. After a 'song', he
executes an excellent if asymmetrical Lancers' quadrille. He clears the
wardroom floor, but perhaps not in a good way.

16 JULY 1911

ORIANA – HILTON, ENGLAND

It is early morning, Oriana has just returned from the eight o'clock at
St Mary Magdalene and already it is too hot to sit in the sun. It has
been an exceptionally sunny month – hardly a drop of rain, with the
temperature rising to 31 degrees. She is in the walled rectory garden
at Hilton, the tall sash windows already wide open behind her. The
croquet lawn is turning brown; the climbing rose scents the air. Ory
spreads the *Morning Post* on the table beside her cup of tea. On 4 July,
Prime Minister Lloyd George sent a note to Germany. The Kaiser wants
France to cede its colony in the French Congo in return for a German
withdrawal from Morocco. Lloyd George has told him that Britain must
be consulted. From the *Morning Post*, it seems that he has still not
received a reply.

From across Hilton Green, the church bell tolls the hour. The birds
have stopped singing in the heat, though shadows hop through the ivy
on the opposite wall. Ory is looking forward to getting back to the
cool interior of the flint church. Her father, Reverend Souper, took the
early service and will take the next two. Ory will go to all three on
this the tenth anniversary of the day she 'gave herself away' to Bill in
that very church.

1901

Ory remembered the heady scent of trumpet lilies in her bouquet and the black mourning rosettes on her dressing table for the bridesmaids to pin to their dresses – a mark of respect for the recently deceased Queen Victoria. Her sister Constance helped her into a swan suit of tight white satin. Swans, they reminded her, bonded for life, but this time their migration would be staggered. Bill would be leaving in three weeks for Antarctica. His lungs were scarred by tuberculosis but Scott offered to take him at his own risk. 'If the climate suits me I shall come back more fit for work than ever, whereas if it doesn't, I think there is no fear of me coming back at all.'[353] Ory sat in front of the dressing room mirror while her bridesmaids fixed the tulle veil and arranged orange blossom in her soft brown hair. She was taking a big risk. Bill's mother believed that they should have waited until he returned, *if* he returned, to get married. The old Mrs Wilson worried that they might incur 'responsibilities', by which she meant children. Ory decided she would rather be a single-handed mother than wait. If it came to it, she would rather be a widow than a spinster.

Thinking back to her wedding, she remembers the gravel crunching under the wheels of the open landau that pulled up to her father's church in a peal of bells. At 4 p.m. Mr and Mrs Wilson left for Cambridge with all their luggage and got to Pinner, via King's Cross and Euston, by 10 p.m. 'A late arrival but a very happy one.' Their first night as a married couple . . . 'And so began our life together before God.'[354]

16 JULY 1911

BILL – CAPE CROZIER, ANTARCTIC

As they lie shivering violently side by side, Bill tells Birdie and Cherry that he will call their rough stone igloo 'Oriana Hut, and the ridge on which it is built, Oriana Ridge'. It is Sunday 16 July and, he writes with frost-cramped hands, 'a date not easily forgotten'.[355] They are halfway through the six weeks allotted to this journey to Cape Crozier to collect emperor penguin embryos. It is the first journey ever attempted in a polar winter, and it is colder and darker and frankly worse than the worst journey any of them could imagine. Bill has been lent these two men by Scott on condition that he brings them back alive.

Three weeks ago, they set out from the comfort of their hut at Cape

Evans with a couple of sledges and a tent. Now the thermometer is heading to minus 27 degrees (mild by comparison to 30 July when the temperature will plummet to minus 63) and it is beginning to blow hard. Cherry's glasses have shattered, his teeth are cracking.

He is beginning to realise that 'men do not fear death, they fear the pain of dying', but not Birdie.[356] He is still cheery – he offers Cherry his spare eiderdown sleeping bag lining. He hasn't used it yet. Hasn't felt the need.

They've retrieved five eggs, but on the way back up the crevasse cliff in the moonlight, they broke two. That night Bill cooks using penguin blubber for fuel. 'I got a spurt of burning oil in my eye and it gave me great pain for a good many hours.'[357] His eye burns, his body freezes. In the morning Cherry and Birdie try to persuade Bill to pick somewhere more worthy of his wife's name but he assures them that this stone hut has been a 'Useful Help' and besides, it would be 'a top hole dwelling place in any other land'.[358]

It may be dark, but sometimes the moonlight is fairly good and besides, darkness is not necessarily unpleasant. Birdie speaks for them all when he says, 'The same old moon smiles down on us as you see so far away.'[359] They sing all the songs and hymns they know to keep warm. Birdie begins composing a poem celebrating the return of the sun on 23 August – it has a catchy rhythm and fits quite well to the tune of a hymn they all know: 'Thou Whose Almighty Word', the first line of which is 'Chaos and darkness heard' and the last 'Let there be Light!'[360]

EMILY – BUTE

From the wooden pulpit, unusually centred in the nave, the Reverend Dewar peers at his flock. He and May have had some interesting discussions about 'spiritualism & telepathy' recently; 'Mr Dewar believes in it. Told me some interesting things.'[361] But that is not the theme of today's sermon. Instead he seems to be addressing himself to Emily. He tells her that in a healthy congregation, everyone takes responsibility for being ambassadors for Christ, not just the minister. It is 'call-to-arms' sermons like these that precipitated Emily's move from the safety of her position as a headmistress in England to the unknown reaches of Penang and Further India in her youth. When the sermon finishes, the hymn reinforces Dewar's point.

One of the best features of Emily's childhood in the tailor's workshop at number 29 was its proximity to the Evangelical church and the passionate Christianity of the Reverend Francis Close. That is where she had first encountered the American hymnists Sankey and Moody, and been made aware of the close connection of souls and minds, Christianity and education.

May, standing beside Emily in the pew, associates hymns with her childhood routine. Even now Emily begins each day with a watered-down school assembly: prayers, Bible readings, a Sankey and Moody hymn. Music encourages what Emily calls 'pulling together'. Now in St Ninian's, the choir process back down the aisle and Reverend Dewar reads the banns of marriage. Will Emily's children ever have their marriage banns read?

She looks down the pew at May. Albert Armitage pursued May for some time, but it seems May didn't encourage him. Emily is aware that she is still trying to overcome the disappointment. '*Il faut battre le feu tandis qu'il est chaud* (One must fan the fire while it's still hot),' May tells herself sternly in her diary. She finishes with: 'Wish I had!'[362] Dr Moore had called upon Edie more than once, but that relationship had not ended in marriage either. Emily thinks of her husband Captain Alexander, of his chastity until his marriage in his early fifties, his integrity and resilience. She wonders if Birdie might take after his father.

1877

From the day of her wedding, in St Andrew's Cathedral in Singapore, Emily's marriage was happy, however unlikely it seemed – Captain Bowers was surely a man of the world, not somebody that nice evangelical Christians from Cheltenham went about marrying. But in Further India, Captain Bowers had made a name. His father was a carpenter from Scotland and yet Alexander had become a Fellow of the prestigious Royal Geographical Society. And to Alexander, Emily, in starched white dresses and radiant with her newfound calling, must have seemed what their son might call 'a pukka memsahib to [her] fingertips', regardless of her own start in life.[363]

By the time Birdie was born, 'Empire Emily' had had enough of adventuring, and was living back in Scotland in Greenock in a large stone villa built by Alexander on the seafront. It was the genteel life she had been hoping for, but Alexander's business drew him back to the East. In February 1887 he cabled her to come to Mergui. He was ill. Leaving May and Edie with her mother-in-law in the stone villa, Emily left England with her toddler son. She arrived in Singapore to a message. She was too late.

Alexander's business had been so harried by the East India Company that he'd died leaving her little to live on. She wrote to May and Edie and prayed. Friends from her colonial days, fellow British traders the Fouchars, came up with a plan. Emily was the kind of person that people trusted with their children. They could set Emily up in a house in England so that the Fouchar children could have a British education. That was the beginning.

Emily sailed on to Penang and took Birdie up Penang Hill. She showed him the tree ferns that she and his father used to sit under. She fed him strawberries and sang to him about Greenock: 'I'll sing a song about a toon . . .'

23 JULY 1911

BIRDIE – CAPE CROZIER, ANTARCTIC

. . . a wee toon upon the Clyde,
It is the toon whaur I was born, it fills my heart with pride.
My mither often telt me as she crooned me on her knee,
That Greenock took its name frae the Green Oak Tree.

Birdie is shout-singing above the noise of a furious force 11 storm. Partly he is doing it to cheer himself and partly to let the others know that he is still alive. Every so often he stops and, taking his gloved hands out of his sleeping bag, slaps Bill in the bag next to him on the back just in case he can't hear Birdie bawling his way through all the songs he knows a few inches from Bill's ear.

They have anchored the green canvas roof sheet on the outside with large stones, stones they could hardly carry. Now the wind is acting on the canvas to joggle the stones about like so much gravel so that they are shifting out of place.

Suddenly the canvas rips out all along the lee end of the hut with a noise like a battery of guns going off. In a second it is ripped in about ten places and the ragged edges start 'bang, bang, banging . . . the noise was most distressing and we hardly noticed the rocks that fell in, or that the sledge was at once flapped off and fell in also across our three bags.'[364]

Now they are completely exposed to an Antarctic winter night. Shouting over the wind, Birdie assures Bill that he is still as keen as anyone to look for 'hen's teeth' (or at least penguin eggs with embryos that might have teeth) and prove Bill's evolutionary theory. Cherry wonders if extreme shivering has ever broken bones.

The next day, when the wind drops from storm force 11 to a croonin' gale force 9, Birdie tries to persuade the others to have another 'crack' at those eggs. They only have three. Is it enough? On 25 July, when Bill insists they start their retreat, Birdie ties himself to the tent pole, determined that if it should blow away this time, he will go with it.

AUGUST 1911

LOIS – PORTSMOUTH

Arthur Thomas is thirty-three and the man Taff has chosen to be executor of his will. Arthur is a brass moulder. He works in the brass foundry in the dockyard. All day he is surrounded by the hiss of steam and the heat of molten metal being poured into moulds. After work he might go round to see Lois and the children, to check that everything is shipshape in Taff's little family. After a day at the foundry, he could probably do with some refreshment too. Lois is used to cooking man-sized meals for Taff and knows how to satisfy the appetite of a hungry working man.

When the census man comes to Chapel Street, he adds, '1st Shipwright' in pencil after Lois has written her name. There are no female shipwrights registered in Portsmouth until 1914. Since there are no men named in the census, apart from 'Norman Edgar [aged] 5' and 'Ralph, 2', Lois hasn't taken in a shipwright as a lodger. Is Lois the first female shipwright in Portsmouth? If that's the case, why isn't it 'news'? Perhaps Lois was working as an assistant for Arthur's shipwright brother Walter Thomas? Is Walter's childless wife Ellen minding Ralph? Although the form must be filled in in ink, the census man never confirms 'Shipwright' with pen. And so Lois hands the form back to him and sets off to the post office to draw her 'allowance' from Taff's British Antarctic Expedition salary as usual.

After a visit to Chapel Street, Arthur can walk the mile back to Landport, where he lives at 393 Commercial Road next door to Charles Dickens's house. Since Dickens's death in 1870, the house has become a museum and lending library open to the public free of charge. Lois can borrow books so that when Taff is reading *David Copperfield* in the Antarctic, she can read it out loud in Chapel Street.

Lois is a do-er, but if she ever stops to think about Taff's choice of executor, she might wonder whether he has made some deeper arrangement with Arthur. Lois never needs to ask for help when Taff is around, he can do anything from mending furniture to repairing the children's leather boots, but when he is away things are different. If anything should happen to Taff, is Arthur the person Taff has set up to look after her? How far has her husband imagined the future? Arthur is not one of Taff's 'Swansea Tars'. He is a sensible bachelor. He has a good trade and no dependants. Arthur Thomas is the kind of man that could be trusted to do the right thing with your will and your wife.[365]

AUGUST 1911

TAFF – CAPE EVANS HUT, ANTARCTIC

Dr Wilson, Lieutenant Bowers and Mr Cherry-Garrard may be back from the 'weirdest birding trip in history' in one frozen piece, but those sledges have taken one hell of a battering. Taff runs his forefinger along the length of the elm wood sledge runners. He can feel the texture of the grain, making it resistant to splitting. The main body is ash wood. It is strong and durable and the grain lies straight and smooth, cool to his touch. As Taff sands the elm runners smooth, he can smell the faint faint scent of sawdust in Walter Thomas's workshop back in Portsmouth. The wooden runners need to flex enough not to break, but not so much that they go out of balance. Any resistance will be transferred straight through to the men's harnesses. Spliced together the elm and ash are, Taff sincerely hopes, invincible.

The sledge is based on the Inuit komatik translated through Fridtjof Nansen, but it is the shipwright's skills that mean he will be able to strip the sledge down once they are en route to the Pole. It is easy enough to do this in the hut, but what will it be like in the deep freeze after a day's sledging?

Taff's job, as he sees it, is to keep the equipment functioning for the race. The distance of the Antarctic 'stadium' – there and back – is 1,530 miles. The whole return journey should take 144 days. Taff breaks it down. The race out. Fire the gun or at least run the Union Jack up that most southerly pole. The race back to the *Discovery* hut. Cape Evans. New Zealand. Chapel Street. Finish. Taff wants this sledge to sail through the snow like one of Walter's perfectly wrought skiffs.

15 JULY 1911

KATHLEEN – DARTMOUTH, ENGLAND

The Vickers monoplane climbs into the blue sky. Beside her on the grassy runway, a man drops to the ground, kneeling. It is one of Captain Herbert Wood's mechanics. He puts his hand behind his ear 'to hear if the motor was missing'. Suddenly it seems to lose steerage and flutter out of the sky, but just before it hits the ground the wings level out: 'He had a narrow shave at one moment,' Kathleen tells Scott in her diary, 'and I thought it was his last.'[366] The monoplane landed beautifully. Kathleen is enchanted. This is witchery.

She is sure that she would be fine. She is lucky, Scott is not. Recently she confided to Compton Mackenzie, who is sitting for her, that she did not believe that Scott would reach the South Pole. 'He has always been unlucky. If he has an important engagement, the train or the bus breaks down, and he misses something that might have made all the difference. I try to put away this doubt but it's no use. I cannot somehow believe that he will reach the Pole.'[367]

She has taken to spending afternoons at airfields chatting to the lions of the air. She talks to their engineers and tries to learn about engines. She is determined to fly in spite of Scott's relations, his mother and sisters, who think she has a responsibility to Peter to stay safe.

'What nonsense that "virtue is its own reward"! What reward have I for refraining from getting my pilot's certificate? There is nothing I want so ardently to do as to learn to fly. Almost every day I have to actively restrain myself. Everybody is shocked at my flying, even as a passenger . . . My duties to you two! I see their point.'[368] Kathleen is working on a sculpture of the late Charles Rolls, who died flying, but there is still something utterly irresistible about the sensations flight offers: the increased gravity, the corresponding sense of weightlessness, the rush of air in her face. She has seen the danger, but why should

Scott have the monopoly on risk, on danger, on fun and excitement? 'But I want to fly, and what reward have I? Worse – I believe you'd like it if I did fly. Damn!' A few days later a Mr Sopwith invites her to fly his new dual-control aeroplane. If she accepts his invitation and takes the controls, she will be only the second woman in England to fly. How can she resist?

SCOTT – CAPE EVANS HUT, ANTARCTIC

Scott brushes away the powdery drift with his mittened hand. He must not touch the metal of the motor – it's cold enough to burn – but he has come to the motor's 'stables' to check on his investment. He wants to embrace technology, and in terms of cost and confidence he has spent seven times more on the motor sledges than on the ponies and dogs combined. Motor engineer Bernard Day has been exercising them, as Oates has the ponies, but the motors play up in the cold. Scott consoles himself that even 'a small measure of success will be enough to show their possibilities'.[369] Perhaps there will be some other use for an all-terrain vehicle with caterpillar tracks if there is a war?

At some point man will probably be able to fly to the Pole. In the hut they joke about a future where tourists will come from 'the effete centres of civilisation. At Cape Evans mountaineers will land to tackle Erebus, and aeroplanists will descend for refreshment on their arrival from New Zealand.' When? To illustrate the point, someone has painted a watercolour of a 'Flyer', a flimsy bi-plane flying over snowy Antarctic peaks, in the *South Polar Times*.

What kind of Antarctic will those airborne tourists be visiting? The scientists in the hut do not know whether the world has even finished with the Ice Age. 'If as seems possible still warmer conditions supervene, we shall arrive at a topography like that of the Himalayas.' They imagine forests and populations and fertile glacial soil. They can't agree on when there will be 'summer motor trips to the South Pole'. Scott and Day trudge back to the hut wondering: 'Judging the future by the past, about 200,000 AD.'[370]

8

'We Can Do Without You'

BILL – CAPE EVANS HUT, ANTARCTIC

I am fed up with having written this journal for so many days on end. Every now and then I have had to go and play the pianola to work off my writer's cramp, mental chiefly . . . Our winter life has been very quiet, as may be judged by the regularity of our horse exercising, my continual painting and drawing, and the lack of exciting incident to put into this old journal of mine.[371]

Bill's idea of 'quiet' is a relative term, not one that usually encompasses near-death experiences or world firsts, as he has faced on the Winter Journey to Cape Crozier. But he is frustrated in spite of the fact that he has only just recovered sufficient feeling in his frozen fingers to hold the paintbrush. 'Men don't improve when they live together alone,' he believes, 'cut off from all the better half of humanity that encourages decency and kindliness. Some of our mess have quite dropped the mask and are not so attractive in their true colouring.' Now he is struggling to maintain his own 'mask' – the pianola helps.[372]

In the twilight when the sun skims just beneath the horizon, Bill realises that his watercolours are not perhaps his best work. Ory is his only chance at guaranteeing a little leeway: 'In looking at them,' he tells her, 'you must remember that they were all done by artificial light, acetylene and so they look queer in daylight. The blues and yellows are apt to go wrong.'[373] He trusts her with his artistic reputation – if anything has to be done, 'Ory will have the doing.'

He doesn't have time to redo them – there is far too much to do. Clissold, their cook, is laid up. He was posing for Ponting and fell on hard ice and hurt his back badly. Hooper, their 'wardroom servant', is working on the motors and so, Bill tells Ory, 'we have to do the cooking and housework ourselves.'[374] [Dr] Atkinson and Seaman Pat Keohane do the baking and cooking, while Birdie and Cherry do the sweeping, fire-lighting, table-laying and what not.

All morning they have been trying to telephone the *Discovery* hut where Meares has gone with the dogs (the line was laid between the huts some time ago, but hitherto there has been no communication). Now two more men set off south to see whether the telephone wire is broken. Bill knows that Ory despises the telephone, but sometimes it is useful. He wishes he could call her to check that 'my dear old Ory [is] getting through the time without any sorrows or sickness or sadness of any sort. I always have the feeling before me that although I ought to be the most uncomfortable . . . it is you who are having all the more difficult part of uncertainty and doubt.'[375] The telephone rings.

ORIANA – CHELTENHAM

Ory hears it from the Westal garden. Bill is not due back for months and yet she always wonders, when the telephone rings, if it is Central News calling about him. Her nerves are jangly. Bill's father refers to the telephone as a useful servant – it is all about usefulness in this household, and yet she is at the moment beyond use.

Ory is lying under a tartan rug in a canvas deck chair that can be levered out into a reclining position with a footrest. She is, as usual, reading the *Morning Post*. Ory likes to be able to keep her husband up to date on world news in the letters to be sent south with the *Terra Nova*. Right now it is all mind-boggling numbers. Plans are outlined for an impossibly lavish Durbar in Delhi in December, where King George V will be formally proclaimed King-Emperor of India before an audience of 80,000. He will soon have 315,000,000 subjects; the population of the British Isles is only 45,370,530.

Under the rug she wears her thick woollen winter coat with the fur-trimmed collar but no hat. Under her left eye, there is a semi-circular cut like a smile. The rose that blooms over an arch in the summer is almost leafless, its thorny crown hovering over her head. What ails her? Is it just the slow erosion of living in 'uncertainty and doubt'? Has she had treatment for her infertility? Does the problem concern her tendency to anorexia or her 'bad headaches'? Is it simply that she has lost her way? Her purpose is predicated on her husband's presence or at least on the data he collects. Ory's mother died of pneumonia shortly after the birth of her eighth child. When Bill left her for the Antarctic the first time in July 1901, Ory contracted pneumonia. If things had been different, the medical student that she met in Battersea all those years ago might have become a rural GP like his father. He would have been able to tend to the cut under her eye, her pneumonia-weakened lungs, her infertility and her present need to recline in a rug in the garden on a chilly morning.

TAFF — CAPE EVANS HUT, ANTARCTIC

Captain Oates has chosen Taff to be on his football team. He compares the slippery ice pitch they are about to play on to the manicured playing fields of Eton. Taff has heard about those fields. Didn't the Duke of Wellington say, 'The Battle [of Waterloo] was won on the playing fields of Eton'? Taff learned his football first on Rhossili beach and then on the rough ground on the outskirts of Swansea. Does anyone know where they won the Battle of Trafalgar?

Taff passes the alpine rope on to the next player waiting in line. They are standing in the hut, ready to jog out of the door-tunnel and up past Ponting's camera onto the 'pitch'. Taff uses idle moments like this to show the others how to tie a one-handed clove hitch. Maintaining dexterity is not just a trick – with frost-nipped fingers 'handy men' need a decent margin for error. And in addition to ropes and knots, Taff is responsible for the sledges and the shoes – it is not glamorous or 'academic' work, but the devil is in the detail and he is determined to win that race.

It is not ski boots they need for football on an ice rink, however, it's 'naily boots', at least that is what the cockle fisherwomen call them in Gower. Ponting is ready. They line up in teams. Taff 'jogs' down the tunnel and emerges, blinded by the low sun. He jogs past the camera and onto the pitch, where they have set up two goals by sticking poles into the snow. They take their positions. The whistle blows.

'Break 'em up, Taff,' says Oates.

'Right oh, Sir', says Taff, striding out.[376]

LOIS – PORTSMOUTH

It's a disaster. The previous season, Portsmouth Town had been relegated after winning only eight of their thirty-eight games. Now, in the second tier of the Southern League, Merthyr Town are the victors. Lois is Welsh. If things get awkward, she can explain that although rural Gower is less than 40 miles southwest of industrialised Merthyr, there's no cockling in Merthyr and barely any coal mining in Gower; they could be different countries.

When Taff left Gower at the age of ten (twice the age that Norman is now), he began work as a telegram boy at the Swansea Post Office. In his smart uniform, Taff explained to his cousin that collecting stamps from different countries was a way that she could travel with him without leaving Gower. And there were people who'd got rich through stamps. Even the king devoted hours every afternoon to his stamp collection. And what's good enough for the king . . .

Lois takes one of Taff's precious letters from the mantelpiece in the front room. She tells the children that since Taff licked this stamp and placed it on this envelope in the Antarctic in February, it has travelled all the way around the globe. At school they have a world map on the wall. All the pieces of red on the map – large swathes of Africa, the whole of India, all those islands across the Pacific – they are theirs. They may not be as rich as the king but they are like centurions.

Most countries seem to have their own figurehead – versions of Britannia. On this stamp 'New Zealandia' descends from a plinth in a white dress with her hair loose. In the background, framed in scrolls and pearls, there is a globe on her right and, on her left, a ship, a coastal steamer. Taff has told Lois that in a new country like New Zealand, there aren't many roads or railways yet, so the coastal steamer is the main form of transport. In the corners of the stamp there is an orange cut in half, with six segments like the spokes of an organic wheel. It takes Lois back to her childhood in Swansea before they inherited the Ship Inn and moved to Middleton. Back then her father William was a greengrocer and her mother Jane and Aunt Margaret worked in the shop. Cutting an orange in half encouraged people to buy them and meant she and her siblings could eat the display. The stamp makes her mouth water.

BIRDIE – CAPE EVANS HUT, ANTARCTIC

Yes, they all know about limes. Birdie's audience in the hut have just watched one of Ponting's magic lantern shows from his pre-Antarctic travels, and the kimonoed Japanese ladies are a tough act to follow. Birdie persists. Around the world, the Brits are known as 'limeys', but what about the 'Esquimaux'? Perhaps the preventative for scurvy is in seal meat. Even Dr Atkinson admits that the dread disease scurvy is not yet fully understood. Science has still not ruled out the possibility that it may be contagious.*

Birdie adjusts his makeshift blackboard. It is a table comparing allowances for seventeen items of food and fuel taken by ten expeditions from Parry to Scott. It is thorough and detailed. He has given a similar lecture on clothing: people who tend to rely on dog sledges use fur because it protects against the cold when the wearer is seated on the sledge. (He knows that Scott has 'a sneaking feeling that [the fur clothing of the Esquimaux] may outclass our civilised garb'.[377] But they cannot get hold of quantities of reindeer skin now, and anyway, they are not Esquimaux.)

Birdie doesn't know about the others, but he is here to prove that, as Leonard Darwin said, 'The manhood of their nation is not dead' – man-hauling (men dragging the sledges rather than dogs or ponies) will contribute to that proof, but it is hot work. Layering natural fibres such as wool and cotton under a windproof layer seems to work best. He concludes that Messrs Wolsey, Burberry and Jaeger have done them proud; that man-hauling is more manly, requires less clothing but more rations; and that dog sledging is 'native' and requires warmer clothing, but dogs can be killed and fed to the other dogs.

Only to Emily, Birdie mentions 'the bad boy in the orchard'.[378] For Amundsen, who has overwintered just down the coast in the Bay of Whales, it will be 'dog eat dog', with over 100 to choose from. But it is difficult for Britishers to think of dogs as 'rations'. Dogs for them are really pets.

---

* Not until Vitamin C was isolated in 1928 was scurvy effectively conquered at its source. For more details, see: Carpenter, K. J., 'The Discovery of Vitamin C', *Annals of Nutrition & Metabolism*, 61(3), 2012, pp. 259–64.

OATES – CAPE EVANS HUT, ANTARCTIC

Oates's hand hovers over the chequebook. He wants out and he does not want 'small change' to get in the way. 'Myself, I dislike Scott intensely and would chuck the whole thing in,' he tells his mother. But it is strange to see the civilised page of his chequebook open here in his blubber-grimed hands at the back end of the world.[379] He wants to pay Scott for his expenses and return home at the first opportunity.

It has been building all winter. It is not just Scott's 'rows' with Teddy, Debenham and Meares. Oates has been taken on for his knowledge of things equine and yet Scott ignores his advice. The only piece he's followed is Oates's suggestion to order Indian mules. Even that might benefit from a spot of nepotism. In the past he has asked his mother to pull strings, 'talk to the wives of the Generals'.[380] In general it was the wives – the old boys' network via the 'old girl' – that got him anywhere sensible in life. The problem is that if those blessed mules do make it from Shimla to Cape Evans for the next season, he will have to stay to look after them.

Oates shifts on his bunk. Frank Debenham has hobbled over to the chessboard and played his move. Deb is one of the men aware of Oates's immanent resignation. He has tried to persuade Oates to stay, not to chuck it all in with the goal in sight, especially since he hasn't injured his knee playing football or had the subsequent 'row' with Scott like Deb has. Caroline plays patience. Her son plays chess. Oates realises that the mules may have been a false move. He sets his pen on the chequebook and after 'Pay' writes: 'British Antarctic Expedition'.

CAROLINE – GESTINGTHORPE

'£200'. She tears off the cheque and puts it in an envelope addressed to Sir Edgar Speyer, the expedition treasurer. So far Caroline has not contributed, except by releasing the money Laurie promised in the first place. At the last Antarctic lunch, she learned the extent of the debt and worries that it might mean dangerous corner-cutting. She opens her accounts book, picks up her pen and dips it in the inkwell again.

There is one ruled space left. She writes 'Telegram to Laurie £1.10.00'. She runs her pen down the columns of figures on the right-hand page, then the left. She turns the page:

Carried over	£1176.16.01
Waifs and Strays (Bishop of London)	£0.10.00
Warren for Clergy Charity	£0.10.00
A & N Bowl for Mr Travers	£1.8.00
Shoreditch Mission	£0.10.00
Bishop of Falkland Islands	£0.10.00
British Antarctic Expedition	£200.00.00

The seventeenth-century Oates ancestors look down from their portraits. A single hyacinth on the slim-legged occasional table in front of her scents the air. Caroline has a dog at her feet. He has chosen to sit on the carpet Laurie had sent back from India. In the accompanying letter he had warned her to keep the blinds down lest the carpet fade. She has the blinds up; she does not think that there will be much danger in the watery light leaking over the sash windowsills in Essex.

The carriage she sent to meet Mrs Wilson, Oriana, at Sudbury Station is due back at any minute. 'Wilson is a first-rate chap,' Laurie told her, 'perhaps you remember him, he has a very nice wife.'[381] Nice or not, when she thinks of Mrs Wilson her mind goes to that misspelt 'Chicargo slaughterhouse' and its 'blood and hair'.[382] There may be blood and hair in England too. Back on 2 April, suffragette Emily Davison hid in a cupboard at Westminster to avoid being recorded on the 1911 census (refusing to be counted as an individual while being discounted as a voter). For Caroline, Davison's action is not mischievous, but unladylike and even bloody-minded; a sign of the lengths the suffragettes are willing to go. Caroline plans her trips to London around avoiding the Women's Social and Political Union demonstrators marching through the city.

Oscar Minchin announces Mrs Wilson. Caroline gets up to welcome her across the 40-foot room. After tea they can look at Laurie's Mhow 'treasures' in the hall. Either side of the great stone fireplace and vast gilt-framed pictures there is a vertical line of mounted animal horns of diminishing length. But Ory is drawn to a tall case of birds that stands like a glass wardrobe on the stone-flagged floor. Caroline tells her that it is her late husband's collection. The slim woodwork is painted in black and gold, and the corners angled to minimise reflection. The flock of birds inside has alighted, it seems, on a leafless tree, so that every branch flashes with colour: a scarlet macaw, a yellow-crowned parrot, a pale-billed woodpecker, a keel-billed toucan, a rufous-tailed jacamar and a collared aracari. Oriana counts twenty-eight different birds and, at the bottom, an armadillo hiding in the leaves.[383]

KATHLEEN – LONDON

For Kathleen, the days seem to layer and overlap, sliding and reversing like the sea ice her husband has described. She knows that this is about the time that Scott should be leaving for the Pole but perhaps it was last week, or in a week's time. She hopes that coming to the Royal Geographical Society's lecture on Norsemen in America might bring her husband's reality a little nearer. Kathleen tries to focus on tonight's speaker, Fridtjof Nansen, but his Norwegian accent is impenetrable. She'd met him with Scott at the motor sledge trials in Norway. '[The lecture] was stiff and his delivery dull,' she told Scott in her diary, 'but I enjoyed it very much.'[384] He is fifty years old with a craggy face – perfect for sculpting. She has seen photographs of him as a younger man. Spiked blond hair, the same moustache and blue eyes – a Viking lion. Afterwards Major Darwin reintroduces her to Nansen and she becomes suddenly shy.

Kathleen alternates lectures like these with more bohemian artistic salons like the ones hosted by Mabel Beardsley. 'Flirtation: is it a legitimate amusement?' asks Mabel: 'As in all games, the amusement is in proportion to the degree and interest with which it is played. It is not within the capability of everyone, but then neither is croquet – and to some it is hardly more amusing.'[385] In the Bechstein Hall, as Kathleen becomes shy, Nansen loses his reticence. It may not be flirtation, but something has changed.

Sir Ernest Shackleton arrives at her side and her conversation with Nansen ceases. 'I was asked before whether I minded meeting [Shackleton],' Kathleen tells Scott later, 'and I said no. I hope I was right.'[386] Kathleen is determined not to hide in the leaves, to run from Shackleton, though she notices that the geologist explorer, Douglas Mawson, has just hotfooted it out of the back door.

Shackleton asks if Sir Lewis Beaumont told her that he had supported a move to increase the grant the RGS proposed to give the British

Antarctic Expedition at their last meeting. 'You know,' says Shackleton, 'everyone expected me to get up and discourage the grant. They were awfully surprised when I did just the other thing.'[387] Kathleen cannot stop the stream of Shackleton's talk. 'You know, I know your husband very well, perhaps better than any man. I have never seen him hesitate; he is the most daring man I ever met, extraordinarily brave.' Kathleen is trying to leave. What lies under this obsequious, ostentatious flattery?

'Yes', says Kathleen, 'he is brave morally as well as physically.' She turns to leave.

'Yes,' says Shackleton after her. 'I agree.'

SCOTT – CAPE EVANS HUT, ANTARCTIC

Scott will have to stay a second year if he is to have a proper shot at the Pole. He only has funds for one. He lists his assets: 'the ship, cinematographic rights, authorship, lectures, commemorative stamps, press releases, donations, a signed indemnity relieving the expedition of his own and his officers' salaries.' He realises that he will have to ask for an overdraft. He knows the idea gives Kathleen the sensation of going down in a lift, but there is nothing else for it. Scott tells the expedition treasurer Sir Edgar Speyer, 'My wife is entirely with me.'[388] Are the officers' wives and mothers entirely 'with' them too? Will any of the sailors forego their salaries too?

As Teddy later puts it, 'About this time he called on us severally to relieve him if we could of the responsibility of paying us for the second season. Most of us signed the document but not all could afford to do so.'[389]

Scott retires to his cubbyhole and writes to Kathleen: 'All this in one sense seems to be asking you to sacrifice your own interest and the boy's to the expedition – but I know you would wish it that way, so we can act straight to ourselves and the world. But you must understand the whole case, for after due consideration I have myself signed the indemnity document referred to in Speyer's letter; that means that my salary from the expedition will cease to be paid, over and beyond the term which it would have been paid had I returned in the *Terra Nova* in 1912.'[390]

In the inside pocket of his jacket he has a letter given to him by Teddy on 2 September, their third anniversary. The writing is Kathleen's. This is the other side of the one-sided conversation. It is an answer of sorts to his questions about profit and cost:

I left off just where I was going to tell you a very difficult thing. Look you – when you are away South I want you to be sure that if there be a risk to take or leave, you will take it, or if there is a danger for you or another man to face, it will be you who face it, just as much before you met Doodles [Peter] and me. Because dear man we can do without you please know for sure we can. God knows I love you more than I thought could be possible, but I want you to realise that it won't [crossed out] wouldn't be your physical life that would profit me and Doodles most. If there is anything you think worth doing at the cost of your life – do it. We shall only be glad. Do you understand me? How awful if you don't.[391]

9

'If Anything Should Happen to Me'

29 OCTOBER 1911

CAPE EVANS HUT, ANTARCTIC

It is less than forty-eight hours to go before they set off in earnest for the South Pole and the men are dressing up to pretend. From behind a picturesque iceberg – which Ponting has scouted as representative 'scenery' – there is the sound of talking and laughing. Of the twenty-five men who overwintered in Cape Evans hut, sixteen will be chosen for the Southern Party. They will take motor sledges, ponies and dogs. They will carry a heavy burden of supplies. Once they pass the most southerly of the depots, One Ton, they will begin laying new ones, then one by one, three four-man relay teams will peel off from the party to return to Cape Evans, until only four men remain. No one knows who Scott will choose for the final push to the Pole. All winter they have been trying to outdo each other in order be selected – friendly competition. As far as they know, Taff, Birdie, Bill and Scott have been chosen randomly by Ponting to form this 'quartet in some amateur theatricals' – they do not think they have been chosen for their acting ability, but they are pretty sure they can all act eating, cooking and sleep![392] The resulting film will be sent home with the *Terra Nova*, which is due to return any day now, to share a slice of Antarctic life with an eager nation. With any luck it will be screened in the (British) summer of 1912, by which point the Polar Party should be safely back at Cape Evans, Pole conquered.

Ponting assures Scott that the film will record the transfer of familiar activities to an unfamiliar environment 'in such a manner that when you have seen it, I hope you will personally feel that you have taken part in a great adventure'.[393]

He sets the Prestwich Model 5 Kinema Camera vertically on its wooden tripod, careful not to touch it with bare skin. Once, while he had been focusing, he'd run his tongue over his moustache and the tip had come into contact with the metal, instantly freezing. Falling backwards in shock, he'd lost the tip of his tongue, frozen to the camera.

Keeping his tongue well inside his teeth, he shouts 'Action' and starts the Prestwich's crank handle.

In one movement, the quartet lean into their harnesses and drag a loaded sledge diagonally across the snow from upstage left. When they get to a predesignated spot in the foreground, they unharness and begin to unpack, their movements practised and efficient.

Ponting has already sketched out the 'inter-title' script that will accompany this: 'The routine was always the same,' the script will read, 'first to lay the floor cloth of the tent.'

Taff is enjoying himself. He has his favourite wide-brimmed tam o' shanter sun hat on over his balaclava. The major difference between this and his performance in the Boer War re-enactment in 1906 is that in London this would be accomplished to deafening cheers, with Lois and the children in the stands. Here the only noise is of banter and the clicking whirr as Ponting turns the crank.

'Having made everything weatherproof,' Ponting's script continues, 'they go inside and immediately prepare for the evening meal.'

For this sequence they have pulled the tent cover back on itself so that one side is open. Bill removes his finnesko, then layers of thick socks, and wiggles bare toes. It is difficult not to overact his part, but they have been told to be natural. His watercolours, together with his journal and letters, will enable Ory to imagine his experience of Antarctica more completely than any film.

Ponting is toying with the title; will it be *Scott, First to the South Pole* or *The Great White Silence*? There is nothing silent about Birdie, who sits beside Taff chirping merrily. The sole audience Birdie cares about is his family, though isn't averse to 'making a splash in the public eye'. He thinks Emily will appreciate the film's educational element. Ponting has declared that: 'The Kinematograph, properly applied, is the greatest educational contrivance ever conceived by the mind of man.'

On the other side of the tent, Scott holds his hands over the steam billowing from beneath an inverted saucepan covering the stove. Suddenly he bursts out laughing and looks across at Taff. Over the years he has come to value Taff's dry humour, his ability to reach into his deep store of anecdotes to break the monotony of camp life. And Scott knows that laughter will convince Kathleen that he has defeated the black moods, at least for now.

While the four men act for the camera, there is a serious undertone. Oates curses the 'bloody Norskies', but he is back at the hut stables, preparing the ponies, so there is no danger that 'London' will lipread that. Together with the quartet, Oates knows that Amundsen may, even now, be on his way to the Pole. He does not have ponies – dogs can stand lower temperatures. Ponting reserves judgement, but he could cut the film reel at this point and splice it to a still of Amundsen just to make the point.

SCOTT – CAPE EVANS HUT, ANTARCTIC

Back in the hut after filming, as the men eagerly finish any letters to be sent home with the *Terra Nova*, Scott reminds them that they must include the typed confidentiality notes he has handed out. These swear both the writers and recipients of the letters to silence about all things expedition. Scott's experiences with false news, and their contract with Central News Agency, mean that he is wary of the media. Censorship and self-censorship preoccupy him. He reveals that Central News Agency have paid £2,500 for world newspaper rights (excluding the USA). He reminds the men that it was the CNA who broke the news of General Gordon's death twelve hours before Reuters and its other rivals in 1885, and it was the CNA who received a letter purportedly from 'Jack the Ripper' in 1888. Without exception, every single letter must be accompanied by a BAE caution notice.

Scott eases himself behind his desk and starts writing to Kathleen. As he does so, he is handed a letter. Seeing that bold looping hand is the nearest thing to welcoming her into his cabin cubby-hole to change her stockings. On the envelope is written, 'The eve of departure'. It is exactly a year to the day since he last held her in his arms. Scott treasures all her notes, even the harsh ones, 'because they express the inspiriting thoughts which I would have you hold'.[394]

'It seems a woeful long time since I saw your face and there is the likelihood for a woefuller time ahead, and then what,' he writes. He thinks 'woefuller' is a good word. With his other letters, to the

wives and mothers of the men, he makes a point of writing gram-
matically, but intimacy allows for informal inventiveness at a time
loaded with uncertainty. 'I am quite on my feet now,' he continues,
'I feel both mentally and physically fit for the work, and I realise that
others know it and have full confidence in me. But it is a certain fact
that it was not so in London or indeed until we reached this spot.'
Scott has mentioned her face and his feet. As 'the Boss', he is so
removed, so isolated from physical touch in this hut, that it is almost
dehumanising. The men might 'Furl the Topgallant Sails', but he
cannot join in. To the men he would lead, Scott never suggests that
he is not 'on his feet'. But to her, he confesses, 'The root of the
problem was that I had lost confidence in myself.'[395] In his breast
pocket he has her letter, as if to absorb her confidence, her positivity.
He acknowledges that they will send themselves mad if they worry
about things that might never happen. 'It thrills me most to think
of your courage. It is my greatest comfort to know that you possess
it, and therefore by nature can never sit down and bewail misfortune.
I can imagine you nothing but sturdily independent and determined
to make the most of the life you possess.'

KATHLEEN — LONDON

Kathleen is proud that Scott thinks her an 'antithesis of the pathetic
grass widow' and agrees with him that 'happily I am not often silly'.
But right now she is feeling disempowered, irrational and on the verge
of tears which she believes makes her 'very silly'.[396] 'An infuriating thing
has happened,' Kathleen writes on the day that she knows Scott is due
to leave for the South Pole:

> The people who were cinematographing Peter for you sent down
> on Sunday after I'd gone and took miles of photos of him and
> have made a glorious advertisement for themselves without asking
> my permission at all. They have published pictures of him in all
> the rags with a story to say they are to send a special messenger
> to catch the mail or if necessary, push on to [the Antarctic] to
> take the films to Captain Scott. The whole thing is so vulgar and
> horrid, and I cannot bear him to be lent to this sort of thing. It's
> beastly and I want to cry.[397]

OATES – CAPE EVANS HUT, ANTARCTIC

Oates folds the BAE caution notice and slips it into the envelope. It is absurd to tell his mother not to gossip when for her 'talking outside the family' is a crime punishable by disinheritance. He is at the ward-room table, his back to The Tenements. Deb is standing over him. Oates hates writing letters at the best of times, and this is not the best. He cannot see why Deb is making him write this letter when there are ponies waiting to be exercised, or groomed, or fed, or otherwise got ready for the unlikely task required of the 'old crocks'. But Deb insists. Oates reluctantly agrees with Deb that the Mater does deserve a letter and that it cannot be his usual 'disgraceful note'.[398]

'If you get this without hearing of the return of the Polar Party and I happen to be in the party,' he writes, 'there is no cause for anxiety as the only dangerous part of the journey is the ascent of the glacier and you will have heard if we get up that safely, the coming back is not nearly so bad.' No living creature had been to the South Pole before, but this sounded good and reassuring. He turns over the paper. His mother insists that his notes, however 'disgraceful', always reach the second page. 'Please give my love to all the family,' Oates wraps it up quickly, adding, 'I often wonder how Lilian and [Frederick Ranalow] are getting on in their new house and if Violet has got fixed up and settled.' Oates's thoughts speed home – racing up the driveway to the imposing front door of Gestingthorpe Hall. He can't bear the thought that even Violet, his youngest sister, might be a fully paid-up grown-up before he returns.

'I have half a mind to see Scott and tell him I must go home on the ship,' he writes, as waves of homesickness crest with every familiar name. Family and Eton have instilled in him a belief that self-mastery is life's goal. He checks himself: 'but it would [be] a pity to spoil my chances of being on the final party especially as the regiment and perhaps the whole army would be pleased if I was at the Pole.'

Oates has arrived at the 'possibility of non-return' moment he has been dreading. Is there a way around it? Perhaps the best thing to do is to refer Caroline to the writing he has already done, rather than essaying 'sentiment', which neither of them can abide. 'If anything should happen to me on this trip, which I don't think likely, ask for my notebook. I have written instructions on the flyleaf that it is to be sent to you.' He is in too much of a hurry to get back to the stables to remember how unguarded he has at times been in his notebook, particularly in his appraisal of Scott.

Scott has also written to Oates's mother, although he plays his cards so close to his chest that Oates can only guess at Scott's opinion of him. Memories of the dreaded school report threaten. 'Please remember,' Oates scribbles to warn his mother off, 'that when a man is having a hard time he says hard things about other people which he would regret afterwards.'

TAFF – CAPE EVANS HUT, ANTARCTIC

Generally, Taff's letters home follow a practised formula: enquiry after health, the weather, sea/snow conditions – but the formula refuses to fit the present requirements. He sits at the table by the galley and writes the address on the envelope in careful copperplate. Lois won't give a brass farthing about the weather if he doesn't come home. Taff could be indiscreet, particularly after a drink, but his wife is naturally reserved. As he folds the caution notice and slides it into the letter, he can remember their wedding in 1904. Taff had left in 1901 for the Antarctic on Scott's first *Discovery* expedition, with an 'understanding' that he would marry Lois on his return, but she had never let on while he was away.

Although the last letter that Taff wrote to Lois from Cape Evans no longer exists – Lois will later quote the line: 'A year will soon pass and then I shall be with you and the children once again.'[399] The rest of the letter might have resembled his Cardiff speech at the *Terra Nova*'s farewell dinner. The last time he'd seen Lois was just before he'd given it (he still doesn't remember much about after it, except what the six men who carried him aboard ship had told him). Was it easier to serve the family as a husband and father from a distance of half a world away? When he was in the Antarctic, he couldn't be side-tracked by the public houses along Chapel Street and the likes of Beatrice Pharaoh.

'Whatever I have to say I'll say it in as few words as possible (Cheers),' ran the newspaper report quoting Taff's speech. 'Every man in the ship has confidence in Captain Scott. I know him well and he knows me very well (Laughter) . . . Every man in the Expedition is heart and soul in the business, and it has got to be a success this time – (Cheers) –

every man will do his best.'[400] The sentiment and perhaps the rhythm, the thrice repeated 'Every man' is Nelsonian – a message flagged across the years. The cheers belong to the crowd at the Cardiff Chamber of Commerce, but Lois is a proud patriot, a stalwart support, her 'cheers' are understood. Besides, Taff's feelings have not changed and neither, he hopes, have hers. He has come down here to get that D.O.P. (the Damned Ol' Pole), and he'll be damned if he goes home without it.

If he wants Scott to make an unprecedented move, to take someone other than an officer to the Pole, he needs to put everything, his salary and his life, on the line. Lois is not one to 'sit on a cushion and sew a fine seam', but Taff doesn't want her life to be as hard as it is for some of the women in Gower, particularly those widowed by the sea. He trusts her to remember that he is three years from getting his Royal Naval pension and then they can retire. If he wins this race they can buy that pub and Lois can sing all day.

BIRDIE – CAPE EVANS HUT, ANTARCTIC

'My dearest Mother,' writes Birdie on the plank across the mattress of his 'comfy bed'. His handwriting leans forward. There is never anything retrospective in his attitude to life, but this letter is by its very nature retrospective, which makes it difficult to begin.[401]

As he writes, instead of the cheery plink plonk of Cecil Meares on the piano, or Nellie Melba and Caruso taking turns on the gramophone, all is quiet, but for the scratching of pencils on paper and the occasional muffled expletive through the packing-case wall.

'We are just away for the Southern journey', Birdie begins. He knows Emily is anxious about his adventure, but she is also his inspiration: 'I would not belong to the family of Bowers if I did not attempt the apparently impossible.'[402] For him this expedition is the ultimate test of manliness, proof that the effete edges of the Empire can be properly hemmed before the fabric collapses. He slides the caution notice into the envelope.

'We are going forward knowing what we have got to face, and I for one am sure that the journey will be no school-boy's picnic, but as hard as any that have ever been and that the Pole will not be gained without a terrible struggle.' Birdie likes the word 'picnic', a short, upbeat tick of a word. The sledge journey he undertook with Scott the previous season to make supply depots had been 'a jolly picnic'; the Winter Journey to Cape Crozier was 'a weird picnic'. But, he tells Emily, their journey to the Pole will be 'no picnic' at all.

He finishes with qualified optimism: 'What a glorious return we shall have with all our letters & news waiting & the fellows on the ship to see again. Well, if we only succeed it will be a happy return indeed.'

BILL – CAPE EVANS HUT, ANTARCTIC

In order to continue his journal-letter to Oriana, Bill has to move the paint box to make space. Although he had promised his wife that he would not set off until he knew she was 'in good health', they are going to have to leave for the Pole before the *Terra Nova* gets through the sea ice with home letters. With the clock ticking, Bill ponders how any decision to go before receiving Oriana's letters will hold up to scrutiny? He hates to break his promise.

Agonising over how to tell her, he begins a letter to the Smiths instead:

McMurdo Sound, 29 October 1911

It is not happy to think of Ory's disappointment when the ship gets back – no news perhaps of our journey and no news of us perhaps since October or November. That's a hardship bigger than I have ever had to put up with anywhere before – and it's one I can't help inflicting on Ory as well.

[What if the letters that come down with the *Terra Nova* should contain news which would] hurry one back at all costs and that one can only read them when it is too late to act on them – and then sit down for a year and wonder whether one could have done otherwise.[403]

As a rule, Bill draws his way out of a conundrum. He captures and labels it, then moves on. The pictures he sketches of Oriana hut serve to illustrate Bill's last long journal-letter to her. His first drawing of 'her' shelter was done on the march, a scrappy pencil sketch with frost-numbed fingers. The second, done in comfort in Cape Evans hut after their return, is destined for the 'official report'. The third, for the *South Polar Times*, is full comic strip. The men are two-dimensional loin-cloth-wearing Egyptian slaves, with Oriana hut a stone pyramid. These drawings are really his last letter home. They will give his wife more of an insight into his state of mind than any amount of prose.

He has enlisted the Smiths to help Ory; now he tries to recruit Kinsey too: 'You have helped her so often in the past that I know you will again.' He sends two packages of sketches to Ory through Kinsey. They are clearly marked 'Sketches' on the outside, he tells Kinsey, 'so you needn't be afraid of opening love letters! Oh yes, there is a package of those – but I don't think they would interest you, Kinsey.'[404]

'I don't see any other course open to me than to carry through the job,' he tells Ory. Scott needs him and he will have to go.

> *L'homme propose mais le bon Dieu dispose* is an honest creed, and in this case *l'homme* hasn't decided to do anything from first to last that he isn't convinced will be approved by his infinitely better half, so *le bon Dieu* will have to do the rest. Whatever happens . . . even if it's worse than anything one can bring oneself to imagine . . . There is no more to be done than this.[405]

He folds the confidentiality notice and slides it into the envelope. Life without her is painful to contemplate, as he knows that life without him is for her. And yet he has a strong sense that this is their future. It makes him 'inexpressibly sad like autumn days with their early-closing, dark, cold, wet, grey evenings, cheerless to a degree, most suggestive of what my life would be in its latter half if I had to finish it without you'.[406]

IO

'Just for Your Sake'

BIRDIE — ANTARCTIC

There is a moment of calm after a storm of violent activity. Birdie, with his pony Victor, sets off at 11.30 a.m. on 1 November from Cape Evans. He is the last to leave. Christopher, the pony Oates has allocated himself, has as usual behaved like a demon. The corrective methods are harsh. Emily would never discipline a child or even a dog in this manner. First they trice Christopher's front leg up tight under his shoulder, then throw him down on his side. He is harnessed to the sledge while his head is held down on the snow. But despite this, when he rises up, still on three legs, he starts off galloping as well as he is able. After several violent kicks his foreleg is released, and after more watch-spring flicks with his hind legs he sets off. After all the shouting of the past hour, it is a relief for Birdie to walk beside Victor and listen to his breathing, the soft crunch of hoofs on snow, the sledge runners sliding after.

OATES — *DISCOVERY* HUT, ANTARCTIC

Oates stirs heated water into pony mash. He is in the temporary shelter outside the *Discovery* hut, but he breathes in the comforting smell of the Gestingthorpe yard. He predicted that leaving with this cavalcade – dogs, ponies, motors – would be 'a bit of great circus', and this is what has happened.[407] No one has remembered the Union Flag to be flown at the South Pole. Everyone thought someone else had brought it. It is a small oversight perhaps, but on an expedition like this, such omens can be dangerous. The slow-moving motor sledges started off a week ahead of the main party of twelve men with ponies. Meares with the dogs would ferry supplies back and forth along the route. Scott is a man used to boats – now he is preparing an assault on land. Where is the military campaign logic?

SCOTT — *DISCOVERY* HUT, ANTARCTIC

The *Discovery* hut telephone has handwritten pencil messages scrawled on the wooden box on which it has been transported. Beside the phone's crank handle is written: 'Telephone Cape Evans 9 to 9.10 a.m. 0 12: 6 o'clock' – perhaps an instrument reading given over the phone and jotted down.[408] This must be a scheduled call. Scott picks up the aluminium and Bakelite receiver carefully; it is cold to the touch but not dangerously so. It is 4 p.m. when Scott depresses the button on the handset to talk. He asks if the Union Flag can be brought over. He releases the button to listen for a reply. It is a Norwegian accent. The irony of the situation is almost laughable. Tryggve Gran, Amundsen's countryman, is the best skier. He is the obvious person to ski the British Antarctic Expedition's Union Jack over from Cape Evans to the *Discovery* hut for them to take to the Pole.

4 NOVEMBER 1911

BILL — ANTARCTIC

'Yesternight', begins Bill, trying for accuracy in his new journal. The night-time marches remind him of the Winter Journey, where shapes were shadows – but now 'we were coming across derelict cans of petrol, lubricating oil and eventually Day's derelict car itself'.[409] They are barely four marches in and one of the motors has already failed. '£1,000 by the wayside!' writes Bill, with a tell-tale exclamation mark breaking his resolution not to log anything other than facts. He has always said that the Pole is 'a romantic concept' and that once motors can drive there, even the romance will be gone. He is a devotee of Ruskin, watercolours over photography, craft over machine-made, but one should not ignore progress – it just helps if it actually progresses.

TAFF — ANTARCTIC

Over the winter Taff has voiced his support for the motors: 'Lord, sir, I reckon if them things can go on like that you wouldn't want nothing else.'[410] Taff does not envy the motor-less motor party. A week in and already they are beasts of burden, dragging the sledges themselves. He hopes that the wooden sledges he has been refining all winter will withstand their 700-lb loads. Captain Scott still believes in Taff's ability: 'He looks after the sledges and sledge equipment with a care of management and a fertility of resource which is truly astonishing.'[411] Has Taff overhead Oates and Meares in the stable? 'We both [Meares and Oates] damned the motors,' Oates told his mother. 'Three motors at £1,000 each, nineteen ponies at £5 each. Thirty-two dogs at 30 shillings each. If Scott fails to get to the Pole he jolly well deserves it.'[412] One motor costs as much as thirty years' worth of Taffs, but Taff himself keeps his head down. He thinks of the snowshoes that he has modified – since he is employed by Scott, the credit will probably go to him. 'We have designed new ski boots and I think they are going to be a success,' writes Scott. 'Evans, P.O. has arisen well to the occasion as a bootmaker . . . [The] seal skin overshoes for ski made by Evans seem to be a complete success. He has modified the shape of the toe to fit the ski irons better. I am very pleased with this arrangement.' Later Scott goes further and admits: 'P.O. Evans, the inventor of both crampons and ski shoes, is greatly pleased, and certainly we owe him much.'[413] Taff is sure he can improve the ponies' snowshoes too, but Captain Oates doesn't believe in shoes for ponies. Taff walks beside his pony, Snatcher. He thinks of Lois and of the children, and occasionally he thinks of the fat that rises to the top of a cup of hot water when you put pemmican in. Pemmican, that rich mixture of tallow, dried meat and dried berries. They come across the last abandoned motor shortly after.

5 NOVEMBER 1911

KATHLEEN – LONDON

An old school friend of Kathleen's is waiting for the cramps in her abdomen to begin. 'You were right when you recommended me not to mix myself up in it. It's rather sordid and endless and one can't help much. One can't put things into people when they haven't got the elements in them.' The school friend is not married and has just taken medication to induce an abortion. Kathleen knows the man responsible, but she doesn't blame him.

Sometimes she has to remind herself that her diary is not, in fact, her husband. She tries to put the record straight – talking to oneself is the first sign of madness after all: 'But of course,' she tells her husband, 'you weren't here, and didn't recommend anything; but you would have done it if you had been here, being wise.'[414] If the girl had the right 'elements' in her she wouldn't have got herself into this position. Kathleen wishes she was the one who was pregnant. She'd 'called to the gods' for a brother for Peter, but instead, now, she is suffering period pain and takes to her bed.

The pain is familiar but it is her finances that are causing her more trouble. She has gone overdrawn for the first time and it makes her stomach lurch. Unlike most husbands, Scott confides business matters to Kathleen because 'your head is so well adapted for business when you like', and now it is a matter of necessity rather than liking.[415] The Scotts are liable – everything they own or earn is on the line – they 'stand or fall by the expedition'. The expenses seem endless. The least they need, Sir Edgar tells Kathleen, is another £15,000.[416]

Even from their bedrooms, people with 'the body of weak and feeble women' can reach out to the heart of a man. 'I want to thank you in the absence of my husband so very much for your very great kindness in reviving the Antarctic Appeal,' she writes to Sir Arthur Conan Doyle, that lion of detective literature and supporter of polar exploration. 'It was very good of you to give an hour of your so valuable time and I know how immensely my good man will appreciate it.' She changes the pronoun to 'I'. 'Mrs Reginald Smith tells me too that you are going to subscribe most generously and I cannot tell you how good I think that is of you.' And again now, to 'we'; the weak and feeble woman is also joint leader of the expedition. 'You know your speech at the Mansion House has meant an immense amount to us and we never forget our gratitude to you.'[417]

17 NOVEMBER 1911

SCOTT – ANTARCTIC

Scott is in his sleeping bag at Camp 13. He has had a horribly cold wind on the march, minus 18 and force 3. 'It is early days to wonder whether the little beasts [ponies] will last; one can only hope they will, but the weakness of breeding and age is showing itself already.'[418] The dogs seem to be thriving and Scott confesses, 'I had a panic that we were carrying too much [pony] food'. Birdie argues that they should take enough to feed all the ponies. Scott overrules him. The ponies are food.

KATHLEEN — LONDON

'I meant to go to Paris to-day, but went to meet Fridtjof Nansen at lunch instead.'[419] Nansen is being understandably reticent about talking to the RGS about his fellow countryman, Roald Amundsen. Kathleen decides to squeeze him herself. Nansen reveals that he had no idea what Amundsen was planning but wondered why he was taking so many dogs. Kathleen tells her husband that Nansen 'hopes you will meet [Amundsen] and go on together. He said the most popular thing Amundsen could do would be to let you get there first and then go on himself.' But, Kathleen concludes, 'I think that's silly.'

AMUNDSEN — ANTARCTIC

At 2 p.m. Roald Amundsen calls a halt and notes, 'Passed *Discovery* expedition's southernmost latitude 82 degrees 17'.[420] He spies a rock to the side of a steep snow slope. He skies over. He wants to put a foot on solid ground after months on ice and snow, but instead of executing a perfect telemark turn he falls head over heels. His men politely pretend not to notice. After so long riding on the dog sledge, Amundsen's legs have lost muscle and are easily tired. He is managing the dogs ruthlessly. If one comes on heat, it is shot, lest it confuse the others. If any are found to be pregnant, likewise. One dog is shot for laziness. They camp – as intended – at 82 degrees, 20 minutes for the night. They have 45 dogs and 8 degrees of latitude to go.

24 NOVEMBER 1911

SCOTT — ANTARCTIC

'Just a note from the Barrier to say that I love you,' Scott writes to Kathleen.[421] He has just told Hooper and Day that they will be the first relay team to turn back, and they are all in the tent scribbling notes to be taken back with them. 'There are long hours in which to think of you and the boy,' writes Scott. 'Everything is going pretty well for the present, though we had a bad scare about the condition of the ponies last week.' Kathleen demands such optimism that he is sometimes obliged to lie. 'The animals are not well selected. I knew this in New Zealand, though I didn't tell you.' It will not put him into a 'black mood', but it has led him to appreciate Oates's efforts. He tells Kathleen that Oates is, in fact, a 'treasure'.[422] However badly selected the ponies are, he is determined to drive them further south than Shackleton did. He is determined to beat every point of Shackleton's *Nimrod* expedition record. He has Kathleen's 'inspiriting' letter in his breast pocket. He leaves camp each day as if he is being chased; it is all the others can do to keep up with him.

OATES – ANTARCTIC

Oates strokes Jehu's soft, frostbitten muzzle. He smells the hot equine sweat – the result of extreme exertion. He holds his hand flat under the pony's mouth and the soft lips move in his palm. They are 90 miles from the Beardmore Glacier. With his left hand on the pony's bridle, he removes a revolver from his belt with his right and holds it against the pony's temple. The shot echoes around the camp. Dogs are carnivores, ponies are not. Each pony equals four dog feeds. 'Gave Jehu the bullet,' begins Oates boldly in a note to his mother to be taken back with Hooper and Day. Later he confesses, 'It is a brutal thing killing these poor ponies. The sad part is that Jehu had plenty of march left in him.'[423] But Scott had panicked that they were carrying too much pony food and this is the result. He knows that his mother will sympathise – shooting an animal at the end of its natural life is one thing, this is quite another. Scott, Oates tells his mother, wears a face like 'a tired sea boot'.[424]

TAFF – ANTARCTIC

Taff writes to Lois. He is sharing a tent with two of the officer class and one fellow rating, Tom Crean. Taff knows that Crean feels more comfortable with his own kind – he assumes that Taff too would feel isolated if he were with only officer types. But within the tent, class distinctions blur. Every night the ratings make camp, but they all share cooking duties. Mercifully Captain Oates, like Taff, is a good, straight-forward cook – no ruining the food with hot spices.

Taff thinks of Lois's brothers and the Gower Princess, their prize filly for which they have been offered a lot of money. The Princess has fine lines, elegance and poise. Snatcher, Taff's stalwart pony, is more like Taff, broad, muscular and workman-like. Even though Taff is used to working animals on his brother Charlie's farm, it is difficult to force a dumb animal like Snatcher through suffering towards its execution.

BILL – ANTARCTIC

Bill persuades himself that he is going to the Pole just for his lady; he is just the knight in the frozen ice helmet his balaclava has become. He is executing her wishes to the best of his ability. 'Nov 20th Lat 80 30 – I just hope I shall be one of the four to be chosen to go all the way to the Pole – just for your sake.' He is fit and, in spite of the balaclava, sunburnt and happy, but mostly he is longing for her letters. 'I live now for that, not for the Pole, I'm afraid, half so much.' He has taught himself to let his mind wander forwards and backwards in time so that the march itself becomes automatic and he hardly notices that he is still putting one foot in front of the other:

> Lat 81 15 . . . My mind is much occupied with a hope that we shall be able sometime to go to Japan together. I have a longing to sketch there and see the country and the people more than any other place in the world . . . I have such happy hours – on the march and in my sleeping bag, when I lie awake at all (not very often) – [thinking] about our many happy times together . . . My heart goes out to you.[425]

BIRDIE – ANTARCTIC

Birdie tears out pages one to twenty-three from his journal notebook and writes, 'Strictly confidential. For personal friends & relations only', on the front page. This is how he will write to Emily, sending his journal pages back with each returning party. He tells Emily the scheme:

> Namely to arrive at the foot of the Beardmore Glacier with twelve strong men & twenty-one weeks' provisions for a four-man unit. This will enable one unit to go to the top of the Glacier & return & a second to go forward two weeks beyond the first & return, the last unit being left at that point with its return food depoted & six weeks' food to go to the pole & return to that spot.[426]

He has just taken a series of photographs and written captions – a magic lantern show for Emily to see what he can see, albeit with a time delay of a few months. He assures her that although there will be long periods of silence, any news he hears from her will be good news and he promises her that she will never hear anything to make her ashamed.

II

'I Love You'

SCOTT – ANTARCTIC

Four days after Scott's 'I love you' note begins its slow sledge journey north back to Cape Evans and thence across the world to Kathleen, Scott is in his sleeping bag. She will not get that note until late spring, early summer reaches the northern hemisphere. He is heading south, in the opposite direction, and has just made Camp 24 in a snowstorm. The day has been swirling drift and freezing cold – 'thick as a hedge'. But tonight, he has at least chewed the texture of fresh pony meat. 'Plucky little chap [Chinaman], he has stuck it out well and leaves the stage but a few days before his fellows.'[427]

Kathleen might flicker through his almost unconscious mind for the last couple of hours of sleep, but it is the ghostly pace setters, Shackleton and Amundsen that preoccupy him. Scott wakes for a 4 a.m. start and he is layering up into sledging gear just as the Norwegian explorer, Fridtjof Nansen, Amundsen's mentor, knocks on his front door.

KATHLEEN – LONDON

Kathleen is expecting him. She walks up the short hall to answer the door of 174 Buckingham Palace Road. It is 1.30 p.m. precisely. Fridtjof Nansen is a man of precision and thoroughness and, she believes, honesty. Amundsen did not tell Nansen about his change of plans from the Arctic to the Antarctic so, however the Royal Geographical Society feels about it, she is determined to play the game.[428] She turns the handle with some trepidation. The last time she saw this man she was suddenly shy.

Kathleen has been desperate for male company. She'd hired a cottage in Sandwich in Kent and taken Peter and his nurse there for a seaside holiday. She swam in stormy seas, slept out on the beach, everything to try to control her urge to ask a man down to join her: 'I rather need a man down here, but I hesitate to ask one because I am afraid I should make love to one if I had one.'[429] And yet now, a day short of a year since she waved Scott off from Port Chalmers, she has asked Nansen to lunch. She could have asked others too. A conventional luncheon party. She did not. She wants a man, singular.

She cannot imagine meeting a man like this as she met Scott, at a fashionable salon, at Mabel Beardsley's. Nansen takes up too much room. He is as big as a bear. She feels very small and feminine beside him. She introduces him to Peter. Nansen has five children and very particular ideas about child rearing. Peter is scantily clad for November, he has cold baths and feeds lustily. Nansen approves. He disapproves of anything warm, weak and 'feminine'– a point of view that chimes so precisely with Kathleen's sentiments it lends instant depth and recognition to their encounter. Peter is forgotten, whisked out of sight by his nurse.

Socialism, Nansen tells her between mouthfuls of cold meat, is 'a feminine movement'.[430] He agrees with Leonard Darwin about the implications of natural selection and extrapolates into politics: socialism 'is an inconceivable contravention of the fundamental principles of the living world. It is the religion of all incompetence. Nature and society require that incompetence must sink to the bottom . . . Nature has only given the strong the right to live.'

Scott's father was indolent; Kathleen's husband's urge to explore is in part an exculpation of this inheritance. Hard living, Nansen agrees, is a cure-all. While it is a good thing to bring up nice, well-behaved children, it is not enough. 'It is just as important to form character and willpower [which] are often developed by harsh treatment.'[431]

Nansen has been at Buckingham Palace Road for five hours. He shows no sign of leaving. As the winter sun sinks in the London sky, Nansen sits in profile in Kathleen's studio. She scrapes a slab of clay and massages it between her fingers. He asks her questions. She answers that it would be a year tomorrow since she last saw her husband. She misses his physicality. She misses the stimulation of masculine conversation. She is afraid; she tells Nansen that she is growing trivial and houseproud so that when Scott comes back he will find her 'settle[d] down into the most conventional of middle-aged matrons'.[432] Nansen does not share her fear. He has never met anyone like her: 'It is nice to know,' he writes in halting English the following day, 'that there is a woman so like what one has dreamt of but never met.'[433] 'I am inclined to think,' Kathleen tells her husband 'that explorers are a comprehending race.'[434]

11 DECEMBER 1911

BILL – ANTARCTIC

There is blood everywhere, slick and bright red against the glaring snow. There is nothing pristine about the foot of the Beardmore Glacier. It is like an abattoir. 'Meares leaves us tomorrow to return with the two dog teams and Dmitri [Girev, a Russian dog driver] – and I must send you just a word,' writes Bill in his sleeping bag.[435] 'Thank God the horses are all dead now. We shot the last five last night as we reached the entrance to the Beardmore, having no more food for them, and having been on the march with them yesterday for eleven hours with no halt and no food ourselves; and when we camped we had to skin them all and cut them up and depot the meat before turning in.'

Writing to Ory allows him to close the door on the gory scene outside and turn instead to the future. Scott has not disclosed who he will take to the Pole. 'But I am as fit as can be,' Bill assures Ory, 'and just thrive on it: I am afraid one or two of the others are not. It is telling on them a bit.' The next party will return in ten or twelve days' time, reducing them to eight. 'I expect to be one of the eight at any rate: but whether I shall have the good fortune to be considered strong enough to be one of the final four or not – why, I don't know. No one knows yet who they will be – but I do hope to be one of them for your dear sake.' If he is one of the magic final four: 'We shall be back to our mails in another ten or twelve weeks, and the time is simply flying. It is good to have been loved by you, and oh, a privilege indeed to have been allowed to love you. God keep you.'

OATES – ANTARCTIC

The ponies are dead. Oates's responsibility is over. He is a cavalry officer without a horse and he has blood, literally, all over his hands. When he flicks back through the journal he is sending back with Meares and the dogs, he can see that even Caroline will be able to tell that it has not been a straightforward business.

Christopher has been the most difficult pony and he was the hardest to kill. At the moment of firing, 'the pony tossed up his head & the bullet entered just below his brain. He charged away . . . & was secured with difficulty, nearly giving Keohane a bad bite. The next shot finished him.'[436] Christopher died as he lived – hard. At least Bill and Scott seemed to appreciate Oates's efforts in getting the crocks this far:

'Well! I congratulate you,' says Bill.

'And I thank you,' says Scott.[437]

Oates has never felt the urge to make such unguarded exclamations of gratitude to Scott. On 4 December Oates was thinking about Shackleton, whose account of this route he had read slowly and laboriously over the winter. 'And now one is here,' he tells his mother, 'one can realise what a wonderful journey his was and the daring which prompted him to strike up the Glacier instead of following the coastline.'[438]

The dogs are about to return north with Meares. When Oates thinks about how well the dogs have performed, it puts him in mind of Amundsen, somewhere out there, perhaps ahead. On 29 November, when the featureless landscape finally gave way to mountains on the horizon, Oates told Caroline in his journal that although they might get to the Pole, 'I think there is a very good chance of the Norskies getting there before us.'[439]

12 DECEMBER 1911

CAROLINE – LONDON

While her son is shooting Christopher, Caroline is at Harding's just south of Hyde Park, climbing the mounting block. She patronises 'Harding for Riding and Driving' horses because it is the establishment that invented the humane rubber bit guard. The flexible brown discs on either side of the bit protect the horses' soft lips. She sets her left foot into the stirrup and lifts herself into the side saddle, her right leg tucked under. The bridle smells of saddle soap. Caroline leans forwards and pats the warm neck of her mare. She watches Mr Harding's groom as he adjusts the rubber guards.

After returning from an invigorating ride, Caroline settles down to her accounts, writing 'Telegram to Laurie £1.10.00'. She wants to make sure there will be a message with up-to-date news from home when the *Terra Nova* leaves New Zealand to take letters from home and fresh supplies through the melting sea ice to Laurie. She feels closest to Laurie's experience when mounted, riding out in the frost of December.

TAFF – ANTARCTIC

Taff knows that his modifications to the pony snowshoes got them this far ('the situation was saved by P.O. Evans,' Scott had noted back on 5 December[440]), but now Snatcher is dead and butchered. There's a lot more blood in a pony than a pig, but otherwise it is not that different to the annual butchering at home each winter. With the ponies gone, they will have to start man-hauling – there will be no more pony steaks for a while.

Taff is looking forward to an increase in rations to allow him to keep up his strength for the climb up the glacier. He knows exactly what they will be: 16 oz biscuit (made by Huntley & Palmers), 12 oz pemmican, 2 oz butter, 0.57 oz cocoa, 3 oz sugar and 0.86 oz tea per day. The rations are calculated by Birdie, who, though precise in his measuring of them, is nearly half Taff's size.

Taff is pleased that Scott has chosen him for his sledge team with Oates and Bill. Scott keeps a nice, neat tent with a homely atmosphere and an efficient routine. Is this a hint that they are the ones Scott will select for the Pole? It's like poker; Scott plays his cards so close to his chest. 'Petty Officer [Taff] Evans, of course, is a tower of strength,' writes Scott in his journal page within glancing distance of Taff, 'but Oates and [Bill] are doing splendidly also.'[441]

Taff has brought along a couple of novels: 'the library'. Mary Johnston's *By Order of the Company* seems to be most popular. He also likes science fiction, *The Red Magazine* is a favourite, and the others are alternating *In Memoriam* by Tennyson with Dickens's *Little Dorrit*. Taff knows from experience that the entertainment, the distraction, are worth their weight in sledge space. He thinks of the letter Captain Scott told Taff that he sent to Lois to tell her not to be anxious or worried. But what else has Scott said in it?[442]

LOIS – GOWER

The pig is put on a wooden plank and tied down on its side. The women have the warm metal bowl and a wooden spoon ready. The Beynons raise a good pig – the test of good husbandry.

The animal is killed with one precise stab to the jugular vein, and the knife is withdrawn as quickly as it was inserted. The blood flows quickly into the bowl where it is stirred rapidly to prevent it from clotting. The men have done the killing, the women must use all their skills to make sure that every part of the animal can be eaten or preserved. The women rinse the intestines in a bucket of water before cutting them up and putting them through a large mincer. These will be made into large sausages of offal and blood to hang by the fireplace to smoke. The pig blubber is reduced to be spread on bread in the cold months, but the children might have bread and dripping today if they are good. As Lois wipes the blood off her hands onto her canvas apron, she remembers the *Gower Church Magazines*'s modest biography of her:

> His spouse, Miss Lois Beynon, was quite as popular in her own sphere. Possessed of a good voice and fond of singing, she rendered great assistance for years . . . in the local concerts . . . Her services were greatly appreciated, as was evidenced in the numerous and costly presents given her by a large number of friends and relatives.[443]

Now Lois's help rendering the family pig are as 'greatly appreciated' as her singing.

BIRDIE – ANTARCTIC

As he writes to Emily, Birdie tries to remember why exactly he is here. 'We came down here to meet difficulties & if they are too great for man to overcome, we cannot do more than man can do.'[444] He assures her that he is not as depressed as he sounds and feels extremely fortunate that although he does not, as a person, have an 'excessive number of good points', he is privileged to be a part of Captain Scott's expedition. Before he signs off, he acknowledges the threat of Amundsen, particularly now that he has seen how well the dogs have worked.

Amundsen is now less the 'bad boy in the orchard' and more a 'back-handed, sneaking ruffian'.[445] Birdie finishes, 'Hurrah for the glacier!'[446] Beardmore is conquered.

Birdie quickly tears out pages 24 to 46 of his journal and dashes off a last letter to Emily for Meares to take back to Cape Evans with the dog team. Meares will not be there when they return because he is taking the *Terra Nova* back to New Zealand. This is goodbye. Someone else will have to bring the dogs out to meet them on their way home.

> No worry now – only marching, observing, navigating, grooming, cooking, etc – living out one's full allowance of time under conditions that fulfil one's ideas of manliness . . . You may be sure of one thing that though I may not get to the Pole or make a splash in the public eye – I shall do much towards the object in hand & the honour of my mother who deserves to have something better than a rolling stone for a son. All's well for a start. The finish is in the hands of a higher power.[447]

SCOTT – ANTARCTIC

Scott is wondering why the other sledge team is not pulling as fast as they are. Teddy has been man-hauling since the motors broke down. Has he reached a breaking point? He is criticising Scott to everyone but the man himself – Birdie calls it 'sedition'.[448] All Scott knows is that though Teddy is officially his second-in-command, he must not be allowed to tell the story of this expedition. Kathleen must ensure that it is his version rather than Teddy's that reaches the public.[449]

Scott judges his progress south against Shackleton's record, fulfilling Kathleen's desire to annihilate Shackleton by beating his dates and distances. In his breast pocket, Scott still has Kathleen's inspiriting note: 'If there's anything you think worth doing at the cost of your life – do it.'[450]

'Just a tiny note to be taken back with the dogs,' Scott writes to Kathleen. 'Things are not so rosy as they might be, but we keep our spirits up and say the luck must turn. This is only to tell you that I find I can keep up with the rest as well as of old.'[451]

As he watches Meares set off with the mailbag, making for Cape Evans, he sees the dogs pulling strongly north. (Dogs and ponies cannot foresee, Scott reminds himself. They cannot live and support discomfort for a future as humans can.[452]) But right now it is hard not to imagine Amundsen and his dogs somewhere in this snow desert pulling just as strongly south.

12 DECEMBER 1911

KATHLEEN – LONDON

As Scott wakes up for a 4 a.m. start, Kathleen, in 174 Buckingham Palace Road, is writing to the prime minister:

Dear Mr Lloyd George,

On Wednesday evening I have to cable to my husband Capt. Scott the state of his expedition fund. This is the last chance of communicating with him this winter.

£15,000 is required to clear the Expedition.

£5,000 has already been subscribed.

He may reach the Pole this winter, he may need to stay another year. He will have to decide from the information in any cable on Wednesday evening whether this is possible.[453]

She is not above a little coercion: 'As there is a very well-equipped Norwegian Expedition in the field it becomes still more of National importance that England should not fail.' She adds her telephone number, Westminster 5953, in case the prime minister should feel the urge to phone her directly. She receives a handwritten reply by return:

Dear Mrs Scott,

It is with the utmost regret . . . It is not my own money.

D Lloyd George[454]

12

They Also Serve Who Stand and Wait

14 DECEMBER 1911

AMUNDSEN – SOUTH POLE

At 3 p.m., Amundsen on the lead sledge arrives at a featureless white space that dead reckoning tells him is the South Pole. He plants the Norwegian flag and names the plateau 'King Haakon VII Plateau'.

What had he imagined the place to be like? He had never really tried: 'Never has a man achieved a goal so diametrically opposed to his wishes. The area around the North Pole – devil take it – had fascinated me since childhood, and now here I was at the South Pole. Could anything be more crazy?'[455]

14 DECEMBER 1911

ORIANA – LAMER PARK ESTATE, HERTFORDSHIRE, ENGLAND

Apsley's mother Evelyn Cherry-Garrard greets Ory warmly at the wide steps under the classical portico of Cherry's stately home. Robert Adam and Humphrey Repton have both had a hand in making Lamer one of the most impressive classical mansions in the country. Evelyn too has read of Sir Joseph Hooker's recent death. She has traced the HMS *Erebus* voyages on the atlas in the library, Ory must come and see. The famous botanist and zoologist made three trips to the Antarctic with James Clark Ross in the 1840s, before returning to have seven children and die peacefully in his sleep at the age of ninety-four in Berkshire. It was, surely, a perfect life.

There is the scent of freshly ironed newspaper in the library where the family atlas is laid out on a table. The table is in a bay beside a double-height bow-fronted window with a view of the manicured lawn and the undulating fields beyond, studded with clusters of beech. Evelyn shows Ory the dotted lines that mark the coast of Antarctica, where she and her daughters have written the names and dates comparing the BAE progress with the accounts in the library's growing section on polar travel. Both Ory and Evelyn know that, around now, the expedition should be nearing the South Pole. This means they are furthest from civilisation and at their most vulnerable, and yet there is nothing they can do but have tea.

Ory has heard of the Lamer 'cake' – 'looking after the cakes' is how Mrs Cherry-Garrard sees her role. She is the custodian rather than the chatelaine. With only her conventional female upbringing to help her make decisions about 'the cakes', Evelyn tells Ory, she feels her son has 'left me in a place of great trust'. She assumes the seemly, passive age and sex-appropriate dowager role, and hopes that it would not be too long before Cherry 'brought a wife to Lamer'.[456]

As they put on outside coats and stroll out to the hothouses, Evelyn admits that she is praying hard and when she wakes in the night, Cherry is 'her first thought always'. Ory is praying too. She is missing her husband so badly it is difficult to bear. She thinks she will go to New Zealand just in case they come back this year. At least she will be nearer, in the right hemisphere. 'They also serve who only stand and wait,' both Evelyn and Ory know, is a useful quote from 'On His Blindness' by John Milton, to describe their predicament. Ory knows that as far as Kathleen Scott is concerned it is simply blind. Ory was a year early for her husband last time and waited for a year in New Zealand for the Discovery's return. Waiting about in New Zealand like one of the 'pathetic grass widows' Scott disparages, in Kathleen's opinion, 'would be awful'.[457]

But Ory tries to justify her decision. She tells Evelyn that if she is there on the ground in New Zealand, she will be able to relay any news immediately except that: 'no private cables would be allowed to be sent home from NZ until the news of the Expedition had been in the English papers for thirty-six hours [most accounts say twenty-four], that is to say no cables about plans – men would be allowed to cable "all well" or "love" or something of that sort. But they would not be allowed to say what they were going to do – I suppose this is true and if so, it means that I could not cable to you very much about your son until a day and a half after the newspaper cables have been sent back from New Zealand.'[458]

Walking out to the classical temple, a folly, one of Apsley's favourite haunts, Mrs Cherry-Garrard is keen to imagine the world to which their men will return. Only the year before, at the end of 1910, when war with Germany seemed inevitable, Evelyn was 'working up "Voluntary Aid Detachments" in case of war'.[459] The threat has since subsided, but she tells Ory that their offer of Lamer as a hospital in case of invasion has been accepted. They will need a doctor in charge. Through the back window of the Cherry-Garrard motorcar, having accepted a ride back to Wheathampstead railway station, Ory waves goodbye to Evelyn, a small, smiling figure standing beneath a giant classical portico. Bill is a pacifist. He has told her that he 'would rather kill himself than any other man, I simply could not do it.'[460] If there were a war, would he return to a career in medicine? Is there a future with Bill as Dr Wilson strolling the pilastered halls of Lamer, stethoscope around his neck?

21 DECEMBER 1911

BILL – ANTARCTIC

The party of four that Scott has 'told off' to return north in the morning includes a bitterly disappointed Cherry. Bill tries to soften the blow with a glowing report to accompany him, which he hopes Ory will copy out for Mrs Cherry-Garrard to read.

'In another fortnight the next four will return,' he continues.[461] 'I may be one of them. We shall see.' He is fairly confident that Scott will pick him for the Pole, but there is always the possibility of illness or accident.

He luxuriates in the prospect of mail and 'news of my beloved wife. God knows how I long for it.' Ory has become a real presence on this journey, an image that hovers just out of reach. He is nervous about how their grouse enquiry report has been reviewed: 'I hope you will let me know whether my efforts at the Grouse and the British Mammals have been decently reviewed or slated as bad work. I am prepared for either; I only know they were the best I could do under the circumstances, and as you liked them I can swallow anything that is said besides. Only I hope, for Reginald Smith's sake that the Grouse Disease Report is to be a very great success.'

It is getting late. They have less than 300 miles left to the Pole: 'We are over the worst of it all now though, and we come home with light loads from depot to depot. All my love is rolled up in this.'

BIRDIE – ANTARCTIC

'Naturally, none of us like to turn back,' Birdie tells Emily, but 'in another sixteen days or so another four will have to turn back. I am expecting to be in charge of that detachment. But one never knows.'[462]

He is feeling sentimental: 'I am sending this [his journal] by my friend Cherry whose going back I feel muchly, though we cannot all go on, worse luck.'

He reads back over cheerier times before he tears out the pages to enclose with the mail home. He had been thinking of home on 17 December. Sledging through the crevasses is, Birdie tells Emily, 'just like the Scenic Railway' at the Scottish National Exhibition at Saughton in Glasgow, where they had roller-coastered around rickety scaffolding through a maze of twists and turns. Birdie's Antarctic roller-coaster was 'great sport . . . you poised the sledge on a giddy height, aimed her carefully, all four men breking [sic] with their feet & then a shove & down you would fly, often faster than any switchback. Sometimes . . . we would all jump on & let her rip.'

The other source of hope is Christmas in three days' time, for which he has secret plans for a 'great feed which I [have] kept hidden and out of the official weights since our departure from Winter Quarters.'[463] To finish there will be the crystallised squares of ginger from Emily.[464] Increasingly hungry, he wants to 'get hold of all the poor children we can and just stuff them full of nice things'.[465]

TAFF – ANTARCTIC

Taff is relieved that the mad rides through the crevasses have not broken any of the sledges. A broken sledge would be, even Lieutenant Bowers agrees, 'a most serious matter'.[466] Taff writes a short note to Lois for the mailbag the following morning. She must be back in Gower for Christmas. The Mari Lwyd will doubtless be paying them a visit. When he thinks of his children, Norman, Muriel and Ralph, he tries to imagine them a year older. Does he also think of his unofficial daughter, Lillian, who like Muriel will be approaching her fifth birthday?

Taff has long hours in which to reflect on his families. He knows that before the twentieth century it was illegal for illegitimate children to inherit. Prosperous families set up trusts to care for the child's welfare.

Families like his do not, but women can make bastardy claims on the fathers. If anything should happen to him, Lois will get his navy pension. What will happen to Beatrice and Lillian?

CAROLINE – LONDON

Caroline is touring London theatres as is her custom in the short, dark days of winter. She shuttles between Evelyn Mansions and the West End, her opera glasses in her reticule. Now she is sitting in His Majesty's Theatre about to see *Drake*, with Miss Phyllis Neilson-Terry as Elizabeth. The Terry family are a theatrical dynasty including actors with the surnames Neilson, Craig and Gielgud – the idea of ancestry, even theatrical ancestry, appeals to Caroline. Phyllis Neilson-Terry is the niece of Ellen Terry, superstar actress and erstwhile mistress to Charles Dickens. Everyone knows that, but somehow in a theatrical dynasty what Kathleen Scott calls an 'affair *à outrance*' is acceptable.[467] Actress Mrs Patrick Campbell explained it well when she said: 'Does it really matter what these affectionate people do, so long as they don't do it in the street and frighten the horses?' Caroline knows that in her world, only legitimate heirs can inherit, and any other sort should really be hidden away. One must keep one's mouth shut – nothing must risk exposure on the street, let alone in front of the poor innocent horses.

OATES – ANTARCTIC

'My feet are giving me a lot of trouble,' Oates confides to his mother. 'They have been continually wet since leaving Hut Point and now walking along this hard ice in frozen crampons has made rather hay of them, still they are not the worst in the outfit by a long chalk.'[468] Health is competitive. He is not the worst. Oates tells Caroline about the state of his feet, but he does not tell Scott. He does not ask Bill, the doctor, to look at his feet. He might mention them, in confidence, to Dr Atkinson, who receives the impression of a man 'who knew he was done – his face showed him to be and the way he went along'.[469]

The conspiracy of silent stoicism inculcated by everyone from his mother, through his years at Eton, to the Inniskilling Dragoons, means that Oates says nothing. On the rare occasions when his mother calls the doctor to Gestingthorpe, she writes, 'not for self' beside the fee in her accounts book. Physical weakness is something to be ashamed of, to be mastered rather than given in to. Suffering in silence is something Oates has perfected. He does not surrender, especially not with the goal in sight.

Just before Atkinson leaves the next morning with Cherry and the two other men of the penultimate relay team, Scott issues him with fresh instructions, telling him to bring the dogs out later in the season to meet the Polar Party on its way back. Meares, the expert dog driver, will have returned in the relief ship to New Zealand by that time. Scott is aware of the large distance between the first two depots on the return journey: 120 miles separate Mid Barrier Depot from One Ton. Oates is also aware of the distance. It is dangerously large.

21 DECEMBER 1911

SCOTT – ANTARCTIC

'I dreaded this necessity of choosing,' Scott tells Kathleen, 'nothing could be more heartrending.'[470] Grown men weep as he tells them that they will not be in the final team for the Pole. But what can he do? 'I calculated our programme to start from 85 degrees, 10 minutes with twelve units of food [a unit being a week's supply for four men] and eight men.' He can't take everyone. 'For your own ear also, I am exceedingly fit and can go with the best of them. I write this sitting in our tent waiting for the fog to clear – an exasperating position as we are in the worst crevassed region. Teddy and Atkinson were down to the length of their harnesses this morning, and we have all been half-way down. As first man I get first chance, and it's decidedly exciting not knowing which step will give way. Still all this is interesting enough if one could only go on.'

In his mind's eye, Kathleen is nodding approval at his literal following of her instruction that 'if there is a risk to take, you take it.' He is going first. Every step he takes may give way. As he curls up in his sleeping bag, he finishes with the kind of hope she requires of him: 'We ought to get through.'

DECEMBER 1911

KATHLEEN – LONDON

In the tiled hall, there is the smell of pine resin and echoes of whickering excitement as the two-year-old Peter and thirty-three other toddlers await the moment the candles will be lit.

Peter is entranced. He is growing up so fast – Kathleen takes photographs and tucks the corners into specially cut holes in the pages of her diary for Scott to see when he comes back. Peter walks around the house with a framed photograph of 'Daddy'. 'If you could look down through the Earth right under your feet with a great big telescope,' Scott once explained to his niece, 'you would see . . . me at the other end.'[471]

Now, in London, spots of light are reflected in the upturned eyes of the children as an adult approaches the Christmas tree candles with a flaming taper. The flames are a welcome light in the dark days of winter in London, though Kathleen knows that in the Antarctic Scott is basking in the midnight sun. She has just opened Scott's postdated letter:

At Sea
October 1st, 1910

Soon there won't be any post to bring you letters when I am thinking of you so I write to you now . . . As I tramp alone, it will be good to feel the [sun's] rays and think that similar ones are falling on a small lady and a still smaller man who is toddling about with her.

But it is not the rays of the sun that fall on Kathleen and her 'smaller man'. One of the branches is crackling and spitting; the candle flame has set a small fire going. The tree is quickly a tower of flame, with fire leaping across to the curtains. Kathleen has already scooped up Peter. She is running through the crowds of mothers and nannies, their panicked faces a blur passing on either side.

She is inciting her husband to risk his life and yet, 'I regret to say that Peter and I were the first out of the house.'[472] The truth is that she would willingly 'sacrifice Rome' for the safety of her son.[473]

13

The Final Five

SCOTT – ANTARCTIC

Through the canvas Scott can hear the sound of sawing and hammering. The seamen are reducing the length of the sledges from 12 to 10 feet to save weight. When Scott calls through the canvas to ask how much longer, Taff replies that it is nearly done. '[Taff] and Crean are tackling it, and it is a very remarkable piece of work,' writes Scott in his diary. 'Certainly [Taff] is the most invaluable asset to our party. To build a sledge under these conditions is a fact for special record.' Scott and the other officers are 'warm as toast' inside their tent because they have put up the inner lining. The seamen are still outside. They are 9,126 feet up and the temperature outside is minus ten degrees and falling.

OATES – ANTARCTIC

Oates knows that the seamen have done the same distances as the officers and yet they cannot rest until they have done their jobs. He mucks in where he can, but he is an officer with Indian servants still employed for his return. This is his life. He takes off his finnesko – the sennegrass no longer smells of burnt grass, but something fruitier. He does not have a batman here, so he is his own responsibility.

For some reason Oates finds himself talking. He tells the others about Eton, of caning and fagging and practical jokes. The end of his anxiety over getting the crocks to the foot of Beardmore has left him feeling strangely careless. He goes on and on – favourite horses, funny anecdotes, pet dogs at home – Scott reaches over and squeezes his shoulder. 'You funny old thing,' he says, 'you have quite come out of your shell, Soldier. Do you know we have all sat here talking for nearly four hours?'[474]

Oates has told only Caroline of his respect for Shackleton and Amundsen and the fact that at times he 'dislike[s] Scott intensely'. He'd nearly resigned, nearly written that cheque to go home, and yet here is Scott squeezing his shoulder. Surely by now Scott must have noticed that Oates's feet are raw and he is favouring his strong leg to the point of limping. Since 26 December, he has confided to Caroline in his diary that 'the back tendon of my right leg feels as if it has been stretched about 4 inches.'[475] He will surely be sent back with the next return party soon, tomorrow perhaps. He hopes he'll make the ship.

TAFF – ANTARCTIC

The light is failing. Taff's hands are cold. It is nearly eleven o'clock at night after a day spent in the harness pulling over a surface of yielding snow. Taff can tie a clove hitch with one hand, but here in sub-zero temperatures with frostnipped fingers, dexterity eludes him. He knows the new sledge must be perfect. Scott is about to choose the final team for the Pole. He cannot afford to make any mistakes.

His friend Tom Crean coughs his pipe-smoker's cough. Tobacco is an appetite suppressant, a taste more than a smell, but it is no substitute for hoosh. William Lashly, another rating, has experience; he too was on Scott's first *Discovery* expedition. The only cards Taff has to play are his 'inexhaustible fund of anecdotes' and his exceptional ability as a handyman. But is he fitter and stronger than Crean and Lashly? If he were Scott, who would he choose?

Taff grasps the woodworking blade. Like the others, he has two layers of woollen gloves snug to his hand and, when marching, fur mitts over – but some parts of sledge stripping are fiddly and it is easier to be accurate with bare fingers. Suddenly he feels a sharp pain. He tries not to curse out loud. His blood tastes warm and metallic as he probes the wound with his tongue. He can hide the cut inside his glove. He hopes it will heal quickly. Have the other two men seen?

EMILY – BUTE

The Ascog Fernery, on the slope above Rothesay, is an excellent, if brief, poor man's holiday at a time when funds do not extend to 'abroad'. Inside, large hot pipes run horizontally around the low glass wall supporting the glasshouse, filled with the warm smell of damp humus and luxuriant green plants. It is just the sort of place where Birdie's Ceylonese butterflies would have thrived, fluttering their iridescent wings among the waxy palms.

Emily can hear the water trickling through brick channels in the floor, brushing aside the delicate fronds of the maidenhair ferns and spotting the whisks and liquorices. The careful labelling with 'country of origin' means that Emily can travel from Bute to Australia to Burma in a couple of paces. But it is an idealised version of 'abroad'. There are no mosquitos here, no danger of sunburn or heatstroke. There is no language barrier, no clash of religions, no danger of misunderstandings that can escalate, so quickly, into tragedy.

Does she think of Birdie in these moments?

3 JANUARY 1912

SCOTT – ANTARCTIC

Three days into the New Year and Scott has made his final selection. Taking Teddy aside, he tells his second-in-command that he will go no further south. This is despite the fact that Teddy had raised funds for his own expedition but, on Sir Clements Markham's advice, thrown his lot in with Scott. He even carries a flag from Hilda to fly at the South Pole. As an additional blow, Scott tells Teddy that he has decided to take five men instead of four to the South Pole. He will need Birdie – Teddy, with Crean and Lashly, will be one man down on the way home.

Crean is next. Scott approaches the tent.

'You've got a nasty cough, Crean, you must be careful with a cold like that!'

'I can understand a half-sung song, Sir,' says Crean.

Then there is Lashly. Scott needs only one Jack Tar and it is not him.

Birdie is 'a treasure'. Scott relies on his brain. His mathematical ability is astounding. No task that Scott has thrown at him has been accomplished with anything less than excellence. He may have 'very little in the shop window . . . but the goods inside were pure gold.'[476]

Oates opened up after the ponies were killed, and that night he and the other men had 'warmed to each other in a way that we had never thought of [before,] quite oblivious to cold, hardship, scant ration, or the great monotony of sledge-hauling'.[477] And aside from any newfound regard for the man, Oates is cavalry and Scott doesn't want to be accused of making this an exclusively naval exercise. And Bill? Bill is his right arm. Bill is the voice of reason. He is the staunchest friend Scott has ever had.

In Taff he has a working-class Welshman, and alongside Birdie from Scotland, Oates from the army, Bill a civilian scientist and himself, it is the most representative team he can imagine. On the flyleaf of his diary Scott scribbles, 'Ages: Self 43, Wilson 39, Evans (P.O.) 37, Oates 32, Bowers 28. Average 36.'[478]

Scott gives the devastated Teddy verbal instructions that the dogs should be brought further south to meet them. As Teddy understands it, the object is to hasten the Southern Party's return rather than to succour them.[479]

Having sown hope and bitter disappointment, Scott begins a note to Kathleen:

Lat 87 32. A last note from a hopeful position. I think it's going to be all right. We have a fine party going forward and arrangements are all going well. So this is simply to say that I love you and that you needn't be ashamed of me, or the boy either. I have led this business – not nominally but actually – and lifted the other people out of difficulty – so that no man will or can say I wasn't fit to lead through the last lap that is before us.

I shall have to keep wondering how you are, and thinking of you constantly as I have done all along. But it will be good to see you when this business is through.[480]

This is the last letter he will send home.

OATES – ANTARCTIC

'Dear Mother, I have been selected to go to the Pole with Scott as you [will have] seen by the papers,' Oates tells Caroline.[481] 'I am of course delighted but I am sorry I shall not be home for another year as we shall miss the ship. We shall get to the Pole alright . . . We are now within 50 miles of Shackleton's Farthest South.' They are 148 miles from the Pole – it will be a 296-mile round trip back to this point.

'The last supporting party takes this home – I am now lying writing this in my bag, we had minus 20 degrees last night.' Although he tells Caroline he has lost 'less condition' than most, he means fat and he had none to lose. The cold seems to be a constant presence deep in his bones. So far he has dreamed of beefsteaks, but increasingly he dreams about warmth and the fire in his room at home:

> I hope the alterations at Gestingthorpe have been carried out I mean the archway between Violet's & my room and my gear is in the room opposite the bath room, it will be nice in there as I can have a fire at night better than in my old one – my clothes I left in the ship for returning to Lyttleton are in a fearful state from damp I am afraid so I have enclosed a list of things I should like sent out for me if you will, also I enclose a note for Brujum [Bryan] it is about the filly. Can you please also send me ½ doz books so I can start working for my major's exam on the way home? These things should be addressed to the *Terra Nova* at Lyttleton. What a lot we shall have to talk about when I get back. God bless you & keep you well until I come home.

It is the only time he has ever mentioned God.

Oates encloses a wishlist of clothing, tobacco, cigarettes and a big box of caramel creams. He wants the rush of sugar, he wants to be warm and cosy in his bedroom looking over the south lawn with a fire in the grate. The Amazon adventure with Birdie had sounded interesting on the voyage out, but now he wants candy-flavoured comfort.

BILL – ANTARCTIC

'Tomorrow . . . the last supporting party returns to the winter quarters – and they will take this note home, arriving probably in time to catch the ship,' Bill tells Ory.[482] 'I am one of the five to go on to the Pole. So this may be the last you hear of me for another whole year . . . Only I am glad for your sake that I am one of the five.'

Bill senses that the last decade's worth of effort is accumulating in this tent. Throughout his marriage the South Pole has been a theory; now with only 148 miles to go, 'It seems too good to be true that this long journey to the Pole should be realising itself – we ought to be there in less than a fortnight now.'

After all the competition and the tearful disappointment of those sent home, he is happy with the selection. They are all good men. 'Our five are all very nice together and we shall be a very happy party.'

This means that he will definitely not be back this year. The final chance of a reunion in three months' time goes with this letter. He hopes that Ory will be able to readjust to the extra year's wait without any damage to her health. 'You know my love for you – it's just myself and all I do and all I pray for is your good. Be strong in hope and in faith if you hear no more of me after this till next year . . . I believe firmly that we have a lot to do together when we meet again. I am full of plans and possibilities as we stolidly plod along with our sledges – but oh, how I long to be with you again!'

TAFF – ANTARCTIC

Until now, Taff is not sure whether the South Pole will be an entirely officer-class affair. Birdie has told him how impressed he is with the Jack Tars, Scott has told him that the expedition could not manage without him, but why would Scott sacrifice a place for a rating? But Scott hasn't. He has made an extra place. There will be five of them in a four-man tent. How will they manage? Taff's kit maintenance has been almost perfect (apart from that careless mistake with the blade, which he has not disclosed). He can almost taste success and yet he has sledged to this point in the certain knowledge that if he is ordered home, he will have to obey.

The other two ratings, Lashly and Crean, are friends. Ever since Taff offered to sacrifice hammock space for storage space on the way out from New Zealand on the *Terra Nova*, these men have followed his lead, but there are two distinct differences. The first is that Taff has not been man-hauling for as long (the other two were in the advance depot party), the second is that he still has skis and sticks. It is as if Scott willed him to be the fittest Blue Jacket, the strongest Jack Tar left when the decision for the Polar Party had to be made.

But neither Lashly nor Crean have an injury like the one Taff is hiding inside his glove. Taff does not want to risk becoming the Jonah, bringing bad luck to the expedition, but as he sees it, the security of his future with Lois, his retirement plan, depends upon the Pole.

What will Lois be doing now? Taff often tries to imagine his children running on Rhossili beach – even the baby will be able to run by now. Are they warm enough? Is Arthur Thomas helping to keep Chapel Street in good order? Are the neighbours looking out for her? Taff writes his last note to Lois in the knowledge that his wife is not just a 'pizened critter', a grafter, but his 'right hand'. At this moment, if he were left-handed, he would not even be able to hold the pencil.

BIRDIE – ANTARCTIC
87 degrees and 32 minutes South

My dearest Mother,
I am sending you a note from what is perhaps the bleakest most unutterable spot in this round world. We have arrived here on our flat feet & dragging our means of livelihood etc as usual . . . but you will be pleased to hear that Captain Scott has selected your offspring to accompany him to the Pole or as near it as we are destined to go.[483]

In his sleeping bag Birdie realises that he is about to jump off a diving board into the unknown. He has been longing for the comforting presence of his mother. After the Christmas feast he wrote, 'In fact I should have liked somebody to put me to bed.'[484] He is, perhaps for the first time in his life, 'thin', and the lack of insulation makes a difference. All his life he has been obsessed with a man's work but never really defined what that constitutes. Now he knows:

It is terribly hard work this marching in harness for over nine hours a day through yielding snow. To add to it the wind blows incessantly against us as if to bar us to the confines of the apex of the Earth, & we are going up & up . . . we are about 10,000 feet high now & God alone knows how high the Pole will be.[485]

He reassures her that though he is thin, he is fit and strong, and 'The Pole should (D.V.) be pulled off in a fortnight's time and then we should be able to get this wind behind our backs & streak for home.' Birdie is aware that Scott has altered his instructions again concerning the dogs, telling Teddy that they should meet the returning team at the 82nd or 83rd parallel and do the 'streaking' for them. That way they will be sure to deliver their news to the ship. 'I shall be able to send you word & the remainder of my journal then,' Birdie tells Emily.

It would be dishonest to give his mother false hope, so he admits that 'nothing is absolutely certain in a land of such extremes. I think we are going to reach the Pole. I think the British flag will be the only one to fly there. I shall . . . thank God that our country has the honour it deserves . . . I am no party to record breakers but I realise that the polar business must be cleared up – once & for all – & may the Lord grant that I shall be one of the ones to see it done.'

4 JANUARY 1912

Scott calls a halt. They have only covered a short distance, but it is enough to see that it will work having Birdie on foot instead of ski and that the departing team can manage as a three.

Here on the snowy plateau they say farewell. Teddy and Birdie are not on skis. They walk towards each other. Teddy gives Birdie a little silk flag. It is the one that Hilda gave him to fly at the Pole. Birdie attributes Teddy's bitter disappointment to letting her down. He never thought Scott would select Teddy for the Pole, but realises that Teddy had convinced himself that as second-in-command he would be offered a place in the final party.

Teddy walks over to Oates, who asks him to send out tobacco and sweets with the dog teams. 'I'm afraid, Teddy, you won't have much of a slope going back,' says Oates, 'but old Christopher is waiting to be eaten on the Barrier when you get there.'[486]

Teddy calls three cheers, and Crean and Lashly manage to rouse themselves, punching the air with their mittened fists.

The two teams leave in opposite directions. Scott leads, Taff behind him, Bill and Oates slide their skis forward, Birdie makes sure his trace is not slack and plods along on his 'flat feet'. They are going south, their letters are going north. They do not stop to look back, but Teddy turns around frequently 'until we saw the last of Captain Scott and his four companions – a tiny black speck on the horizon'.

EARLY JANUARY 1912

KATHLEEN — BERLIN, GERMANY

That day they'd strolled up snow-cleared streets framed by bare lime trees and scented with roasted chestnuts from barrels. They'd visited an art gallery and Kathleen had, again, modelled Nansen's head. They have returned to the Hotel Westminster, a Beaux Arts affair on Unter den Linden in Berlin where they are staying. Nansen is lecturing. Her ear is so tuned to his accent these days that she wonders why she ever found it difficult to understand.

Now Kathleen wants, needs, to go dancing. She does not want anything sedate or conventional, she wants 'improper dancing' – like that loose new music from America with a beat. Isabella maintains that jazz isn't American music, it's savage music. Savagery. Can Nansen dance that? They meet in the hotel's white-domed lobby, with its large chandeliers and wall sconces lighting shallow classical stairs. When they get to the club she finds all the German officers to be 'spotty and poor-looking creatures'.[487] They do not seem to have the right 'elements'. But the music is thrilling and she likes to stay out late. 'She was a mad dancer,' wrote another friend later.[488] Mad dancing is a kind of opiate perhaps for a teetotaller, and 2.30 in the morning is a suitable time to return to the hotel. If Nansen, nearly fifty, begins to tire, she has her cousin Benji, some Americans, Charlie Rolls's sister and the painter Harrington Mann to keep her company to dance the night away.

But watching Kathleen dancing is invigorating. Nansen thinks back to that first memorable lunch at Buckingham Palace Road: 'I feel like a Faust, who has got a draught of the fountain of life, and has become young again,' he tells her.[489] Kathleen knows precisely what it is like to be 'mad crazy in love' – 'hundreds of men experience [this] about me.'[490] But now she wrestles with her instincts. In an attempt to be completely open, she tells her husband: '[Nansen] really is an adorable person . . . and I will tell you all the lovely times we had together when you get back. He thinks you are marvellous, and me still more!'[491]

Nansen seems to understand her. She belongs to a long line of 'great women who could forget themselves and their vanity for the man they loved'.[492] But that does not stop him trying. He is the assertive Scandinavian *skáld*: 'The only star I see now is you, whom my longings seek.'[493]

14 JANUARY 1912

SCOTT – ANTARCTIC

It is minus 18 degrees in what even Scott admits is a 'congested tent' – five of them squashed in a space meant for four – but they have reached Camp 66.[494] 'Very often I could see nothing,' Scott tells Kathleen scribbling with his pencil in his sleeping bag, 'and Birdie [sitting] on my shoulders directed me.' They are all cold, colder than normal, particularly their feet. The finnesko boots are balding. Scott rubs some grease on the sole of his foot. 'Oh for a few fine days.'

KATHLEEN – BERLIN

In Germany the weather is fine but the cold is intense, particularly high up in the Etrich Rumpler in which Kathleen is sitting. She is wrapped in woolly caps, mufflers, goggles and gloves. As they take off from the grassy strip she feels the tug of gravity but now, as they level out, she sees that the complicated duty-demanding conventional world has been replaced with the shining sinuous river, foreshortened trees and the flattened roofs of railway stations. It is a refreshing perspective and as a rule she does not give in to the weak feminine 'shiver' – but now high up in the Rumpler she is deeply cold, far colder than she ever thought possible, but perhaps no colder than her husband, who must be nearing the South Pole.[495]

She has chosen to fly with an older man rather than the younger daredevil who offered to take her first. This is her nod to risk aversion, of doing her duty to stay safe for her husband and young son. Flying is surely a legitimate form of excitement, of physical sensation, and now Kathleen indulges wholeheartedly and deliberately in her ardent desire to fly. She is a sensual being, and flying and 'mad dancing' are her attempts to channel that desire into legitimate sensations. She is aware that if she were a man, it would be simply laddish to embrace risk or to have an 'affair à outrance'. Nansen is a perfect specimen for a mate and she knows she can only stay up in the sky as long as the fuel allows. She returns to the hotel where Nansen is waiting. He speaks half a dozen languages – his grasp of English is excellent, his grammar, rhetorical. Now he asks her, 'Is it passion you are afraid of?'[496]

14

'This Is an Awful Place'

SCOTT — SOUTH POLE

'The worst has happened,' Scott tells Kathleen. 'Or nearly the worst.'[497] They are at least still alive. But the Norskies have stolen the prize. Amundsen's flag planted right in the centre of his dreams. 'Great God,' says Scott, 'this is an awful place and terrible enough for us to have laboured to it without the reward of priority.' After seventy-seven days and almost 800 miles, they are here at the South Pole, but they are not the first. The snow around is pocked with dog shit.

TAFF — SOUTH POLE

Taff stands on Scott's left as instructed. Somehow he is in the centre of the line of five men – a self-promotion. Taff has never forgotten his place – he should have insisted on swapping with Scott, but he is struggling to think clearly. He stands, head tipped slightly back, the fold of his balaclava shading his eyes. Dr Wilson has run a piece of string from the camera back along the snow. Taff listens for the click of the shutter.

The photograph is familiar, a team photograph, but this is not like other photographs after matches or races or feats of endurance. This one is a record of defeat. It is a possibility that Taff has never considered, never experienced. He is part of the British Empire, the dominant force on earth – Norway is a new nation – this reversal of the natural order will take some adjusting to.

They have been beaten by dogs. Those dumb animals. During the winter Taff had found dogs with their tongues stuck on tins of dog food. The only way to release the animal was to heat up the tin. He had been hoping for the euphoric taste of victory – the sensation that charges the muscles and dulls the appetite. The taste of failure is bitter and wholly unsatisfying. Those dogs with their stuck tongues have out-sledged them. Human muscle is no match.

Where will Lois put this photograph? Will it be tucked behind the letters guarded by New Zealandia on the mantelpiece in the front room at Chapel Street? It cannot be put with the other team pictures of Taff with his field gunners. Bill gives the signal. He pulls the string carefully, trying to pull the shutter without jogging the camera. Ponting told Taff he would be 'conspicuous in any company', but at this moment Taff would gladly be behind the camera rather than in front of it.[498]

OATES – SOUTH POLE

Oates turns from the photograph and looks at the flags – none of which sports his family crest. He tries not to favour his good leg. His gloves are heavy, he leans forward. He tries to angle the lip of his hat, to shade his pupils from the glare of the sun. It is difficult to believe that they are having have their likeness taken with no one behind the camera – perhaps if Ponting were here Oates would brace himself, stand up straight in the manner of an English cavalry officer. Is that the last photograph to be taken? Can they go home now?

From the 15th, Oates has been feeling physically homesick. He uses the word 'very' sparingly – it doesn't go well with his natural tendency to understate but he has been, he admits to Caroline in his journal, 'very depressed and homesick'.[499] To keep his pride intact he attributes it to the pemmican. Was the pemmican off? Had it smelled a bit odd? It must have disagreed with him at breakfast.

Oates has become detached. He observes Scott objectively, but instead of recourse to 'intense dislike', he credits Scott's self-control. He is, Oates tells his mother, 'taking his defeat better than I expected'.[500] Oates isn't part of the 'defeat', that is his leader's business. He has done his job, his duty.

He is even more impressed with Amundsen. The Norskies have beaten them to it with dogs. Oates does not think it is cheating – that is what animals are for. 'I must say that man must have had his head screwed on right. The gear they left was in excellent order.'[501] They understand transport – no need for the shilling book here – 'and they seem to have had a comfortable trip with their dog teams. Very different to our wretched man-hauling.'

If dogs could get five men all the way to the Pole, surely dogs can come halfway to help them back. It will not matter that One Ton Depot has been left north of 80 degrees if the dogs can bring supplies south. All they have to do is meet those dogs.

BILL – SOUTH POLE

Standing with his right shoulder to the wind, Bill sketches a wooden sledge runner that has been pushed into the snow. The dog tracks are a month old. 'The Norskies had got to the Pole on December 16th.'[502] They should get back before the sea ice freezes so that they will be able to sail away.

Scott sees a sledge runner with a black flag about half a mile away and sends Bill to fetch it: 'I found a note tied to it showing that this was the Norskies actual final Pole position. I was given the flag and the note with Amundsen's signature and I got a piece of the sledge runner as well.'

For his own sake, he must be scientific, forensic in his attention to detail to protect against this now transparently 'romantic' enterprise. Without stopping to ask himself why, he bends forward and takes a 'sample', a biopsy of the sledge runner. He also takes a 'spirit lamp . . . for sterilizing and making disinfectant lotion of snow', found left behind in the tent that Amundsen named 'Polheim' ('Home at the Pole'). Taff's hand will not heal. The medical supplies are dwindling.

Finally Bill concedes that Amundsen has beaten them only 'in so far as he had made a race of it'.

BIRDIE – SOUTH POLE

'We have fixed the exact spot of the South Pole today & left the British flag here,' Birdie tells May.[503] 'I have navigated the party here.' He is proud of his navigation, the sextant has become a friend. 'Amunsden's [sic] people left a tent . . . [T]hey were here exactly a month ago – I am awfully sorry for Capt Scott who has taken the blow very well indeed. . . . We now head for home & all it means – news from my own home is my first thought . . . You will be glad to hear I have been to this spot I am sure.'

'Our ration is an excellent one, but we could all eat far more', he tells Edie.[504] 'As you will have heard, the Norwegians' dogs brought them here long before our feet could bring us . . . If ever a journey has been accomplished by honest sweat ours has. We will have man hauled over 1,200 miles before we reach home again.'

'It is sad that we have been forestalled by the Norwegians,' Birdie tells Emily as he puts down the sextant, 'but I am glad that we have done it by good British man haulage.'[505]

Birdie is thinking of Emily and of home and of the invisible bond between mother and son. 'I am nearer to you here than at Winter Quarters, in fact a rapid flight up the Greenwich Meridian would be my shortest way home.' That is his mark now. For the first time since he ever heard of polar travel, his compass has swung through 180 degrees. 'Now the great journey is done it only remains for us to get back . . . Every day will now bring me nearer to your letters & all I want to hear & know.'

SCOTT – SOUTH POLE

'Now for the run home and a desperate struggle. I wonder if we can do it.'[506]

15

'Our People'

SCOTT – ANTARCTIC

Scott knows that Kathleen would tell him not to 'make life into Hell by anticipating things that may never happen'.[507] His pencil is getting very short but he scrapes the tip with his penknife and writes with a cold hand: 'It's no use meeting troubles halfway.'

Flicking back through his journal, he sees that on 8 January he told her that 'Evans [is a] a giant worker with a really remarkable headpiece.' He closes the journal. He lies down, wriggling his body deep into the bag and pulls the flap over his face; the bedraggled reindeer fur door brushes his cheek, shutting out the world. It is difficult to ignore Taff's clumsy movements beside him. It started with 'the accident' a fortnight earlier, when he and Taff fell into a crevasse. Taff seems to have struck his head on the way down and now the 'strong man' has become the 'sick man'.

Scott's uncensored frustration is seeping into his journal. To start with, a fortnight ago Taff was just 'rather dull and incapable', then 'very stupid about himself' and by the 13th, three days ago, he was incapable of assisting with either making camp or sledge-hauling, just a 'great nuisance and very clumsy'. That evening as they camped in 'the worst place of all', Taff had made the final transformation. He 'changed from his normal self-reliant self and has become impossible'. He is becoming a dangerous burden to them all.

17 FEBRUARY 1912

TAFF – ANTARCTIC

Taff cannot get his foot into his shoe, the finnesko boot that he had designed to be easy to put on. His fingers are raw where all the finger-nails have fallen off and the tips are open blisters. Scott asks him how he is feeling.

'Quite well,' Taff answers.[508] He has never said anything else.

Somehow he puts the canvas sledge harness on and takes the strain on the traces. After half an hour one of his finnesko boots comes adrift. He has to unharness. He asks Birdie to lend him a bit of string. Scott tells Taff that they will go on ahead and cautions him to come on as quickly as he can.

'Yes, Sir,' Taff replies, and watches the other four men pull away into the dull swaying light.

Taff takes off his glove and tries to pick up the bit of string. Despite his usual dexterity, the string is very thin and difficult to hold. He tries to get his foot into the shoe. The flesh of his left hand smells bad – there is a lot of pus. The fabric dressing sticks to the open wounds. His nose has been badly frostbitten for weeks. His skull hurts where it cracked against the ice in the accident and he can't seem to think straight.

At some point he gets up and tries to follow the others. He finds himself lying on the snow. He gets up. He falls down. He begins to remove his coat. It is difficult to work the buttons. He tries to stand but falls to his hands and knees and crawls slowly in the direction that he thinks the others have gone. All around him it is the same colour, like a foggy day on Rhossili beach where the sea and the sky are one.

Captain Scott and the others reappear and ask Taff what has happened. When Taff tries to talk, his voice is slow. He tries to answer Captain Scott in the correct manner but he does not know what to say. He thinks perhaps he's fainted. Scott orders Oates to stay with him while he takes Bill and Birdie back to retrieve the sledge from where they left it a mile or so on.

Taff drifts in and out of consciousness, but when he is conscious he knows that Captain Oates is there beside him. It is difficult to remember where they are or why. Perhaps Oates is talking. Perhaps he is asking Taff about his plans for the future – his wife, his children. Perhaps Taff vaguely remembers a football match.

'Go on, Taff, break them up,' Oates is saying.

'Right-o, Sir.' Taff jogs onto the icy football pitch outside the Cape Evans hut and does just that.

By the time Scott, Bill and Birdie get back with the sledge, Taff is unconscious. They pitch the tent and lift him inside. Taff dies at 12.30 a.m., two hours later.

17 FEBRUARY 1912
LOIS – PORTSMOUTH

Whatever happened, it was an awful way to die. There is much discussion on Chapel Street. Had they died of drowning or run out of air and died of suffocation? Why hadn't they been able to open the escape hatch? Was the weight of water too much to push against? Of all the fourteen men on board the submarine HMS *A3*, twelve were ratings. It was the Jack Tars, that willing breed, husbands and fathers of people like them, who were paying for decisions made high up in the Admiralty. The navy would have problems recruiting submariners now.

Lois has seen the submarines – they look like long metal cigar cases floating out of the mouth of Portsmouth harbour. Their propeller shafts are powered by the same make of engine that powers the motorised sledges in the Antarctic, Wolseley engines. From what Taff has told her, those Wolseley motor sledges would pull three tons of supplies. In Chapel Street, they joke that Taff will be chauffeur-driven to the Pole – perhaps Captain Scott will walk in front with a flag to make sure they don't exceed the Antarctic speed limit.

Lois knows that one of the three sledges is not going to the Pole. In one of those letters guarded by New Zealandia on the mantelpiece in their front room, Taff tells her that one of these blessed machines is 120 fathoms deep. Apparently Taff and the men tried to hold her on the rope but it was no use, 'she took charge at a gallop.'[509] It was as if Taff had watched £1,000 in paper notes float out to sea. This was not information she discussed. Taff had enclosed the expedition's confidentiality note with his letters.

Recently, the news in Portsmouth was that the submarine tragedy wasn't due, as they suspected, to the malfunctioning Wolseley engine. Just as HMS *A3* was surfacing on 2 February, it was rammed by the depot ship HMS *Hazard* near Portsea Island off the Isle of Wight on the other side of the Solent from Portsmouth. Apparently the submarine had been quickly tidied out of sight on the same day that it sank.

The timing is bad. The disaster happened to coincide with the premiere of the film of the king and queen at the Durbar in India as a prelude to celebrations for their triumphant return. The film was being screened in full Technicolor at the Scala in London while the submarine, with its fourteen dead men, was being surreptitiously towed to Portland Bill.

18 FEBRUARY 1912

KATHLEEN

'Very taken up with you all evening, I wonder if anything special is happening to you. Something odd happened to the clocks between 9 and 10 p.m.'[510] The next day Kathleen is still unsettled: 'As you ought about now to be returning to ship I see no reason for depression. I wonder . . .'

19 FEBRUARY 1912

SCOTT – ANTARCTIC

'I wonder what is in store for us, with some alarm at the lateness of the season.'[511]

3 MARCH 1912

TERRA NOVA – CAPE EVANS

The sea is freezing around Cape Evans. The *Terra Nova* is preparing to leave Antarctica, where, two months ago, she arrived with the mail from home, fresh supplies, fourteen dogs and seven mules from Shimla in India.

6 MARCH 1912

AMUNDSEN – HOBART, TASMANIA

The *Fram* sails into harbour at Hobart. Amundsen disembarks and, disguising his identity and that of his ship, walks straight to the post office in civilian dress and sends three coded telegrams to Norway. The first is to his brother Leon, the second to his mentor Fridtjof Nansen, the third to King Haakon VII.

6 MARCH 1912

KATHLEEN – LONDON

'Rumours began to-day that you had got to the Pole,' Kathleen tells her husband, 'and reporters began to flock and telephone; but apparently there is no sort of foundation, so I pursued the even tenor of my ways.'[512] She is writing in her diary at Scott's desk, which she has had moved downstairs in Buckingham Palace Road. Peter scribbles with fat crayons on an old sketchpad on the floor beside her. His obliviousness is a balm.

6 MARCH 1912

FRIDTJOF NANSEN – OSLO, NORWAY

Nansen is in his study on the first floor when a servant tells him that the post office has a telegram. They will dictate it to him over the phone. It must be to him. Leaving Kathleen mid-sentence, Nansen puts down his pen, descends to the hall and picks up the receiver. The message is from Roald Amundsen. Leon Amundsen, his brother, has already made Nansen aware that he will be told the news in advance but must keep it to himself for twenty-four hours.

Nansen's caller seems to have dictated Amundsen's message: 'THANKS FOR EVERYTHING OBJECTIVE REACHED ALL WELL.'[513] Nansen walks back up to his room and his letter to Kathleen. 'I wish that Scott had come first,' he tells her. 'Yes, life is very complicated indeed!'

7 MARCH 1912

KATHLEEN – LONDON

'Today came the clash and turmoil, writes Kathleen. There were cables right and left to say, "Amundsen arrived Hobart; states Scott has reached the Pole." Thank all the gods – I was not taken in; and while the posters shrieked, "Scott at South Pole – Brilliant victory", I was certain there was something wrong.'[514]

What is wrong? Scott has warned her, warned them all, to be sceptical when it comes to headlines. Chinese whispers. False news. Hearsay. All of it bundled into a commercial incentive to shift newspapers. Kathleen ignores the persistent ringing of the telephone. She will not be taken in by bells or shrieking. Instead, she unfolds the flimsy telegram that has just been delivered to the door of Buckingham Palace Road. She angles it to the window for light. There is movement on the edge of her vision. A man. Men. Outside she sees 'gentlemen of the press' hovering on the opposite side of the street by the Victoria Station shunting yard. She looks back down at the telegram. No signature. She must not trust it.

The telephone rings again. This time Kathleen picks it up and tells the caller that 'those cables are worthless and unsigned – [your news-paper will] only make [itself] and everybody else ridiculous by publishing them.'

Two newspapers have been delivered. She has avoided all interviews, but one paper, she notices, claims to have interviewed her. She picks up the telephone and asks the exchange for *The Times*. Is the operator listening in? Across the crackling line, she dictates a short note. She presses the receiver cradle and asks the exchange for the *Morning Post*. She dictates the same note: 'I have no reason to believe the reports and I [am] too occupied to see any reporters whatsoever.'

Slamming the back door behind her, she marches down the garden to her studio. Taking her clay-covered sculpture smock, she loops it over her head. From the bottom shelf around the room she picks up a photograph of her most recent portrait subject, Aubrey Waterfield, and props it in front of the table. Holding a wire at both ends, she draws the damp cloth back from the large lump of clay and slices off a piece. She notices that Aubrey's upper lip and chin are about a thumb's width in front of his recessed forehead. How will she sculpt spectacles? Aubrey is never without them.

She has not thought about the cables for a few minutes. A brief respite. She throws the damp clay onto the wooden surface. The clay is heavy and stiff but the smell is right. She kneads it, pressing the pads of her thumbs into its yielding mass. She pounds it with her fist. With clay-dyed fingers, she takes up her pen. In her journal she writes: 'I had an awful day. The house was a pandemonium – telephone, front door, telegrams, and reporters who worked their way in by saying they had definite and startling news . . . I tasted of hell.'

Later she learns the truth. Amundsen has beaten her husband to the Pole. 'My friends are afraid of me,' she writes, 'I worked badly and my head racked. I am not going to recount what I have been feeling, even if I could it would not make pleasant reading. It is better only to record the gay things of life.'[515] She receives a telegram from Oslo. It is from Nansen. He tells her his thoughts are with her. Nansen feels sure, he tells her later, that Amundsen will go straight to the Arctic and honour his intended work there before returning to Europe. She replies by return, asking if any traces have been seen of her husband, adding: 'Hurrah for Norway in spite of all.'[516]

He replies immediately: 'Noble! No traces have been seen.'

OATES – ANTARCTIC

Oates's leg aches along the Achilles. His left is no better, particularly his old war wound. He can feel the scar, as if that part of his leg is unravelling to the point before the operation to remove the bullet and reset the bone. He had not complained then. He would not complain now. He will say nothing. He will not surrender to anything or anyone, ever.

IO MARCH 1912
APSLEY CHERRY-GARRARD – ONE TON DEPOT

Cherry and Dmitri have arrived at One Ton Depot with the dogs. It is minus 40 and blizzarding. Cherry looks across the wind-battered tent at Dmitri. The Russian appears to be suffering from a progressive form of paralysis. First he'd had a headache, then his right arm stopped working, now he cannot feel his right side. What will happen to him? How far will it spread? If Dr Atkinson was here, he would be able to help. But he is not here because he is treating Teddy who was carried to Hut Point nearly dead from scurvy.*

Cherry listens to the howling gale and tries to think straight. Should he disobey Atkinson's orders, risk the dogs and the Russian and go south into this blizzard in the hopes of meeting Scott, or should he obey Atkinson, save the dogs for the next sledging season and head home hoping? He takes out a pencil and removing his mitten, begins a note to Scott:

> 10 March
> Dear Sir, we leave this morning with the dogs for Hut Point . . .
> Yours sincerely
> Apsley Cherry-Garrard

II MARCH 1912
SCOTT – ROSS ICE SHELF, ANTARCTIC

'Titus Oates is very near the end, one feels. What we or he will do, God only knows.'[517]

Should they abandon him or will Providence intervene as it did in the case of Taff? The third option is that he will 'walk out'. When, after their small breakfast ration, the four of them discuss the matter, Oates

---

* Teddy was saved by Lashly and Crean – the latter made the solo trek of 35 miles to get help and all at the end of an almost 1,500 mile round trip.

'practically asked for advice'. If Scott's last instructions to Teddy to bring the dogs to the 82nd or 81st parallel are followed, he believes he has a chance.* In his diary, Scott writes baldly, 'in point of fact he has none.'

Oates is 'a brave fine fellow'. Following discussions over breakfast, Scott 'practically order[s Bill] to hand over the means of ending our troubles to us, so that any one of us may know how to do so.' Bill hesitates until he realises that, if he refuses, Scott is prepared to ransack the medicine case and do it himself.

'We have thirty opium tabloids apiece,' writes Scott, 'and [Bill] is left with a tube of morphine.'

II MARCH 1912

KATHLEEN — LONDON

'Mummy,' asks Peter, 'is Amundsen a good man?'

'Yes,' replies Kathleen. (She has never talked 'baby'.) 'I think he is.'

'Amundsen and Daddy both got to the Pole. Daddy has stopped working now.' (Peter is two-and-a-half. He has only just learned the words 'Amundsen', 'Daddy', 'Pole' – he has no idea of the power of that configuration.)

Buckingham Palace Road is left behind as Kathleen rushes out of the door into the bracing March wind and marches east. 'I try to give myself no leisure,' of course her husband is 'still working'. Leisure 'surely leads to madness'.[518] Her heels beat the pavement while in the back of her mind drums: 'Is my man unhappy? Will he be unhappy?' She walks quickly towards the epicentre, the Royal Geographical Society.

Major Darwin receives her. He is packing up his office. He tells her that the Society has just sent a cable congratulating Amundsen. She does not stop for an explanation but returns straight home. Shortly after she has closed the front door, a letter drops through the post box. It is from Major Darwin. She writes back immediately: 'But of course. Let us at any rate if we don't win be good losers.' She rewrites the

---

* During their final push across the Ross Ice Shelf, Scott was anticipating his orders had been acted on by Teddy and the surviving men would soon meet the dog teams. By 27 February 1912, Scott and his men had reached 82 degrees south and remarked: 'We are naturally always discussing possibility of meeting dogs, where and when, &c. It is a critical position.' By 10 March, Scott realised the dogs were not coming: 'The dogs which would have been our salvation have evidently failed.'

phrase out for her husband in her journal with the suffix, 'as you would be my only man'. Perhaps she should send a congratulatory telegram to Amundsen herself? She asks the wise publisher, Reginald Smith. He says 'no'.

Confronting the Amundsen issue head on is not working. Kathleen tries displacement. Lately she has been battling with Mrs Cobb about woman's suffrage. 'You know the brutes have been breaking all the shop windows,' she tells her husband. 'I find myself launching deeply into these issues.'

16 MARCH 1912

CHERRY – *DISCOVERY* HUT

The door of the hut opens. An icy wind blows in and a man peers in at them with a myopic stare through the slit in his iced balaclava. From the open door, Cherry feels the heat of the room on the small exposed area of his face. They were obviously expecting him to be Scott, but move quickly into action, bringing the paralysed Dmitri in and untethering and feeding the dogs, who seem to be starving and suffering from frostbite.

For the last month Atkinson has exerted the full force of his medical skill to keep Teddy alive. He now turns his attention to the latest frozen returnees: 'Both men [are] in exceedingly poor condition,' he notes, 'Cherry-Garrard's state causing me serious alarm.'[519]

16 MARCH 1912

CAROLINE – LONDON

Caroline is at the New Theatre, where Juliet and Romeo 'wherefore art thou' within plain sight of each other in front of a handsome Italian hilltop town. Occasionally, when actors enter and exit, the hilltop ripples. It is warm and dark in the auditorium, there is the faint rustle of taffeta. The New Theatre is a good place to be seen but also an excellent place to lose oneself.

The tragedy before her now is happening precisely because the message never got through. If Juliet had been able to say 'I'm asleep not dead,' there would have been a different ending. In real life, is there ever a time when 'saying nothing' is the difference between life and death?

Miss Phyllis Neilson-Terry wakes to hope and, when that is dashed, staggers about in a picturesque manner before collapsing elegantly backwards across Vernon Steel, her head down stage right. She has her eyes closed, as one would expect. But Mr Steel has his eyes open. Surely the urge to blink is instinctive, like the urge to swallow, to breathe, to survive.

17 MARCH 1912

OATES – ROSS ICE SHELF

Two days before Oates had asked to be left in his sleeping bag. The idea of trying to get his boots on, let alone help with the camp, was beyond imagination. His three companions had 'induced him to come on'.[520] It wasn't an order, it was an inducement. What if the dogs were just over the horizon with food and fuel? How could he 'surrender' when the dogs were expected at any minute?

He asked Bill if he had a chance. Bill said that he did not know if he had a chance, he must just 'slog on, slog on'.[521]

The others make camp. Still no sign of the dogs. On his frozen hands and knees, Oates crawls in. It is minus 40 and getting dark. Scott is writing in his journal. Does anyone know what day it is? Is it Friday the 16th or Saturday the 17th of March? Oates does not know, but he does know that if it is the 17th of March, it is his birthday. He is thirty-two.

He has not written in his journal for weeks. He has not been able to hold a pencil. He tries to sleep, hoping not to wake. As he drifts towards unconsciousness, he can hear that it is blowing a blizzard. The tent canvas is cracking and bending with the strain, the noise is deafening. In the morning he wakes. He is still alive.

'I am just going outside and may be some time.'

Oates leaves the tent. He does not take his sleeping bag. He does not even put on his shoes. He must walk far enough from the tent to make sure that the others do not have to trip over his frozen body on their way home.

BILL – ROSS ICE SHELF

Inside the tent Bill picks up Oates's journal and, turning to page 56, writes across the top 'To Mrs Oates – from E. A. Wilson', and underlines it.

Dear Mrs Oates,

This is a sad ending to our undertaking. Your son died a very noble death, God knows. I have never seen or heard of such courage as he showed from first to last with his feet both badly frostbitten – never a word or a sign of complaint of the pain. He was a great example – Dear Mrs Oates, he asked me at the end, to see you and to give you this diary of his – You, he told me, are the only woman he has ever loved . . . These diaries will be found and this note will reach you some day . . . Our whole journey's record is clean and though disastrous – has no shadow over it. He died like a man and a soldier without a word of regret . . . except that he hadn't written to you at the last . . . not

God comfort you in your loss. [522]

18 MARCH 1912

ORIANA – WELLINGTON, NEW ZEALAND

Oriana stands for a photograph in front of Fern Grove to the west of Wellington. In spite of the devastating news about Amundsen, or perhaps because of it, Ory is determined not to be 'shoddy'. She wears a pristine white long-sleeved blouse and white skirt. She tips her head to the left and smiles. She must have been leaving Hobart just as Amundsen's *Fram* was sailing in, victorious. Now she concentrates on the camera – she knows how much Bill values photographs of her. He has told her that he keeps them in his prayer book; 'they have been well used & a very great joy to me.'[523] Her husband will only need an up-to-date picture of her if he has stayed in the Antarctic. She has come all the way out to New Zealand hoping that he has not, that he will not need this photograph, which is why she agrees for it to be taken.

In the trunk that Ory has brought out from England, she has two volumes with sage green canvas covers and the title *The Grouse in Health and in Disease* picked out in gold. The frontispiece is a wonderful picture of a pair of red grouse in summer with young chicks low in the tussocky grass of Fort Augustus. She remembers that picture emerging from the page in the drawing room of Lord Lovat's shooting lodge. It is just one of sixty full-page colour illustrations under tissue guards. Reginald Smith spared no expense – Ory suspects he might have paid for it out of his own wallet.

From his letters she knows that Bill is anxious about reviews, but she has brought along a copy of *Nature* from 26 October the previous year: 'This magnificent piece of work . . . a unique example of what can be done by the combined efforts of sportsmen, gamekeepers, field-observers, and biological experts . . . gratitude of naturalists and sportsmen, not only in the British Island, but throughout the world'. As she stands for the photographs, she smiles. It will be so exciting to see his face when he sees his grouse book. It is 'their baby'. The sensation is similar to seeing that bluebell wood at the Crippets. It is difficult to see something so beautiful, so linked to Bill, and not be able to share it with him – the suspense is difficult to bear.

23 MARCH 1912

LONDON

Scott Keltie
Royal Geographical Society

23rd March 1912

Dear Sir,

As no news has arrived of Captain Scott's expedition, it occurs to the Editor that to be on the safe side, it might be well, in case of accidents, to have an obituary of Captain Scott and his principal assistants prepared . . . The editor would be glad to know whether the absence of news is beginning to excite anxiety in geographical circles. Perhaps the suggestion is premature, but will you kindly inform the Editor whether there is likelihood of the partys [sic] meeting with disaster?

C. W. Brodwill (signature unclear)
The Times[524]

23 MARCH 1912

BIRDIE – ROSS ICE SHELF

They are just over 11 miles from One Ton Depot. They have been in this tent since the evening of Monday the 19th, when the blizzard began. The tent canvas is flapping and crackling in the wind; the noise is loud and unremitting, a continuous gale from the southwest. Every day they have been ready to start out for One Ton. Between singing songs and keeping up cheery conversation about exactly what they will do when they reach Hut Point, Birdie makes use of the time:

My own dearest Mother,

As this may possibly be my last letter to you am sorry it is such a short scribble. I have written little since we left the Pole but it has not been for want of thinking of you & the dear girls. We have had a terrible journey back . . . we have had terribly low temperatures on the Barrier & that and our sick companions have delayed us till too late in the season which has made us very short of fuel & we are now out of food as well. Each depot has been a harder struggle to reach, but I am still strong & hope to reach this one with [Bill] & get the food & fuel necessary for our lives. God alone knows what will be the outcome of the 23 mile march we have to make, but my trust is still in Him & in the abounding grace of my Lord & Saviour whom you brought me up to trust in & who has been my stay through life. In his keeping I leave you & am only glad that I am permitted to struggle on to the end. When man's extremity is reached, God's help may put things right & although the end will be painless enough for myself, I should so like to come through for your dear sake. It is splendid to pass, however, with such companions as I have & as all five of us have mothers & wives, you will not be alone.

H. R. Bowers[525]

Birdie tries to focus his starving mind on his last logistical problem. Scott's foot is frozen. He knows that amputation is the best he can hope for. Should they leave Scott in this tent, sledge to One Ton and come back with food? If they do, they will have to make the journey three times. Should they put Scott on a sledge and try to pull him to One Ton? It will be more difficult to pull, but they would only have to make the journey once and if they die, they will all be together. Would it be better if one of them set out alone but perhaps did not make it to One Ton and back, in which case two men would starve to death in the tent?

Somewhere in his thoughts there is a short, bearded sea captain lashed to the wheel of his ship. A storm rages but in the centre of it the man is steadfast. Birdie retreats into his sleeping bag. The man became master of his own ship at nineteen, nine years younger than Birdie, his son, is now.

23 MARCH 1912

SCOTT – ROSS ICE SHELF

My dear Mrs Bowers,

I am afraid this will reach you after one of the heaviest blows of your life.

I write when we are very near the end of our journey, and I am finishing it in company with two gallant, noble gentlemen. One of these is your son. He had come to be one of my closest and soundest friends, and I appreciate his wonderful upright nature, his ability and energy. As the troubles have thickened his dauntless spirit ever shone brighter and he has remained cheerful, hopeful, and indomitable to the end.

The ways of Providence are inscrutable, but there must be some reason why such a young, vigorous and promising life is taken.

My whole heart goes out in pity for you.

Yours R. Scott.

To the end he has talked of you and his sisters. One sees what a happy home he must have had and perhaps it is well to look back on nothing but happiness. He remains unselfish, self-reliant and splendidly hopeful to the end, believing in God's mercy to you.[526]

23 MARCH 1912

EMILY – BUTE

To keep warm, Emily has to sit close to the fireplace, where a modest pile of coal glows in the grate, filling the room with a pleasant smokiness.

There is the very real possibility of a coal famine in Rothesay. Already the coal strike means that the supply of the village of Kilchattan Bay has practically run out and the villagers are having to do without fires. The Marquess of Bute sent Mr Howe, his forester, to tell the people of Kingarth near Mount Stuart that they were at liberty to take fallen timber from the woods free of charge. Everyone knew that they had already 'taken French leave', stacking their timber quietly under the stairs.

Emily hopes the strike will come to an early end. The word in Ardbeg is that they have another week to go. The Glasgow merchants say that coal could be got but at the prohibitive price of 45 shillings per ton, which, with added charges would make it out of the question for Emily and May. Emily does not want to accept charity, even from the ever-generous William Maxwell upstairs.

She hopes that Birdie is warm back at the expedition base hut. It is so fortunate that he has inherited her tendency to be well covered. 'I feel proud of my parentage,' he has told her. It is partly their adventurous example but also his physique. Emily and Alexander combined 'ha[ve] given me a constitution & physical strength to stand such a test'.[527]

She and the Maxwells are hoarding back copies of the *Buteman*. They can be folded as dense as briquettes. Emily tries to be thrifty; she depends upon her allowance from Birdie's salary, but she does not want to be a burden to him. One copy of the *Buteman* features: 'A remarkable feat': it concerns a female scientist who was in San Francisco when an earthquake caused the stairs of her building to fall down, leaving only the portions to which the banisters had been attached.

'Upon this precarious remnant (being an experienced mountain climber) she made her way to the eighth floor and brought down a collection of rare specimens of Californian plants of priceless value. A young man who was with her offered to undertake the job but she said "No. You have a family. Nobody depends upon me. I will go." And she did.'

23 MARCH 1912

BILL — ROSS ICE SHELF

'Don't be unhappy,' Bill tells Ory, '– all is for the best. We are playing a good part in a great scheme arranged by God himself, and all is well . . . I am only sorry I couldn't have seen your loving letters, and Mother's and Dad's and the Smiths', and all the happy news I had hoped to see, but all these things are easily seen later, I expect . . . God be with you – my love is as living for you as ever.'

On a fresh page he writes to Reginald and Isabel Smith – they will be important friends for Ory: 'I have valued your friendship and your example, and how I and my beloved wife have loved you both . . . I should like to have seen the Grouse book, but it is not allowed to me.'[528]

He resumes the final letter to Ory. 'I would like to have written to Mother and Dad and all at home, but it has been impossible. We will all meet after death, and death has no terrors . . . We have done what we thought was best . . . My own dear wife, good-bye for the present.'

The tent canvas is tugged violently by the wind, but Bill does not think that it will fly off like the roof of Oriana hut did, on the Winter Journey. The inner lining is still free from snow. He wants to make sure that everything is neat and tidy. He is confident that these diaries will be found.

As he becomes weaker, Bill realises that through his medical ministrations on this journey, often at the expense of his own health, he has reached a point of self-forgetfulness and suffering that is the sublimation of all his Christian ideals. He repeats Julian of Norwich's mantra, 'All Shall be Well'. Ory is his anchoress, the woman who has set herself apart for him. When he thinks about her, he still wonders how 'the deuce such a girl came to give herself to me'.[529] But lately he has begun to wonder whether Ory has already died. Perhaps God is bringing him to her in heaven? 'God may have even now closed [your life] before mine and I may be coming to you by a quicker way.'[530]

With his remaining strength he checks himself. It is presumptuous to second guess God, and if she is still alive she must not kill herself to reach him. It is *le bon Dieu* not *l'homme* who decides when to close a life.

To my Most Beloved Wife.

I leave this life in absolute faith and happy belief that if God wishes you to wait long without me it will be to some good purpose. All is for the best to those that love God, and oh, my Ory, we have both loved Him with all our lives. All is well . . .

We have struggled to the end and we have nothing to regret. Our whole journey record is clean, and Scott's journal gives the account . . . The Barrier has beaten us – though we got to the Pole.

God knows I am sorry to be the cause of sorrow to anyone in the world, but everyone must die – and at every death there must be some sorrow . . . My only regret is leaving you to struggle through your life alone . . . All is well . . .

Bill lies back in his sleeping bag and folds his arms over his chest.

28 MARCH 1912

SCOTT – ROSS ICE SHELF

My Dear Mrs Wilson

If this letter reaches you Bill and I will have gone out together. We are very near it now and I should like you to know how splendid he was at the end – everlastingly cheerful and ready to sacrifice himself for others, never a word of blame to me for leading him into this mess. He is not suffering, luckily, at least only minor discomforts.

His eyes have a comfortable blue look of hope and his mind is peaceful with the satisfaction of his faith in regarding himself as part of the great scheme of the Almighty.

[As he is writing, Bill stops breathing.]

I can do no more to comfort you than to tell you that he died as he lived, a brave, true man – the best of comrades and staunchest of friends.

My whole heart goes out to you in pity.

Yours truly,
R. Scott[531]

27 MARCH 1912

KATHLEEN – LONDON

All the downstairs rooms still have chairs pushed back around the walls to make room for a hundred and ten people who were there last night to help her celebrate. There are ashtrays, stale smoke competing with the fresh scent of daffodils in the air. Brand, the servant, is still clearing up.

'I think my party was a great success,' she tells her husband in her journal. It was her thirty-third birthday, and Scott would be forty-three by now. 'It seems an odd moment to choose to give a party, but I went through with it rather on principle. I am very glad I did. I was expecting your news hourly, but determined to go through with the party anyhow.'[532]

The day before she had been to a dance at the Savoy: 'Yes I did and it did me a world of good – one's mental feelings vanished away and one's blood circulated happily.'[533] Now she takes out her latest letter from Nansen: 'Of course you may still have to wait some weeks. It would be like [Scott] to wish to use the ship for completing his previous discoveries of the coast . . . But your time of indescribable joy and happiness will soon come. People here take much interest in Scott, but I forgot to tell you when I first spoke to the King [of Norway] after Amundsen's telegram, the first thing he said was that he thought of you, and that he only wished it had been Scott.'[534]

29 MARCH 1912

SCOTT – ROSS ICE SHELF

Scott has already written a letter to Kathleen, beginning 'Dearest darling . . .'.[535] Now he writes above the first line 'To my widow' and underlines it. His eyes skim the words he wrote just a few days ago:

'We are in a very tight corner and I have doubts of pulling through . . .'

There is optimism in those words . . . just a few days ago he wrote them, hoping to be able to tear them up one day in London, a ritual fire perhaps in the grate of 174 Buckingham Palace Road. He tells her that his first and last letters are to her 'on whom my thoughts mostly dwell waking or sleeping – if anything happens to me I shall like you to know how much you have meant to me and what pleasant recollections are with me as I depart.'

'We have decided not to kill ourselves but to fight to the last for that depot but in fighting there is a painless end, so don't worry.' They are not going to take the opium or the morphine but they've agreed to assure their relatives that they will not have suffered any pain. Scott goes further; Kathleen's pathological positivity demands it and he will not fail now: 'Leave the world fresh from harness & full of good health & vigour . . . splendid physical condition . . .' He describes their appetites as compensation for all discomfort, not as the animal appetites of starving men, and assures her that the hot food 'is so wonderfully enjoyable that one would scarcely be without [such an appetite]'.

'How much better has it been than lounging in too great comfort at home.' Surely he has proved the master of 'the inherited vice from my side of the family . . . indolence'. He tells Kathleen to guard Peter against that. 'I had to force myself into being strenuous as you know – had always an inclination to be idle. My father was idle and it brought much trouble.'

He knows that she admires his 'big nature', his trust, his lack of petty jealousy. 'Dearest . . . you know I cherish no sentimental rubbish about remarriage – when the right man comes to help you in life you ought to be your happy self again – I wasn't a very good husband but I hope I shall be a good memory . . . and I like to think that the boy will have a good start in parentage of which he may be proud.'

He is anxious for his son. He checks over a letter he has already written to Sir Edgar Speyer. Perhaps Speyer or Barrie can support his family: 'If this diary is found,' he asks Speyer, 'will you please do your best to have our people looked after? I have my wife & child to think of. The wife is a very independent person but the country ought not to let my boy want an education & a future.' And not just his wife. Bill, he tells Speyer, 'the best fellow that ever stepped who has sacrificed himself again & again to the sick men of the party leaves a widow entirely destitute. Surely something ought to be done for her and for the humbler widow of Edgar Evans.' He should mention Birdie's family and perhaps Oates's – but he cannot give Speyer a list. He must trust him and his 'dear kind' wife Leonora. Now Scott turns back to the letter to Kathleen:

'Make the boy interested in natural history if you can,' he tells Kathleen. He has spent long hours with Bill discussing the system of compulsory games in British public schools, designed to get fitter recruits for the Boer War. Bill has convinced him to steer Peter towards the study of nature. 'It is better than games. They encourage it at some schools. I know you will keep him in the open air. Try and make him believe in a God, it is comforting . . .' He is concerned lest Kathleen is too proud to accept help for their son's sake. 'I think he and you ought to be specially looked after by the country for which after all we have given our lives with something of the spirit which makes for an example.'

He starts on a fresh page. These are words for people he has never met, words he has been juggling day after endless day – now he has them by heart. Deliberately he heads the page: 'Message to the Public'.[536] When he finishes, he is aware that he has written his epitaph.

He stops and changes key. 'Oh dear me,' he writes to Kathleen, 'you must know that quite the worst aspect of this situation is the thought that I shall not see you again.' He feels himself weakening, giving in to 'sentimental rubbish'; he checks himself, he must be 'a good memory.'

'You must know that quite the worst aspect of this situation is the thought that I shall not see you again. The inevitable must be faced, you urged me to be a leader of the party, and I know you felt it would be dangerous. I have taken my place throughout haven't I?'

He never signs the letter. Like Kathleen when the *Terra Nova* left Port Chalmers, he never says goodbye.

Scott looks right at Bill and left at Birdie. The temperature outside has risen. Inside the tent it is horribly warm. His frozen leg is thawing. The pain is unbelievable. He must bear it alone. It is almost as bad as not knowing whether his family will be saddled with his failure and debt. He opens his coat. He fumbles for his pencil and opens his journal at the page titled 'Message to the Public'. With a hand made clumsy by cold and pain, he turns to the end and scribbles:

'For God's sake look after our people.'

29/30 MARCH 1912

BIRDIE – ROSS ICE SHELF

Perhaps Scott is asleep or unconscious, or perhaps he has already died when Birdie reaches out of his sleeping bag and puts two of Bill's sketchbooks in the instrument box. He is capable and thorough, and he is not about to let a little thing like death change that. He reaches out for one of Scott's letters, and on the back he writes: 'Dr [Bill] Wilsons note to Mrs [Oriana] Wilson is in the satchel in the Instrument Box with his journal & two sketchbooks HRB.'[537]

16

'As Safe Down South as at Home'

31 MARCH 1912

TERRA NOVA – AKAROA, NEW ZEALAND

The *Terra Nova* anchors off Akaroa on the east coast of South Island. A boat rows out from the shore. A man boards the ship briefly. He is handed the message Scott wrote before he left Cape Evans hut for the South Pole. He rows back to shore and walks straight to the cable head. He translates the message into the agreed Central News Agency 'Hereward' code for the British Antarctic Expedition and sends eighteen words: 'I am remaining in the Antarctic for another winter in order to continue and complete my work. RFS'

Once the CNA agent is confident the message has reached London, he telephones Joseph Kinsey's office in Christchurch. He is told that Kinsey is at Te Hau, his country cottage in the suburb of Clifton. He asks to be put back to the exchange and patched through to Te Hau.

ORIANA – CHRISTCHURCH

One of them has to pick up the thing and Mr Kinsey has just left for the office. Ory and Mrs Kinsey look at each other. The telephone continues to ring. Outside the window, Ory can see the Southern Ocean stretching to the horizon, the morning sun sparkling off it.

Minutes later, Mr Kinsey is panting back up the hill with Ory in hot pursuit. Above them gulls skim the cliff edge on stiff wings. Once inside, Ory knows that she should allow Mr Kinsey a private conversation, but she can't. 'I felt this must be something really about the ship & waited to see the expression on his face.'[538] Ory knows about the Central News Agency contract, but surely Mr Kinsey will tell her something? He finishes the call, replaces the receiver and sets off immediately for the office.

A few moments later, the telephone rings again. Ory feels the Bakelite cool against her right ear. The line is bad but through the whooshing and static, a low voice. The same man. She tells him she is Mrs Oriana Wilson, wife of Dr Bill Wilson. She asks if everyone is back. Has the *Terra Nova* arrived back from its latest resupply trip to the Antarctic? Is Bill nearly back? 'And then I heard that all the Expedition had not come back – that [Teddy] was on board. [Bill] was not.'

The line crackles with silence. Is this how it ends? A disembodied voice? The shock is difficult to master. She tries to speak. She must understand if she has heard the man correctly. The automatic mantra that she and Bill use as a shorthand code comes to her: 'For a moment I had a shock as he put it in a way that I did not understand, so I asked if "all was well" & he said yes & that [Bill] had remained South.'

She tries to replay the brief crackled message accurately in her head. CNA have exclusive rights to the news for either twenty-four or thirty-six hours, she's still not clear which. The man's message was guarded, presumably because the exchange might be listening in. Kinsey is the only person with whom she can check that she heard right, that Bill has remained South. It is a walkable distance from Te Hau to Kinsey's office in Christchurch. She sets off at a run.

She does not need her binoculars. If an aviary of exotics were to fall out of the sky, she would not care. As she rushes across the tusky grass that covers the Port Hills, she tries to adjust to the implications of that man's words. Bill is not about to sail back into her life. The grouse book with its gold lettering will remain wrapped in tissue for another year. She cannot afford a ticket back to England.

Sometime later, flushed and breathless, she walks into the office of Kinsey & Co. Kinsey has a telegram and more news. '[Bill] was in the final Southern Party.' Ory masters her 'selfish grief'. Bill is one of the lucky few that Captain Scott has chosen for the final journey. She focuses on the exclusivity and privilege of that choice rather than the forestalling disappointment – by the afternoon she has achieved temporary self-mastery: 'It was an exciting day.'

KATHLEEN – LONDON

'Central News rang to say you were staying another year.' Kathleen accepts that the terms of the lucrative exclusive news contract gives a disinterested journalist the right to tell her that she must wait another year before she can hope to see her husband and her son, his father. 'I didn't enjoy the rest of the night very much . . . it is difficult to bear the thought of your disappointment.'[539] Outside the bedroom window of Buckingham Palace Road, the wind blows through the still leafless London plane tree.[540] She cannot be sure of the impact of Amundsen's flag. Lesser things have precipitated her husband into one of his 'dread thunderclouds'.

She wonders whether Peter's psychology shows symptoms of his father's tendency to depression. Every night when she puts him to bed she says, 'More fun tomorrow.'[541] It is alchemy. Those three words erase, transform and precipitate problems into optimistic 'fun'. Through what she knows of Hannah, Scott's mother, she worries that her husband's upbringing laid down expectations that were limited and economic, rather than grand and iconic. Peter will not be an unhappy man if she has anything to do with it – which she does. Even Scott can't infect his son with 'black moods' from the Antarctic. Will her post-dated letters be enough to save her husband from himself? As she tosses in bed, she wondered why she can't seem to 'more-fun-tomorrow' herself.

The wind rattles the sash window. The dates don't work. The date Scott was last seen heading south is later than the ideal date he gave her for heading north. Why so slow? 'It's hard to think of you out so late in the season, but there I suppose you know your job and wouldn't take too awful risks.'[542]

I APRIL 1912

ANTARCTIC

Dr Atkinson, nominally in charge of the expedition in the absence of Scott and Teddy, arrives back at the *Discovery* hut after having sledged south dangerously late in the season. He has been out laying supplies at Corner Camp between Hut Point and One Ton. He has put them there in case Scott and his team can use them on their return. He has done this on principle, although he is 'morally certain' that the Polar Party must have perished on their return.

EMILY – BUTE

The telegram arrives in Ardbeg early on 1 April. The weather is terrible, a 'tempest', 'fierce blasts', 'bitter coolness' – Emily tries to find the strength to deal with the reversion to winter. 'My laddie' would not

RIGHT: *Terra Nova* on the point of departure from New Zealand for the Antarctic. L–R on board: Bill (sitting far port stern obscuring Oriana who is sitting on his left); Hilda and Teddy (facing each other, port side of wheel); Kathleen (broad brimmed hat starboard of wheel); Scott (white peaked cap second in from dockside). (Photograph by Herbert Ponting, © Scott Polar Research Institute, University of Cambridge)

BELOW LEFT: Captain Robert Falcon Scott takes command of the *Terra Nova* from South Africa, for the journey to the southern hemisphere, then on to Antarctica. (KGPA Ltd / Alamy Stock Photo)

BELOW RIGHT: *Terra Nova* anchored to the sea ice unloading supplies using a gantry. Shortly after this was taken, they unloaded a motor sledge which 'took charge at a gallop and is now resting on the bottom at a depth of 120 fathoms'. (Photograph by Herbert Ponting, © Scott Polar Research Institute, University of Cambridge)

ABOVE: Oriana and Bill, both *c*. 1901. (Left: Magite Historic/Alamy Stock Photo; right: Family album, private collection)

BELOW: The Wilson wedding group at Hilton, Cambridge, 16 July 1901. L–R: Polly Wilson (Bill's sister), Bill, Oriana, Constance Souper (Oriana's sister). '[I] wonder how the deuce such a girl came to give herself to me.' (Family album, private collection)

ABOVE: Press photograph, L–R: unknown, Teddy, Hilda, Oriana, Bill and Joseph Kinsey aboard the *Terra Nova* in Lyttleton, November 1910. (Otago Heritage Books, from Church, 1997)

BELOW LEFT: Oriana Wilson at the New Zealand War Contingent Association Office in London, with Bill's watercolours on the wall behind her, *c.* 1917. (Private collection)

BELOW RIGHT: Bill at his desk in the Cape Evans Hut painting a Paraselena, 1911. 'He trusts her with his artistic reputation – if anything had to be done, 'Ory will have the doing.' (AA Images/Alamy Stock Photo)

ABOVE: Kathleen Bruce's marriage to Robert Falcon Scott at the Chapel Royal, Hampton Court on 2 September 1908. *The Times* report of the wedding ended, 'The marriage will make no difference to Capt. Scott's future plans with regard to Antarctic exploration.' (Royal Geographic Society)

BELOW: Scott at his desk in the Antarctic, photos of Kathleen and Peter on the wall behind him. (Photograph by Herbert Ponting, Pictorial Press Ltd/Alamy Stock Photo)

ABOVE: Kathleen with Scott and Captain Oates (bowler hat) on Quail Island, New Zealand, inspecting the dogs, November 1910. (Private Collection, similar by photographer S. F. Webb)

BELOW LEFT: Kathleen with a selection of her work in the studio gallery, 1933. L–R: *The Kingdom is Within*; Adam Lindsay Gordon; William of Wykeham. (Photograph by Stuart Hamilton, John Murray, from Kennet, 1949)

BELOW RIGHT: Kathleen in her sculpture studio with Peter, working on statuette 'Veronica' in 1912. (Press photograph *Daily Mirror*, Bridgeman Images)

ABOVE AND RIGHT: Caroline Oates, together with all her children, hunted with the East Essex. L–R: Bryan, Lawrence, Violet and Lilian Oates outside Gestingthorpe Hall, early 1890s. (Left: Gilbert White's House & Gardens; right: Gestingthorpe Hall Archive)

BELOW: The Gestingthorpe Hall south facade. The two middle windows on the first floor are Oates's bedroom where Caroline slept after his death. Beneath them are the external awnings that shaded her study windows. (Gestingthorpe Hall Archive)

ABOVE: Captain Lawrence 'No Surrender' Oates (Photograph by Herbert Ponting, Pictorial Press Ltd/Alamy Stock Photo)

LEFT: Caroline Oates in the Gestingthorpe garden with a parasol, *c.* 1912. (Gestingthorpe Hall Archive)

BELOW: Oates on the *Terra Nova* with the expedition's ponies and dogs. (Photograph by Herbert Ponting, Pictorial Press Ltd/Alamy Stock Photo)

ABOVE: Miss Emily Webb, trainee teacher at Cheltenham Teacher Training College, *c.* 1886 (second from right front row). (University of Gloucestershire Archives and Special Collections)

LEFT: Emily shortly following her wedding in 1877, Singapore. 'I have not forgotten,' Birdie tells his mother, 'that you once said you hoped you would be dead before I started on anything so foolhardy [as an expedition to the South Pole].' But 'I would not belong to the family of Bowers if I did not attempt the apparently impossible.' (© Scott Polar Research Institute, University of Cambridge)

ABOVE: The Bowers sisters beside the *Terra Nova* at London's West India docks in 1910. Birdie is fourth from right and the women are L–R: Edie, May and Mrs George Wyatt (wife of the London expedition agent, who is at the centre in a boater hat). (© Scott Polar Research Institute, University of Cambridge)

BELOW LEFT: Detail of Birdie from a group photograph on point of departure from the Cape Evans hut for the Cape Crozier Winter Journey to collect penguin eggs, 27 June 1911. (Photograph by Herbert Ponting, GL Archive/Alamy Stock Photo)

BELOW RIGHT: Bill and Birdie, detail from a group photograph taken by Herbert Ponting used as a frontispiece for *'Birdie' Bowers of the Antarctic* by George Seaver. (John Murray, from Seaver, 1938)

ABOVE: Press photograph: Lois Evans with her children, L–R: Ralph, Muriel and Norman, 1913. (Trinity Mirror/Mirrorpix/Alamy Stock Photo)

LEFT: Lois shortly after learning that she is a widow, 11 February 1913. Image for *Cambrian Daily Leader*. L–R: William Beynon, Lois's father, Ralph and Lois. The journalist will describe her as 'quite a superior and refined little woman'. (Photograph by Sam Chapman)

ABOVE: Taff (P.O. Edgar Evans) dressing Dr Atkinson's frostbitten hand in Cape Evans hut, 1911. 'Ever sat on a wasp nest? No? Well it's like that, only worse. You don't feel any pain at the time but when the blood begins to circulate…' (Photograph by Herbert Ponting, The Print Collector/Alamy Stock Photo)

BELOW: Taff (right) and Tom Crean mending the reindeer sleeping bags. Taff is responsible for all the 'housewifes', the sewing kits that each man carries to keep his gear in good repair. (Photograph by Herbert Ponting, Popperfoto via Getty Images/Getty Images)

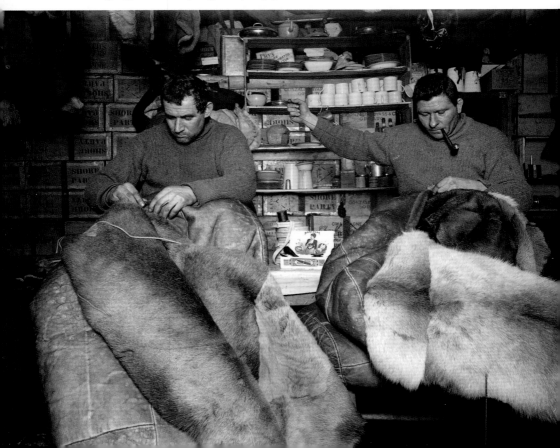

VOL · III · PART · I.

THE SOUTH POLAR TIMES · 1911 ·

THE ONLY MAN WHO COUNTS "

" ATTACH A HOOD TO YOUR SHIRT-WAIST. "

The cover of the 1911 edition of the *South Polar Times*, the expedition's magazine, produced over the Antarctic winter. Far left is an illustration of 'Titus' Oates, 'the only man who counts', and near left, society style icon, 'Madame Berde'.
(Bute Museum archive copy of the *South Polar Times*, presented to the Bowers family by Cherry-Garrard)

ABOVE: Scott's birthday celebration, 6 June 1911. L–R: Oates (standing), Atkinson, Meares, Cherry-Garrard, Taylor, Nelson, Teddy, Scott, Bill, Simpson, Birdie, Gran (standing), Wright, Debenham, Day. Behind Oates's head is his portrait of Napoleon. The sledging flags decorate the room. 'Down the centre of the crisp white tablecloth are silver soda siphons, bottles of wine and champagne.' (Photograph by Herbert Ponting, Heritage Image Partnership Ltd/Alamy Stock Photo)

BELOW: 'The Tenements', where the creed is: 'Down with Science, Sentiment and the Fair Sex'. L–R: Cherry, Birdie, Oates, Meares (above) Atkinson. (Photograph by Herbert Ponting/Scott Polar Research Institute, University of Cambridge/Getty Images)

LEFT: The last page of Captain Scott's diary:
We shall stick it out to the end, but we are getting weaker, of course, and the end cannot be far. It seems a pity, but I do not think I can write more.
R. SCOTT
For God's sake look after our people

OPPOSITE: British Antarctic Expedition map of the main southern journeys of Scott and Amundsen's expeditions to the South Pole.

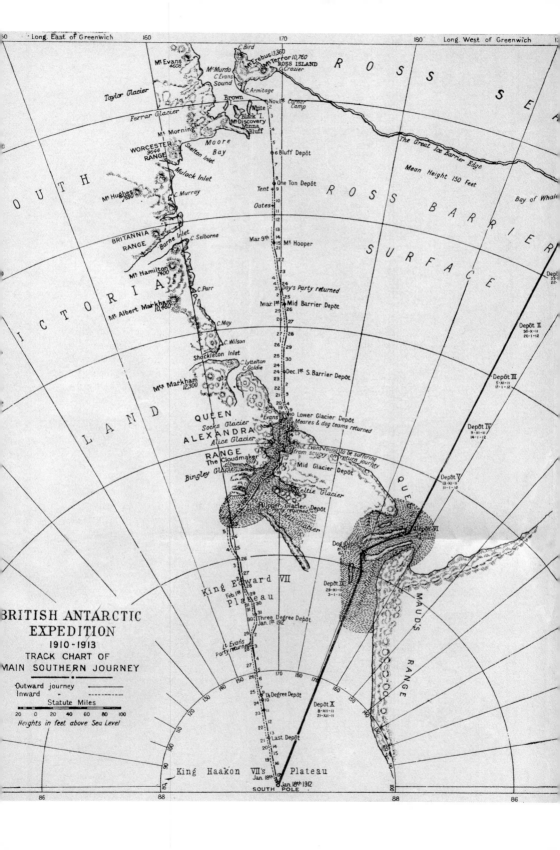

BRITISH ANTARCTIC
EXPEDITION
1910-1913
TRACK CHART OF
MAIN SOUTHERN JOURNEY

Outward journey ————
Inward ‑ ‑ ‑ ‑ ‑ ‑
Statute Miles
20 0 20 40 60 80 100
Heights in feet above Sea Level

"A Throne of Rocks, a Robe of Clouds, a Diadem of Snow."

DAILY SKETCH.

THE PREMIER PICTURE PAPER. ONE HALFPENNY.

NATION'S REQUIEM FOR THE ANTARCTIC HEROES.

LEFT: 'Nation's requiem for the Antarctic heroes'. The *Daily Sketch* reports on the memorial service at St Paul's cathedral, held on 14 February 1913. Inset clockwise from top left: Kathleen, Scott, Peter, Bill, Taff, Oates, Birdie. (© British Library Board. All Rights Reserved/ Bridgeman Images)

BELOW: A feature on the families left behind, in the *Daily Mirror*, 21 May 1913. Clockwise from top left: Hannah (Scott's mother); Ralph, Norman and Muriel (Taff's children); Lois; Emily; and Oriana.

Mrs. Scott, the mother of the famous explorer.

Mrs. Wilson, widow of Dr. E. A. Wilson, chief of the scientific staff.

The three children of the late Petty-Officer Evans and Mrs. Evans. They are: Muriel, aged five; Norman, aged seven; and Ralph, aged four.

Mrs. Evans, the widow of Petty-Officer Evans.

Mrs. Bowers, the mother of Lieutenant R. H. Bowers (Royal Indian Marine).

be back for another year.[543] Next year she will go south, Rome perhaps. She simply cannot endure another Scottish winter of uncertainty. Kathleen Scott may not have told her that on 27 October the previous year, Birdie revealed that he is glad that Captain Scott is 'letting me stay down here another year. I feel that I should enjoy several, though if I overdo it my Mater may have something to say on the subject.'[544]

LOIS – PORTSMOUTH

Adverts for the White Star Line are up all over Portsmouth. It is the hottest ticket in town. The mood is springlike, full of possibility. After all the hardship of the coal strike and the unemployment, the world's most luxurious liner has begun recruiting crew. Men have travelled from all over Britain to join the queues in Portsmouth and Southampton. The ship's arrival signals a welcome boom for local firms: Oatley and Watling are supplying crates of fresh fruit and vegetables, and F. G. Bealing's vast nursery at Highfield is providing 400 potted plants – trees, palms and ferns. They have also received an order for buttonhole flowers for every first-class passenger.

The *Titanic's* crew would only come on board a few hours before she sailed. They still have vacancies across all three departments: Deck, Engine and Victualling. The money will be good. The passenger lists are starry: socialites, suffragettes and sports stars. Even the lower-paid vittlers can expect hefty tips. Perhaps Lois and the family should go and watch this unsinkable monster leave for America? In the middle of the excitement, a telegram boy pedals along Chapel Street looking for No. 52.

CAROLINE – LONDON

Caroline spends £1.10/- on the London Telephone Service.[545] She cannot ask why Laurie has had to stay in Antarctica. Why Scott miscalculated the time it would take to make the return journey. Central News has sold different excerpts of Scott's expedition report to different newspapers. She will buy all the papers and piece the story together. Caroline has just been to see *Die Fledermaus* by Johann Strauss. In the opera, Eisenstein and his lawyer, Dr Blind, arrive fresh from a session in court arguing because Blind has bungled the court hearing and the prison time has been extended. Caroline is hoping that Scott is not a bungler. Her son's time under him has now been extended by a year.

3 APRIL 1912

ORIANA — LYTTLETON

The alarm clock rings at 3 a.m. Oriana rises and wakes her sister
Constance, who has come out to join her in New Zealand. There is a
hiss and the smell of sulphur as Ory lights a match. She touches the
flame to the methylated spirit in a stove beneath a tiny kettle. This
stove will only make two cups. The little flame throws vague human
shadows around the chilly room. The fuel runs out before the kettle
boils. They light some candles and set the kettle over them. The shadows
multiply with each new source of light.

Cradling their cups of tea in their hands, they hear footsteps on the
pavement outside. A soft knock at the door. The night watchman has
come to collect them. Together with Teddy's wife Hilda, they follow
him to the harbour, where a dirty streak rises from the chimney of a
tug. As soon as they motor out beyond the heads, they see the familiar
silhouette: 'the dear old ship coming in slowly, with a gorgeous red
sunrise behind her'.[546]

Sitting beside Hilda in the tug, Ory can see Teddy hobbling up to
the bridge of the *Terra Nova*. Even from a distance through the binoculars, he does not look well. His body is bloated, his Royal Navy coat
flapping open in the light breeze. He stumbles and sits. The women
board the boat and greet the crew. Teddy cannot stand for long without
fainting. Ory leaves Hilda and Teddy to a reunion bathed in the rose-
tinted sunrise.

The crew immediately tell Ory about her husband's Winter Journey
to collect the emperor penguin eggs in Cape Crozier. It is an unprecedented feat of human endurance, a true world first. They have three
eggs carefully wrapped in the hold to prove it. They also have Bill's
letters and journals. They have everything, in fact, apart from the man
himself, but Ory must be proud, very proud.

Teddy tells Ory that he last saw Bill on 4 January alive and well
and pulling strongly for the south. There is little doubt that party
of five would have made the South Pole. Ory can be pretty confident about that. He tells her that Bill was in a quandary about
going at all – he was concerned for Ory's health – he had apparently
told her that he would wait for news that she was well before he
set off.

Ory is suddenly deeply tired, but overwhelmed with relief. The letters she had sent south with the *Terra Nova* in December told Bill she was happy and well and quite prepared to wait another year: 'for by now I trust he is safely back in the hut enjoying all his letters & presents.' They sail back into Lyttleton over a pink sea as calm as silk. The dock is empty, as empty in fact as it was full when the *Terra Nova* left for Antarctica sixteen months earlier. It is proof that they have all managed to keep to the contracted twenty-four-hour news deal with Central News. The ship's arrival has been kept secret.

The autumn sun slants through the carriage windows of the 7.30 a.m. train back to Christchurch. Ory is sleepy – it was 'the longest morning I have ever spent'. Bill's letters sit on the seat beside her, the metallic scent of Antarctic ice seeping into the worn upholstery. She must read the journal first and copy out passages to keep her memory accurate. The journal has to be sent to London. Teddy and Hilda are due to take it by liner when he is sufficiently recovered. She must save those precious letters, forcing herself to read only a little at a time. They need to last her a year.

KATHLEEN – LONDON

Kathleen has the typesetter's proof of her husband's expedition report. She has been working on the manuscript, but she is experiencing a rare case of self-doubt: 'It is a difficult job, and not in my line. I find it very difficult being your wife. I hope none of my blunders will make indelible marks. I am quite a good mother, and a moderate sculptor; but beyond that I seem rather a failure.'[547]

She is trying to read the report with him, her pen in her right hand hovering over her diary to him, the sheaf of his words in her left hand. Like an alchemist, she must convert failure to success. Kathleen will not get Scott's letters to her for over a month, but she is glad that her husband will not come back in Amundsen's shadow. 'The more one reads,' Kathleen tells her husband, 'the more apparent the splendid achievement against awful odds appears, and the smaller the value of Amundsen's dash to beat you.'

She has tried to keep any mention of a race out of her communication with Nansen and the RGS, but somehow the newspaper terminology, to 'beat', seems to have leaked through her pen nib.

'I'm so glad, so very glad, you are staying another year. It would have been a thousand pities to return with such opportunities before you.'[548]

5 APRIL 1912

ORIANA — CHRISTCHURCH

Ory is 'quite annoyed' that some of her New Zealand friends have phoned to commiserate. 'I asked them if they had read the paper & they hadn't – so I told them that when they had done so – they would see why I was glad he had stayed South.'[549]

The excitement of the *Terra Nova*'s return has subsided and she is easily irritated by ignorance. How can these people pity her when Bill is one of the chosen five? Through gritted teeth she explained 'that I was so very proud of his work & to think that he had been chosen to go on the final journey to the Pole & that no one else in the world had ever done such a Winter Journey as those three men did'. She does not need their sympathy, Hilda does. 'I am so sorry for poor [Hilda] – it must be such a bitter blow to have her Teddy sent home ill, he is bad.' Hilda's husband has been invalided out of the picture – Bill is, if her New Zealand friends could be bothered to read the paper, centre stage.

Ory is determined not to give way to disappointment. She telegrams Westal: 'Last news from South Pole Plateau [Bill] absolutely fit exceedingly happy Ory.'[550] On the following day the *Cheltenham Echo* reports that their local hero Dr Edward Wilson was fit, happy and advancing. But Mary Agnes, Bill's mother, has a painful attack of nettle rash when she hears that her son is not coming home for another year. It is so bad that her doctor husband injects her with morphine. Ory knows that mind and body are connected. 'I shall feel very ill [next spring] for I shall know for a certainty that [Bill] will be coming unless anything has gone wrong . . .'[551]

There are two packets from Bill 'c/o Kinsey'. There is a fat envelope addressed to her, which Kinsey tells her is 'love letters'. He knows because Bill has warned him against opening them. But there is also a letter to Ory from Captain Scott:

Winter Quarters,
October 1st 1911

My dear Mrs Wilson,

As you will know before this reaches you we are in doubt as to the ability of the Southern Party to return to McMurdo Sound before the *Terra Nova* has to leave for New Zealand. Under these circumstances it has been decided to occupy this station for a second year. If things go as I expect I shall remain here and in that case your husband intends to stop unless his home letters recall him.

This letter is important only if you are robbed of your good man for a second year. I don't forget that it is for the second time and that it must be a heavy tax on your patience but I hope it will be some comfort to know how evidently this life here suits him from a physical point of view – I never saw him looking fitter than he does at this moment after the winter's darkness and one of the hardest sledge journeys on record . . .

Even to you I have no words to express all that he has been to me and to the expedition – the wisest of counsellors, the pleasantest of companions and the loyalist of friends.

In this time of doubt as to the future I have a sort of conviction that whatever happens your husband will come out sound and well and will benefit. If this letter fulfils its mission I trust it may help you to face circumstances with that same hopeful conviction,

With my warmest regards and wishes,
Yours sincerely,
R. Scott[552]

Herbert Ponting brings a box of photographs to show her. They lay them out on a table in Kinsey's shed at the townhouse in Warimoo, Christchurch. Ponting picks up a black-and-white image of three men standing side by side. The image is clear, taken with a flash outside the hut at midday but it might as well be midnight. Bill stands between Birdie on his right and Cherry on his left. To Ory it seems as if Bill is looking straight at her and he is smiling. The men look purposeful and healthy, well dressed in fur hats and mitts. This, Ponting tells her, is before the famous Winter Journey to Cape Crozier. He lifts another photograph from the box. This is after.

Three men sit around a table. Bill is, again, looking straight at the camera. His eyes are swollen, his face bearded. His index finger is thick and stiffly hooked through the handle of a mug from which steam rises, partly blurring his features. There are slabs of bread on a wooden board. He holds one piece in his left hand, a splodge of jam on the end. Birdie, sitting beside him, is entirely focused on his cocoa. Cherry seems to be holding his teeth in with his lips. The contrast between the two photographs, taken just a few weeks apart, is, Ory admits, 'quite painful to see'.[553] Ponting assures Ory that her husband recovered quickly. He and Birdie were the least affected. Perhaps it was the snow baths they took every morning when they were in the hut 'in a state of nature' that had somehow inured them to the worst effects of the cold. Bill is, Ponting assures her, a 'marvellous man made of piano wires! Not an ounce of superfluous flesh on him.' Ory is relieved to learn that when Bill first left for the South, he had 'weighed over 11 stone with nothing on!' Ponting is talking about her lover, a man whose nakedness she is familiar with. She remains scientific and talks weights and measures.

'You may be proud of your son,' Oriana writes to Mrs Cherry-Garrard, 'it seems as if they cannot do without him down South.'[554] This letter will not arrive until early May but Ory has already sent a telegram to Lamer.

> I am nearly bursting with pride in [Bill] . . . I am so thankful [he] has stayed South . . . and your son will come back with full honour and glory and if he has got through the really great dangers of a Winter Journey which no one else in the world has ever done . . . I think you may feel that God will keep him safe to do even more and better work.
>
> I think it is marvellous . . . I know that really they are every bit as safe down South as if they were at home – God is with them & no harm can come to them unless He wills it – Therefore we can all be peacefully happy & proud of our dear ones and look forward to a meeting next year.

CAROLINE – LONDON

Caroline has just become a grandmother to Erica Sheila Mary Ranalow. It is a welcome distraction from Antarctic affairs. Erica is not a son but they call Frederick 'Eric' and she is his firstborn. Caroline is not sure about the name – she spends £1.15.9 on 'frocks for Sheila'.[555] It is odd to make the transition from mother to grandmother in a moment, but Sheila is a substitute for Laurie and she receives the full force of Caroline's fierce love and protectiveness. She lavishes Lilian with flowers and Sheila with baby presents, and pays for a well-qualified nursery nurse to be installed at Lilian's home in Argyll Road, Kensington.

9 APRIL 1912

ORIANA – CHRISTCHURCH

Roald Amundsen stands in the beam of the lantern projector, looking up at the operator on the balcony. Ory blinks. In the flickering light she sees the long, lean figure and the picture of a penguin. Amundsen puts his hands on his hips. The projected image is upside down again. What is the operator doing up there?

The Christchurch Club on Latimer Square, founded by twelve gentleman farmers in 1856, is the city's venue of choice. Women are only admitted on special occasions. Kinsey has issued the invitation to his usual list – the guests that flutter in the breeze at his garden parties at Te Hau. They have all answered summons to 'play the game', acutely aware that Christchurch is Captain Scott's 'stronghold'. This lecture is a deliberate show of sportsmanship. Kinsey has taken great pains to ensure that there is no excuse for a repetition of the controversy that plagued the American counter-claimants of the North Pole, Robert Peary and Frederick Cook. He is determined to show that the British Empire is capable of being even-handed.

They sit quietly, waiting for the Norwegian explorer to resume his lecture, while up on the balustrade balcony, the projector clunks twice. Oriana is at the front between Lieutenant Harry Pennell, the man who captained the *Terra Nova* back from the Antarctic, and Mrs Kinsey. They sit patiently, willing the operator to competency. Is that the slight smell of burning? A double click and the hall is suddenly lit by the electric light without an image to filter the brightness. Is the projector operator deliberately trying to sabotage the lecture? Is he drunk or is this some misplaced attempt at solidarity with Scott's team? Amundsen's hands are deep in his pockets.

The lantern slide, when it appears finally, the correct way up, is dull.

The detail is blurred, the scene abstract and very like the last slide. There is the *Fram*, tied to the ice, but the sky looks unlikely, two ochre streaks bleeding in from the left like London smog. The 'smog' colours the top of the ice barrier. The pristine Antarctic seems streaked with pollution and the sea slicked with a sulphurous yellow. 'He showed bad slides.'[556]

Ory had steeled herself to endure this demonstration of sportsman-like behaviour, but now she feels herself sympathising – the audience are shuffling in their seats. 'Poor man he was very handicapped . . . the Operator at the lantern was apparently tipsy,' concludes Ory. 'It was appalling.' At the end of the travesty, Kinsey tries to rescue the situation with a summing-up speech but Amundsen wants out. He paces like wild animal in a trap and leaves by the back door, as soon as it is feasible to do so.

The crowd has dissipated by the time Amundsen re-emerges. The pavements are covered with leaves. Ory and Pennell have been instructed to 'cheer him up', to take him back to Warimoo. Like Bill, Amundsen does not appear to be capable of adjusting his speed to walk beside someone in a long skirt. Ory strides alongside, trying to distract him with science. What does he think the Ice Barrier is comprised of, precisely?

'For parts of his journey to the Pole the Ice barrier is on land as the Hypsometer registered 800 feet & they were apparently going up a gentle rise.' Apart from meteorological observations, which he claims were 'very interesting', it was the most he could tell her.

Ory concludes that there is nothing much to tell 'but his dash to the Pole'. She finds him 'quite pleasant but personally I am not prepossessed by him – & I don't think it is all prejudice!' The best thing about the encounter is his respect for Bill's Winter Journey. Anyone who can survive that, Amundsen assures her, can probably survive anything.

14 APRIL 1912

NORTH ATLANTIC

The *Titanic* strikes the iceberg shortly before midnight. But there is no need to panic, the ship is unsinkable. In order to be sure, the radio operator Jack Phillips depresses the ship-to-shore Morse transmitter again, spelling out 'CQD'. The band is playing on the upper deck while lifeboats are lowered into the sea on creaking pulleys.

15 APRIL 1912

LOIS – PORTSMOUTH

The early reports have been trickling in. Apparently, the *Titanic* met with an accident on her maiden voyage to New York and everyone on board has been saved. Family of crew members begin to gather outside the White Star Line offices in Canute Road, Southampton, hoping for confirmation that there are no casualties.

16 APRIL 1912

THE TIMES

April 16th 1912, 1.01 a.m. . . . An ocean disaster, unprecedented in history, has happened in the Atlantic. The White Star liner *Titanic*, on her maiden voyage, carrying nearly 2,400 people, has been lost near Cape Race, and according to the latest messages there is grave reason to fear that less than 700 of the passengers and crew have been saved. Early yesterday evening the messages gave no indication of a catastrophe of such terrible magnitude, but later they became more and more serious.

KATHLEEN – LONDON

The press have vanished from outside Buckingham Palace Road. The *Titanic* disaster has knocked 'Amundsen v Scott' right off the front pages. Kathleen knows that her friend Guglielmo Marconi has just sailed for New York. After some enquiries, she is relieved to hear that he took the RMS *Lusitania*. He had been offered a free passage on the *Titanic*, but he had some paperwork to do and preferred the company of the public stenographer aboard the *Lusitania* to Jack Phillips and Harold Bride, the radio operators posted to the *Titanic*.

The British wireless operator on nearby RMS *Carpathia* had noticed Marconi's distress signal: 'Seek You, Danger' 'CQD' among the twenty-four-hour chatter of social telegrams from the HMS *Titanic*. 'Those who have been saved, have been saved through one man, Mr. Marconi,' says Britain's post-master general, 'and his marvellous invention.' Kathleen remembers that Marconi had tried to persuade Scott to take one of his machines on the *Terra Nova*, but they were large, and space was limited. She has continued to see Marconi, a smooth Italian fascinated by women and science, and particularly fascinated by women who like science.

As Peter plays on the floor, Marconi talks Kathleen through the refraction of long-wave radiation in the ionosphere. Ships and light-houses can use this system, but it can only transmit messages for about 300 miles. Radio waves are invisible. Kathleen is not the only person who compares radiography to séance . . .

Earlier in the week Peter had walked to the front door as if someone were coming through it and raised his arms. Kathleen did not hear him say 'Daddy' but she had a guest who seemed to have got the impression he had. Kathleen is wary of Peter being used as a cipher for 'ghost work'. She dismisses the incident and hopes the guest will too.[557]

LOIS – PORTSMOUTH

All over Portsmouth, flags are flying at half mast. Many children are absent from school. At Northam School near the Southampton docks, 120 out of 250 pupils have lost their fathers. For one local man, Arthur May, and his son, also Arthur, it was the first time they had worked at sea together. Between them they are leaving two widows and eleven children. With so many breadwinners lost, hundreds of families will be plunged into poverty. Most seamen have no kind of insurance; their employment only lasts as long as they are on board ship.

23 APRIL 1912

DISCOVERY HUT, ANTARCTIC

It is dark in the *Discovery* hut, but during the daytime a trickle of twilight leaks through the only window. Cherry is hearing bells. There are no bells. The trip to One Ton nearly did for him. Now he 'hardly cared what happened'.[558] They cannot get back to the relative luxury of the Cape Evans hut until the sea ice freezes hard enough to take their weight. Besides, if they stay here, there is a chance that the Polar team will come in and they will be able to minister to them – water, food and warmth.

Dr Atkinson had already sent Teddy home with scurvy.* Now he is

---

* Teddy Evans was the only member on the expedition with a confirmed case of scurvy. He claimed to have 'subsisted all that time on a diet consisting almost wholly of pemmican' (*The Advertiser*, 18 May 1912, p. 20). Vitamin C wouldn't be isolated until 1928, but later Debenham observed: 'We did know that seal meat was a preventative [from getting scurvy], and only one member of our expedition got scurvy in severe form: Teddy Evans . . . Teddy really was a very naughty boy and wouldn't eat his seal

nursing Cherry. From his symptoms, Atch thinks Cherry must have strained his heart, but the lethargy and carelessness speak of dangerous depression.

Atch is morally certain that the Polar Party have perished, but that is only 'moral' certainty. They all know that two of the men out there have survived the Winter Journey. They go through the motions of their days chasing away the image of their frozen corpses swinging from harnesses in crevasses on the Beardmore. They will go south when the sun comes back at the end of August and try to find the bodies.

Suddenly both Cherry and Atch hear knocking at the window. Was that 'bells' or real?

'Hullo! Cherry, they're in,' Seaman Pat Keohane yells. 'Who's cook?'

They rush out of the door, hearts pounding. They stare out into empty darkness.

27 APRIL 1912

KATHLEEN – DOVER, ENGLAND

Kathleen watches the cloth. Behind her waves crash on the pebbles. Charles, or perhaps that charming footman she'd hired to model for him, stands behind that cloth with his hands behind his back, head forward. Charles was a tall man, very tall, and tall men have a tendency to stoop. He is not idealised in a classically heroic pose. There is no need for that. The bronze Charles looks intently across the English Channel to Sangatte.

The Duke of Argyll releases the string. Lady Llangattock, Charles's mother, lets out a loud sob. No one claps. The Pathé cameras whirr. Kathleen wills the woman to stop weeping. Does she want her grief to be so public, recorded for the world to see?

Kathleen does not know what it would be like to lose a son, but if she ever has to stand and watch a statue unveiled to Peter, she hopes she will not sob like that. Doesn't the woman understand that her son is now immortalised?[559]

On the way back to London in the motorcar, the duke is kind about the 'wonderful qualities' of Kathleen's statue, but she wonders whether he really understands her modernist approach.[560] The surface of the bronze

---

meat. It's not fishy, but it is black, and tastes like very poor steak, and the rest of us ate it.' (*Sydney Morning Herald*, 27 January 1959, p. 2, quoted in Turney, 2017, pp. 498–511)

is deliberately textured, no detail. It is just 'form expressing essence', as Rodin taught her – just the essence, the essential lion in the man.

MAY 1912

CAROLINE – GESTINGTHORPE

Caroline looks out of the window. Her study is directly under Laurie's bedroom. The view from the room where she conducts her morning's business has the same view as his bedroom except from a lower angle, and the letter she has in her hand was written from his view, but from a higher latitude, and in temperatures of 20 below. He has enclosed an order for clothes including '3 pairs drawers – medium' and '1 pair black shoes (brogues) size 10 with broadest toes'.[561] Why does he have to say 'medium', he is her son, she knows what size clothes he takes. And what is all this about 'broadest toes'? What is wrong with his feet? 'I wish I could see you for a week,' writes Laurie, '& then get back here.' Caroline's accounts book does not have space for the figure she would give to see him.

ORIANA – CHRISTCHURCH

In her thickest tweed suit from Fort Augustus days, with her winter coat wrapped around, Ory sits under the flagpole on Sumner Cliff at Te Hau – 'such glorious views all round of sea & sand dunes & snow mountains' – and looks south across the ocean. 'I think & hope that this time I shall keep well. I know it will be a long wait when all the present excitement has gone & the winter is coming on,' she tells Isabel Smith.

Ory would rather be at home, or at least to have somewhere she could be that was hers. Without Bill's expedition salary, she will not be able to afford hotels. She thinks of 'Oriana Hut' on 'Oriana Ridge' at Cape Crozier, christened by Bill on 16 July 1911 – 'a date not easily forgotten'.[562] If the journal is an official expedition document, does that make the entry Bill made on that day 'official'? Is there a ridge called after her in the Antarctic?

It is not clear when Ory first notices the planks piling up. Perhaps she sees the mules breathing hard as they drag the loaded carts up Sumner Hill. It is, Kinsey tells her, a kit hut. It is in fact the kit hut that Scott ordered as an observatory. It was taken to the Antarctic but returned 'surplus to requirements' and he has purchased it. Partly this is to allay the expedition debt and partly he hopes to make a 'comfortable little cottage and home' for her.[563] They could name it 'Uncle Bill's Cabin' – a play on Uncle Tom's cabin from the bestselling American novel.

Ory is moved beyond words by the generosity and kindness of this gesture. This will be their first ever home. She sits on the bench under the flag pole while Constance sews and reads out Evelyn Cherry-Garrard's letters describing spring at Lamer: 'It makes me rather homesick to have letters telling me about all the bulbs and fruit flowers coming out at home!' Ory tells her, but perhaps she can plant a garden, a rockery with the volcanic stone from Mount Erebus that has been brought back in the *Terra Nova* as ballast. And she would rather be here in Uncle Bill's Cabin than anywhere else but his hut at Cape Evans, down in the southern hemisphere. 'It is easier to realise here what they are going through in the Antarctic . . . and I like to think that my morning begins when theirs does and that we are hearing the Service read at the same time on Sundays and I know that really they are quite happy and busy all through the winter in spite of the dark and cold.'[564]

EMILY – BUTE

'Dear Mrs. Bowers.' Emily has just received Scott's letter, written in October the previous year. She has already received the news that Birdie will be staying an extra year, telegrammed from New Zealand, but the post comes by ship and this letter was written six months ago, before they left the hut. She is proud of her son's ability but not surprised:

[Birdie] Bowers is all and more than I ever expected of him. He is a positive treasure, absolutely trustworthy and prodigiously energetic. He is about the hardest man amongst us, and that is saying a good deal – nothing seems to hurt his tough little body and certainly no hardship daunts his spirit. [When Emily thinks of Birdie's letters peppered with the word 'manliness', she might agree that if this were a school subject report, Scott is awarding him full marks, maybe even the class prize.] I shall have a hundred little tales to tell you of his indefatigable zeal, his unselfishness, and his inextinguishable good humour. He surprises always, for his intelligence is of quite a high order and his memory for details most exceptional . . . He has such a happy knack of coming

through difficulties with a smiling face that I haven't any doubt
he will be as flourishing in health and spirits when you see him
next as he is while I write.
With kind regards,
Yours sincerely,
R. Scott'[565]

Emily has memorised Scott's letter – why the word 'surprise'? It is a
fine assessment, but a letter from Commander Pennell is even more
heartfelt: 'Of all the members who so envied him his position in [the
final five] there is not one who grudges it him, or who has not acknowledged his choice as being the most suitable.'[566]

In an effort to focus on pride rather than anxiety, Emily seeks activity.
The songbirds are singing up a storm in Skeoch Wood but they can
hardly be heard for the shrieks of bathers entering the sea on West
Bank. May sports a fashionable flannel shorts one-piece with a sailor
collar. For a matron of Emily's splendid dimensions, a serge costume
that will not float on the water or cling to the figure is appropriate: a
long, belted tunic with a high collar paired with mid-calf bloomers with
buttons, trimmings and ruches and, if desired, a hat. For the feet –
low-cut leather slippers, laced to the bottom of the bloomer. For Emily,
swimming is medicinal – a treatment for chronic rheumatism – for her
son, it is a joy. At least in the Antarctic she does not have to worry, as
she had when he was in the tropics, about sharks. But on receipt of his
letter about that lethal game of hopscotch with the killer whales snap-
ping at his heels, Emily now has to add them to the list of hazards.

Emily will not go too far, but it was in these very waters that Birdie
swam out to a Royal Naval vessel with a visiting card in his teeth. After
boarding the ship and presenting the card, he saluted and, running the
full length of the ship, dived off the end and was back home for breakfast. Emily misses scolding him into a hot bath. She would like to ask
how he liked the swallow-tailed sledging pennant she sewed to his
precise specifications. She would like to ask whether the woollen socks
May knitted are protecting his feet.

Emily makes a respectable round trip, returning to the beach. Bathing
is Rothesay's food and drink. In May the boarding houses and tourist
attractions are just building up for the onslaught. The pier will soon be

groaning under the strain of tourists, and Emily may have to take in paying guests herself. She has received notice that Captain Scott asked all the officers if they would forego their expedition salary to allow them to overwinter for a second year. Emily knows that she cannot stand another winter in Bute. She plans to go abroad, to Italy. She knows that her son will approve. 'I hope to goodness you won't look worn out, and ill when I come back,' Birdie wrote a decade before. 'I want to see you laughing and jolly, you understand.'[567] Her children could be so bossy – 'One would think I was a child or in my dotage & I am neither the one nor the other.'[568]

KATHLEEN – LONDON

With her husband's letter beside her, Kathleen braces herself for a letter to 'Mummy', as Hannah Scott insists on being called. She lists the assets Scott has signed over to the expedition: 'He has put all the moneys from whatever source (book, cinematograph, articles, photographs, lectures, stamps, newspaper news, etc.), all with no qualifications into the Antarctic Fund, and he is to cease to have an Antarctic salary – this I think is splendid.'[569]

Kathleen is fully aware that Scott's late father was an indolent bankrupt and that Captain Scott supports his mother and unmarried sisters. In the past, Scott's sisters have been obliged to stoop to 'trade', to nursing and discreet seamstress work to support themselves and their mother. Scott refuses to believe that his sisters have suffered: 'They have gained in a hundred points, not to mention appearance and smartness.'[570] Enforced leisure expected of eligible 'nice girls' led to boredom and torpor.

'Scott', Kathleen now tells Mummy, 'once said he believed one did one's best work when there was no question of financial gain.' 'I believe he was right,' she continues, 'and it gives me great pleasure to think that he [by which she means we, including Hannah] won't make anything out of it at all.' There was no way that Hannah could whine about her son's irresponsibility after the word-plinth Kathleen is constructing for him, or at least if she did, it would prove her unworthy of such a son. Kathleen does not tell Hannah that she is making £300 a year from her sculpture. She does not tell her that Scott disliked her having to sell her art for 'sordid gain'.[571]

'I have as you know,' Kathleen continues in an attempt to avoid anything sordid, 'known many men of many nations [her mother-in-law probably rather wishes she hadn't], but I think I have never met a man one can so wholly admire as your son. He astounds me.'

LOIS – PORTSMOUTH

Lois is on her way to the post office to draw her weekly allowance. She and her *Titanic*-widowed neighbours in Portsea follow the repercussions of the disaster in the news. Portsmouth and Southampton have suffered the heaviest losses, but around the world donations are flooding in. A relief fund has been set up, and gradually they realise that the widows might expect a dependable income for the first time in their lives. Not only that, but apprenticeships for their children.

Standing in the queue for the counter, she is reminded that there are still queues outside the White Star offices. Some employment records show dead crew as being 'discharged at sea'. A few men have survived. They are not eligible for the fund. Many plan to go straight back on the ships. They have no choice.

Lois reaches the end of the queue and requests her allowance as usual. The postmistress checks the account. There is no money. As Taff advised in similar circumstances: 'If you want to kick up a shindy, go on the upper deck and fight yourself!'[572] Lois does not want to 'kick up a shindy', she does not want to draw attention to herself, but she asks the postmistress to check. She checks. None.

Lois is already thrifty; what can she afford to do without? If she were working for that pencilled 'Shipwright' on the census form, she would not have to worry, but she does worry. Back in Gower it was more straightforward. As Lois's relative Wilf Beynon remembers it: 'No real poverty then. I have no recollections of ever being hungry.' In Gower you could 'put [in] a few manders and swedes – grind flour, bake the bread, kill a pig and live off the land. What [we] had besides, a bullock or two, sold to pay for clothes.'[573]

Even after the Penrice Estate and the teetotal Methodists had refused to renew the Ship Inn's licence, her father had kept the family going from his smallholding. But going home would be giving up, it would lead to questions and perhaps breach that confidentiality note Taff had enclosed with the stack of letters. Lois remembers Taff's proposal joke about the 'pizzend critter', the mate who 'kin kip yourself and help me a bit too'.

CAROLINE — LEEDS, ENGLAND

'There is a possibility that your son may not return to England this year,' wrote Scott in the letter Caroline has just received. 'Under these circumstances, I think you may be glad to have a word of him from a companion . . . We might have kept our ponies alive but we certainly should not have had them in such fit and promising condition for the journey to come.'[574] Caroline compares this with her son's assessment that they are 'the greatest lot of crocks', a fact that Scott still does not seem to accept.[575] 'Everything depends on the successful work of these [ponies],' Scott continues, 'and your son kindly took charge of them . . . besides personally leading the least tractable of them. To this really great service his welcome personality is a great addition. He has been and remains one of the most popular and cheery members of our small community.'[576]

The train draws into Hunslet. Laurie has obviously said nothing to betray his intense dislike, though Scott says: 'I realise how keen a soldier he is and that it will not do for him to drop out of the running.' Caroline knows that Laurie was fed up with the army, but now Laurie's concern for army promotion would be a legitimate excuse to leave. It is not one he has taken. Six months ago Scott assured her that 'He seems in excellent spirits and he is certainly in excellent health.' Is that still the case now?

Through the train window Caroline sees the railway works serving the Midlands Goods Station, and the printing works, both on Butterley Street, and beyond them the foundry on Meadow Street. Having roots in trade does not sit easily with Caroline's image as lady of the manor of Gestingthorpe. It is not something that she talks about outside the family. But it is important to be visible here, as it is in Gestingthorpe.

Following Willie's death, Caroline made frequent trips up to her in-laws in their stately home at Meanwoodside, but her roots are in Chapel Allerton and Hunslet, the 'workshop of Leeds'. Caroline's father, Joshua Buckton, described himself as 'Engineer – Machine Works' rather than 'Gentleman'. He established Buckton & Co. in 1842. A decade later he was employing 80 people, and a decade after that 190 men and 66 boys. Shortly after her marriage to Willie, Caroline's family business had incorporated as a limited company.

Caroline's father's foundry is an enormous shed covering three and a half acres of land. It echoes with the sound of machinery, the air heavy with the smell of oil and sweat. It was her father's idea to glaze most of the roof – this is not a dark Satanic mill, but a place filled with daylight, noise and pride. The sound of steam-driven tools, the hiss of water, the tooth-rattling bang of metal rams on metal sheets. The biggest non-transport machines in the British Empire, Caroline's late father had assured her, sported the green and gold 'J. Buckton & Co. Ltd Leeds' metal plate.

The National Insurance Act, passed the previous year, is a new system of health insurance for industrial workers based on contributions from employers like her. Lloyd George is just 'putting ourselves in this field on a level with Germany; we should not emulate them only in armaments.' It replaces the Poor Law, or Poor Relief, as they call it in traditional Gestingthorpe. Caroline, an 'employer', must be visible while the implications of the National Insurance are established among the Buckton & Co. workers. Laurie has the common touch – he is second generation – the Etonian confidence around 'the working man'. Caroline is financially secure but socially less so. Walking around the foundry in her long dress, Caroline would recognise the Crank Web Slotting Machine. She'd been ten when her father came home with the drawings, fine technical pictures in shaded pencil – here before her now in three dimensions and cold, hard metal. A sturdy square metal column of iron is bolted to the factory floor. This machine made Joshua's fortune. To him it was a great oak, the industrial equivalent of the Gainsborough oak in Essex. It is reliable, dependable, the sort of thing one might have one's portrait photograph taken against in the manner of Isambard Kingdom Brunel and his giant chain-link backdrop.

Returning to the station, Caroline glimpses dull-eyed men and women and miserably clad children down the side streets. She can comfort herself with the thought of her annual donations to Leeds-based Reverend A. Powys's 'The Poor Box'. Caroline straddles both worlds, the receding factories and the country of Meanwood opening out before the train window. If she were Mrs Andrews with the unfinished hands, Gainsborough would probably paint her accounts ledger onto her lap.

JUNE 1912

LOIS – PORTSMOUTH

28 October 1911

Dear Mrs Evans,

Although I have never met you, your husband told me a great deal about you so that I can imagine that you and the children will be wanting to see him home again next year, and will be very disappointed if he isn't able to come.

So I write to tell you that he is very well indeed, very strong and in very good condition. It is possible we may not finish our work this year, and in that case he will stop with me for a second season. If so you must try and remember that he is certain to be in the best of health and that it will be all the better when he does come home. When that time comes I hope he will get some good billet and not have to leave you again. He is such an old friend of mine, and has done so well on this Expedition that he deserves all I can do for him. So I must hope you won't be anxious or worried.

Yours sincerely,
R. Scott[577]

Scott's letter is accompanied by fifty letters that Taff wrote over the winter. A letter a week from a busy man? It shows impressive commitment to his role as husband and father. Putting food on the table is normally the man's role. What is Taff eating in the Antarctic? If Teddy has scurvy, does Taff too? Harry Pennell has written separately to reassure Lois: 'This case was very exceptional – as he was the only one of the main party out sledging just before they started, and so was on sledging rations while all the others (including your husband) were on fresh food in the hut . . . The last reports of your husband are that he was in the very best of health and spirits, and I heartily congratulate you.'[578]

Lois's job is to keep Taff's family in the same state, 'the very best of health and spirits', but how? One could always live off the wealth of the land and sea in Gower. But how could she stave off real poverty in Portsmouth?

Before Miss Talbot of Penrice Castle declined to renew the licence in order to counter drunkenness in the village, the Beynons brewed their own beer. In Portsmouth the bench that grants public house licences refuses to entertain applications from married women because the family rather than business should be their concern. But what about married women whose husbands' expeditions have run out of funds but who still need to buy their growing children new boots?

Lois may have become a singer, but it seems that for the moment her singing was focused in the choir at St Mark's, Portsmouth, where Muriel was christened. When Taff is home, he loves the music halls. Perhaps Lois could work at the theatre? Portsmouth's largest and most modern theatre, the New Vaudeville, is just finishing an epic run of Charles Dickens. Should she take to the stage like the impoverished theatrical family the Crummells in *Nicholas Nickleby*, said to be based upon a troupe that had visited Portsmouth in Dickens's youth?

Lois does not want to give away the extent of her financial distress. If she isn't able to work in a pub, perhaps she can work in the corsetry business, sewing at home while minding Ralph. She knows that some women feed their children laudanum to keep them quiet while they sew; some even supplement these legitimate wages with prostitution.

Perhaps she will go back to Gower for the summer and help with the harvest on Taff's older brother Charlie's farm at Singleton or her cousin Will Tucker's at Pitton Cross?

If Taff comes back with the Pole, things will improve.

'Do you think the South Pole will ever be reached?' an interviewer from the *Cambrian Daily Leader* asked Taff back in 1904.[579]

'No. It would take an expedition four years to deposit stores and another couple of years to get over the mountains if ever they do. I believe it's all land at the Pole and no open sea as has been suggested.'

In the backyard of Chapel Street in the summer sun, Lois pegs out the washing in the knowledge that Taff probably has a fair idea whether it is land or sea at the South Pole now. She looks forward to welcoming him home. Not 'a frozen pinched and anaemic derelict from the Pole', but, as the columnist from the *Cambrian* once described him, a man who would 'fill the little house completely, and his health and strength radiated from every pore of his burly frame'.

22 JUNE 1912, MIDWINTER'S DAY

ANTARCTIC

Another headache. 'It is of some scientific interest to be a living blizzometer,' writes Cherry, 'but I wouldn't recommend it even to my enemies, if there are any about.'[580] He is less concerned about his enemies than his friends. Two of the best he has ever made, Bill and Birdie, are still out there somewhere. The bunk above his is empty, as is the one diagonally across. Where Birdie had yawned, 'Morning, Farmer – how's the hay?' and Oates had delivered his crushing replies, there was now a loud silence and yawning space. Cherry knows he isn't alone. Deb feels that the scenery has lost its beauty: 'Auroras are cheap and the cold rather colder.' And yet Dr Atkinson is keeping them to a routine. They put up the remaining flags as bunting for the midwinter day's feast and they plaster on smiles for a menu that includes 'charlotte russe glace à la Beardmore'.[581]

26 JULY 1912

KATHLEEN – LONDON

There are rumours that Bonar Law is boiling for a fight. On Monday he will declare Prime Minister Asquith's cabinet to be 'a revolutionary committee'.[582] Kathleen knows she is just one of Asquith's 'harem'; at least that is how Mrs Asquith describes the intelligent women that her husband seeks out between parliamentary sessions. Unlike some of them, Kathleen doesn't even have the encumbrance of a husband around. It seems that 174 Buckingham Palace Road has become a refuge for Asquith, and, since she doesn't approve of alcohol, from his tendency to use that as a refuge instead. (Peter immediately christens the newcomer 'Squiff'.)

When they first met at a lunch back in February, Kathleen found the prime minister to be 'extraordinarily pleasant'.[583] Now, as she removes the damp cloth from the clay on top of her sculpture table, she tells Mr Asquith that she is still working on Captain Scott's journals, typing them up. It is a man's business – not really in her line. The maquette is a three-dimensional sketch done as Asquith paces the room. She presses her thumbs in to warm the clay, trying to capture his off-duty face rather than his dispatch-box oratorical. His grey hair is swept to the right. He wears a wing collar, dark tie and waistcoat.

Asquith exhales smoke and taps his ash into the ashtray provided. What has she been doing with herself since they last met, a few days before? Kathleen tells him that she has been to the Women's National Anti-Suffrage League demonstration at the Albert Hall. Several people were carried out kicking. She knows that suffragettes have thrown a hatchet at the prime minister. They are 'brutes'.[584] Imagine giving people like that the right to vote. It is preposterous.

Kathleen needs to raise funds for her husband's expedition but she does not want to ruin her relationship with Asquith by begging. Had he heard that Lord Curzon, newly elected as president of the RGS, is in the process of purchasing Lowther Lodge from the Speaker? Asquith knows of the building, a Norman Shaw-designed villa on the corner of Kensington Gore, near the Albert Hall. The Society can spend a small fortune on a new headquarters after giving Scott a paltry £500 towards the expedition to which it has attached its reputation. By September, Keltie writes to Scott that the Council have guaranteed an additional £1,000.[585]

Asquith's brain works fast – he assesses the other 'Knights of your Tea Table'. It turns out that Fridtjof Nansen 'thought of writing to *The Times* in answer to [Lord] Curzon's criticism of Amundsen'. Kathleen 'wrote him an earnest appeal to do nothing of the sort, as it would only be the signal for the overflowing of pent-up feelings and the very type of controversy one must at all costs avoid'.[586]

Kathleen is determined to finish her bust of Asquith before she leaves for New Zealand to welcome her husband home. Asquith sits in her studio with her other busts, her other 'men'. On a wooden shelf there is one particularly curious sculpture. A thick finger of wet clay rises from a wooden board; there is a slight kink in the middle of it. What is that? Kathleen tells him that, since he asks, it is a false nose she is making for Nigel Playfair for his part in Arthur Wing Pinero's new play. 'You see I do anything from false noses to Prime Ministers.'[587]

17

Campo Santo

KATHLEEN – NORFOLK, ENGLAND

Kathleen feels the thrill of wavelets caressing her ankles, the sound of pebbles rattling under the receding wave. Perhaps she is wasting her life, her youthful body, her fertility: 'When one is young one is always preparing and waiting for the unknown, unguessed great happenings, which – never come . . . Oh dear me!' she tells Scott in her diary: 'How I hope you will come back next year.'[588] The waves are breaking against her thighs. The shorts of her woollen swimming costume are becoming heavy with seawater. She sinks into the cold embrace and pushes off into a strong crawl.

Once Kathleen had focused on sex as a means to an end – 'a father for my son' – but it's not just about procreation for her anymore. Scott always claimed that it was the women who kept 'the sex question' in the forefront – of course it was, agreed Kathleen – 'it is their life, however intellectual they are'.[589] It is the women who have the babies. In the case of an 'affair à outrance', it is the woman who has to pray that her period comes on the day that she has written in her diary that she is expecting it. No amount of intellectual thought can influence the situation. Kathleen prefers to look at the thing scientifically, like Marie Stopes.

'If a swimmer comes to a sandy beach when the tide is out and the waves have receded,' Marie Stopes wrote, 'does he, baulked of his bathe, angrily call the sea "capricious"?' Kathleen knows Stopes's theory of 'sex tides'. When a woman's 'sex tide' was at its highest level: 'With an ardent man, wholly devoted to his wife and long deprived of her,' Stopes maintains, 'the time will come when it will be sufficient for him to be near her and caress her for relief to take place without any physical connection.'[590] Kathleen turns for home.

At that moment her husband could not be further from her, but his name has brought a delectable pride of lions – Nansen, Asquith, Marconi – to her door.

Kathleen enjoys splashing about in the waves with Peter, but when she swims out this deeply, he and his nurse stay safely on the shore. Kathleen battles with her desires, which, she supposes, must be natural. She loves her son, she would like to have more. 'I wonder if I am not permanently maiming myself by denying myself a baby.'[591] But unfaithful thoughts are surely followed by 'a punishment' (generally a headache the next day, so no great disaster).[592]

Kathleen receives a telegram signed by the expedition secretary Francis Drake. One of the *Terra Nova* sailors, Lead Stoker Robert Brissenden, has drowned during routine hydrographical work in New Zealand. Kathleen must inform the family.

Shortly thereafter, the motorcar in which Kathleen and Drake are sitting draws up to a small house near Sandwich. A boy of about seven is playing in the garden. '[Scott] dear, it was just terrible! We told [Mrs Brissenden's] mother as best we could and told her to tell her daughter, but she dare not, and so eventually I had to. She was a dear, quiet little woman with a fine boy . . . I don't suppose anybody could have felt her blow more poignantly than I, but I doubt if my sympathy was any help.' Kathleen had tried to break the news directly, as she would like it. It was an accident. Kathleen has no details. 'It seems so terrible to descend on her gay, neat little house, to drop a bombshell like that, and depart.' The boy was still playing in the garden as they drove away.[593]

27 AUGUST 1912

ANTARCTIC

Cherry packs Bill's and Birdie's possessions into wooden boxes, listing the contents as he goes in one of his slim hardback notebooks. When he has finished, he nails down the lids.[594]

20 SEPTEMBER 1912

LOIS – GOWER

All morning small groups of men and animals have walked from farms over Gower, heading for the castellated towers of Penrice Castle. Miss Talbot has put up £300 of prize money. The competition is fierce.

Sarah Evans wears her good Welsh lace cap, and Lois, her bolero jacket. 'I suppose you saw plenty of Lois and the children while they were home,' Taff says, 'I expect Lois had a job to get them back to school when she got back.'[595] School has started but the Gower Show is an exception and they are all ready to enjoy the hospitality of the estate owner, Miss Talbot, in spite of her position on the license for the Ship Inn.

For the last month there have been advertisements for the Gaumont Company films, *With Captain Scott, R.N. to the South Pole*. Part I will be released in ten days' time on 30 September with 1,500 feet of film, and Part II on 14 October. It is billed as 'The Greatest Attraction of the Day'. Taff is the Gower superstar and his young family move around the show in his reflected glory. If Miss Talbot approaches, Mr Beynon would doff his cap. Lois's father takes Taff's role as spokesperson. His son-in-law is, he always says, 'a fine boy . . . a good husband and a good son to his old mother'.[596]

Taff's older brother Charlie is a high-profile farmer in the family. He is good with animals, but he is not a writer: 'I had a letter from Charlie today,' Taff said, '– quite a spasm for him, wasn't it?'[597] Lois is private and proud, and unlikely to disclose the full details of her financial situation to Sarah and Charlie. The Gower Show is a welcome distraction from financial anxieties. Apart from prizes, after the long strenuous days of harvest, the Show offers relaxation, entertainment and food. By mid-morning the delicious smell of spit-roasting lamb and pork drifts across the show ground to where Lois's brothers, Enoch and Stanley, are showing the fabled 'Gower Princess'. They have been offered over 120 guineas for the Princess. It is a lot of money but they have refused it, preferring to put her in foal rather than sell their golden goose.

There are many ways to make money. In one letter to Lois, Taff described the Antarctic: 'Not a sign of life, no bird to speak of, only a melancholy seal to look at, and his blessed hide not worth a cent in a European market.' When Taff first came back from the Antarctic in 1904, he was wary of people making money out his 'hide'. One interviewer quoted him saying, 'By the way, this isn't a patent medicine advertisement, is it?' Showing the Gower Princess in the ring under Penrice Castle is a way of increasing her value. It is better than the bad old days of wrecking. They all know the story of the girl from the Ship Inn: Kate, like Lois, was the publican's daughter of the Ship Inn. Her job was to carry the lantern that ignited false flares to lure unsuspecting ships onto the rocks so the wreckers could plunder their cargo. Kate set alight a warning beacon instead. Before he died, a local man told the then rector that he had struck Kate with his boathook and flung her body over the cliff. The Beynons aren't wreckers but there are no local families without a few secrets in their cellars. Even their own Reverend Lucas's relatives were involved in smuggling at Port Eynon and Culver Hole. But now Lois's family are involved in rescuing. Lois and Taff grew up playing around the small shed that houses the Rhossili Life Rocket with its lines and breech buoys for attending shipwrecks around Worms Head.

Lois walks into 52 Chapel Street after a summer harvesting in Gower, to be greeted by a letter. It is addressed in a curious loose hand in thick black pen. The address takes up most of the envelope. The stamp has been franked in Sandwich in Kent on 19 August 1912.

My dear Mrs Evans,

Captain Scott has sent his diary back from the Antarctic & I think you will be glad to hear how well he speaks throughout it of your husband & his work. Apparently he has made himself more than useful, he has worked so hard & so willingly through every sort of difficulty – & finally been chosen to go on to the Pole.

I am sure you will like to hear how indispensable he has made himself to Captain Scott & how fit and hardworking & thorough he has been. My husband asked me to tell you how splendid he has been.
Sincerely yours

Kathleen Scott[598]

30 SEPTEMBER 1912

EMILY – LONDON

Emily, May and Edie have come to London for the 'The Greatest Attraction of the Day', the premiere of *With Captain Scott, R.N. to the*

South Pole. As the relatives gather for the luncheon before the screening, they might meet Teddy. Teddy was the last person to see their sons and husbands. Having recovered fully from scurvy, Teddy has been promoted from lieutenant to commander and been given an audience with the king.

Emily realises that Birdie is just three years younger than Teddy and that both trained on HMS *Worcester*. Perhaps Birdie will be promoted as Teddy has been – a change in status and salary, and the financial security for Birdie to 'keep a wife'.

From his letters home, Emily knows what Birdie thinks of the other wives. An Antarctic lunch is the perfect opportunity to see whether she agrees with her son's opinion. Is Oriana 'without a particle of frivolity'? Is Hilda the perfect image of a 'womanly woman'? Does Kathleen's presence precipitate 'an awkward silence'?[599] What kind of wife will Birdie choose? Lilian Oates, Caroline's daughter, arrives fresh from the fashionable London tailors and milliners. She has a new outfit and a new 'Madame Emile' hat for every occasion. Lilian is the kind of client that Emily's family would have nurtured as a secure way of putting bread on the table.

Caroline Oates and Emily are separated by a generation from the wives, but lunch gatherings offer an opportunity to exchange letters; Emily might tell Caroline about Oates giving Birdie the 'wink' to persuade Scott to take linseed pony meal. Caroline might tell Emily that their sons are planning another trip after this one, to the Amazon perhaps.

Birdie had not asked for his mother's approval before he applied for a place on the expedition – neither had Laurie. Sometimes Emily marvelled at her son's thoughtlessness, but she knew it was not intended to hurt her: 'I have great sympathy with the thoughtlessness of sailors, being the wife of one & the mother of another.'[600] Caroline hopes that, with a sailor and a solider between them, the Antarctic is at least safer than war – at that moment, war is looking likely but she is curiously reticent on Germany. Emily agrees with her son: 'No they don't love us,'[601] but May is a linguist and, ironically, German comes naturally to her. Birdie joked that he couldn't think how 'unless you have been gargling a lot lately'.[602]

Caroline might change the subject from 'gargling' Germans to ask

if Emily is in touch with Oriana in New Zealand. Oriana had come to
Gestingthorpe a year before and they'd discussed what was best to send
south with the *Terra Nova*. Since their boys would be coming straight
back with the ship, there was no point sending 'many things'. 'I am
sending one or two books and also the weekly *Times* from June,' offers
Oriana from New Zealand, along with 'letters and photographs! . . .
Only six months more now – but oh, they do go slowly. Still everything
comes to an end sooner or later.'[603]

Caroline and Emily find they have a great deal in common, not least
an interest in education: Emily is a professional educationalist, Caroline
owns a school. Caroline and Emily will become friends for life, but for
the moment they brace themselves for the reality of their sons on
screen.

Wives and mothers at the Antarctic lunch all agree that 'March
will be the worst month of all. When every telephone ring will
make one jump to the conclusion there is news of the *Terra Nova*.
It makes one feel quite sick with excitement & anticipation to think
of it even & what it will be when the month is really here I can't
imagine.'

8 OCTOBER 1912

KATHLEEN – LONDON

The tiny theatre of Gaumont Company holds only twenty-four
people. Kathleen has invited guests strategically: 'Very elect indeed!!!'
she tells her husband. 'I'll tell you who they were & will you please
say I'm a good wife.'[604] Kathleen's success in being the 'nice little
wife' has been mixed, but she is triumphant as she reels out the guest
list to Scott: 'There was Lord Curzon & Prince Louis of Battenberg
& his Princess & his son . . . [Kathleen makes no mention of the fact
that Battenberg's German loyalties mean his reputation is in the
descendent] & Sir Francis and Lady Bridgeman & Sir George & Lady
Egerton [Sir George is the admiral in charge of HMS *Vernon*, the
torpedo school where Scott and Taff had trained] & Mrs McKenna
(an excitement in the House of Commons prevented Mr McKenna
[Reginald McKenna, home secretary and future chancellor] & Winston
Churchill [First Lord of the Admiralty] coming, the latter sent a nice
telegram) & Sir Henry Clissold & Gertrude Bell & Leonard Darwin

& Mr Longstaff & Willy and Ettie [Scott's sister and her husband] & the Baroness Erlenger & Sir Henry Galway & Admiral Parry Cust and Mr Newell and Peter!!'

It would not have been possible to squeeze a greater concentration of admirals into a room smaller than the Gaumont private cinema. Whatever Admiral Poore and his wife said about lunching wives, there is surely no better route to one's husband's promotion. 'Don't you think that was a nice party,' Kathleen asks Scott, '& everybody was so thrilled. They [the films] are the most wonderful thing I ever saw, the ones in the tent are so splendid.' The pictures in the tent appeal to Kathleen because of their reality. Like her sculptures, they seem to bring out the essential elements of the expedition, and Scott's laughter assures her that – at least when this footage was taken – Scott was not victim of a black mood.

'Sir George Egerton was so excited he could scarcely contain himself, & Prince Louis hopped about & asked questions.' Moving pictures are still such a new technology they make princes hop. 'I got Ponting to come & introduced him to everyone & made a great fuss of him.' Kathleen knows that quite apart from Ponting, the admirals and hopping princes, it is Peter that interests Scott most: 'It was really lovely, & Peter was so adorable & sensible. He said "the motor sledge" – can't imagine how he knew.'

It was unconventional to have three-year-old Peter up so late, but he thrilled everyone halfway through the film by pointing to the screen and saying, 'That's my Daddy.' The evening finished at 11.30 but Kathleen kept him close. She tells her husband that Peter looks fitter than ever, 'apparently he is like his mother & thrives on dissipation.'

Having built him up so high, she feels that it is finally safe to mention the unmentionable – Amundsen.

Lambie dear, there is another thing I want to impress upon you [she has never called him Lambie in writing before]. I don't know whether you have just heard the Amundsen news or whether you learnt it at the Pole (neither bear thinking of) but I want to tell you with six months knowledge of it upon one that it matters very, very little – so far less than one thought at first – indeed in some respects it has done good for it has laid great stress on the

differences of the two ventures & the greater scientific importance
of yours is percolating in to the public mind . . . I don't think it
has made a scrap of difference.

Kathleen is determined that Scott must be grand, not reduced by petty
jealousy. She tells him that where the chief aim is being the first, men
do not generally apprise others of their intentions. 'You are not going
to let the little Amundsen pin prick (upon my word it's no more) worry
you, are you?'

Her stance on Amundsen's silence is justified or at least understand-
able. Kathleen uses reductive nouns like 'scrap' and 'pin prick'. She
hopes that, like a lump of clay, it is just something that requires cutting
down to size. But she has called the South Pole 'a little thing to be
done' before – it worked in so far as it convinced her husband to go
'and leave no stone unturned', but has it actually reduced the enormity
of the task itself? It is the best she can do to save him from himself.
'Don't ever be sad, my darling.' It was an order, not a suggestion.
Kathleen believes sadness a contaminant. She demands happiness,
hedonism, elation: 'Oh my darling, how I love you and long to talk
with you and know that you are content.'

As she draws her letter to a close, she longs for the physical presence
of her husband – the cinema version has brought him tantalisingly
close: 'To see your little face in the Cinematograph last night, almost
like a stranger after all these years, and your dear toes when you took
off your socks, then to feel that in a few short months!'

18 OCTOBER 1912

CAROLINE – LONDON

Four days after the premiere of Part II, Caroline buys a return ticket
from Sudbury to Liverpool Street and a ticket for a matinee screening
at the Coliseum. Her son does not feature much in the film, according
to Ponting. Perhaps it is just as well. When Caroline met Lieutenant
– now Commander – Teddy at the Antarctic lunches, she learned her
son is referred to as 'The Farmer'. Apparently a seaman, P.O. Taff
Evans, 'had words' with some visitors to the wharf in Lyttleton when
they refused to believe that someone so scruffy could possibly be a
gentleman. Perhaps Kathleen has already mentioned the 'indescribable

hat' Caroline's son wore to the Christchurch races when the obvious uniform was a topper? Laurie's downward mobility is at least consistent with the character she knows. She will smarten him up. The clothes she'd sent out from Derry & Tom's would be leaving New Zealand on the *Terra Nova* in December.

Caroline likes photographs – she has just commissioned a society portrait photographer, to take her granddaughter's baby likeness. She has also had a rather 'Gibson Girl' portrait taken of herself, a girlish, swaying 'S' shape from the top of her parasol to the bottom of her new chiffon gown. On Oriana's recommendation, she's commissioned the portrait artist Alfred Soord to paint her likeness, but she now wonders whether she shouldn't have chosen an artist prepared to idealise. She has seen the portrait photographs of Laurie that Ponting has taken and ordered copies. There is the vaguely respectable Captain Oates of mid-winter's day and the rather grimier flash photography in the stables.

The train from Sudbury to London cost 16 shillings and sixpence and the theatre tickets just over £1. Caroline wants to be anonymous but is obliged to turn up in style. She hires a motorcar and chauffeur for the day to transport her to and from St Martin's Lane, as she would if this was a proper theatre show. (What kind of hat does one wear to a cinema show?) The motor and driver cost more than the theatre tickets, but arriving in a common cab would, for Caroline, have been as bad as arriving without one's corset or, at the very least, one's hat.

What would Laurie make of all the show, the advertising, the organ music, the 'fuss'? There is a hush before an announcement: '*With Captain Scott, R.N. to the South Pole*, Part II'. The lights go down. A hush settles.

'I recall a remark made by Captain Scott at the time,' Ponting later wrote. 'He turned to the others and said, "What fun it will be when we are home and see this at the cinema."'

EMILY – LONDON

In the Picture House, the credits roll, the lights go up, the audience rustle and stand up. Just for a moment, Birdie has been in the same room, walking and talking across the great white projection screen. Emily, Edie and May all know that Ponting's film, all 1,500 feet of it, is designed to make them feel as if they have actually been there, and it has succeeded. They have.

Emily tries to appreciate the educational potential of the film. It is strange that the tent sequence, which must have been shot the previous year, suggests that Scott selected the four of the five men in advance. Does Caroline mind that her son was not included? When had Scott decided to add Oates, or Laurie, as Caroline calls him? All she knows is that while it is wonderful to see Birdie, it is also very difficult to watch the son she last saw over two years earlier with anything approaching objective academic detachment. Birdie looks cheery and healthy. The men in the tent look happy, content, purposeful, and yet it is a world of dangers that she cannot share.

Emily has booked serviced apartments at Whitehall until she must head back up north to Bute. She is looking forward to going to stay with friends in Rome for the winter, but when she returns, she hopes Caroline will visit her in Rothesay. And when she does, Emily writes to her friend: 'Be sure you remind me to show you [Birdie's] collection of butterflies and moths . . . finished in Ceylon about four years ago.'[605]

If only their sons could have walked right out of the cinema screen, Laurie might take his hat off; Birdie would sweep Emily clean off her feet. It is an image almost too painful to imagine.

END OF OCTOBER 1912

ANTARCTIC

Twelve men set off from Cape Evans. They have dogs and the new Indian mules brought down with the *Terra Nova*. They are prepared to go to the Beardmore if necessary to haul up those bodies that have been twisting and turning, dangling all winter in the fissures in their minds.

15 NOVEMBER 1912

KATHLEEN – LONDON

Kathleen creeps into the back of the Queen's Hall with Sir Matthew Nathan, a friend and long-time admirer, leading the way. It is dark and stuffy in the top gallery as they take their seats at the very back. She's sent back her council ticket for Roald Amundsen's lecture on principle – she cannot afford to be recognised, but how could she possibly miss this?

On the platform, Kathleen can see Lord Curzon – even the name sends her into the ditty: 'My name is George Nathaniel Curzon, I am a most superior person.'[606] Looking down from her eyrie, she sees that Curzon has thinning hair, a preposterously round head and looks better with the hefty, befurred robes of office conferring weight and gravitas. She knows that he has recently taken up with a mistress, the racy novelist Elinor Glyn. Ms Glyn caught his attention, and that of all the males of London's clubland, with her description of sex on a tiger skin in her banned 1907 novel *Three Weeks*. Curzon, having read it, presented her with a gift of a tiger-skin rug, by way of an invitation. Now Curzon's face is the expressionless mask of his class.

Scott Keltie, the moustachioed RGS secretary, is fiercely loyal to Captain Scott and is very sensitive about Amundsen. He is employed to be the voice of diplomacy but tells Scott that 'there is certainly a considerable feeling in the country against Amundsen, and his Norwegian friends realise that and have some sort of fear that this may find expression at these meetings.' The RGS cannot refuse Amundsen (though they have taken the Queen's Hall rather than the Albert), because the RGS gave the man a grant of £100 for his reported 'Arctic expedition' – an iniquitous link which comes with an obligation to provide him with this lecture opportunity.

This is the same dais from which, two years earlier, Elgar conducted his Violin Concerto premiere. Amundsen's premiere does not require an orchestra, he can play an audience. Many people, he tells them, ask what is the use of trying to get to the South Pole. He pauses. 'Little minds,' he says, 'have only room for thoughts of bread & butter.'[607] The Queen's Hall is flattered. They do not, self-evidently, have little minds, or they would not be here. It is a clever tactic of Amundsen's in a potentially hostile environment.

Kathleen is aware of the angry letters that have flashed between the RGS and Amundsen's 'Norwegian friends', as Keltie tactfully refers to Nansen. Kathleen has been treading carefully to offend neither, but even Curzon, via Darwin, seeks her permission to 'dine at the Norwegian embassy' these days. Nansen has, with Kathleen's knowledge, encouraged Amundsen to come. If Nansen and Kathleen can be 'noble' and 'sportsmanlike' in their praise of the winner, surely so too can the establishment.

Kathleen takes mental notes for Scott's benefit: '[Amundsen] did not mention you except just to say you were at McMurdo Sound.'[608]

She can see that beside Curzon on the stage is Leonard Darwin, balding, with white hair and a luxuriant moustache under his pince-nez, and beside him, Sir Ernest Shackleton. Kathleen knows Shackleton loves a platform. It is difficult to stomach his self-satisfaction – if the South Pole is not to be his, at least it is not Scott's.

Kathleen thinks Amundsen's speech 'dull and of a dullness!' But the Queen's Hall is full and the applause 'moderately enthusiastic'. Curzon gives the closing address and, Kathleen is pleased to note, '[he] was very decent and paid a goodly tribute to you'. She does not mention that Curzon asked for three cheers 'for the dogs' while patting the air as if to say, 'There, there' in Amundsen's direction.[609] Is Curzon's patronising, not to say disparaging, toast clumsy or brilliant? Either way, Amundsen seems suddenly unsettled. The audience titters. Kathleen leaves quickly by the back door before the house lights give her away.

'I do not think that it is likely,' writes Scott Keltie after the lecture, 'that there will be any further recognition of Amundsen.'[610]

NOVEMBER 1912

ORIANA – PEEL FOREST

It is a sunny day in early summer and the collies are working the flock into the shearing pens. There is the reek of lanolin, urine and droppings, and the persistent cacophony of bleating. But the Dennistouns are right, it is proper southern hemisphere entertainment. It is a show of skill with the atmosphere of a country fair. 'I heard of a man shearing 160 sheep by hand in a day!' says Ory. 'And another shears 240 by machinery in a day. One and a half minutes for each sheep.'[611]

The shear buzzes like a bored bee, the metal clippers blur at the end of the shear where the combs cross and recross. To start with, shears were cranked by hand but the introduction of electricity means that only the shearer is required to do hard physical work. 'The country life out here is so much nicer than the town life,' says Ory. Town life 'seems very small in some ways. There are no big things to take people's attention off little everyday gossipy things.'

Ory has been rationing Bill's letters, reading them slowly to make them last, to make 'him' last. In the last one, he talked about gossip in the Antarctic, though the traffic is only one way: 'My goodness! I had hours of it yesterday; as though I was a bucket, it was poured into me . . . it's a very great thing to know what is going on in the minds of everyone here . . . Grievances there are bound to be and disagreements, but as long as everyone can keep them from boiling over.' Keeping the peace is the job he feels he was sent by God to do. 'I think having a wife who is all the world and all the next world too to me, makes it impossible for me to want another person to confide in . . . Be assured I am content to feel that I was really wanted here after all, as you assured me I was and would be when we parted . . . I feel I am here for some better purpose than to merely get to the Pole.'[612] Ory's role is to be the bucket into which he pours his bucket, and as she leans over the fence watching the shearing, she is aware that even though she is not beside him, her role is essential. She is still his 'U.H.'.

HILDA EVANS – CHRISTCHURCH

Hilda prefers town life, or at least, Christchurch society. In Christchurch she is 'somebody', her father is a wealthy and influential man. Hilda has just heard that Kathleen Scott intends to come out to Christchurch to meet the *Terra Nova* the following spring. Their relationship has not improved since the 'blood and hair' of Dunedin in 1910. Both Hilda and Ory are in touch with Caroline: 'I do wish you were coming,' says Hilda, 'instead of that horrid Mrs Scott.'[613]

12 NOVEMBER 1912

ROSS ICE SHELF

It is six o'clock in the morning when the glaciologist Charles Wright's sledge swerves sharply right – the Indian mules kick up a cloud of drift that powders the air. Wright points to a snow-covered mound to the right of last year's track. He and Cherry walk nearer. The others join them. The men are silent. The dogs and mules shuffle and whinny in the snow. 'It's the tent,' says Wright.

A man breaks away from the group and, leaning against the top of the mound, brushes the snow away with a fur mitt. Under the snow is green canvas. They all recognise the flap of the tent ventilator. There is utter silence. It is as if they have walked into a cathedral and found themselves with their hats on.

I must own I shed a few tears [writes Petty Officer Thomas Williamson] and I know the others did the same, it came as a great shock to us all, although we knew full well for months past that we should meet with this sort of thing everyone seemed dumfounded [sic] . . . we just stood there wondering what awful secrets the tent held.[614]

Who is in that tent? Are they all there, all five? Or none of them. Perhaps they have already walked over the snow-covered bodies of their former teammates on their way to this point where the tent is pitched.

Dr Atkinson takes charge. They clear the tent's funnel entrance. Together with Petty Officer Williamson, Atkinson drops to his knees and crawls up the funnel. The tent has been pitched well but the entrance is shut from the inside, and since it is covered in snow it is too dark to see anything. They retreat. The snow is cleared from the canvas. They crouch down and crawl back in.

Inside the tent it is a 'ghastly sight', says Williamson, 'those sleeping bags with frozen bodies in them. The one in the middle I recognised as Capt. Scott . . . the other two bodies I did not see, nor did I care to.'

Atkinson orders every man to go into the tent to witness the scene inside. 'All gastsly [sic], says Gran the Norwegian in halting English. 'I will never forget it so long I live – a horrible nightmare could not have shown more horror than this.'[615] Scott is in the middle, half out of his bag. Birdie is on one side, his sleeping bag over his head. Scott's face is a frozen mask of agony. His arm is flung out across Bill. 'The frost had made the skin yellow & transparent & I've never seen anything worse in my life. [Scott] seems to have struggled hard in the moment of death, while the two others seem to have gone off in a kind of sleep.'

Birdie lies on Scott's left, his bag zipped over his head. Their skin is translucent, the colour of parchment but mottled with frostbite. Everything is tidy. Cherry unbuckles Bill's watch from his wrist to give to his widow.

Gran wonders whether Amundsen and his Norwegians have suffered a similar fate. Suddenly, there is a noise like the report of a gun shattering the silence. The men look at each other. From inside the tent, Atkinson tells them that it was not a gun. He had to lift Scott's arm to retrieve the diaries. It snapped off in his hand with a loud crack.

They find everything following Birdie's carefully written instructions: the diaries, letters, film and even 35 lb of rock specimens dragged hundreds of miles from the Beardmore. In the front of Scott's diary is an instruction for the finder to read the diaries, then bring them home. The men pitch tents, and Cherry and Atch share one. 'Hour after hour it seemed to me,' Cherry later wrote, 'Atkinson sat in our tent and read . . . When he had the outline, we all gathered together and he read to us the 'Message to the Public' and the account of Oates's death, which Scott had expressly wished to be known.'[616] The diaries must now be taken back to base, sealed with wax and presented to the relatives.

Twelve bareheaded men stand in a circle outside the tent, their balaclavas folded in their hands in spite of temperatures of minus 20. Atch reads the burial service from Bill's prayer book. They leave a record: 'November 12, 1912, Latitude 79 degrees, 50 minutes South'. They collapse the tent canvas over the bodies and build a 12-foot snow cairn over them. Gran has just learned that Amundsen beat Scott to the Pole. He offers his skis to make a cross on the top of the cairn. In their place he takes Scott's skis and fastens them to his feet. Whatever happens, these skis will complete the journey.

'I do not know how long we were there,' Cherry wrote later, 'but when all was finished . . . it was midnight of some day.'[617]

They do not find Oates's body, but build another cairn in his memory with a small cross and a record: 'Hereabouts died a very gallant gentleman.' Taff is too far south to reach.

DECEMBER 1912

LOIS – PORTSMOUTH

Will Tucker walks down Chapel Street, his breath clouding the air. His walk is uneven, he limps, an old injury – but at least he has kept the leg unlike his uncle, Taff's father, whose leg was amputated below the knee. In his leather jerkin, knee-length trousers and leather chaps, Will Tucker stands out as a landsman. There are those who go to sea, his

uncle, Taff and Stanley Beynon, and there are those like Taff's brother
Charlie Evans and himself who make their living from the land. He is
one of the Tuckers of Pitton Cross Farm and he is here to see how
cousin Lois is doing.

Chapel Street seems to be full of public houses. Lois must feel at
home. In the early morning there is the clinking of glass bottles as the
landlords clear up after the night before. Men in dark navy blue overalls and flat caps emerge from the houses either side and pause to cup
their hands around short pipes before walking west towards the docks.
Will walks up to the door of No. 52 and knocks. He has not seen Lois
since harvest. She has always been the most beautiful woman in Gower.
Last time he saw her she was tanned and laughing, her children playing
with his around the hayricks.

Lois opens the door. Will tries not to be shocked by her appearance.
She welcomes him in and shows him Taff's letters – fifty of them. The
envelopes are thick, with the *Terra Nova* crest on the back and a plump
New Zealandia descending from her plinth on the dark pink stamp.
Lois's clothes hang on her frame.

Will can see that the house is a good size, six rooms. There is a nail
over the mantelpiece with the faint trace of a light patch where a round
object, like a large coin perhaps, used to hang above a smoky fire. Lois
begins to get Norman and Muriel ready for school. Will tells her that
she is coming home with him. They are all coming with him. They
will get the next train back to Gower. She will live with him and his
daughter Lily at Pitton Cross Farm until Taff comes home. It is not a
suggestion.

NEW YEAR'S DAY 1913

ORIANA – RANGITATA, NEW ZEALAND

The countryside around Rangitata is becoming familiar now, and in
midsummer they motor to picnic at local beauty spots, having a 'really
delightful time'. Ory has spent Christmas with her sister Constance
and the Dennistouns in Peel Forest. On the first day of the New Year,
1913, she writes to Cherry's mother Evelyn, telling her not to send
money for a cable from her with the expedition news because Cherry
will be back and able to send one himself.

'Isn't it lovely to be able to say "this year" now – I do hope they will

all get back & will not be stopped by ice – or any further big journey,'
Ory tells Evelyn.[618] 'I try to be prepared for every eventuality.' She thinks
Cherry will probably go back the quick way across Canada or America
and have a quiet reunion at Lamer rather than the kind of reunion
that followed the *Discovery*'s return in 1904 – 'one continual rush &
feting & there is not much satisfaction in that'.

When Bill comes back they can retreat to Uncle Bill's Cabin in
Sumner for a few days' privacy before the 'rush & feting'. She is looking
forward to showing him their first home. Ory has made curtains, framed
Bill's watercolours and hung them on the walls. They can climb to the
platform on the roof for sunsets or sit on the bench in the garden
under the Kinseys' flagpole, spotting gulls.

11 JANUARY 1913

KATHLEEN – NEW YORK, USA

Kathleen waits for the lift as it begins clanking down to reach her floor.
She has sailed to New York, from where she will cross America and
set off for New Zealand across the Pacific from California. She is determined to make the most of the journey – not to repeat the same old
route of 1910, when she and Scott went out together via the Cape and
Australia. Now Kathleen stands by the lift with her friend Adolf
Hofbauer ('You remember my French painter'), who has just picked
her up from the Colony Club.

Asquith had come to see her before she sailed for New York. An
admiral arrived while he was there and said: 'I am sure Mr Asquith will
see that your man gets a Peerage.' It still made her wince. It reduced
her relationship with the prime minister to something tawdry, to social
climbing. 'I hated it.' The worst of it was that Asquith doubted her:
'Oh!' he said, '– do you think that would meet the case?'[619] Even the
flowers and free Marconigrams that Guglielmo Marconi showered her
with as her ship left Liverpool have done nothing to lift her spirits.

Now in New York with Hofbauer, she seeks oblivion or at least
distraction. The lift is descending in the shaft. It clanks alarmingly like
the sound of a liner that has just hit an iceberg. The *Titanic* is fresh in
all their minds – Kathleen is reading a book on the disaster by way of
ensuring uneventful Atlantic, and then Pacific, crossings. Soon she will
be going up to the top of one of the highest skyscrapers in Manhattan.

At the top is a conference room, halfway down, Martin's, 'a sort of Maxims's', a nightclub Hofbauer assures her has a reputation for that kind of 'improper dancing' he knows she loves.[620] They are on Liberty Street, New York, after all.

The lift door opens. The bellboy clicks open the metal gate and steps out. A man arrives and, tipping his hat to Kathleen, asks the bellboy for the conference room at the top. Kathleen knows that face, that luxuriant moustache. It is the face of the man who claims to have been first to the North Pole. The RGS commissioned her to produce a portrait to be rendered on the obverse side of their Arctic medal. She was pregnant with Peter at the time. It was four years ago. With luck, he may not remember her.

'Mrs Scott,' he says.

Automatically, she introduces Robert Peary to Hofbauer, 'a friend of mine from Paris', and braces for the inevitable pity and platitudes. The bellboy presses the button for Martin's and the lift begins to ascend. Peary looks confused.

Why is she getting out at Martin's?

Isn't it obvious? She wants to dance.

To dance?

To dance.

Peary looks from Hofbauer to Kathleen. What is going on? Surely this woman is not going dancing with a single man 'from Paris' on the eve of her husband's return? The lift door clanks. In the cramped space, Kathleen is forced to tip her head back. Peary is tall. She blusters.

But 'apparently', Kathleen later told Scott in her diary, '[Peary] was going to a supper to Amundsen upstairs and I didn't understand that he didn't understand that I wasn't, so we were rather muddled.'

The lift jerks to a halt. The door opens to loud music. Peary is telling her that she must look in on them. Kathleen rushes past the bellboy into Martin's and straight onto the dance floor. What is the opposite of serendipity? Is the whole building booby trapped with polar explorers? Kathleen dances herself to distraction, knowing as she does so, that the Norwegian nettle must be grasped. Kathleen takes the lift up to the Amundsen banquet. Flushed from dancing, she enters the victorious lion's den. The men turn around at their banquet table, stumbling to their feet to greet her awkwardly. Who is less pleased to see whom?

The Norwegian Minister is placed between Amundsen and Peary. Getting home at 2 a.m., she tells her diary-husband that the whole lugubrious gathering was even duller than that 'dull and of a dullness!' lecture in London.[621]

18 JANUARY 1913

ANTARCTIC

The sear of the floe against the greenheart sheathing that protects the *Terra Nova* is, for Teddy at least, the ice-hissing sound of the Antarctic sea. The ship has waited from April to November in New Zealand safely away from the sea ice. Now the ice is thawing, Teddy will be bringing the ship south to Cape Evans to bring the expedition team home. After recovering from scurvy, Teddy had sailed with Hilda to England for the summer, where he met the king and was promoted to the rank of commander. The *Terra Nova* is scrubbed and cleaned, yards squared, ropes hauled taut and neatly coiled down, and best Jacks and Ensigns hoisted in gala fashion. Even the figurehead has been tied up, ready to meet Captain Scott. Aboard the ship, the men have prepared a feast, the table in the wardroom now decked with flags and silk ribbons. Letters are done up in neat packets for each member and champagne is chilled, chocolates, cigarettes, cigars all placed in readiness.

Through binoculars they see men running around on the beach. The shore party give three cheers, echoed by those on board.

'Is everyone well?' shouts Teddy through the ship's megaphone. On the shore there is a stillness, a moment's hesitation.

'The Southern Party reached the South Pole on 17 January, last year,' is the shout back, 'but were all lost on the return journey – we have their records.'

On the shore, on the boat, nobody moves. The silence is broken by the splash of an anchor, followed by the rattle of its heavy chain.

28 JANUARY 1913

KATHLEEN – DIAMOND BOX RANCH, CALIFORNIA, USA

The sun is low in the sky. They are looking for a suitable place to set up camp although, Kathleen notices, they have brought no tents. She has come across America from New York. Diamond Box Ranch could not be further from Martin's if it tried. Surely there are no polar explorers here. There are just five cowboys, Frank, Tim, Walk, Mack and Win, who hold their horses back as she passes through the gate with her eiderdown tied to the back of her saddle. It is obviously 'ladies first'. She rides through on her horse, sitting astride, holding the reins loosely in her right hand, as the cowboys do. There is the smell of cattle, the herds driven before them, lowing and jostling for position.

After sunset, her horse, hobbled, grazes quietly beside the rug they have laid out for her on the ground. Frank hangs a lantern up in the tree. Beside her is a calf's ear, blood congealing furthest from the tip where it was severed from the animal. It is a trophy, a gift, a chivalrous gesture from the cowboys after roping and branding calves that afternoon. As Kathleen scrapes stewed corn off a plate with her metal spoon around the campfire, she tells the men about riding in the engine of the train via New Orleans and El Paso, 'rushing through the prairies . . . at 120 kilometres an hour . . . throwing off with the cow catcher any cattle that were too slow getting off the line'.[622] Kathleen wanted to ride on the cowcatcher, but the train driver thought she'd be killed by a flying cow.

The cowboys tell her she should just 'stay right here with us and make your old man come and fetch you'. She is tempted. The cowboys in their leather chaps and belts with guns, are 'such darlings'. That night she sleeps, still in her divided skirt, under the stars as the horses stamp and the cowboys snore. Her eiderdown, one of Scott's, gathers frost as the stars sparkle.

10 NOVEMBER 1910

QUEEN'S HALL, LONDON

On the manuscript of his score, just after cue 53, Elgar has written a new metronome mark as the pace quickens for the central part of the Andante. This is the heart of the concerto, the enshrined soul of '. . . . .'. Elgar has told his wife that he would like the five-bar 'nobilmente' to be inscribed on his tombstone.

Fritz Kreisler is playing out the Andante's narrative section. He is approaching that impassioned crescendo, leading to the climax that closes the second movement. But the character of the piece is one of restraint. He must play with a kind of reckless passion, yet all the while keeping to an even beat – tick, tock, tick, tock, tick, tock . . .

18

'They Must Be the First to Hear'

10 FEBRUARY 1913

OAMARU, NEW ZEALAND

It is midnight and in the moonless dark, the *Terra Nova* lies at anchor off Oamaru harbour. The men are summoned below decks – Teddy, as second-in-command, is now in charge. He is about to read out the telegram he has composed. The telegram will be sent from Oamaru to the Central News Agency in London in the morning. As the major sponsor, CNA has exclusive rights to distribution of expedition news for the first twenty-four hours. The expedition is in considerable debt. It is in their interests not to jeopardise that contract.

As the crew emerge onto the *Terra Nova*'s blacked-out deck, a beam of light sweeps across it. It is the Oamaru lighthouse. The message, in Morse code, reads: 'What ship?' Another beam of light and the Morse question is repeated. Should they respond?

At 1.30 a.m. the dark bulk of the *Terra Nova* slides nearer the land and cuts its engines. A dinghy is lowered on creaking pulleys and three men scramble down a rope ladder. One of them takes the oars. The boat moves off, pulling steadily towards the wharf on the south side of the harbour, Sumpter Wharf. As they get nearer, a voice demands that they identify themselves. Tying up, two men in seaboots climb the wooden ladder to find the night watchman, Neil McKinnon, standing at the top. McKinnon is expecting the arrival of the *Ngatoro*. Who are they? Why have they ignored his signals? He could arrest them. The two men are escorted to McKinnon's hut. He telephones the harbour master, Captain James Ramsey who says he will meet them on Arun Street. The men identify themselves to Ramsey and the port's medical officer, Dr Alexander Douglas, but swear them both to secrecy. Tom Crean, who rowed them to the wharf, has returned to the *Terra Nova*. They can hear the ship's engine start up. It will sail northeast and hide over the horizon, out of sight of land.

ORIANA – DUNEDIN

Seventy miles to the south, Oriana Wilson wakes. She is staying at Vernard, a guest of William and May Moore. Outside, day is just dawning and she hovers in the liminal place before full consciousness. Suddenly she has a strong sense of the presence of her husband. She is fully awake. She sits up and looks around the turreted bedroom in the dim light. 'I felt [Bill] so near . . . & wondered whether he was specially thinking of me.'[623] But it isn't an anniversary, when she knows he thinks of her. Why can she feel him so near?

OAMARU

At 9 a.m. a ship, the *Ngatoro*, drops anchor outside the harbour and reports that it passed what it thinks was the *Terra Nova* sailing north.

The two men in seaboots leave the harbour master's house, where they have spent the night on the floor. At the Postal and Telegraph Office in Oamaru, they explain to the cable operator that the information they are about to give him to send is sensitive.

> Captain Scott reached the South Pole on 18 January last year. The party was overwhelmed in a blizzard on the return journey, and Captain Scott and the entire Southern Party perished.[624]

After he has sent the message, they ask whether he will kindly agree to be confined to his room for the rest of the day.[625]

The two men walk out of the office in the direction of the station. Instead of waiting there for the train, they settle down to wait on the grass verge beside the track. The grass is green and luxuriant, the sun is warm. They are back in civilisation, home.

Some of the *Ngatoro*'s crew who saw the *Terra Nova* have come ashore. Rumours have begun. The telegraph lines between Oamaru and Christchurch begin buzzing but the Oamaru telegraph operator on the early shift is strangely absent.

CHRISTCHURCH

At Kinsey's shipping office in Christchurch to the north, he tells journalists that he has heard nothing concerning the arrival of the *Terra Nova* beyond the news that the papers have received: 'You know as much as I do,' he tells them. The journalists are confident that 'When the return party left [Captain Scott] on January 3rd, he still had five men and large supplies of food, quite sufficient to take him to the Pole and back again to the depots. If he covered only 8 miles a day he would do it easily but as a matter of fact he was doing 15.'[626] Perhaps they are back so early because Scott has had enough of the ice and snow. And who can blame him!

OAMARU

When the Christchurch Express leaves Oamaru station for Christchurch, two men in seaboots emerge from beside the track and climb aboard.

RANGITATA

A reporter from the *Ashburton Guardian* is sent to catch the Christchurch Express at Rangitata. When he finds the two men in a carriage he questions them. One replies that his orders are to say nothing. 'Don't mind you asking,' he says, 'those are your orders. Ours are to say nothing.'[627] But the rumour starts. None of the passengers are entirely sure what Captain Scott looks like, except from photographs in the newspapers two years earlier. With an Antarctic beard, it would be difficult to recognise anyone. The report goes out that two men have landed, 'supposed to be Captain Scott and one of his officers'.

ASHBURTON, NEW ZEALAND

In Ashburton, Hugo Friedlander, Chairman of the Lyttleton Harbour Board, confronts the two men. They do not give their names or purpose, but smile and talk animatedly. Friedlander later concludes that 'from their cheerfulness and the buoyancy of their spirits, it may have been readily concluded that [Scott had been first] to the Pole'.

CHRISTCHURCH

It is late afternoon when the two men arrive at Christchurch. A press man from the *New Zealand Times* who has been sent to cover the story notices that they have only small bags for luggage. One of them turns slightly round and the reporter recognises Lieutenant Pennell, who has spent a lot of time in New Zealand, as he was in charge of taking the *Terra Nova* to and from the Antarctic with fresh supplies.

'You know,' Pennell explains to the reporter, 'the only man who can give you any information is Captain Scott.' The reporter asks Pennell if the other man who is now walking through one of the exits into the street and hailing a taxi is Captain Scott. 'I can't even tell you that,' says Pennell. 'As I said before, Captain Scott is the only one who can tell you the story, and I can only tell you this: that Captain Scott has arranged to supply an account of the expedition to the New Zealand papers.'

'When?' asks the reporter.

The other man has got into the back seat of the taxi. Pennell stands patiently shaking his head in a manner that signifies there will be no reply, before climbing in and being driven away.

Kinsey is at his town house on Papanui Road when Pennell and Atkinson knock on the door. They hand over a British Antarctic Expedition embossed envelope with Kinsey's name on it. It is from Teddy.

'At Sea' 10 February 1913

My Dear Mr Kinsey,

Pennell and Atkinson are bringing the Central News Telegram. I know you will find things run smoothly this way from what you told me before we sailed. I will bring the ship in on Wednesday . . . I hate bringing home such bad news, but however disastrous the end of the Southern Party was, the nation's heart will swell with pride at the heroism displayed . . . I have written to all the relatives of the Southern Party that I know of. I am very worried about poor Mrs Wilson. I feel somehow that the blow to her will be far worse than to the others. Mrs Scott has her son, but Uncle Bill was all the world to his wife. The shock to us has been very great but every member will strive to end the expedition in a manner that will reflect to the lasting credit of Scott & [Bill] particularly.[628]

Kinsey sends a short cable with the full names of those lost before sending the report. 'This information [is] intended for bereaved relatives and friends.'[629]

The services must contact the relatives of their respective servicemen. Pennell and Atkinson are Royal Navy officers. Their telegram to the Admiralty reads: 'Regret report deaths of Captain Scott and Edgar Evans, petty officer first class O.N. 160,225 29th March and 17th February 1912 respectively.'[630] They must do the same to the War Office for Oates and the Royal Indian Marine for Birdie. A general suffix to be included with each of the five notifications reads: 'Members wish to express deepest sympathy in your sad loss. Commander [Teddy] Evans.'[631]

Kinsey suspects that this action will be 'hotly resented by a certain section of the press', but he is quite prepared to accept the responsibility.

Lieutenant Pennell wants to tell Mrs Wilson in person. Kinsey tells him that Oriana is staying with his daughter May in Dunedin. Like the rest of them, she is not expecting the ship back until March or even early April.

LONDON

The day has just dawned in London at the Central News Agency offices on 5 Bridge Street. The street runs from Fleet Street where all major newspaper offices are based, down to the icy Thames. The nerve centre of Central News is the Private Telegram Room. Here the telegram officers work through the twenty-four hours in shifts. The telegram officer on duty sits facing the wall. He wears large metal headphones. Above his desk of indexed drawers, there are wall-mounted black wooden boxes with minutely indexed dials. On the wall beside the dials is a world map showing the principal intercontinental cables and radio transmitters. The ticker-tape machine is in the middle of the room with a wooden table to itself. As the telegram officer works, the machine behind him springs to life. The ticker tape begins spewing out. The message contains the word 'Hereward', the code for Scott's expedition.

The telegram officer alerts the director John Gennings who composes a telegram to Kinsey demanding the full word quota. The reply is almost immediate.

NEW ZEALAND

[To Gennings] I shall telegraph message tomorrow morning in one section only, consisting of 2,500 words. Calamity explains brevity. Telegraph instructions immediately with regard to Australian Press Association. Kinsey.[632]

LONDON

[To Kinsey] Replying to your telegram. Telegraph immediately nature of calamity, whatever occurred. Will be disastrous our contract if you do not cable at least 7,000 words, other papers will obtain fuller account on arrival of *Terra Nova*. Imperative you should prevent leakage until you have telegraphed fullest. Insertion of 2,500 entirely inadequate. Gennings.

NEW ZEALAND

[To Gennings] Regret unable to increase cable. Surely this contains enough sensation without describing distressing details. Feelings of friends and relatives must be considered. Kinsey.

LONDON

[To Kinsey] Quite appreciate your feelings but must emphasise we owe paramount duty public and also memory Scott. He would have sent us last year scientific details etc. In addition to personal details. Earnestly request you do the same. Must have text of Scott's diary continuing account from last year to the disaster. Scott would have desired this. If you do not personally feel equal to the undertaking make arrangements admit our correspondent Drummond Times Christchurch aboard, and ensure him twelve hours start with information procurable by him. Gennings.

DUNEDIN

They are just finishing dinner at May Moore's house in Dunedin. The summer days are so long that it is still light. Oriana is particularly weary because she woke before dawn with a strong sense of Bill's presence. In the hall the telephone rings. May takes the call. It is her father Joseph Kinsey on the other end of the line. The operator at the exchange in Dunedin has put the call through, but both May and her father know that sometimes they are 'overheard'. The line between Christchurch and

Dunedin thrums with wind in the wires, but the message is clear. May's houseguest must take the first train north to Christchurch in the morning.

LONDON

[To Kinsey, Christchurch] Your silence inexplicable. Please reply immediately to our telegram of this morning. Where is ship? Gennings.

ROYAL GEOGRAPHICAL SOCIETY – LONDON

Sitting in the secretary's office at the Royal Geographic in Lowther Lodge just off Hyde Park, Scott Keltie is writing a letter. He has just received a call from the Central News Agency with the news that the ship is back. Nothing more. Lord Curzon, who has taken over the presidency from Sir Clements Markham, is pleading sick at Montacute House in Somerset. It is all very well that Scott has returned to New Zealand, but the first group of sixteen women are to join the Fellowship tonight. Since Curzon is pleading sick (he doesn't object to the 'guineas' that these globetrotters will contribute, but he does not feel inclined to endorse the spectacle with his presence), it is up to Keltie to stage manage this seismic shift.

10 February 1913

Dear Lord Curzon,

I see in *The Times* this morning that you are laid up and won't be able to be at the House of Lords for some time. If this is so I trust there is nothing serious . . . The Central News has telephoned to me that Scott has arrived in New Zealand, at Wellington. They are the agents for his Press communications. There are no details as yet but there may be in the afternoon. I propose to cable Scott in your name as follows if the further communications justify it: 'Warmest congratulation on success of great expedition. Cable when arrive England. Invite lecture Albert Hall' signed by you as President. This will go at half rate if we agree to the delay of a few hours. Nobody expected him for another month at least . . .

There will be 16 ladies elected [to the RGS] today, with 9 men making a total of 25; there will be 16 ladies proposed with 12 men, making a total of 28 in all. I am cutting off Mrs Weinberg's

name. I am sorry Miss Sykes won't join . . . You might return the
cards with the addresses I sent you when convenient.

Keltie[633]

NEW ZEALAND

[To Gennings CNA London] Regret must decline inspect or take
extracts of sacred diaries belonging to those perished without instructions from Speyer [the expedition's treasurer] Evans concurs. Fullstop.
Hope to be able to telegraph few further particulars tomorrow [11
February] morning, but your proposal with regard to Drummond
quite impracticable. I am anxious to assist every reasonable way, but
while endeavouring to serve public I must regard memory of Scott.
Ship arrived this morning. Kinsey.[634]

LONDON

Sir Edgar Speyer and his wife Leonora are well into their morning
routine in 44–46 Grosvenor Street, Mayfair. Speyer breakfasts in
the morning room in 44, while his wife goes through her scales on
her violin in the music room in 46. A uniformed servant brings in a
telegram on a silver tray. It is from New Zealand, from Joseph Kinsey.
Has Scott returned?

[To Sir Edgar Speyer] Central News are making unfair and impracticable suggestions to me in order to obtain certain news. I would
like you to understand that Evans and I are alive to necessity
carrying out agreement and we will do everything reasonable
assist them. Stop. Ship arrived this morning. Kinsey.

Owing to the secrecy of the situation, Gennings might choose to
take a cab round to Speyer's mansion in Mayfair rather than discuss
the matter over the telephone. Gennings and Speyer are in the same
time zone, the same country and on the same page. Gennings tells
Speyer that he understands the expedition is badly in debt. Gennings
will only honour his side of the contract if Speyer gets Kinsey and
Evans to honour theirs. Speyer is a successful financier. He is used to
tough negotiations.

NEW ZEALAND

Teddy's report is encoded into the 'Hereward' cipher before being sent to CNA, London.

> From [Lieutenant Evans], of the *Terra Nova*, Christchurch, NZ, Monday – Captain Scott reached the South Pole on January 18 of last year, and there found the Norwegian tent and records. On their return [a word here is indecipherable] the Southern Party perished. Scott, Wilson, and Bowers died from exposure and want during a blizzard about March 29 when 11 miles from 'One Ton Depot', or 155 miles from the base at Cape Evans. Oates died from exposure on March 17. Seaman [Taff] Edgar Evans died from concussion of the brain on February 17. The health of the remaining members of the expedition is excellent. (Signed) [Teddy] ERG Evans, Lieutenant RN.[635]

All of them are concerned that the speed of reception on the ground cannot match the accelerating new technology. Pennell is determined to tell Oriana Wilson himself. But Kinsey knows from his exchange with Gennings that they cannot hold off the newspapers for long – three more hours perhaps?

LONDON

Gennings phones the RGS, a courtesy call. In Curzon's absence, the call is put through to his deputy, Douglas Freshfield. Freshfield is deeply shocked. Scott Keltie told Curzon that Scott had arrived back to New Zealand. What can have happened? 'No Arctic or Antarctic party was . . . ever sent out better equipped.'[636]

MONTACUTE HOUSE, SOMERSET, ENGLAND

Lord Curzon receives a telegram sent from Freshfield to Montacute House in Somerset, where he is 'laid up' with Elinor Glyn. After reading it he immediately realises that he is too far away from the action. Damn the women. He does not want history to be made without him. He tells Freshfield to summon a meeting for which he will telegram a speech. He, personally, will make sure that the king is informed.

LONDON

In the House of Commons, Winston Churchill, the First Lord of the Admiralty, has received Teddy's telegram. Churchill has to explain to MPs that the government has no further information about the disaster.

At his offices in the Strand, Guglielmo Marconi is still working on increasing the range of his radio transmitters, but progress is frustratingly slow. In confidence, he is asked whether he can contact Kathleen Scott. In order to do that, Marconi would need to know when she left San Francisco. What route is she taking to New Zealand? What is the name of her boat? What kind of boat is it and what type of radio equipment does it carry?

The last message has caused a sensation in the CNA office. Inside the newsroom, men in three-piece suits sit behind their wooden desks. 'Want'. 'Exposure'. 'Concussion'. All excellent headline words. In a separate room, the telegram office, the operators sit silently, waiting at their machines. They have been told that the 2,500 words will come in one section. This is what they have been trained for. Gennings paces his office. He has left it to the last-minute-deadline print time for the 10 February London evening papers. They now have over 100 words, still nothing approaching the 8,000 they are due, but the agency cannot sit on such an explosive story and wait for the official report to arrive while their rivals swarm over New Zealand, hoping to steal an exclusive. They must start making worldwide distribution deals with what they have.

Finally, 2,487 words of pure newspaper gold begin spewing out of the ticker-tape printer over the telegram operator's desk. This is the exclusive report the newsmen have been waiting for, even if it is over 5,000 words short. They have twenty-four hours – but when do the twenty-four hours start from? Now or from when they got the first 31-word message? The editor summons an extraordinary meeting. This agency was founded in 1863 and on its 50th anniversary it has been offered the most valuable news exclusive in the world. There is frenzied activity in the newsroom.

MONTACUTE HOUSE, SOMERSET

Curzon is just finishing an intimate dinner with Elinor when he is presented with a telegram by his butler. It was handed in at 7.30, received half an hour later, but has arrived at Montacute House at 9 p.m. It is from Buckingham Palace:

Earl Curzon

I am deeply grieved to hear the very sad news which you give me of the loss of Captain Scott and of his party just when we were hoping shortly to welcome them home on the return from their great and arduous undertaking. I heartily sympathise with the RGS in the loss to science and discovery through the death of these gallant explorers. Please send me any further particulars.

George R[637]

11 FEBRUARY 1913

THE PACIFIC

Kathleen is five days out of port en route from San Francisco to New Zealand. Lying in her bunk, she remembers the scent of horses, a wood campfire and those cowboys who were 'dear, thoughtful, gentle, naïve and altogether touching'. It has been a long, long time since she has found a life so entirely to her taste 'and [she] would fain go back'.[638] But for now she is confined to her cabin, the sick bucket her companion, the outside world reduced to a porthole framed with rivets.

NEW ZEALAND

'Loss of Captain Scott Perished in a blizzard after reaching the Pole By Electric Telegraph – Copyright (Received Feb 11 8 a.m.)' The CNA news release has reached the New Zealand press offices. It is too late for the morning papers but it will appear on posters advertising the evening ones: 'News has been received that Captain Scott and the four men with him perished in a blizzard after reaching the Pole on 18 January. The news has caused a sensation in London.'[639]

LONDON

It is dark as Douglas Freshfield walks up the stairs to the minstrels' gallery, which gives onto the smoking room. The RGS council has postponed the

Society's regular evening meeting, delaying the election of a new group of women fellows.* Freshfield is being briefed by Scott Keltie, who tells him that they have been besieged by phone calls. Everyone wants to establish a personal connection to the expedition. Keltie has even received one call from Dr Thomas Barnardo, who wants to know if there were any of his boys involved. Freshfield asks which of the committee members will be present. Keltie tells him that Sir Lewis Beaumont 'felt too keenly to be present or speak' and Sir Clements Markham is in Portugal. The meeting will be a 'difficult and painful task'.[640]

As the men take their seats around the French-polished table, there is a hush. Freshfield rises to read out the telegram Lord Curzon has sent from Somerset. Outside he can hear voices, then a knock on the front door. He finishes reading the telegram while Scott Keltie goes down to investigate. Outside the window, the committee members see a crowd gathering. Between Lowther Lodge and Hyde Park there is a confusion of headlights: motor cabs, horse-drawn cabs and men on bicycles.

Downstairs, Scott Keltie opens the door. The journalists burst in – 'a swarm of press'. Keltie is soon overwhelmed. They want answers, interviews, pictures . . . 'What became of the fuel? Why was the Relief Party at One Ton ten days before the end not provisioned to stay on there some time and make sallies along the S Road? How came . . . provisions . . . cut so fine that delays by bad weather led to starvation? What . . . distance between the depots as compared with Amundsen's? . . . How did it happen?'

Freshfield strides out onto the balcony and looks over the balustrade into the hall below. Keltie is obviously quite unable to cope. The journalists look up to see a man descending the stairs. He reaches out and pulls something off the wall. What is it? A geographical artefact, a tribal weapon hung on the stair wall, a stick, a spear? Brandishing the article, Freshfield descends the stairs and lunges towards the swarm, 'until at last I drove them all out at the point of a [word unreadable]'. Freshfield chases the swarm out of the building and instructs the doorman to let 'no man in'.[641]

---

* With the news of Scott's death, the council postponed the election of the first women fellows for twenty years.

ORIANA – DUNEDIN

From the marbled halls of busy Dunedin Station, Ory moves out onto the platform. At the midway point there is raised decking leading to the southbound Invercargill train. Slatted trucks carrying cattle, horses and bleating sheep all make for a place teeming with life. Open carriage trains with wooden benches for the suburban services to Mosgiel and Port Chalmers wait next to rail cars to Palmerston and the Otago Central Railway. The station includes a huge shunting yard to the south, with goods carriages piled with timber, coal and ore, all rattling back and forth.

Ory negotiates the crowds and animals and finds her steam engine, black with smoke pouring out of its forward funnel. Kinsey's daughter May and her husband William Moore help her into her carriage. It is difficult to be heard as they call their goodbyes over the noise. The guard blows his whistle and with a hiss of steam, the train wheels revolve on the narrow-gauge track taking her north. She has over 220 miles to go.

The carriage is upholstered in brocade and smells of horsehair. The morning sun glances off the ocean. All she has is a summons from Kinsey to return to Christchurch. Nothing more. She has waited over twenty-six months to be reunited with her husband – the wait is nearly over. She will not reach Christchurch until that sun is on her left, in the early evening. 'Isn't it wonderful how they come through safely?' she has just written to Mrs Pennell. 'It makes me realise how they are as safe on the sea and in the Antarctic as at home and I feel full of hope.'[642]

TERRA NOVA

A little steamship appears to be making straight for the *Terra Nova*. It is the coastal steamer that runs daily between Akaroa and Lyttleton. It comes alongside. Looking down, the men catch their first glimpse of civilised life. The British Antarctic explorers are half changed into shore-going clothes, their creases three years old. They wear boots for the first time – Cherry thinks them 'positive agony'. Their beards are freshly shaved.

'Are all well?' asks the captain of the steamer. The passengers wait expectantly for a reply. 'Where's Captain Scott? Did you reach the Pole?' The men on the *Terra Nova* look down at the boat – their answers are unsatisfactory. The boat leaves.[643]

ORIANA – GERALDINE, NEW ZEALAND

Oriana's train is just drawing out of Geraldine Station. It is a warm afternoon and she has the window open. Outside there is the buzz of excited chatter and she can't help noticing a crowd around a news poster in the station. As the train begins to ease out, the door of her carriage opens and her friends, the Dennistouns from Peel Forest, tumble in.[644] They are breathless and windswept from galloping from their homestead to try to catch up with the train, hoping it would be the one she was on.

LOIS – GOWER

The early morning light glistens on the icy wet expanses of Oxwich Beach along the southern coast of Gower. Lois Evans and her youngest son Ralph have been given a jolting lift down here by Will Tucker on his cart. The tide is going out and the cockling ladies are arriving bareback on their ponies. Will has told Lois he will come back in the afternoon to take them home.

Lois stops every so often to shake her hand to prevent it becoming so numb that she can't hold the rake or the riddle sieve properly. Planting her legs astride, she bends as far forward as she can with a straight back, and, holding the rake, draws its teeth firmly through the wet sand. If she stands upright, she can look for her son Ralph and Will's daughter, Lily, whom she is minding – Muriel and Norman are at school. Lois casts her eyes systematically from St Illtyd's church, tucked into the bare branches of the woods to the south, and sweeps around the horseshoe of flat sand. She can usually spot the children playing with the serrated clam shells that lie in drifts further up the beach, Lois knows these sands, but the tides are fickle and they come in fast.

PORTSMOUTH

It is a bitter February and the telegram boy can see his breath as he slips the telegram back into his leather satchel and begins cycling back to the post office. The addressee at 52 Chapel Street, a Mrs Edgar Evans, has moved. One of the neighbours has scribbled a forwarding address in Wales.

GESTINGTHORPE

At the same time, deep in the Essex countryside, the pony cart swings left off the main Sudbury road and up a frosty drive. The drive is lined with majestic leafless trees and leads towards Gestingthorpe Hall. The maid-of-all-work answers the door to the servants' entrance. The senior servant, probably Oscar Minchin, writes a new address on the telegram. The addressee, Mrs Caroline Oates, the lady of the house, is at her London residence at Evelyn Mansions, South Kensington.

BUTE

Four hundred miles away, in Ardbeg on the Isle of Bute, the telegram boy pants up the steep icy hill looking for Caerlaverock. A lady opens the front door of the downstairs flat. The telegram is for her mother, Mrs Emily Bowers, but Mrs Bowers is not here. She is staying with friends in Rome.

SWANSEA, WALES

The telegram addressed to Mrs Edgar Evans reaches Swansea Post Office. It is carried along a hall lined with framed 'team' photographs of employees past. Taff looks down from the wall. He started out as a telegram boy in this office. There is some confusion over the delivery address. To Pitton Cross Farm with a Mr W. Tucker or West Pilton Cottage with a Mr and Mrs W. Beynon? Both are right out on the Gower peninsula. The road doesn't reach all the way. The delivery boy will have to walk the last few miles or take a pony.

LONDON

In the gilt mirror at Evelyn Mansions, Lilian is pinning on her latest Madame Emile hat. Her mother's apartment is reflected in the glass. It is decorated in the late-Victorian style – fringed lamps, velvet uphol-stery, ferns – the overall impression of a scaled-down country house. It smells of beeswax, the grand piano is polished to a mirror sheen. Caroline was at the Queen's Hall the night before, where Lilian's husband was singing. Now Caroline is preparing for the day, sitting at her desk, her accounts book open, pen poised. Later, perhaps, she might order a mount from Harding's and ride out in Hyde Park.

Taking the cage lift to the ground floor with baby Sheila and Sheila's uniformed nurse, Lilian walks out of the building. Her daughter is suitably swaddled inside the Silver Cross pram, but a cold wind funnels down Lower Grosvenor Street. At the newspaper kiosk, the vendor is weighting newspapers lest they fly off the stand. As Lilian approaches, she sees the news written across the poster headline.

BUTE

May has read the telegram. She has contacted Edie. They are grief-stricken but trying to focus on how best to tell Emily. They decide that one of them should go out to Italy. It will probably be May. She must arrange to leave the dogs and organise a ferry and train from Glasgow to London Euston, Paris, Lyon and finally Rome. They have sent a telegram ahead to let Emily know that one of them will be with her as soon as possible.

LONDON

Lilian Ranalow is breathing hard. She is not given to running but she is rushing back to her mother at Evelyn Mansions, where she knows that Caroline Oates is just getting ready for the day. Lilian is praying that the headlines are wrong. They often are. Just this time last year the headlines screeched, 'Scott at the Pole, Brilliant Victory'. The sensible reaction now would be to phone some well-placed contacts and ask them to check with their sources. As she opens the door to the apartment, she sees her mother with a telegram. She can stop Caroline seeing the newspapers, but she cannot stop the news.

In the Strand, Marconi has just learned that Kathleen Scott is on the SS *Aorangi*, an ordinary mail boat. She is five days west of San Francisco, way out in the Pacific Ocean. The boat is due to stop in Tahiti, but that is no use. The cables go across the Pacific, they link in Fiji, not Tahiti. In fact, the radio transmitter capable of reaching Kathleen's boat has not yet been invented, as Marconi, who invented them, should know.

LOIS – GOWER

Lois Evans looks in the direction that Lily Tucker is pointing. A man is walking towards them across the beach, that familiar limping gait. But Will was due to pick them up when the tide came back in. The sea is still right out. He has only been gone a few hours. He carries an envelope. Opening it, Lois finds a telegram: 'Members wish to express deepest sympathy in your sad loss. Commander Evans.' What does it mean?

EMILY — ROME

The telegram boy has a message for a Mrs Emily Bowers, *cura di*, 'care of', but Emily is at All Saints, the English Church, where the service has just finished. The organ plays. Emily walks out of the tall redbrick building, back onto the Via Babuino, where the Italian shopkeepers brush their pavement frontages clear of snow. Emily makes her way towards the British Library. She will read the noticeboard as usual and then attend to her other commitments. As she alights from the cab and climbs the echoing white marble stairs, she draws her reading glasses out of her reticule and approaches the notice board. A man is busy pinning up a new notice.[645] Emily never remembered much about what happened next.

KATHLEEN — THE PACIFIC

Kathleen is still looking for 'anything human' on board the *Aorangi* without much success, though there is a promising young South American man who speaks no English. The best solution is distraction. There are language lessons on offer and luncheon parties and 'deck quoits'. She thinks of her cowboys. She does not relish the thought of being 'the nice little wife of a naval officer', either in this swaying goldfish bowl or in New Zealand.

ORIANA — CHRISTCHURCH

It is still light when Oriana's train draws into the station in the late afternoon. Some of the rumours seem to report that 'Captain Scott and one of his officers' are ahead of her on this train. As the time nears for a reunion, she doesn't know how she has been able to stand the wait. She alights from the train. Hissing steam brakes, footsteps of disembarking passengers, doors banging – the noises echo off the station walls. She walks slowly up the platform before she hears it. The *Evening Post* is for sale on the main concourse. A newspaper hawker is shouting out the news. 'Antarctic Tragedy'. A list of names. Her husband is not there waiting on the platform to meet her. He is dead.[646]

LOIS — GOWER

The *Cambrian Daily Leader* sends a journalist and a photographer to interview 'the widow'. Will Tucker has taken Lois in the farm cart straight from Oxwich beach to her parents at West Pilton Cottage. Lois is still in her cockling clothes, yet poised and dignified. She tells the *Leader* journalist that she has had two telegrams. The first is one of condolence from Commander Teddy Evans, Scott's second-in-command. The second is from her brother Stanley Beynon, who is in the navy and is at present stationed at Devonport. 'Just read terrible news. Try and bear up. Will write. Stan.'[647]

Lois knows that something dreadful has happened, but isn't clear what. As she said later to the journalist from the *South Wales Daily Post*, 'I received a bundle of letters last May, which had been brought to New Zealand by Commander Evans when he left the party. They were about fifty in number and covered the period of a whole year. The last one . . . stated that he was only 150 miles from the Pole and that the party were in good health and very confident of success. Since then I heard nothing until this morning.'[648]

In the absence of any other facts, it is left to the journalist to tell Lois Evans that her husband died from concussion on 17 February 1912, a year ago. Lois asks him to tell her everything he knows. He tells her that the five men did reach the South Pole on 17 January. That her husband was the first to die but that the others did not abandon him. She concludes, 'I have this consolation; my husband died bravely and it seems he did not have to undergo such suffering as the other members of the party went through.'[649] The journalist will describe her as 'quite a superior and refined little woman'.

A photographer, a Mr Sam Chapman, has been setting up his camera outside the front door. Lois changes out of her cockling clothes into her best bolero jacket and stands in the doorway. It is a modest rough stone cottage with a narrow door and a stone step down to a dirt track. Her father stands outside the door on one side, with his four-year-old grandson Ralph beside him. Lois cannot look at the camera. As the photographer clicks the shutter, she stares to the side.

NEW YORK

'I cannot believe it is true,' says Sir Ernest Shackleton. 'It is inconceivable that an expedition so well equipped as Captain Scott's could perish before a blizzard.'[650] He tells journalists that curiously, he is the only survivor from the three that achieved 'Furthest South' on Scott's first *Discovery* expedition in 1903. He telegrams his wife to expect his return. Lady Shackleton, in Eastbourne with their three children, reminds him that his *Nimrod* expedition did not lose a man. He replies that except for a Trans-Antarctic expedition – crossing the continent from coast to coast – there is nothing much left in the Antarctic.

At the Royal Geographical Society headquarters, they receive a message of condolence from Lady Shackleton, and 'calls from the Swedish and Norwegian Ministers to express their profound regret and sympathy'.[651] Scott Keltie tells Lord Curzon that the Central News Agency 'feels very sore' that the king's telegram has not been sent to them, as it evidently has been, they think, to other agencies and papers. Since they have the monopoly on the news and the funds depend on exclusivity, Keltie asks Lord Curzon if he would 'care to write a soothing letter to the Editor, Central Bridge Street, EC'.[652]

ORIANA – CHRISTCHURCH

Oriana has just arrived at Papanui Road, where she discovers the identity of the 'men in seaboots'. Pennell is upset. He and Atkinson never disclosed the news of her husband's death; they had not even given their own names! How has this happened? How could she have heard it, alone, from an anonymous newspaper hawker in the station? Ory tells them that she was not alone. God sent her husband to her room the previous night and then sent the Dennistouns galloping to catch up with her train on the off chance she might be on it. These are not coincidences.

All Ory wants for now is the scientific facts. How exactly had Bill died, what did his frozen body look like, did it show signs of scurvy, was it very badly frostbitten? What evidence do they have to support their opinion? Atch gives Ory his medical opinion and into her hands he places Bill's journals, sealed with wax. The men tell Ory that they have retrieved the camera the five men took to the Pole. They need a photographic studio they can trust to get that film developed – Ponting is in London.

MADISON, WISCONSIN, USA

Amundsen has just finished a lecture on his attainment of the South Pole in Madison when he is told. 'Horrible, horrible . . .' 'I would gladly forego any honour or money,' he tells a journalist, 'if thereby I could have saved Scott his terrible death.'[653] He cannot conceal his emotion: 'And to think that while these brave men were dying out there in the waste of ice, I was lecturing in warmth and comfort in Australia.' Later he composes a formal response: 'Captain Scott left a record for honesty, for sincerity, for bravery, for everything that makes a man.'

WORLD

By the end of Tuesday, 11 February, 767 newspaper articles across the world's time zones have covered the disaster. The New Zealand press is especially unhappy at the way news was withheld.

A Dreadful Shock

Not even the barest hint of disaster was allowed to leak out yesterday and the news this morning came as a dreadful shock . . . Indeed the earliest rumours were received with flat incredulity, it being assumed that if such a great calamity had befallen the expedition those concerned were sure to have mentioned it when the vessel called at Oamaru. That [the] secret could be so jealously maintained was, in the circumstances, incredible.[654]

The *New York Herald Tribune* journalist sums up the situation: 'Cable networks around the world are pulsing with signal. This is like a new *Titanic*.' Many years later, people will be able to recall exactly what they were doing when news of the Antarctic tragedy first reached them.

Kathleen Scott is still mid-Pacific – the news of her husband's death is tracing to and fro across the ocean floor under her ship. She does not know that Scott's 'Message to the Public', written in a frozen tent in Antarctica a year before, is about to be published, to reach its intended audience:

MESSAGE TO THE PUBLIC

For four days we have been unable to leave the tent – the gale howling about us. We are weak, writing is difficult, but for my own sake I do not regret this journey, which has shown that Englishmen can endure hardships, help one another, and meet death with as great a fortitude as ever in the past. We took risks, we knew we took them; things have come out against us, and therefore we have no cause for complaint, but bow to the will of Providence, determined still to do our best to the last . . .

Had we lived, I should have had a tale to tell of the hardihood, endurance, and courage of my companions which would have stirred the heart of every Englishman. These rough notes and our dead bodies must tell the tale, but surely, surely, a great rich country like ours will see that those who are dependent on us are properly provided for.

For God's sake look after our people.[655]

19

'Courage Indeed'

It's nearly 8 o'clock in the morning when Atkinson and Pennel climb into a tug and make their way out from the Lyttleton docks to meet the *Terra Nova* just outside the harbour entrance. Coming along on the lee side, they climb up the rope ladder onto the familiar deck. Their crew mates, shaved and changed into their shore clothes, are eager for news. Has the British expedition been eclipsed by Roald Amundsen's success? Is it regarded as a failure? Have the relatives of the deceased been informed? Have they managed to honour the confidentiality terms of the Central News Agency contract? Atch is a man of few words. How can he communicate to them the extent of the reaction around the world? They will find out soon enough. 'It's made a tremendous impression,' he tells them, 'I had no idea it would make so much.'[656]

The *Terra Nova* sails back into Lyttleton, its flag at half mast. When Cherry steps off the boat onto the crowded, silent dockside, he finds the whole civilised world in mourning. It is as if they've all lost close friends.

GOWER

Taff Evans's mother is being interviewed for 'The Mother's Story' by the *Cambrian Daily Leader*. She is standing in the cold outside the lime-washed Welsh longhouse in Pitton Cross that she shares with her sister Mrs Powell. Both are dressed in full-length dark dresses, with their widow's caps fastened to the crown of their heads. Sarah Evans has only just learned that her son is dead, and now she is being asked to deliver his obituary. What on earth is she supposed to say to the *Leader* journalist? She tries to think of the highest compliment in Gower: 'He was always a very venture-some boy,' she says, 'but from the time he left me until he went away on the last occasion with the expedition, I never heard a word of complaint pass his lips no matter what amount of hardships he had to endure.'[657]

When the journalist goes on to ask about her daughter-in-law Lois, Sarah hasn't had time to adjust her standard defensive answer. It is the same one that she gives to those who infer that her son has neglected his duty to look after his family, the people who ask why Lois has suddenly had to leave her house in Portsmouth. 'On the occasion of his last visit home,' begins Sarah, 'I gave him some good advice, and told him to take care of himself and do the right thing by his wife and children.' But Taff is not coming home. What will happen to his wife and children? The journalist decides to leave the quote hanging in the air and asks Sarah for a final comment: 'I was always proud of my boy,' she continues, 'and I am prouder than ever to know that he died the death of a hero.'

Just over the hill at the Beynons' West Pilton Cottage, the secretary of the British Antarctic Committee arrives and asks to see Lois. He offers his condolences. Is Lois in any 'want'? Before he leaves he gives her 'sufficient money to provide her and her children with mourning dress'.[658]

LISBON, PORTUGAL

Sir Clements Markham sits at his desk in the Grand Hotel d'Italie, Mont Estoril, Lisbon. He is not due to return to England until 30 March. He has just seen the news reported in *The Globe* newspaper. He is not inclined to believe it, but 'if it is true . . . we have lost the greatest Polar explorer that ever lived without any comparison except McClintock . . . We can never hope to see his like again.' If, indeed, the news is true he would like to take this opportunity to remind the newly appointed president of the RGS, Lord Curzon, that the expedition was his, Markham's, idea, and that he, Markham, appointed Scott, 'never was the result so well justified'.[659]

While Curzon was playing at being Viceroy of India, Markham, as president, was rescuing the RGS from the ignominy of the female membership controversy. As the only person who knows the full story, he proceeds to enlighten Curzon with an unpunctuated stream of consciousness. First, Amundsen: 'When he [Scott] heard of Amundsen's action, all he said was "I hope and think that it would have been outside my code of honour under any circumstances."' Second: 'Shackleton who owed everything to Scott and would never have been heard of if it had not been for his kindness gave a written promise ('+I have it') not to go to Victoria Land as Scott was preparing to go there again yet went straight there, and tried to forestall his old chief to whom he owed so great a debt of gratitude yet Scott has never mentioned that broken promise.' And third, he urges Curzon to ensure Scott is properly honoured: 'He would of course have received a KCB as Captain Nares did. Mrs [Kathleen] Scott a worthy wife of such a man should receive the rank of a Knight Commander's wife. There are precedents (we gave Lady Franklin our medal).' He is, he is sure Curzon understands, the father of Antarctic exploration, the one who started all this and it would be only proper that any memorial service be delayed for his return.

LONDON

At the office of the RGS, Scott Keltie is drowning under 'shoals of telegrams and letters'.[660] The deluge is a result of Scott's 'Message to the Public'. They are queuing up at the newsstands for their copy. Curzon, returned now to full vigour at his London residence, 1 Carlton House Terrace, recognises that this frozen 'Message' is the core of the legend. Public sentiment is 'quickened by this tale of mingled heroism and disaster as by no other event in my time'.

In Buckingham Palace there is intense discussion as to the appropriate royal response. Should there be some kind of state ceremony to commemorate the dead, a funeral without bodies, a memorial, as for the *Titanic*? Already the outpouring of public grief has exceeded that disaster. Perhaps the king should break with protocol and attend this memorial in person?

Sergeant Major Williams of the Inniskilling Dragoons is making his way to the Cavalry Club on Piccadilly. His regiment is stationed in India, but a cable has been sent. 'I was in London on the 12th February,' Williams later recalled, 'and everybody was talking of Captain Oates, in train and tram and tube one hears it, and I sitting and knowing him so well simply swelled with pride and had difficulty in restraining myself from joining in every conversation I heard.'[661]

MHOW, INDIA

The atmosphere in London has not translated through the cable. At their barracks in Mhow, the Inniskillings hear the news with stunned disbelief. 'For hours we hoped there was a mistake somewhere, but as cablegram after cablegram came in from all sources, a distinct gloom was noticeable throughout the regiment.'[662]

SWANSEA

The *Cambrian Daily Leader* is a regional newspaper, but after a day of frenzied activity the editor is in a self-congratulatory mood. He notes that 'Mr Sam Chapman['s] . . . admirable portraits of Mrs [Lois] Evans, her father and son . . . appeared exclusively in our 5.30 and 6.30 editions. A print of this picture was handed into the "Leader" Office at a quarter to three. It was given over to our artists, who prepared it for the process department and before four o'clock the block was ready for use. This constitutes a record in local journalism.'[663]

13 FEBRUARY 1913

CHRISTCHURCH

At 8 a.m., the third message of 1,381 words is telegrammed from Christchurch to the Central News Agency; it 'followed up the first dispatch by getting those members of the Expedition together at [Kinsey's] house, who could relate their individual experiences'. Some newspapers have run their stories without going through the Central News Agency. Kinsey knows who the culprit is. 'I regret to say, that outside these interviews and against my implicit instructions, one individual would "talk", and has continued to "talk", though constantly and amusingly reminding the public he must not "talk", being anxious to observe the traditions of the "Great Silent Navy".'[664] At his desk in London, John Gennings does not find Teddy's indiscretions amusing. He begins composing a cable to Kinsey to this effect.

LONDON

A memorial service is scheduled for the following day. The London Underground commissions a special poster. The blue and white graphic image shows an androgynous figure clad in a white cloak holding two laurel wreaths in a snowy landscape. A sledge trail with footprints in the snow leads in a sinuous line from the foreground to the figure's feet. The poster declares that the memorial service will be held at St Paul's Cathedral at noon the following day and that bookings should be made through the Mansion House.

Even before the posters go up on the station walls, the Mansion House is overwhelmed with callers. They are already dealing with an outpouring of donations following the publication of Scott's 'Message to the Public' and his final request to 'look after our people'. Newspapers declare that subscriptions may be sent to the Lord Mayor at the Mansion House or to the Bank of England. The funds will be used to provide for the widows and children of the men who died, to pay off the £16,000 debt still owing of the £40,000 to £60,000 expedition cost, and to erect a memorial. Kathleen Scott is a sculptress, and it is suggested that when she is finally apprised of the situation she might be commissioned to create this.

Sir Edgar Speyer, the expedition's treasurer, still has Scott's last letter about funds. Speyer feels Scott's loss on a personal level and is not sure how much money the public will raise. He has attended Kathleen's parties at 174 Buckingham Palace Road and begun sitting for a portrait by her. He has just received a telegram with the words of Scott's letter to him, which laments 'the women we leave behind'. He declares that he is prepared to take personal responsibility for a share of the liabilities himself.

Lord Curzon instructs Freshfield and Scott Keltie to be sure to reserve a block of seats at St Paul's for RGS Fellows. He is thinking along viceregal lines when he suggests that they must all arrive and enter the cathedral together for maximum ceremonial impact.

14 FEBRUARY 1913

CHRISTCHURCH

It is 8 a.m., but after another sleepless summer night Kinsey stumbles into bed, believing that this last cablegram of 2,280 words exceeds and concludes the expedition's contractual responsibility. John Gennings – who receives the message at the Central News Agency offices in London ten minutes later – does not agree.

It is Valentine's Day. Instead of being inundated with orders for red roses, the florists have been trying to keep up with orders for wreaths to be delivered to parish churchyards, 'In memory of . . .'.

LONDON

The solid tyres of the Oateses' limousine trace the light covering of snow on the Mall. Entering Fleet Street, Lilian can see crowds walking steadily towards the cathedral. By the time the car gets to Ludgate Hill, the crowds block the road. Is Caroline in the car too? What should they do? No one knows who they are. At this rate they will miss the service. Eventually, the crowds are cordoned back behind temporary railings and, as the road becomes passable again, the dome of St Paul's looms out of the smog. Somehow they make their way to the front entrance of the cathedral, where there are two mounted policemen.

Only Lilian alights, and she is directed up the staircase of limestone steps that stretch the width of the enormous classical building. Arriving at the top by the west door, she sees that there is a notice, 'Church Full'. The man on the west door tells her that it has been full since 9.30 a.m. From the road level comes the sound of hooves and the jangle of harnesses. The Oateses' chauffeur must clear the road, but he will be back after the service. Lilian tells the man on the west door that she is Captain Oates's sister. The man does not know what to do. Eventually the wife of the organist, Lady Martin, offers to escort Lilian up to the organ loft.[665]

Caroline's cousin Mary Oates is representing the family at St Mary's Gestingthorpe, where a private service is being held simultaneously. Would Caroline rather be there? St Paul's is dramatic, but public and impersonal. Did she bundle into the organ loft with Lilian, or did she mourn alone? In Cheltenham, Bill Wilson's mother and father are holding a private family service at Westal.

A carriage stops outside the main entrance to St Paul's and sheriffs in gold-braided full ceremonial regalia emerge to line the wide steps. Another carries a large gold mace, from a third the Lord Mayor alights, and finally the royal coach draws up with the king. It is 11.55 a.m. precisely and snow falls lightly. The Pathé cameras mounted at the head of the stairs whirr. The camera operator tries to shield the lens from the snow to record 10,000 people standing silently outside the cathedral, as the neatly bearded figure of George V in his admiral's uniform makes his way slowly up the steps.

From the organ loft, Lilian has a bird's-eye view of the king as he makes his way to his chair at the end of the central aisle to the accompaniment of Beethoven's 'Funeral March'. Scott's sister Grace and

Birdie's sister Edie are among those watching him take his place. As the service at St Paul's begins, there is a rustle of paper. The ink has barely dried on the black-bordered order of service, six pages hastily printed by R. E. Thomas & Co. of Moorfields. The service starts with Hymn No. 184, 'Rock of Ages, Cleft for Me', with the line 'When I soar through tracts unknown' in the last verse sung with particular emphasis by the cathedral choir.

After the reading of 1 Corinthians 15:20 there is a roll of drums from a military band. The sound reverberates into the silent streets outside. As the drum roll becomes a single beat, the band begins Handel's 'Dead March' from *Saul*. Grace Scott, Scott's sister, who is sitting near the king under the central dome, feels the music rising up through the building. The last hymn concludes the service, a thousand voices singing Hymn No. 193, 'Jesu, Lover of my Soul', and finally the cathedral doors are opened and the king processes out. A solitary voice begins to sing the first line of the national anthem, 'God Save our Gracious King', the whole congregation join in the second line, 'Long Live our Noble King', until the crowd outside catches on and ten thousand voices standing around the cathedral unite in grief and renewed patriotic fervour.

In the pews around the bereaved relatives, journalists compose their pieces for the evening newspapers. The *Evening Standard* feels it speaks for many when observing that the service, though magnificent and moving, was 'rather unreal'. Everywhere they are keenly aware that the key figure is absent, the 'one who is still ignorant of the frightful tragedy, that hapless woman, still on the high seas, flushed with hope and expectation, eager to join her husband'. Grace Scott, however, 'never imagined anything so wonderful and uplifting'. The *Daily Chronicle* journalist is going to claim that it is a citizens' tribute, in spite of the fact that there were no working-class people in the congregation: 'all classes, rich and poor . . . knew best of all the inner meaning of this tribute to courage and to sacrifice. They knew that it is sweet and beautiful to die for one's country's honour.'[666]

LOIS – GOWER

Lois returns from the beach to find a man in gold-braided uniform and a bicorne hat standing outside West Pilton Cottage. Admiral Lord Beresford is tall and imposing, the highest-ranking naval officer she has ever met, as well as being a Conservative MP. He has come to offer his condolences to Lois.[667] Lois had never even met Captain Scott. For an admiral to call on her is a reversal of the natural order – has she had time to spend the money brought by the BAE secretary to enable her to wear correct mourning?

15 FEBRUARY 1913

CAROLINE – GESTINGTHORPE

Veiled in full mourning, Caroline arrives back at Gestingthorpe. The fires have been lit in anticipation, but the air inside the hall is still. The builders have left. At his request, Caroline has finished Laurie's bedroom alterations as he had desired in anticipation of his return. Now she orders that his bed should be made up for her. Downstairs there must be fresh flowers placed under his portrait, but all the other paintings must be turned to the wall, ornaments and photographs veiled in black crêpe. As the servants begin to carry out her orders, she sees one of her son's regimental epaulettes on his dressing table and places it in her handbag. Looking out of one of the two south-facing sash windows, she can see the pristine, white-frosted lawn.

LOIS – GOWER

In New Zealand the reasons for the tragedy were widely discussed under headlines such as: 'Rumours at Christchurch, Fate of Petty Officer Evans – Could the Explorers have been saved?' Lois can only read the New Zealand reporting where it is quoted in British papers: 'It would seem from what has escaped some of the survivors that the unfortunate man Evans lost his reason for the time being under great stress of fatigue and privation, and was incapable of obeying orders or assisting in the weary work of pulling the sledge. Indeed it became necessary in the end to lay him on it.'[668]

16 FEBRUARY 1913

ORIANA – CHRISTCHURCH

Oriana passes under the green canopy made by an avenue of oriental plane trees in Hagley Park. She believes that Bill is walking alongside her: 'he is here helping me now.' She must accept that this is what *le Dieu* disposes and that any resistance would be faithless. She wills herself to live up to her husband's expectation not to wallow in 'selfish grief' but to comfort others. She tells those near her that should her husband's saintly example have more influence if he is dead than alive, she can relinquish him.

To Anne Hardy, her friend in Rakaia, she writes: 'Our life together was so absolutely perfect. We just had a little fore-taste of heaven – and his life, which was entirely Christlike, will have helped many hundreds – and he will be very near me.'[669]

Where the Avon river bends around Christ's College, 'they' head due east towards the earthquake-damaged cathedral, designed by the English architect Sir Gilbert Scott. It is already beginning to heat up outside but inside the stone building it is refreshingly cool. As she walks in, she sees that in the nave there is standing room only. She attends her husband's memorial service with Bill by her side.

She does not blame anyone. She is secure in Bill's high personal regard for Scott: 'There is nothing,' Bill once told her, 'that I would not do for him. He is a really good man, and a perfect marvel in brain power: the cleverest man all round I have ever known.'[670]

LOIS – GOWER

A memorial service has been speedily arranged in the tiny stone church of St Mary's, Rhossili. The cold onshore wind buffets the congregation as they arrive, summoned by St Teilo's bell. The pews are filled mostly by relatives, and Lois is at the front with her family. She is dressed in black, with a high crêpe collar and black embroidered flowers on her blouse. She stands quietly just a few paces away from the spot where she and Taff were married nine years before. In his address, the Reverend Lewis Hughes says that 'rich and poor have sent messages of heartfelt sympathy [to] those who have been stricken with grief and have suffered such a loss.' He tells them that at this very moment, prayers are being offered for the 'bereaved of the Gower' in Swansea's Albert Hall and in chapels and churches throughout Wales. The editor of the *Gower Church Magazine* tells Lois that he is going to write a piece on her husband. He quotes Scott's 'Message to the Public', in which Taff is described as 'the strong man of the party – the man whom we had least expected to fail'. Lois is aware of a contradictory theme – strength and failure. She can trust the *Church Magazine*, but can she trust the nationals?

17 FEBRUARY 1913

KATHLEEN — TAHITI, PACIFIC

Kathleen Scott's ship docks in Tahiti into an earthly paradise of coconuts, mangos and tropical vegetation. 'I had a wonderful drive . . . bananas, guavas and vanilla everywhere, profusion of bright coloured flowers, flamboyant hibiscus, oleander and pomegranate, all very lovely.'[671] Now she wants to walk barefoot on the sand, to paddle in the surf. The young South American man she met on board (Gallinal, although she does not name him) holds the camera as she poses in the shallows, her long white dress hitched out of the waves. In the evening the passengers from the *Aorangi* are all taken to a cinematograph show 'a great event'. The locals shout, clap, boo and hurrah; 'in the most delicious way'. Kathleen is charmed by Tahiti. The colours are brighter, the whooping louder, contrasting with the protracted endurance of life aboard. She sleeps that night in a wooden hut, in a bed that neither rocks nor sways, with the windows and doors wide open to the night breeze.

LOIS — GOWER

A rumour has reached Taff's mother, Sarah Evans, in her cottage near Pitton Cross. 'I'm worried because I feel that if he hadn't broken down they – Captain Scott and the rest of them – would have been alive today.' She tells the *Leader* journalist that she can't help thinking about it: 'all the time ever since I read about them being – forced to wait for him . . . Perhaps it would have been better if they have left him behind.'[672] The journalist notes that despite his best efforts, 'the worthy old dame refused to be comforted.'

Lois Evans realises that Taff's 'failure' is being blamed on some sort of mental incapacity, madness, insanity. Some reports blame Taff's working-class education. The officers were more mentally resilient, better able to cope with the monotony, with being beaten to the Pole. The reports suggest that the other four could shrug off defeat and draw stimulation and comfort from the well furnished classical libraries of their minds. Lois defends her husband, but increasingly the press is divided between her husband-hero and her mother-in-law's failure-son.

LONDON

Caroline's telegram is handed in at 12.40 p.m. to the post office in Sudbury. An hour later the telegram boy knocks on the service door at the bottom of the basement stairs at 1 Carlton House Terrace. The telegram is brought to Lord Curzon.

'Please accept my very grateful thanks for your letter and also for your kind appreciation of my son. Caroline Oates.'[673]

18 FEBRUARY 1913

KATHLEEN – BETWEEN TAHITI AND RAROTONGA, PACIFIC

Partly due to Marconi's contacts and instructions, the SS *Talune* has been sent out to communicate with the *Aorangi* when the latter is one night out from Papeete. The message is conveyed at night but is withheld from Kathleen Scott until the next morning.

LONDON

At Buckingham Palace, Lieutenant Colonel Arthur John Bigge, 1st Baron Stamfordham, has been tasked to react to honours suggested for Captain Scott's memory. Addressing Lord Curzon merely as 'Curzon' rather than 'Earl Curzon' as his boss, the king, has in his telegrams, Bigge asks for precedents: 'Were Capt. Scott to be gazetted as having earned, say, a KCB, would this legally make his widow Lady Scott – I hardly think so – the wife's title is only derived from that of her husband unless she is made a Peeress.'[674]

At the RGS, Keltie answers a question from Curzon about Petty Officer [Taff] Evans. Keltie tells him that 'His wife' (they are not sure of her name – they do not even call Lois 'Mrs Evans' so it is just 'His wife') 'states that her husband always told her that he would go out again with Capt. Scott towards the Pole if asked; he was very ambitious to get there. He had been with Scott on his first expedition.' There was little more to the biography. He 'belongs to Portsmouth and had been Instructor in gunnery on HMS *Vernon*.'[675]

CAROLINE – GESTINGTHORPE

Caroline sits at her desk and opens her faithful accounting book. She still has three children. She gives Lilian £5, Violet £10 (for telegrams), and Bryan his allowance and a gift amounting to £135. Bryan's wife has just been delivered of a son, Edward. Neither Edward nor Sheila will ever meet their uncle now. According to the law of primogeniture, Bryan is now the heir, and Edward, his. A few days later she gives £160 as a gift to Frederick Ranalow. She is not yet decided about the Oates succession – the next lord of the manor. Looking back through the numbers, she realises that on 12 February, when she heard the news of Laurie's death, she made an error. She goes back and writes £40 in the margin in pencil after 'General Expenses'. She must not become 'dishevelled' in her accounting or her dress. She orders a black 'Toque' from Madame Emile for £1.9.9.

19 FEBRUARY 1913

KATHLEEN – BETWEEN TAHITI AND RAROTONGA, PACIFIC

Kathleen sits on the recently swabbed deck, which is beginning to steam in the heat. Focusing her eyes on the horizon and breathing deeply, she is concentrating on keeping her breakfast down. Out of the corner of her eye, she notices that the captain has left the bridge and is walking up the wooden deck towards her. Turning, she notices that his hands seemed to be trembling. He tells her that he wants to speak to her in his cabin. Kathleen is better in the open with the sea air blowing on her face. She has no idea why she's been summoned in this way, and has no desire to leave the fresh air of the deck, 'but I went.'[676] Once in the cabin, she tries to get the interview over with as fast as possible.

'I've got some news for you,' he says, 'but I don't see how I can tell you.'

'The expedition?' says Kathleen.

'Yes.'

'Well,' Kathleen says, 'let's have it,' and he shows her the message: 'Captain Scott and six [sic] others perished in blizzard after reaching South Pole January 18.' 'I remember,' Kathleen wrote in her diary later, 'I said, without the least truth, "Oh well, never mind! I expected that. Thanks very much. I will go and think about it."' She asks the captain to discuss the news with no one but the officers who already know.

The hot tropical air is oppressive and yet she cannot be on the crowded deck. It is the hour at which she sometimes has a Spanish lesson. She goes to her lesson for an hour and a half and acquits herself well. She walks to the dining room for lunch. She sits with a group and discusses American politics. She tries to concentrate on the 16th Amendment to the United States constitution which was ratified a fortnight before. There is also the issue of 'La Decena Trágica', a revolution in Mexico. None of her fellow diners suspect.

After lunch she is still not sure that she can control herself. She begins to write her diary – her writing small and upright rather than her customary loose, leaning hand. Halfway through the writing deteriorates as if she has swapped to her left hand, or begun dictating to a child who has just learned to hold a pen. She makes herself read her book on the sinking of the *Titanic*. She has been commissioned to sculpt a monumental portrait of the *Titanic*'s Captain Smith on her return – the man who went down with his ship.

20 FEBRUARY 1913

KATHLEEN – RAROTONGA, PACIFIC

When Kathleen's ship arrives in Rarotonga in the Cook Islands, the other passengers see the news posted in the post office window in the port. Kathleen stays on board and writes letters. Late in the afternoon, she goes ashore with the young South American. Since he speaks no English, he does not know. From the land she can smell the scent of frangipani. She heads along the white sandy beach towards the rocks, away from people. She sits with her back to the volcanic peak and looks out over crystal waters, pocked with rain. She watches the breakers curl in over the reef. She is still watching as it gets dark. She thinks about her son. It is almost midnight when she returns with the South American, picking their way back across the slippery rocks in the moonlight, wet to the skin.

ORIANA – CHRISTCHURCH

Oriana plans to go to Wellington to meet Kathleen. Sitting at her desk in Uncle Bill's Cabin – the home she shares with his presence – she is beginning to master the past tense. She tells Mrs Cherry-Garrard that 'My future is all uncertain – but I hope to be able to make some use of my life – I know my husband would not have me lead an idle one & I am strong enough . . . & work is such a help.'[677]

21 FEBRUARY 1913

KATHLEEN – BETWEEN RAROTONGA AND NEW ZEALAND, PACIFIC

Kathleen is too hot to stay in her cabin but there is no privacy on board. She plays five games of deck-golf and reads 'violently. Anything to get the awful, haunting picture out of my head.' She notices that the third officer is almost always on duty and suspects he's been tasked to make sure she doesn't jump. 'It is good that I do not believe firmly in life after death,' she confides to her diary that evening, 'or surely, surely I would have gone overboard to-day. But I am afraid my [husband] has gone altogether, except in the great stirring influence he must have left on everyone.'[678]

She thinks of the 'great stirring influence' he has had particularly on her. 'I think he has made me twice the man [sic] I was. Certainly I couldn't have faced this with complete self-control but for his teaching. Ever since I knew him I have worked striven and strained that he might applaud ever so little . . . Can I keep to it without the hope of his applause?'

She cannot sleep, and paces the moonlit top deck. 'Always only his pain, his mental agony, boring into my brain', she writes. 'How one hopes his brain soon got numbed and the weight of his responsibility left him.'[679] She writes to Nansen to ask him not for comfort, but for his expert knowledge on what a death like that would be like.

23 FEBRUARY 1913

'These have been the strangest nights,' Kathleen writes, as they sail west across lines of longitude and the hour of day is continuously reset. She has taken to sitting in the wireless room. The operator is an Irishman. They never converse. He just hands her the papers as soon as he has finished writing them. When she gets too tired she goes to her room, and for the rest of the night the third officer ('the only human I have to turn to') goes backwards and forwards, bringing her the messages.

At about eleven or twelve midnight the wireless messages begin and go on till about 3 a.m. . . . A few words come and then a stop at the most critical moment. Messages of condolence, lovely messages, keep coming through, coming and coming without ceasing, but thus blocking the line and preventing me getting press news. It is of course necessary for the operators to send through paid messages before sending press news, and so without knowing it my kind friends, and so kind some of them, are baulking my news and keeping me absolutely in ignorance except of the main fact.

ORIANA – CHRISTCHURCH

Oriana thanks the Kinseys for their extraordinary hospitality and moves from the spare room in Papanui Road to 1 Park Place in central Christchurch. She is determined not to hide but to be independent, and she welcome visitors while answering every message of condolence. But sometimes when all the visitors have left, she pauses, fountain pen poised above the page, and realises that a new idea is creeping in. Whichever way she reads them, Bill's last letters from the Antarctic are all written as if he knew he wouldn't return. It is not just an insurance against the 'worst-case scenario', it is more than that. He had once written that 'It is no sin to long to die, the sin is in the failure to submit our wills to God to keep us here as long as He wishes.'[680]

LORD CURZON

Curzon submits his manuscript to Keltie for the RGS journal, suggesting that it had 'better be printed or typed at once'. He has no objection to being budged up by extracts from Scott's journal but objects strongly to being kept in ignorance about being budged up by anyone else. No one told him that 'Markham was coming in with 3 ½ pages.'[681]

24 FEBRUARY 1913

KATHLEEN – BETWEEN RAROTONGA AND NEW ZEALAND, PACIFIC

'All night messages came,' writes Kathleen in her cabin. 'One from [Oriana] crossed mine. One came yesterday sent by Marconi, to say Peter is well.'[682] Kathleen is grateful that at least she has her son. She thinks of that note she wrote for Teddy to give her husband. She remembers it verbatim with corrections: 'I want you to realise, that it won't [crossed out] wouldn't be your physical life that would profit me and Doodles [Peter] most.' Had Teddy given it to him? Had it influenced his decisions – the final outcome?

LOIS — GOWER

Lois is aware of the outpouring of funds but she is not sure whether the ratings class is eligible. She continues to scratch a living from Oxwich beach every low tide. She takes the children sometimes to play on the tide line. She wants to make sure they do not suffer any more than necessary.

Relatives in Swansea try to keep her abreast of developments in the newspapers. 'How Much Are You Sorry?' is the heading over J. M. Barrie's feature on the front page of the *Daily News & Leader*. Apparently there are four collection centres: the BAE committee, London's Mansion House, the *Daily Chronicle* and the *Daily Telegraph* but the king has declared that he would only make a donation once the campaign was properly coordinated. When the Lord Mayor hurriedly proposed to combine the four funds into the Mansion House Fund, the king donated £200.

There are rumours that the five 'Antarctics', as they are increasingly being described, will be decorated posthumously. Although Lois would be relieved if Taff were included rather than ignored, or even blamed for holding them back, there is a problem. Her husband has already earned an Antarctic Medal from the *Discovery* expedition of 1901 to 1904 and will only be given a metal clasp to add to the ribbon above with this subsequent expedition. The problem is that Lois doesn't have the medal or its ribbon anymore. She has sold it for cash.

25 FEBRUARY 1913

KATHLEEN — BETWEEN RAROTONGA AND NEW ZEALAND, PACIFIC

'Last night there came through the last words of [Scott's] diary,' writes Kathleen in her diary.[683] She has changed out of her day clothes into her nightdress and crept back down to the wireless operator's room. As Kathleen steps barefoot onto the moonlit deck with Scott's 'Message to the Public' in her hand, she realises that it must have been starvation that killed them. 'I thought it was exposure . . . I didn't want to hear any more.' But once in her cabin, Kathleen reads Scott's now famous 'Message' for the first time: 'That was a glorious, courageous note, and a great inspiration to me. If he in his weakness could face it with such sublime fortitude, how dare I possibly whine? I will not. I regret nothing but his suffering.'

'It is cowardly to sit down under trouble.' Kathleen is stern with herself. She knows she has to stand up to what is coming, and it is coming fast: 'This day is 180 degrees and so we miss it out. There is no Wednesday.' They are racing through time to the moment when she will have to face the world.

EMILY – ROME

'What can I say,' writes Emily. 'My boy was my only son & fatherless from infancy & his loss is a great sorrow for we were more to each other than ordinary mother and son.'[684] Now Emily and May Bowers are setting off for home. When Emily has suffered bereavement in the past, May describes her as 'smitten with paroxysms of grief'.[685] It makes her 'very poorly'.[686] But Emily is now strong enough to begin the long journey north, and their luggage sits on the marble tiles in the hall. Emily has several leather suitcases and hatboxes. May has only a small travelling bag, the result of her hasty departure from Bute. As people call at the house to say goodbye, May realises that her mother Emily has become a reluctant celebrity. The British ambassador and a number of Italian dignitaries come to offer condolences. The Italians' grief is not the reserved emotion of northern Europe but the warmth and empathy of the Mediterranean. Their farewells are long and heartfelt, and often accompanied with food and gifts. Emily has made friends in high places. She tries to respond to them all with her customary warmth, but she is still stricken. The congregation of the English Church have done all they can to offer her comfort and community, but she cannot yet bear to sing those hymns. She is struggling to accept God's decision to take her only son, so young, with so much before him. The cab arrives. Emily and May are escorted across the city to Roma Termini station – the pain of bereavement is sharp and unrelenting.

CAROLINE – GESTINGTHORPE

Caroline is determined to be grand. She is trying to rise above her own grief. She thinks of Kinsey and his desperate attempt to get the news to the relatives before the newspapers: 'This tragic disaster has touched the whole world. May I say that I have thought a good deal about you personally – and felt for you. It must indeed have been a terrible ordeal to welcome the return of *Terra Nova*, bringing as she did the sad tidings.'[687] And what was it like for those waiting at the base? 'All those weary months, when they must have known that the Southern Party had perished.' Caroline thinks particularly of Oriana: 'Poor Mrs Wilson . . . she took luncheon with me very shortly before she left for New Zealand. I could see clearly what she and her husband were to each other.'

27 FEBRUARY 1913

KATHLEEN AND ORIANA – WELLINGTON

The *Aorangi* arrives off Wellington in the evening. On the wharf, Oriana and Dr Atkinson are waiting. '[Oriana],' notes Kathleen, 'is behaving very well, poor, poor soul . . . She of course has had more than a fortnight to get used to it. I only a few hours.'[688]

Dr Atkinson places a small black leather notebook in her hand. She weighs the book in her hand. It is familiar, its rounded corners, its heft. Scott had bought it at the Army & Navy Co-operative in Victoria Street, London, before they left in 1910. She feels the uneven texture of the leather against her fingertips. When he was alive, she told him categorically that it was not his physical self that she needed, but when she holds, held, his hand, she felt reassured. She always insisted that instead of her whole hand, he hold just her index finger in his. This book was in his pocket. There is physicality there. Her diary and his journal are Kathleen and Scott. Two parallel monologues, about to intersect. She breaks the seal.

PART THREE

Allegro molto

QUEEN'S HALL, LONDON

At the end of this piece, Leonora has told her husband Sir Edgar, there is a false ending. She knows because she played it for Elgar in the music room at home. The Speyers prepare to enjoy the last movement. It begins with a quiet but strenuous violin passage, accompanied by the orchestra. There are many double stops and fast arpeggios. The music reaches back into the past to themes from the first and second movements. And then, as the movement seems to be heading for a conventional finish, the past is buried and an exciting present returns. And to top it all, Elgar has invented a new sound, a revolutionary thrumming effect, *pizzicato tremolando*, a trembling. On the manuscript, Elgar has written, 'The soloist thinks over the material sadly.'

Elgar and Kreisler have synchronised – they are on the same journey now, after the false ending. How does the story really end?

20

Body of Evidence

KATHLEEN – NEW ZEALAND

[Atkinson] told me the details of how he found you,' she writes to Scott, 'but not enough. I didn't like asking so I still ache to know more.'[689] If Kathleen's pen hesitates after the word 'you', she can flick back to her diary entry of 4 September the previous year, in which she declared her agnosticism: 'My own tendency is to believe that the whole business is body. It is sad to me to see people striving after what they desire against the opposed weight of all that they know.'[690] In February 1913 she knows that the whole business is body, and yet she cannot help herself addressing that deceased, frostbitten corpse as 'you'. Why does she ache to know more? It is just a body, after all. And yet she suspects that Atkinson is holding something back. What is it about Scott's body that he wants to spare her from? She has already posted the letter she wrote to Nansen on board the *Aorangi*, Nansen won't spare her, she can trust him.

What of the other four? Two, already widowed, have now also lost their sons – they are five widows now. What of the bereaved mothers? 'Mothers have finished their work. They have had their glory. They've made their miracles. But boys, cut short before they've made their miracles –!'[691] For Kathleen, that is where the real tragedy lay, and Mrs Oriana Wilson is the only one of the five who has not made miracles. And yet in spite of this, 'she was sweet and gentle. I am so glad we could be nice to each other; it is comforting for us both.'[692] Before the expedition, Kathleen thought Ory 'not much use'; now she admires her. 'Hers is courage indeed.' Kathleen will bring Peter up 'to live for' Scott. Returning to her diary, she tries to resist the urge to continue her conversation with 'you' and deliberately changes pronoun. 'Within I shall be exultant. My god is glorious and could never become less so. Loneliness is a fear that I have never known. Had he died before I had known his gloriousness, or before he had been the father of my son, I might have felt a loss. Now I have felt none for myself.'[693]

Before leaving for home, Oriana and Kathleen (now Lady Scott) compose a piece for the New Zealand newspapers – it is a 'Message to [their] Public'.

> Before leaving this country we would like to express our very real gratitude to the Government and people of New Zealand for their sympathy and thoughtful help to us. The forethought for our welfare has touched us very deeply, and will not readily be forgotten. [Signed] Kathleen Scott. Oriana Wilson.[694]

MARCH 1913

EMILY – BUTE

From Rome to Bute. Station signs in Italian, French and finally English. Grey seas. London smog. Scottish accents. Trains, ferries and finally, after forcing the door open against the large drift of envelopes, a coal fire in their front room.

Sitting beside May and Edie in her usual chair, Emily begins to go through the mail. Many of the letters are from children, from former pupils and old school friends of Birdie's. All seem to have been impressed by Arthur Machen's address, which was read out in morning assemblies at the same time that the memorial service Edie attended was conducted at St Paul's. Many of the correspondents tell Emily that they will never forget that assembly as long as they live. In one of the envelopes, Emily finds a copy, a cutting from the *Evening News*.

Emily has an almost religious belief in the power of a good morning assembly – whether it be an assembly read out to the whole school, to her scholar lodgers or just to which ever of her children happened to be at home. These days it was sometimes just the dog, Pete. This assembly text was read at Ardbeg Primary, at the Rothesay board school, all the way down the country at Birdie's old school in Sidcup, in the imposing neo-Gothic chapel at Bill's old school Cheltenham College, Oates's Eton, Taff's St Helen's School, Swansea, and Scott's Stubbington House in Fareham. It is an unprecedented step, and the impact of it, Emily knows, will be deep and long-lasting.

Standing in the front room of Caeverlock with a copy of the text in her hand, Emily can picture headmasters and headmistresses in the cold, echoing chapels and assembly halls as they step up to their lecterns with 'Scott's Expedition – How Five Brave Englishmen Died'. 'Children,' begins Machen's assembly text, 'you are going to hear the true story of five of the bravest and best men who have ever lived on the earth since the world began.' Emily wonders what age group Machen is aiming at.

> So Captain Scott sailed down till he came to the frozen sea, and then when the right time came he and four of his companions left the ship and started in sledges for the South Pole. They found it, and they marked the place, and they found out all that there was to be found out, and then they turned back, hoping to go on the ship again and so sail safely to England. Then their troubles began . . .

It is a comfort for Emily to be able to retreat to the academic theory behind the prose. The text has been translated into many languages already. It is so difficult to appeal to all children from primary to secondary, to be accessible without being patronising, simple without being *simpleste, semplicista, simpel*. But there are the elements that comprise what Marie Montessori refers to as 'foundational stories'. Like Marie, Emily has always used a story as a vehicle for teaching – to communicate vocabulary, comprehension, sequencing, memory and creative writing. A story that endures in the heart and mind would be a fitting memorial, but where is God in Machen's text? No mention. Isn't Machen the newspaper's religious correspondent? Who advised him to leave God out, and why?

'You are to hear about five great men' – the cadence and the repetition are intimate and engaging, designed to be read out loud. In Emily's imagination, thousands of headteachers pause, 'Their names are: Captain Scott, who was their leader, Captain Oates, Lieutenant Bowers, Doctor Wilson and Petty Officer Evans . . . These men are all dead,' Machen's piece tells the children, '. . . and they died after dreadful pain, in a dreadful place, called the Antarctic Region.'

'Dreadful pain'? Perhaps she should put Machen's school assembly aside until she has Birdie's expedition journal in her hand. She is aware that Christ died in pain, but there is no overt sense of Christian justification in Machen's text. Why is it a necessary part of human greatness that it has been arrived at, not just through manly striving, but through 'dreadful pain'? What was Machen's point? What are the children supposed to take from this?

'And people who have not got something of this spirit in them are very little good either to themselves or to anybody else.'[695]

KATHLEEN – SYDNEY

This is the biggest public monument she will ever sculpt – her image must be so bold and convincing that she can silence the detractors in spite of the newspapers and in spite of Teddy's head start. 'Dear Keltie,' writes Kathleen from the desk in the guest bedroom at Government House, Sydney. 'They could have pulled through had they not stayed by their dying and so one is very glad they did not pull through!' She tells Keltie to 'see to it that none of the ridiculous reports of dissension, lack of support, tampering with depots or other harmful fabrications of detrimentalists be allowed to have weight. There is no blame anywhere.'[696]

Kathleen's brief reprieve on dry land is nearly over. She must catch the P&O for the next leg of her journey home. Oriana will arrive home a week after her, Teddy and Hilda, a week after that. But as Kathleen's pen skitters on, she knows she has many more dams to plug. She must make sure that her in-laws do not let the side down. How to do this within the conventions of condolence? 'Mummy', she writes to Scott's mother, 'I wonder if anything he could have done in life could give my Peter a better start in life than that heroic story.'[697]

MARCH 1913

ORIANA – PACIFIC

Now the deck of the SS *Remuera* is silent. The ship has turned east; behind it the sun makes orange patterns on the surface of the sea. Uneven gold rings join and split and re-join. The coffin floats for a moment in the white splash, and then tips and slides suddenly under. A black plume of smoke from the funnel streams behind them. Through her feet, Oriana can feel the engine throb, the mechanical heart of the ship.

Ory has been up all night with a passenger who fell gravely ill, a Mrs Malet, and now her eyes are gritty from lack of sleep. Last night,

Dr Gibson had injected digitalis into Mrs Malet's heart but the patient did not respond. As she and the doctor stand there looking at the smoothed surface of the sea, Ory reveals that before she died, Mrs Malet told her that it was the first anniversary of her husband's death. She wanted to die. She wanted to join him. It was something she willed. Is it possible to resist digitalis? The doctor thinks it is. It is the first time Ory has seen someone pass from 'this life' to the next. It was not as peaceful as Bill claimed his death would be. Is it possible to have a truly peaceful death? She consoles herself with the evidence

> In one of my husband's last letters from the tent (I can only quote from memory as I am away from home) he said 'the barrier has beaten us – but our record is clean, we have nothing to be ashamed of' – shows that no sense of failure entered his head – and his beautifully neat writing up 'til the very last, showed his self control – and his strong faith helped him to meet death without fear or unhappiness – he knew it was all right.

No sense of failure, neat writing, strong faith; surely the sum of this evidence supports the argument for a peaceful death 'without fear or unhappiness'.[698]

But there is still the biology of dying, of ceasing. Leaving the group, Ory walks around the side of the ship to a birdcage. The shadow of the bars falls across a small bird inside. Carefully, Ory unhooks the door of the cage. She reaches in. It is a little diving petrel blown on board when they were four days out from Cape Horn. Captain Greenstreet wants to present it to the Natural History Museum, but that would mean killing it and preparing the skin, just as she has done with thousands of dead grouse. It would ensure its immortality. She cups the bird gently and brings it out of the cage. Its warm feathered body flutters against her palm. Holding it still, she can feel the tiny heart beating. Its wings are tucked in, it is peacefully alive, 'such a dear, fat, comfortable little thing'. She notes its colouring, its markings, despite herself: 'with a blue-black back and head and white breast and pale blue legs'.

She hears laughter. Constance, Ory's sister, is conducting a glee to entertain the other passengers. They start again, practising a tricky musical phrase with Constance demonstrating first. Suddenly Ory raises her arms and releases the bird into the sky. 'I am glad,' she tells Captain Greenstreet later, 'that it "got away".'[699]

LOIS — GOWER

A letter with a BAE emblem, dated 5 February, is delivered to Pitton Cross. It is the first post that has arrived back from New Zealand and it provides Lois with a valuable piece of reassurance in a tilted world.

'Your husband,' Teddy tells Lois, 'died a gallant death, on the return march from the Pole, after faithfully serving his leader, Capt. Scott, through the most trying time. He lost his life for the honour of his country, and the British Navy will be proud of having possessed such a brave man. His "grit" will for ever be an example to the lower deck, his ability was remarkable and I wish to convey to you from the whole Expedition our sorrow.'

Lois will never know that Frank Debenham regards the letter as characteristically disingenuous. Deb believed Teddy 'never quite forgave [Taff] for one of his "drinking too much" occasions in New Zealand'.[700] But for Lois, Teddy is a fellow Welshman. Teddy's brother has visited her. His parents feel kinship in the name 'Evans', even though they are not related to Taff. They send condolences, particularly because they feel it could just as easily have been Teddy that died. 'It is only the Will of Providence that one Evans was taken instead of another.'[701]

'I will see that you and yours never want,' Teddy concludes. 'If you are in any immediate need write at once to:

Mr Wilkinson Greene,
Secretary to Sir Edgar Speyer Bart.
7 Lothbury London E.C.

I cannot tell you how sorry I am for you,
Believe me,
Your sincere friend
Edward G. R. Evans
Commander R.N.'[702]

Lois thinks about her 'immediate need'. She has been 'in need' of an allowance for some time now. It is strange that when she lived with Taff, she never felt vulnerable. To be protected by Taff was to be safe. He was 'the strong man', 'the biggest, heaviest and most muscular man' of the people she saw visiting the *Terra Nova* back in 1910.[703] She looks across at the bundle of letters she had received last May from Commander Evans when he left the party early.[704] Taff had never left a party early until now. She misses his strength.

14 APRIL 1913

KATHLEEN – LONDON

Kathleen has been picked up by Lord Curzon's car and is on her way to 1 Carlton House Terrace for tea and interrogation – she is expected to divulge 'nothing but the truth' of what really happened in the Antarctic. She has prepared as if for an examination, and perhaps she is feeling slightly stronger. Nansen's reply, that now familiar handwriting, was waiting to comfort her at Buckingham Palace Road:

'You should not think so much of [his pain and suffering],' wrote Nansen. 'I have some experience . . . One gets so tired and weak and worn out that one becomes more or less indifferent to physical as well as mental pain. And then at last one falls asleep and does not wake again.'[705] Nansen's polar exploration experience – although he obviously did 'wake again' – is the best reassurance available. (Nansen had tele-grammed his condolences the day after his youngest son Asmund died after a long illness, but he never mentioned it, not wanting to add to her sorrow.)

As she watches the long facade of Buckingham Palace flash past on her left, she has time to reflect on her change of status. When Captain Scott had first seen her and asked Mabel Beardsley who she was, Kathleen was confident that Mabel would have described her as 'a nobody'.[706] There are those who recognise their nobodyness and those that recognise only their importance, but Lord Curzon does not have Scott's journal, and that knowledge empowers. As she arrives, she is announced as 'Lady Scott'. She does not know, though she is sure that Lord Curzon does, whether she is entitled. She knows, as he does, that no one will challenge it.

From the vast reception room window, Kathleen can look left to

Whitehall and the government, or right to Buckingham Palace and the king. Straight ahead, St James's Park Lake glints between the leaves just coming out on the trees that line the fashionable rides. A large tiger-skin rug dominates the floor. It is curious to sit at the epicentre of the British Empire, between the government and the king, and yet to imagine its stiff-backed representative 'gyrating and purring' on the floor with Ms Glyn. Was there a chance that Curzon had not heard the popular ditty:

'Would you like to sin with Elinor Glyn on a tiger skin?
Or would you prefer to err with her on some other fur?'

The room abounds in 'other fur' but Curzon's expressionless face gives nothing away. His voice is strangely slurred and monotone, as if slightly bored and dictating to a minion, perhaps one of his army of gold-braided servants. In one of his letters Curzon used 8 e's in the word 'remember' and this is how he speaks.[707] Kathleen sits. Curzon sits and draws a pad of headed paper and a pencil towards him.

Kathleen knows of Curzon's opinion of globetrotting women, those 'horrors of the latter end of the nineteenth century'.[708] And, to a certain extent, she agrees, but she is not one of those women – she is not expecting to be 'treated as an outsider as regards expedition affairs'.[709] Her husband never excluded her, and neither should Curzon.

Kathleen begins. She is direct; she has never been anything else. She sees Curzon scribbling notes as she speaks: 'Scott's words in his diary on exhaustion of food and fuel in depots on his return' writes Curzon. '. . . lack of thoughtfulness and even of generosity . . . It appears that [Teddy] – down with scurvy – accompanied 2 men with him on return journey have . . . consumed more than their share.' Fuel, Curzon must realise, is as important as food, for without fuel, the snow cannot be melted to drink.* [710]

That is the main secret she has to divulge. She suspects Teddy of

---

* It has also been suggested that the fuel shortage may have been caused by cracked lids, evaporation or pressurized leakage. And the fuel shortage by itself will not have doomed the party, only caused additional discomfort as it would have had to be carefully rationed, so fires simply for warmth would have become impossible and drinking water would have to be melted only at mealtimes. (Fiennes, 2012, chapter 16) greed and thoughtlessness at the expense of the Polar Party, who, she is quite certain, died from starvation. This is awkward. Since Teddy returned to England the previous year – promoted to commander by the navy, given an audience with the king – he has received the establishment's unconditional blessing. It will take some fancy footwork to demote him without revealing the establishment – Curzon and the king included – to have been gullible.

The tiger skin is apparently from Bengal. It has large yellow glass eyes and fluffy fur in rounded, upright ears. The mouth is open, the teeth, whiskers and claws, real. (Neither Kathleen nor Curzon know that years later Dr Atkinson will reveal that starvation was caused by the ration which generated 50 per cent less than the calories they required. The chief reason for the shortage of fuel was leakage through freeze–thaw action on the stoppers.)

As Kathleen talks, Curzon scribbles: 'No doubt [Taff] gave out at the Pole. Lost heart because all in . . . did not perform his share of work. Late behind hand . . . Not . . . till just before . . . when he became delirious and lost his senses . . .'

The death of a rating is one thing (the loss of the senses, of sanity perhaps a feature, in the Curzonite worldview, of his class), but the death of Captain Oates, an upper-class landowner, is quite another. Curzon takes another sheet of paper: 'Oates no doubt took opium and then killed himself. All . . . had a supply and a hypodermic.'

Captain Oates's journal has been sealed and sent to Caroline. Why is the fact that Oates and his pills are missing from the final tent now taken as hard 'no doubt' proof that Oates took them? Neither Kathleen nor Curzon deal in 'doubt', with the exception of that shameful scourge, 'scurvy':

'[Taff] may have had scurvy . . . tho no reference to it,' writes Curzon. 'Oates developed frostbite . . . He had not to be carried on the sledge but could not pull . . . Had he not failed they could have got through.'

Rightly or wrongly, Kathleen, and now Curzon, believe that if Captain Oates had not failed at that point, the others could have got through. This might not fit with the popular legend of the timely self-sacrifice of the officer class, but from reading her husband's journal, it is what Kathleen believes. Oates did not have to be carried – Kathleen is emphatic about that. Scott's account of the ignominious 'carrying' of our 'invalid' Ernest Shackleton in 1903 had precipitated dangerous resentment. Oates had never stooped to taking a ride.

Curzon's final notes include Kathleen's acknowledgement that 'the men indeed all . . . terribly disappointed at [being] anticipated [by] Amundsen'. But Kathleen seems to communicate that only Taff 'gave out . . . lost heart' as a result of the Norwegian flag.

Curzon asks her about Scott's diaries. He hopes, one day, they will be kept at the new headquarters of the Royal Geographical Society at Lowther Lodge, opening in a few days' time. Kathleen tries to be non-committal. (She will not be bullied even by the ex-Viceroy of India himself.) She is still reading them – they make difficult reading. Curzon is looking for a straight answer, a promise. Instead, he receives the distinct impression that her support for the RGS is conditional. He reminds her that the Society wants her to accept a casket with the Founder's Medal on behalf of her husband. It is, as he is sure she realises, a great honour. Sitting in silence, Curzon scribbles a final note, a summarising list:

I asked Lady Scott about
    a. . . . picture in . . . she is to try and get artist
    b. . . . exhibition of relics tent
    c. . . . exhibit clothes skis etc
    d. . . . his last message
    e. She promised to lend it [Scott's journal] to RGS with however recall and she so desired

As Kathleen is ushered towards the door, they discuss the idea of taking down evidence from the expedition's members. Curzon wonders whether Sir Lewis Beaumont and George Goldie might be on a special Antarctic Committee to effect this 'enquiry'. Kathleen tells Curzon that if there is to be an enquiry, she would like to be present. The gold-braided servants swing into action, the doors open and she descends through the spacious lobby to the portico where her 'carriage' awaits. Kathleen may suspect that she is a perfect example of why Curzon did not want to elect females to membership of the RGS. She is not a doormat; she is not even a tiger skin. She will not prostrate herself before him with glass eyes. She is no longer 'nobody'.[711]

LOIS – GOWER

In the playground of Rhossili village school, Player's cigarette cards are a form of currency. These trade cards are issued by tobacco manufacturers to stiffen cigarette packaging and advertise the brand. The most popular to date is a series 'Ships' Figureheads' – twenty-five cigarette cards issued in 1912 by John Player & Sons with historical information on the reverse. Like stamps, these are a form of democratic art and culture that can expand horizons.

Now there is a new series, 'The South Pole'. There is one card for each of the four gentlemen that reached the South Pole but, Lois notes, no card with a picture of Taff. There is even one of Teddy, one of 'An Adélie Penguin & His Mate', and a picture of just four men, in 'A Sledge Team'. Norman and Muriel wonder when they'll release the one of their father. Lois cannot give her children an answer. Perhaps the Player's artist has muddled their father P.O. [Taff] Edgar Evans with Commander Teddy Evans – many people do.

Lois cannot do anything about the Player's cigarette cards, but she can assure the children that the memorial she has planned for Rhossili church will be far better. Perhaps she'll take the children to see the mason in his dusty yard. He has already sketched out a design. It will be a low-relief carving of five men pulling the sledge. Five men. Under it will be some lines by Tennyson. And do the children remember what the rector said in church last Sunday? He said that all the explorers had 'taught afresh to a world growing more luxurious and effeminate, the glory of a soldier's endurance and capacity for strenuous duty and the possession of scientific courage to the last'.[712] But, the children wonder, did the rector mean sailor and soldier, or just soldier?

For the children's sake, as well as of all their relatives on Gower, Lois must somehow quell rumours that Taff held the others back with fatal consequences. That Scott's journal comments that he 'has nearly broken down in brain, we think' denoted insanity, madness. That though he was the strong man, he became the weak man, the sick man, the first to 'fail'. One British newspaper, quoting New Zealand *Daily Chronicle*, claims that: 'Great surprise is expressed here at Captain Scott's references to Seaman Edgar Evans. He accompanied Captain Scott on his first attempt to reach the Pole ten years ago, and the leader then praised him highly.'[713]

Herbert Ponting's portrait of Taff in sledging dress outside the hut, rather than the final pictures at the South Pole, shows Taff as the strong man he was. Lois can assure her children of the photographer's opinion of their father: 'In the mess deck Petty Officer Evans was the dominant personality. His previous polar experience, his splendid build, and his stentorian voice and manner of using it – all compelled the respect due to one who would have been conspicuous in any company.'[714] Lois hopes that the weight of praise will reassure the children or that it will at least be enough to prevent playground taunts.

With their Portsmouth accents, Norman, Muriel and Ralph already stand out. Right now they need their father to be a hero – the kind of man that could take on two difficult men at a time outside the Ship Inn and make sure they thought twice before coming back.

17 APRIL 1913

HILDA – MEDITERRANEAN

Hilda Evans's stomach is tender and swollen. She feels nauseous. Could she be expecting, finally? She is sitting in a stuffy cabin on board the *Otranto* in the Mediterranean. Hilda is sailing away from her friends and family in Christchurch, and into the hostile waters that swirl around the BAE headquarters in London. It is her third trip between New Zealand and London in a year. Kathleen's ship is a fortnight ahead, Oriana's a week ahead. Teddy is second-in-command, and yet Kathleen and Oriana seem curiously reticent about involving him.

On the *Otranto*, their principal sources of information are gleaned from Marconi's ship-to-shore radio. Newspapers send bulletins to be pinned up on the ship's noticeboard. That morning they'd heard a report suggesting that Sir Ernest Shackleton should bring the three bodies in the tent home. The high commissioner of New Zealand has apparently offered the steamer *Hinemoa* for the purpose. Rumours are buzzing around the deck and, to distract herself, Hilda tries to take an interest. The bodies are, after all, frozen, and there are freezer ships that sail regularly with lamb and mutton from New Zealand to the UK. 'While Westminster holds the bones of those who have lived for us,' observes the *Daily Telegraph* news notice, 'St Paul's has become the garner of the fame of those who have gone to their deaths in our service.'

There is frenzied speculation, but at the captain's table they discuss the precedents. Jane Franklin, wife of Northwest Passage explorer Sir John Franklin, sent many expeditions north precisely to find his body in order to refute charges of cannibalism. When Hilda leaves the table she can hardly walk. The ship's doctor is called for. She is helped back to her cabin.

EMILY – BUTE

Emily does not know how the other relations might feel about it, but she thanks God for that final blizzard. It is basic mathematics. When they set up camp they had two days' food. The blizzard was nine days long. If Birdie was going to die, she was glad he died in the tent with his companions near. She pities Lois and Caroline, whose menfolk died alone, whose bodies were never found. And on the subject of the bodies – Birdie was navy. Like all the other cadets he trained with on the *Worcester* he was taught that in 1805 Admiral Horatio Nelson's body was brought back to the UK upside down in a barrel of brandy on the *Victory*. The level of brandy in the barrel was found to be considerably lower on arrival in London. Had the sailors been sipping their hero? Nelson was buried at St Paul's Cathedral, but in Emily's opinion, Birdie should not be moved from his cosy companionable resting place, however much glory and status a tomb at St Paul's might confer.[715]

HANNAH SCOTT – HENLEY-ON-THAMES, ENGLAND

Scott's mother Hannah writes to Lord Curzon to tell him that 'where they made their tragic deaths should be their resting place to us; any other thought seems desecration and in this I have every reason to think my beloved son's wife will agree.'[716]

ORIANA – LONDON

Both Bill and Ory's families have Christian missionaries in their ancestry. She knows that David Livingstone died in 1873, the year before she was born. Livingstone's servants buried his heart in Africa under a mvule tree and then proceeded to carry his body over a thousand miles until it was returned by ship to Britain. The body lay in the map room of the RGS prior to internment at Westminster Abbey. What kind of basic native form of specimen preservation, Ory wonders, had Livingstone's body gone through in order not to have rotted on that march across the dark continent? Something like the Indonesian shrunken heads? It hardly bears thinking about. She wants nothing of the sort: 'I hardly need say that on no account would I wish my Husband's body to be touched. I feel that it could not have a more fitting resting place.' Ory is reacting to yet another article on the subject, this time in a Canadian newspaper – she wants to put an end to the months of grisly speculation by taking the responsibility as spokeswoman, adding, 'and I know [Kathleen] feels the same about Captain Scott's and also [Emily] about her son's body.'[717]

18 APRIL 1913

HILDA – MEDITERRANEAN

The ship-to-shore radio on board the *Otranto* reports that Lord Curzon has ended speculation. With one imperial gesture he has swept aside the brandy barrel, the cannibalism and the mvule tree. The bodies will be left where they are, 'with the snow as their winding sheet, the eternal ice as their tomb, and the solemn Antarctic wastes as the graveyard in which it has pleased God that they should sleep'.[718]

Hilda's abdomen is badly swollen and she is vomiting. The pain is terrible. The ship's doctor diagnoses acute and dangerously advanced peritonitis. The operation will be severe and it will have to be done immediately if her life is to be saved. The doctor lays out his instruments and calls for soap and water.

20 APRIL 1913

ORIANA – LONDON

Isabel Smith walks her friend straight through their Mayfair house – Oriana's 'London home' – past the white marble staircase and out into the large private square. They are in a green oasis protected on three sides by stately stucco villas. Reginald is there. Ory gives them the letter her husband wrote in the back of his journal:

My Dear Good Friend and my Dear Mrs Smith,

This looks like a finish to our undertaking for we are out of food and oil and not able to move now for 3 days on account of the blizzard. We have had a long struggle . . . I want to say how I have valued your friendship and your example, and how I and my beloved wife have loved you both from first to last. God be thanked for such as you. We shall meet in the hereafter . . . I should like to have seen the Grouse book, but it is not allowed me. God's will be done. I am only hopeful that this note may reach you some day to tell you how your goodness has helped me and my beloved Ory. I know she will come to you in her trouble and find consolation, thank God . . .

Your loving [Bill] Wilson[719]

And here she is. She has come to them. The three friends stand in silence in the garden, the birds sing while Bill's words fall in drifts like the apple blossom around them.

Later, in the panelled drawing room, Ory sets Bill's journals on a cloth-covered table and turns the pages one at a time. Reginald has been chosen as the expedition publisher. Leonard Huxley will be the editor. With his glasses on the end of his nose, Reginald looks more closely at the faint pencil script. The handwriting, Ory points out, shows no sign of stress, starvation or delirium. Reginald and Isabel know that script. They have read it in prose, in tables, up the side of graphs, in drafts of the grouse enquiry report – they 'should like [him] to have seen the Grouse book' too.

Reginald pauses with '11th February 1912' open. Until this point, his friend Bill has used every line of the journal. After that date, there are gaps. He flicks on, to the 24th of February, where there is half a line of blank space and then three words, 'Fat pony hoosh', followed by two and a half lines of space. The words are written in pencil. Someone has rubbed them out.

Ory has been called to the front door. A telegram. She left a forwarding address with her in-laws, the Wilsons at Westal in Cheltenham. Oriana opens the envelope. Hilda Evans is dead.

APRIL 1913

LORD CURZON – LONDON

Oriana walks around the tiger-skin rug. What breed of tiger? What age? Had Lord Curzon shot it himself? Which taxidermist had he used? Edward Gerard and Sons? Curzon mumbles his answers, hoping that this tall, thin, impeccably dressed woman will be easier to tame than Scott's wife.

If Curzon offers his condolences on the recent death of Mrs Evans, Ory might tell him that Hilda was her friend. She probably would not add that Hilda was the 'real brick' that had helped her to keep Bill sane on the liner over to Melbourne, the lady she had defended from Kathleen through all that 'blood and hair' before the *Terra Nova*'s departure from Port Chalmers.[720] But Curzon quickly understands that it does not follow that because Oriana admired Hilda's character, she admires her husband Teddy's. Taking a seat, Curzon draws out his Carlton House Terrace embossed notepaper and his sharpest pencil.

Mrs Wilson told me later there was a passage in her husband's diary which spoke of the 'inexplicable' shortage of fuel and provisions on the return journey related . . . depots . . . had not been touched by Meares and which could only . . . to an unauthorised subtraction of one or two . . . the returning parties. This passage however she proposes to show to no one and to keep secret.

C.[721]

It is at least corroboration, but although she has given him the information, she has not given him permission to use it. How had an all-male expedition to the bastion of masculinity empowered 'globe-trotting females' in this manner? Why do they feel they can dictate the terms? Before she leaves, Oriana makes him promise that the notes would be locked in a safe. Curzon mumbles. Will madam take his word as a gentleman, or is that not sufficient? Perhaps she requires written confirmation from George Nathaniel Curzon, 1st Marquess Curzon of Kedleston, KG, GCSI, GCIE, PC, FBA, that these notes will not be revealed in her lifetime?

When Oriana has left, Curzon realises that he could still have his enquiry if only he could get the expedition members, all men, to re-iterate what the 'globetrotters' have told him. But Admiral Sir Lewis Beaumont is not keen: 'the rumour would certainly go the rounds of the papers that the Royal Geographical Society had held an enquiry – they would probably say "a secret enquiry". I think with regard to Lady Scott attending a Committee Meeting that it would be best to wait – we should spare her if we can do it without her.'[722]

Curzon agrees with 'sparing' Kathleen; would that they could 'spare' all females. Beaumont assures Curzon that Kathleen sees sense, 'and would rather that nothing happened to mar the splendid record of her husband's work'.[723] Beaumont is careful not to mention Teddy by name. He does not want to leave a paper trail. 'I cannot in a letter give you my reasons,' states Beaumont. Instead he suggests that Curzon, as president, should decide what attitude to take by himself, rather than wait for an informal meeting with Teddy to decide.

22 APRIL 1913

KATHLEEN – LONDON

Kathleen meets the Southampton boat train in London. She suspects, though she cannot be sure, that Teddy might be responsible for the fatal shortage of oil; that he failed to deliver the revised instructions about bringing the dogs south of One Ton; that he fabricated Scott's intention to back his promotion to commander. Teddy is slippery and self-promoting yet deserving of sympathy. He faces that 'emptiness' Scott referred to – Hilda has not left a child. Kathleen has recently learned that Isadora Duncan's two children have drowned, and Nansen's son has died of a chronic illness. These are tragedies. Both Hilda and Scott have at least lived adult lives.

Teddy walks onto the station platform where a handful of reporters in trilbies and dark suits watch from a respectful distance. They have their headline, 'Widow meeting Widower – A Touching Scene', they just need a bit of copy to go underneath. They do not realise that Kathleen and Hilda were never friends, that Kathleen thought Hilda 'lacked any erudition', was 'ignorant' at best and 'puerile' at worst. Similarly Kathleen has no idea that Hilda called her 'that horrid Mrs Scott'. Kathleen and Teddy make sure that their greeting is appropriate to the circumstances so that the trilbied gentlemen have no idea of what Kathleen knows and Teddy suspects. Kathleen is about to knock Teddy off his pedestal or, at least, slice him down to size.

Kathleen learns how Hilda died. She'd been diagnosed with peritonitis on 15 April. She'd recovered from the operation but in the early hours of the morning of the 17th she suffered from an embolism as a result of the operation and died just after midnight on the 18th. Teddy is going to add 'Russell' to his name. It is Hilda's maiden name. After their 'touching scene', Teddy retires directly to his hotel. He intends to continue writing up his expedition report.

Kathleen arrives at the offices of Smith & Elder. She needs to make sure that her version will be out first. How is Huxley doing with the excisions – 'seventeen substantial alterations . . . but the alteration or excision of only sixty-eight words in a sixty-page account' – it can't take that long, can it?[724] Kathleen is assured that the report will be produced as quickly as possible. As per her instructions, Teddy will not be allowed access to Scott's journal. Sir Clements Markham is writing the preface, J. M. Barrie, the introduction. It will fill two volumes, be priced at two guineas, and appear simultaneously in English, French and German.

Kathleen notes that Teddy has not brought Hilda's body home. For while the bodies of the five men who died at the South Pole are forever frozen, in the Mediterranean heat Hilda's body had to be buried immediately in Toulon.

4 MAY 1913

LOIS – MORRISTON, WALES

Commander Teddy Evans RN is at the door of Falmouth House in Morriston, where Lois is staying with her sister Beatrice Faull. He has motored down from Cardiff with a naval friend, Percy Lewis, who is waiting outside. He wishes to deliver Lois's husband's journals to her in person. Lois welcomes him in. She wears her thick brown hair parted slightly to the left. She wears a full-length black dress with a high collar. She is small and slight but upright. Ralph wears long flannel shorts and a sweater. He has socks up to his knees and sturdy lace-up boots. He leans against Lois's knee. Lois tells Commander Evans that Taff 'was such a good husband and how fond he was of these dear children'.[725] She has a last letter, written in pencil, undated, in which Taff tells her that he is only 150 miles from the Pole. Where is his body now? Teddy listens to her Welsh accent, to her suffixing sentences with 'you see'. He and Hilda had never been able to have children. What would it be like to have a child like Ralph, your child, leaning against your knee?

Teddy remembers Taff bandaging Pennell's frostbitten fingers, his dexterity and care. Such a burly man with such a gentle touch. But Taff will not see these children grow up. Teddy gives Lois a letter from

Pennell: 'Your husband on many occasions has shown me very great kindness, and if in any way I can replay it, it would give me great pleasure . . . his diary from the South Pole will be sent to you.'[726]

Teddy is charmed by Lois and Ralph. When he leaves Falmouth House, he will describe Lois as 'the brave widow of a brave man'. Lois appreciates the visit. Although she may appear to be brave, she is worried about the children. They are being bullied. The word in the playground is that their father was insane – 'the unfortunate man lost his reason' – and that while Captain Oates sacrificed himself to release the others from the burden of having to care for him, their father had not.

APRIL 1913

CAROLINE – GESTINGTHORPE

Caroline is sleeping in Laurie's bedroom. She carries one of his epaulettes with her wherever she goes. When she descends every morning down the oak staircase, she can stop to look at the jewelled light in the heraldic stained glass. Each emblem is the symbol of a dynasty. And yet heraldry is really a breeding chart for humans; the acceptable presentation of a visceral history of successful legitimate sexual relationships. However committed Caroline has been in tracing the Oates genealogy thus far, one cannot continue to breed without a body. Laurie's bloodline stops here. Or does it?

Caroline descends to the flagstoned hall presided over by Laurie's horned beasts. These animals are mounted, but the family's dead dogs are buried just outside the high brick garden wall. She can visit their graves and know that their canine remains are just under the turf. To visit Willie, she can go to Madeira. But Laurie has no place she can visit. She has read accounts of the snow cairn over the three men found in that tent. The relief expedition had moved on to look for Laurie and recovered his sleeping bag where it had been discarded, but his body was nowhere to be found. Near the place they erected a memorial: 'Hereabouts died a very gallant gentleman.' But 'hereabouts' isn't precise enough. She needs to know precisely where Laurie lies, a specific point on the earth's surface where she can visit his frozen body, somehow in her mind.

Caroline often finds herself seeking the equine atmosphere of the

Gestingthorpe stable yard. She inhales the sweet-smelling hay, the burnished leather saddles; even the straw mound of mucked-out horse manure is just processed grass. Can she feel his presence here? 'He had a wonderful personality; no one could have said an unkind thing or lost their temper in his presence,' she says. 'Truly he inspired one with the highest ideals – just to be with him was such a help in life's perplexities.' Climbing the mounting block, she arranges the long skirt of her riding habit over the side saddle and leans forward to strokes the animal's firm neck. She can feel the warmth, even beneath her gloved hand.

She tries to grapple with 'life's perplexities': why is it acceptable for any man or woman to show affection for a horse, even in public? Laurie was always smoothing the horse's flank. A horse can be petted, plaited and pawed over even by strangers, without comment. But when it comes to showing affection to other humans, the rules are different. Caroline and Laurie belong to a class that is so restrained, they cannot bring themselves to say goodbye.

Caroline's horse walks through the short tunnel out to the drive, the sound of hooves on paving echoing off the roof. Steering her onto the driveway, Caroline remembers Laurie on a horse, he was always a 'dashing, & quite fearless rider – very clever with horses'.[727] Caroline might hack out of the village and right out across verdant spring fields to the Gainsborough oak. No one forgets to doff their cap now.

21

Defiance & Cowardice

25 MAY 1913

KATHLEEN — LONDON

Kathleen is on the telephone in the narrow hall of 174 Buckingham Palace Road. She is often on the phone these days. While listening, she can use the time to deal with her correspondence. This letter is from a news editor, who writes to ask if she 'would affirm or deny a report . . . that she was married to Sir J. M. Barrie six weeks ago. The news editor hesitates to trouble Lady Scott in this matter, but on account of the many rumours which have been in circulation . . .'.[728]

Kathleen answers distractedly into the voicepiece. Lord Curzon is on the other end, a monologue that only requires the occasional confirmation that she is still there. Slipping the letter back into the envelope, she makes a mental note that she will have to tell the news editor that no, she is not Mrs Barrie, Mrs Nansen, Mrs Asquith nor Senora Marconi. They will have to 'hesitate to trouble' someone else to fill their pages. Perhaps she can delegate this nonsense to the secretary she's been obliged to employ to keep on top of such rubbish.

She knows how the Mrs Barrie rumour started. Barrie confided to somebody that Scott had entrusted Peter's future to him. Even if Scott had, which is unlikely, it did not follow that Kathleen is part of that package. She has recently been elected to Mrs Humphrey Ward's anti-suffrage committee, but it does not follow that she thinks wives, widows even, are chattels.

The only really 'hungry love' Kathleen can feel for the present is for babies, for Peter specifically, but for future babies too should they appear. 'How absurd,' she observes, 'that I, able bodied and self-supporting, and having proved my capacity, am debarred from producing babies without binding myself to some man I don't want.'[729] She does not rule out remarriage but she needs something altogether more robust than the diminutive author of *Peter Pan*.

Perhaps the news editor should contact Lois Evans, the petty officer's wife. In Scott's dying letter he'd alerted Barrie to P.O. Evans's wife: 'a widow in humble circumstances. Do what you can to get their claims recognised.'[730] Lois has not one but two 'lost boys', Norman and Ralph, and Muriel, a 'lost girl', if that counts? Mrs Lois Barrie?

As Curzon's 'eeeeee's pour down the telephone, Kathleen tries to respond without always having to 'beg your pardon?' She does not want to beg for anything from Lord Curzon. He is in the middle of outlining the grants to relatives. Kathleen knows that the Mansion House Fund sum has reached £60,000 and money is still being donated. Why is Curzon proposing to give the relatives so little? It is indefensible.

Curzon becomes even less coherent when interrupted, but she really cannot listen to any more. She blames the line. It is a bad line. Sorry. In the background she can hear the typewriter. Kathleen scribbles a reply to the news editor and places it at the top of her secretary's in-tray. She needs to dictate a new letter.

Dear Lord Curzon,

What I meant on the telephone about not making the grant to relatives too small is that I think there would be a great outcry from the public if only £12,000 (one fifth of the sum subscribed in response to my husband's message) be devoted to the object he wrote about.

I have heard already the rather mannerless criticisms on suggestions for applying much of the money otherwise. I wish it were otherwise but feel it would be a sad pity to have any controversy on the subject after it be decided. Already I have had to restrain people writing to the papers although nothing has been determined. I write in great haste and probably without discretion, but thought I'd better tell you what you couldn't hear and I do all the time.

How should she end it? His grateful servant? His dutiful servant? She is not his servant. She would end it politely but uniquely:

Sincerely and most gratefully

Kathleen Scott[731]

The park is heavy with blossom, the grass a startling green and she has just lied to Lord Curzon. Surely the sky will now fall down. He wants to restrict the amount of the Mansion House Fund that the relatives get but at the same time to get her to come to the RGS to accept a casket on behalf of her husband. On both counts it is absurd, but she has told him that 'I will come [to the RGS] this afternoon in defiance of my cowardice.' She will not. She will not be summoned to pay homage to the RGS while accepting just one fifth of the monies her husband's 'Message to the Public' has raised. She will use the 'bad line' along with Curzon's expectation of womanly cowardice as 'deniability' – she can play the game as well as he can, perhaps better. She will walk outside, briskly and defiantly, and she will remain sane.

25 MAY 1913

ORIANA – LONDON

Oriana watches the door of the new Royal Geographical Society head-quarters to see whether a miracle will occur. Has her letter to Kathleen been sufficiently persuasive? Their relationship has changed as much as her status from wife to widow, from white to black. 'Frankly,' she'd told Kathleen, 'I could not have said this 18 months ago, but I feel it very truly & honestly now – that I want to be with you at these times & I would have given much to have you, as it won't be at all easy to go alone. I have my people [relations] there – but that is not the same as having you.' She'd even tried to reduce the business of accepting the blessed casket to its component parts: 'after all it only means standing for about 3 seconds at the most.'[732] Ory does not have a choice. In her reply to Keltie's letter of condolence, which reached her on her way home in Tenerife, she told him that 'I believe I would like to receive the Patron's Royal Medal myself if possible. I should feel proud to be at the meeting for my husband's sake.'[733] The time for that meeting, the presentation, is now upon them. But Kathleen is nowhere to be seen.

The building has only just been opened and still smells of paint and plaster overlaid with the faint whiff of cigars. The hall is lofty and handsome, the members mostly mutton-chopped and shod in spats. Someone asks her about the exhibition she is organising at the Alpine Club of Bill's drawings and watercolours. *The Times* declared that they 'tell us more than words could . . . they are not to be judged as works of art, but as records of fact.'[734] Now that Bill is dead, she is the custodian of his artistic reputation. She believes his paintings have more poetry than simply scientific records, but she is focused on more prosaic matters. She negotiated a much better deal on the gallery's commission than Bill had after the *Discovery* expedition. Even before his death, Bill wrote that if there was anything to be done with his paintings, Ory will 'have the doing', and she has.

As the members begin to take their seats for the presentation, Keltie asks Ory why her husband hadn't become a member himself – surely he'd been invited? She tells him that he had, but he could never afford the membership fee. There is a polite pause. Is this a clubland faux pas?[735]

Ory needs reinforcements. If Kathleen doesn't appear soon, Ory will have to climb those stairs alone. She has saved a seat beside her, just in case. She begins to fear that her letter to Kathleen was too harsh: 'Well my dear, if you can't make yourself . . . I certainly can't! & I am only terribly disappointed.'[736]

26 MAY 1913

KATHLEEN – LONDON

Curzon is displeased. He is not accustomed to having the telephone call ended at the opposite end of the line and he is not in the business of having his invitations, or his caskets, refused. And now the male Fellows have written to Scott Keltie to ask if they could bring their ladies with them. 'I think, we had better say no,' writes Keltie to Curzon, trying to think of a reason why: 'If many Fellows bring ladies with them the place won't hold them.'[737] Keltie could sugarcoat it all he liked but Curzon replied: 'No male Fellow can bring lady guests.'[738] Some are unavoidable. Mrs Workman is 'a bit of a bounder & does rub people up the wrong way', agrees Keltie, 'but I think you will find she conducts herself beseemingly at the dinner.'*[739]

When Curzon's displeasure percolates through Keltie's diplomacy to Kathleen, she responds with 'a soothing letter'. She is not completely sure how craven she is expected to be but she tries to stay the right side of downright parody. Curzon has dealt a casket, she raises him 'about a dozen . . . gold medals on very long loan [to the RGS]?' Scott has been awarded so many she can't even count them.[740]

Curzon is hardly mollified, but there is more to come. Soon he will have to offer Scott Keltie's suggestion that they should make Lady Scott a Life Member of the Society. At least they do not have to update the statute book for Life Members, but 'under Chapter 3, number 6 of our Bye Laws, the words are as follows: "Where it may be found desirable to elect gentlemen to the Fellowship who are distinguished for their services to geographical science."'[741]

EMILY – BUTE

Emily is proud to see that it is not only her son mentioned in the newspapers but her husband's role as a Fellow of the RGS: 'Captain Bowers's distinguished record of exploration in China and the Bhamo expedition'.[742] But in the same newspapers, there is some controversy about Emily's eligibility for an Indian government pension. Cherry is instantly defensive on her behalf. It is so like Birdie's 'outraged from the Royal Indian Marine' letters that she responds in her mother voice, telling him to ignore the bullies and have the courage of his moral conviction: 'Never mind what the press says or doesn't say – those who know him loved him . . . He was all the world to me – my only son – but I cannot write about it.'[743]

Emily knows that Cherry is 'rich beyond dreams of avarice', as Birdie had described him. Cherry is, to be sure, a person from the other side of the Cheltenham Promenade fence, but there is something about his righteous indignation, and the affection it implies, that makes her want to mother him.

---

* *Two Summers in the Ice-Wilds of Eastern Karakoram* by Fanny Bullock Workman describes mapping the Rose Glacier in the Karakoram between 1911–12. Fanny organised and led the expedition, accompanied by her husband William who took a photograph of her on a glacier holding a newspaper with the headline 'Votes for Women'.

My dear Cherry,

You see I am taking a great liberty but I am so used to 'my friend Cherry' that I never think of you in any other way . . .[744]

. . . I write freely to you because somehow you seem a little bit of [Birdie] left to me – you don't mind do you?[745]

. . . of course you must come to Rothesay . . . he would like you to do so – it will be a small house [about the size of the cook's larder at Cherry's family seat at Lamer] & a very hearty welcome.[746]

She did not say 'but', she said '&' – Emily is precise about grammar and the balance of status it confers.

Would Emily like to see Ponting's film? 'I do not feel,' she tells him, 'I could see the Antarctic pictures again'. It was like getting a telegram followed by a letter. The first time she'd seen those moving images it had filled her with joy and anticipation. But thinking back it seemed cruelly ironic that while she'd been sitting in the cinema watching him talk and laugh with his companions, he was already dead. Instead she tells Cherry that she would like him to have Birdie's rifle '& there may be something else you would like though I know you will need nothing to remind you of your friend "Birdie".'[747]

With sensitivity and prescience she anticipates the impact on Cherry's mental health. 'I have so often thought what a dreadful winter it must have been for you all in the hut – knowing what must have happened & yet powerless to do anything – We have all suffered & those who were left behind not the least.'

LOIS – GOWER

Lois has received a 'generous offer' from the board of managers of the London Orphanage Asylum.[748] They will admit, free of charge, one of Edgar's children, in recognition of the bravery and heroism of their father. The child would be maintained and educated until the age of fifteen. Norman? In an orphanage? Norman is not an orphan. Norman is only just eight. She knows that the officer class often send their children away to public schools at that age, but that is not the Gower way.

Lois stands up and empties her raked sand into the sieve riddle. Her back aches. When she thinks about Taff's physical labours – the heavy going across crushed snow – she might remember his comment 'makes one swear'.[749] Bracing herself again, she leans down to scoop seawater and shake the riddle so that the cockles are left glistening on the sieve. For the moment she is shuttling between her sister's in Morriston and her parents on Gower, part of a stalwart community of husband-less women who work the sands to provide for their families.

When Lois was young, she was friends with the rector's daughter, who had left Gower for boarding school. Was Taff at boarding school in that segregated hut – half boarding school, half asylum? William Lashly, Taff's rating friend, worries that Taff might have been isolated in the final five – the only member of his class. The isolation might have contributed to his demise. One of the officer class, Raymond Priestly, seems to agree: 'The psychological effect of being, in those days, a rating among four officers, placed a heavy burden on poor Evans. He was in a thought compartment by himself, and was naturally the first to crack.'

Lois looks up to check the children further up the beach. They at least are well fed again, but there are persistent threats of a medal presentation from the Royal Geographical Society in London. Soon she will have to admit that she's sold Taff's medal. Will it be taken as a typically lower-class understanding of the worth of a thing, its worth in cash? Recently, the *South Wales Daily Post* has requoted Taff's assessment of the Antarctic: 'only a melancholy seal to look at, and his blessed hide not worth a cent in a European market.'[750]

Meanwhile, who is supporting Beatrice Pharaoh and Taff's illegitimate daughter, Lillian? Are they in any immediate need? Beatrice put Taff's full name and rank on Lillian's birth certificate. How hard would it be for a journalist to track her down? Lois's address is mentioned in every newspaper. Perhaps Arthur Thomas, Taff's executor, knows something she doesn't. Was Taff already paying some form of bastardy tithes? Had he always?

EMILY – BUTE

As Emily scrapes butter onto her toasted teacake, she tells William Maxwell from upstairs that the public nature of the Mansion House

Fund means that she is responsible to that public. It is like being accountable to the donors towards the Mission School she'd worked at in Burma thirty years before. Like the Mission, this is a Christian initiative, 'God' having been one of the seven words in Scott's final message – 'for God's sake'. She feels that her mission now is to honour Birdie's name and share his inspiration throughout the educational establishments of the Empire. It will be her Duty with a capital 'D'.

Passing the sugar, William studiously avoids the word 'charity' in Emily's presence. He has always believed that the sense of common purpose can be harnessed to achieve far more than any single individual is capable of and this Mansion House Fund is proof. He is glad that Emily will be financially secure, although in the back of his mind he's already begun to form other plans for making sure of that himself.

For Emily the fund is a godsend, one that she has spent time on her knees at St Ninian's giving thanks for. She will not have to accept the money from individuals ('charity'); she will not have to accept the money from lectures (though Teddy wants all the proceeds of the lecture he gave in Rothesay to go to her).[751] They are now middle middlers – they are independent, capable women – they may choose to work but they don't have to.

For Birdie's sake, she will accept the Mansion House money that he has earned through 'honest sweat'. She knows it would have pleased him in the same way that it had pleased him to be able to send them money from his Royal Indian Marine salary when he was abroad. It would also have pleased him to know the title of an evening lecture by the Rev. T. R. Thompson, in the East Kirk at Greenock: 'The Finest Features in Manhood'.[752] There can be no doubt that he proved himself there. Ironically the money would have enabled Birdie to keep a wife, to marry and have a family of his own.

Emily has been in frequent correspondence with Cherry, who refers to the public as 'the yelling pack', trying to bleed landowners like him dry.[753] But Emily had grown up among that pack and is indebted to them for their generosity – for money given unconditionally for her welfare. She does not feel she has the right to make her response conditional.

CAROLINE — GESTINGTHORPE

It had taken courage to break the seals upon Laurie's journals. They were all that remained of her son, new thoughts Caroline had not yet encountered. Once she read them, he would cease to talk to her, cease to live as a correspondent, cease to exist. Impossible. And yet, she had to know. On page 56 of the last journal she found Bill Wilson's letter to her, describing her son's death: 'My wife has a real faith in God,' Bill wrote to Caroline, 'and so your son tells me have you – and so have I – and if ever a man died like a noble soul and in a Christlike spirit your son did'.[754]

Caroline notices that the vegetables of the kitchen garden are coming through in gratifying straight rows, the first green shoots pushing through the chocolate-coloured earth. She'd ordered those seeds a week after Laurie's death. They symbolise the fact that life must go on but, as Kathleen put it to Emily Bowers, 'one misses one's mankind more all the time, I expect you find that too.'[755]

Under the pear blossom, Caroline sits on a garden bench with Oriana Wilson. She'd found a letter written in Laurie's journal that Bill asked if she would tear out and send on to his wife. At first Oriana was delighted. She told Kathleen, and perhaps Caroline, that it was 'wonderful' to get a new letter from Bill, albeit one written on 21 March 1912, 'just wonderful'.[756] But when Oriana came to visit Caroline at Gestingthorpe, there were long pauses where a hand-kerchief had to be used, and Caroline later wrote, 'I felt deeply and heavily for her . . . not dissimilar to [that which] God handed to me.'[757] It was so difficult to know when grief would strike.

Caroline found the horses a comfort. Perhaps a visit to the stables? Did Ory confide in Caroline that even Bill could tell that Oates had been handed an impossible load of crocks in the Antarctic? 'I am very anxious about Titus Oates, who has had a great string of rotten unsound ponies thrown on his hands,' wrote Bill back in 1911, 'and who is spoken to rather as though he was to blame whenever anything goes wrong with them, and of course he doesn't like it.'[758]

It is difficult to think of Laurie being blamed for the crocks, but corroboration of her own opinion of Scott is also somehow important for Caroline. She encourages confidences. At some point during her visit, Oriana confides to Caroline that she felt Bill knew he would not return. Both Caroline and Ory know that premeditated death and sacrifice – as opposed to suicide – have Christian endorsement. 'Their deaths were necessary to God's great purpose,' observed one Christian writer at the time. 'There seems so much to me like our dear Lord's death in a way.'[759]

Oriana returns to the slop and plaster of Westal, where her in-laws are creating a separate flat for her. Caroline returns to the practicalities, the Mansion House Fund – she hopes that the accounts for that fund will be properly managed. She does not need or want the money. She is on the giving end of largesse, not now, and not ever, on the receiving end. 'Largesse' defines any lady of the manor – she will not be demoted by Scott to a charitable case, whatever else she has to endure.

What she needs is information not cash. The king's donation of £200 to the Mansion House Fund shows an unquestioning acceptance of the heroic myth, but she cannot forget her son's letter: 'Scott has put two or three people's back up lately,' Laurie told her at the end of the winter, 'and Meares, who looks after the dogs and is a pal of mine, had a regular row with him. Myself I dislike Scott intensely and would chuck the thing if it were not that we are a British expedition and must beat the Norwegians – Scott has always been very civil to me and I have the reputation of getting on well with him but [these next words are crossed out] the fact of the matter is he is not straight, it is himself first and when he has got all he can out of you it is shift for yourself.'[760] It would be disloyal to her son for her to be passive. What did he mean with, 'when he has got all he can out of you'? She wants facts, hard facts, and she will not rest until she has them.

Caroline decides to refuse the RGS summons to Buckingham Palace, while 'keeping [her] mouth shut'. It will be the most elegant way of expressing her suspicions and disapproval to those who matter.

22

Mansion & Palaces

14 JUNE 1913

The June sky is overcast, there are no shadows and no particular breeze to animate the flags. In three days it will be precisely three years since the ship left this dock in Cardiff to a deafening roar of cheers, bands, flag waving and sirens. Now it is returning in silence. The crowd standing around Bute Dock is still, bare-headed men and women in dark clothing, like people attending a funeral. Smoke issues from the large chimney of the tug towing Scott's ship a boat's length behind. The tug's engine chugs. One of the huskies chained to the foredeck of the *Terra Nova* barks and wags its feather tail. There is the sound of the slap of water as a shallow bow wave breaks against the dock. The whirr of the Pathé cameras seems loud.

Suddenly, a single voice from the crowd calls out: 'Three cheers for little Peter'. It is as if a signal has animated the dockside. A sudden wall of sound breaks free, a unanimous cheer moves out, sound waves rippling out over the water towards the boat. On board the *Terra Nova*, a small boy runs to the side. A man in the uniform of a commander of the Royal Navy picks him up and holds him out for the crowd to see. Now that the silence has been broken, the cheers are given again and again. A woman joins him. She is smiling. The cheering from the dockside becomes a roar.

Oriana joins Teddy, Peter and Kathleen. Ory looks down, focusing the attention on Peter. Scott's dying message to 'make the boy interested in Natural History' is surely directly from Bill. Oriana may not have children, but Bill's legacy will live on through Peter. Kathleen is glad to see that it is not to be a funeral procession but a Roman *triumphus*, a civil ceremony to celebrate and sanctify success. She knows that she can trust the Christian Oriana to fall in. Grief is selfish. Both widows, for different reasons, exalt their 'dead lions', however 'Victorian' the older generation might choose to be. On the dockside, Lois realises that three-and-a-half-year-old Peter is the same age as her youngest, Ralph. Should she have brought him? *John Bull* suggested that a replica of the *Terra Nova* should be made for Peter Scott, a 'toy' to help him learn about his father's heroism. One reader wrote in to ask if Taff Evans's children should be offered one too for the same purpose?[761]

Mrs Wilson makes a point of talking to Lois. Lois looks over to where five young sailors lean against the rigging. Gradually, they notice that the Pathé camera is rolling. They grin briefly, then, remembering the sombre occasion, resume appropriate expressions and look away.

Lois has been invited to sit in the front row at the Cardiff Exchange with the Lord Mayor, Alderman Morgan Thomas and the Lady Mayoress his wife. If there were no controversy surrounding Taff, she could decline the Mayor's invitation. She does not.

The Pathé cameras positioned on the dockside have recorded the return of the ship. The newspaper journalists who stand near them note that the *Terra Nova*'s return coincides with suffragette Miss Emily Davison's funeral. On 4 June she'd tried to intercept Anmer, the King's horse. She died of a fractured skull. The moment of impact was caught by three news cameras covering the Epsom Derby, but still there are comparisons with these five men who died a world and over a year away.

Emily Davison's death is being treated by the suffragettes as a 'sacrifice'. Drawing an equivalence with the South Pole deaths, Votes for Women hopes that Davison's death will 'bring home to all the men and women united in service to this movement the realisation that in sacrifice it was created, in sacrifice it has thriven and by sacrifice alone it will triumph'.[762]

The Tablet eschewed the suffragettes in favour of women in general: 'A million wives and mothers, devotees of duty . . . are exemplars of a heroism not inferior to that of the man of adventure. Daily drudges mated to monotony, and with no aid or inspiration such as comes from the knowledge that their deeds are to make history . . .'[763]

Emily Bowers arrives on the dockside, hot, bothered and rather put out. Oriana wrote to discourage her from coming to Cardiff at all.[764] Emily sees that both Oriana and Kathleen have not only come, but arranged to be on board the *Terra Nova* as it sailed in. When Emily asks Teddy if he can think of a reason that she and Caroline might have been 'discouraged', he has no idea. Emily wants to shake the hand of Petty Officer Tom Crean. His extraordinary walk to save the life of Teddy has made him a hero in his own right, and Birdie did admire the British bluejackets.

Emily stayed in Cardiff last night, at the home of a school friend of Birdie's who 'sent me a most warm invitation. I knew him very well as a boy.'[765] Caroline is staying at the Park Hotel, a new luxury Beaux Arts affair in the centre of Cardiff. It offers rooms for servants. One of the kennelmen she has brought with her from Gestingthorpe will take a husky back to their kennels the next day. Emily does not think she can keep a husky in the flat in Ardbeg – 'I dare not have one because of the sheep all about the island in the winter.'[766]

Both Caroline and Emily are keen to see the bluejackets. Caroline wants to give out presents of cash, 'largesse'. Emily has socks to distribute. Caroline is determined to take down names and addresses. She has her notebook and needs interviews, but the crew is about to be paid off, after which they will disperse and be difficult to trace. Together, the two mothers make their way through the crowds to the *Terra Nova*.

The Pathé camera cuts back to the ship, where the five women stand together on the deck, looking up as Teddy addresses them from the bridge. It will be, he tells them, just a short speech.

JUNE 1913

SCOTT KELTIE – LONDON

From his window, Scott Keltie watches Curzon's liveried motorcar sweep out of the drive heading east towards the Mansion House. Lowther Lodge was, they all agreed, a bit 'far out' of the centre and it didn't sound as good as their old headquarters at Savile Row. Perhaps they should drop the 'Lodge' bit, and the 'Lowther' while they were at it? 'Very well,' agreed Curzon, faintly relieved to have sidestepped the preposterous suggestion of 'Lowther House'. Anything 'House' was terribly common. They would just call it 'No. 1 Kensington Gore', or even just 'Kensington Gore' in the same way that Lord Curzon's residence was referred to as 'Carlton Terrace'.[767]

Keltie could open the Norman Shaw lead light and lean out towards the May sunshine bathing Hyde Park. Fresh spring air. Today the RGS president would be attending to business at the Mansion House. They must decide on how to apportion the fund, which had been closed at £75,000 (£4.5 million today), and they can then archive the Royal Geographical file.

Keltie might go back to his desk and flick back through his correspondence with Curzon over the last five months to make sure he'd briefed him correctly. On the top, an undated stiff blue postcard, headed '1 Carlton House Terrace, SW', with one of Curzon's typical messages: 'I have written to Mrs Oates. You might do Mrs Evans & Bowers.'[768]

Curzon had written to the 'superior persons', the Royal Navy wife and the doctor's wife, Kathleen and Oriana. He had now also written to Mrs Oates. Who even were the others? A rating and a merchant sailor? Really, Keltie could soak up the rest.

It isn't just widows and money that the RGS secretary has to deal with – frankly, the actual cash is the least of it.

Feb 17th 1913

My dear Lord Curzon,
I enclose a poem from a working man which is addressed to you [and] another curious letter from a working man who wants to sell his violin in order to contribute to the fund. Freshfield thinks we ought to be cautious about it.'

Feb 17th 1913
Hackwood, Basingstoke,

Keltie,

Please acknowledge these verses! Lord, what rubbish.

C.

Curzon as arbiter of taste is a familiar figure. He does not trust one single detail of the RGS to anyone else. He pronounces on everything

from the address ('"House" anything – frightfully common') to the posi-
tioning of 'cloak rooms' and the design of the garden railings. Keltie
closes the file. The men have kept their poem and violin respectively, but
Keltie suspects that the distribution of the Mansion House Fund will not
escape a Curzonesque scale of qualification. This will be ameliorated,
however, by a more disinterested approach with pensions and the BAE
salary to date, to be taken into account and included in a 'Table of
Incomes' that will be titled 'Circumstances of Dependents'.

When the car sweeps back in later that afternoon, Keltie is apprised
of the final reckoning: Kathleen Scott (who had apparently given
Curzon an earful down the phone) would get £8,500. Peter would get
a separate portion of £3,500. Together the Scotts will have £12,000 of
the total £75,000. 'There art thou happy?' Was that delivering on her
husband's request to 'look after our people'? Curzon felt that surely
even that volatile artiste must agree it was more than enough money
for housekeeping.

Oriana Wilson was considered to be the next most important. She
would also be given £8,500. She had no children, no dependants.

The only real aristocrat, Caroline Oates, had, Curzon noted, bowed
elegantly out of the race for cash long before. Caroline was a wealthy
woman of private means – a country estate and an apartment in South
Kensington. She did not want money – rumour had it that she'd given
handouts to the ratings when the *Terra Nova* returned to Cardiff –
'largesse'. He can also see that on 7 June 1912, Mrs Oates paid £45 for
her son's Fellowship to the Society, ignorant of the fact that he had
been dead for some time. Friends of Mrs Oates want that membership
to be transferred to her.

Emily Bowers qualified, in Curzon's mind, for about half the Scott/
Wilson fraction. She was allocated £4,500. She had two grown-up
daughters – apparently they both worked for a living. The money was
Mrs Bowers's to share if she so chose. She would also receive her son's
Royal Indian Marine pension.

Then came the rating. Lois Evans, the petty officer's wife, was given
£1,250. Lois's was the only fund that would be paid weekly (to
encourage her to spend it responsibly), and it was dependent upon her
proving each year that her children were still alive. The government
pension was 12 shillings sixpence a week, plus 3 shillings a week for

each child until the age of eighteen (which amounted to £56 per year). She had been made the 'generous offer' of a place in the London Orphanage Asylum for her eldest son.[769] There was no indication that this generosity had been accepted. The figure for Mrs Lois Evans may have been less than half the amount they had allocated to Peter Scott, but Curzonites were sure that £1,250 would be 'riches' to the Welsh woman, and they are not in the business of meddling with the classes.

27 JUNE 1913

ORIANA – LONDON

Oriana takes the escalator down to the Piccadilly Line platform southbound. She is on her way to the 'Imperial Services Exhibition' at Earl's Court. It was Sir Clements's cousin Albert Markham's suggestion that they exhibit Antarctic artefacts. Partly this was considered an appropriate gesture of thanks to the public for their generous donations to the Mansion House Fund. The Antarctic exhibit is the main attraction drawing the crowds.

Once through the turnstile, Ory passes a diorama of the Northwest Frontier, a province of British India in miniature. The stage is set for 'Saving Prince Kishan'. Miniature pith helmets with swords stand across a rail track from a group of miniature turbans with sabres, a model steam locomotive stands on the slope above, small plumes of steam emerging from its chimney. She walks on past 'an engagement off the coast' – a model town on a flooded stage, with model flying machines on rotating wires, crumbling fort walls and miniature explosions.

Finally she arrives at the 'Antarctic Section'. There is a tent, and alongside it, a sledge, skis, a theodolite, the camera, empty provision bags, a thermometer and a book, *By Order of Country*, labelled 'The book that they were reading'.

Is this the lining of the tent in which her husband had actually died? Is this sacred artefact really erected here, in the Empress Hall, among all these callous strangers on summer holiday?

After an impromptu visit from Oriana, Kathleen acts quickly and decisively. She telephones 'that disgraceful creature [Teddy] Evans'.[770]

In reference to our conversations just now over the telephone, I am writing to say that I consider the exhibition of the Tent, wherein the Explorers died, their skis and a novelette purporting to have been ready [sic] by them, is singularly out of place and in very bad taste exhibited as they are side by side with manne-quins dressed in Wolseley underwear, advertising the firm. I hope you will be kind enough to see that the above named articles (Tent, skis, book) be removed today from the exhibition.[771]

The typewriter keys clack. 'Notices were put up to say that the exhibition had been given with my consent,' dictates Kathleen. 'My consent was neither asked nor given and I had no knowledge of it whatsoever.'

21 JULY 1913

LOIS – GOWER

Dear Mrs Evans,

The Admiralty have advised Commander Evans that His Majesty the King has graciously decided to present Antarctic Medals to members of this Expedition and the relatives of the deceased members, on Saturday next at Buckingham Palace.[772]

Should Lois sell the cockles to raise the train fare and find someone with a typewriter in order to reply?

She stands up and stretches her back, looking for her children playing up in the dunes. Will the British Antarctic Expedition ask for Taff's *Discovery* medal? Will this 'Antarctic Medal' be an entirely new one or, as she suspects, a *Terra Nova* band to add to the ribbon of the *Discovery* medal? Who can she ask? The letter writer does not seem to invite queries.*

Will you, therefore, please be at this office at ten o'clock on Saturday next 26th inst., to recieve further instructions as to the ceremony before going to Buckingham Palace to get your husband's medal.

---

* A duplicate medal was made and given to Lois in 1914.

Please acknowledge this by return post as we have to advise the Admiralty,

Yours faithfully

Francis Drake
Secretary

22 JULY 1913

CAROLINE – LONDON

Caroline rides out of Harding's on Petersham Mews up Elvaston Place in South Kensington. She has nearly finished her investigations. 'I was never satisfied with the accounts,' she told her BAE member interviewees. 'I have persevered in trying to obtain all the information possible from reliable sources re the causes of the failure. Distressing as it very much is, I would rather know.'[773] The sound of the metal horseshoes on the cobbles provides a familiar rhythm.

She has settled her financial accounts – she paid Humphrey's for the new suit she had finished ready for Laurie's return, Hatchards for his boots, Jaeger for his coat and new combinations – if only it were as simple to settle Laurie's BAE account. But she has made the first strategic move in his defence. Caroline has just informed Francis Drake that she will not be 'at this office at ten o'clock on Saturday next 26th inst.' She has declined the invitation to Buckingham Palace. She does not feel the need to expand, to give a reason. Teddy tells her he will receive Oates's medal on her behalf. The gesture is strong and decisive. It is not every day one refuses an invitation to meet the king.

The horse walks Caroline past the 'nibs nobs and snobs' at Kensington Gore. On 24 March, Caroline wrote on the black-edged paper she had ordered with the 14 Evelyn Mansions address. She wrote to 'Sir', at the RGS, asking for fifty copies of the March copy of the *Geographical Journal*. 'I am quite willing of course to send a cheque . . .'[774] The Society sent her fifteen copies four days later – as many as they could spare. Caroline suggested that they might put a 'little notice' in the April edition to ask for anyone who did not 'care to keep them' to send them to her because she knew many people who would 'greatly prize' one. She took care to retain aristocratic manners: 'I trust that I am not giving undue trouble . . .'[775]

Upon receiving life membership of the Society (unbeknown to her, Howard Payne, a family friend, prompted the RGS to do the honourable thing), she writes: 'I confess it came to me quite as a surprise and a pleasant one,' for which she wanted to 'express my sincere thanks to the President and the Council for the honour which they have conferred upon me'.[776] The RGS Memorial Medal, which Francis Drake received on her behalf, also required a thank you: 'It will always be chief in value amongst the family treasures . . . How exquisitely the photograph of the Southern Party has been worked into the obverse side.'[777]

Aristocratic business is conducted with 'I trust that I am not giving undue trouble' etc, and sentences starting 'I don't suppose it would amuse you to . . .' but Caroline is her father's daughter. She must categorise, corroborate column by column, adding or subtracting from the received story. Kathleen, it seems, is determined to whitewash failure with a broad brush of heroism – there would be no enquiry – Caroline must conduct her own.

The first entries in Caroline's notebook are from conversations on board the *Terra Nova* at Cardiff. While on board, she gave Tom Crean £1 and the crew £4. Prizes spoke for her, but her son did not need props – as they told her, Captain Oates was beloved. He spoke to them all as if they were the king himself.

Dr Atkinson and Cecil Meares both visited Evelyn Mansions. Atkinson told her that Laurie was not sufficiently fit, when the time came, to go on to the Pole – 'that man-hauling was so terrible', she concluded.[778] When the search party tried to find her son's body they had found his 'fur boots were . . . slit up the back, showing how bad the feet must have been'.

Meares talks animals, though his speciality is dogs rather than horses. Scott was sentimental about animals. Herbert Ponting agreed that 'Scott did not like the idea of employing dogs and then having to kill them.' Was it Scott's squeamishness that had cost Laurie his life?

'One cannot state facts plainly when they reflect on the organisation,' confided Teddy to Caroline on returning to the British Antarctic Expedition office in 1913: 'I cannot find in one [expedition contract] anything that is not contradicted in another,' he told her. 'I personally would never have embarked on the expedition had I known.'[779] Was it incompetent leadership that had finished Laurie?

Caroline was devastated when Frank Debenham told her that during the Antarctic winter, Laurie had very nearly written a cheque to pay his way out – just when she was writing one for £200 to enable him to stay. He had so nearly come back with the ship. Was it Laurie's inability to give up, to surrender his soldierly ambition, that had been his own undoing?

It was almost as bad as when Ponting told her about their conversation in the darkroom. They shot sick animals at Gestingthorpe, but Laurie was not just a sick animal, he was her son. He had not used a gun, but Captain Scott had ordered Bill to hand out the morphine pills, the means of ending it all.

Although she has not seen Nansen, she's read his opinion that 'Captain Oates's illness must surely have been scurvy also. Frostbitten hands and feet are just what scurvy patients are liable to, because their circulation is impaired.'[780] Shackleton agreed.[781] Was it scurvy that had killed her son?

Caroline has been to visit Lady Shackleton in Eastbourne. Lady Shackleton corroborated the reports of her husband's scurvy on Scott's first expedition, and Scott's unreliable temper.

If Caroline turns her horse up towards Marble Arch and Speakers' Corner, she can see patches where the grass suffered from the thousands of marchers from the National Union of Women Suffrage Societies who had attended 'The Great Pilgrimage' in June and July. Caroline has just donated £10 to the Anti-Suffrage League in an effort to keep the NUWSS in check. She is about to pay a call on Lady Scott. The League is, perhaps, something that she and Kathleen can agree upon.

She reaches the southwest gate of the park and heads back to Harding's stables. She has reached her conclusions and she will not be silent. Caroline believes that her son was 'disgusted with the way in which the whole thing was done'.[782] In a letter she says: 'It is pretty ghastly when you think of the fourteen fresh dogs and seven well-trained Indian mules over which my boy took so much trouble – ready there at the base – and no transport officer to make use of them – while the Southern Party were deserted and dying. Horrible.'[783]

26 JULY 1913

LOIS – BUCKINGHAM PALACE, LONDON

Lois walks on carpet from outside the BAE car to inside the building. The men, about forty of them led by Teddy, have marched here from the Caxton Hall. She and Mrs Brissingden, the two ratings widows in their best widow's weeds, follow Lady Kathleen Scott, Mrs Oriana Wilson and Mrs Emily Bowers. They emerge into a huge open space. Lois saw the artist's impressions of the ballroom of the *Titanic* in the newspaper the year before. This space seems as big.

The broad central staircase rises and splits with ornate golden balustrades around three sides of the room. Looking up, Lois can see a glass chandelier. A strong chain holds it to the ceiling, from which it drips cut-glass crystals for several storeys.

A palace official explains the protocol. They must not attempt to make conversation with the palace staff or, when they met him, with the king and his attendants. They must answer questions briefly, curtsey and retire walking backwards four paces and then turning, follow the liveried footman out of the room.

Looking across at Kathleen Scott, Lois remembers that nice letter passing on Scott's praise for Taff a year before. It was written at a time when neither she nor Kathleen knew that their husbands were already dead. How does Kathleen feel about Taff now? Does she think Taff 'failed' her husband? Does she wish Captain Scott had abandoned him when he became a burden, as Taff's mother Sarah suggested? Quite apart from the Polar journey, Lois wonders if Taff made a spectacle of himself before he left New Zealand. What had they seen?

The men return with their medals. The women are informed that the king wishes to see each of the widows entirely alone. A uniformed footman opens double doors. Lady Scott naturally goes first. She is breezy, the palatial surroundings not seeming to impress her. Her clothing is loose and artistic. She is going to ask the king if she can bring her son Peter to see the queen next time.

Sitting now in among the plush and gilt, Lois could not be further from those last weeks of want in Portsmouth. But however bare her cupboards, her want was as nothing to Taff's. If Beatrice Pharaoh suffered from 'want' as Lois had, how could Lois deny her? Is she the only one of the South Pole widows to have 'skeletons' like this? Lois notes that Caroline Oates is not here, but she has asked Lois to crochet an altar cover for St Mary's Gestingthorpe. Could one refuse an invitation from the king? Lois's husband died on 17 February, Caroline's son had dragged his poor frostbitten body on for another month.

It is Lois's turn to meet the king.

AUGUST 1913

CAROLINE – LONDON

The door opens. Kathleen Scott is determinedly bright. Caroline is ushered into the drawing room, where she sees evidence of one, perhaps two servants. Kathleen's brother Wilfred Bruce is introduced, he is obviously staying. The house is chilly, though nearly-four-year-old Peter, who is playing on the drawing room floor, is scantily clad. Through an open door, Caroline sees a typewriter.

Caroline waits for Peter's nurse to take him away. It is unusual for the children to be so visible when adults call. Gradually, she realises that Peter's nurse is not coming. His presence, and Mr Bruce's, are strategic.

'She [Lady Scott] was not at her ease and evidently embarrassed throughout the visit, perhaps quite naturally.'[784]

Caroline tries to commit the visit to memory.

'I asked Lady Scott whether she realised the risks and dangers, which indeed I had not, and she said she knew they were considerable.'

Kathleen is using words like 'considerable'; they are carefully chosen, as if she knows that Caroline is recording the conversation in a notebook. She is on her guard.

'I contrived to ask her what she considered was the cause of the whole disaster.'

Kathleen broad-brushed, as Caroline had predicted. 'She said everything had gone against the expedition from first to last and there were difficulties on every hand and a condition of weather which it was absolutely impossible to battle against.'

Caroline sips her tea, trying to 'contrive' questions that will deliver the information she desires. It is difficult. Long silences result. She wants to ask why Scott didn't postpone the Pole venture for a year after losing so many ponies on the depot trip in early 1911. Why didn't he wait for the mules that Laurie had told him to get to replace the 'crocks'?

She wants to confirm what she already knows, which is that 'Laurie was never dragged on the sledge.'[785] What does Kathleen think of Shackleton's remark that 'There is something behind it and in my opinion that something is scurvy'?[786] A remark corroborated, incidentally, by Fridtjof Nansen, whom Caroline believes Kathleen is acquainted with.

Caroline takes another sip, the only sound apart from Peter's babbling and the sound of wooden brick upon wooden brick. Will Peter's distracted mother dare to ask her what she thinks? Kathleen will never know Caroline's candid opinion that '[Scott] had too many sideshows, [his] base was denuded once when relief should have been sent [and] there was seemingly no one to take the initiative. Scott overworked his men from the outset.'

The silence thickens with unsaid words. Caroline cannot even press Kathleen for answers in the same way that she did the other interviewees in her investigations. Is Caroline afraid that Scott's insidious implication that the 'sick' are to blame will begin unravelling her son's reputation?

Caroline rises to leave. Her fur coat is brought. As she is helped into it, she retreats to the safe neutral ground of social platitudes. She thanks Kathleen for the tea. She thinks of something suitable to say about Peter, who is just a little older than her own grandchildren, Lilian's daughter Sheila and Bryan's son Edward.

The exit assumes a predictable pattern, the meeting is nearly over. But as Caroline follows Kathleen to the front door, Kathleen turns and looks at Caroline directly for the first time. 'You must realise, there could have been no better outcome in the circumstances . . .'*

II SEPTEMBER 1913

EMILY – WEMYSS BAY (A FERRY RIDE FROM BUTE)

Waiting for Caroline now at Wemyss Station, Emily reflects that sometimes neither of them can actually believe their sons are dead, so accustomed are they to Birdie and Laurie being posted abroad for years at a time in the service of their Empire. 'At times the whole

---

* In 1929 Kathleen authorised Stephen Gwynn to write in Scott's biography that, like Agamemnon in Homer's *Iliad*, her husband abhorred the idea of a return 'with his deed unachieved' at whatever cost. Caroline (and perhaps her son) may not have been aware of Scott's Homeric attitude towards risk. (Gwynn, 1929, p. 194)

thing seems to me impossible.'[787] May cannot believe Birdie is gone either. She has been to a 'a little séance' or two. She does not see 'much harm'.[788] More recently, the Marquess of Bute, president of the occult Psychic Society, held séances at his home in the south of Bute at Mount Stuart. Had Birdie sent them messages from beyond the grave? Would he and the rest of the men speak through a séance? May has a message from Birdie through a different route. She has a photograph of HMS *Worcester* mounted on a card in her room at Caerlaverock. On the back is written: 'This photo was handed to me in a dream on the night of Nov 18th by my brother Henry who perished with Capt Scott . . . with the words I am so glad to remember "the flesh is nothing."'[789]

Birdie existed in letters with such vitality, they keep half expecting the postman to bring a new letter. It isn't such a forlorn hope. Emily received a new letter in July. May had found it addressed to her and 'not to be opened unless he did not return'. Back then, Emily had been briefly in London but wrote to Cherry, 'You see I cannot stay – I must see if there is anything he wishes to be done.'[790] She'd invited Cherry to stay, to come up and see Birdie's collection. Caroline may have tiger skins at Gestingthorpe but Emily has butterflies and moths.

As the station begins filling up with porters and taxicab drivers eager for custom, she wonders whether Caroline's expectations of the visit will be delivered upon. She has begun investigating the tragedy of their sons' deaths in a way that concerns Emily. Caroline is coming to Bute to copy out sections of Birdie's diary and letters as 'evidence'.

Perhaps it is because Caroline's son had committed suicide. (Suicides are not buried in the High Kirk above Rothesay, where Emily has bought a plot for her Bower birds.) More and more, Emily thanks God for 'the blizzard that shut them in & kept the three together at the last'.[791] 'I do not for a moment regret he went,' she tells Cherry, 'for he was so happy among you all.'[792] She would like copies of the more cheerful photograph of the Polar Party at the Pole.[793]

Emily realises that she and Caroline – the two mothers – start from different positions on many things. Caroline, for example, is not beholden to the Mansion House Fund. Emily is. The other widows, Kathleen and Oriana, had expected some solidarity with their revulsion at the tastelessness of the Earl's Court exhibit, but she surprised them all. She is used to wrong-footing people. 'It is so difficult to say and do the right thing,' Emily tells Cherry. 'Often enough I find one has to put feelings etc on one side & do what seems right . . . the public have most generously contributed a large sum to the British Antarctic Fund & I think it is only right that they should . . . have an opportunity of seeing these things . . . [so] they will have a better idea of the work etc of the Expedition.' She knows that the others disapprove but that does not mean she has to: 'Mrs Oates has the right to say what she likes,' says Emily. 'She takes nothing from the Expedition but I do.'[794]

Emily hugs her coat around her. Her arm is playing up. It is the damp. Caroline has suggested that they should take a trip to Worthing on the south coast, a wholesome change, and the weather down south is so mild. The rails began to hum. The train wheezes slowly into the station. Steam collects in the curved glass roof and curls around the hanging baskets. Emily, the tailor's daughter, walks up the platform looking for her friend, the lady of the manor of Gestingthorpe. What will Caroline make of Birdie's journal, the parts she wants to copy out? Will Caroline be disarmed by Birdie's obvious unswerving loyalty to Scott? Caroline descends from the train in a beautifully cut Jaeger mackintosh.[795]

23

Memoria

LOIS — ROATH PARK, CARDIFF

The *Terra Nova* figurehead is set on a modest plinth in the middle of a newly planted formal garden – a classical shrine to a goddess, perhaps. On either side of Lois are 'gentlemen of the press'. (Lois and Sarah Evans, Taff's mother, are in their Sunday best. Mr Sam Chapman and his *Cambrian Daily Leader* camera will not catch them off guard again.) Around the base of the three-quarter-length wooden lady, the herbs dotted in the earth are little more than plugs – 'make believe'. Perhaps this figurehead is now Taff's lady – Taff's '*cwtch*' – an appropriate memorial to a man who could charm the birds off the trees.

Lois stands silent, listening to the man in the bowler hat. It is the man from the dockside in Cardiff, the man watching the *Terra Nova*'s return. Mr Frederick Bowring tells them that Bowring & Co. sold the *Terra Nova* to Scott for £12,500 and bought her back for £5,000, but Bowring had put £500 towards the expedition and encouraged the brokers David Bruce and Sons to hand over the better part of their commission too. Mr Bowring has been generous, but perhaps strategically so. The audience may be interested to know that he intends to stand as Liberal Party candidate.

The figurehead wears a serene expression, definitely more Shakespearean than music hall, a young Sarah Bernhardt rather than a Marie Lloyd. The wooden figure puts the *Cambrian* reporter in mind of Handel's courtly song, 'Did you not hear My Lady'. Lois still follows all the famous singers in Wales. The baritone David Ivor Davies, known outside his native Cardiff as Ivor Novello, could just step from his childhood home into Roath Park and 'go down the garden singing'. Lois has begun taking part in concerts again in Morriston, singing duets with her sister, with her niece Ida Faull accompanying on the piano. Lois will not be singing 'Three little girls' nowadays, but perhaps 'O'er life's dark sea'.[796]

Bowring tells the crowd that the figurehead sustained some damage in the ice, but it has been repaired and repainted. They might have heard of the famous shipwrights to the Admiralty, Messrs Hellyer of Portsmouth. Lois knows the Hellyers; shipwrights like Walter Thomas regard them as the top woodcarvers of their trade. They have produced comely ladies for the navy for over a century, but why have they changed the position of the right arm? It is no longer stretched forwards but held across the chest.

The crowds might be interested to hear that in 1796, the Admiralty had tried to abolish figureheads on new ships, but the order was not complied with – many sailors felt a ship without a figurehead would be an unlucky vessel. The *Terra Nova* had not been unlucky. This figurehead, this woman, should inspire them all to face the trials ahead.

Lois regards the wooden half-woman. In the peaceful setting it is difficult to imagine the 'mighty shocks' she has endured on the other side of the world. Could the 'trials ahead' be anything resembling the trials behind? Although Lois is living in Morriston, she still receives navy news. The latest German ship, the SS *Imperator*, is said to sport a large bronze figurehead of an eagle, the Imperial German symbol, standing on a globe. Folk say that from the beak of that eagle to the stern, the *Imperator* would stretch from end to end of Roath Park. As a result, the *Imperator* is the longest naval ship in the world, but it's only because of the extra length afforded by that blessed eagle.

8 JULY 1913

EMILY – GREENHITHE, KENT, ENGLAND

Emily completes her stately progress to the upper deck of HMS *Worcester*, anchored in the Thames off Greenhithe, where Sir Clements Markham is waiting with Cherry-Garrard and Teddy Evans. Teddy is ex-*Worcester* and Cherry is ex-*Winter* Journey. Both are here to support her. The wooden planks under her leather lace-up boots are holy stoned and newly swabbed, a clean smell rising. Glancing down, Emily can imagine Birdie with the *Worcester* boys now positioned across the deck in straight lines. In their hands they hold flags on short poles. On the order of the master on the bridge, the display begins. Semaphore is still a useful way of communicating, in spite of the cables that run under the sea and the radio waves that undulate above it. The boys are quick and precisely choreographed, the flags making a ripping sound as they are drawn swiftly through the air from one position – both arms apart parallel to the deck – to the next – one arm straight up, the other arm across and down. They crack through the alphabet. Above, gulls wheel and cry, barges chug past beside them, the chain ferry links rattle.

After the semaphore display there are knots tied along a thick piece of taut rope that is secured at either side of the deck. Walking along the row, Emily is called to admire a bowline, a reef knot, a clove hitch, a round turn and two half hitches, and a figure of eight. Birdie's favourite was the monkey's fist, the knot of friendship. Emily knows that one of the bluejackets, an exceptional petty officer they called 'Taff', taught Scott's team a one-handed clove hitch. Can any of the boys do that?

Finally, Emily is called to stand at the base of the middle mast. After Sir Clements Markham's speech about 'Cadet Bowers', in which he reads out Captain Scott's last letter to Emily, the plaque she has come here to open is unveiled. The top is a medallion with a bas-relief bust of Birdie in Royal Indian Marine uniform. Emily steps forward and looks through her round glasses to read the inscription beneath it: '. . . sincerely mourned by old shipmates and friends who cherish the memory of his achievement and devotion and his gallant and heroic end. Erected by "Worcesters" 1913.' Emily has deliberately been acting the headmistress, but it is difficult. The memorial is so personal, so heartfelt.

Sir Clements asks her about the other memorials to Birdie. The Royal Indian Marine has erected identical memorials in her local church, St Ninian's in Rothesay, and in Bombay Cathedral. The Rothesay memorial, unveiled by Captain H. B. Simpson with prayers by Reverend Dewar, had ended with the national anthem and a bugle playing the 'Last Post'. The Worcesters prepare to do the same. The sound is impossibly moving.

Perhaps Emily is called to make a speech? George Bernard Shaw's *Pygmalion* has just premiered at His Majesty's Theatre in town. The flower seller Eliza Doolittle has captured the public imagination and the idea has a relevance here. These boys are not rich, but the training they receive here gives them a chance to achieve officer status on merit, rather than social class. If Emily does give a speech, she might find her morning assembly voice. Captain Scott deliberately sought out men who had been through the HMS *Worcester* training, a training that she believes made Birdie the man he became. He will be 'sincerely mourned' by many of the old Worcesters, including Commander Evans, but it heartens his mother to see that he has touched the hearts and minds of Worcesters to come – boys whom he has never met. Birdie's favourite song was 'Hearts of Oak'. He must have learned it here with that wonderful refrain: 'Steady, boys, steady'.

Rationally, Emily realises that now Birdie is dead, safely tucked up in heaven, the anxious days should be over. But it has never been just about Birdie. She is a headmistress, her reach extends beyond her family, and the boys that stand to attention on the *Worcester* singing 'Hearts of Oak' are, somehow, her boys. She suspects that Sir Clements Markham thinks they are his boys too.

What is in store for these sons of Empire who raise their narrow-brimmed hats in unison to echo the call for three cheers as Emily prepares to leave? How will they manage if called to serve in a war against the Imperial German Navy? Around the time of Emily's visit, the airship Zeppelin LZ 14 has just crashed in the North Sea and the disaster is pulsing through the news – the Imperial Navy has, it seems, taken to the skies. Can this ultra-traditional *Worcester* education – its semaphoring, knot-tying innocents – ever hope to defeat a nation prepared to send its men up under gas-balloons in a thunderstorm?

ORIANA – CAMBRIDGE, ENGLAND

Frank Debenham inserts a screwdriver between the wooden lid and the side and pushes down on the handle. The nails squeak as they are drawn out and the cover is levered off. The final collection of 35 lb of rocks found on the sledge near the tent is of the utmost interest to his team. Deb stands in his geology classroom where the lecturer would stand with the blackboard behind him. Ory is behind the desks where the university students sit. The camera is before her. The shutter clicks again. Is the camera still focused? Is it still pointing the right way? They have captured Stage 1 (box closed) and Stage 2 (lid off). Would Oriana like to leave her post for a moment, come round to the lecturer's side of the desk and look in?

Leaning her head over the top of the box of Antarctica, there is the smell of coal – metallic, musty, mineral, dead – but to Frank Debenham and to Ory's husband Bill, this box contains 'gold'. They are not looking for gemstones, for real gold or even commercially valuable coal, they are looking for facts, for data from which to understand creation.

The rocks rustle as Deb unwraps the paper they've been so carefully wrapped in and places them on the table. He places a dark stone into Ory's hand. It is about the same size as her palm and less than an inch thick, a sort of irregular rectangle. Ory traces the impression of tongue-shaped leaves with her fingertip. Deb suspects this stone might provide valuable evidence to support Edward Suess's theory of a supercontinent that existed during the late Palaeozoic and early Mesozoic eras. If it does, it would also be valuable proof of a more recent theory of something that increasingly is being referred to as 'continental drift'.

Ory still finds it difficult to believe that her husband's work on earth is finished. 'There seemed so much for him to do in the future . . . I only hope and trust that the scientific results may be edited by some really good man – as a lasting memorial. At his wish they went on dragging the geological specimens up till the last.'[797] While they lift the remaining rocks carefully out to set across the lecturer's desk, Deb tells her that of all the members of the British Antarctic Expedition, 'If I were asked to pick out the best all-round men, I should place [Bill] easily first.' The work he is doing, he tells Ory, is really 'in memory of Bill'. Most of the time Deb is tongue in cheek, so that when he speaks in earnest the effect is devastating. Ory tries to be her brusque, scientific self. Deb punctuates his profoundly emotional declarations with profoundly practical qualifications. He has ambitions to use part of the Mansion House Fund to create a 'Wilson Polar Research Institute' – a memorial to her husband and a way that Deb hopes to 'wangle' himself a job.[798]

8 NOVEMBER 1913

CAROLINE – GESTINGTHORPE

'A brilliant dash of colour' – red and white plumes above polished silver guardsmen's helmets move in the wintry air. The newspaper reporters have already been spotted by the Gestingthorpe chauffeur at Sudbury Station. They note 'the scarlet uniforms and gold facings of the dragoon officers and the richly gold-embroidered blue uniforms of the naval officers who had been Captain Oates's companions on the Expedition.'[799] Dr Atkinson and Cecil Meares, both of whom visited Caroline at Evelyn Mansions, have come up for the ceremony.

Caroline knows that six trumpeters of the Queen's Bays will line up at the porch. The 'Last Post' travels on the air towards Laurie's home. Inside St Mary's, Caroline knows that Major-General E. H. H. Allenby will be unveiling the tablet – the service will follow. If Caroline has chosen not to attend, this will be the first time for months that she is not being watched for her reaction – her family, her domestic staff and her villagers are all crowded into the church.

Caroline has deliberately kept busy. She's joined Newton Golf Club about seven miles from Gestingthorpe and continues to take regular lessons. She seems to be permanently travelling from one end of the country to the other to be grateful for memorials. She was in Colwyn Bay at the end of October, in Eastbourne on the 2nd of November and Leeds on the 3rd. She only just got back to Gestingthorpe in time to welcome Captain King. The navy have presented the Inniskillings with a silver statuette. Part of the Antarctic is to be named Oates Land. The Cavalry Club have commissioned a large oil painting. Where will it end? Does she want it to?

Now she plans to spend a few days at Gestingthorpe for her most ambitious project. If she walks across the south lawn she can see the strings skewered to the lawn marking a large rectangle to the west of the house. She has commissioned a new private chapel in memory of Laurie. It will be built on the first floor of a new west wing designed by Arthur Bloomfield Jackson. Sudbury-based Theobold Building and Joinery Company has already made a start. Ernest Beckwith (who carved the chancel screen in St Mary the Virgin in 1907) is going to build the staircase and will also design a lych gate for the church, to be dedicated at an evensong by the Bishop of Chelmsford.[800]

Walking on round the house to the Gestingthorpe kennels, Caroline finds the husky dog she adopted from the pack brought back to Cardiff on the *Terra Nova*. This is one of those that Laurie was listening for as he stumbled forward on frostbitten feet. But the dogs never came. As she strokes the thick fur, smells the meaty breath, sees its glistening pink tongue, she thinks of the fact that if properly managed, the dogs could have met Laurie and brought him home. Has Cecil Meares already been by the kennels on his way to church? This dog has no idea that he is a living memorial for her animal-loving son. But he will not last forever. The brass plaque – that must by now have been unveiled – will.

The bells sound the end of the service. Caroline has probably ordered her staff to set out refreshments in the hall – a fire in the large fireplace under animal trophies some of the Inniskillings might recognise from Mhow. Caroline can retire to her office, her accounts. The bell ringers, who are still pulling their ropes in the ringing chamber, will need to be paid £1 16s for the day's work.

Later, taking the polish from her handbag, she tips it onto the cloth. She has to stand up on the wooden pew seat inside the empty, silent church to reach the top of the plaque. She begins polishing the Inniskillings' motif, a castle, and under it, a ribbon with their motto: 'Inniskilling'. She pauses over the word 'gallant' – that word was also written a piece of paper in a cylinder near where her son's body lay in the Antarctic – then continues down, polishing horizontally along each line: 'When all were beset by hardship he being gravely injured went out into the blizzard to die in the hope that by so doing he might enable his comrades to reach safety. This tablet is placed here in affectionate remembrance by his brother officers AD 1913.'[801]

9 JULY 1914

KATHLEEN – CHELTENHAM

Kathleen and Oriana sit on either side of Mrs Mary Agnes Wilson, Bill's mother. (Both Ory and Mary Agnes have already seen the statue in London. Kathleen did not want to risk a repeat of the Rolls unveiling and the wailing mother.) Kathleen's dress has a loose artistic white collar – only Ory 'the widow' is dressed entirely in full mourning. Kathleen turns and looks over her shoulder. The crowd stretches back as far as she can see. There are men and women, young and old, a gaggle of Cheltenham Ladies' College girls, some Boy Scouts.

Mr Kinsey and his daughter May have sailed over from New Zealand for this unveiling. The Kinseys represent New Zealand, where the Mayor of Christchurch, Henry Holland, has already collected £1,000 for a memorial statue of Scott. The plan, originally, was to duplicate the London statue, but that has stalled. The London Parks will not sacrifice 'one blade of grass' for statuary.[802] This plays to Kathleen's advantage – they will not sacrifice a blade of grass and she will not trust her 'lion' to them anyhow.

Finally, Sir Clements releases the string and the sheet billows down. There is Bill, Dr Edward Wilson, in his full bronze glory. There are gasps in the crowd. Kathleen notices white fluttering handkerchiefs on the edge of her vision. She glances across at Ory looking up into the face of her dead husband, composed, serene. It is the face of a woman who believes her husband is still beside her demanding Christian resignation and unselfish grief.

As the crowd begin to talk, Kathleen listens. Do they think it is a good likeness – the pointed nose, the head slightly forward, just as in the full-length portrait photograph taken outside the Cape Evans hut by Ponting in 1911? Kathleen wonders if they like the sledge dress. Can they see the sketchbook pouch?

In her studio she already has a maquette of Scott in baggy sledging dress with his right arm out horizontally, holding a ski pole – this will be finished in bronze. Many admiral types argue that being portrayed in 'working clothes' lets the side down, especially when the other naval chaps on plinths in London are attired properly in dress uniform.[803] (Out of her earshot they agree that Scott's wife may be an admirable woman in many ways, but she has 'no artistic sense'.[804]) Kathleen suspects that they do not understand Rodin's impressionistic approach and assures them that neither her husband, nor his teammates, need to rely on props.

22 OCTOBER 1913

LORD CURZON – LONDON

Curzon prowls around his tiger-skin rug. On 26 May he made a promise to the Royal Geographical Society, one based on a conversation with Kathleen Scott. (He might refer her to 'Item e' in his notes taken during their conversation at his home on 16 April earlier that year.) Now he is being made to look a fool. When he looks out of his window towards St James Park, fashionable ladies flutter behind half-veiled riding habits. These fluttering women are reminiscent of the 'Fishing Fleet' of women Queen Victoria had encouraged to come out to marry the men of Empire to keep them from marrying native. He has had quite enough of them. 'Dear Keltie,' he wrote in June,

'Is there any need for me to do this? I am tired of all these endless functions & wonderful ladies.'[805]

Kathleen is one of the 'wonderful ladies' he is tired of. Curzon has heard that Markham unveiled her statue of Edward Wilson in Cheltenham. If Kathleen has her way, the capital cities will be covered in statues of men in working clothes rather than in formal dress. She will reduce Scott to a manual worker rather than a member of the upper classes – 'The Top 10,000', as King Edward VII called them – who are 'above all that'.

Back in May, Curzon had, he felt confident, pulled off the ultimate coup, more than justifying his position as president, perhaps even future prime minister. Kathleen Scott assured him that she would place her husband's original journal on permanent loan with them at the Royal Geographical Society, 'where she may be sure that we will cherish it as a treasure beyond price'. As an afterthought, following his announcement, he sent a letter to Kathleen to check that she remembered 'promising me for Museum at RGS loan of your husband's priceless diary and also gift of some personal effects to put in a glass case in Museum?'[806] Curzon didn't feel inclined to bother with the definite article where lesser mortals were concerned.

Now, pacing around his gilded cage, Curzon tries to understand what has just happened. In the letter his butler brings in, he learns that Kathleen understood his desire 'to have some further memento of my husband at the R.G.S. . . . [but] I really made no promise as to his journals, and after very careful reflection think I want them (if out of my own keeping) to be in the British Museum.'[807]

Curzon will not be cheated. What about 'Item e'? He fires off a letter to be driven round to Buckingham Palace Road: 'You said that you could not [loan the journals] at once because you wanted the diary for purposes of the book,' he roared, peppering his notes with definite articles. 'I reported this conversation at once to Keltie and mentioned it at the next meeting of the council.'

Curzon looks out over the square to the backs of the all-male clubs along Pall Mall. The Reform, The Travellers, The Athenaeum. Why had his RGS committee ever thought that it would be a good idea to let anyone but a man anywhere near the inner sanctum of Empire – the map room of the world?

Of the other 'wonderful ladies' he is obliged to deal with in this Antarctic business, Mrs Oates seems to be the only one who knows her place. She recognises the attentions of the council of the RGS as an 'honour . . . conferred upon me'.[808] Oriana, a vicar's daughter married to a doctor and therefore several rungs down the social ladder, is almost as bad as Kathleen. She presumes to drag her heels on a promise to donate her husband's sketches and watercolours to the RGS as she'd promised.

'Has Mrs [Oriana] Wilson sent the other sketches?' Curzon had written to Hinks, Keltie's replacement as secretary. 'Do you want me to stir her up? C'[809]

'Mrs [Oriana] Wilson has not sent any more sketches and I should be very glad if you could give her a reminder of her promise,' Hinks tactfully replies.[810]

But Mrs [Oriana] Wilson is refusing to be stirred up or anywhere. She tells the RGS that she has 'not forgotten my suggestion to Lord Curzon long ago', but she has a price. She wants cards for special RGS meetings. 'Other Societies have been most kind.'[811] Even when she's received the aforementioned cards, she still isn't satisfied. Now she wants the RGS to promise that her husband's sketches will not under any circumstances 'be stowed away in the archives! This is the reason why [my husband] never sent any to the old building as he knew they would only be put away in cupboards, where they would be of no interest to anyone.'[812]

At least the suffragettes are obvious – one could get a clean shot at a suffragette, marching in plain sight in green and purple plumage. These 'wonderful women' lurk in the shadows, disguised in subservient, demure camouflage. There is a rumour that George Bernard Shaw has at least flushed Kathleen out: 'No woman ever born had a narrower escape from being a man,' he says. 'My affection for [Kathleen Scott] is the nearest I ever came to homosexuality.'[813] And yet Asquith, Marconi, Barrie and Nansen still beat a path to her very modest front door.

It is a mystery to George Nathaniel Curzon but surely Kathleen – half man, half woman – can see that once a president of the RGS has made a statement like the one he made about depositing Scott's journal (he included a quote from that statement to make sure she understood his position), one could not retract one's word.

24

War Widows

EMILY — BUTE

'I always think well of Germany for producing a man like Luther,' Birdie told Emily just before he left for the Antarctic in 1910. 'In spite of the fact that they are bursting themselves to wipe us out they are not bad chaps. Next ourselves they are the best going. They will let themselves in for a terrible hammering (D.V.) someday though, if they overreach themselves . . . It will be many years before she can attack us with any degree of certainty . . . I hope to be a commander then.'[814]

It is a clear bright day when, four years later, Germany attacks. Birdie is not a commander. He is dead, but Emily hopes they will give those Germans a 'terrible hammering' too, D.V., *Deo volente*, God willing. Edie, ever practical, isn't about to leave it to 'D'. She is off to help.

Nursing suits Edie Bowers. She trained at St George's Hospital in East London, fielding random punches from lunatic patients like flicking off troublesome flies. As a full-time nursing sister, she recently answered an advertisement for nurses to join Lady Paget, wife of Britain's former ambassador to Serbia. During the Balkan War, Lady Paget had helped to create a military hospital in Belgrade. Now she plans to replicate this in Nish, a small city in the southern part of the country.

Emily, still adjusting to the reality of her son's absence, now prepares to adjust to her youngest daughter's. Among the blood and bandages Emily foresees no end of flirting. Edie's excitement is strangely contagious. Both Emily's daughters have done a course at the Marchioness of Bute's Voluntary Hospital in the south of the island, but Edie has the edge, with a decade's hospital experience. Trying to remember pre-war etiquette, Emily inquires if George Wyatt might act as Edie's chaperone. George had helped Birdie reload the *Terra Nova* in Lyttleton. He would be delighted to meet Edie, escort her across London and onto the boat train to Southampton. After that she will be on her own.

Now as the Bowers women rush around packing Edie's Paget trunk, Emily wonders whether she will ever get her 'sea-legs' at Aros na Mara. She is almost 'lady of the manor' – she's even been lent a gramophone. She has purchased a 'most lovely old jewel table – really beautiful antique' for Birdie's medals.[815] She is ridiculously house proud, of course, because she is furnishing 'that house on the front', the pretty classical one with the decorative fretwork she's always had her eye on. It is double fronted, with a balcony between double-height bay windows and a big front garden practically down to the sea. A high diving board and a shallow dive, and Birdie could have begun his epic sea swims right from the garden fence. It is the kind of place Emily dreamed of living when she was growing up. A house, not a 'shop'. Emily wouldn't even have to take any scholar-boarders – for the first time in her life she does not have to worry about 'chink'. Birdie has been as good as his word. He has provided for them.

'Now, dears, don't worry about me,' says Edie, folding starched linen aprons into her campaign trunk. 'I am afraid I am not one to die an untimely death.' Edie has so much experience of death and counselling relatives that Emily could sometimes be just another one of her patients, but Edie is really good. Physical assault, amputations, former beaus and the like following her around the beds – nothing phases Edie. As Birdie said in similar circumstances, 'In a show like this we have no scared namby pambys, thank goodness.'[816]

Emily is not the only mother seeing a child off to war at Wemyss Bay Station the following day, but she does not have the awful presentiment of death that accompanied Birdie's farewell. Most of the other mothers grasping hands through the train windows are saying goodbye to sons. Edie insists on cheer. As one of the five most famous pre-war bereaved, Emily has a responsibility – there must be no namby-pambying. Imagine that poor 'widow Queen' Victoria, she must be fairly spinning in her grave! As for the Kaiser her nephew, he is now the 'bad boy in the orchard' and must be punished. When the steam clears there are only two stiff-upper-beaked Bower birds left on the platform.

CAROLINE – GESTINGTHORPE

It is a cloudy midsummer morning as Caroline takes her patriarchal place in the middle at the back of the group of villagers. She and Bryan are the only people not in uniform. Caroline adopts an alert, positive expression, her lower right lip slightly loose now on the right. She wears her black-feathered hat, its broad brim tipped right. She has her black velvet choker and layers of long necklaces over her Edwardian bosom, encased in its usual black lace. This group photograph is 'evidence' of her allegiance. She has already made several donations to the navy – to the Dreadnought Hospital, to Admiral King Hall and to Lady Jellicoe. As soon as she heard about Edie Bowers's plans, she sent money to the Serbian Relief Fund, to the Serbian Red Cross Fund and, specifically, to 'Miss Bowers' herself for 'War Comforts'.

As the photographer adjusts the tripod, Caroline looks down at the backs of the heads of 'our boys' – some of whom are actually 'our girls'. Gestingthorpe's latest volunteers include four uniformed women, who sit cross-legged on the ground in front of six uniformed men. Mostly, the women wear light khaki belted coats, leather knee-length boots and rounded broad-brimmed hats.

Most people believed that Laurie had a contempt for dressing up but when Laurie's Inniskilling uniform first arrived from the London tailors he confessed that 'When no-one was about, like any bride I used to examine my trousseau.' But later he told his mother that 'You will be sorry to hear that the whole of the British Army is going to wear khaki in the spring. It is a great shame I think as they will never be able to recognise us from the Hussars or Dragoon Guards.' Laurie wondered how far the khaki reforms would go; 'If they do too much they will drive a lot of people out, as it won't be much fun to spend £600 a year and be treated like the Germans are.'[817]

Caroline pulls her narrow shoulders back, bracing herself for the photograph. It will not be much fun to be treated as the Germans are now, in fact it will be downright dangerous. If Caroline's Kremnitz connections are made public, she might suffer the same hate campaign as the Speyers. Lilian has 'Dusseldorf' on her birth certificate. Caroline went out to Germany to have her first child near her sisters Mary and Marion Kremnitz. Caroline thinks of her late brother-in-law Hermann, who was in the German VII Army Corps. Will her nephews be drafted into the German army? Prime Minister Herbert Asquith has promised that he will not conscript married men. Caroline tries not to imagine the unthinkable possibility that compulsory conscription might mean Bryan ends up fighting his cousins.

The world has gone mad, and yet Caroline's son-in-law Frederick Ranalow knows that the composer Edward Elgar supports Speyer,* a rare 'mark of confidence at a time when [a] sense of fairness and proportion and logic seems to have forsaken a section of the people.'[818] But Fritz Kreisler has exchanged his violin for a gun in the Austrian Army. Elgar cannot save Speyer, who has asked Asquith to accept his resignation as a Privy Counsellor and to rescind his baronetcy: 'Nothing is harder to bear,' Speyer claims, 'than a sense of injustice that finds no vent in expression.'[819] Caroline is already living with 'a sense of injustice that finds no vent in expression'; her never-mentioned German connections have merely caused that 'injustice' to be channelled into the context of war.

LATE SUMMER 1914

EMILY – BUTE

Edie, like Birdie, pens dispatches from the departing train. She is still in England and yet she has 'arrived'. She is writing from a plush first-class saloon carriage. '. . . all the Serbian Legation & a hundred other Lady's Lord's & Sir's arrived to shake hands,' writes Edie, mostly for her mother's benefit, '. . . & promised us the dinner of our lives when we all returned . . . the reporters from the Sphere, Mirror & Sketch were trying to take photos, notes, etc.'[820]

Emily and May feel that 'the dinner of our lives' is a good incentive for Edie ('she does enjoy her meals') to stay safe and come home – the hullabaloo is reminiscent of the *Terra Nova*'s send-off from Cardiff in June 1910. It seems extraordinary to Emily that another of her children is to appear in the newspapers. Edie takes over the role of cheery

---

*A letter from Elgar to Speyer was cited in his trial under the Aliens Bill in 1921. Elgar cited the considerable indebtedness of the English people to Speyer as 'a great uplifting force in the nation's musical life'. The minutes of the trial, which have only recently become available, show no evidence that Speyer was a spy, and yet his British citizenship was revoked.

correspondent from the danger zone, picking up the baton where her brother left off: 'We have about 1,000 Tommies on board & a couple of hundred officers. We are the only ones of the opposite sex, one of the officers told me they were not expecting any Ladies & were high pleased to see us arrive.'[821]

Emily is beginning to be nervous of things other than Germans. She hopes Edie remembers her advice: '. . . not to allow any flirtation but . . . if she saw [a man] was in earnest of course it would be a different matter.'[822] Caroline's third grandchild is on the way – Lilian is pregnant again. Neither May nor Edie show any signs of 'getting spliced' but Emily hopes there are still Christian men like her husband, who can appreciate a well-built intelligent woman.

Edie's dispatches keep them abreast of the news: 'We are going to such funny places . . . it really is an experience that I am very glad to get . . . You will be greatly relieved to know that we are not going up the Adriatic but going through Greece instead to Salonika . . . I believe we have been through one mine-field after we left Southampton; at any rate we got through it alright.'[823]

And later: 'We really are having an awfully good time . . . there is a regular scramble amongst the men to take us out & it is so funny to see how jealous some of them are when they get left behind without anybody.' (Emily is less than impressed with the sailors that obviously took advantage of the gangplank to try to look up the girls' skirts, however amusing Edie obviously found it.) Edie finishes: 'It seems so funny to think of the cold & wet in this hot climate with everybody wearing the thinnest of clothing & solar topees.'

May leans into the horizontal Scottish rain. She looks down at Tai Tai, the bedraggled new dog. It is difficult not to think of the 'regular scramble' of men Edie is fending off. Minefields notwithstanding, sometimes May would rather like to be in that sunny Mediterranean too.

5 NOVEMBER 1915

KATHLEEN – LONDON

Kathleen sits at a bench with a large pile of electric coils in the box beside her. The bench stands on a rough concrete floor. The vast shed in which she sits is 'a perfect inferno of noise', as her fellow Mutinette

Joyce Read describes it, 'and the noise intensified by the roaring of the furnaces, by the metallic clanging of the steel shells as they are flung upon one another in heaps'.

Kathleen's strong sculptor's hands are becoming more dexterous, picking up the tiny components that make up the coil. This is a different type of creativity. Her foreman has told her that they must increase productivity from forty coils a day. The Vickers machine gun, a water-cooled .303 (7.7mm), is in demand – they must deliver a daily average of at least 120.

Her mind strays.

The clock on the factory wall tells her that Mr Balfour will be unveiling her statue of Scott in Waterloo Place at any minute. She has deliberately stayed away. She wonders how it looks. She knows the proportions will be right because she made a dummy figure and pedestal in situ in June, but the light is different, the contrasts less pronounced. As she puts the completed coil into the box, she looks up to see cold daylight flooding in through large windows reaching from the roof almost to the floor. How does her 'Scott' look in this wintry light? Perhaps it is more in keeping with his polar sledging attire. She is glad to have won through with 'working clothes'.

If Kathleen looks up from her bench between coils, she sees a row of girls in their working clothes. Kathleen is well aware that it is the first time that middle-class women have done dirty jobs for the public good. They are all, regardless of their class, working under a company entitled 'The Women Munitions Workers Ltd'. What will the 'Muntinettes' mean for enfranchisement? The mechanics are all men and most of the labourers, but otherwise A3 is filled with girl workers. They wear a brass 'V' for Vickers on either side of their collars and have become nicknamed 'Vickers Virgins'. On a whim, Kathleen decides to reward them for their usefulness her own way – she will hire a charabanc and take the forty 'V.V.s' on her bench to see Barrie's *Peter Pan* in London's West End. As for the men, Kathleen applies her expedition-honed brand of tough love. When a young man confesses his fear of dying in the war to her she says: 'I would have liked to have taken him in my arms and comforted away the horror, but I only said "Oh that's rather absurd".'[824]

DECEMBER 1915

VIOLET OATES — ROUEN, FRANCE

Violet Oates is buttering a slice of bread. Beside her is a stack. Beside that is a stove with a large cauldron of boiling water and in the cauldron are eggs. Boiled eggs are incredibly popular in the café and the room is full of steam. This is the warmest place to be in the early mornings in Rouen. Caroline has asked Violet to write a letter home to be published in the *Gestingthorpe Village Church Monthly*. Violet should describe her job with the Women's League of Service in Rouen to underline the fact that 'Miss Oates has gone "to do her bit" at Rouen.'[825]

Violet is boarding in a French house where she doesn't understand a word of what they are saying (French is not her second language), so they think she is 'mad'. Or perhaps they think she is mad because she wants to keep the window open, even in December. At least the language barrier makes it easy not to give away secrets. Violet knows that 'No end of men have lately gone off from here to the new ground,' but she does not say who the men are or where the new ground is. She knows exactly which soldiers have come and gone because of their badges. The badges, like heraldic devices, are the only colourful thing in the otherwise gloomy city where all the French women wear deep mourning, 'even for distant relatives'. It is gloomy, except of course for the exquisite stained glass in Rouen Cathedral.

As Violet composes her dispatch, she peels an egg in her fingers and slices it on a wooden board. She is in the kitchen behind the café on the ground floor of the club. Upstairs there are three rooms for writing, reading and games. In spite of her mother's insistence that nice girls do not cook, Violet has become adept at buttering, peeling and slicing, and can cut sandwiches into triangles quite quickly now. This is 'not an idle life'; it is still not paid work, but volunteers work six-hour shifts six days a week to serve soldiers of all ranks refreshments and Player's Navy Cut cigarettes. Violet must hurry; she has to finish the egg sandwiches before the lunchtime rush at 1 p.m. Perhaps by tea time, the post will have arrived with the Christmas parcels. The boxes were Violet's suggestion, but it was her mother's that they append a list of subscribers to the

December issue of the *Church Monthly*. Since no one wanted to be unpatriotic, the amount raised was a hefty £9 5s 3d, and parcels were made up 'as follows: ½ lb tin of tobacco, 2 lb tin of Christmas pudding, 1 lb ginger chips, 1 lb brandy balls, 1 tin Vaseline, cigarette papers'.

In her first letter home, Violet told Caroline of the extraordinary coincidence that the first soldier she ever served in the café was a sergeant in the Inniskilling Dragoons. Caroline is not sure that it is a coincidence, but then neither is she sure about the word combination 'served' and 'sergeant'. Caroline suspects that Violet's connection to her hero-brother has been discovered. She knows that Ponting's film of the expedition is being shown in the trenches. 'The thrilling story of Oates's self-sacrifice, to try and give his friends a chance of "getting through"', claims the Reverend F. I. Anderson, Senior Chaplain to the Forces, 'is one that appeals so at the present time.'[826] Caroline knows that 'getting through' alludes to an altogether muddier and bloodier No Man's Land and that reaching the German trenches will require the self-sacrifice of many thousands of sons. 'We all feel,' concluded Anderson, '[that] we have inherited from Oates a legacy and heritage of inestimable value in seeing through our present work.' But for Caroline, Laurie should be there in the flesh, not just in celluloid. It is wrong that his stumbling death should inspire rather than his military career. If he had been awarded that Victoria Cross for his No Surrender in South Africa, the balance would be easier to redress.

I JULY 1916

ORIANA – LONDON

Oriana Wilson marches along the pavement towards the New Zealand War Contingent Association office on Southampton Row. She's cut her hair short and wears a uniform, a fitted two-tone jacket with brass on the shoulders, a badge saying 'Assistant Hon Secretary' and a tie. 'What I would not give to be able to start nursing!' she'd written to Cherry at the beginning of the war.[827] But instead of patrolling the wards at Lamer, she's found herself in charge of an office in London. She arrives at her desk, dusts herself off with the clothes brush, answers the hateful telephone and wonders what Bill – in the travel frame on her desk – would make of her now. In rare moments of quiet, she turns and disappears into the two water-coloured seascapes by her husband that she has framed on the wall of her office.

To start with, Ory had been in charge of 'comforts', of liaising between the injured soldiers and their New Zealand families. But after the evacuation from Suvla Bay on the Aegean coast of Gallipoli on 7 December when 46,000 people died, she was given a more managerial role. Instead of deferring to men as she has done all her life, she now finds herself managing them, sometimes even firing them: 'The great Classey has been sent away,' she tells one of her secretaries. 'I felt a brute – but he was too lazy and naughty to keep.'[828]

Sometimes, Ory wonders what Bill would have done in the war. More than once he told her that 'I would rather shoot myself than someone else by a very long way, I simply could not do it [829] Perhaps Bill could have combined his art and medicine to make prosthetics? An injured soldier had recently come into the office to show Ory his new leg, 'a very special one . . . & I'm not sure if the New Zealand government will pay for it as they only sanction one kind apparently – but I told him I should much enjoy presenting him with one – such a nice & useful present to give.' The friend now wanted to join the new Flying Corps: 'apparently they do take one legged men sometimes as Pilots – thought it seems impossible.'[830]

With the pandemonium in the office it is sometimes difficult to get through the workload. The bevy of girls are now discussing condoms. New Zealand nurse Etta Rout, serving in Egypt, has suggested that venereal disease should be treated as a medical issue, not a moral one. She has designed prophylactic kits to give out to troops. The idea has caused such outrage that her name is forbidden to appear in print on pain of a £100 fine. Ory looks at the thing scientifically. Absenting herself from the bevy, she writes to one of her old secretaries who has left to become a Land Girl: 'The French letter business is very big now & really is one person's work.' She glances up from her letter at an office awash with condoms. She has been dealing with clothes and cleanliness, but really! Is this the kind of thing Bill had in mind when he assured her that God left her in this world for some purpose?

1917

LOIS – SWANSEA

Lois sits in the front room of Slate Street cursing her stupidity.

She has Taff's Royal Geographical Society medal and the medal from the Reale Societe Geografica. She has reassured the RGS that she will not sell these: 'I need hardly state that [the medals] will be carefully treasured by my children and myself'.[831] Those words 'need', 'hardly', and 'state'. She has been hard up, in a needy state again but she has promised the RGS that she will treasure them. It was because she couldn't sell those medals that she had tried to find another way to raise some funds. She remembers sweating over that letter to the RGS back in 1915.

1915

Putting down her knitting, Lois picks up the heavy typewriter she has been lent and lugs it over to the table. She can delay it no longer. Lois is good with her hands, her fingers strong from knitting, but she has never been taught to type. The smooth, continuous clicking of knitting needles is replaced an uneven 'clack' as metal letters flick forwards to leave their mark on the page. Slowly '5 Slate Street, Morriston' appears, but the 'o' and 'i' tend to stick together and over-type. She tries to disentangle them, getting metallic-scented ink on her fingertips. She starts again but she must not waste paper. She winds the roller on and with one finger carefully taps out: '1st June 1915'.

Dear Sir,

Included in the effects of my late husband, Petty Officer Edgar Evans, which were returned to me after his death . . . was a diary chronicling the various details of the journey to and from the South Pole . . .

Shortly after the announcement of [Taff]'s death, I was approached by the representative of an American newspaper and asked if I would permit him to publish the contents of the diary . . . Commander Evans, R.N. [Teddy], to whom I mentioned the matter, stated that the Royal Geographical Society desired that no part of the diary should be published until two years elapsed from the date of the death. I therefore retained the diary. Now that the period of two years has expired, I should be glad to be informed whether there would be any objection, so far as the Society is concerned, to the publication of the contents of the diary. I should be grateful for information on this point,

Yours very truly,

Lois Evans.[832]

DECEMBER 1917

EMILY – BUTE

May Bowers arrives at Mount Stuart House to take over from the night staff at 6 a.m. It is still dark. When she enters the ward, she sees the lanterns throwing the shadows of the night staff around the marble walls. They are adjusting the bed coverings to neaten everything up before handover. The room echoes. It is difficult to move patients, chairs and beds quietly on the shiny surface. This room was Mount Stuart's fabled 'Marble Hall'; now there are fifty beds ranged around the walls with a double line down the middle.

May approaches the nurses' station. It smells of starched linen and antiseptic. She knows that it will not be so pleasant when she embarks on her first task, the ablutions of the morning.

The chief surgeon is Sir William Mcewen, a pioneer of brain surgery. May helps to prepare patients for the operating theatre that has been set up just off the dining room. Many of the new arrivals are victims of German gas attacks, their burns are terrible, some are blind. Some of May's patients are haunted by the memory of greenish-grey clouds sweeping down upon them, turning yellow as they blow over the battlefield, shrivelling vegetation in their path before seeping down to collect in the trenches.

What would Birdie make of the war? Both Emily and May know that he hated submarines. It was so ungentlemanly to creep up on the enemy and torpedo him from beneath the waves. 'The spirit is against all our national traditions.'[833] But the gas attacks are surely the most ungentlemanly form of warfare yet invented. Moved by the sight of May's injured boys, many of them the same age as Birdie would be,

Emily has swung into full headmistress mode, rallying the fundraisers at a sale for the Red Cross to raise £200. She is about to start collecting specifically for 'The Blinded'.

Watching the submarines nets going up across the mouth of the Clyde, Emily still finds time to write to Cherry. When he first signed up he'd been like a boy in a sweet shop, believing it would be 'Kipling in real life!' The enthusiasm was so like Birdie. But now Cherry has been invalided home with colitis. He blames it on the suffering he endured in the Antarctic, both mental and physical. He lies in bed at Lamer, now a hospital. He recently received a white feather in the post.

1917

LOIS – SWANSEA

Finally Lois has the RGS's answer to her 1915 letter, but she also has the journal in question. Taff's journal. It is just bigger than her hand, maroon, smooth leather, bound and beautifully preserved. Back when she'd sweated over the typewriter to ask if she could publish it, she'd assumed it was Taff's record of the journey to the South Pole. How could she have been so stupid? Taking a pile of letters, she flicks through her expedition correspondence. She still has that letter from Pennell from 1913 somewhere: '[Taff's] diary from the South Pole will be sent to you.' The book was handed to her, sealed, by Teddy in April 1913.

Lois has followed the fortunes of that other Evans, Commander Teddy. She knows that in 1916, he remarried, a Norwegian, Elsa Andvord. More recently on 20 April, his destroyer HMS *Broke* deliberately rammed a German destroyer in Dover Strait in a sensational victory. He has become something of a hero. The Welsh newspapers are claiming him as their hero, together with the nationals, the *Cambrian Daily Leader* refers to him as 'Evans of the *Broke*'. But even Evans of the *Broke* seems also to have assumed that Taff's journal was a record of his final journey to the South Pole.

Since Teddy handed it over, it has been in the trunk under Taff's mother's bed. As the bank for his salary, it was the obvious place for Sarah to keep her son's precious journal. But now Lois realises that since Sarah can't read, she couldn't correct the misunderstanding. Lois puts down Pennell's letter. It's no use blaming anyone else.

Lois can flip Taff's leather journal open to 28 February 1911 – the paper smells musty – 'a most depressing day'.[834] She could not have put it better herself. This maroon book is not, after all, worth its weight in gold, even though it is precious to her. It is not a journal of the journey to the South Pole – Taff never kept one. This journal begins on 27 January 1911 and ends on 15 March the same year – it is his record of that dry geological expedition to the Dry Valleys.

Taff is one for curses. As Lois flicks through the pages of her husband's writing, she finds that on 30 January and 2, 6 and 17 of February, he wrote: 'cussed plenty' or 'I've cussed a bit today' or 'cussed a good deal'. Now in Slate Street, as Lois realises what a fool she must seem, she may well invoke those 'blind beggars of Egypt'. What would Taff do? Taff had the grace to admit when he was in the wrong. On 27 February he wrote, 'I got a frostbitten ear through having only my Tom a' Shanta [sic] on, pure carelessness on my part.' But Taff and Lois do not have the monopoly on mistakes, even if not everyone confesses to them as her husband did.

The first of the RGS's replies came from 'Hinks', Scott Keltie's replacement, informing her that he had 'referred the enquiry on'.[835] Although Lois doesn't know it, straight after posting that letter to her, Hinks wrote at once to Captain H. G. Lyons: 'I do not know anything of the Society having expressed a desire that no part of the diary should be published, but perhaps you do . . . At any rate, you are in a position to form the best opinion as to whether anything should be done now to hinder the publication . . . I dare say that the diary is worth a considerable sum of money to the widow.'[836] While Lois has been trying to work out how to keep afloat at Slate Street, Hinks and Lyons were trawling the archived *Terra Nova* paperwork to find any record of the requirement for a two-year delay. Had Scott stipulated it before he left? Had Teddy made it up? The RGS is not in the confession business. The only thing left to establish was if it would suit them to find a new reason to 'hinder the publication'. Neither man could think of one. All Lois knows of it is that she now has a letter telling her to go ahead.

MAY 1916

KATHLEEN – LONDON

Kathleen opens the gate and walks up the path. If Kathleen's admiring men, the 'Knights of your Tea Table', are there, the prime minister will order his chauffeur to drive him around the block until the coast is clear.[837] Kathleen opens her front door. As the prime minister strides through to the studio at the end of the modest back garden, Peter may call out 'Squif?' Summer and winter, barefoot and scantily clad, the seven-year-old Peter now sports a layer of fine hair on his legs and arms.

The atmosphere between Kathleen and the prime minister is strained. At the end of April, Asquith sent Kathleen 'a frivolous note', possibly a love letter. Kathleen has assumed that 'harem' is not a literal term and confronts him about the note. Asquith asks, 'Did I want him to write always about conscription.'[838] There is the hiss of sulphur as Asquith strikes a match. As the smell of tobacco curls across the unheated studio, Kathleen loops the tape of her sculptor's apron over her hair, rolled up loosely around the nape of her neck. And what, pray, asks Kathleen, is on Asquith's mind today?

Briefly he sketches the problem. They are swiftly back to conscription. Asquith had promised that only single men need volunteer for active service. It was their duty to 'go first'. Married men who have volunteered were deemed 'bounders' for volunteering despite their responsibilities as husbands and fathers.[839] What can Kathleen say? In her opinion, men with the 'right stuff' – and who have passed that 'stuff' on – have a responsibility to do their patriotic duty. Asquith knows that Kathleen urged Scott, a husband and father, to take risks because he had passed his genes on. As for herself, Kathleen's mother 'went blind when I was born and died soon after . . . How glad I am I have no parents.'[840] Parents are expendable, limiting. She is living proof of that.

She has, Asquith tells her, 'the best brain of any woman he knows'. Is he being frivolous again? Kathleen places her strong hands on the top of her clay bust of Asquith's head and presses the pads of her thumbs gently into the damp clay at the nape of his neck as she asks him to 'say that again'. He does.[841] 'I am glad I am a woman, that is, being born into the class I am,' Kathleen says. 'Nothing is expected of a woman in my class, neither brains, energy or initiative and you have merely to display the modicum of any of these things to get fantastic kudos.'

Kathleen decides on a strategy. The thing she admires about men like Asquith is 'moral courage' – that elusive quality that she believes

Scott had and Shackleton lacks. Asquith, on principle, has refused to accept Sir Edgar Speyer's resignation from the Privy Council – but the public are out for German blood and there are demands to 'Intern them All'. Asquith tells her that the king is outraged. '"Intern them all" indeed,' he exclaimed privately. 'Then let them take me first! All my blood is German. My relations are German. Let me be interned before . . . Speyer.'[842] Kathleen knows that Asquith, like Scott, will not abandon his friends, even though it may be the death of his political career.

Eventually, Asquith tells her about his day. The chancellor of the exchequer, the president of the Board of Trade, the foreign secretary and the home secretary have all resigned over the issue of reneging on his promise not to conscript married men. He has their resignation letters with him. Kathleen's endless days on the Vickers production line are forgotten as she changes gear into 'inarticulate comforting'.

'You,' Asquith tells her later, 'did me more good than you can know.'

EARLY 1917

CAROLINE – GESTINGTHORPE

A frosty morning at Gestingthorpe for the East Essex Hunt meet. There is much discussion as to the horses – the Suffolk Punches have been drafted to pull the heavy guns in France – and Caroline's largest war expenditure will be a donation towards helping wounded horses. As the master of foxhounds gathers his hounds, Caroline remembers Major Richardson of the 13th Hussars – 'I was so sorry to hear about poor Oates, I did not know him well, but I do know that he was a right fellow to hounds, and other things generally follow.'[843]

If Caroline detects a flicker of awkwardness at any casual mention of 'the Hun', she can immediately bring up the Inniskillings, the cavalry regiment who famously came to unveil a brass plaque right here in Gestingthorpe. There is also the entire family tree in coats of arms glowing from the stained glass in the Gestingthorpe Hall. It would be no trouble to take anyone who cared to know through the Oates manorial claim in coloured lights. Such distractions are like throwing down decoys for a hound, leading the hunt away from the scent – from the trail in their minds that might lead to her Kremnitz relatives, might lead them to question her allegiance.

As she watches the horses set out from her trap, Caroline mulls over the recent news of the Kremnitzes. In 1896, Mary Kremnitz was widowed and reverted to British citizenship along with her sons. They have both been trained as engineers in Leeds, but when war broke out, were visiting their mother in Wernigerode and were interned. On 6 June 1916, Franz Kremnitz, Lilian's age, was declared 'a poor specimen', unlikely to be a threat to Germany, and released to England with the news that his brother Harry wasn't so lucky and is being held at the Ruhleben Internment Camp, a civilian detention centre housed in a racecourse near Berlin. The camp has a printing press producing a magazine in the manner of the *South Polar Times*. Caroline and her family are surely not the only people to consider the similarities between the camp and a hut in the Antarctic, albeit with Germans rather than weather keeping men locked up.

What should Caroline's sisters the Frau Kremnitz do? Parliamentary Counsel discussed the matter: '[Mary Kremnitz née Buckton] lives a very long way from Ruhleben and, as far as sentiment goes, she might as well return here and be near her repatriated son.'[844]

But on 30 January 1917, in a file referenced 'Trading with the Enemy Ref No 977', Harry Kremnitz is still in Ruhleben. Caroline is related to Liberal MP Professor Arnold Lupton through her stepmother. Lupton is a pacifist and is anti-conscription He is regarded with some suspicion by the government, but in the case of pleading for repatriation for her nephews, he is an influential public figure. 'Harry is getting into a very nervous state . . . that he will break down if he remains a prisoner much longer.' Harry is not alone. Several men have attempted to escape or to commit suicide.

Someone, sensitive to the term 'suicide' and with the mind of an accountant, attempts to balance the books between the 'In' and 'Out' columns headed 'English' and 'German'. Someone suggests that Harry Kremnitz could be exchanged for a Dr Hugo Rosenberg, No 525, now interned at Lofthouse near Wakefield, who has a wife and children in Berlin.[845] The following year the Prisoner of War Dept, Downing Street, will send Harry a passport. Secrecy will be fastidiously maintained. Caroline understands that her son's example of going over the top is vital to the war effort, and that supressing the Oates link with Germany is not only in her interests, but her family's.

After the day's hunt, Caroline stands by the warm fire in the new memorial west wing and runs her thawing fingers over the text she's had carved into the new mantelpiece:

When you sytte by ye fyre to keep Yrslfes Warme

Take heede leaste Yr Tongues doe yr nay bourse noe Harm[846]

Caroline is still careful to advertise her patriotism and her financial support for the war effort. It is no crime to keep 'Yr Tongues' still, or as Laurie had put it, to 'keep your mouth shut'.

1 JULY 1916

ORIANA — LONDON

Ory rushes back to her flat in Fitzjames Avenue. She is anxious about her brother, Noel Souper. He and his wife Rosalie returned from their home on Vancouver Island to help with the war effort. But Ory has just heard that there has been a massive offensive in the area of Picardy where Noel's regiment, the Royal Berkshire, has been posted.

The poky flat smells of stale cigarette smoke. Ory takes off her polished shoes and walks across the only carpet that she's laid in her 'ward room'. There are New Zealand girls living with her now. They have come over to England to help and Ory enjoys their company. At one point it looked like they would have the flat to themselves, when the Red Cross prepared to post Ory to northern France. She joked that she might slip into speaking German 'and that would never do.' But Ory's in-laws preferred her safe on 'the Home Front'. She is all they have left of Bill.

Ory and Rosalie do not feel like joking now. They light 'Smokes for Soldiers' and watch blue tits pecking shards of coconut on the window sill. They cannot distract themselves from discussing Noel. The last they heard he was in the newly dug trenches in northern France with his twenty fellow officers. They have tried to read between the censored lines of his letters home. From them they might know that the Berkshires have 20 officers and 656 men at a place called Casino Point. Everyone knows that the objective is to capture the German trenches.

Both women have both spent all day praying that God has spared Noel. Praying that the telegram will not come. Rosalie thinks of the farm that she and Noel will return to in Vancouver Island, where the American sycamore still reaches its branches out over the bright blue waters of Vancouver Sound, where the orcas blow and their friend's boat, *The Nancy*, bobs on its mooring, awaiting their return. But the telegram comes all the same.

Bill had been one of five, Noel is one of 19,000 men that lost their lives in a single day. Noel, like Bill, was thirty-nine years old. But Ory is no longer the same woman who was widowed in that prehistoric, pre-war time. She can no longer accept that a loving God can allow mechanised warfare, slaughter on this scale. She cannot comfort Rosalie. Until now Bill was with her, just out of sight. Now she realises that he is just a photograph in the travel frame on the desk in her office. Her life, since 1913, has been lived as if Bill is watching her. But he is not. He never has been.

In the days and months that follow Ory's life begins to unravel – 'L'homme propose mais le bon Dieu dispose', the phrase that explained everything, is a self-indulgent platitude, a delusion. If God doesn't exist, then Noel is just a body lying out in No-man's Land. Bill is just a frozen body even further out of reach. They have not passed over from this life into the next, they have simply ceased. Ory's new bereavement is as private as losing Bill was public. Where that was heroic, this is taboo. Her grief is disguised in an increasing brusqueness lest her ultra-Christian relatives – four of them clergymen – suspect the truth. She clings to empirical facts, to medicine, to science and to her trunk of Antarctic letters – she has been loved.

NOVEMBER 1916

KATHLEEN – LONDON

Kathleen sits in the cold church, watching the coffin – a body in a box. It is absurd. The body belongs to Reginald Smith, Scott's publisher, Bill and Ory Wilson's great friend. But Reggie had not wanted that body and had thrown it out of the window to crumple on the pavement below his bedroom window in Green Street. Why then would they carry it about in a box? Kathleen is sitting beside Cherry, whom she has been trying to cheer up. What he needs is a jolly good party at the Ritz, not a dirge-y church. But she knows that suicidal tendencies are real and that even great men are not immune.

Eleven years in office, Asquith told Kathleen at their last meeting, and he is 'heartily sick of it'. 'I'm like a rat in a trap.'[847] When Kathleen says that 'it really is a ridiculous world', Asquith tells her 'seriously that he often wished he could get out of it'.[848]

The prime minister is replaceable. They both know that. Kathleen, also, is replaceable. In June she went to a dinner of ten people and wished she hadn't. The man who sat next to her opened the conversation by saying: 'You must be tickled to death by the news about your husband.' It turned out that Shackleton had just returned from a second trip to Antarctica – he had not lost a single man. Kathleen left the party as soon as she was able.

After Reggie Smith's funeral, Kathleen approaches Ory, sitting stiffly in a pew in her New Zealand War Association uniform. Asquith has found Kathleen a position in the Pensions Office. Isn't office work deadly dull? Kathleen would rather work in the 'Tin Noses' shop, making masks for maimed soldiers.* Perhaps Kathleen mentions their mutual acquaintance, Lord Curzon. Apparently poor Elinor Glyn was staying at Curzon's residence, Montacute House, when she read of his engagement to American heiress Grace Hinds in the newspaper over breakfast. Curzon's private and public lives have never been properly introduced, rather like his private opinion of 'globetrotters' and his presidential opinion of the 'first batch' of female members who, he still publicly claims, are 'at least equal and in some cases superior, to those of any corresponding number of men'.[849]

Whatever they discuss, Curzon, Speyer, war work, Peter, the ex-BAE team, Oriana's expression is fixed into the same sphinx-like mask as it was on the tug, the *Plucky*, back in 1910. Kathleen and Cherry leave the 'party'. Kathleen has no time for Oriana. The woman is quite simply 'an absurd prig'.[850]

16 NOVEMBER 1918

LOIS – SWANSEA

The war has been over for five full days. Swansea is still en fête. Lois is enjoying a brief moment of fame, and her fingers, a well-earned rest. She has finished Caroline's altar cover and knitted her way into the local papers: 'Among the hard and consistent war workers may we

---

* Which she will, in fact, go on to do: 'Surgery calls art to its aid', said surgeon Sir Harold Gilles, and Henry Tonks, Kathleen's art professor at the Slade School of Fine Art enlisted her help.

mentioned the name of Mrs Edgar Evans, widow of the late Petty Officer Edgar Evans, of Captain Scott's Antarctic Expedition fame. She has knitted on an average, one pair of stockings every weeks since the war began, the total number she has knitted being 230 pairs. This is in addition to other war work of a similar nature.'[851]

1918

ORIANA – LONDON

Outside Buckingham Palace, Ory walks towards a crowd of friends, her black feather boa lifting in the light breeze. She is beginning to master her loss of faith, at least in public, though she still wonders what Bill would make of all this if he could see her now. She knows that as a widow she is now in the majority. She holds out the turquoise enamel medal, given her by the king, towards expectant, smiling faces: 'A CBE – I think how amused and pleased Bill would have been.' Oriana's honour has been awarded on the recommendation of the New Zealand government. She regrets that the king was not told who she was. She told her waiting friends that she had been ushered into the throne room, with a line of people. Suddenly the king looked at her as if he had seen her before: 'and he had of course – but I moved on and it was over.'[852]

Anne Hardy, one of her New Zealand friends, amuses her by asking if it makes her a Dame. 'No my dear, but I would rather like to be,' Ory replies. But she is 'electrified by it all'. She knows of one lady whose husband is 'most annoyed to think that I would take precedence of [sic] him on any public occasion'. A suited man approaches the group with a camera. He tells them that he is the photographer for the *Daily Sketch*. Ory poses in her boa and then talks to the reporter. 'I am very pleased,' says Ory, 'to be identified with New Zealand in this way ... When the Order of the Empire was first instituted I thought it would be a very nice thing to have – but never dreamt it would come to me & certainly not the Commandership!'

25

Worst Journeys

ORIANA — AUSTRALIA AND NEW ZEALAND

Oriana listens to the rhythmic slapping of paddles. She resists the urge to trail her hand in the water as she might from a punt in the Cambridge backs. It is hot and humid up here in the Top End of Australia and the colours are so vivid: splashes of bright orange and deep green, luxuriant white flowers hanging between trees. Ory holds her binoculars ready with one hand and steadies herself against the motion of the canoe. She has come here to Darwin, Australia, en route to New Zealand. She wants to thank the people of New Zealand for recommending her for a CBE, but first she will do some work for Bill's friend, the mammologist Michael Oldfield Thomas.

Oldfield Thomas has asked her to send specimens back to the Natural History Museum in London and Ory intends to try, 'unless I am collected by a crocodile or a cannibal!' Oldfield Thomas urges her to be careful, to link up with a contact of his, a Mr Sherrin. Perhaps he has sensed a spirit of reckless adventure, a woman with nothing to lose, or perhaps he is adjusting to this reversal of pre-war norms where the man adventured and the woman urged him to take care.

In the upper storeys of the trees that overhang the East Alligator River there is a flash of pure turquoise. It is the hooded parrot. But there is already a specimen in South Kensington and besides, a parrot is not a mammal. Ory's canoe glides past white beaches and through rock gorges. She is the first white woman ever to travel this far upstream, her destination a place 150 miles from the nearest outpost and out of communication with the outside world. In her rucksack she has Bill's dissection kit, the one they used for eviscerating all those grouse back in Scotland. Carefully wrapped beside it, she has cyanide and arsenic preserving fluid in glass bottles. Oldfield Thomas has given her a packet of stiff paper specimen labels and string. She tells him that: 'So far I have not been successful in catching small mammals. There seem to be none here.' She hopes she will amuse the scientist at his desk in London – 'What? No mammals in Northern Australia!' – and then surprise him with a find.

The canoe arrives at the entrance to a karst limestone cave. Inside it is dark, darker than any wartime blackout, but the guides light torches and hold them aloft. They flare in the cool air, illuminating ancient paintings high up on the walls. Ory follows flickering light along powdery pathways through a stone forest of stalactites and stalagmites until, deep in the cavern, she becomes aware of a chirruping. Looking up, she sees black clumps clustered across the cavern ceiling. Bats.

Weeks later, Ory arrives in New Zealand and heads for Christchurch, where a stack of mail awaits her. She takes it to Uncle Bill's Cabin and climbs the external stairs to the roof lookout. She leans into the briny onshore breeze, her hands on the rail which is, after years of guano and sea spray, slightly less than sturdy. She has come to find Bill, in much the same way that he used to climb the rigging to find her in the crow's nest of the *Terra Nova*. She looks towards the familiar southern horizon. It is just as it has always been. Bill is still there in the frozen South, still the same age. 'I am so happy to be back in N.Z. again,' she tells her friend Anne Hardy from Rakia, 'but find it very difficult in Christchurch, owing to all the many associations with the expedition – I wish I could stay in any other place.'[853]

She tries to resume her traditional role as a 'Useful Help'. Cherry is writing a book about the Winter Journey to Cape Crozier for penguin eggs, and he has asked her to read through an early draft. Ory knows that Cherry handed the eggs in to the Natural History Museum for their analysis before the war, but there has been nothing since. Haeckel's theory, ontogeny recapitulates phylogeny, which Bill had set out to prove, is under suspicion (apparently Haeckel deliberately fudged the data).* Is there some tactic behind the delay? Cherry, not a scientist, is determined and has enlisted Scott's sister Grace to stir them up: 'I certainly sound a fire eating person!' Grace says of Cherry using her as a threat. [854]

---

* C. W. Parsons, who was eventually assigned to study the eggs, concluded in 1934 that the Cape Crozier emperor penguin embryos collected in 1911 by Bill, Cherry and Birdie were too close in age to make a decisive impact on penguin embryology.

Now at the desk in the main room of Uncle Bill's Cabin, Ory looks at the first page of Cherry's manuscript. 'Is the title of the book to be The Worst Journey in the World? I am not sure what the second word is.'[855] Even with her new reading glasses, Ory believes that second word still looks like 'Worst' – 'if it is this & if you will forgive my saying so, it does not seem to me a happy title.'

Ory can appreciate a joke. Before the war, Cherry and Dr Atkinson found and named a troublesome species of tapeworm after her: *Tetrabothrius (Oriana) wilsoni*.[856] A worm, a hut and a ridge – it is an amusing and eclectic collection of Orianalia that they know will appeal to her sense of the ridiculous. But where Antarctic things are concerned, she has not, as Birdie had once observed, 'a particle of frivolity'.[857]

Ory leans back and takes off her glasses. She wonders if Cherry ever understood Bill. 'I am interested to read that you think Scott was the most highly strung man in the little party of five,' writes Ory, 'whereas I think & know that [Bill] was that – but he had far more self-control than Scott – how much control, no one but myself knows, he was an absolute marvel in that way.'[858]

Cherry may have shared a tent and an Antarctic winter with Bill, but he has not shared a marital bed or a grouse moor. Ory knows that her husband had a temper. Bill always regarded the Antarctic as a 'hard school', but had forced himself not to 'give way' so successfully that Cherry seems to have reached the wrong conclusion.[859]

Cherry asks Oriana if she minds him publishing extracts from her husband's journal. Ory assures him that there is nothing private in Bill's journals. Her husband's caution (and her eraser) saw to that. Her private letters from him are a different, though parallel, story. Cherry only has the public version and Ory does not intend to give him the other. The long-suffering Christian gentleman and the hot-tempered lover are selves that Bill took pains to keep discreet, and she has no intention of betraying him.

Secrecy has become increasingly important to her. Ory decides to use money she's raised from the sale of prints of Bill's artwork to create a secret fund. She wants to help New Zealanders suffering from 'war epilepsy' (shell shock). She starts with the painter Esmond Atkinson: 'It was so pathetic to see his expression as it was coming on,' she wrote after Esmond had broken down in front of her at a smart Wellington tea party, 'and so terrible to hear his cries.'[860]

Perhaps Cherry's Worst Journey will be a useful metaphor for sufferers like Esmond – Bill's peaceful contribution to the war from beyond his snowy grave? Although she has lost her faith in God, she has almost replaced it with Charles Baudouin's philosophy of 'auto-suggestion'. Bill schooled himself not to 'give way' in the Antarctic – perhaps this is something scientific and medical that could also be applied to the New Zealand soldiers?

By ANZAC Day on 25 April, to celebrate the southern hemisphere's veterans, Ory can stand Christchurch no longer and has escaped to stay with war friends in Auckland, where there is a letter waiting from the Natural History Museum. 'I am much complimented,' she tells Oldfield Thomas, 'by your calling a bat [*Miniopterus orianae*] after me! . . . I long to go back to Darwin again . . . or the Sudan . . . or Dutch New Guinea: is that a useful place to collect in? . . . I fancy bats more than anything.'[861] According to the experts at the Natural History Museum, Bill was 'a dreamer of great dreams' but it was sometimes necessary to call him down to earth.[862] He 'revolted against the minute detail inseparable from mammalogy' and yet his widow, it seems, does not.

As Ory reads through Cherry's manuscript again, she realises that dreamer though he might have been, Bill is the hero of the piece. He inspired such affection that Cherry and Bowers would have followed him anywhere. Frank Debenham wants to name the new Polar Research Institute for Bill. He obviously felt the same.

Like Bill, Ory is finally a recognised collector, a scientist in her own right. Her organisational abilities, focused during her marriage on Bill, earned her a CBE. On paper this amounts to Bill's promise that she had been left 'for some purpose', but no amount of success and recognition can replace Bill.

1923

EMILY – BUTE

In her seventies now, Emily holds on carefully with her right hand to the banister as she descends the elegant stairs of Aros na Mara. In her other hand she has a private bank cheque, 'To Mrs Emily Bowers £100', signed, with a flourish, 'A. C. Garrard'. The cheque is for copyright of Birdie's journal, his unique account of the Winter Journey to Cape Crozier. Despite becoming a homeowner, she cannot shake off her suspicion of charity. How does one judge what the copyright of a piece of writing is worth? And there is something strangely possessive about it – Cherry demands exclusive rights.

As she eats her breakfast in the dining room, Emily might reflect that she has had to tap Cherry on the wrist once or twice before – if she accepts this cheque, will she also be accepting his often volatile version of events? She is at least sure of one thing, Birdie's journal is an excellent piece of prose: 'Is it not well written? I think so anyway but I am his mother you see.'[863] Emily likes the idea of Cherry making Birdie come alive. She still loves to read Birdie's accounts: 'How clearly one sees it all – he is a living personality still!'

Emily looks out across the mouth of the Clyde and thanks God that she never cashed the cheque. She had decided to put it on deposit so as not to spend it until after the book was published. Now, two years later, she has retrieved it from the bank in Rothesay.

Cherry has written to ask her if she has already given the information, which, he emphasised, he had bought the copyright to, to anyone else? Has she ever given it to Teddy, Lt Teddy Evans? Emily leaves the table and crosses the hall to the library. Perhaps her once sharp mind is becoming muddled. One thing is clear. Money solves as many problems as it creates. She does see 'the seriousness of the situation'.

Caroline Oates has tried to help. After one of their regular short breaks to Worthing, she sent Emily a copy of Teddy's book *South with Scott*. Emily, flicking through, sees that it states that: 'I [Emily] gave [Teddy] the extract.' In her neat teacher's hand Emily admits to Cherry, 'I have not the faintest idea or remembrance of the circumstances . . . I am more sorry than I can say about this . . . please let me return the £100.'

The postman is waving from the end of the garden. He does not like to come in these days. May is breeding Pekinese and one gave him a nasty nip. Smiling in the brisk onshore wind, Emily accepts her mail over the stone garden wall. The regulation red Post Office bicycle leans against the railings on the opposite side of the promenade and beyond that, black and white oystercatchers poke their bright red beaks into the rock pools. Cherry, she learns once back inside, does not care a hoot about the £100, it is small change. But he is determined to get to the bottom of this copyright issue. He will be damned if Teddy gets away with publishing without permission.

Emily knows that Cherry is disparaging about those who treat exploration like a job: 'No shopkeeper,' writes Cherry in his book, 'will look at research which does not promise him a financial return within a year . . . Those with whom you sledge,' continues Cherry, 'will not be shopkeepers; that is worth a good deal.'[864]

Emily has visited Lamer, the Cherry-Garrard family seat, and walked in the orangery. Many of her father's tailor shops would fit in there. But walking straightens the mind and now she too has the space – the end of the stair rail curls round like the rail of a witness box. While a bewigged Cherry paces his marble floor in Hertfordshire, Emily leans on the rail with her elbows and composes her careful replies:

CHERRY: Do you believe you ever gave him leave to publish?
EMILY: I think not.
CHERRY: Could you state definitely that you never gave him leave to publish?
EMILY: I could not say – cannot remember.
CHERRY: Could you undertake (crossed out) state definitively that you have never taken money or other consideration from Evans in return for leave to publish Bowers's diary of letters?
EMILY: I never received money or other considerations.[865]

It is exhausting and rather belligerent legalese – worst of all, Emily worries that Cherry is enjoying himself. 'None of these publishers know anything about copyright', he says. 'It is fun to teach them, but just at present I have bigger fish to fry & these sprats need worry neither you nor me at all.' She imagines Cherry strutting on his way to the silver post tray. Lamer is a magnificent place, but he is not being magnificent. It is not acceptable to disparage 'sprats'. It is arrogant and myopic.

Emily reads Cherry's manuscript a second time: 'To those accustomed to judge men by the standards of their fashionable and corseted drawing-rooms,' writes Cherry from his vast experience of standards other than those held in fashionable and corseted drawing-rooms, '[Birdie] appeared crude.' [866] Emily is not sure she likes this assessment. Birdie would approve of the manly implications and Emily can appreciate the prose, but Cherry seems to think that there was 'nothing subtle about him'. It would be transformed into a compliment – a rhetorical technique she is familiar with. 'But give me a sledge-party almost shattered,' Cherry continues, 'or one that has just upset their supper on to the floor, and I will lie down and cry for [Birdie] to come and lead me to food and safety.'

Emily draws herself up to her diminutive height. She will use the witness box as a lectern. The moment has arrived for a morning assembly: 'At the time the expedition arrived [Teddy] was in real trouble.' Emily peers over her half-moons, reminding the boy, Cherry, of his humanity. '[Teddy] had just lost his wife . . . he was doing his best for us & I saw more of him then than I have done since – the thing may have occurred at this time but I honestly do not know . . . They [the extracts] must have been given in quite a friendly way. The only thing I ever received from [Teddy] was a Christmas present in 1913.'[867]

Back then, Teddy had come up to Rothesay with his mother when giving a lecture on the island. They stayed with Emily. Perhaps it happened then: 'He wanted me to take the proceeds of his lecture here & that I absolutely refused to do in spite of all his arguments.'

Emily does not like Cherry's aggressive, bullying tone. She hopes he has got the message. She wants, in spite of or perhaps because of Cherry's inquisition, to 'do justice to [Teddy] as well as to myself'. But she does not want to discourage Cherry entirely. Bill is obviously Cherry's idea of the perfect hero, as he was for her son. And Cherry also highlights Birdie as an example of resourcefulness and stalwart cheer: 'I do hope you are going to publish your book about the expedition,' she tells him, 'even though the RGS think it "too readable" . . . Nothing appeals to that parched up body unless it is dry and of a soporific nature.'[868] Solidarity is followed by encouragement: 'I wish you every success with your book.'[869]

Emily turns to deal with the rest of her post. Among the letters is the Alumni leaflet from Cheltenham Teaching College. She had enrolled precisely because, as the main feature confirmed, all the teachers trained there were guaranteed posts after graduating. But why exactly had Emily become a teacher? A route to independence and a better social position certainly, but also, irresistibly, a ticket to adventure. And en route to that adventure, Emily and her fellow CTC alumni had influenced the shape of young minds, many of whom went on to hold positions of responsibility across the Empire. The article concludes that

11 million people had been educated CTC-trained teachers. Half the teachers were female, therefore, five and a half million people in the British Empire had been educated by CTC-trained female teachers. Emily is proud of her small part in these astonishing numbers. Whichever way you look at it, five and a half million is a lot of people.

30 JULY TO 2 AUGUST 1923

KATHLEEN – LONDON

It is a hot day and Kathleen has decided to go for a walk. It will be more like a waddle. She is forty-five years old and nine months pregnant with a child that, since conception, has been christened Wayland. Nansen is not the father – in 1919 she'd finally had things out with the Norwegian. 'It's quite absurd from my point of view. He's fifty-seven and – well I am not.'[870] The father is her second husband, the politician Edward Hilton Young, a year her junior. She has promised him a son, and assuming she survives the birth, this will be her second biological masterpiece. She has created real and metaphorical plinths for all her menfolk, she has preserved them in clay, bronze and stone, and yet she feels that people she was once fond of have begun hacking at one of them.

Approaching her statue of Scott in Waterloo Place, she thinks of the changes she wants to make to the plaque. To fit all her husband's companions on one line, she needs to strip out titles, ranks and qualifications: 'E.A. Wilson, H.R. Bowers, L.E.G. Oates, E. Evans' will be all on the same line, equals, that 'band of brothers'. She touches the cold metal, running the pads of her fingers over the raised letters – while she is at it, she can 'better the lettering'.[871]

Kathleen wanted to take her sculptor's hammer to Cherry's monument, but a book will not smash as a statue might. She refuses to read it but has heard that Scott is described as 'weak' and 'peevish', which she believes is the 'silly opposite of the truth'.[872] She asks George Bernard Shaw, her friend and Cherry's neighbour, to read it for her and give it to her straight.

'Cherry's narrative does, I think, convict [Scott] of two mistakes,' Shaw tells her.[873] 'The fatal one being the sentimental one of taking five men on a journey planned and provisioned for four and, as it proved, under-provisioned even for four. The second was taking a big man like [Taff] instead of Lashly. Cherry evidently believes that if they had gone without Oates and with Lashly instead of [Taff] they would have got back to One Ton before the blizzard, and that the fatality was in [Scott]'s character.'

'Amundsen', Shaw tells her, translating Cherry's opinion, 'was no scallywag but a very great explorer . . . With the exception of one false start too early in the season he had not made a single mistake, not lost a single life, nor overdriven a single man of his party.' Mistakes, lost lives, overdriven men . . . Kathleen does not need to read the book. She has asked for Shaw's blunt response and been taken literally by Literature himself. Bill Wilson's leadership of the Winter Journey has been praised at the expense of her husband's of the final journey. Bill has been put on a higher pedestal than Scott and there is nothing she can do about it. 'There!' concludes Shaw, 'that is the worst of it. If you can stand this, very much less bluntly put by a man very much more [Scott's] partisan than I am, you will be able to read the book without distress or resort to your hammer.'

But there is more. Shaw tells her that this assessment of Scott is not original. Cherry is only the second person to portray her husband in this way. Shaw has just seen Kathleen's bronze statue of Bill in Cheltenham's Promenade. Comparing the statues of Scott in Waterloo Place in London and Bill on the Promenade in Cheltenham, Shaw tells her that he 'suddenly realised that the sort of contrast made between [Scott and Bill] by Cherry in his book had been exactly anticipated by you in bronze!!!'

Kathleen feels weak pains cramping her stomach. She looks up at the statue with its right arm extended to grasp the top of a ski pole. The expression is surely noble. How can Shaw read 'fatality of character' into that face? Perhaps the replica she made for Christchurch is better. It is easier to achieve a serenity in marble, which she'd used due to the rising cost of metal during the war. She turns to leave. A pain pinches her abdomen so that she has to lean on the plinth and breathe through it. She thinks of her statue of Bill on the Cheltenham Promenade, his hands on his hips, his expression less formal.

As the cramping releases its grip, she turns to leave Scott and walks back home, 'a terrible walk'. But the pains fade and next day she hears strange metallic noises in the hall and finds an operating table being wheeled in. She is in her mid-forties. It would be irresponsible to let her go overdue. The surgeons, she is told, are arriving at four. The surgical instruments on the operating table are very like the sculpting tools she keeps in her studio, but these will be used not on clay but on live flesh, hers. Quite apart from the pain, Kathleen believes there is a good chance she might die. The thought of leaving Peter is unbearable. That blond replica of Scott, with newts and caterpillars and natural history pouring out of his blazer pockets. All her life she has maintained that it is 'cowardly to sit down under sorrow', and this situation is no exception.

'Little Sweetheart', writes Kathleen, 'I want the person who tells you I am dead to give you this letter. I am writing it before I die, because I am afraid I may. I want you to take it very sensibly.'[874] It is her version of the letter Scott wrote her. She sometimes suspects he can see her. 'And remember,' she tells Peter, 'if I can see you in any way after I'm dead (and tho' I don't think one can one can't be too sure), if I can see you I want to see you gay and merry and funny, working hard and playing.'

Kathleen has spent her life trying to create the perfect man. As the chloroform is prepared in the drawing room, she concludes that there is no such thing: 'The perfect man does not exist. He doesn't, so there it is; and at . . . two score years, one should have learnt that.'[875] She had given birth to Peter in a violent thunderstorm with her bed pushed up against an open window. But that was twelve years ago. This time she is much less certain, and if she dies, who will wield her hammer, who will be the fierce she-lion to protect her cubs?

Kathleen inhales the chloroform in the early hours of the morning of 2 August.

1904

It is 1904 and Kathleen is in her early twenties. The cool night breeze blows across her face. She is sleeping on a mattress on a trestle table on a terrace overlooking the Ponte Vecchio. The terrace is just two rooftops away from Rex, another young artist at the beginning of their career. She wakes with the distinct sensation that something, someone is very near her. She lies absolutely still and opens her eyes very slightly. She sees Rex kneeling beside her bed with hands together like a mediaeval saint. His hair and clothes look white under the moon. Her 'heart knocks, thumps and roars' in her ears, but she lies deathly still until eventually he tiptoes away.[876] She does not think he knew she was awake. Later, in the daytime, Rex calls round in a more conventional manner to tell her he is going on a walking tour, pack on back, sleeping out at night.

'Pity you aren't a boy,' he says. 'You could come too.'

'Let me be a boy,' says Kathleen, then immediately regrets it. She does not want to be a boy, she wants to make boys and to be worshipped by boys. She wants that heart-knocking, blood-thumping, roaring sensation that will cause her to worship the worshipper right back with all her talent, with all her body and soul.

At 6.30 a.m., Kathleen surfaces in a haze of anaesthesia. The face of Dr Menzies hovers white like a moon above her.

'You've got another boy.'

'Is he. . .?' begins Kathleen, but everything is somehow very blurred and she feels sharp pain where she has been sculpted. 'Is he bad in any way?'

He is not. He is like all the other men she loves, has loved and will love – he is perfectly imperfect. 'What amazing things men are,' says Kathleen.[877]

1934

CAROLINE – SPRI, CAMBRIDGE

Caroline walks into the newly opened Scott Polar Research Institute (SPRI), a classical building designed by Herbert Baker on Lensfield Road in Cambridge. The smell of barely dry paint wafts from the colourful murals that decorate the inside of twin domes. Caroline has, as usual, eschewed the public opening. Frank Debenham, Laurie's chess opponent in the Antarctic, now the Institute's first director, offered to give her a private tour. She accepted. Deb is not really what her friend Lady Shackleton calls 'a Scottite'.[878]

If Caroline stands under the Antarctic dome and looks up from the echoing entrance lobby, she can see Scott's ship and Shackleton's ship, chasing each other around the Pole. A decade before, Caroline had read 'Shackleton's *Nimrod* book. How thrilling when they climb Mount Hope and find the "Highway to the South".'[879] Laurie had concluded that it was Shackleton, not Scott, who had discovered that way through. 'I find the characters of Shackleton and Scott to be a most interesting study,' is all Caroline will say on the matter.

It has taken some courage for Caroline to come here. Since the publication of Cherry's *The Worst Journey in the World*, there are rumours. 'I was never satisfied with the accounts of Scott's book,' Caroline says.[880] On 11 March, in 'Scott's book', Scott claims that 'Oates is very near the end,' and writes of 'discussing the matter' with her son: 'He is a brave, fine fellow and understands the situation.' What had Scott said to Laurie? George Bernard Shaw is perhaps not alone in his opinion that 'there is no getting away from the fact that Scott . . . had finally . . . to give Oates silent hints that he should go out to perish for a day or two before he did – too late [to save his companions' lives] – Poor Oates.'[881] Is this Caroline's opinion too?

Caroline, however, will not force a public enquiry: 'I always felt that my boy's military career was a little overshadowed by subsequent events, and not sufficient was made of it.'[882] She'd hoped the military would redress this, but in 1913 the Cavalry Club commissioned John Charles Dollman's picture of him stumbling blindly out of the tent to his death. That 'little overshadowing' has been neutralised to a certain extent by Kathleen Scott's bronze plaque of Laurie at Eton, which is 'quite good'. But Caroline directs everyone to the 'excellent lifelike portrait of my son in oils (posthumous)', by John Newman Holroyd, where Laurie is in his military uniform, straight-backed, clear-eyed and very much alive. She can do nothing about the Dollman, but she has given the Cavalry Club a replica of her preferred portrait.[883]

As part of his private tour, Deb might try to distract Caroline from the Cavalry Club commission and her counter commission, with an amusing cartoon: 'The Soldier Leaving Cardiff'. In the cartoon, Laurie stands in profile on the deck of the *Terra Nova*, his hands deep in his pockets. His eyes are obscured with a working man's flat cap, pulled down low. His lower lip juts forward until it is in line with the tip of his nose. When Caroline sees that lip, it might conjure up a memory, eight years old.

1926

It is a crisp January day when Caroline's butler Oscar Minchin announces that there is a young woman, a Kathleen Gray, 'Kit', at the front door.

She is mid-twenties, slim, handsome and neatly dressed. She has even features, her lower lip protrudes slightly, and she wears her wavy brown hair in a side parting. She has a brooch at the top of her ironed shirt, under a carefully pressed woollen jacket. Standing on the doorstep, she tells the butler that she would like to see Mrs Oates. If she is asked why, she might say that she had been brought up in north London in the care of Blanche Wright and Ellen Kingsford, two former nurses who ran a home for the unwanted children of unmarried mothers. The home was in Fallow Corner on Finchley Road.

Caroline knows that area of London. She was a pupil at a girl's school in the parish of Hampstead St John. There was no orphanage in Fallow Corner when she was there. Miss Kathleen would not expect her to know it because the home started out as the Wright-Kingsford refuge in Hersham, Surrey, but moved when she was two to Finchley Road. She recently married a Mr Jack Sayers and was obliged to produce certificates for the official records. She took the opportunity to look into her parentage. Miss Kathleen's mother was Henrietta McKendrick, known then as Etta. Her father, she believes, was Captain Oates.[884]

1934

CAROLINE — SPRI, CAMBRIDGE

Leaving the 'The Soldier Leaving Cardiff' behind, Caroline follows Deb out of the gallery on the first floor of the Institute. The cartoon exaggerates that lip, but there is no mistaking it. Eight years ago, Caroline turned the young woman away. With a surname like 'Oates' and the facile prefix 'Wild', Caroline is sure that there are rumours that both Laurie and Bryan have sewn illegitimate children far and wide.[885] But there has been no call for money, no blackmail, no further communication at all from the woman on the doorstep. Does Caroline ever wonder whether her reverence for ancestral pedigree caused her to miss an opportunity to secure Laurie's line? Miss Kathleen Gray / Sayers 'Something' must not be talked about.

Deb continues his tour. He is Australian, warm, friendly and chatty. He talks of his wife, his brood of six children, two sons and four daughters. He knows that since 1915, Caroline has become close to the Shackletons. She has the Shackleton children to stay for the school holidays at Gestingthorpe, and Lady Shackleton stays with her at Evelyn

Mansions when she comes up from Eastbourne to London. She even helps with the Shackleton children's school fees. After Sir Ernest's death in 1922, Lady Shackleton introduced Caroline to her husband's biographer, the distinguished polar historian Dr Robert Mill. 'What a charming man,' says Caroline. It is not only his charm but his discretion that appeal. When Lady Shackleton asked Mill whether they should mention the wife of one of the explorers in Shackleton's biography, he dismissed the matter out of hand: 'If we were to do the like for every [wife] mentioned we should have "husband of Miss Kathleen Something or other the famous sculptress" . . . and so on!'[886] The idea that any of the explorers should be associated with 'Miss Kathleen Something' is, Caroline is reassured to know, so ridiculous it merits an exclamation mark.

Deb stands aside at the Institute's library to allow Caroline through first. Does he dare to ask her about Oates's Polar journal? He knows that Caroline lied when she told Louis Bernacchi (who wrote Laurie's unauthorised biography) that it did not exist.* Now that she has perjured herself, it would be difficult for any of them to hark back to that journal.[887] Deb might argue that since Taff Evans did not keep a diary, if Caroline was somehow mistaken and Laurie had kept one, it would be one of only three possible narratives with which to balance Scott's official account.

But Caroline stands firm on what she sees as personal items. Like Lady Shackleton, she believes they should be burned. 'I take great objection to the publication of Scott's love letters and others which he counted private,' Caroline says, referring to Stephen Gywnn's biography of Scott. 'His views as to his wife's possible remarriage should never have been printed . . . Surely such things are sacred . . . It is not right to give his letters to the world – I suppose [Kathleen] furnished them – or copies thereof – They should have been burnt on her remarriage!'[888] But Caroline's intense indignation hides the real reason for her objection – that sentence in Gwynn's book: 'When Oates in his turn failed on the return journey, the fate of all was settled.'[889]

Deb continues his tour of the Institute, pouring oil on Caroline's

---

*After her mother's death, Violet admitted that '[Laurie's journal] was brief and entirely personal', and Caroline did 'not want it published'.

terrible disapproval. His words are intended to comfort – 'hero', 'gentleman', 'courage', 'example' and 'inspiration' – for Caroline they are like a blizzard, a blizzard she must walk through every day. As the words pile up in drifts around her, Caroline tries to detach herself. Frank Debenham offers her his arm as they leave. Perhaps he is concerned that she is unstable. They descend the steps between the Antarctic and the Arctic domes, out onto Lensfield Road, but Caroline pauses. On the right in the garden between the Institute and the road is a bronze statue of a naked man, just smaller than life size. His arms are thrown out to the side, his face tipped back to the sky. A fully naked male nude, obviously one of Kathleen's, donated to the Institute. Deb seems a bit embarrassed. He's thinking of a fence, or a wall, or some other way of screening it from Lensfield Road. (Mind you, he is not as embarrassed as the man on whom it is modelled, the brother of Lawrence of Arabia, who is now a lecturer at Cambridge and has to bicycle past his naked self every day!) But embarrassment is a slight emotion alongside the storms building inside Caroline. Kathleen has called her statue *Youth*. Its gesture of exaltation and self-sacrifice, and its position outside the Scott Institute, seem to draw a pointed comparison.

Caroline's chauffeur opens the car door for her. The cold November air is still. Caroline pauses and looks back at the classical proportions of the creamy stone facade. Above the door is the bust of Captain Scott that Kathleen made for a special circular niche. Caroline thinks about Laurie's youth; he was only thirty-two when he died on the Ross Ice Shelf. He had his whole life ahead of him, and the lives of his descendants as well. Caroline observes Scott's cleft chin, strong jaw and noble brow. Is that the face of the man she 'never warmed to', or an idealised classical hero? Back in 1913, one of Laurie's army colleagues told her of 'commanding officers [who are guilty of] sacrificing numbers of valuable lives from sheer obstinacy . . . Men who would not listen to the advice of their officers.'[890] It is an opinion that has followed her ever since.

She turns to Deb. She should thank him for the tour. She should wish him luck with his directorship. She should say something about the 'worth of it all', the contribution to science, to the moral fibre of the country. She does not. Something has cracked inside her. Perhaps it was the cartoon of Laurie with the lip and Deb's talk of children. Perhaps it is Kathleen's celebratory bronze of young male self-sacrifice. Caroline gestures to the bust in the central niche.

'That man,' she tells Deb, 'killed my son.'[891]

29 NOVEMBER 1948

LOIS – LONDON

Lois braces herself. She must do this not just for Taff but for his family. She walks out of the London fog, past the crowds and up the red carpet, through the flare of flash bulbs. She is still that girl from Gower with dreams of singing on a stage, but this is not how she dreamt it. The press photographers standing on the other side of the cordon at the entrance to the Empire on Leicester Square are professionals, and if she is on the carpet she must be someone.

Inside the cinema's foyer, Lois is asked to pose for the camera. She pushes her black round-rimmed glasses back up the ridge of her nose with her finger and adjusts her black felt trilby over her snow-white hair. She has a long winter coat with two big buttons on the front and a thick scarf carefully crossed and tucked in the top. It is not as glamorous as the 'picture hat' of her wedding day, but it is her best post-war austerity wardrobe. Norman towers over her in his suit, a mackintosh loose on his broad Evans shoulders, and Ralph follows behind.

Muriel is accompanied by her cousin Sarah Owen, who was the last member of the family to see Taff alive. Twenty-two in 1910, Sarah had gone to Cardiff to see Uncle Taff off. She was shown around the *Terra Nova* and met Captain Scott (who gave her a biscuit from the sledging rations). Muriel, with her mother and brothers on the Gower cliffs at the time, did not share stories of biscuits and glory. She'd rather have had a living father than a dead hero.

Lois knows about the bullying. A 'living father' would have dealt with bullies. But Lois is 'a tiny woman', a Sunday School teacher, and she can only protect them with words.[892] Taff's descendants should memorise Scott's assessment of their grandfather as 'a giant worker with a truly remarkable headpiece'.[893] It is the beginning of a glowing report that Lois still knows by heart.

Now, in the centre of London's West End, as Lois progresses into the cinema, she looks up at the poster on the wall, which promises

'Technicolor'. It shows five men in full sledging gear against a snowy background. Three of the men pull a sledge to one side; they look co-ordinated, strong and purposeful. On the other side there are two men, one helping the other, who is almost prostrate. This is Lois's husband, the father, the grandfather, 'broken down in brain', his ungloved hand reaching out of the frame towards her.[894]

As flash bulbs continue to pop around her, Lois is taken back to a time when she and the children were plucked from obscurity into the limelight and exposed to the full force of speculation. Now she is the only one of the five snow widows still alive to tell of that time, nearly beyond memory, before not one, but two devastating world wars. Together with her boys, Lois moves into the lobby and she sees the familiar faces of the actors, John Mills and James Robertson Justice.

When John Mills, who is playing Scott, made a special visit to her bungalow on Heol-y-Fedw Road in Morriston (which she has christened, 'Terra Nova') to ask Lois what Scott was like, she couldn't say. Mills was four when Taff died. How can she explain that back then everyone was expected to know their place? Professor Frank Debenham maintains that Taff 'was quite at ease with officers . . . though always very correct in addressing them'.[895] When some joker on the quay at Lyttleton had doubted the dishevelled Captain Oates could be a gentleman, Taff had to be restrained from leaping to his defence. The petty officer, ready to demand respect for Captain Oates. Lois had never wanted to be 'above herself', never presumed to ask to meet her husband's boss, but Captain Scott had written to her once. She showed Mills the letter written in October 1911 telling her not to worry, Taff would come home.

John Robertson Justice is playing Taff. He is about the right size, but Scottish; he is not going to try a Welsh accent. Kathleen Scott gave John Mills the watch found on Scott's body before she died the previous year. Lois did not have anything from Taff's body to give – she is holding on tight to his replacement Antarctic Medal and the clasp. Lois is sure that James Robertson Justice will make a good Taff. He has not always been an actor. He was 'a giant worker' and, like Taff, willing to 'pig it' anyhow if the goal was worth it.[896] He had worked his passage back from Canada on a Dutch freighter, washing dishes in the ship's galley to pay his fare. He is sporty like Taff – a keen ice hockey player with the London Lions – and a Labour Party supporter planning to stand for North Angus and Mearns in the next general election. With the earnings from the film, he hopes to realise his dream and buy a distillery on the Isle of Skye.

There is a burst of applause from outside the Empire – the royals must be on their way. Lois recognises many of the film stars that have been assembled here from seeing them at the cinema in Swansea, including Glynis Johns, Sid Field, Vivien Leigh, Laurence Olivier, Jean Simmons and Elizabeth Taylor. From inside the cinema, they hear another loud cheer, with flashes bouncing off the glass foyer door. Queen Elizabeth (who in a few years will become the Queen Mother) sweeps in with Princess Margaret. They wear full-skirted ball dresses glittering with sequins, ermine wraps and white gloves. On their heads are tiaras of sapphires and diamonds that sparkle in the light of a double-height electric chandelier. Child star Bobby Henry steps forward and presents a bouquet of ferns and lilies to the queen. A little girl presents a bouquet of roses to Princess Margaret. She bobs a curtsey, turns to walk away and then bobs another to the delight of the crowd.

Lois and her family follow the procession into the auditorium and stand in front of their seats. The cinema is scented with flowers; everywhere there is lush red velvet and gilded woodwork. The royals take their seats, signalling that everyone else can take theirs. The royal family are the top of the class system, no one sits before them, but Lois feels solidarity as well as deference now. Princess Elizabeth (not in attendance tonight due to the recent birth of her son, Charles) trained as a driver and mechanic. Margaret was a Girl Guide and later joined the Sea Rangers. Lois knows that the king is too ill to leave the palace, but the Duke of Edinburgh accompanies the royal ladies. The duke is Royal Navy; he fought alongside men like Taff and was mentioned in dispatches for bravery.

The royals sit, and Lois and her family take their seats. The lights dim. The film starts. The first screen is just text: 'This film could not have been made without the cooperation of the survivors and the relatives of late members of Scott's Last Expedition. To them . . . the producers express their deepest gratitude.' The film begins with Captain Scott's visit to Fridtjof Nansen, who urges him to rely on dogs. What would Caroline Oates have made of this? The Technicolor is so realistic that Lois would not have guessed, though she knows, that most of it was shot in Ealing Studios. She sits back in her seat and is transported from London to Antarctica.

James Robertson Justice looks believable as Taff. Lois has Ponting's portrait of Taff in the front room of her bungalow in Morriston. His fur mittens are crossed over the top of a long ski pole. It was this picture that caused her to make the mistake on Taff's memorial. She'd told the sculptor that they only used one pole, but that was the earlier *Discovery* expedition; actually, on the *Terra Nova*, they'd used two. There is also the mistake in the Tennyson quote from 'Ulysses', which should have read 'To strive, to seek, to find and not to yield', but someone swapped the seeking and striving around. It is literally 'in stone', too expensive to correct but still galling. How will Justice portray Taff, dishevelled and crawling in his final hours?

At the end of the film, Lois and her two sons stand and wait for the queen and the rest of the royal party to leave. They walk back down the red carpet, out of the glare of royalty and flash bulbs, and find themselves on the dark grey platform of Paddington Station. Trundling west on the last mail train of the night, Lois thinks of Kathleen Scott, played by Diana Churchill. While sculpting a bust, she tells her husband that she isn't jealous of him going to the South Pole. Harold Warrender played Bill Wilson, with Anne Firth as Oriana Wilson. She wasn't so happy about Bill going back to Antarctica but was persuaded by it being worth it for the science. No one had been cast to play Lois. Her attitude to her petty officer husband leaving for Antarctica cannot have been thought significant enough to portray.

The city lights are left behind, but the music of Ralph Vaughan Williams's stirring film score endures. Lois has followed Vaughan Williams in the newspapers. His score has specific musical themes for Kathleen Scott and Oriana Wilson. He is developing the score into an independent piece to be called 'Sinfonia Antarctica'. It will require a small chorus of soprano and alto women's voices, but the women will not have any words. For the first performance all the singers, the wordless women, will be positioned off stage.[897]

It is the early hours of the last day of November. Fog still hangs over London, but in Wales it is clear and the pavement is frosted white. A tiny figure in a trilby, a winter coat and a scarf walks between pools of light from the lamps along Heol-y-Fedw. The figure turns off and, unlatching a garden gate, walks into a bungalow and closes the door. At the bottom of the garden path, a sign with the house name reads 'Terra Nova'.

EPILOGUE

Son of old Laertes –
mastermind – what a fine, faithful wife you won!
What good sense resided in your Penelope –
how well Ikarios's daughter remembered you,
Odysseus, the man she married once!
The fame of her great virtue will never die.
The immortal gods will lift a song for all mankind,
a glorious song in praise of self-possessed Penelope.

Homer, Odyssey

QUEEN'S HALL, LONDON

'[Kreisler] played superbly . . . all went well and the ovation at the
end was tremendous. Kreisler and [Elgar] shook hands for quite a
long time.'[898] They walk off stage but the applause continues.
'Performance wonderful,' notes Alice Elgar. 'Enthusiasm unbounded.
Shouts.'

Elgar knows that there will be even more frenzied speculation about
the five dots now. He has no intention of revealing who they represent.
It allows the audience to find themselves in the music, on the scroll,
in the story. To become those five dots.

EMILY BOWERS

Emily stayed in close contact with schools in New Zealand and
England, and used part of her Mansion House Fund to donate to
Waitaki High School and Sidmouth Parish School. At home, Emily
and May supported William Maxwell, reading his books in manuscript
and taking it in turns to nurse his terminally ill wife, Agnes, whom
they all loved. On 25 September 1924, May Bowers, aged 46, married

the widowed William Maxwell. William had been knighted for his services to the international Co-operative alliance in 1919, and so May became Lady Maxwell.

According to her niece, 'Aunt May' always maintained that Emily had a letter confirming that Birdie was actually the last of the five to die. Emily felt that Birdie would not have wanted to challenge the legend that the 'Captain of the Ship' was the last to go down, even if it were the truth, so this was never made public. Some of Birdie's relations regard this omission as his 'biggest sacrifice'.[899] Reverend George Seaver, who wrote biographies of both Birdie and Scott, worked closely with May, and knew about this, but agreed to end the story as May directed and dedicated Birdie's biography to Lady Maxwell.

In her chosen profession, Edie Bowers was quickly promoted to the nursing equivalent of headmistress. She served with Lady Paget's unit in Skopje, volunteering to work on dangerous infectious diseases wards with the typhoid and typhus patients. When returned to work in London, she was appointed Sister-in-Charge at Croydon Hospital, where Matron E. E. O'Connell found her 'good tempered and willing', even under great stress.[900]

Emily was a proud alumna of Cheltenham Teacher Training College and retained a passionate interest in teaching theory throughout her life, but her children, her nest of Bower birds, were her pride and joy. A warm obituary appeared in the *Buteman* after her death, celebrating 'a lady of wide experience of travel . . . survived by her two daughters'.[901] She was described as the widow of 'Captain A. Bowers [who] had a distinguished record of exploration in China', and the mother of not Henry, or Birdie, but '"Little Bowers". . . one of that band of heroes.'

CAROLINE OATES

Caroline continued to gather facts as if a sufficient accumulation would make everything right. She wanted to know the precise location of her son's memorial cairn. Cherry couldn't be sure, justifying to himself that 'anything written then was done at a time of great mental distress.'[902] This lack of precision over the location of her son's body relative to the tent, was increasingly difficult for Caroline to bear.

Caroline became increasingly private and solitary following the publication of Bernacchi's biography of Captain Oates. Bryan Oates told Bernacchi (with whom he served in the navy during WWI) that the 'very few details I have gladly given you will most probably be placed at my door'.[903] And indeed, 'Violet and Lilian were left Gestingthorpe Hall by their mother on her death.'[904]

Violet never married but dutifully adopted the role of companion to Caroline in old age. She promised her mother that she would burn all of Laurie's papers immediately on Caroline's death, but thankfully she did not keep this promise. Instead she copied out sections and hid them in a trunk. Violet was the last Oates to live at Gestingthorpe Hall, and when she moved out to a cottage in 1948 the trunk came too. On the opposite side of the country, Sue Limb, a sixteen-year-old schoolgirl with a fascination with the Scott story, sent Frank Debenham, Director of the Scott Polar Research Institute, a Christmas card in the style of the *South Polar Times*. Deb, utterly charmed, introduced Sue to Violet, then in her eighties. As Deb had suspected, Violet was as charmed as he had been. Violet let Sue see the contents of the trunk and in her will left the girl £150 to write her brother's biography.

On 26 November 1937, the pantry boy at Gestingthorpe found Caroline collapsed after a sudden haemorrhage. She was eighty-three. Caroline's body was taken to Ipswich crematorium. The villagers were asked not to talk about her death – no cars followed the hearse. It is as if Caroline fought the public obsession with her son's death with her own: 'When I die,' she had decreed, 'I wish to die alone and no one must know.'[905]

LOIS EVANS

The fifty letters that Lois received from Taff in May 1912 no longer exist. Taff was not able to write a last message for Lois just before he died, and unlike Oates, he did not ask Bill to write one for him. But Teddy Evans wrote anyway. Teddy never told Lois that Taff's drunken fall into Lyttleton Harbour when the *Terra Nova* left in 1910 had nearly precipitated mutiny, though Deb maintained that Teddy had never really forgiven him. Taff's relatives are still involved with ensuring his posthumous reputation with statuary and perhaps a feature film. For a family who have endured bullying and vicarious blame from the public, the tide has certainly turned.

In 1964 HMS *Excellent*, the Royal Naval gunnery school at Whale Island, Portsmouth, named an accommodation block for petty officers 'The Edgar Evans Building', the first to be named for a petty officer rather than a famous admiral.

John Evans still celebrates his grandfather Taff and his grandmother Lois today. John remembers her as a 'tiny woman'. She was a 'lovely lady', with whom he used to catch the Number 26 bus every Tuesday to go to Aunt Muriel's for tea. Lois continued to follow the fortunes of the ship after which her house was named. In 1913, after the expedition, the *Terra Nova* re-joined the Bowring fleet and went back to whaling, but the figurehead was removed and placed in Roath Park, Cardiff. In the late 1930s, the *Terra Nova* foundered off Greenland. The crew were rescued, but the 58-year-old ship was not considered to be worth salvaging. It was set on fire and sunk by gunfire.

Lois died at the age of seventy-three on 23 April 1952 in Gorseinon Hospital near her daughter's home. The *South Wales Evening Post* ran a short obituary: 'Mrs Evans was a member of St David's Church Morriston. She leaves two sons Norman and Ralph, and one daughter Muriel.'[906] Recently her relations have visited her grave, registered as No. 8515 in Morriston Cemetery. It is unmarked at her request.

KATHLEEN SCOTT

Wayland Kennet, Kathleen's second son, remembered a lot of laughter in his mother's house. James Lees-Milne, Kathleen's friend, decided that she left for posterity the worst parts of her character – parts that in life were overridden by energy, optimism and fun. Louisa Young, her granddaughter (whom she never met), wrote those parts into the family-approved biography: *A Great Task of Happiness*.

Kathleen was the only one of the five widows who ever married again. Her son Wayland became a writer and a politician, focusing particularly on clean air. (Scott always said he could not breathe 'twice-breathed' London air.) Kathleen supported her second husband Edward Hilton Young around the political hustings while trying to maintain a separate artistic career for herself. Mark Stocker, the New Zealand art historian, suggests that her hostility to modernists – Jacob

Epstein, Frank Dobson and Henry Moore – may explain why her work has been largely overlooked. He believes she might have been the most significant and prolific British woman sculptor before Barbara Hepworth.

Kathleen, the Right Honourable Lady Kennet FRBS, died of leukaemia on 25 July 1947 aged sixty-nine. Kathleen's second husband offered the Royal Geographical Society her bronze bust of Fridtjof Nansen, a clear statement that he believed that she had not had an 'affair à outrance' with him in Scott's absence – a position robustly defended by his family. Kathleen referred to their relationship as 'a divine friendship', and she kept all Nansen's letters to her (not hers to him) and had them professionally bound in gold embossed leather. Within those covers is the record of a sustained pitch of incendiary flirtation. Having immortalised 'the men of many nations' in bronze, Kathleen neglected to create a plinth for herself. Instead she left instructions for a tiny gravestone with the epitaph: 'No happier woman ever lived.'

ORIANA WILSON

Oriana burned all the letters between her and her husband after George Seaver, Bill's biographer, had read them. Ory's words only exist in the attic trunks of those who received her letters all over the world and in the memory of those who actually knew her. Eleanor Bantoft remembered 'Aunt Ory' well. Her overriding impression was of a bossy, well-meaning lady who wheeled barrows full of presents into their house on Christmas Day.

Ory continued in her role as a collector for the Natural History Museum, but if the increasing speed with which her specimens were examined and named for her had ever made her think twice, she need not have worried about eclipsing Bill. One of the penguin's eggs collected on the Winter Journey is the most visited exhibit at the museum today. Her bats (perfectly preserved) are hidden in a drawer.

Ory never married again (the Wilsons discouraged it), but she fell head over heels in trust with Seaver and the books they produced together – *Edward Wilson of the Antarctica* and its sequel *Edward Wilson: Nature Lover* – were bestsellers. With the proceeds, Ory sponsored New Zealand artists, particularly those suffering from post-traumatic stress disorders after the First World War. Ory may have lost her faith, but she continued to believe in what Seaver called 'an immanent spirit of goodness alive in the world'. She died of a stroke in a blitzed London on ANZAC Day at the end of the Second World War. Upon her death, Seaver received many letters citing her inspirational 'good courage'.

Uncle Bill's Cabin in the garden of Te Hau was nearly destroyed in the 2011 Christchurch earthquake, but it was plucked from the cliff edge by a crane and removed to Godley Head, where it has been restored and is open for visitors. It is, perhaps, a fitting monument not only to Ory but to all the Snow Widows, an important symbol of resilience in the face of disaster.

PETER SCOTT

It is not until January 1966 that fifty-seven-year-old Peter Scott visits the Antarctic, and he arrives, predictably, with a television crew. He's already founded the Wildfowl & Wetlands Trust at Slimbridge, helped to found the World Wildlife Fund and lent his signature to the Antarctic Treaty, but he has never actually been to the Antarctic himself. He has avoided it.

After some initial filming, dogs, sledges and a tent are assembled, and they make camp. It is 'all for show', writes Peter in his journal, 'as if we had been doing it for months in some long and rugged journey. It is bogus, and hard not to feel a charlatan.'[907] A few days later they fly to the Pole in a Hercules aircraft. A journey that had taken his father forty-seven days took him three hours. 'What a way to arrive!' Peter writes, 'sweaty hot in an overheated aircraft'.

There are film crews with them. 'I remembered that fifty-four years ago, my father had also been involved in taking photographs at the Pole. It made the whole distasteful business a fraction more bearable.' But for that famous picture – the last of his father and the others alive – there had been nobody behind the camera. Who are the ghosts behind the camera now? What are they expecting of him?

Peter knows that his father only made the final selection of the five men in that photograph about 150 miles north of the spot where Peter is standing now. After choosing his South Pole team, Peter's father scribbled a last message to his mother:

January 3rd 1912
Lat 87.32

A last note from a hopeful position. I think it is going to be all right. We have a fine party going forward and arrangements are all going well. So this is simply to say that I love you and that you needn't be ashamed of me, or the boy either.[908]

Can 'the boy' – named after Peter Pan, that fictional boy who never grew up – wind back the clock? Peter is fourteen years older than his father was when he stood on this spot half a century ago, but can he create a different ending?

At the South Pole in 1966, Peter continues to humour the photographers and, when they are finished, they reboard the Hercules for the flight back to his father's base camp. Once inside Cape Evans hut, Peter is asked to pose in his father's place. This is what he has been dreading most. He sits and, trying to block out the sound of camera shutters, begins to write in his journal: 'It [is] a strange feeling in [here], shelves stacked with tins of still edible food, beds with blankets', he writes. 'It [doesn't] need much imagination to hear the crunch of men's boots and the hiss of sledges, the door flying open with a rush of wind and a flurry of snow as a party returned.'

As he is writing, something happens – he changes tense to the future conditional. 'Soon the hut would be warm and full of noise and talk again with those famous larger-than-life ghosts from the past.' This tragedy, he realises, has been superimposed by history. He must, like his mother, reject the 'contamination of sadness' because behind every one of those men who trudged away, there was a woman living as hopefully and courageously as they were in this very hut.

'Goodbye to the Antarctic,' he writes, after he has climbed back into the Hercules bound for New Zealand. 'I wonder if I shall see it again. I wonder if I could have kept away from it if I had allowed myself to go there as a young man . . . Cold and inhospitable it may be, but oh the exquisite beauty of it.'[909]

Instead of avoiding his father's shadow, he has somehow become the figurehead. He goes back to the Antarctic four times (he cannot keep away), but every time the sprawl of McMurdo Station looks more depressing. Against the grandeur of the snowy volcano of Erebus and the jewellike refraction from icebergs, it is 'an ugly manmade conurbation, rusting machinery, middens'. Peter's father once told his mother than he wanted 'not only to love you but to conquer the world with you', but surely not like this.[910] Moving forward, the base-line data collected by the *Terra Nova* expedition in the Antarctic must be used to push for conservation not just there, but on an unprecedented world-conquering scale.

The move to use the Antarctic to calibrate world ecology continues today. DNA sequencing and other new technologies mean that century-old collections can be analysed in ways that Peter's father and his companions could never have imagined. A hundred years ago, the Snow Widows could visit the expedition's specimens at the Natural History Museum in London, now much more can be learned. Dr Anne Jungblut, who is researching the Antarctic data at the Natural History Museum today, suggests that 'Scott would not have thought about climate change and yet his data provides us with a vital piece in the puzzle.'[911] Now we can look at the *Terra Nova*'s legacy from an entirely different perspective. We can ask new questions of an old story to extract information on which to build a better future.

The legacy of *the* five, and *their* five might be to deliver on Scott's 'hopeful position'. To hope.

ACKNOWLEDGEMENTS

When I first started researching the Snow Widows over a decade ago, they were invisible. I was looking for inspiration at the time because my husband was about to climb Everest (our children were nearly five, nearly three and nearly one). He climbed it and came home, but by then I had discovered the treasures that are Oriana, Kathleen, Caroline, Emily and Lois. They have continued to be inspiring companions for me over the years as I hope they now can be for you.

ORIANA

Oriana's niece, Eleanor Bragge, was in a nursing home when her nephew Nicholas and his wife Christina Bantoft first took me along to visit. Ory was bossy, of that Eleanor was in no doubt, but she and Ory shared a prescient and almost pantheistic regard for the conservation of the natural world. Dr David Wilson FRZS is the keeper of the Wilson flame and his help, over the years, has been invaluable. Other relations include Toby Garfitt and Kit Bowen, who have been charming and generous in their praise and with their photographs. Ory fell in trust with her husband's first biographer, George Seaver, and Peter Seaver has helped to bring that relationship to life. Ory nearly emigrated to New Zealand where, as a result of long periods of waiting for her husband to return from the Antarctic, she had as many friends as in the UK. Among those friends, the Studholmes are treasures guarding treasures. My extraordinary aunt and godmother Jane Bannister found Oriana's bats in the Natural History Museum belfry, thereby redefining Ory's identity from 'wife-of' to scientist. Nick Smith (conservation minister and minister for housing in New Zealand) saw the importance of saving 'Uncle Bill's Cabin' at a time when the Christchurch earthquake had created a housing crisis. Together with the owners of the garden in which it teetered, he has brought that 'historic monument' back from the brink of destruction, an appropriate symbol of Ory's extraordinary resilience.

KATHLEEN

In the course of researching this book, I discovered that Mary Ann Shaffer, the American author of the bestselling *The Guernsey Literary and Potato Peel Pie Society* had always wanted to write about Kathleen Scott using Kathleen's papers at Kennet Collection in Cambridge. Arriving from the other side of the Atlantic she found them 'nearly unusable' and got on the first plane out, which happened to be to Guernsey. And the rest, as they say . . . (In relating the experience to me, her niece and co-author concluded: 'that's why I write fiction'.) The source material used in *Snow Widows*, sourced and cross-checked from the Kennet collection, has already been published both in Kathleen's candid autobiography and in her fascinating biography written by Louisa Young, her granddaughter (whom she never met). Perhaps Kathleen is not to be found in an archive, but in the opinion of others. 'There is no consistency about her,' wrote her husband's biographer Stephen Gwynn: 'She will argue by the hour on the personal inferiority of women, yet in practice can seldom refrain from confuting her own argument . . . If her conduct is too often unladylike, I have always found her to act like a gentleman.'[912]

EMILY

It was hailing upwards when I stood on the doorstep of Emily's old flat in Bute on a *dreich* winter's night, but Bobby and Beck Reid inhaled me in. (I hadn't even knocked.) Emily's Bowers relatives, the Lauries, are no less accommodating. On an academic level Emily exists in the well-indexed SPRI archive collection on 'Bowers', as a lively, intelligent clucking hen. In Apsley Cherry-Garrard's *Worst Journey*, he concluded that though Birdie might have 'appeared crude' in London's clubland, he was the man you would lie down and cry for when a crisis loomed. The same might be said of his mother.

Anne Strathie gave me a file labelled 'Emily' from her work on Birdie's biography. More than a start, it was a vote of confidence that I have tried to deserve. Cherry gave a beautiful copy of the *South Polar Times* to Emily, which her daughters Edie and May left to the Bute

Museum. Jean McMillan, the archivist, is a worthy custodian of that book. Emily as an active alumna of Cheltenham Teacher Training College was a revelation. Archivist Lorna Scott found a picture of Emily, the tailor's daughter, emerging from her chrysalis in an immense crinoline. It is the kind of costume from which one could sew a different future, and she did.

CAROLINE

Meeting Sue Limb, who knew Violet Oates, has been one of the great joys of this project. Patrick Cordingley is 'the cavalry' without whose arrival Captain Oates's biography might never have been written. I was honoured to have Patrick as my tour guide around the Oates collection in Selbourne. Ashley Cooper is a busy Gestingthorpe author, farmer and antiquarian. In meeting him, I stumbled upon a gentleman researcher of the very highest calibre. Andy Craig is the Chair of the Gestingthorpe History Group and the country's history groups would all benefit if, like the St Mary's Gestingthorpe's Lych Gate, he was reproduced around the British Isles. Peter Nice discovered Violet Oates 'doing her bit' for the war effort in the *Church Magazine*, an amazing find. My tour of the privately-owned Gestingthorpe Hall by Michael and Elaine Sharp convinced me that the place could not be in better hands. Kimberley at Gilbert White House Museum allowed me to see Caroline's diary with the entry which encapsulates her eyewatering stoicism: 'Baby boy born'. Due to a project clash, Bryan Oates politely and understandably declined to discuss his play, *What Mrs Oates Knew*, about Caroline, but he kindly gave his permission to include a photograph in the Oates Collection.

Caroline was a formidably becorseted horsewoman, but more accessible as a brave but broken-hearted mother.

LOIS

Thank you to polar historian Gary C. Gregor and his wife Jane, who heard that Lois received the telegram on Oxwich beach from Lily Tucker herself. John Evans is succeeding in the great task of statuary, and he is on first-name terms (almost) with Taff's greatest fan, Princess Anne. John's memories of taking the bus with his grandmother Lois are still touchingly tender. Sharon Holder, daughter of Ray Burton, has shared equally heartfelt memories of her father finding out that Taff was probably his grandfather. His mother never told him, but on her death, her sister, Ray's aunt, revealed the truth. Like the Evanses, Ray's children are proud of their ancestor and have attended several polar commemoration events. As a doctor–biographer, Isobel Williams has covered both Bill and Taff in fantastic medical detail. It is incredible that antibiotics and vitamin C were not discovered until around 1928, and therefore postdate the *Terra Nova* expedition. I was relieved to find that Lois's is not the only unmarked grave in Morriston cemetery. I would hate to think she died anxious that it might be vandalised. May her ascent to full recognition be as steep and steady as her husband's.

SIR EDGAR SPEYER AND EDWARD ELGAR

The musical structure behind this book began with the combination of Elgar's mysterious five-dot dedication and Speyer's sponsorship of both him and Captain Scott. Speyer – a fascinating man – is also responsible for the London Underground. Thank you to Antony Lentin for detailing Sir Edgar Speyer's fall from grace and the hysteria that characterised anti-German sentiment in World War One. Fritz Kreisler's own book *Four Weeks in the Trenches* has been a revelation. Many thanks to musician Imogen Seth Smith, BBC Radio 3's David Owen Norris and Yehudi Menuhin's grandson, Lin Siao Fou-Menuhin, for helping me to understand how Fritz Kreisler might have approached playing Elgar's Violin Concerto. When I was standing in Elgar's birthplace (minding my own business) someone put on a record of Elgar conducting Yehudi Menuhin. The sound played through Elgar's own gramophone.

GENERAL ACKNOWLEDGEMENTS

For general archive help, I would like to thank the following: Jane Ridley, Biographers' Club; Elizabeth Haylett Clark, Society of Authors, London; Naomi Boneham and Lucy Martin from SPRI, Cambridge; Anne Jungblut and Douglas Russell at the Natural History Museum, London and Tring respectively; Eugene Rae and Julie Carrington at the Royal Geographical Society Archives, London. (For the record, the RGS is now the, dare I say, polar opposite of the early twentieth-century organisation that Emily Bowers described as a 'parched up body' which judged manuscripts 'too readable' to be worthy of its august institution – the archivists have been outstandingly helpful.) Thank you very much indeed to Frank Bowles, archivist at the Department of Modern Manuscripts at the Cambridge University Library. Thank you to Charles Wright for his translation of Homer's Greek script in Stephen Gwynn's authorised biography of Scott – a revelation.

The warp and weft of this story are the mail boats and the undersea cables. Many thanks to Bill Burns, communications historian, for his help in piecing together the jigsaw of telegrams. I am grateful to the staff of the fantastic Museum of Global Communications in Porthcurno, Cornwall and to the experts at the Postal and BT Archives in London for a glimpse into that fascinating era at the centre of a Venn diagram where pigeon post and cables intersected with radio waves. And thank you to Jennifer Protheroe Jones for introducing me to the *Terra Nova*'s figurehead in Cardiff.

My heartfelt thanks to the giant-shouldered writers who have been so generous supporting me over the years, including Robert Macfarlane, Peter and Leni Gillman, Neil MacKenna, Alexander Masters, Alice Jolly, Sue Limb and Sara Wheeler. Thank you to David Crane who read the manuscript (and perhaps thought it anti-Scott) and to Roland Huntford, with whom I corresponded briefly years ago (who thought my approach pro-Scott). Thank you to Nicola Kearton for perspective on historical binarism and for her suggestion that the women might introduce shades of grey. Thank you to the lecturers and guest speakers at Kellogg College – particularly to the poet and biographer, Jon Stallworthy for his thoughts on intersecting time. Thank you to Carol O'Brien for her research at the National Archives and for reading the first draft along with the stalwart and wise sounding boards that are Frances House and Nico Jackson. Thank you to the Symmetry & Blisters group for long-distance walking and chat, and to the Shepherdesses of Uley for sketching and more chat.

Limitless thanks to my incredible parents Patrick and Hilary MacInnes, the Bowmans, Zlattingers, Bullocks and (Huntley&)Palmers and to Dave Rutherford. With love to Freddie, Flora, Kit, Amelie, Charlie, Billy, Clara, Alex, Gabriel, Milo, Olly, Alice, Jamie and Hattie.

At HarperCollins, Hazel Eriksson took on this polar world with humbling enthusiasm, rigour and clear-sightedness. It was amazing to have someone so invested in the complexity and detail of the story. (If time investment and talent were represented in font size, her name would take up this page.) Myles Archibald's first reaction to the original script has motivated me when the enormity of the task seemed impossible. Thank you both for the whole adventure. Thank you to Lucy Kingett and Mark Bolland for their copyediting, fact-checking and proofreading. Their careful eyes and thoughtful suggestions have been invaluable. And thank you to publicist Alison Menzies and to my agent Charlie Viney for their belief in the project and for making it happen.

Most importantly, thank you to my husband Sebastian and our children Xander, Jago and Claudie for everything else. Sometimes words just fail. This is one of those times.

REFERENCES

Unpublished material

EMILY BOWERS

Bowers, May, 1910 diary copied by her niece Ida Florence Ramwell (née Aldridge), private collection

CB 9, 1911–1920, Emily Bowers and RGS, Royal Geographical Society, London

Edith Bowers Nurse Report for Queen Alexandra's Imperial Military Nursing Service Reserve Exhibit, Bute Museum, Bute

Edwards, Horace, 'The Royal Cheltenham and County Directory 1872–1873', University of Gloucestershire Special Collections and Archives, Cheltenham

Envelope dated January 1913 addressed to 'Mrs Bowers', sale 1020, lot 1866, Spinks, London, 2010

Gibbons, G., 'Sidmouth, A History', Sidmouth Museum, Sidmouth, 1987

King, H. G. R., ed., Henry Robertson Bowers Papers Catalogue, Scott Polar Research Institute, 1990, 1505/7/2/9

Laurie, J. (née Ramwell), conversation with the author, 11 April 2021

St Mary's College Reports 1847–94, St Mary's College Archive, Cheltenham

GEORGE NATHANIEL CURZON

Curzon, Lord, Correspondence, Box No 2. Royal Geographical Society, London

Curzon, Lord, Correspondence re BAE, British Library, London, MSS Eur. F112/51

Lois Evans

CB 9, 1911–1920, Lois Evans and RGS, Royal Geographical Society, London

Evans, J., conversation with the author, 27 January 2021

Ford, A., conversation with the author, 27 January 2021

'Gower dialect: Mrs B talks about cockle picking', sound recording, British Library, London, C1314/11/10

Gregor, G., Talk on Edgar Evans, Swansea Museum Archives, D/D HSV 10S/100

Hardy, Dudley, Royal Naval & Military Tournament Poster, 1911

Holder, S., conversation with the author, November 2021

Howard, D. V., 'Yard Memories 1956–1964', Royal Dockyard Historical Trust

Kelly's Directory Portsmouth, 1911–1912

Lay, C., Letter to the author, Portsmouth Royal Dockyard Historical Trust, 4 October 2019

Lewis, D. I., 'Married to the Navy', MA dissertation, Thames Polytechnic, London, 1988

Mansel Thomas, J., Tape recordings of Gower people, Wilf Beynon and George Tucker, c.1970s, West Glamorgan Archive Service, GB 216 T 3 T3 33a

Official opening of Edgar Evans building, invitation addressed to Mrs Sarah Owen, 1964, private collection

Player's Polar Exploration cigarette cards, Archives, Royal Museums Greenwich, London, ID ZBA2283

Scott of the Antarctic Royal Command Performance invitation, 30 December 1948

Caroline Oates

Accounts book of Mrs Caroline Ann Oates, Essex Record Office, Chelmsford, D/DOa A7 and D/DOa A8

Bank passbook of Mrs Caroline Ann Oates, Essex Record Office, Chelmsford, D/DOa A9–11

Catalogue description for The Polar Sale, sale 6544, lot 178, Christie's, London, 25 September 2001

CB 9, 1911–1920, Caroline Oates and RGS, Royal Geographical Society, London

Cooper, A., letter to the author, 17 December 2019

ESE Accounts 7 September 1918, Prisoners of War Agricultural Depot, The Workhouse, Halstead

Gestingthorpe History Group, gestingthorpehg.co.uk

Kremnitz file FO 382 and 383, National Archives, London.

Limb, S., conversations with the author, 2020–2021

Memories of resident Arthur Mears, Gestingthorpe History Group

Oates, Caroline, diary, Oates Collections, Gilbert White's House, Selborne

Oates, V., 'History of the Parish of Gestingthorpe', manuscript undated c.1932–48

Preachers' Book Essex Record Office, Chelmsford, D/P 1720/17

Receipted bills of Mrs Caroline Ann Oates, Essex Record Office, Chelmsford, D/DOa A12

Ruhleben Internment Camp record, 1917, Imperial War Museum, London, LBY 106

St Mary the Virgin, *Gestingthorpe Church* magazine, Essex Archive, Chelmsford Record Office, Chelmsford

Seaver, George, typewritten pages bound after page 228 into his personal copy of *The Worst Journey in the World* (Apsley Cherry-Garrard), vol. 1 1922, 'Oates', SPRI MS 1012

Spinks Polar Medal Display Catalogue, 18–24 November London, 2019

KATHLEEN SCOTT

Captain Robert Falcon Scott Collection (RFS), Royal Geographical Society, London, RGS213513

CB 9, 1911–1920, Kathleen Scott and RGS, Royal Geographical Society, London

Conan Doyle, A., general correspondence to MS, British Library, London, 88924/1/48

Curzon BAE correspondence, British Library, London MS F112

Howard, E. J., conversation with the author, 2008

Kennet Papers, D1-15 1910–1924, Cambridge University Library (CUL), Cambridge

Kennet, W., conversation with the author, 14 May 2007

Murray, C., 'Scott of the Antarctic: The Conservation of a Story' PhD thesis, University of Tasmania Open Access Repository, 2006

ORIANA WILSON

Bantoft, Nicholas, tribute at the funeral of Constance E. Bragge, Yeovil Crematorium, 15 March 2016

Bragge, Constance E., conversation with the author, Sherbourne, 21 March 2012

Bragge, Constance E., letters to the author, 2012–2016

Bragge, Constance Mary, death certificate, Axminister, 31 August 1931, General Register Office, Birkdal

British Seamen's Orphan Boys' Home records, Brixham Museum, Brixham

Edward Wilson, RGS Special Collection, Royal Geographical Society, London, C8/Wilson EA/278

Hilton War Memorial, Huntingdonshire

Interview by Evelyn Forbes of David Wilson, 11 August 1995, 10 Summerfield, Cambridge, sound recording, The Wilson, Cheltenham Museum

'Life of Copthorne Preparatory School', *The Old Copthorne School Chronicles*, Copthorne School Archives

Mandate for Induction of Francis Abraham Souper, Hilton Parish Records

Painter, Gillian, letter to the author, 17 March 2013

Slater, Ralph, conversation with the author, The Old Rectory, The Green, Hilton, Huntington, September 2012

Thiepval Memorial to the Missing of the Somme, Authuille, Pier F11 D

UK Incoming Passenger Lists 1878–1960, Board of Trade: Commercial and Statistical Department and Successors, National Archives, London

Vandenberg, Maarten, 'Souper Family Tree', private collection

Wilson, David, correspondence with the author, 2008–2018

OTHER

South Polar Times, Bute Museum, Bute, and Royal Geographical Society, London

Published materials

Airey, E., *The Taming of Distance: New Zealand's First International Telecommunications* (Wellington: Dunmore Publishing, 2005)

Amundsen R., *The South Pole: An Account of the Norwegian Antarctic*

Expedition in the Fram *1910–1912*, tr. A. G. Chater (Edinburgh: Birlinn Ltd, 2002; first published London: John Murray, 1912)

Antarctic, quarterly publication of the New Zealand Antarctic Society, Christchurch

Ashburton Guardian, 'Hardy's Stores Catered for Everyone' (Ashburton, 7 January 1989)

Beeton, Isabella, *Mrs Beeton's Book of Household Management* (London: Chancellor Press, 1861)

Bell, Y., *The Edwardian Home* (Oxford: Shire Publications Ltd, 2010)

Beynon, L., *Rhossili: The Land, Landscape and People* (Swansea: West Glamorgan Archive Service, 2008)

Booth, Charles, *Life and Labour of the People in London*, vol. 1 (London: Macmillan, 1902)

Bryce, R. M., *Cook & Peary: The Polar Controversy, Resolved* (Mechanicsburg: Stackpole Books, 1997)

Cambrian Daily Leader, accessible from the National Library of Wales

Cecil, R., *Life in Edwardian England* (London: Batsford, 1969)

Cherry-Garrard, A., *The Worst Journey in the World* (New York: Dover, 2010; first published London: Constable, 1922)

Christensen, K., 'Hidden Lives, Hidden Wives', *The Author*, autumn 2019, pp. 92–3

Church, I. N., *Last Port to Antarctica, Dunedin and Port Chalmers: 100 Years of Polar Service* (Dunedin: Otago Heritage Books, 1997)

Clark, B., *Gourock to Largs Coast Through Time* (Stroud: Amberley Publishing, 2013)

Clark, C., *The Sleepwalkers: How Europe Went to War in 1914* (London: Penguin, 2012)

Clarke, A.C., *Voice Across the Sea* (London: Frederick Muller Ltd, 1958)

Conefrey, M. and Jordan, T., *Icemen: A History of the Arctic and Its Explorers* (London: Boxtree, 1998)

Cooper, A., *Heart of Our History: 500 Years of Village History along the Suffolk–Essex Border* (Essex: Bulmer Historical Society, 1994)

——, *Our Mother Earth – Of the Furrow Born: 300 Years of Countryside History along the Suffolk-Essex Border: Heart of Our History*, vol. 2 (Essex: Bulmer Historical Society, 1998)

Country Life, Feature on Over Hall, Gestingthorpe Hall, Essex, 30 August 1946

Crane, D., *Scott of the Antarctic: A Life of Courage and Tragedy in the Extreme South* (London: Harper Perennial paperback edition, 2012)

Crow, D., *The Edwardian Woman* (London: George Allen & Unwin, 1978)

Daly, R. W., *The Shackleton Letters: Behind the Scenes of the Nimrod Expedition* (Norwich: The Erskine Press, 2009)

Davies, B. E., *Mumbles and Gower Pubs* (Stroud: The History Press, 2008)

Dawes, F., *Not in Front of the Servants: Domestic Service in England 1850–1939* (London: The History Book Club, 1973)

Edwards, E., *Women in Teacher Training Colleges, 1900–1960: A Culture of Femininity* (London: Routledge, 2001)

Eliot, George, *Scenes of Clerical Life* (London: Blackwood & Sons, 1857)

Ervine, St John, *Bernard Shaw: His Life, Work and Friends* (London: Constable, 1956)

Evans, E. *Happy Adventurer: An Autobiography* (New York: Wilfred Funk, 1951)

——, *South with Scott* (London: Collins, 1921)

Evans, S., 'The Prisoners of War Who Made Little Britain in Berlin', BBC News, 29 July 2014, www.bbc.co.uk/news/magazine-28420676

Fiennes, R., *Captain Scott* (London: Hodder & Stoughton, 2003)

Galicki, M., *Victorian & Edwardian Stained Glass* (Swindon: English Heritage, 1987)

Gee, M., 'The Monstrous Regiment of Women', *The Author*, autumn 2019, pp. 94–5

Gestingthorpe Parish magazine, 1914–1918

Gower Church magazine, accessible from the National Library of Wales

Greenock Telegraph and Clyde Shipping Gazette, accessible through british-newspaperarchive.co.uk

Gregor, G. C., *Edgar Evans of Gower (1876–1912): From Rhossili to the South Pole* (Swansea, The Gower Society, 2008)

——, *Swansea's Antarctic Explorer Edgar Evans, 1876–1912* (Swansea: Swansea City Council, 1995)

Gwynn, S., *Captain Scott* (London: Penguin, 1929; 2nd edn, 1940)

Hackney, R., *200 Years of Polar Exploration 1891–2019* (London: Spink, 2019)

Harwood, J. A., *Portrait of Portsea 1840–1940* (Southampton: Ensign Publications, 1990)

Heacox, K., *Shackleton: The Antarctic Challenge* (Washington, DC: National Geographic, 1999)

Herbert, K., *Heart of the Hero: The Remarkable Women Who Inspired the Great Polar Explorers* (Glasgow: Saraband, 2013)

Herbert, W., *The Noose of Laurels: The Discovery of the North Pole* (London: Hodder & Stoughton, 1989)

Howard, E. J., *Slipstream: A Memoir* (London: Macmillan, 2002)

Huntford, R., *Nansen: The Explorer as Hero*, (London: Abacus, 2001; 2nd edn, 2005)

——, *Scott and Amundsen: The Last Place on Earth* (London: Abacus, 2000)

——, *Shackleton* (London: Cardinal, 1989)

Jones, M., *The Last Great Quest: Captain Scott's Antarctic Sacrifice* (Oxford: Oxford University Press, 2003)

'Joshua Buckton and Co', *Grace's Guide – British Industrial History*, www.gracesguide.co.uk/Joshua_Buckton_and_Co

Kennet, K., *Self-Portrait of an Artist, from the Diaries and Memoirs of Lady Kennet, Kathleen, Lady Scott* (London: John Murray, 1949)

Lane, H. *et al.*, *Last Letters* (Cambridge: SPRI, 2012)

Leach, A. F., *A History of Bradfield College* (London: Frowde, 1900)

Lear, E., *Nonsense Songs, Stories, Botany and Alphabets* (London: R. J. Bush, 1871)

Lee, L. G., ed., *Boulton & Paul Ltd: 1898 Catalogue, Rose Lane Works, Norwich* (Almonte: Algrove Publishing, 1998)

Lentin, A., *Banker, Traitor, Scapegoat, Spy? The Troublesome Case of Sir Edgar Speyer* (London: Haus Publishing, 2013)

Limb, S. and Cordingley, P., *Captain Oates: Soldier and Explorer* (Barnsley: Pen & Sword, 1997; first published London: Batsford, 1982)

Lucas, R., *A Gower Family* (Market Harborough: The Book Guild Ltd, 1998)

MacInnes, K., *Love and Death and Mrs Bill: A Play About Oriana, Wife of Polar Explorer Edward Wilson* (Snow Widow, 2013)

——, *Woman with the Iceberg Eyes: Oriana F. Wilson* (Cheltenham: History Press, 2019)

McMillan, J. *et al.*, *Bute Connections* (Bute: Buteshire Natural History Society, 2011)

Mallinson, A., *1914: Fight the Good Fight: Britain, the Army and the Coming of the First World War* (London: Bantam Press, 2013)

Mankelow, S., 'Well-Travelled Antarctic Cabin Rides Again', Conservation Blog, Department of Conservation, 20 March 2013, blog.doc.govt. nz/2013/03/20/scotts-antarctic-cabin/

Marshall, H. E., *Our Empire Story* (London: Thomas Nelson and Sons Ltd, 1908)

Meyric Hughes, S., 'Captain Oates' Saunterer Returns to Help Heroes', *Classic Boat*, July 2011, pp. 9–14

Monk, R., *Edward Elgar: Music and Literature* (Hampshire: Scolar Press, 1993)

More, C., *The Training of Teachers 1847–1947: A History of the Church Colleges at Cheltenham* (London: Hambledon Press, 1992)

Nicholson, J., *The Perfect Summer: Dancing into Shadow in 1911* (London: John Murray, 2006)

Nicolson, V., *Singled Out: How Two Million Women Survived without Men after the First World War* (London: Penguin, 2008)

Patchett, A., *Notes on the Parish of Gestingthorpe, Essex* (London: F. E. Robinson and Co, 1905)

Peary, J., *My Arctic Journal: A Year Among Ice-fields and Eskimos* (New York: Contemporary Publishing Co., 1893)

Peary, M. A., *The Snowbaby's Own Story* (New York: Frederick A. Stokes, 1934)

Petrocelli, P., *The Resonance of a Small Voice: William Walton and the Violin Concerto in England between 1900 and 1940* (Newcastle: Cambridge Scholars Publishing, 2010)

Pound, R., *Scott of the Antarctic* (London: World Books, 1966)

Richards, J., *Imperialism and Music: Britain 1876–1953* (Manchester: Manchester University Press, 2001)

Riffenburgh, B., *Shackleton's Forgotten Expedition: The Voyage of the* Nimrod (London: Bloomsbury, 2004)

Riley, R. C. and Eley, P., 'Public Houses and Beerhouses in Nineteenth Century Portsmouth', *The Portsmouth Papers*, No. 38 (Portsmouth: Portsmouth City Council, September 1971)

Rosove, M. H., ed., *Rejoice My Heart: The Making of H. R. Mill's 'The Life of Sir Ernest Shackleton'* (California: Adelie Books, 2007)

Sargeant, H., 'A History of Portsmouth Theatres', *The Portsmouth Papers* No. 13 (Portsmouth, Portsmouth City Council, September 1971)

Scott, P., *Observations of Wildlife* (Oxford: Phaidon Press, 1980)

Scott, R. F., *Journals: Captain Scott's Last Expedition*, ed. Max Jones (Oxford: Oxford University Press, 2006)

Seaver, G., *Birdie Bowers of the Antarctic* (London: John Murray, 1938)

——, *Edward Wilson of the Antarctic: Naturalist and Friend* (London: John Murray, 26th repr. ed. 1959)

——, *Edward Wilson: Nature-Lover* (London: John Murray, 1937)

——, 'Mrs E. A. Wilson, CBE', *Polar Record*, 4(30), 1945, p. 290

——, *The Faith of Edward Wilson of the Antarctic* (London: John Murray, 1948)

Shackleton, E., *The Heart of the Antarctic: The Farthest South Expedition 1907–1909* (London: Penguin, 2000)

Shackleton, J. and MacKenna, J., *Shackleton: An Irishman in Antarctica* (Dublin: Lilliput Press, 2003)

Sidmouth Observer, 3 October 1934

Smith, H., *The Norwegian with Scott: The Antarctic Diary of Tryggve Gran, 1910–13* (London: The Stationery Office, 1984)

Smith, M., *An Unsung Hero: Tom Crean – Antarctic Survivor* (Cork: The Collins Press, 2009)

——, *I Am Just Going Outside: Captain Oates – Antarctic Tragedy* (Stroud: Spellmount, 2002)

South Wales Daily News, accessible from the National Library of Wales

Spufford, F., *I May be Some Time* (London: Faber and Faber, 1996)

Stopes, M., *Married Love: The First Book About Sex Technique for Women* (London: Victor Gollancz, 1995; first published London: Fifield, 1918)

Strathie, A., *Birdie Bowers: Captain Scott's Marvel* (Stroud: History Press, 2012)

——, *From Ice Floes to Battlefields: Scott's 'Antarctics' in the First World War* (Stroud: History Press, 2015)

Swain, Joseph, 'Waiting to be Won', *Punch*, 5 June 1875

Thomas, J. M., *Yesterday's Gower* (Dyfed: Gomer Press, 1982)

Trollope, J., *Britannia's Daughters: Women of the British Empire* (London: Pimlico, 2006)

Turney, Chris, 'Why didn't they ask Evans?', in *Polar Record*, 53(5), September 2017, pp. 498–511

Twaddle, G., *Old Bute* (Mauchline: Stenlake Publishing, 2000)

Weintraub, S., 'Shaw's Sculptress: Kathleen Scott', *The Annual of Bernard Shaw Studies*, 24, 2004, pp. 166–85

Wheeler, S., *Cherry: A Life of Apsley Cherry-Garrard* (London: Jonathan Cape, 2001)

Williams, I., *Captain Scott's Invaluable Assistant: Edgar Evans* (Stroud: History Press, 2012)

——, *With Scott in the Antarctic: Edward Wilson, Explorer, Naturalist, Artist* (Stroud: History Press, 2008)

Wilson, D. M. and C. J., *Edward Wilson's Antarctic Notebooks* (Cheltenham: Reardon Publishing, 2011)

——, *Edward Wilson's Nature Notebooks* (Cheltenham: Reardon Publishing, 2004)

Wilson, E., *Diary of the 'Discovery' Expedition to the Antarctic Regions 1901–1904*, ed. A. Savours (London: Blandford Press, 1966)

——, *Diary of the 'Terra Nova' Expedition to the Antarctic 1910–1912*, ed. H. King (London: Blandford Press, 1972)

Winton, J., *Hurrah for the Life of a Sailor!: Life on the Lower-deck of the Victorian Navy* (London: Michael Joseph, 1977)

Young, L., *A Great Task of Happiness: The Life of Kathleen Scott* (London: HarperCollins, 2014)

Archives

Alexander Turnbull Archive, National Library of New Zealand, Wellington, New Zealand

Ashburton Museum, Ashburton, New Zealand

Bradfield College, Bradfield

British Library, London

Buteman Archive, Bute Library, Bute

Cambridge University Library Archives (CUL), Cambridge

Cheltenham College Archives, Cheltenham

Essex Record Office, Chelmsford

National Archives, London

Natural History Museum, London

Oates Collections, Gilbert White's House, Selborne

Royal Geographical Society (RGS), London

St Andrew's Prep School, Eastbourne

St George's Hospital, London

Scott Polar Research Institute (SPRI), Cambridge

Seaver Family Archive

University of Canterbury Archives, Christchurch, New Zealand

Waitaki Museum and Archive, Oamaru, New Zealand

Wilson Family Collection, The Wilson, Cheltenham

ENDNOTES

Where the same source is referenced multiple times in a row, only the first instance is given an endnote. Annotations here refer back to this book's References.

1   Bell, Morag and McEwan, Cheryl, 'The Admission of Women Fellows to the Royal Geographical Society' in Geographical Journal, Vol. 162, No. 3 (November 1996), p. 302
2   Gwynn (1929), p. 139
3   Oriana to Isabel Smith, 21–26 February 1935, MS 559/145/1–5; D SPRI
4   Seaver (1959), p. 61
5   MS 1505/1/1/3/7 SPRI
6   Birdie to Emily, MS 1505/1/1/3/116 SPRI
7   *Cardiff Times*, 5 November 1910
8   Smith (2002), p. 78
9   Kennet Papers D2 CUL, quoted in Young (2014), pp. 118–119
10 Kathleen to Scott, Young (2014), p. 98
11 Kathleen to Rosslyn, Young (2014), p. 98; Kennet (1949) p. 84
12 Monk (1993), p. 80
13 Petrocelli (2010)
14 MacInnes (2019), p. 11
15 Seaver (1959), p. 143
16 David Wilson to the author, Cheltenham, 2011
17 Bill to John Fraser, 27 November 1910, MS 1577/6/22;D SPRI/Wilson
18 MacInnes (2019), p. 151
19 Birdie to Edie, 27 October 1911 (written as 1910), MS 1505/1/1/1/8 SPRI
20 Birdie to Emily, 11 May 1907 quoted in Seaver (1938), p. 66
21 Emily to Birdie, 7 October 1904, MS 1505/1/2/2/17 SPRI
22 Birdie to Emily, letters of 18 and 23 April 1910 MS 1505/1/1/3/83 and 84 SPRI

23 MS 1016/41 SPRI, quoted in Limb/Cordingley (1982), p. 29

24 MS 1012 SPRI

25 Cecil Meares, reported conversation (source unknown), RDG quoted in Smith (2002), p. 83

26 Laurie to Caroline, MS 1016/329 SPRI, quoted in Limb/Cordingley (1982) p. 107

27 Limb/Cordingley (1982), p. 45

28 Cherry-Garrard (1922), p. 637

29 Taff's journal from the Dry Valleys, MS 1487;BJ SPRI

30 Cherry-Garrard (1922)

31 Kennet (1949), p. 119

32 E. J. Howard to the author, 2008

33 Young (2014), p. 137; Kennet (1949), p. 99 Subsequent quotes in this paragraph are also from Kennet (1949), p. 99

34 Kennet (1949), p. 122

35 Kennet (1949), p. 112

36 Young (2014), p. 100

37 Young (2014), pp. 99–100

38 *The Times* Letters, 31 May 1893, Lord Curzon response to a letter from 'A bona fide traveller', quoted in Jones (2003), p. 54

39 *The Times* Letters, 1 June 1893, Lord Curzon, quoted in Jones (2003), p. 54

40 C. R. Markham to Lord Curzon, 9 November 1911, Curzon Papers, India Office, MS Eur F 112/51, quoted in Jones (2003), p. 57

41 Seaver (1959), p. 179

42 Seaver (1959), p. 171

43 Seaver (1959), p. 170

44 Seaver (1959), p. 192

45 Bill's journal, 1 June 1910 to 27 February 1912, including extracts from his letters and those of his wife, RGS C8/Wilson EA/278, quoted in MacInnes (2019), p. 107

46 Wilson (1972), p. 10

47 Bowers, M., diary, 6 June 1910

48 Bowers, M., diary, memoranda after May 1910 entry

49 Bowers, M., diary, 6 June 1910

50 Bowers, M., diary, 28 January 1910

51 Seaver (1938), p. 146; telegram quoted in Bowers, M., diary

52 Letters of 18 and 23 April 1910 to Emily, MS 1505/1/1/1/3/83 SPRI

53 Seaver (1938), pp. 146–7

54 MS 1505/1/1/3/89 SPRI 15/6/1910, quoted in Seaver (1938), p. 150

55 Letters of 18 and 23 April 1910 to Emily, MS 1505/1/1/1/3/83 SPRI

56 Seaver (1938), p. 147

57 Seaver (1938), p. 151

58 Wilf Beynon, quoted in Thomas (1982)

59 Evans (1921), p. 34

60 Wilf Beynon, quoted in Thomas (1982)

61 Limb/Cordingley (1982), p. 118

62 Laurie to Caroline, MS 1016/328 SPRI, quoted in Limb/Cordingley (1982), p. 106

63 Laurie to Caroline, MS 1016/164 SPRI, quoted in Limb/Cordingley (1982), p. 28

64 Caroline quoting 'Vain Questioning' by Walter de la Mare

65 Rudmose Brown Collection, MS 356/79/4 16.4.24 SPRI

66 Kennet (1949), p. 90

67 Kennet (1949), p. 89

68 Young (2014), p. 98

69 Kennet (1949), p. 89

70 Scott to Kathleen, 17 October 1909, quoted in Gwynn (1929), p. 156

71 Kennet (1949), p. 90

72 Kennet Papers CUL, quoted in Crane (2012), p. 412

73 12 March 1912, Kennet Papers D7; quoted in Huntford (1989), p. 531

74 Emily to Birdie, 3 April 1903, MS 1205/1/2/2/3 SPRI

75 Birdie to Emily, 6 and 9 June 1910, MS 1505/1/1/3/86 and 7 SPRI

76 Seaver (1938), p. 152

77 Seaver (1938), p. 144

78 Birdie to Emily, 28 August 1910, MS 1505/1/1/3/94 SPRI

79 Birdie to Edie, 18 December 1910, MS 1505/1/1/5 SPRI

80 Emily to Birdie, MS 1505/7/10/04 SPRI

81 Lear (1871)

82 Emily to Birdie, 9 October 1903, MS 1505/122/10 SPRI

83 Seaver (1938), pp. 150–1

84 Edie to Birdie, 7 June 1910, MS 1505/1/1/1/1 SPRI

85 Birdie to Emly, 9 June 1910, MS 1505/1/1/3/87 SPRI

86 Bowers, M., diary, 1910

87   Birdie to Emily, 9 June 1910 MS 1505/1/1/3/87 SPRI
88   Birdie to Emily, 10 July 1910, MS 1505/1/1/3/91 SPRI
89   Laurie to Caroline, MS 1016/317 SPRI, quoted in Limb/Cordingley (1982), p. 103
90   Limb/Cordingley (1982), p. 20
91   Young (2014), p. 100
92   Gwynn (1940), p. 125
93   Kennet Papers D/2 CUL, quoted in Young (2014), p. 114
94   *Geographic Journal*, 36, 1910, pp. 21–2
95   Young (2014), p. 26
96   Kathleen to Rose Scott, 29 August 1910, MS 1464/14/3 SPRI
97   Seaver (1959), p. 202
98   Young (2014), p. 98
99   Seaver (1959), p160
100 MacInnes (2019), p. 84
101 Seaver (1959), p. 171
102 Wilson (1972), p. 42
103 Letter from Oriana to Westal, 26 August 1910, in Wilson (1972), p. 70
104 Bill to John Fraser, 25 January 1909, MS 1577/6/14 SPRI
105 Wilson (1972), p.44
106 Bill to Oriana, referring to the Smiths' marriage
107 All South Africa quotes are from Bill's journal, 26–28 August 1910, quoted in Wilson (1972), pp. 40–4
108 Limb/Cordingley (1982), p. 119
109 Limb/Cordingley (1982), p. 63
110 On the bell itself, quoted in Smith (2002), p. 66
111 Caroline to H.R. Mill, 15 January 1930, MS 100/88 SPRI
112 Smith (2002), p. 63
113 Caroline's diary at Oates Collections, Gilbert White's House, Selborne
114 The 'No Surrender' story is quoted in the contemporary press and Inniskilling Dragoon records, as well as in Smith (2002), p. 59
115 *Essex & Halstead Herald*, 29 June 1901, quoted in Smith (2002), p. 66
116 All quotes from accounts book of Caroline Oates
117 Gregor (2008), p. 27
118 *South Wales Daily Post*, 20 September 1904
119 Taff to Jack and Beat[rice] (née Beynon), 22 June 1910 SPRI
120 Frank Debenham's journal, 19 January 1911, MS 279/2/;BJp, p. 56

121 Seaver (1938), p. 111

122 Birdie to Emily, 22 August 1910, MS 1505/1/1/2/98 SPRI

123 Bowers, M., diary

124 Bowers, M., diary, memoranda at end of August 1910

125 Emily to Cherry, 9 July 1913, MS 559/31/9 SPRI

126 Strathie (2012), p. 83

127 Peggy Pegrine to Shackleton, 11 January 1914, MS 1537/22/30/5–6–7;D SPRI

128 Lady Shackleton to Mill, 27 March 1922, MS 100/104/4 SPRI

129 Birdie to Emily, 23 and 28 August 1910 MS 1505/1/1/3/92 and 93 SPRI

130 Birdie to Emily, 28 August 1910, MS 1505/1/1/3/93 SPRI

131 Birdie to Emily, 16 August 1910, MS 1505/1/1/3/92 SPRI

132 Birdie to Emily, 28 August 1910, MS 1505/1/1/3/93 SPRI

133 Birdie to Emily, 7 December 1910, MS 1505/1/1/3/104 SPRI

134 Crane (2012), p. 420

135 Birdie to Emily, 20 November 1909, MS 1505/1/1/3/71 SPRI

136 Bowers, M., diary, end of September 1910, memorandum

137 Emily to Birdie, 13 August 1903, MS 1505/1/2/2/7 SPRI

138 Bill's journal, 31 Aug 1910, quoted in Wilson (1972), p. 45

139 Kathleen's diary, 26 August 1910, Kennet Papers D/2 CUL, quoted in Crane (2012), p. 419

140 Kennet Papers D/2 CUL and Young (2014), p.113

141 Young (2014), p. 211

142 Kennet Papers D2 CUL, quoted in Young (2014), p. 113

143 Young (2014), p. 113

144 Young (2014), p. 181

145 Crane (2012), p. 417

146 Young (2014), p. 115

147 Crane (2012), p. 431

148 Bill to Reginald Smith, MS 559/142/6/D SPRI

149 Bill's journal, 31 August 1910, quoted in Wilson (1972), p. 45

150 Leaf from Bill's observations on birds at sea, made on board RMS *Corinthic*, MS 234/2 SPRI

151 Bill to Westal, September 1910, Wilson Archives, Cheltenham

152 G. Gregor letter to the author, 3 December 2019

153 Abbott, G.P., journal, 1 June 1910, MS 1754/ID SPR

154 Bill's journal, 12 October 1910, quoted in Wilson (1972), pp. 48–51

155 Kennet Papers D/2 CUL quoted in Crane (2012), p. 422

156 Young (2014), p. 115

157 Scott's journal, 28 October 1911, MS 1453/127/2 SPRI

158 Bill's journal, 12 October 1910 quoted in Wilson (1972), p. 51

159 Bill's journal, 12 October 1910 quoted in Wilson (1972), p. 53

160 Oriana to Westal, 2 November 1910, quoted in *Edward Adrian Wilson: A Memoir by his Father*, 1995.550.36 Cheltenham Borough Council and the Cheltenham Trust, Wilson Family Collection

161 Limb/Cordingley (1982), p. 123

162 Kennet Papers, D/2 CUL, quoted in Crane (2012), p. 429

163 Kathleen's diary, 30 September 1910, Kennet Papers D/2 CUL; Young (2014), p.113

164 Kennet Papers D/2, quoted in Crane (2012), p. 429

165 Stopes (1918), p. 47

166 Gwynn (1940), p. 101

167 Kennet Papers D/2, quoted in Young (2014), p. 119

168 Birdie to Emily, 11 September–12 October 1910, MS 1505/1/1/3/96 SPRI

169 Birdie to Emily, 23 April 1910, MS 1505/1/1/3/84 SPRI

170 Bowers, M., diary, 21 November 1910

171 Birdie to Emily, 23 April 1910, MS 1505/1/1/3/84 SPRI

172 Birdie to Edie, 23 October 1910, MS 1505/1/1/1/3 SPRI

173 Seaver (1938), p. 54

174 Birdie to May, 1 March 1910, MS 1505/1/1/2/87 SPRI

175 Strathie (2012), p. 29

176 Birdie to Emily, 1909, MS 1505/1/1/3/44 SPRI

177 Birdie to Edie and May, MS 1505/1/1/1/4 SPRI

178 Birdie to May, 25 September 1910, MS 1505/1/1/2/101 SPRI

179 Kennet Papers, D/2 CUL, quoted in Crane (2012), p. 431

180 Young (2014), p. 113

181 Kennet Papers, D/2 CUL, quoted in Crane (2012), p. 431

182 Young (2014), p. 96

183 Young (2014), p. 105–6

184 Young (2014), p. 104

185 Young (2014), p. 105

186 Rudmose Brown collection MS 356/79/4 16.4.24 SPRI

187 Limb/Cordingley (1982), p. 29

188 Smith (2002), chapter 26

189 Gregor (1995), p. 33

190 Williams (2012), p. 112

191 Winton (1977)

192 Beeton (1861)

193 Seaver (1959), p. 154

194 Bill's journal, 28 November 1910, quoted in Wilson (1972), p. 61

195 Bill to John Fraser, 30 July 1901, MS 1577/6/4;D SPRI

196 Seaver (1959), p. 183; Bill's journal, 28 November 1910, quoted in Wilson (1972), p. 61

197 Bill to John Fraser, 25 January 1909, MS 1577/6/13 SPRI

198 Bill's journal, 28 November 1910, quoted Wilson (1972), p. 62

199 Kennet Papers, D/2 CUL, quoted in Crane (2012), p. 436

200 Laurie to Caroline, 17 November 1910, MS 1016 336 SPRI

201 Oates's diary extracts, copied by Violet Oates, MS 1317/2 SPRI

202 Oates to William King, 15 November 1910, MS 1416/3 SPRI

203 Author's capitalisation but otherwise Limb/Cordingley (1982), p.121

204 Kennet Papers CUL, quoted in Crane (2012), p. 436

205 Laurie to Caroline, 'diary' letter dated 23 November 1910, MS 1016/337 SPRI

206 Young (2014), p. 115

207 Kathleen's diary, 28 November 1910, Kennet Papers CUL, D/2, quoted in Crane (2012), p. 436

208 Bill to John Fraser, 25 January 1909

209 Seaver (1959), p. 143

210 James Lees Milne, *Ancestral Voices*, (London, 1975), pp. 31–2, quoted in Crane (2012), p. 412

211 Kathleen's diary, Kennet Papers CUL, quoted Crane (2012), p. 436

212 Birdie to Emily, 28 November 1910, MS 1505/ 1/1/25/104 SPRI

213 Birdie to Emily, 25 January 1911, MS1505/1/1/3/109 SPRI

214 Rudyard Kipling, 'Female of the Species', 1911

215 Birdie to Emily, 28 November and 7 December 1910 MS 1505/1/1/ 25/103 and 104 SPRI

216 Seaver (1959), p. 185

217 Oriana to Westal, 2 November 1910, quoted in *Edward Adrian Wilson: A Memoir by his Father*, 1995.550.36 Cheltenham Borough Council and the Cheltenham Trust, Wilson Family Collection

218 Seaver (1959), p. 242

219 Kathleen's diary, 29 November 1910, Kennet Papers D/2 CUL quoted in Young (2014), p 116

220 Birdie to Emily, 28 November 1910, SPRI

221 Cherry-Garrard (1922), p. 46

222 Scott (2006), p. 10

223 Kennet (1949), p. 90

224 Young (2014), p. 117

225 Kathleen's diary, 29 November 1910, quoted in Young (2014), p. 117

226 Bill's journal, 29 November 1910, quoted in Wilson (1972), p. 62

227 Evans (1921), p. 48

228 Kathleen to Kinsey, 29 November 1910, Kinsey collection, Alexander Turnbull Archive, NZ

229 Young (2014), p. 118

230 Bill's journal, 1 December 1910, quoted in Wilson (1972), p. 63

231 Bill's journal, 1 December 1910, quoted in Wilson (1972), p. 65

232 Limb/Cordingley (1982), p. 112

233 Bill's journal, 1 December 1910, quoted in Wilson (1972), p. 65

234 Birdie to Emily, 10 December 1910, MS 1505/1/1/25/106 SPRI

235 Limb/Cordingley (1982), p. 127

236 All quotes in this section are from Bowers, M., diary, 1 December 1910

237 Kathleen's diary, 29 November 1910, Kennet Papers D/2 CUL, quoted in Young (2014), p. 116

238 Birdie to Emily, 10 December 1910, MS 1505/1/1/25/106 SPRI

239 Bill's journal, 1 December 1910, quoted in Wilson (1972), p. 68

240 Scott (2006), p. 20

241 Taff to Sarah Evans, 3 January 1911, from Cape Crozier

242 Young (2014), p. 119

243 Birdie to Emily, 25 December 1910, MS 1505/1/1/3/105 SPRI

244 Seaver (1938), p. 94

245 'Christmas Dinner on a Wyoming Prairie', *The Buteman*

246 Bowers, M., diary, 10 December 1910

247 Bill's journal, 25 December 1910, quoted in Wilson (1972), p. 83

248 Seaver (1959), p. 214

249 Preston (2012), p. 101

250 Scott (2006), p. 21

251 Seaver (1937), p. 200

252 Gwynn (1940), p. 49

253 Spufford (1966), an homage to Francis Spufford's peerless title

254 Bill's journal, 24 December 1910, quoted in Wilson (1972), p. 83–84

255 Young (2014), p. 119

256 Bill's journal, 1 January 1911, quoted in Wilson (1972), p. 87

257 Scott's letter to Kathleen, 1 January 1911, quoted in Gwynn (1940), p. 132

258 Bowers, M., diary, 1910 Memoranda to last entry

259 Seaver (1938), p. 159

260 Crane (2012), p. 450

261 Huntford (1989)

262 Young (2014), pp. 120–1

263 Priestly, R., diary, 18 January 1911, MS 298/6/ SPRI

264 Bill's journal, quoted in Wilson (1972), p. 93

265 Crane (2012), p. 452–3

266 Crane (2012), p. 454

267 Bill's journal, quoted in Wilson (1972), p. 99

268 Scott elaborates that they found more, 'thick under the veranda & even in the corners of the hut itself. It's extraordinary to think that people could have lived in such a horrible manner.' Scott's journal, 27 January 1911, Scott (2006), p. 459

269 Oriana to Cherry, 13 December 1916, M559/143/1-25 SPRI

270 Seaver (1959), p. 300

271 Oriana to Mr Swinhoe, 21 May 1922, David Wilson copied it at SPRI, 'but no one has ever found it again for me to check back against the original manuscript'.

272 Seaver (1959), p. 300

273 Evans, E., journal, 27 January to 12 March 1911, MS 1487; BJ 03/02/1911 SPRI

274 Debenham to Stanley Richard, 25 May 1962, Swansea Museum, Box 210 (P.O. E. Evans)

275 Evans, E., journal, 6 February 1911, MS 1487; BJ, 03/02/1911 SPRI

276 Debenham's journal, 19 January to 8 March 1911, MS 279/2:BJp, p. 78

277 Taylor, G., *Journeman Taylor, The Education of a Scientist* (Robert Hale, London, 1958), p. 98, quoted in Williams (2012), p. 129

278 Evans, E., journal, 27 January to 12 March 1911, MS 1487; BJ, 03/02/1911 SPRI

279 Debenham's journal, 19 January to 8 March 1911, MS 279/2:BJp

280 Williams (2012), p. 13

281 *Cambrian Daily Leader*, 11 February 1913, accessible from The National Library of Wales

282 *Gower Church Magazine*, January 1905, quoted in Gregor (1995), p. 25

283 Interview with George Tucker, Gower archives T 3–33a Recording

284 Laurie to Caroline MS 1317/1/1 SPRI

285 All quotes in this paragraph from Limb/Cordingley (1982), p. 142

286 Smith (2002), p. 144

287 Huntford (1989), p. 354

288 Gestingthorpe History Group

289 Laurie to Caroline MS 1016/286 SPRI

290 Bill's journal, quoted in Wilson (1972), pp. 105–6

291 Wheeler (2001), p. 95

292 Kennet (1949), p. 95

293 Young (2014), p. 125

294 Young (2014), p. 126

295 Kennet (1949), p. 84

296 Kennet (1949), pp. 75–6

297 Kennet (1949), p. 76

298 Kennet (1949), p. 82

299 Kennet (1949), pp. 81–2

300 Gwynn (1940), pp. 77–8

301 Seaver (1938), p. 185

302 Seaver (1938), p. 188

303 Cherry-Garrard (1922), pp. 138–45

304 Seaver (1938), chapter 13

305 *The Straits Times*, November–December 1878 and June 1879

306 Oriana to Emily, 22 May 1911, MS 1505/7/2/20

307 Young (2014), p. 105

308 Young (2014), p. 124

309 Petrocelli (2010)

310 Bill's journal, quoted in Wilson (1972)

311 Spufford (1996), p. 147

312 Bill's journal, quoted in Wilson (1972), p. 125

313 Bill's journal, quoted in Wilson (1972), p. 127

314 For details of Bill and Ory's wedding and first two weeks of married life as described by Bill, see Wilson (1966), prologue

315 Seaver (1959), p. 81

316 Dr George Levick, 'Sexual Habits of the Adelie Penguin 1910–13' pamphlet, Natural History Museum

317 Seaver (1959), p. 61

318 Oriana to Fraser, 8 March 1904, MS 1577/8/2 SPRI

319 Seaver (1959), p. 50

320 Dr E. T. Wilson, *Edward Adrian Wilson; A Memoir by his Father*, 1995.550.36 Cheltenham Borough Council and the Cheltenham Trust, Wilson Family Collection

321 Wilson el al. (2004), p. 54

322 Seaver (1959), p. 102

323 Seaver (1959), p. 156

324 Petre, Jonathan, 'Wife's Last Letters', 18 March 1912, *Daily Mail*

325 Kennet (1949), p. 102

326 Kennet (1949), p. 93

327 Quotes from Taff in this section are all from 'Antarctic Ice – A Swansea Boy Onboard the *Discovery*', *South Wales Daily Post*, 20 September 1904

328 For more details see Williams (2012)

329 Williams (2012), pp. 104–5

330 Limb/Cordingley (1982), p. 156

331 Smith (2002), p. 158

332 Limb/Cordingley (1982), p. 132

333 Limb/Cordingley (1982), p. 160

334 Limb/Cordingley (1982), p. 48

335 Gestingthorpe Church noticeboard, Gestingthorpe History Group

336 Accounts book of Caroline Oates

337 Seaver (1938), p. 195

338 Birdie to Edie, 27 October 1911, MS 1505/1/1/1/8 SPRI

339 Birdie's journal, 23 November 1911, MS 1501/1/1/3/113 SPRI

340 *South Polar Times*, 1911

341 Seaver (1938), pp. 194–5

342 Birdie to Emily, September–October 1910, MS 1505/1/1/95, SPRI

343 *South Polar Times*, 1911

344 Bowers, M., diary, 1910 Memoranda to September entry

345 Bowers, M., diary, 1910 Memoranda to last entry

346 Bowers, M., diary, 4-5 June 1910

347 Potter, Beatrix, *Tailor of Gloucester*, Frederick Warne & Co: London, 1903

348 Bowers, M., diary, 17–24 June 1910

349 'The Marys of Bute', *Buteman*, 22 June 1911

350 BAE menu, SPRI

351 Cherry-Garrard (1922), p. 237

352 See Lieutenant-General William Bellairs's pronouncements on officers' marriages in 1889, in Trustram, M., *Women of the Regiment: Marriage and the Victorian Army* (Cambridge: Cambridge University Press, 1984), pp. 233–35

353 Seaver (1959), p. 75

354 Wedding and early married life are covered in Bill's journal as quoted in Wilson (1966)

355 Bill's journal, quoted in Wilson (1972), p. 151

356 Wheeler (2001)

357 Bill's journal, quoted in Wilson (1972), p. 155

358 Bill's journal, quoted in Wilson (1972), pp. 153–4

359 Birdie to Emily, 1 November 1911, MS 1505/1/1/3/113 SPRI

360 Bowers, M., diary, mentions discussions re séance with Revd Dewar

361 Bowers, M., diary, 24 October–5 November 1910

362 Bowers, M., diary, 24 January 1910

363 Birdie to May, 20 March 1910, MS 1505/1/1/2/88

364 Bill's journal, quoted in Wilson (1972), chapter 11

365 Artefact Taff's Will, Exhibition/Sale at Spinks London, December 2019

366 Kennet (1949), p. 96

367 Mackenzie, C., *My Life and Times, Sir Compton Mackenzie* (Chatto & Windus, 1965)

368 Kennet (1949), p. 102

369 Crane (2012), p. 505

370 *South Polar Times*, 1911

371 Bill's journal, quoted in Wilson (1972), p. 171

372 Crane (2012), p. 180

373 Seaver (1959), p. 237

374 Wilson (1972), p. 189

375 Bill to Westal, 16 January 1911, 'E. A. Wilson – Journal', typed, bound copy, 1 June 1910 to 27 February 1912, MS 715/2;BJ SPRI

376 Limb/Cordingley (1982), p. 151

377 Scott (2006), p. 289

378 Birdie to Emily, 1 May 1911, MS 1505/3//5/ SPRI

379 Smith (2002), p. 171

380 Limb/Cordingley (1982), p. 30

381 Laurie to Caroline, 23 November 1910, quoted in Limb/Cordingley (1982), p. 121

382 Laurie to Caroline, 'diary' letter dated from 23 November 1910, MS 1016/337 SPRI

383 This is exhibited now with the Oates Collection at the Gilbert White Museum, Selborne

384 Kennet (1949), p. 101

385 Beardsley, Mabel, 'Flirtation: Is It a Legitimate Amusement?', January 1900

386 Kennet (1949), p. 103

387 Kennet (1949), p. 96

388 Scott to Speyer, quoted in Gwynn (1929), pp. 147-8

389 Evans (1921), p. 148

390 Scott to Kathleen, quoted in Gwynn (1929), pp. 147-8

391 Young (2014), p. 157

392 Bill's journal, quoted in Wilson (1972), p. 174

393 This quote and the descriptions in this section are taken from *90° South: With Scott to the Antarctic*, Ponting's 1933 edit of the Antarctic footage. The footage was originally screened in three parts, titled *With Captain Scott, R. N. to the South Pole* in 1911 and 1912, then was edited by Ponting into a feature-length film titled *The Great White Silence* in 1924. The footage was remastered and released by the BFI in 2011.

394 Scott to Kathleen, quoted in Gwynn (1929), p. 150

395 Scott to Kathleen, quoted in Gwynn (1929), pp. 149-50

396 *antithesis*: Scott to Kathleen, October 1911, quoted in Gwynn (1929), p. 204

397 Kennet (1949), p. 101

398 All quotes in this section, Laurie to Caroline, MS 1317/1/3 SPRI

399 Gregor (1995), p. 83

400 Gregor (1995), p. 31

401 All quotes in this section, unless otherwise indicated are from one letter: Birdie to Emily, 1 November 1911, MS 1505/1/1/3/113 SPRI

402 Seaver (1938), p. 122

403 Reginald Smith collection, MS 559/14/1–9 SPRI

404 Bill to Kinsey, 29 October 1911, Kinsey Collection, Alexander Turnbull Archive, NZ

405 Bill's journal, quoted in Wilson (1972), pp. 181–2

406 Seaver (1959), p. 72

407 Smith (2002), p. 173

408 Artefact in the *Discovery* hut, Antarctic

409 Bill's journal, quoted in Wilson (1972)

410 Scott (2006), p. 309

411 Scott's journal, October 1911, quoted in Scott (2006), p. 303

412 Huntford (2005), p. 405

413 'Evans the Resourceful Innovator' quoted from IAATO.ORG

414 Kennet (1949), p. 101

415 Gwynn (1929), p. 204

416 Kathleen's diary, 13 September 1911, quoted in Kennet (1949), p. 100

417 MS 88924/1/4 – ACD Brit Lib 7–9/11/**

418 Scott (2006), p. 325

419 Kennet (1949), p. 102

420 Huntford (2005), p. 423

421 Crane (2012), p. 514

422 Limb/Cordingley (1982), p. 179

423 Cherry-Garrard (1922), p. 360

424 Preston (2012), p. 165

425 Seaver (1959), p. 271

426 Birdie to Emily, 24 November 1911, MS 1505/3/5/9 SPRI

427 Scott (2006), p. 332

428 Quoted from Vitai Lampada by Henry Newbolt

429 Kennet (1949), p. 98

430 Huntford (2001), p. 558

431 Huntford (2001), p. 559

432 Kennet (1949), p. 102

433 Kennet (1949), p. 103

434 Young (2014), p. 136

435 All quotes in this section are from Bill's journal, quoted in Wilson (1972)

436 Birdie's journal, MS 1505 SPRI

437 Cherry-Garrard (1922), p. 209

438 Limb/Cordingley (1982), p. 183

439 Smith (2002), p. 181

440 'Evans the Resourceful Innovator' quoted from IAATO.ORG

441 Limb/Cordingley (1982), p. 184

442 Scott to Lois, 28 October 1911, quoted in Gregor (1995), pp. 50-1

443 Gregor (1995), pp. 25–6

444 Strathie (2012), p. 142

445 Strathie (2012), p. 141

446 Birdie to May, 8 December 1911, MS 1505/3/5/9 SPRI

447 Birdie to Emily, undated, MS 1505/1/1/3/114 SPRI

448 Cherry to Reggie Smith, 15 July 1912, MS 559/40/8 SPRI

449 Crane (2012), p. 528

450 Young (2014), p. 157

451 Scott (2006), p. 344

452 Gwynn (1929), p. 140

453 Kathleen to David Lloyd George, undated letter, MS 1453/158/1 SPRI

454 David Lloyd George to Kathleen, 12 December 1912, MS 1458/158/2 SPRI

455 Langner (2007), pp. 195–6

456 Wheeler (2001), p. 77

457 Young (2014), p. 123

458 Oriana to Mrs Cherry-Garrard, 2 December 1911, MS 559/144/1 SPRI

459 Wheeler (2001), p. 77

460 Seaver (1959), p. 68

461 Bill's journal, quoted in Wilson (1972), p. 219

462 Birdie to Emily, 21 December 1911, MS 1505/3/5/9 SPRI

463 Evans (1921), chapter xiv

464 Seaver (1938), p. 245

465 Strathie (2012), p. 150

466 Seaver (1938), p. 243

467 Young (2014), p. 136

Kathleen carried on a romantic correspondence with Fridtjof Nansen, but she 'felt that anyone reading [their] letters would see that theirs had not been "an affair *à outrance*",' an actual romance.

468 Limb/Cordingley (1982), p. 185

469 Limb/Cordingley (1982), p. 194

470 Scott (2006), p. 335

471 Gwynn (1929), p. 127

472 Kennet (1949), p. 104

473 Young (2014), p. 265

474 Limb/Cordingley (1982), p. 189

475 Limb/Cordingley (1982), p. 188

476 Cherry's introduction to Seaver (1938), p. xv

477 Crane (2012), p. 535

478 Scott (2006), p. 356

479 Evans (1921), p. 245

480 Gwynn (1929), p. 220

481 All quotes are from Laurie to Caroline, MS 1217/1/4 SPRI

482 Seaver (1959), pp. 276–77

483 Birdie to Emily, 3 January 1912, MS 1505/3/5/9 SPRI

484 Seaver (1938), p. 425

485 Birdie to Emily, 3 January 1912, MS 1505/3/5/9 SPRI

486 Evans (1921), p. 211

487 Young (2014), p. 141

488 Young (2014), p. 180

489 Huntford (2001), pp. 567–8

490 Huxley (1994), p. 27

491 Huntford (2001), pp. 567–8

492 Huntford (2001), p. 573

493 Huntford (2005), pp. 566–7

494 Scott (2006), pp. 374–5

495 Kennet (1949), p. 106

496 Nansen to Kathleen, 8 December 1914, Kennet papers, Nansen letters, CUL, quoted in Young (2014), p. 137

Nansen's letters to Kathleen suggest he wanted more than friendship: 'There's only one thing you want to avoid, you say, even at the cost of losing it all. I wonder what it can be. Or do I know? Is it passion you are afraid of?'

But Kathleen maintained that the two never crossed the bounds of friendship, later writing of the 'affair': 'I was going to remain a completely faithful wife, only I was not going readily to throw aside such a divine friendship.' (Young, 2014, p. 137)

497 Scott (2006), p. 376

498 Ponting, H., *The Great White South* (1932), p. 162

499 Violet Oates's notes of Laurie's diary, 15 January 1912, quoted in Limb/Cordingley (1982), p. 195

500 Violet Oates's notes of Laurie's diary, 16 January 1912, quoted in Limb/Cordingley (1982), p. 195

501 Violet Oates's notes of Laurie's diary, 18 January 1912, quoted in Limb/Cordingley (1982), p. 195

502 Bill's journal, quoted in Wilson (1972), p. 232

503 Birdie to Emily, 17 January 1912, MS 1505/3/5/9 SPRI

504 Birdie to Edie, 18 January 1912, MS 1505/3/5/9 SPRI

505 Birdie to Emily, 17 January 1912, MS 1505/3/5/9 SPRI

506 Scott's diary, 17 January 1912, 1503/5/8 SPRI, quoted in Crane (2005), p. 543

507 Young (2014), p. 105

508 Scott (2006), p. 397

509 Raymond Priestly's journal, 8 January 1911, MS 298/6/1 SPRI

510 Young (2014), p. 142

511 Scott (2006), p. 400

512 Kennet (1949), p. 107

513 Nansen to Kathleen, 8 May 1912, Kennet papers, Nansen letters, CUL, quoted in Huntsford (2001), pp. 568–9

514 Kennet (1949), pp. 107–8

515 Young (2014), p. 147

516 Kennet (1949), p. 108

517 All quotes in this section from Scott (2006), p. 409

518 Kennet (1949), p. 108

519 Wheeler (2001), p. 134

520 Scott (2006), p. 410

521 Seaver (1959)

522 Bill to Caroline, MS 482 SPRI

523 Dr. E.T. Wilson, handwritten copy of 'Life of Ted' copied by Oriana, dated 21 March 1912, SPRI

524 RGS Scott Special Collection 1910–24 46 e

525 Birdie to Emily, 22 March 1912, MS 1505/7/2/17 SPRI

526 Scott (2006), p. 415

527 3 January 1912, MS 1505/1/1/3/118 SPRI

528 Ed. Boneman, N., 'Last Letters' SPRI booklet, 2012, pp. 61–3

529 Seaver (1959), p. 143

530 Ed. Boneman, N., 'Last Letters' SPRI booklet, 2012, p. 54

531 Scott (2006), p. 415

532 Kennet (1949), p.109

533 Young (2014), p. 148

534 Kennet (1949), p. 109

535 All quotes from Scott's last letter to Kathleen are from Gwynn (1929), p. 228

536 All quotes from Scott's 'Message to the Public' are from Crane (2012), pp. 567

537 Huntford (2005), pp. 547

538 All Oriana to Mr and Mrs Smith, 7 April 1912, MS 1330/7 SPRI

539 Young (2014), p. 148

540 'Birches' by Robert Frost, 1915

541 Author's conversation with Wayland Kennet, 14 May 2007

542 Young (2014), p. 148

543 *Buteman*, 12 April 1912

544 Letter from Birdie to Kathleen, quoted in Gwynn (1929), p. 211

545 Accounts book of Caroline Oates, 23 April 1912

546 All Oriana to Mr and Mrs Smith, 9 April 1912, MS 1330/7 SPRI

547 Kennet (1949), p. 111

548 Young (2014), p. 148

549 Letter from Oriana to Mr and Mrs Smith, 7 April 1912, MS 1330/7, SPRI

550 Telegram, 3 April 1912, Cheltenham Borough Council and the Cheltenham Trust/The Wilson family collection

551 Letter from Oriana to Mrs Cherry-Garrard, 5 April 1912, MS 1330/6/1 SPRI

552 Scott to Oriana, 1 October 1911, Cheltenham College Archives

553 Letter from Oriana to Mr and Mrs Smith, 7 April 1912, MS 1330/7, SPRI

554 Letter from Oriana to Mrs Cherry-Garrard, 5 April 1912, MS 1330/6/1 SPRI

555 Accounts book of Caroline Oates, 10 May 1912

556 All Oriana to Isabel Smith, 2 May 1912, MS 841/13/1/13 SPRI

557 Gwynn (1929)

558 All quotes in this section from Wheeler (2001), pp. 136–7

559 Young (2014), p. 149

560 Kennet (1949), p. 110

561 Laurie to Caroline, 3 January 1911, MS 1317/1/4 SPRI

562 Bill's journal, quoted in Wilson (1972), p. 151, with sketches and maps

563 Kinsey to Scott, 10 December 1912, MS 1453/127/4 SPRI

564 MacInnes (2019), chapter 23

565 Seaver (1938), p. 225

566 Seaver (1938), p. 227

567 21 February 1900, MS 1505/1/1/3/1 SPRI

568 Emily to Birdie, 2 December 1904, MS 1505/1/2/2/20 SPRI

569 Kathleen's letter to Hannah is quoted from Young (2014), pp. 149–50

570 Gwynn (1929), p. 22

571 Young (2014), p. 102

572 *South Wales Daily Post*, 20 September 1904

573 Mansel T. J., Tape recordings of Gower people, Wilf Beynon and George Tucker, *c*.1970s

574 Limb/Cordingley (1982), p. 173

575 Crane (2012), p. 499

576 Limb/Cordingley (1982), p. 173

577 *South Wales Daily Post*, 13 February 1913

578 Gregor (1995), p. 64

579 'Three Years in Antarctic Ice – Swansea Boy Onboard the *Discovery*', *South Wales Daily Post*, 20 September 1904

580 Cherry-Garrard (1922)

581 Wheeler (2001), p. 139

582 E. E. Reynolds and N. H. Brasher, *Britain in the Twentieth Century*, (Cambridge University Press: Cambridge, 1966), p. 52

583 Kennet (1949), p. 106

584 Kennet (1949), p. 108

585 Keltie to Scott, 19 September 1912, RGS Scott Collection 1910–24

586 Kennet (1949), pp. 111–2

587 Kennet (1949), p. 106

588 Kennet (1949), p. 113

589 Young (2014), p. 103

590 Stopes (1995), p. 112

591 Young (2014), p. 193

592 Kennet (1949), p. 99

593 Kennet (1949), p. 113

594 Wheeler (2001), p. 140

595 Gregor (1995), p. 41

596 *South Wales Daily Post*, 11 February 1913

597 Gregor (1995), p. 37

598 Photocopy of letter given to the author by G. Gregor

599 Crane (2012), p. 435

600 Emily to Cherry, 14 December 1921, RGS Archives

601 Birdie to May, 15 May 1909, MS 1505/1/1/2/65 SPRI

602 Birdie to May, 12 January 1909, MS 1505/1/1/2/81 SPRI

603 Oriana to Mrs Cherry-Garrard, 22 September 1912, MS 559/144/2 Okie, Hawera SPRI

604 All quotes from this section are from: Letter from Kathleen to Scott, 8 October 1912, MS 1835/399 and 389 SPRI

605 Emily to Cherry, 26 June 1913, MS 559/31/8 RGS Archives

606 Wayland Kennet recited this to the author at the mention of Curzon in Kathleen's home, 14 May 2007

607 Bristol schoolgirl who attended one of Amundsen's lectures, quoted in scottvamundsen.blogspot

608 Kennet (1949), p. 115

609 Huntford (2001), p. 558
     For more information, see the RGS Journal, quoted in Cameron, I., *To the Farthest Ends of the Earth: The History of the RGS 1830-1980* (London: MacDonald, 1980), p. 150

610 Keltie to Scott, 19 September 1912, RGS Archives

611 2 May 1912, MS 841/13/1/13 SPRI

612 Seaver (1938), p. 267

613 All Christies descriptions of sale of Oates mementos: Caroline Oates collection of papers – notes of conversations in summer of 1913. This quote is either Oriana or Hilda's – evidence points to Hilda.

614 Huntford (2011), p. 537

615 Evans (1921), p. 252

616 Crane (2005), p. 571

617 Wheeler (2001), p. 145

618 Oriana to Mrs Cherry-Garrard, c/o G. Dennistoun Esq, 1 January 1913, MS 559/144/3 SPRI

619 Kennet (1949), p. 117

620 Young (2014), p. 153

621 Kennet (1949), p. 115

622 All from Kennet (1949), p. 1

623 Oriana to Anne Hardy, 14 February 1913, MS 64.1, Anne Hardy Collection Canterbury Museum, Christchurch

624 *Pall Mall Gazette*, 10 February 1913, MS 1453/40 SPRI

625 Account of meeting the Oamaru telegraphist, from Norman Meikle to the Royal Geographical Society, 23 February 1970, RFS Library, MSS 6 RGS

626 Press Association, Wellington, New Zealand, 10 February 1913

627 All quotes in this section from the *Evening Post*, 10 February 1913 and the *Wanganui Chronicle,* issue 12857, 11 February 1913, p. 5

628 Teddy to Kinsey, 10 February 1913, Kinsey Collection, Alexander Turnbull Archive, NZ

629 Kinsey to Gennings, 26 June 1913
     Kinsey explains that he 'consider[s] it my duty to see they were informed officially, and that the first painful news and details should not be conveyed to them through the medium of the newspaper.'

630 *South Wales Daily Post*, 11 February 1913

631 Gregor (1995), p. 70

632 Murray (unpublished PhD thesis, 2006), p. 81

633 Keltie to Curzon, 10 February 1913, Curzon, Lord Correspondence, Box 2, RGS Collection

634 Murray (unpublished PhD thesis, 2006), p. 81

635 *Daily Express*, 11 February 1913

636 Jones (2003), p. 110

637 Curzon Papers, 10 February 1913, British Library

638 Kennet (1949), p. 11

639 *Taranaki Herald*, vol LXI, issue 144018, 11 February 1913

640 Freshfield to Curzon, 10 February 1913, MS 88924/1/48, British Library

641 Freshfield to Curzon, 12 February 1913, 1 Sirlie Gardens, Curzon Papers, British Library

642 Oriana to Mrs Pennell, 7 April 1912, MS 888/3;D SPRI

643 Cherry-Garrard (1922), p. 638

644 Oriana to Anne Hardy, 14 February 1913, MS 64.1 Anne Hardy Collection Canterbury Museum, Christchurch

645 Strathie (2012), p. 181

646 Oriana to Anne Hardy, 14 February 1913, MS 64.1 Anne Hardy Collection Canterbury Museum Christchurch
647 *South Wales Daily Post*, 12 February 1913
648 *South Wales Daily Post*, 12 February 1913
649 Gregor (1995), p. 70
650 Turney (2017), p. 287
651 Curzon Papers, 11 Februrary 1913, British Library
652 Keltie to Curzon, Curzon Papers, 11 February 1913, British Library
653 Huntford (2005), p. 545
654 *Evening Post*, vol LXXXV, issue 35, 11 February 1913, p. 7
655 Scott (2006), p. 422
656 Wheeler (2001), p. 151
657 *Cambrian Daily Leader*, 11 February 1913
658 *Yorkshire Post* and *Leeds Intelligencer*, 13 February
659 Markham to Curzon, 15 February 1913, Curzon Papers, British Library
660 Jones (2003), p. 102
661 Journal of 6th Inniskilling Dragoons, March 1913
662 Journal of 6th Inniskilling Dragoons, February 1913, D Squadron Notes
663 *Cambrian Daily Leader*, 12 February 1913
664 Kinsey Papers, 17 April 1913, MS 559/164;D PRI
665 Jones (2003), p. 132
666 Jones (2003), p. 135
667 *South Wales Daily Post*, G. Gregor courier script notes to author
668 *Telegraph* and *Clyde Shipping Gazette*, 15 February 1913
669 Oriana to Anne Hardy, 14 February 1913, MS 64.1, Anne Hardy Collection, Canterbury Museum, Christchurch
670 Seaver (1959), p. 266
671 Kennet (1949), p. 120
672 *Cambrian Daily Leader*, February 1913
673 Curzon papers, British Library
674 Bigge to Curzon, 19 February 1913, Curzon Papers, British Library
675 Keltie to Curzon, 19 February 1913, Royal Geographical Society
676 Kennet (1949), p. 120
677 Oriana to Mrs Cherry-Garrard, 20 February 1913, MS 1330/4 SPRI
678 Kennet (1949), p. 121
679 Kennet (1949), p. 122

680 Seaver (1959), p. 72

681 Curzon to Keltie, 23 February 1913, Curzon, Lord Correspondence, Box 2, RGS

682 Kennet (1949), pp. 122–3

683 Kennet (1949), p. 123

684 Emily to Waitaki High School for Boys, MS MS68, Waitaki Boys' School Collection, Canterbury Museum, Christchurch

685 May to Birdie, MS 1505/1/1/2/9

686 Bayard to Birdie, 3 June 1903, MS 1505/1/2/3/2

687 Caroline to Kinsey, 10 April 1913, Kinsey Collection, Alexander Turnbull Archive, NZ

688 Kennet (1949), p. 123

689 Kennet (1949), p. 124

690 Kennet (1949), p. 125

691 Kennet (1949), p. 121

692 Kennet (1949), p. 124

693 Kennet (1949), p. 121

694 *Marlborough Express*, vol XLVII, issue 52, 1 March 1913

695 Arthur Machen's 'Scott's Expedition – How Five Brave Englishmen Died', Dundee Heritage Trust, Online Collections

696 Kathleen to Keltie, RGS Special Collection, Scott 1910–24 RFS 46-e

697 Kathleen to Hannah Scott, 5 March 1913, MS 1464/14/8 SPRI

698 MS 68.2, Waitaki Boys' School Collection, Canterbury Museum, Christchurch

699 Oriana to Kinsey, 20 March 1913, quoted in MacInnes (2019), p. 168

700 Gregor (1995), p. 89

701 Gregor (1995), p. 73

702 Gregor (1995), p. 72

703 Scott (2006); Cherry-Garrard (1922)

704 Gregor (1995), p. 70

705 Nansen to Kathleen, quoted in Huntford (2001), p. 572

706 Kennet (1949), p. 76

707 Curzon to Knight, Frank and Rutley, 24 February 1913, Curzon, Lord Correspondence, Box 2, RGS

708 G. N. Curzon to *The Times*, 31 May 1893, quoted in Jones (2003), p. 54

709 Young (2014), p. 113

710 Curzon re BAE, 16 April 1913, MS F112/51, British Library

711 Kennet (1949), p. 76

712 *Guardian*, February 1913, quoted in Gregor (1995), pp. 75–6

713 'The Polar Tragedy', *Telegraph* and *Clyde Shipping Gazette*, 14 February 1913

714 Ponting, H. G., *The Great White South* (Duckworth: London, 1932), p. 162

715 Oriana to Curzon, 19 May 1913 (See P.S. of Ory's letter), Curzon, Lord Correspondence, British Library

716 Hannah to Curzon, 25 February 1913, Curzon, Lord Correspondence, British Library

717 Oriana to Curzon, 19 May 1913, Curzon, Lord Correspondence, British Library

718 G.N. Curzon, 'Address by the Right Hon Earl Curzon of Kedelston', GL 41 (13) 212, quoted in Jones (2003), p. 134

719 Seaver (1959), p. 292

720 'Real brick' from Bill's journal, 15 August 1910, quoted in Wilson (1972); 'blood and hair' from Limb/Cordingley (1982), p. 121

721 Curzon's notes run on from those taken when interviewing Kathleen Scott, MSS F112/51, Curzon Correspondence, British Library

722 21 April, 1913, Curzon Correspondence, British Library

723 Beaumont to Curzon, 17 April 1913, Curzon Correspondence, British Library

724 Jones (2003), pp. 123–4.
For more detail on the edits to Scott's journal, see Scott (1972), Editor's Appendix III: Significant changes to Scott's original base and sledging journals

725 *South Wales Daily Post*, quoting Lois, 12 February 1913

726 Gregor (1995), p. 73

727 16 April 1924, Rudmose Brown Collection, MS 356/79/4, SPRI

728 Young (2014), p. 163

729 Huxley (1994), p. 25 and p. 20

730 Scott (2006), p. 416

731 Kathleen to Curzon, 25 May 1913, Curzon Correspondence, British Library

732 Oriana to Kathleen, 22 May 1913, MS 1453/190/3 SPRI

733 Oriana to Keltie 20 April 1913, CB8/Wilson EA/278, RGS

734 Jones (2003), p. 190

735 Oriana to Keltie, 26 April 1913, RF Correspondence 1911–20, RGS

736 Oriana to Kathleen, 22 May 1913, MS 1453/190/3 SPRI

737 Keltie to Curzon, 14 May 1913, Curzon Correspondence, Box 2, RGS

738 Curzon to Keltie, 16 May 1913, Curzon Correspondence, Box 2, RGS

739 Keltie to Curzon, 18 October 1913, Curzon Correspondence, Box 2, RGS

740 Kathleen to Curzon, 26 May 1913, Curzon Correspondence, British Library

741 Darwin to Curzon, 20 June 1913, Curzon Correspondence papers, British Library

742 Emily's obituary, 'Death of Mrs Bowers', *The Buteman*

743 Emily to Cherry, 13 May 1913, ACG Collection, MS 559/31/1 SPRI

744 Emily to Cherry, 16 June 1913, ACG Collection, MS 559/31/5 SPRI

745 Emily to Cherry, 9 July 1913, ACG Collection, MS 559/31/9 SPRI

746 Emily to Cherry, 10 June 1910, ACG Collection, MS 559/31/4 SPRI

747 Emily to Cherry, 13 May 1913, ACG Collection, MS 559/31/1 SPRI

748 *Western Mail*, 21 February 1913

749 Taff's Dry Valley diary, 29 January 1911, MS 1487;BJ SPRI

750 *South Wales Daily Post*, vol. DCCLXIX

751 Emily to Cherry, 14 December 1921, ACG Collection, SPRI

752 *West Coast Advertiser*, 21 February 1913

753 Frank Debenham to Cherry, 30 May 1920, MS 559/57/10;D SPRI

754 Bill to Caroline, undated March 1912, MS 482 SPRI

755 Kathleen to Emily, MS 1505/7/2/14 SPRI

756 MS 1453/190/2 SPRI

757 P. Cordingley, conversation with author, 6 December 2019

758 Seaver (1959), p. 263

759 Jones (2003), p. 242

760 Crane (2012), p. 498

761 John Bull, 8 March 1913, quoted in Jones (2003), p. 113

762 Jones (2003), p. 236

763 *Tablet*, 15 February 1913, p. 268, quoted in Jones (2003), p. 249

764 Teddy Evans to Emily Bowers, 21 June 1913 (on BAE-headed paper), MS 1505/7/2/9

765 Emily to Cherry, 28 May 1913, MS 559/31/3 SPRI

766 Emily to Cherry, 15 October 1913, MS 559/31/5 SPRI

767 Keltie to Curzon, 19 March 1913; Curzon to Keltie, 28 March 1913; both from RGS Archives

768 Curzon Correspondence, Box 2, 26 letters, 4 pieces

769 *Western Mail*, 21 February 1913

770 Wheeler (2001), p. 160

771 Kathleen to Teddy Evans, 27 June 1913, MS 1453/153/1

772 '200 Years of Polar Exploration 1819–2019' exhibition catalogue written by Roan Hackney RFGS and co-curated with Marcus Budgen for Spink and the Endeavour Fund, p. 133

773 Caroline to Rudmose Brown, 26 March 1928, SPRI

774 Caroline to the Secretary of the RGS, 24 March 1913, RGS Archive

775 Caroline to the Secretary of the RGS, 3 April 1913, RGS Archive

776 Caroline to the Secretary of the RGS, 18 November 1913, RGS Archive

777 Caroline to the Secretary of the RGS, 15 November 1913, RGS Archive

778 Caroline to Rudmose Brown, 26 March 1928, SPRI

779 Teddy to Caroline, 15 April 1913, MS 1016/345 SPRI

780 *Daily Chronicle*, 13 February 1913, quoting Nansen

781 *Morning Post*, 12 February 1913

782 Wheeler (2001), p. 159

783 Caroline to Rudmose Brown, 26 March 1928, SPRI

784 All quotes in this section, unless otherwise indicated are Caroline's notes from her meeting with Kathleen, quoted in Smith (2002), p. 248

785 Caroline to Rudmose Brown, 26 March 1928, MS 356/79/8 SPRI

786 *Morning Post*, 12 February 1913, quoting Shackleton

787 Emily to Cherry, 15 October 1913, MS 559/31/4

788 Bowers, M., diary, 26 February 1910

789 May to Emily, MS 1505/6/3/1 SPRI

790 Emily to Cherry, undated, 559/31/10 SPRI

791 Emily to Cherry, 16 June 1913 SPRI

792 Emily to Cherry, 13 May 1913, MS 559/31/1 SPRI

793 Emily to Reginald Smith, 16 June 1913, MS 559/32/1 SPRI

794 Emily to Cherry, 9 July 1913, MS 559/31/9 SPRI

795 Oates Collection, MS 83/1-2, copy by Caroline

796 G. Gregor letter to author, 3 December 2019

797 Oriana to Hodgson, 20 February 1913, MS 1181;D Hodgson SPRI

798 Quotes from 'Deb' by Peter Speak, chapter 4, SPRI

799 Limb/Cordingley (1982), p. 211

800 *Church Magazine* 1915, Gestingthorpe History Group notes

801 Plaque in Gestingthorpe Church

802 L. Earle telegram to F. Ponsonby, Royal Yacht, Cowes, undated, Works 20/121 PRO

803 Beaumont to Kathleen, 12 November 1914, MS 2 SPRI

804 Beaumont letter, RGS Archive

805 Curzon to Keltie, 13 June 1913, Curzon Papers RGS Archives BB8 1911–20

806 Curzon to Kathleen, 19 October 1913, MS 4 SPRI, quoted in Jones (2003), p. 144

807 Kathleen to Curzon, 21 October 1913, Scott Correspondence, Block 1911–20 file (b) RGS

808 Caroline to the Secretary of the RGS, 18 November 1913, RGS Archive

809 Curzon to Hinks, undated, RGS Collection

810 Hinks to Curzon, 13 July 1914, RGS Collection

811 Oriana to Hinks, 12 December 1916, RGS Archives

812 Oriana to Hinks, 5 February 1918, RGS Archives

813 Kathleen's diary, 19 September 1929, quoted in Kennet (1949), p. 270

814 Birdie to May, 3 April 1910, MS 1505/1/1/2/86 SPRI

815 Emily to Cherry, 17 July 1916, MS 873/2/3 SPRI

816 Birdie to Emily, 22 June 1910, MS 1505/1/1/3/90 SPRI

817 Limb/Cordingley (1982), p. 45

818 Edgar Speyer to Sir Edward Elgar, 24 October 1914, Worcester Record Office 705/445/5427/5/VI, now in Southampton

819 Speyer to Asquith, 17 May 1915, British Library

820 Edie to Emily, October–November 1914, MS 1505/5/1–3 SPRI

821 Edie to Emily, late summer 1914, MS 1505/5/1–3 SPRI

822 Emily to Birdie, 9 December 1904, MS 1505/1/2/2/21 SPRI

823 Edie to Emily, late summer 1914, MS 1505/5/1–3 SPRI

824 Young (2014), p. 182

825 All references in this section are from *The Gestingthorpe Church Monthly Magazine*, December 1915, pp. 12–13, Private collection

826 Ponting, H., *The Great White South* (Duckworth, 1921), pp. 297–8

827 Oriana to Cherry, 8 October 1913

828 Oriana to Bertha Rayham, 31 May 1917, Private collection

829 Seaver (1959), p. 68

830 Oriana to Cherry, 13 April 1916

831 Lois to the RGS, 13 November 1913, RGS Correspondence Block 1911–20

832 Lois to the RGS, 1 June 1915, RGS Archives

833 Birdie to May, 3 December 1909, MS 1505/1/1/2/77 SPRI

834 MS 1487; BJ Journal, 27 January to 12 March 1911 [Western mountains sledge journey], 1 volume, holograph, SPRI

835 Hinks to Lois, 2 June 1915, RGS Archives, Correspondence Block 1911–12

836 Hinks to H. G. Lyons, 2 June 1915, RGS Archives Correspondence Block 1911–12

837 Young (2014), p. 170

838 Kathleen's diary, April 1916, quoted in Kennet (1949), p. 140

839 Ugolini, L. (2018), 'The "Recruiting Muddle": Married men, conscription and masculinity in the First World War England', *First World War Studies*, vol. 9, issue 1, pp. 73–92

840 Kathleen's diary, 8 January 1918, quoted in Kennet (1949), p. 162

841 Young (2014), p. 182

842 Margot Asquith's diary, July 1918, MS Eng d 3216, British Library

843 Limb/Cordingley (1982), p. 209

844 File FO 383, British Archives

845 Kremnitz documents, September 1916, File FO 38312, British Archives

846 Existing fireplace in Gestingthorpe Hall

847 Kennet (1949), p. 148

848 Kennet (1949), p. 145

849 Mason, Joan, 'The Admission of the First Women to the Royal Society of London' in *Notes and Records of the Royal Society of London*, Vol. 46, No. 2 (The Royal Society: 1992), pp. 279-300

850 Kathleen's diary, 29 December 1916, Kennet Papers, quoted in Wheeler (2001), p. 194

851 *Cambrian Daily Leader*, 16 November 1918

852 Oriana to Sir John Murray, 25 October 1933, DV22/22A Wilson

853 Oriana to Anne Hardy, 20 December 1922, MS 64.5, Anne Hardy Collection, Canterbury Museum, Christchurch

854 Letter from Miss Scott, c/o Mrs Scott Hampton Court Palace, 18 July 1922, MS 873/216 SPRI

855 Oriana to Cherry, 27 February 1921, MS 873/2/21 SPRI

856 Leiper, R. T. and Atkinson, E. L. (1914), 'Helminthes of the British Antarctic Expedition 1910–1913', *Proceedings of the Zoological Society of London*, pp. 222–226

857 Birdie to Emily, 7 December 1910, MS 1505/1/1/3/104 SPRI

858 Oriana to Cherry, 3 March 1921, MS 873/2/21 SPRI

859 Seaver (1959), p. 103

860 Oriana to Isabel Smith, 21 February 1935, MS 559/145/1–5;D SPRI

861 Oriana to Oldfield Thomas, 1 April 1923, 219 Natural History Museum

862 A new introduction for the March 1914 5th edition of Barret Hamilton's *British Mammals*, illustrated by Dr E. Wilson.

863 Emily to Cherry, 4 August 1918, MS 873/2/3 SPRI

864 Cherry-Garrard (1922)

865 Cherry to Emily, 10 December 1921, MS 873/2/3 SPRI

866 Cherry-Garrard (1922)

867 Emily to Cherry, 14 December 1921

868 Emily to Cherry, 20 September 1920, MS 873/2/14

869 Emily to Cherry, 26 January 1919, MS 873/2/3

870 Young (2014), p. 193

871 Kathleen's diary, 30 July 1923, quoted in Kennet (1949), p. 220

872 Young (2014), p. 214

873 All Shaw quotes: Letter from George Bernard Shaw to Kathleen Hilton Young, 23 March 1923, British Library, MS 50519, ff. 29-34

874 Young (2014), p. 215

875 Kennet (1949), p. 199

876 Kennet (1949), p. 57

877 Kathleen's diary, 30 July–2 August 1923, quoted in Kennet (1949), pp. 220–1

878 Lady Shackleton, 27 May 1922, quoted in *The Life of Sir Ernest Shackleton* by H. R. Mill (Heinemann: London, 1933), p. 21

879 Caroline to Rudmose Brown, 1 May 1924, MS 356/79/5 Rudmose Brown Bequest, 1957

880 Caroline to Rudmose Brown, 26 March 1928, MS 356/79/8

881 George Bernard Shaw to Lord Kennet (second husband to Kathleen Scott), 28 February 1948, quoted in Limb/Cordingley (1982), p. 212

882 Caroline to Rudmose Brown, 13 March 1924, MS 356/79/2 SPRI

883 Holroyd never knew Oates, but the portrait is probably based on a photogravure portrait by G. Lekegian & Co., Cairo

884 No birth certificate exists, which is normal in this situation. For further detail, all references are from Smith (2002), pp. 263–70

885 For details see Smith (2002), chapter 26, 'A Second Tragedy'

886 Mill to Lady Shackleton, 19 November 1922, quoted in *The Life of Sir Ernest Shackleton* by H. R. Mill (Heinemann: London, 1933), p. 59

887 Smith (2002), p. 225

888 Caroline to H. R. Mill, 15 January 1930, MS 100/88 SPRI

889 Gwynn (1929), p. 234

890 Caroline to Rudmose Brown, 26 March 1928, MS 356/79/8 SPRI

891 Author's conversation with Sue Limb, 11 November 2020

892 John Evans to author

893 Scott's journal, 8 January 1912, Scott (2006), p. 369

894 Scott's journal, 16 February 1912, Scott (2006) p. 396

895 Frank Debenham, quoted in Gregor (1995), p. 89

896 'Giant Worker' and 'pig it anyhow' quoted in Scott (2006), p. 10 and p. 369 respectively

897 C. Mason (1953), 'Vaughan William's "Sinfonia Antarctica"' *Musical Times*, vol. 94, p. 128

898 Monk (1993), p. 80

899 Jo Laurie conversation with author, 4 November 2021

900 Edith Bowers Hosp. Report, Bute Museum Archive, Copy of National Archive WO 399/804

901 *Buteman*, August 1928

902 Cherry to Mr White, 10 August 1930, MS 1557 SPRI

903 Louis Bernacchi, quoting Bryan Oates to Hugh R. Mill, 14 November 1932, SPRI

904 Note inserted into a copy of *History of the Parish of Gestinghorpe* by Violet Oates

905 *Daily Express*, 29 November 1938

906 Gregor (1995), p. 77

907 Huxley (1994), p. 272

908 Scott's journal, quoted in Scott (2006), p. 157

909 Huxley (1994), p. 274

910 Gwynn (1929), p. 93

911 *Science Daily* 2018 and Anne Jungblut to the author in conversation, 16 October 2020

912 Young (2014), p. 181

INDEX